SOMETHING ABOUT THE AUTHOR®

Something about
the Author *was named
an "Outstanding
Reference Source,"
the highest honor given
by the American
Library Association
Reference and Adult
Services Division.*

ISSN 0276-816X

something ABOUT THE AUThor®

**Facts and Pictures about Authors
and Illustrators of Books for Young People**

EDITED BY
ALAN HEDBLAD

volume 94

GALE

DETROIT • NEW YORK • TORONTO • LONDON

STAFF

Editor: Alan Hedblad
Managing Editor: Joyce Nakamura
Publisher: Hal May
Associate Editor: Sheryl Ciccarelli
Assistant Editor: Marilyn O'Connell Allen

Sketchwriters/Copyeditors: Linda R. Andres, Scott Gillam, Mary Gillis, Johanna Haaxma-Jurek, Janet L. Hile,
Laurie Hillstrom, Motoko Fujishiro Huthwaite, J. Sydney Jones, Sean McCready,
Thomas F. McMahon, Susan Reicha, Gerard J. Senick, Maria Sheler-Edwards, Pamela L. Shelton,
Michaela Ann Swart, Diane Telgen, Crystal Towns, Arlene True, and Kathleen Witman

Research Manager: Victoria B. Cariappa
Project Coordinator: Cheryl L. Warnock
Research Specialists: Andrew Guy Malonis, Barbara McNeil, Gary J. Oudersluys, Maureen Richards
Research Associates: Laura C. Bissey, Julia C. Daniel, Tracie A. Richardson, Norma Sawaya, Robert Whaley

Permissions Manager: Susan M. Trosky
Permissions Specialist: Maria L. Franklin
Permissions Associates: Edna M. Hedblad, Michele M. Lonoconus
Permissions Assistant: Andrea Rigby

Production Director: Mary Beth Trimper
Production Assistant: Deborah Milliken

Desktop Publisher: Gary Leach
Image Database Supervisor: Randy Bassett
Imaging Specialists: Robert Duncan, Michael Logusz
Photography Coordinator: Pamela A. Reed

∞™ This book is printed on acid-free paper that meets the minimum requirements of American National Standard for Information Sciences—Permanence Paper for Printed Library Materials, ANSI Z39.48-1984.

Library of Congress Catalog Card Number 72-27107

ISBN 0-7876-1147-6 ISSN 0276-816X

Printed in the United States of America

10 9 8 7 6 5 4 3 2 1

Contents

Authors in Forthcoming Volumes viii
Introduction ix
Acknowledgments xi

Authors in Forthcoming Volumes

Below are some of the authors and illustrators that will be featured in upcoming volumes of *SATA*. These include new entries on the swiftly rising stars of the field, as well as completely revised and updated entries (indicated with *) on some of the most notable and best-loved creators of books for children.

Brian Burks: A seasoned cowboy and rancher, Burks blends firsthand knowledge of horses, guns, and cattle with careful research and a natural interest in the cultural and historical aspects of the southwest to spin exciting adventure stories for young readers. Apache customs are detailed in his award-winning 1995 novel *Runs with Horses*.

Jamie Lee Curtis: An award-winning actress, Curtis has forged a second career as an author of children's books with *When I Was Little: A Four-Year-Old's Memoir of Her Youth* and *Tell Me Again about the Night I Was Born*.

Nick Earls: Australian novelist Earls broadened his focus to write for a teen audience with the successful young adult novel *After January*. He has been hailed for negotiating the transitional period between adolescence and adulthood with subtlety and humor.

Martyn N. Godfrey: A prolific and accomplished Canadian writer of children's and young adult novels, Godfrey melds humor with often serious subjects in genres ranging from action-adventure to historical fiction. Titles such as *Plan B Is Total Panic, Send for Ms. Teeny-Wonderful,* and *Mystery in the Frozen Lands* integrate real incidents which make them ring true for young readers.

*Trina Schart Hyman: A highly regarded illustrator of scores of books for young people, Hyman is best known for her work with folklore and fairy tales. She has also teamed up with many celebrated contemporary children's authors to produce a body of work that has garnered her a host of honors, among them the coveted Caldecott Medal.

Chris Lynch: Lynch addresses the problems faced by today's urban youth through his gritty, streetwise fiction. Episodic and fast-paced, his novels for young adults, including such award-winning titles as *Shadow Boxer* and *Iceman,* are helping to redefine serious young adult literature.

Victor Martinez: Martinez's fledgling novel, *Parrot in the Oven,* won the 1996 National Book Award in Young People's Literature, the first awarded in that category in more than a decade. This semi-autobiographical rendering of the Mexican-American poet and teacher's youth depicts a tender yet volatile time in everyone's life.

*Lois Ruby: In her novels and short stories for young adults, popular author Ruby confronts and addresses issues that shape many of her readers' lives, offering compelling fiction that is relevant to today's young people.

*David Small: Small is an author and illustrator of picture books for children whose works combine an offbeat and quirky presentation with positive messages and traditional values. Blending vivid visuals with witty text, Small has produced several award-winning titles of his own, including *Eulalie and the Hopping Head* and *Imogene's Antlers*.

Gennady Spirin: Russian-born illustrator Spirin creates beautiful paintings of classic fiction and folktales in such books as *Rumplestiltskin* and *The Children of Lir*. Often framing his pages with architectural elements such as arches and carved borders, Spirin's art lends an otherworldly quality to the retelling of fairy tales.

Colin Thompson: Regarded as a gifted author and illustrator, British-born Thompson is hailed for providing young readers with challenging books that are considered both thought-provoking and entertaining.

David Wisniewski: Winner of the 1997 Caldecott Medal for *Golem,* Wisniewski is a clown and puppeteer turned writer and illustrator of books for young readers. His richly detailed, original folktales set in ancient cultures feature modern messages.

Introduction

Something about the Author (*SATA*) is an ongoing reference series that deals with the lives and works of authors and illustrators of children's books. *SATA* includes not only well-known authors and illustrators whose books are widely read, but also less prominent individuals whose works are just coming to be recognized. This series is often the only readily available information source on emerging writers and artists. You'll find *SATA* informative and entertaining, whether you are a student, a librarian, an English teacher, a parent, or simply an adult who enjoys children's literature.

What's Inside SATA

SATA provides detailed information about authors and illustrators who span the full time range of children's literature, from early figures like John Newbery and L. Frank Baum to contemporary figures like Judy Blume and Richard Peck. Authors in the series represent primarily English-speaking countries, particularly the United States, Canada, and the United Kingdom. Also included, however, are authors from around the world whose works are available in English translation. The writings represented in *SATA* include those created intentionally for children and young adults as well as those written for a general audience and known to interest younger readers. These writings cover the entire spectrum of children's literature, including picture books, humor, folk and fairy tales, animal stories, mystery and adventure, science fiction and fantasy, historical fiction, poetry and nonsense verse, drama, biography, and nonfiction.

Obituaries are also included in *SATA* and are intended not only as death notices but also as concise overviews of people's lives and work. Additionally, each edition features newly revised and updated entries for a selection of *SATA* listees who remain of interest to today's readers and who have been active enough to require extensive revisions of their earlier biographies.

Two Convenient Indexes

In response to suggestions from librarians, *SATA* indexes no longer appear in every volume but are included in alternate (odd-numbered) volumes of the series, beginning with Volume 57.

SATA continues to include two indexes that cumulate with each alternate volume: the Illustrations Index, arranged by the name of the illustrator, gives the number of the volume and page where the illustrator's work appears in the current volume as well as all preceding volumes in the series; the Author Index gives the number of the volume in which a person's Biographical Sketch or Obituary appears in the current volume as well as all preceding volumes in the series.

These indexes also include references to authors and illustrators who appear in Gale's *Yesterday's Authors of Books for Children, Children's Literature Review,* and the *Something about the Author Autobiography Series.*

Easy-to-Use Entry Format

Whether you're already familiar with the *SATA* series or just getting acquainted, you will want to be aware of the kind of information that an entry provides. In every *SATA* entry the editors attempt to give as complete a picture of the person's life and work as possible. A typical entry in *SATA* includes the following clearly labeled information sections:

- *PERSONAL:* date and place of birth and death, parents' names and occupations, name of spouse, date of marriage, names of children, educational institutions attended, degrees received, religious and political affiliations, hobbies and other interests.

- *ADDRESSES:* complete home, office, electronic mail, and agent addresses, whenever available.

- *CAREER:* name of employer, position, and dates for each career post; art exhibitions; military service; memberships and offices held in professional and civic organizations.

- *AWARDS, HONORS:* literary and professional awards received.

- *WRITINGS:* title-by-title chronological bibliography of books written and/or illustrated, listed by genre when known; lists of other notable publications, such as plays, screenplays, and periodical contributions.

- *ADAPTATIONS:* a list of films, television programs, plays, CD-ROMs, recordings, and other media presentations that have been adapted from the author's work.

- *WORK IN PROGRESS:* description of projects in progress.

- *SIDELIGHTS:* a biographical portrait of the author or illustrator's development, either directly from the biographee—and often written specifically for the *SATA* entry—or gathered from diaries, letters, interviews, or other published sources.

- *FOR MORE INFORMATION SEE:* references for further reading.

- *EXTENSIVE ILLUSTRATIONS:* photographs, movie stills, book illustrations, and other interesting visual materials supplement the text.

How a SATA Entry Is Compiled

A *SATA* entry progresses through a series of steps. If the biographee is living, the *SATA* editors try to secure information directly from him or her through a questionnaire. From the information that the biographee supplies, the editors prepare an entry, filling in any essential missing details with research and/or telephone interviews. If possible, the author or illustrator is sent a copy of the entry to check for accuracy and completeness.

If the biographee is deceased or cannot be reached by questionnaire, the *SATA* editors examine a wide variety of published sources to gather information for an entry. Biographical and bibliographic sources are consulted, as are book reviews, feature articles, published interviews, and material sometimes obtained from the biographee's family, publishers, agent, or other associates.

Entries that have not been verified by the biographees or their representatives are marked with an asterisk (*).

Contact the Editor

We encourage our readers to examine the entire *SATA* series. Please write and tell us if we can make *SATA* even more helpful to you. Give your comments and suggestions to the editor:

BY MAIL: The Editor, *Something about the Author,* Gale Research, 835 Penobscot Bldg., 645 Griswold St., Detroit, MI 48226-4094.

BY TELEPHONE: (800) 347-GALE

BY FAX: (313) 961-6599

BY E-MAIL: CYA@Gale.com

Acknowledgments

Grateful acknowledgment is made to the following publishers, authors, and artists whose works appear in this volume.

ANASTASIO, DINA. Cover of *The Case of the Glacier Park Swallow,* by Dina Anastasio. Roberts Rinehart Publishers, 1994. Reproduced by permission.

ATTEMA, MARTHA. Attema, Martha, photograph by Marla J. Hayes. Reproduced by permission of Martha Attema.

BENNER, JUDITH ANN. Benner, Judith Ann, photograph by Gary Powell. Reproduced by permission of Judith Ann Benner.

BENNETT, PENELOPE. Bennett, Penelope, photograph. Reproduced by permission of Penelope Bennett.

BLAKEY, NANCY. Blakey, Nancy, photograph. Reproduced by permission of Nancy Blakey.

BLATCHFORD, CLAIRE H. Blatchford, Claire H., photograph. Reproduced by permission of Claire H. Blatchford.

BOHLMEIJER, ARNO. Lebenson, Richard, illustrator. From a jacket of *Something Very Sorry,* by Arno Bohlmeijer. Houghton Mifflin, 1996. Jacket art © 1996 by Richard Lebenson. Reproduced by permission of Houghton Mifflin Company. / Bohlmeijer, Arno, photograph by S. H. Valcke. Reproduced by permission of Arno Bohlmeijer.

BRANCH, MURIEL MILLER. Branch, Muriel Miller, photograph by Reid Carter. Reproduced by permission of Muriel Miller Branch.

BROOKS, RON. Brooks, Ron, illustrator. From an illustration in *Old Pig,* by Margaret Wild. Text © 1995 by Margaret Wild. Illustrations © 1995 by Ron Brooks. Reproduced by permission of Dial Books for Young Readers, a division of Penguin Books USA, Inc. In Australia/New Zealand by Allen & Unwin Pty Ltd.

BROWNRIDGE, WILLIAM R. Brownridge, William R., photograph. Reproduced by permission of William R. Brownridge.

BRYANT, JENNIFER F. Furnèss, William Henry, Jr., illustrator. Friends Historical Library of Swarthmoire College. From a cover of *Lucretia Mott: A Guiding Light,* by Jennifer Fisher Bryant. William B. Eerdmans Publishing Company, 1996. Reproduced by permission. / Bryant, Jennifer F., photograph. Reproduced by permission of Jennifer F. Bryant.

BUTLER, GEOFF. Butler, Geoff, illustrator. From an illustration in *The Killick,* by Geoff Butler. Tundra Books, 1995. © 1995 Geoff Butler. Reproduced by permission of the author. / Butler, Geoff, photograph by Tegan Butler. Reproduced by permission of Geoff Butler.

CAREY, PETER. Jacket of *The Unusual Life of Tristan Smith: A Novel,* by Peter Carey. Knopf, 1994. Reproduced by permission of Random House, Inc. / Chesworth, Michael, illustrator. From a cover of *The Big Bazoohley,* by Peter Carey. PaperStar Books, 1996. Cover art © 1996 Michael Chesworth. Reproduced by permission of The Putnam & Grosset Group.

CARON, ROMI. Caron, Romi, photograph. Reproduced by permission of Romi Caron.

CASANOVA, MARY. Casanova, Mary, photograph. Reproduced by permission of Mary Casanova.

CHOYCE, LESLEY. Choyce, Lesley, photograph by George Georgakakos. Reproduced by permission of Lesley Choyce.

CLAYTON, ELAINE. Clayton, Elaine, photograph. Reproduced by permission of Elaine Clayton.

CLEMENTS, BRUCE. Lewin, Ted, illustrator. From a cover of *The Treasure of Plunderell Manor,* by Bruce Clements. Sunburst Books, 1991. Copyright © 1987 by Bruce Clements. Illustration © 1987 by Ted Lewin. Reproduced by permission of Farrar, Straus and Giroux, Inc. / Norman, Elaine, illustrator. From a cover of *Tom Loves Anna Loves Tom,* by Bruce Clements. Aerial Fiction Books, 1992. Copyright © 1990 by Bruce Clements. Illustration © 1992 by Elaine Norman. Reproduced by permission of Farrar, Straus & Giroux, Inc.

COALSON, GLO. Coalson, Glo, illustrator. From an illustration in *On Mother's Lap,* by Ann Herbert Scott. Clarion Books, 1992. Text © 1972 by Ann Herbert Scott. Illustrations © 1992 by Glo Coalson. Reproduced by permission of Houghton Mifflin Company. / Coalson, Glo, illustrator. From an illustration in *Hi,* by Ann Herbert Scott. Philomel Books, 1994. Illustrations © 1994 by Glo Coalson. Reproduced by permission.

COHEN, SHOLOM. Cohen, Sholom, photograph. Reproduced by permission of Sholom Cohen.

COOK, JEAN THOR. Cook, Jean Thor, photograph. Reproduced by permission of Jean Thor Cook.

CRAIG, HELEN. From an illustration in *The Town Mouse and the Country Mouse,* by Helen Craig. Walker Books, 1992. © 1992 Helen Craig. Reproduced by permission. / Craig, Helen, illustrator. From an illustration in *Charlie and Tyler at the Seashore,* by Helen Craig. Candlewick Press, 1995. Copyright © 1995 by Helen Craig. Reproduced by permission. / Craig, Helen, illustrator. From an illustration in *Angelina Ice Skates,* by Katharine Holabird. Clarkson Potter, 1993. Text © 1993 Katharine Holabird. Illustrations © 1993 Helen Craig. Reproduced by permission of Random House, Inc. / Craig, Helen, photograph by Geoff Shields. Reproduced by permission.

CREECH, SHARON. Desimini, Lisa, illustrator. From a cover of *Walk Two Moons,* by Sharon Creech. HarperCollins, 1996. Cover art © 1994 by Lisa Desimini. Cover © 1996 by HarperCollins Publishers, Inc. Reproduced by permission of HarperCollins Publishers, Inc. / Burckhardt, Marc, illustrator. From a jacket of *Chasing Redbird,* by Marc Burckhardt. Joanna Cotler Books, 1997. Jacket art © 1997 by Marc Burckhardt. Reproduced by permission of HarperCollins Publishers, Inc. / Creech, Sharon, photograph by Matthew Self. Reproduced by permission of Sharon Creech.

DANAKAS, JOHN. Danakas, John, photograph. Reproduced by permission of John Danakas.

DAVIS, TIM. Davis, Tim, photograph. Reproduced by permission of Tim Davis.

DOLAN, EDWARD F. Jacket of *Teenagers and Compulsive Gambling,* by Edward F. Dolan. Franklin Watts, 1994. Reproduced by permission. / Jacket of *The American Revolution: How We Fought the War of Independence,* by Edward F. Dolan. The Millbrook Press, 1995. Reproduced by permission.

DOYLE, CHARLOTTE. Doyle, Charlotte, photograph by Margery Franklin. Reproduced by permission of Charlotte Doyle.

DUGGLEBY, JOHN. Duggleby, John, photograph. Reproduced by permission of John Duggleby.

DURRELL, JULIE. Durrell, Julie, illustrator. From an illustration in *The Lettuce Leaf Birthday Letter,* by Linda Taylor. Dial Books for Young Readers, 1995. Pictures © 1995 by Julie Durrell. Reproduced by permission of Dial Books for Young Readers, a division of Penguin USA. Reproduced by permission of Greenwillow Books, a division of William Morrow and Company, Inc. / Durrell, Julie, photograph by Jill LeVine. Reproduced by permission of Julie Durrell.

EASLEY, MARYANN. Easley, MaryAnn, photograph. Reproduced by permission of MaryAnn Easley.

ERDRICH, LOUISE. Minor, Wendel, illustrator. From a cover of *The Beet Queen,* by Louise Erdrich. Bantam Books, 1989. Cover art © 1989 by Wendel Minor. Reproduced by permission of Bantam Books, a division of Bantam Doubleday Dell Publishing Group, Inc. / Harrington, Glen, illustrator. From a cover of *Love Medicine,* by Louise Erdrich. Bantam Books, 1989. Cover art © 1989 by Glen Harrington. Reproduced by permission of Bantam Books, a division of Bantam Doubleday Dell Publishing Group, Inc. / Harrington, Glenn, illustrator. From a jacket of *Tracks,* by Louise Erdrich. Harper & Row, 1989. Cover illustration © 1989 Glenn Harrington. Reproduced by permission of HarperCollins Publishers, Inc. / LaMarche, Jim, illustrator. From an illustration in *Grandmother's Pigeon,* by Louise Erdrich. Hyperion Books for Children, 1996. Illustrations © 1996 by Jim LaMarche. Reproduced by permission. / Erdrich, Louise, photograph. © Jerry Bauer. Reproduced by permission.

FLEMING, CANDACE. Fleming, Candace, photograph. Reproduced by permission of Candace Fleming.

FRANK, LUCY. Frank, Lucy, photograph. Reproduced by permission of Lucy Frank.

GERINGER, LAURA. Gore, Leonid, illustrator. From an illustration in *The Pomegranate Seeds,* by Laura Geringer. Houghton Mifflin Company, 1995. Illustrations copyright © 1995 by Leonid Gore. Reproduced by permission of Houghton Mifflin Company.

GLASER, ISABEL JOSHLIN. Glaser, Isabel Joshlin, photograph. Reproduced by permission of Isabel Joshlin Glaser.

GOLDBERG, JACOB. Goldberg, Jacob, photograph. Reproduced by permission of Jacob Goldberg.

GOODMAN, JOAN ELIZABETH. Catalano, Dominic, illustrator. From an illustration in *Bernard's Bath,* by Joan Elizabeth Goodman. Boyds Mill Press, 1996. Illustrations © 1996 by Dominic Catalano. / Goodman, Joan Elizabeth, photograph. Reproduced by permission of Joan Elizabeth Goodman.

HADDIX, MARGARET P. Haddix, Margaret P., photograph. Summit Photographics. Reproduced by permission of Margaret P. Haddix.

HAMILTON, CAROL. Hamilton, Carol, photograph. Reproduced by permission of Carol Hamilton.

HAYNES, BETSY. Bacchus, Andy, illustrator. From a cover of *The Great Dad Disaster,* by Betsy Haynes. Skylark Books, 1994. Cover art © 1994 by Andy Bacchus. Reproduced by permission of Skylark Books, a division of Bantam Doubleday Dell Publishing Group, Inc. / Haynes, Betsy, photograph. Reproduced by permission of Betsy Haynes.

HEO, YUMI. Heo, Yumi, illustrator. From an illustration in *The Green Frogs,* by Yumi Heo. Houghton Mifflin, 1996. Copyright © 1996 by Yumi Heo. Reproduced by permission of Houghton Mifflin Company. / Heo, Yumi, illustrator. From an illustration in *The Lonely Lioness and the Ostrich Chicks,* by Verna Aardema. Knopf, 1996. Illustrations © 1996 by Yumi Heo. Reproduced by permission of Random House, Inc.

HIGH, LINDA OATMAN. Marchesi, Stephen, illustrator. From a jacket of *Hound Heaven,* by Linda Oatman High. Holiday House, 1995. Reproduced by permission. / Himler, Ron, illustrator. From a jacket of *Maizie,* by Linda Oatman High. Holiday House, 1995. Reproduced by permission. / High, Linda Oatman, photograph. Reproduced by permission of Linda Oatman High.

HIMMELMAN, JOHN C. Himmelman, John, illustrator. From an illustration in *Wanted: Perfect Parents,* by John Himmelman. Troll Medallion, 1993. Copyright © 1993 John Himmelman. Reproduced by permission. / Himmelman, John, illustrator. From an illustration in *Lights Out!,* by John Himmelman. Troll Associates, 1995. Copyright © 1995 John Himmelman. Reproduced by permission. / Himmelman, John C., photograph. Reproduced by permission of John C. Himmelman.

HO, MINFONG. Bonners, Susan, illustrator. From a jacket of *Rice Without Rain,* by Minfong Ho. Lothrop, Lee & Shepard Books, 1990. Jacket illustration copyright © 1990 by Susan Bonners. Reproduced by permission of Lothrop, Lee & Shepard Books, a division of William Morrow & Company, Inc. / Bonners, Susan, illustrator. From a cover of *The Clay Marble,* by Minfong Ho. Sunburst Books, 1993. Copyright © 1991 by Minfong Ho. Illustration copyright © 1991 by Susan Bonners. Reproduced by permission of Farrar, Straus & Giroux, Inc. / Meade, Holly, illustrator. From an illustration in *Hush! A Thai Lullaby,* by Minfong Ho. Orchard Books, 1996. Illustrations copyright © 1996 by Holly Meade. Reproduced by permission. / Tseng, Jean and Mou-sien, illustrators. From an illustration in *Maples in the Mist,* translated by Minfong Ho. Lothrop, Lee & Shepard Books, 1996. Illustrations copyright © 1996 by Jean and Mou-sien Tseng. Reproduced by permission of Lothrop, Lee & Shepard Books, a division of William Morrow & Company, Inc. / Ho, Minfong, photograph. Reproduced by permission.

HOESTLANDT, JO. Hoestlandt, Jo., photograph by Gerard Percicot. Reproduced by permission of Jo Hoestlandt.

HOOKS, WILLIAM H. de Kiefte, Kees, illustrator. From a jacket of *The Girl Who Could Fly,* by William H. Hooks. Macmillan, 1995. Jacket illustration copyright © 1995 by Kees de Kiefte. Reproduced by permission of Simon & Schuster Books for Young Readers, an imprint of Simon & Schuster Children's Publishing Division. / Hooks, William H., photograph by Elaine Wickens. Reproduced by permission of William H. Hooks.

HOWARTH, LESLEY. Sibthorp, Fletcher, illustrator. From a jacket of *Weather Eye,* by Lesley Howarth. Candlewick Press, 1995. Jacket illustration © 1995 by Fletcher Sibthorp. Reproduced by permission. / Day, Rob, illustrator. From a jacket of *Maphead,* by Lesley Howarth. Candlewick Press, 1996. Reproduced by permission. / Sibthorp, Fletcher, illustrator. From a jacket of *The Pits,* by Lesley Howarth. Candlewick Press, 1996. Jacket illustration © 1996 by Fletcher Sibthorp. Reproduced by permission.

HURD, THACHER. Hurd, Thacher, illustrator. From an illustration in *Little Mouse's Birthday Cake,* by Thacher Hurd. HarperCollins Publishers, 1992. Copyright © 1992 by Thacher Hurd. Reproduced by permission of HarperCollins Publishers, Inc. / Hurd, Thacher, illustrator. From an illustration in *Tomato Soup,* by Thacher Hurd. Crown Publishers, Inc., 1992. Copyright © 1992 by Thacher Hurd. Reproduced by permission of Random House, Inc. / Hurd, Thacher, illustrator. From an illustration in *Art Dog,* by Thacher Hurd. HarperCollins, 1996. © 1996 by Thacher Hurd. Reproduced by permission of HarperCollins Publishers, Inc. / Hurd, Thacher, photograph by Eliot Khuner. Reproduced by permission

JINKS, CATHERINE. Jinks, Catherine, photograph by Peter Dockrill. Reproduced by permission.

KANOZA, MURIEL CANFIELD. Kanoza, Muriel Canfield, photograph. © Glamour Shots. Reproduced by permission.

KELLER, DEBRA. Keller, Debra, photograph. Reproduced by permission of Debra Keller.

KILWORTH, GARRY. Couch, Greg, illustrator. From a jacket of *The Electric Kid,* by Garry Kilworth. Orchard Books, 1995. Jacket illustration © 1995 by Greg Couch. Reproduced by permission. / Kilworth, Garry, photograph by Annette Kilworth. Reproduced by permission of Garry Kilworth.

KONIGSBURG, E. L. From an illustration in *Amy Elizabeth Explores Bloomingdale's,* by E. L. Konigsburg. Atheneum, 1992. Copyright © 1992 by E. L. Konigsburg. Reproduced by permission of Atheneum Publishers, a division of Simon & Schuster, Inc. / Konigsburg, E. L., illustrator. From a jacket of *The View from Saturday,* by E. L. Konigsburg. Atheneum Books for Young Readers, 1996. Jacket illustration © 1996 by E. L. Konigsburg. Reproduced by permission of Atheneum Books for Young Readers, a division of Simon & Schuster, Inc. / Konigsburg, E. L., photograph. The Florida Times-Union. Reproduced by permission of E. L. Konigsburg.

LANDAU, ELAINE. Mastelli, Rick, photographer. From a jacket of *The Beauty Trap,* by Elaine Landau. © 1994 by Elaine Landau. Published by New Discovery Books, an imprint of Silver Burdett Press, Simon & Schuster Education Group. Used by permission. / Greenberg, J., illustrator. From a cover of *Teenage Drinking,* by Elaine Landau. Enslow Publishers, Inc., 1994. Reproduced by permission. / Landau, Elaine, photograph by Devon Cass. Reproduced by permission of Elaine Landau.

LINDBLOM, STEVEN. Hall, George, photographer. From a cover of *Fly the Hot Ones,* by Steven Lindblom. Houghton Mifflin, 1991. Cover photo © 1991 by George Hall. Reproduced by permission of Houghton Mifflin Company.

LISANDRELLI, ELAINE SLIVINSKI. Lisandrelli, Elaine Slivinski, photograph. Prestwood Studios. Reproduced by permission of Elaine Slivinski Lisandrelli.

MacDONALD, MARGARET READ. Jacket of *Slop! A Welsh Folktale,* retold by Margaret Read McDonald. Fulcrum Publishing, 1997. Reproduced by permission. / MacDonald, Margaret Read, photograph. Reproduced by permission of Margaret Read MacDonald.

MATHIEU, JOSEPH P. Mathieu, Joe, illustrator. From an illustration in *Brewster's Courage,* by Deborah Kovacs. Simon & Schuster Books for Young Readers, 1992. Illustrations © 1992 by Joe Mathieu. Reproduced by permission of Simon & Schuster Books for Young Readers, a division of Simon & Schuster, Inc. / Mathieu, Joseph P., photograph by Joe M. Mathieu. Reproduced by permission of Joseph P. Mathieu.

McDEVITT, JACK. McDevitt, Jack, photograph. Miller Photography. Reproduced by permission of Jack McDevitt.

McGUIRE, LESLIE. Cover of *Anastasia, Czarina or Fake?* by Leslie McGuire. Greenhaven Press, Inc., 1989. Reproduced by permission.

MEAD, ALICE. Young, Ed, illustrator. From a jacket of *Adem's Cross,* by Alice Mead. Farrar, Straus, Giroux, 1996. Jacket illustration © 1996 by Ed Young. Reproduced by permission of Farrar, Straus and Giroux, Inc. / Mead, Alice, photograph. Reproduced by permission of Alice Mead.

MOLONEY, JAMES. Moloney, James, photograph. Reproduced by permission of James Moloney.

MUNSINGER, LYNN. Munsinger, Lynn, illustrator. From an illustration in *Underwear!* by Mary Elise Monsell. Albert Whitman & Company, 1988. Illustrations © 1988 by Lynn Munsinger. Reproduced by permission. / Munsinger, Lynn, illustrator. From an illustration in *Hugh Pine and Something Else,* by Janwillem van de Wetering. Houghton Mifflin, 1989. Illustrations © 1989 by Lynn Munsinger. Reproduced by permission of Houghton Mifflin Company. / Munsinger, Lynn, illustrator. From an illustration in *Three Cheers for Tacky,* by Helen Lester. Houghton Mifflin, 1994. Text © 1994 by Helen Lester. Illustrations © 1994 by Lynn Munsinger. Reproduced by permission of Houghton Mifflin Company / Munsinger, Lynn, illustrator. From an illustration in *Princess Penelope's Parrot,* by Helen Lester. Houghton Mifflin, 1996. Illustrations © 1996 by Lynn Munsinger. Reproduced by permission of Houghton Mifflin Company.

PARTON, DOLLY. Sutton, Judith, illustrator. From an illustration in *Coat of Many Colors,* by Dolly Parton. HarperTrophy, 1994. Text © 1994 by Dolly Parton Enterprises. Illustrations © 1994 by Judith Sutton and Byron Preiss Visual. Reproduced by permission of HarperCollins Publishers, Inc. / Parton, Dolly, photograph. © Ken Settle. Reproduced by permission.

POE, TY. Poe, Ty, photograph by Misty Poe. Reproduced by permission of Ty Poe.

RATHMANN, PEGGY. Rathmann, Peggy, illustrator. From an illustration in *Good Night Gorilla,* by Peggy Rathmann. G. P. Putnam's Sons, 1994. Text and illustrations © 1994 by Peggy Rathmann. Reproduced by permission. / Rathmann, Peggy, illustrator. From an illustration in *Officer Buckle and Gloria,* by Peggy Rathmann. G. P. Putnam's Sons, 1995. Illustrations © 1995 by Peggy Rathmann. Reproduced by permission. / Rathmann, Peggy, photograph. Reproduced by permission of Peggy Rathmann.

ROBBINS, KEN. Robbins, Ken, photographer. From a jacket of *Make Me A Peanut Butter Sandwich and a Glass of Milk,* by Ken Robbins. Copyright 1992 by Ken Robbins. Reprinted by permission of Scholastic Inc. / Robbins, Ken, photographer. From a photograph in *Rodeo,* by Ken Robbins. Henry Holt and Company, 1996. Photographs © 1996 by Ken Robbins. Reproduced by permission. / Robbins, Ken, photograph. Reproduced by permission of Ken Robbins.

ROJANY, LISA. Rojany, Lisa, photograph. Reproduced by permission of Lisa Rojany.

ROOT, PHYLLIS. Speidel, Sandra, illustrator. From an illustration in *Coyote and the Magic Words,* by Phyllis Root. Lothrop, Lee & Shepard, 1993. Illustrations © 1993 by Sandra Speidel. Reproduced by permission of Lothrop, Lee & Shepard Books, a division of William Morrow and Company, Inc. / Cornell, Laura, illustrator. From an illustration in *Contrary Bear,* by Phyllis Root. Laura Geringer Books, 1996. Illustrations © 1996 by Laura Cornell. Reproduced by permission of HarperCollins Publishers, Inc. / O'Malley, Kevin, illustrator. From an illustration in *Rosie's Fiddle,* by Phyllis Root. Lothrop, Lee & Shepard Books, 1997. Text © 1997 by Phyllis Root. Illustrations © 1997 by Kevin O'Malley. Reproduced by permission of Lothrop, Lee & Shepard Books, a division of William Morrow and Company, Inc.

RORBY, GINNY. Lewin, Ted, illustrator. From a jacket of *Dolphin Sky,* by Ginny Rorby. G. P. Putnam's Sons, 1996. Jacket art © 1996 by Ted Lewin. Reproduced by permission. / Rorby, Ginny, photograph by Joan Emm. Reproduced by permission.

SANDIN, JOAN. Sandin, Joan, illustrator. From a jacket of *Snowshoe Thompson,* by Nancy Smiler Levinson. HarperCollins, 1992. Jacket art © 1992 by Joan Sandin. Reproduced by permission of HarperCollins Publishers, Inc.

SCHMIDT, KAREN LEE. Schmidt, Karen Lee, illustrator. From an illustration in *A Nickel Buys a Rhyme,* by Alan Benjamin. Morrow Junior Books, 1993. Illustrations © 1993 by Karen Lee Schmidt. Reproduced by permission of Morrow Junior Books, a division of William Morrow and Company, Inc. / Schmidt, Karen Lee, illustrator. From an illustration in *Going to the Zoo,* by Ron Paxton. Morrow Junior Books, 1996. Illustrations © 1996 by Karen Lee Schmidt. Reproduced by permission of Morrow Junior Books, a division of William Morrow and Company, Inc. / Schmidt, Karen Lee, photograph. Reproduced by permission of Karen Lee Schmidt.

SCOTT, ANN HERBERT. Lewin, Ted, illustrator. From an illustration in *Cowboy Country,* by Ann Herbert Scott. Clarion Books, 1993. Text © 1993 by Ann Herbert Scott. Illustrations © 1993 by Ted Lewin. Reproduced by permission of Houghton Mifflin Company. / Coalson, Glo, illustrator. From an illustration in *Brave as a Mountain Lion,* by Ann Herbert Scott. Clarion Books, 1996. Illustrations © 1996 by Glo Coalson. Reproduced by permission of Houghton Mifflin Company. / Scott, Ann Herbert, photograph. Reproduced by permission of Ann Herbert Scott.

SHANNON, GEORGE. McLean, Meg, illustrator. From an illustration in *Laughing All the Way,* by George Shannon. Houghton Mifflin, 1992. Text © 1992 by George Shannon. Illustrations © 1992 by Meg McLean. Reproduced by permission of Houghton Mifflin Company. / Aruego, Jose, and Ariane Dewey, illustrators. From an illustration in *April Showers,* by George Shannon. Greenwillow Books, 1995. Text © 1995 by George Shannon. Illustrations © 1995 by Jose Aruego and Ariane Dewey. Reproduced by permission of Greenwillow Books, a division of William Morrow and Company, Inc. / Zeldis, Malcah, illustrator. From an illustration in *Spring: A Haiku Story,* by George Shannon. Greenwillow Books, 1996. Illustrations © 1996 by Malcah Zeldis. Reproduced by permission of Greenwillow Books, a division of William Morrow and Company, Inc. / Shannon, George, photograph by David Holter. Reproduced by permission of George Shannon.

SHWARTZ, SUSAN. Goodfellow, Peter, illustrator. From a cover of *Empire of the Eagle,* by Susan Shwartz and Andre Norton. Tor Books, 1993. Reproduced by permission. / Shwartz, Susan, photograph. Bachrach Photo Studios. Reproduced by permission of Susan Shwartz.

SMITH-REX, SUSAN J. Smith-Rex, Susan J., photograph. Reproduced by permission of Susan J. Smith-Rex.

SPUDVILAS, ANNE. Spudvilas, Anne, photograph. Reproduced by permission of Anne Spudvilas.

STEELE, MARY. Steele, Mary, photograph. Reproduced by permission of Mary Steele.

STEVENS, DIANE. Stevens, Diane, photograph. Reproduced by permission of Diane Stevens.

SWANSON, HELEN M. *"Mother of the Groom,"* painting of Helen M. Swanson by Jean London. Reproduced by permission of Helen M. Swanson.

SZYDLOWSKI, MARY VIGLIANTE. Szydlowski, Mary Vigliante, photograph. Reproduced by permission of Mary Vigliante Szydlowski.

TATE, ELEANORA E. Cover of *Front Porch Stories at the One-Room School,* by Eleanora E. Tate. Yearling Books, 1992. Reproduced by permission of Yearling Books, a division of Bantam Doubleday Dell Publishing Group, Inc. / Griffith, Gershom, illustrator. From a cover of *A Blessing in Disguise,* by Eleanora E. Tate. Yearling Books, 1996. Reproduced by permission of Yearling Books, a division of Bantam Doubleday Dell Publishing Group, Inc.

TIEGREEN, ALAN. Tiegreen, Alan, illustrator. From a jacket of *Six Sick Sheep: 101 Tongue Twisters,* by George Shannon. Morrow Junior Books, 1993. Jacket illustration © 1993 by Alan Tiegreen. / Tiegreen, Alan, illustrator. From a jacket of *Why Did the Chicken Cross the Road? And Other Riddles Old and New,* by Joanna Cole and Stephanie Calmenson. Morrow Junior Books, 1994. Jacket illustration © 1994 by Alan Tiegreen. Reproduced by permission of Morrow Junior Books, a division of William Morrow and Company, Inc.

TURNER, MEGAN WHALEN. Smith, Jos. A., illustrator. From a jacket of *Instead of Three Wishes,* by Megan Whalen Turner. Greenwillow Books, 1995. Jacket art © 1995 by Jos. A. Smith. Reproduced by permission of Greenwillow Books, a division of William Morrow and Company, Inc. / Gaffney-Kessell, Walter, illustrator. From a jacket of *The Thief,* by Megan Whalen Turner. Greenwillow Books, 1996. Jacket art © 1996 by Walter Gaffney-Kessell. Reproduced by permission Greenwillow Books, a division of William Morrow and Company, Inc.

TWEIT, SUSAN J. Shattil, Wendy, photographer. From a jacket of *City Foxes,* by Susan J. Tweit. Denver Museum of Natural History/Alaska Northwest Books, 1997. Reproduced by permission of Wendy Shattil. / Tweit, Susan J., photograph by Pamela Porter. Reproduced by permission.

VAIL, RACHEL. Raymond, Larry, illustrator. From a jacket of *Wonder,* by Rachel Vail. Orchard Books, 1991. Jacket illustration copyright © 1991 by Larry Raymond. Reproduced by permission of the publisher, Orchard Books, New York. / Johnson, Doug, illustrator. From a jacket of *Do-Over,* by Rachel Vail. Orchard Books, 1992. Jacket painting copyright © 1992 by Doug Johnson. Reproduced by permission. / Conrad, Sarah, illustrator. From a jacket of *Daring to Be Abigail,* by Rachel Vail. Orchard Books, 1996. Jacket painting copyright © 1996 by Sarah Conrad. Reproduced by permission. / Vail, Rachel, photograph by Bill Harris.

VICKERS, SHEENA. Vickers, Sheena, photograph. Reproduced by permission of Sheena Vickers.

VOGT, GREGORY L. Aldrin, Edwin E. Jr., photograph by Neil A. Armstrong. NASA.

WALDMAN, NEIL. Waldman, Neil, illustrator. From a jacket of *Nessa's Story,* by Nancy Luenn. Atheneum, 1994. Jacket illustration copyright © 1994 by Neil Waldman. Reproduced by permission of Atheneum Publishers, a division of Simon & Schuster, Inc. / Waldman, Neil, illustrator. From an illustration in *Quetzal: Sacred Bird of the Cloud Forest,* by Dorothy Hinshaw Patent. Morrow Junior Books, 1996. Illustrations © 1996 by Neil Waldman. Reproduced by permission of Morrow Junior Books, a division of William Morrow and Company, Inc. / Waldman, Neil, illustrator. From an illustration in *Next Year in Jerusalem: 3000 Years of Jewish Stories,* by Howard Schwartz. Viking, 1996. Illustrations © Neil Waldman, 1996. Reproduced by permission of Viking, a division of Penguin USA. / Waldman, Neil, illustrator. From an illustration in *The Never-Ending Greenness,* by Neil Waldman. Morrow Junior Books, 1997. Copyright © 1997 by Neil Waldman. Reproduced by permission of Morrow Junior Books, a division of William Morrow and Company, Inc. / Waldman, Neil, photograph. Reproduced by permission of Neil Waldman.

WASSERSTEIN, WENDY. Jackness, Andrew, illustrator. From an illustration in *Pamela's First Musical,* by Wendy Wasserstein. Hyperion, 1996. Text © 1996 by Wendy Wasserstein. Illustrations © 1996 by Andrew Jackness. Reproduced by permission. / Wasserstein, Wendy, photograph. AP/Wide World Photos. Reproduced by permission.

WHYTE, MARY. Whyte, Mary, photograph. Reproduced by permission of Mary Whyte.

WOODSON, JACQUELINE. Dillon, Leo and Diane Dillon, illustrators. From a cover of *Last Summer with Maizon,* by Jacqueline Woodson. Yearling Books, 1992. Reproduced by permission of Yearling Books, a division of Bantam Doubleday Dell Publishing Group, Inc. / Cover of *The Dear One,* by Jacqueline Woodson. Laurel-Leaf Books, 1993. Reproduced by permission of Bantam Books, a division of Bantam Doubleday Dell Publishing Group, Inc. / Dillon, Leo and Diane Dillon, illustrators. From a cover of *Maizon at Blue Hill,* by Jacqueline Woodson. Yearling Books, 1994. Cover illustration © 1989 by Leo and Diane Dillon. Reproduced by permission of Yearling Books, a division of Bantam Doubleday Dell Publishing Group, Inc. / Cover of *I Hadn't Meant To Tell You This,* by Jacqueline Woodson. Laurel-Leaf Books, 1995. Reproduced by permission of Bantam Books, a division of Bantam Doubleday Dell Publishing Group, Inc.

something about the author®

ANASTASIO, Dina 1941-

■ Personal

First name is pronounced *Die*-nah; born October 9, 1941, in Des Moines, IA; daughter of William H. Brown (a sportscaster) and Jean (a writer; maiden name, Stout) Kinney; married Ernest J. Anastasio (a director of research), June 30, 1964 (divorced); children: Kristine, Trey. *Education:* Rutgers University, B.A., 1973.

■ Career

Author, 1971—; Sesame Street Publications, New York City, editor of *Sesame Street* Magazine, 1980-84. *Member:* Authors Guild.

■ Writings

FOR CHILDREN

My Own Book, Price, Stern (Los Angeles), 1975.

(Editor) *Who Puts the Care in Health Care?,* illustrated by John Freeman, Random House (New York City), 1976.

(Editor) *Who Puts the Plane in the Air?,* illustrated by John Freeman, Random House, 1976.

My Secret Book, Price, Stern, 1977.

My Special Book, Price, Stern, 1978.

A Question of Time, illustrated by Dale Payson, Dutton (New York City), 1978.

Conversational Kickers, Price, Stern, 1979.

My Private Book, Price, Stern, 1979.

My Personal Book, Price, Stern, 1980.

My Own Book, Number Six, Price, Stern, 1981.

My School Book, Price, Stern, 1981.

My Wish Book, Price, Stern, 1981.

My Family Book, Price, Stern, 1981.

Count All the Way to Sesame Street, illustrated by Richard Brown, Western Publishing (New York City), 1985, published as *Sesame Street Counting Book,* 1985.

Big Bird Can Share, illustrated by Tom Leigh, Western Publishing with Children's Television Workshop (New York City), 1985.

The Romper Room Book of 1, 2, 3s, illustrated by Nancy Stevenson, Doubleday (New York City), 1985.

The Romper Room Book of ABCs, illustrated by Nancy Stevenson, Doubleday, 1985.

The Romper Room Book of Colors, illustrated by A. O. Williams, Doubleday, 1985.

The Romper Room Book of Shapes, illustrated by A. O. Williams, Doubleday, 1985.

Baby Piggy and Giant Bubble, illustrated by Tom Cooke, Muppet Press (New York City), 1986.

The Best Nickname, illustrated by Tom Garcia, Golden Book (New York City), 1986.

The Fisher-Price Picture Dictionary, illustrated by Dick Codor and Carol Bouman, Marvel Books (New York City), 1987.

(Compiler and adapter) *Bedtime Stories,* illustrated by Lucinda McQueen, Grosset & Dunlap (New York City), 1987.

Pass the Peas, Please: A Book of Manners, illustrated by Katy Keck Arnsteen, Warner Books (New York City), 1988.

Roger Goes to the Doctor, illustrated by Cathy Beylon, Marvel Books, 1988.

(Adapter) *Walt Disney's Mickey and the Beanstalk*,
illustrated by Sharon Ross, Western Publishing,
1988.

(With others) *Cars and Planes, Trucks and Trains:
Featuring Jim Henson's Sesame Street Muppets*,
illustrated by Richard Brown and others, Western
Publishing with Children's Television Workshop,
1989.

Twenty School Mini-Mysteries, illustrated by George
Parkin, Hippo, 1991.

Ghostwriter: Courting Danger and Other Stories, illustrated by Eric Velasquez, Bantam (New York City),
1992.

(Reteller) *Joy to the World: The Story of the First
Christmas*, illustrated by Bettina Paterson, Platt &
Munk (New York City), 1992.

It's about Time, illustrated by Mavis Smith, Grosset &
Dunlap, 1993.

The Teddy Bear Who Couldn't Do Anything, illustrated
by Karen Loccisano, Penguin Books (New York
City), 1993.

*Dolly Dolphin and the Strange New Something: A Book
about Cooperation*, illustrated by William Langley
Studios, Third Story Books (Bridgeport, CT), 1994.

Kissyfur and His Dad (tie-in with television specials),
illustrated by Phil Mendez, Scholastic, Inc. (New
York City), 1994.

Virtual Reality Magician (based on teleplays for the *VR
Troopers* series), Price, Stern, 1994.

Virtual Reality Spy (based on teleplays for the *VR
Troopers* series), Price, Stern, 1994.

The Case of the Glacier Park Swallow, Roberts Rinehart,
1994.

The Case of the Grand Canyon Eagle, Roberts Rinehart,
1994.

(Adapter) *Apollo 13: The Junior Novelization* (based on
the motion picture screenplay by William Broyles,
Jr., Al Reinert, and John Sayles, and the book *Lost
Moon* by Jim Lovell and Jeffrey Kluger), Grosset &
Dunlap, 1995.

Flipper: Junior Novelization (based on the motion
picture screenplay by Alan Shapiro), Price, Stern,
1996.

Dark Side of the Sun, HarperCollins (New York City),
1996.

The Enemy, HarperCollins, 1996.

Pirates, illustrated by Donald Cook, Grosset & Dunlap,
1997.

Fly Trap, illustrated by Jerry Smath, Grosset & Dunlap,
1997.

"WRITE-IT-YOURSELF" SERIES

*Dear Priscilla, I Am Sending You a Pet ... for Your
Birthday*, Price, Stern, 1980.

Everybody's Invited to Dudley's Party Except ... !!,
Price, Stern, 1980.

*Georgina's Two ... for Her Own Good, and Someday
She's Going to Be Very Sorry*, Price, Stern, 1980.

Somebody Kidnapped the Mayor and Hid Her In ... !!,
Price, Stern, 1980.

Watch It Sarah!! The ... Is Right behind You!!, Price,
Stern, 1980.

*Crazy Freddy's in Trouble Again and His Parents Are
Going To ... !!*, Price, Stern, 1981.

Careful Melinda, That Footstep Belongs To ... !!, Price,
Stern, in press.

*Something Weird Is Happening to Matthew, and He's a
Little ... !!*, Price, Stern, in press.

OTHER

Contributor to *Sesame Street Parents Newsletter*, *Parents*, and *Ladies' Home Journal*.

■ Sidelights

Dina Anastasio has written books for children of all
ages, from simple board books for pre-readers to ecological mysteries for teens. In *A Question of Time*, a novel
for children, she focuses on the adjustment problems of
Sydell Stowe, who reluctantly moves with her family
from her beloved New York City to the rural Minnesota
town where her great-grandfather had grown up. Unhappy and isolated in her new environment, she stumbles
on an apparent mystery when she finds a set of antique
dolls in a toy shop and subsequently meets Laura, who
inexplicably resembles one of the dolls. Her investiga-

In this ecological mystery from her series featuring
environmental sleuth Juliet Stone, Dina Anastasio once
again introduces villains who threaten nature by their
self-serving actions. (Cover art by Birgitta Saflund.)

tion of this coincidence leads to a connection between the dolls, the dollmaker, a long-ago murder, and her own family ghosts. Barbara Elleman wrote in *Booklist* that "the mystery-ghost element snags attention, and Syd is a likable heroine." A reviewer in the *Bulletin of the Center for Children's Books* noted, "The fantastic and realistic elements are nicely meshed," and added, "the writing style is capable." A *School Library Journal* critic found the denouement "well handled" and describes the book as "briskly written and plotted."

Anastasio's *The Case of the Grand Canyon Eagle* and *The Case of the Glacier Park Swallow* introduce seventeen-year-old Juliet Stone, an amateur detective and aspiring veterinarian. Mary Harris Veeder commented in *Booklist,* "If Nancy Drew had wanted to be a veterinarian, she'd have been Juliet Stone." In these works, Anastasio tackles ecological mysteries, in which "the settings play prominent roles," according to Sister Bernadette Marie Ondus in *Kliatt.* In *The Case of the Grand Canyon,* Juliet must identify the culprit who has stolen an eagle's eggs, while in *The Case of the Glacier Park Swallow,* Juliet attempts to determine the person responsible for disturbing the behavior of certain bird species. Cheryl Cufari observed in *School Library Journal* that each of the mysteries "has a degree of suspense and adventure that will keep readers intrigued." Ondus stated that Juliet's "excursions into nature and her encounters with the denizens of the wild, animal and human, are the heart of the stories."

■ Works Cited

Cufari, Cheryl, review of *The Case of the Glacier Park Swallow* and *The Case of the Grand Canyon Eagle, School Library Journal,* October, 1994, p. 118.

Elleman, Barbara, review of *A Question of Time, Booklist,* October 1, 1978, p. 287.

Ondus, Sister Bernadette Marie, review of *The Case of the Grand Canyon Eagle* and *The Case of the Glacier Park Swallow, Kliatt,* November, 1994, p. 4.

Review of *A Question of Time, Bulletin of the Center for Children's Books,* March, 1979, p. 109.

Review of *A Question of Time, School Library Journal,* December, 1978, p. 68.

Veeder, Mary Harris, review of *The Case of the Glacier Park Swallow, Booklist,* December 1, 1994, p. 669.

■ For More Information See

PERIODICALS

Booklist, July 1, 1977, p. 1649; May 15, 1988, pp. 1601-602.

Books for Keeps, November, 1991, p. 10.

Horn Book Guide, spring, 1993, p. 88; fall, 1993, p. 357.

Kirkus Reviews, November 15, 1978, p. 1246.

Publishers Weekly, July 3, 1978, p. 65; April 25, 1986, p. 79; September 7, 1992, p. 67; March 29, 1993, p. 57.

School Library Journal, April, 1986, pp. 67-68; March, 1988, p. 180.*

ATTEMA, Martha 1949-

■ Personal

Born December 22, 1949, in Menaldum, the Netherlands; immigrated to Canada, 1981; daughter of Wilke (a farmer) and Romkje (a homemaker; maiden name, Noordenbos) Hoogterp; married Albert Attema; children: Romkje, Sjoerd, Rikst. *Education:* Attended a teacher's college in the Netherlands, 1966-70; Laurentian University, B.A., 1986, B.Ed., 1989. *Hobbies and other interests:* Sewing clothes, crafts. "My future goal is to obtain a master's degree in children's literature from Simmons College in Boston."

■ Addresses

Home—376 Voyer Rd., Corbeil, Ontario, Canada P0H 1K0. *Electronic mail*—martatte @ ViaNet.on.ca.

■ Career

Kindergarten teacher in Giekerk, the Netherlands, 1969-73; teacher of kindergarten and grade one in North Bay, Ontario, 1987—. *Member:* Canadian Society of Children's Authors, Illustrators, and Publishers; The

MARTHA ATTEMA

Writers' Union of Canada, North Bay Children's Writers Group; North Bay Writers Club.

■ Awards, Honors

Blue Heron Award for young adults, 1996, and shortlist, Geoffrey Bilson Award for Historical Fiction, Canadian Children's Book Centre, 1996, both for *A Time to Choose.*

■ Writings

The Unhappy Pinetree (picture book), privately printed, 1992.
A Time to Choose (young adult historical novel), Orca Book Publishers (Victoria, British Columbia), 1995.
A Light in the Dunes (young adult novel), Orca, 1997.

Contributor to periodicals.

■ Work in Progress

Research on the Germanic people in Northern Europe during prehistoric times.

■ Sidelights

Martha Attema told *SATA:* "Writing has always been part of my life. In my teenage years I wrote poetry to sort out the world and my personal problems and to find an outlet. During those years I began to envy my grandfather, who was a published playwright and poet. When I became a teacher and later a mother, I wrote stories, poems, and puppet plays for my students and for my own children. My writing was all in the Frisian language. Friesland is one of the northern provinces in the Netherlands. The Frisians are a proud and stubborn people who have their own language (not a dialect).

"After I moved to Canada with my family in 1981, I continued to write in my mother tongue. Several years later I felt myself between languages. I didn't get enough exposure to the Frisian language, and I wasn't proficient enough in English to feel comfortable writing stories and poems in this language. A creative writing course at the local college inspired me. The instructor and my other classmates gave me hope and encouraged me to market my stories.

"I knew what I wanted to write about. After I came to Canada, I decided to share some of my Frisian background and culture with young people here. My first book, *Is That You, Sinterklaas?,* is a novel for middle graders about the legend and traditions surrounding Saint Nicholas. To this day, I haven't been able to publish this story.

"*A Time to Choose* is a young adult historical novel, based on facts and stories from survivors of World War II. I am pleased that I was able to preserve some of the stories from a generation of people who will not be here much longer to tell their own stories. It gives me great satisfaction that *A Time to Choose* is a contribution to

the evidence that this war was real. I am glad to be able to tell young people not to forget this war or any other war, that in every war the conflicts are not just between the good and bad guys, that war is much more complex and conflicts occur within families and among friends.

"The Frisian language is a rich language, full of sagas, legends, and folktales. In my young adult novel *A Light in the Dunes* I have used an old legend from one of the islands off the coast of Friesland and have woven this legend through a contemporary story of a young girl who is unhappy about the fact that she was named after the witch in the legend. I owed our youngest daughter this story, for she was also named after the witch in the legend.

"In my future writing I hope to preserve more history, folktales, and legends by giving these tales and facts new life in young adult novels and picture books. Besides writing, I enjoy research and reading. I collect folktales and legends from Friesland and I love to read about the history of the area where I grew up. As a teacher of grade one, I'm exposed to many excellent picture books. By sharing these picture books as well as my own stories and poems, I hope to foster a love for reading and writing in my students.

"I never dreamed that I would actually become a published author. I always thought the language would be a major handicap and a drawback. Now that I have become an author, I encourage young people never to give up their dreams, but to be determined and try hard to fulfill them."

■ For More Information See

PERIODICALS
Quill and Quire, January, 1996, p. 369.

* * *

AWDRY, Wilbert Vere 1911-1997

OBITUARY NOTICE—See index for *SATA* sketch: Born in June, 1911, at Ampfield, near Romsey, England; died March 21, 1997, in Stroud, Gloucestershire, England. Vicar in the Church of England and author of children's books. Awdry has been hailed as an English institution for creating the Railway Series of picture books in which he develops an entire folklore and typography while celebrating the age of the steam engine. The stories are set on Awdry's island of Sodor, a fictional setting in the Irish Sea between Barrow-in-Furness and the Isle of Man, and characteristically feature anthropomorphic trains and buses with distinctive personalities and universal attitudes and behaviors. Awdry is perhaps best known as the creator of Thomas the Tank Engine, a little train who reforms after his impatience and playfulness cause a series of accidents, becomes a Very Useful Engine, and receives his own branch line as a reward. Throughout the series, Awdry introduces young readers to several other characters, engines and buses in a variety of hues who learn their lessons after similar instances of pride, insolence, laziness, and irresponsibility. *Thomas the Tank Engine* and related works became popular in the United States in 1989, when PBS created an animated television series based on Awdry's work. Several *Thomas* characters were also licensed for merchandise. The series won an Emmy Award and was one of PBS's most popular children's shows. Awdry's son, Christopher (for whom the stories were originally written), took over much of the work on the Railway books in 1972 when Awdry retired. The last book was *Thomas' Christmas Party* in 1984. Awdry was honored with the Order of the British Empire in 1996.

OBITUARIES AND OTHER SOURCES:

BOOKS

Children's Literature Review, Vol. 23, Gale Research, 1991, pp. 1-7.
Twentieth-Century Children's Writers, Fourth Edition, St. James Press, 1995, pp. 46-48.

PERIODICALS

Books for Keeps, May, 1997, p. 14.
Chicago Tribune, March 24, 1997, sec. 4, p. 7.
Los Angeles Times, March 23, 1997, p. B3.
New York Times, March 23, 1997, p. 46.
Washington Post, March 23, 1997, p. B6.

B

J. A. BENNER

BENNER, J(udith) A(nn) 1942-

■ Personal

Born August 8, 1942, in Herrin, IL; daughter of Herbert, Jr. (an United States Air Force warrant officer) and Dorothy (an accountant in the federal civil service; maiden name, Stewart) Benner. *Education:* San Antonio College, A.A., 1963; Southwest Texas State College (now Southwest Texas State University), B.A., 1965; Trinity University, San Antonio, TX, M.A., 1967; Texas Christian University, Ph.D., 1975. *Hobbies and other interests:* Reading, walking, music, movies, jigsaw puzzles.

■ Addresses

Home—San Antonio, TX. *Office*—Bethesda Christian Institute, 2210 Basse Rd., San Antonio, TX 78213.

■ Career

Trinity University Press, San Antonio, TX, editorial assistant, 1967-68; Texas Christian University, Fort Worth, instructor at Evening College, 1972-74; Bethesda Christian Institute, San Antonio, instructor, 1976-81; *Heritage* magazine, Duncan, OK, editor, 1981-84; *Seventh Trumpet* magazine, San Antonio, editor, 1984—; Bethesda Christian Institute, instructor, 1985-96, interim librarian, 1995, publications secretary, 1996—. *Member:* Sigma Tau Sigma, Beta Phi Gamma, Pi Gamma Mu, Alpha Chi, Phi Alpha Theta.

■ Awards, Honors

Award for best historical publication of 1983, local history division, Texas Historical Commission, 1983, for *Sul Ross;* Book Publishers of Texas Award, Texas Institute of Letters, 1996, for *Uncle Comanche.*

■ Writings

(With George H. Paschal, Jr.) *One Hundred Years of Challenge and Change: A History of the Synod of Texas of the United Presbyterian Church in the U.S.A.,* Trinity University Press (San Antonio, TX), 1968.

Fraudulent Finance: Counterfeiting and the Confederate States, 1861-1865, Hill Junior College Press (Hillsboro, TX), 1970.

Lone Star Rebel (young adult novel), illustrated with woodcuts by R. B. Dance, John F. Blair (Winston-Salem, NC), 1971.

Sul Ross: Soldier, Statesman, Educator, Texas A&M University Press (College Station), 1983.

Uncle Comanche (young adult novel), Texas Christian University Press (Fort Worth), 1996.

Contributor to books, including *Ten More Texans in Gray,* edited by W. C. Nunn, Hill Junior College Press, 1980, and a new *Handbook of Texas.* Contributor to periodicals, including *Military History of Texas and the Southwest.*

■ Work in Progress

Two sequels to *Uncle Comanche;* a story of a white boy raised by Indians; a story of the "Reservation War" in Texas; a story about the Third Crusade; editing Civil War letters; research on the Trojan legends of the Celts.

■ Sidelights

J. A. Benner told *SATA:* "I loved books and stories even before I learned to read, and then I read everything I could get my hands on, especially history, horse, and adventure stories. In middle school I started writing western stories and poetry, although I didn't really become serious about being a writer until I took journalism in high school. At the same time, I became interested in the research and writing of history, and over the years I have tried to combine the two interests. My book publishing career started in 1968 when I coauthored a book with a blind professor. (My book writing career had begun when I was sixteen and wrote my first but never published novel, a Civil War western).

"While working on my master's degree, I ran across a mention of counterfeiting and the Confederacy that aroused my curiosity. There was no detailed study of the subject available, although it was a serious problem during the Civil War. I made it my thesis topic, and in 1970 Hill Junior College Press published my book on counterfeiting.

"About the same time I became fascinated with the life of a popular nineteenth-century Texan, Lawrence Sullivan 'Sul' Ross—Indian fighter and friend, ranger, Confederate general, peace officer, constitutional convention delegate, state legislator, governor, and college president. As with the case of counterfeiting, here was a subject worthy of a detailed study but lacking one. I began serious research on Ross before I entered Texas Christian University to work on my Ph.D.

"During this time I combined my background knowledge on counterfeiting and Ross to write my first published novel for young people, *Lone Star Rebel.* It is the story of a fourteen-year-old Texas boy who leaves home during the Civil War to join Sul Ross's Sixth Texas Cavalry and helps to bring a band of counterfeiters to justice. I had a lot of fun writing this book, particularly as I had vowed in high school to write a book someday with guns and horses in it. It turned out the dogs were in somewhat short supply, but there were plenty of guns, and my own registered Galiceno, Capitan, appeared in it as the young hero's mustang pony. A lot of the fictional Bugler's antics were those pulled by Capitan in the years when I rode almost every day. *Lone Star Rebel* is out of print now but still selling nicely, I

understand, on the rare book market. Someday I hope to write the sequel to *Lone Star Rebel* which brings Rob and Bugler safely home at the end of the war.

"At Texas Christian University my major professor's retirement forced me to limit my projected biography of Ross to his military career. After receiving my Ph.D. I went into teaching, and in 1979 the Association of Former Students of Texas A&M University gave me a grant to complete my biography of Ross. It was published in 1983 and won the Texas Historical Commission Award for best historical publication of that year in the local history division.

"My research on Ross's relationship to the Indian tribes here in Texas opened up a whole new world of information on little known Texas/Indian affairs. For example, as a young ranger captain in 1860, Ross was threatened with lynching by a lawless white element because he was an 'Indian-lover.' (Ross's father had been an Indian agent and Ross had more or less grown up among the friendly reservation tribes.) My second young adult novel, *Uncle Comanche,* grew out of this research and the new material about Ross's childhood that came to light after my adult biography *Sul Ross* was published.

"At the same time I wanted to explore the complex white/Indian relations on the pre-Civil War Texas frontier, so in my mind *Uncle Comanche* was only the first of what I hoped would be a series of books on the subject. I had at least four others in mind. The immediate sequel relates an adventure with Sul's Comanche friend Runs Fast. The next book completes the Sul/Runs Fast trilogy and chronicles the deteriorating white/Comanche relations of the time. It is a story of friends from two different worlds wanting to understand each other and yet being pulled apart by events over which they have no control.

"When I write a novel, the important scenes come to me first. (In *Uncle Comanche,* the first scene I 'saw' was Sul riding slung over Sergeant Mason's saddle saying, 'I think I'm going to puke.') I write these scenes down and put them in a ring binder along with any notes that come to mind in the order in which I think they will appear in the story. The ring binder makes it easy to move the pages around and add to them. Then I join the major scenes with notes and ideas, although these sometimes change during the writing process.

"What really fascinates me is the way the characters interact, sometimes seemingly on their own, and often change the direction of the story itself. What also interests me is the way that created characters have of developing a life of their own. Hanse Mason was the hard-bitten sergeant who gave the young hero of *Lone Star Rebel* a hard time and, later, friendship. In *Uncle Comanche* he developed into the boyhood mentor of Sul Ross, and now I am doing research for a novel that is Hanse's own story and chronicles his life with the Comanches. There's a lot of my late father, a career military man, in Sergeant Mason.

"I have several other history monographs for which I am doing research, and I would certainly like to continue writing historical novels for middle school students. One of the reasons I chose to write for this age group was that I wished to avoid the adult themes of so many modern novels. However, I do have a historical novel for adults rolling around in my mind, and perhaps someday I will actually have a chance to write it."

■ For More Information See

PERIODICALS

American Historical Review, October, 1984, p. 1162.
Fort Worth Star-Telegram, May 25, 1997, p. D-8.
Library Journal, May 15, 1972, p. 1910.
Review of Texas Books, summer, 1996.
Voice of Youth Advocates, October, 1996, p. 205.

* * *

BENNETT, Penelope 1938-

■ Personal

Born September 22, 1938, in London, England; daughter of Christopher Dillon (an actor) and Margaret Upton (a musician and painter; maiden name, Slack) Bennett. *Education:* Attended University of Leeds, Goldsmith's College, London, and Putney College of Art. *Politics:* "Liberal Democrat—Labour." *Religion:* "Eclectic." *Hobbies and other interests:* "Roof gardening, cooking, slow cycling, seeing snow."

■ Addresses

Home and office—41 Sydney St., London SW3 6PX, England.

■ Career

Writer. Potter. Volunteer for horticultural therapy. *Member:* PEN, Society of Authors, Royal Society of Literature.

■ Awards, Honors

PEN short story award.

■ Writings

An Endangered Happiness (adult novella and stories), Hamish Hamilton (London, England), 1990.
Town Parrot, illustrated by Sue Heap, Walker (London), 1994, Candlewick Press, 1995.

Contributor to magazines, including *Atlantic Monthly, Mademoiselle, New Mexico Quarterly, Financial Times, Contemporary Review, Encounter, Harpers,* and *Queen.*

■ Work in Progress

Two children's books, one about two umbrellas; adult articles and short stories; research for children's books

PENELOPE BENNETT

about rain and wormeries; research in France on truffles.

■ Sidelights

Penelope Bennett told *SATA:* "I should like to convey enthusiasm and excitement to children, concerning even the smallest things, from watching a potato sprouting to counting the different types of rain. I would prefer to write this in a lyrical way. I greatly enjoyed being a potter, but clay couldn't say everything I wanted to say. Instead of potting, I now make bread, which is a form of edible pottery.

"My advice to aspiring writers is: never give up. If I need to be refreshed—to return to a particular sort of sanity and loveliness, I reread *Alice in Wonderland,* Walter de la Mare, Beatrix Potter, A. A. Milne, or Hans Christian Andersen. Just a few hours in this world of children's books restores me."

■ For More Information See

PERIODICALS

Books, July, 1990, p. 12.
Horn Book Guide, fall, 1995, p. 354.
School Librarian, February, 1995, p. 25.
School Library Journal, June, 1995, p. 98.
Times Literary Supplement, August 17, 1990, p. 868.

BETTS, James
See HAYNES, Betsy

*   *   *

BLACK, MaryAnn
See EASLEY, MaryAnn

*   *   *

BLAKEY, Nancy 1955-

■ Personal

Born October 12, 1955, in Moscow, ID; daughter of Charles D. (a potato broker) and Betty (a homemaker; maiden name, Burns) Holt; married Gregory B. Blakey (an owner of a fish processing company), August 12, 1976; children: Jenna, Ben, Daniel, Nick. *Education:* Attended Washington State University, 1974-75, and the University of Washington, Seattle, 1984-86. *Politics:* "Independent (left leaning)." *Religion:* Episcopalian. *Hobbies and other interests:* Hiking, skiing, golf, kayaking, "anything that keeps you moving, outdoors."

■ Addresses

Home and office—15890 Euclid Ave., Bainbridge Island, WA 98110.

■ Career

Author, journalist, columnist. Worked as able-bodied seaman on ferry boats in and around Seattle, WA, 1974-84. Professional model in Australia and in Seattle, 1978-80. *Member:* Bainbridge Astronomical Association.

■ Writings

The Mudpies Activity Book: Recipes for Invention, illustrated by Melissah Watts, Northwestern Parent Publishing, 1989; reprinted by Tricycle Press (Berkeley, CA), 1994.
More Mudpies: 101 Alternatives to Television, illustrated by Watts, Ten Speed Press/Tricycle Press (Berkeley, CA), 1994.
Lotions, Potions, and Slime: Mudpies and More! illustrated by Watts, Tricycle Press, 1996.

Author of "Mudpies," a column in *Seattle's Child,* also syndicated nationally, 1987—. Contributor to *Reader's Digest.*

■ Work in Progress

Monstercide, about a boy who has trouble with monsters and how he solves his problem; *A Graduate's Guide to Life,* a life skills book for graduating seniors.

NANCY BLAKEY

■ Sidelights

Nancy Blakey told *SATA:* "I was not born a natural writer; that is, I never bowled the teachers over with talent. My essays and papers were stiff with prose, too full of enchanting words I had discovered. No, any seeds of future talent lay in the river of ideas that ran through my head. The ideas would keep me awake at night. They ran headlong and unchecked for as long as I can remember. It was the momentum of these ideas that led me to write science, art, and craft projects. There is nothing else in my background to explain it. I never took an art class in high school or college. I did not consider myself particularly imaginative or creative. Science bored me. I kept the writer inside alive with small writing jobs, but I did not have a clear idea of what was before me.

"In the years that our four children were born, the idea possessed me that I could help our daughter defy the cultural odds stacked against girls. I would raise her to love science. I began to adapt science experiments and projects to tickle the interests of toddlers. With nothing more than the unmeasured energy of four small children and a few ideas, we collected rocks and blew bubbles in winter air. We popped. We fizzed. We soaked chicken bones in vinegar. We measured and planted and took small machines apart. We asked 'What if?' What if we lit twelve candles under the jar instead of one? What if we froze a balloon? What if we took a newly lost tooth and soaked it in vinegar? I was not a scientist. I was often unable to answer the children's questions. I decided to follow their curiosity willingly to the answer. At times it led to nothing more than a mess—a puddle, Jello between fingers, solutions that stank, and broken eggs. Most times we learned something, a germ of something, that we took with us into our lives. We grew to love science.

"This newly born love was instrumental when I applied for a job as a columnist writing science and art activities for children in a regional magazine. The column was called 'Mudpies.' The river of ideas forever chasing me had found a home.

"Trying out projects with four small children restricted my range (so many little pairs of hands and restless energy!) but, in the end, worked in my favor. Most of the activities I wrote about were great fun, but very simple. They were so simple, in fact, that the projects required very little adult supervision. Through this, I discovered that the most successful art and science projects, the ones that children love, that live beyond the time they take to create, were those that surrendered all stages of the activity to the child. The more I interfered or 'helped,' no matter how wonderful the end product, the less interested my children were in doing them. They scattered, refused to participate, sighed and snorted, and declared the project *boring!* The column absorbed these tenets cast by my children. Process was everything. The column evolved. Books were born. Mudpies sprang from a mother, not a professional, and that is where the heart and soul of my writing lies.

"In my books and columns, I want to find the words to convince parents that creativity is vital for children, for all human beings. A well stretched and limber imagination leads to positive risk-taking and fresh discoveries for solving old problems. It leads to larger thoughts and ideas for a better life. There is no room for hopelessness and resignation in imagination. Imagination is a place where possibilities are entertained, possibilities that can change the course of a life, the same possibilities that fostered dreams in a young girl from Idaho that she could become a writer. If it can be imagined, it can be."

■ For More Information See

PERIODICALS

Parents Magazine, April, 1994, p. 184.
Publishers Weekly, March 11, 1996, p. 66.
Small Press, spring, 1994, p. 351.

*   *   *

BLATCHFORD, Claire H. 1944-

■ Personal

Born January 3, 1944; daughter of John I. (a banker) and Nelda A. (an artist) Howell; married Edward W. Blatchford (a headmaster), April 6, 1968; children: Laurel, Christa. *Education:* Bennington College, B.A., 1966; Adelphi University, M.A., 1968; Columbia University, M.A., 1970. *Hobbies and other interests:* Pottery, weaving, tennis, gardening, hiking, canoeing, "tak-

CLAIRE H. BLATCHFORD

ing groups of young people on backpacking trips, studying contemporary young adult literature."

■ Addresses

Home—113 Sam Hill Rd., Guilford, CT 06437.

■ Career

Caritas Day Classes for Deaf Children, Rockville Center, NY, teacher of kindergarten and art, 1970-72; writer, 1972—. Arts and crafts teacher at elementary schools and public libraries, 1980-94; has also worked as a substitute teacher.

■ Writings

Listening: Notes From a Kindergarten Journal, Alexander Graham Bell Association for the Deaf (Washington, DC), 1972.
Yes, I Wear a Hearing Aid, illustrated by Barbara Rothenberg, Lexington School for the Deaf (New York City), 1976.
All Alone (Except for My Dog Friday), David C. Cook (Elgin, IL), 1983.
Down the Path, illustrated by Mike Eagle, Dushkin Publishing (Guilford, CT), 1992.
A Surprise for Reggie, illustrated by Eagle, Dushkin Publishing, 1992.

Shawna's Bit of Blue Sky, illustrated by Eagle, Dushkin
   Publishing, 1992.
Nick's Mission, Lerner Publications (Minneapolis, MN),
   1994.
Full Face, Butte Publishers (OR), 1997.
Many Ways of Hearing, J. Weston Walch (Portland,
   ME), 1997.
Going With the Flow, Carolrhoda (Minneapolis), 1997.

Work represented in anthologies, including *No Walls of
Stone: An Anthology of Literature by Deaf and Hard of
Hearing Writers,* edited by Jill Jepson, Gallaudet University Press (Washington, DC), 1992, and *Of Cabbages
and Kings 2: The Year's Best Magazine Writing for Kids,*
edited by Kimberly Olson Fakih, Bowker (New Providence, NJ), 1992. Contributor of stories and articles to
magazines, including *Spider, Hip, Catholic Digest, Flyf-
isher, Cricket,* and *Better Health.*

■ Work in Progress

A sequel to *Nick's Mission.*

■ Sidelights

Claire H. Blatchford told *SATA:* "I lost my hearing
overnight at the age of six when I had the mumps. My
parents put me back in public school, and I stayed there,
even though I didn't get a hearing aid until I was twelve
(because there was nothing powerful enough). There
were no oral or signing interpreters in those days. No
one took notes for me, and there was no closed
captioning on television or TTYs (telephone typewriters
for the deaf), so I read a lot to keep up with my
classmates. I was also a pretty good bluffer!

"At age eleven I knew I wanted to write, in fact *had* to
write. When I read, and when I wrote, all the hassles of
being deaf were instantly removed. I could understand
what everyone said without having to ask people to look
at me or repeat what they were saying. I could hear
animals, plants, angels, elves, gnomes, and other mysterious creatures speak. Words took me all over the world,
out into space, deep down in the chambers of the heart,
high up in the towers of the mind, forward and
backward in time. They still do. I feel privileged to work
with words and hope the ones I use ring true and call
forth the best in others."

■ For More Information See

PERIODICALS

Booklist, November 15, 1995, p. 559.
School Library Journal, October, 1996, p. 120.

*   *   *

BOHLMEIJER, Arno 1956-

■ Personal

Born May 21, 1956, in the Netherlands; married Marian
van der Haar (died, 1992); children: Rosemyn, Phoebe.

ARNO BOHLMEIJER

Education: Nymegen University, M.A., 1981. *Religion:*
"Universal." *Hobbies and other interests:* Music, dance,
film, photography, psychology, reading, gardening, "but
no time for any."

■ Addresses

Home—208 De Waarden, 7206 GN, Zutphen, Netherlands.

■ Career

Sprengerloo High School, Apeldoorn, Netherlands,
teacher of English and French, 1978-92; freelance
writer, 1993—.

■ Awards, Honors

Charlotte Kohler Award (Netherlands), 1997.

■ Writings

FOR YOUNG PEOPLE

Something Very Sorry, translated into English by the
   author, Houghton Mifflin (Boston, MA), 1996.

OTHER

The Intruder: A Jungian Study of Henry James, Encounter (London), 1987.

Also author of a dozen novels, both for adults and for children, appearing in various European languages.

■ Work in Progress

New works both in Dutch and English, including a sequel to *Something Very Sorry.*

■ Sidelights

Dutch author Arno Bohlmeijer has penned several novels that have been published in his native land as well as in other European countries. Due to his studies and stays in Great Britain, he was able to translate one of his books, a novel for middle-graders entitled *Something Very Sorry,* for publication in English-speaking countries in 1996.

Something Very Sorry is a true story. Bohlmeijer tells it through the eyes of his daughter Rosemyn, who was nine years old when her entire family was involved in an automobile accident. Bohlmeijer suffered severe injuries, Rosemyn's badly broken arm necessitated a long hospital stay, and Rosemyn's younger sister, Phoebe, suffered brain damage. Her mother lapsed into a coma and eventually died when she was removed from life support. Despite the overwhelming tragedy related by *Something Very Sorry,* however, the book offers hope and encouragement. The doctors and nurses who take care of Rosemyn do a great deal to lift her spirits, and the novel ends with the surviving family members leaving the hospital, determined to rebuild their lives. *School Library Journal* contributor Cheryl Cufari hailed the book as "a poignant, sensitive account of a traumatic family situation," while a *Publishers Weekly* commentator praised "the subtle beauty of the author's prose and its life-affirming message." Bohlmeijer plans to translate many of his other books—for all ages—into English.

Bohlmeijer has commented: "The sudden death of my wife, Marian (thirty-seven), broke my heart. But when a heart breaks, it may open—if you let it, if you're not afraid.

"In my case, it was such an overwhelming fusion of heaven and earth, that I wanted to write about fear and faith, about fighting, surrender and conquest, which has become a profound way of communication—a great joy.

"So to me, writing is a kind of nourishment. It means widening my emotional scope, finding the balance between mind and heart—finding the essentials of life. I love the craft, the literary and psychological tension between form and content, which is necessary to achieve the impossible; convey the unsayable."

■ Works Cited

Cufari, Cheryl, review of *Something Very Sorry, School Library Journal,* July, 1996, p. 82.
Review of *Something Very Sorry, Publishers Weekly,* April 1, 1996, p. 77.

During her hospital stay, nine-year-old Rosemyn tells of the tragic auto accident that has taken the life of her mother and critically injured her sister in this novel based on the Bohlmeijer family's actual experiences.

■ For More Information See

PERIODICALS

Bulletin of the Center for Children's Books, March, 1996, pp. 219-20.
Kirkus Reviews, January, 1996, p. 132.

*   *   *

BRANCH, Muriel Miller 1943-

■ Personal

Born April 10, 1943, in Montclair, NJ; daughter of Frank Adolph and Missouri Walthall Miller; married Willis L. Branch, Sr., 1974; children: Willis, Jr., Kenneth, Chery A., Margaret Lewis, Sonja Evette. *Education:* Virginia State University, B.S., 1964, M.Ed., 1978; additional studies at Appalachian State University, Virginia Commonwealth University, James Madison University, and the University of Virginia. *Religion:* Baptist.

■ Addresses

Home—9315 Radborne Rd., Richmond, VA 23236.

■ Career

Richmond Public Schools, Richmond, VA, library media specialist, 1967—. Maggie L. Walker Historical Foundation, secretary, vice-president, and president. *Member:* National Storytelling Association, Society of Children's Book Writers and Illustrators, Virginia Breast Cancer Foundation, Virginia Historical Society, Virginia Area Chapter Pi Lambda Theta International Honor Society, Virginia Educational Media Association, Richmond Story League.

■ Awards, Honors

Rudolph and Esther Bonsal Award for Teaching Excellence, Greater Richmond Community Foundation, 1991; Virginia Hero, Virginia Heroes Incorporated, 1996; "Children's Book of the Year" citation, Bank Street Child Study Children's Book Committee, 1996, for *The Water Brought Us: The Story of the Gullah-Speaking People;* 1997 Cable Educator of the Year.

■ Writings

(With Dorothy Rice) *Miss Maggie: The Story of Maggie Lena Walker,* Marlborough House, 1984.
(Compiler, with Earlene G. Evans) *Hidden Skeletons and Other Funny Stories,* illustrated by Dennis R. Winston, Brunswick, 1995.
(With Earlene G. Evans) *A Step Beyond: Multimedia Activities for Learning American History,* Neal-Schuman, 1995.
The Water Brought Us: The Story of the Gullah-Speaking People, photographed by Gabriel Kuperminc, Cobblehill, 1995.
Freedom Day: The Story of Juneteenth, Cobblehill, 1997.
(With Dorothy Rice) *Pennies to Dollars: The Story of Maggie Lena Walker,* Linnet Books, 1997.

Articles published in professional journals.

■ Sidelights

Muriel Miller Branch grew up in rural Cumberland County where she didn't have access to a library or bookstore. The stories she grew up with were told by her father, brothers, and cousins. The family would gather in the living rooms about once a week and swap stories. Many of the stories were about her great-great-grandmother who had been a slave.

When Branch finally did see the insides of a library, she made up for lost time by staying up late at nights to read as many books as she could. Her deep appreciation for the library influenced her to become a librarian, while her love for the historical stories she heard as a child convinced her to try her hand at writing. After publishing *Miss Maggie: The Story of Maggie Lena Walker,* she collaborated on two other books before writing *The Water Brought Us: The Story of the Gullah-Speaking People,* her first solo work.

MURIEL MILLER BRANCH

In 1991, Branch won an award for teaching excellence from the Greater Richmond Community Foundation that allowed her to travel. Among the places she visited was the Sea Islands. There she conducted research on the Gullah-speaking people, descendants of slaves whose isolated island communities have developed a unique culture based in large part on traditions of handcrafting and storytelling handed down from their West African forebears. Branch's book *The Water Brought Us* draws on formal resources as well as the author's experiences among the people of the Sea Islands "to explore the history, heritage, and culture of these descendants of slaves," a *Kirkus Reviews* critic observed.

The book's "very ambitious aim," Kay McPherson said in *School Library Journal,* is to relay the distinctive history, culture, and language of the Gullah. Despite admitting "the writing often substitutes adulation for detail," Roger Sutton remarked in the *Bulletin of the Center for Children's Books* that "the historical chapters are strong." McPherson likewise praised the historical section, but noted that Branch fails to successfully incorporate her anecdotal material with her objective tone in the sections on contemporary life on the islands. A reviewer in *Booklist,* whose response to *The Water Brought Us* was also mixed, nonetheless concluded that the merits of Branch's subject matter outweighed the flaws in her presentation, saying "many readers will find the place and people of compelling interest."

■ Works Cited

McPherson, Kay, review of *The Water Brought Us: The Story of the Gullah-Speaking People, School Library Journal,* October, 1995, p. 143.

Sutton, Roger, review of *The Water Brought Us: The Story of the Gullah-Speaking People, Bulletin of the Center for Children's Books,* November, 1995, p. 85.

Review of *The Water Brought Us: The Story of the Gullah-Speaking People, Booklist,* September 15, 1995, p. 149.

Review of *The Water Brought Us: The Story of the Gullah-Speaking People, Kirkus Reviews,* August 1, 1995, p. 1107.

■ For More Information See

PERIODICALS

Companion, May, 1996, p. 36.
Voice of Youth Advocates, February, 1996, p. 405.

* * *

BRIQUEBEC, John
See ROWLAND-ENTWISTLE, (Arthur) Theodore (Henry)

* * *

BRITTON, Louisa
See McGUIRE, Leslie (Sarah)

* * *

BROOKS, Ron(ald George) 1948-

■ Personal

Born April 12, 1948, in Pambula, New South Wales, Australia. *Education:* Attended Bairnsdale Technical School, Swinburne Technical School, Swinburne Institute of Technology, and Royal Melbourne Institute of Technology, Australia.

■ Career

Author and illustrator of books for children, 1972—. Has also worked as a free-lance designer and illustrator for advertisers and publishers.

■ Awards, Honors

Best Picture Book of the Year, Children's Book Council of Australia, 1974, for *The Bunyip of Berkeley's Creek,* and 1978, for *John Brown, Rose, and the Midnight Cat;* Picture Book of the Year, Highly Commended, Children's Book Council of Australia, 1975, and Best Children's Visual Arts Book of the Year Award, 1976, for *Annie's Rainbow.*

■ Writings

SELF-ILLUSTRATED

Annie's Rainbow, Collins, 1975.
Timothy and Gramps, Collins, 1978.

ILLUSTRATOR

Joan Phipson, *Bass & Billy Martin,* McMillan, 1972.
David Martin, *Hughie,* Blackie, 1972.
Jenny Wagner, *The Bunyip of Berkeley's Creek,* Kestrel, 1973.
Wagner, *Aranea: A Story about a Spider,* Kestrel, 1975.
Wagner, *John Brown, Rose, and the Midnight Cat,* Kestrel, 1977.
(Contributor of illustrations) Mitsumasa Anno, *All in a Day,* Philomel, 1986.
Maurice Burns, *Go Ducks Go!,* Scholastic, 1987.
Rosalind Price and Walter McVitty, *The Viking Bedtime Treasury,* Viking, 1987.
Price and McVitty, *The Bedtime Story Book,* Orchard Books, 1992 (published in Australia as *The Macquarie Bedtime Story Book,* 1987).
Julia McClelland, *This Baby,* Oxford University Press, 1993, Houghton Mifflin, 1994.
Wagner, *Motor Bill and the Lovely Caroline,* Viking, 1994, Ticknor and Fields, 1995.
Margaret Wild, *Old Pig,* Allen and Unwin, 1995, Dial Books, 1996.

■ Sidelights

In 1974, author-illustrator Ron Brooks received the top honor from the Australian Children's Book Council for his illustrations *The Bunyip of Berkeley's Creek* written by Jenny Wagner. This initial success convinced him to concentrate his efforts on children's literature full time. Since then, he has illustrated many books by other well-known authors and written two of his own, *Annie's Rainbow* and *Timothy and Gramps.*

Brooks was born in Pambula, New South Wales, Australia, in 1948. He lived in several remote locations in Australia during his childhood years, including the Gippsland Lakes region on the continent's south coast. In comments provided to Grace Allen Hogarth for *Illustrators of Children's Books, 1967-76,* Brooks noted that the freedom he experienced as a boy strongly influenced his decision to write and illustrate books for children: "When I wasn't in school, I was out on the sand dunes, creeks, lakes, islands, exploring the miles of beautiful coastline." He recalled building numerous forts and tree houses, and floating on nearby rivers and lakes using homemade rafts and canoes.

At the age of fifteen, Brooks moved to Melbourne to study art. He attended several art schools and colleges in Australia over the next six years. After working as a free-lance designer in the advertising and publishing industries, he began writing and illustrating picture books in 1972 and never looked back. The most satisfying aspect of writing for children, as he explained to Hogarth, was that his young readers had the ability to enter and become a part of his stories. "I like to view my art as like that of a maker of windows," he noted, "which each reader, once having entered, is then able to explore, use and reapply his experiences in his own individual way."

Brooks's first self-illustrated book, *Annie's Rainbow,* was published in 1975. In this fantasy story, Annie is a prim little girl in a white dress who longs to capture a rainbow. She spends most of her time in the garden, waiting for a rainbow to appear and then trying in vain to catch it. One day, she sees a particularly beautiful rainbow and ventures into the woods to find its source, a shining fountain. There she meets a sympathetic artist who helps her to achieve her dream by giving her a picture of the rainbow. A *Publishers Weekly* reviewer praised Brooks's "simple story" and "lovely paintings," noting that "misty colors accentuate the dreaminess" of the tale. Similarly, a *Booklist* commentator called *Annie's Rainbow* "a visual treat plus a curiously satisfying tale."

Brooks's next self-illustrated work, 1978's *Timothy and Gramps,* tells the story of a young boy who feels like an outsider at his school in Dorset, England. Timothy finds relief from the loneliness and isolation by taking long walks with his lively grandfather and exchanging imaginative stories with him. Finally, Timothy persuades his grandfather to accompany him to school and speak to his class for "show and tell." After his grandfather entertains the class with colorful tales, Timothy begins to feel more comfortable relating to the other children, and they begin to accept him. Although *Timothy and Gramps* did not prove as popular as Brooks's previous works, it did earn some positive reviews. Janet French of *School Library Journal* claimed that the book "lacks action or deeply felt emotion," but nonetheless praised Brooks's pen-and-ink drawings, noting that they were "warmed with the soft colors of the English country-side." Writing in *Growing Point,* Margery Fisher also

commended the illustrations in *Timothy and Gramps* for their "elegant precision" and their success in communicating the "zest and richness" of the relationship between the two main characters.

Brooks has also illustrated a number of well-received books by other authors, including *This Baby* by Julia McClelland, published in 1994. The story concerns a family of bear-like wombats who are preparing for the arrival of a new baby. Andrew—a toddler and the only child up to this point—is alternately angry, frightened, and jealous as his parents' attention is diverted to the upcoming event. He reacts by throwing tantrums, sulking, and having bad dreams, while his loving parents try to reassure him. Finally, when they make Andrew realize how small and helpless the infant will be, he begins to look forward to becoming a big brother. In a review for *School Library Journal,* Susan Hepler praised Brooks's decision to show the family from a position above their den in his watercolor illustrations, which gave "the fat ursines an even more compressed and cozy look. It's as if readers are looking in on this family drama." Jo Goodman of *Magpies* called *This Baby* a "sheer delight," adding that the "text and illustrations complement each other perfectly."

Brooks also received high praise for his pastel watercolor illustrations in 1996's *Old Pig,* by Margaret Wild. The poignant story, which a *Publishers Weekly* reviewer called "a winning addition to the many books that help children cope with the loss of a loved one," follows a grandmother pig as she prepares to face the end of her life. After living happily with her granddaughter for many years, one day Old Pig has trouble getting up in the morning to begin the day's routine. When she realizes that her death is near, she prepares herself by returning books to the library, closing her bank account, and paying her bills. Then she takes a walk with her

So Granddaughter switched off the lights, and opened the window to let in the breeze and opened the curtains to let in the moon.

Old Pig **is the sensitive story of a grandmother pig who, knowing her time left is short, shares her last days with her granddaughter in a sensuous enjoyment of nature.** (Written by Margaret Wild and illustrated by Brooks.)

granddaughter in order to enjoy the wonders of nature—such as the play of light on the trees and the taste of rain—one last time. The book's final picture shows the granddaughter alone. In a review for *Booklist,* Ilene Cooper noted that "the soft watercolors are entirely childlike and unpretentious, but Brooks manages to mix the everyday with a beauty that transcends chores and meals." Likewise, Betsy Hearne of the *Bulletin of the Center for Children's Books* noted that Brooks's illustrations "cast a golden glow over this gentle farewell to life and love," while Christina Dorr of *School Library Journal* added that the drawings "successfully extend the unspoken portions of the story."

■ Works Cited

Review of *Annie's Rainbow, Booklist,* January 1, 1977, p. 663.

Review of *Annie's Rainbow, Publishers Weekly,* December 13, 1976, p. 62.

Cooper, Ilene, review of *Old Pig, Booklist,* May 15, 1996, p. 1587.

Dorr, Christina, review of *Old Pig, School Library Journal,* April, 1996, p. 121.

Fisher, Margery, review of *Timothy and Gramps, Growing Point,* January, 1979, p. 3448.

French, Janet, review of *Timothy and Gramps, School Library Journal,* September, 1979, p. 104.

Goodman, Jo, review of *This Baby, Magpies,* July, 1993.

Hearne, Betsy, review of *Old Pig, Bulletin of the Center for Children's Books,* March, 1996, p. 247.

Hepler, Susan, review of *This Baby, School Library Journal,* August, 1994, p. 140.

Kingman, Lee, Grace Allen Hogarth, and Harriet Quimby, compilers, *Illustrators of Children's Books, 1967-1976,* Horn Book, 1978.

Review of *Old Pig, Publishers Weekly,* June 3, 1996, p. 82.

■ For More Information See

PERIODICALS

Booklist, March 15, 1994, p. 1374; January 15, 1995, p. 940.

Bulletin of the Center for Children's Books, May, 1994, p. 293.

Growing Point, March, 1976, p. 2857.

Junior Bookshelf, April, 1979, p. 92; April, 1995, p. 68.

Kirkus Reviews, May 1, 1996, p. 695.

Publishers Weekly, January 9, 1995, p. 62.

School Library Journal, April, 1995, p. 119.*

* * *

BROWNRIDGE, William R(oy) 1932-

■ Personal

Born October 14, 1932, in Rosetown, Saskatchewan, Canada; son of Roy Harper (a railroad station agent) and Theresa Vivian (a teacher; maiden name, Cochlan) Brownridge; married Barbra Irene Orsted (an artist), September 6, 1960 (divorced, 1984); children: David,

Leanne, Nancy, Beth, Boyd. *Education:* Southern Alberta Institute of Technology and Art (now Alberta College of Art), Graphic Arts Diploma. *Politics:* New Democrat. *Religion:* Unitarian. *Avocational interests:* Painting, hockey, nature, books, music.

■ Addresses

Home—705 145 Point Dr. N.W., Calgary, Alberta, Canada T3B 4W1.

■ Career

KB Graphic Design, Calgary, Alberta, partner for fourteen years; Francis, Williams & Johnson (advertising and public relations firm), Calgary, associate creative director for twenty years. Artist. *Exhibitions:* Work represented in a national touring exhibition, 1978-79, at Burnaby Print Show, Young Contemporaries of Canada, Red River Exhibition, National Museum of Science and Technology, and at Canada House Banff, 1996; work included in Calgary's print and film presentation for the 1988 Olympic Winter Games; designer of uniforms for the Calgary Flames hockey club, 1993. *Member:* Art 17 Society (chairperson of arts committee, 1992-95).

■ Awards, Honors

Canada Council grant, 1975-76.

WILLIAM R. BROWNRIDGE

■ Writings

The Moccasin Goalie (self-illustrated children's book), Orca (Victoria, British Columbia), 1995.

■ Work in Progress

The Final Game, a sequel to *The Moccasin Goalie; Tracking the Iron Horse.*

■ For More Information See

PERIODICALS

Quill & Quire, September, 1995, p. 72.
School Library Journal, January, 1996, p. 76.

* * *

BRYANT, Jennifer F(isher) 1960-

■ Personal

Born May 13, 1960, in Easton, PA; daughter of Charles Holcombe (a mortician) and Elizabeth (a homemaker; maiden name, Starczyk) Fisher; married Neil Bryant, June 12, 1982; children: Leigh. *Education:* Attended Rutgers University, in Tours, France, 1980; Gettysburg College, B.A., 1982; Beaver College, 1996—; also attended West Chester University, and University of Iowa. *Politics:* Democrat. *Religion:* Presbyterian. *Hobbies and other interests:* Swimming, cycling, cross-country skiing, bird-watching, travel.

■ Addresses

Home—Glenmoore, PA. *Office*—P.O. Box 816, Uwchland, PA 19480.

■ Career

Writer, 1989—. Substitute high school teacher of English and foreign languages; writing instructor for public school gifted education programs; Pennsylvania Council on the Arts, artist in residence. *Member:* Society of Children's Book Writers and Illustrators, National League of American Pen Women, Philadelphia Children's Reading Round Table, Phi Beta Kappa.

■ Awards, Honors

Books for the Teen Age, New York Public Library, 1995, for *Louis Braille: Inventor;* Young Alumni Achievement Award, Gettysburg College, 1997.

■ Writings

"WORKING MOMS" SERIES; PHOTOGRAPHS BY PAMELA BROWN; PUBLISHED BY TWENTY-FIRST CENTURY BOOKS (FREDERICK, MD)

Anne Abrams, Engineering Drafter, 1991.
Ubel Velez, Lawyer, 1991.
Sharon Oehler, Pediatrician, 1991.
Zoe McCully, Park Ranger, 1991.

JENNIFER F. BRYANT

Jane Sayler, Veterinarian, 1991.
Carol Thomas-Weaver, Music Teacher, 1991.

"EARTH KEEPERS" SERIES; PUBLISHED BY HENRY HOLT

Marjory Stoneman Douglas: Voice of the Everglades, illustrated by Larry Raymond, 1992.
Margaret Murie: A Wilderness Life, illustrated by Antonio Castro, 1993.

"PHYSICALLY CHALLENGED" SERIES; PUBLISHED BY CHELSEA HOUSE

Louis Braille: Inventor, 1994.
Henri de Toulouse-Lautrec: The Artist Who Was Crippled, 1995.

"GREAT ACHIEVERS" SERIES; PUBLISHED BY EERDMANS (GRAND RAPIDS, MI)

Lucretia Mott: A Guiding Light, 1996.
Thomas Merton: Poet, Prophet, Priest, 1997.

OTHER

Birds of a Feather (adult nature anthology), Peter Pauper Press (White Plains, NY), 1993.

Contributor to periodicals, including *Earth's Daughters, Kinesis, The Schuykill Valley Journal, The Pegasus Review, The Forum, Disabilities Digest*, and *Highlights for Children.*

■ Work in Progress

A book of poems; several articles on historical women.

■ Sidelights

A nonfiction writer for middle graders and high schoolers, Jennifer F. Bryant has written an array of biographies on people of achievement from various walks of life. Included in this league are women's rights activist Lucretia Mott, environmental advocate Marjory Stoneman Douglas, inventor Louis Braille, and nineteenth-century artist Henri de Toulouse-Lautrec. Bryant's well-received *Louis Braille: Inventor* was commended by *School Library Journal* contributor Margaret C. Howell as a "solid reference resource on the history of handicapping conditions as well as a biography of a man who overcame a challenge." *Booklist* reviewer Karen Simonetti maintained that "Bryant ... meticulously chronicles Braille's profound optimism, tenacity, and commitment to making the world more accessible for the blind."

Bryant's 1996 biography *Lucretia Mott: A Guiding Light* has also drawn a favorable response from critics. *Voice of Youth Advocates* contributor Joyce Hamilton praised the author's study of the abolitionist and women's rights advocate, calling the book "informative and highly readable." Bryant's "Men of Spirit" series entry *Thomas Merton: Poet, Prophet, Priest* was similarly cited as a "remarkable biography" by a *Kirkus Reviews* commentator, who added that young people "may come away from this book not only with a real sense of the man and his writings, but courage enough for their present and future struggles as well."

In addition to these more famous figures, Bryant has also written about everyday heroes, specifically working moms. Within the "Working Moms" series, Bryant presents women pursuing their career—from an engineering drafter to a veterinarian—while also raising children. Each volume allows readers to ride along with the featured mom for a day, so they can understand the rewards and demands of balancing work and family. When needed, Bryant provides additional material, such as information about the woman's field, its ups and downs, and training requirements. In a review of *Sharon Oehler: Pediatrician,* a critic in *Kirkus Reviews* commented, "There's a substantial amount of information here, well-organized and appealingly presented." "As career guidance," noted Denise Wilms in *Booklist,* "the books give positive examples of how young women might look forward to pursuing careers and motherhood."

Bryant told *SATA:* "Human behavior has always fascinated me. The choices people make, their fears, fantasies, struggles, and achievements provide an endless pool of stories for nonfiction writers and biographers. Researching and writing biographies gives me a chance to explore the lives of unique individuals and to share their stories with young readers. When they read biographies, children inevitably absorb important lessons and

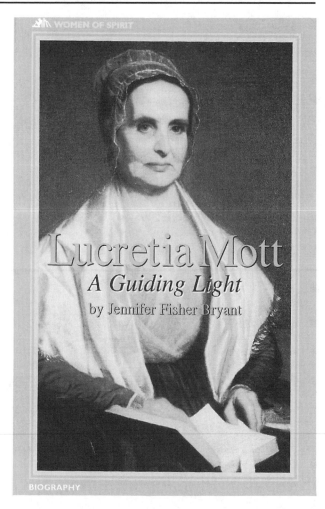

Bryant wrote this biography of the Quaker minister, abolitionist, and women's rights activist as part of the "Women of Spirit" series documenting the lives of outstanding women who have been motivated to action by their powerful faith in God. (Cover illustration by William Henry Furness, Jr.)

concepts from history, science, philosophy, and even religion.

"Most well-written biographies also present positive role models for service and achievement, thereby counteracting some of the negative images presented through the media. Readers also learn that no one leads a charmed life or begins with perfect circumstances, and that all great achievers encounter failure, frustration, and setbacks. Every biography I've written has taught me something new. Each one has given me a deeper appreciation for what it means to be human."

■ Works Cited

Hamilton, Joyce, review of *Lucretia Mott: A Guiding Light, Voice of Youth Advocates,* October, 1996, p. 226.

Howell, Margaret C., review of *Louis Braille: Inventor, School Library Journal,* August, 1994, p. 160.

Review of *Sharon Oehler: Pediatrician, Kirkus Reviews,* May 1, 1991, p. 602.

Simonetti, Karen, review of *Louis Braille: Inventor, Booklist,* July, 1994, p. 1938.
Review of *Thomas Merton: Poet, Prophet, Priest, Kirkus Reviews,* May 1, 1997, p. 717.
Wilms, Denise, review of "Working Moms" series, *Booklist,* June 15, 1991, p. 1958.

■ For More Information See

PERIODICALS

Appraisal, autumn, 1992, pp. 48-49.
Booklist, May 1, 1996, p. 1496.
Children's Book Watch, May, 1991, p. 12; February, 1992, p. 7; April, 1992, p. 5.
Kirkus Reviews, June 1, 1992, p. 726; December 1, 1995, p. 1700.
Main Line Today, January, 1997, pp. 16-17.
MultiCultural Review, March, 1993, p. 28.
School Library Journal, June, 1991, p. 114; July, 1991, p. 77; June, 1992, p. 128; July, 1993, p. 89; June, 1996, p. 154.
Science Books and Films, May, 1992, p. 116; August/September, 1992, p. 181.
Skipping Stones, summer, 1995, p. 30.

* * *

BURTON, Leslie
See McGUIRE, Leslie (Sarah)

* * *

BUTLER, Geoff 1945-

■ Personal

Born January 13, 1945, in Fogo, Newfoundland, Canada; son of Isaac (a clergyman) and Julia (a homemaker; maiden name, Earle) Butler; married Judith McClare (a teacher), August 17, 1976; children: Tegan, Kirsten, Leah, Sean. *Education:* Memorial University of Newfoundland, B.A., 1966; Syracuse University, M.A., 1969; attended Art Students League, New York City, 1972-73.

■ Addresses

Home—P.O. Box 29, Granville Ferry, Nova Scotia, Canada B0S 1K0. *Electronic mail*—gbutler @ aura-com.com.

■ Career

Artist and writer, Granville Ferry, Nova Scotia, 1980—. Soccer coach, Annapolis Royal, Nova Scotia, 1994—. *Member:* Writers Federation of Nova Scotia, Visual Arts Nova Scotia (member of board of directors, 1995-96).

■ Awards, Honors

Ruth Schwartz Children's Book Award, picture book category, Canadian Booksellers Association and Ontario Arts Council, 1996, for *The Killick; The Killick* was also shortlisted for the Governor General's Award and the Amelia Frances Howard-Gibbon Award in 1995 and 1996, respectively.

■ Writings

Art of War: Painting It out of the Picture, privately printed, 1990.
(Self-illustrated) *The Killick: A Newfoundland Story* (children's book), Tundra Books of Northern New York (Plattsburgh, NY), 1995.

ILLUSTRATOR

Peter Wyman, *Dear Don,* privately printed, 1985.

Creator of book cover illustrations.

■ Work in Progress

The Hangashore, "a children's story set in Newfoundland, relating how a magistrate and an intellectually challenged boy regard their respective front pews in church"; *Mouth Music,* a children's story about a fiddler set in Newfoundland; *Wise Acres,* a story set in Nova Scotia contrasting outdoor pond hockey with organized indoor rink hockey; a portfolio of songs, poems, and stories to accompany the author's angel paintings, titled *Angels: Behind the Picture.*

GEOFF BUTLER

Butler's award-winning book, *The Killick,* portrays the indomitable courage of Newfoundlanders, who resolutely adapt when the sea can no longer provide them with their livelihood. (Written and illustrated by Butler.)

■ Sidelights

Geoff Butler told *SATA:* "Someone with natural talents in a particular field is said to be born, not made, that way. It was not until I was in my mid-twenties that I attended an art class for the first time, so, in terms of technique at least, I am a 'made' artist; or, perhaps I just took a long time being born. For some reason, I did feel some kind of kinship with painting, and so I pursued it as a career. For more than twenty years now I have been a visual artist in the fine arts. Only recently have I turned to writing and illustrating children's books.

"For me, the process involved in creating a painting or forming a story is very similar. It involves striving toward that indefinable quality that makes something work. In *The Killick,* my training in visual arts helped to determine the course of the narrative. As the story was about dehumanization and calling names, I used the children's verse about sticks and stones. A killick, being a homemade anchor, is also sticks and stones, and this became the focal point of the story. The killick at the beginning of the story is not what it is at the end, however. It is given a new life. What was a simple anchor becomes, as the story unfolds, a memorial to the innocent victims of war.

"I sometimes used to bemoan the time I thought I had lost in being a late bloomer. I realize now that there is more to becoming an artist than just learning the techniques of art. One must have something to paint and write about. That is largely determined by the experiences one has had in all facets of life, and by the type of person one has become and continues to be. So, time growing isn't really lost.

"I relish the privilege I have in being an artist, but I am mindful also of the responsibility that goes with it: to be creative and open-minded, to follow one's voice without being egotistical about it, and to strive to do one's best. In my case, I use art as a means of self-expression. Particularly I think, when one reaches middle age and gets a sense of one's own mortality, one is driven to do only what is meaningful and not to waste what time one has left on things that don't really matter.

"For most of the 1980s, I worked on a series of paintings on the subject of war and militarism. It was summarized by a tombstone I made to celebrate the death of war. This mostly satirical project culminated in my self-published book *Art of War.* I am reminded of someone's comment that Picasso's feelings about war that he expressed in his large painting, *Guernica,* were probably not much different from those that General Sherman expressed in his short, simple phrase, 'War is hell.' Each of their expressions, however, carries its own impact. Since there is always a need to voice our opinions on such issues, I also decided to offer mine in the form I thought could best express it.

"I do not hold the view that profundity can only be expressed by dealing with negative issues. My second series of paintings dealt with the subject of angels. For me, they are but one of the symbols we use to represent our search for enlightenment. Perhaps even a worldly matter like warfare can be brought to heel by an enhanced spiritual dimension to our lives, by what is otherwise known as art."

■ For More Information See

PERIODICALS

Atlantic Books Today, fall, 1995.
Canadian Materials, March, 1991, p. 110.
Globe and Mail (Toronto), December 23, 1995.
Maclean's, December 11, 1995.
Quill and Quire, November, 1995, p. 46.
Times Educational Supplement, December 8, 1995, p. 12.

C

CANFIELD, Muriel
See KANOZA, Muriel Canfield

*   *   *

CAREY, Peter 1943-

■ Personal

Born May 7, 1943, in Bacchus Marsh, Victoria, Australia; son of Percival Stanley (an automobile dealer) and Helen Jean (an automobile dealer; maiden name, Warriner) Carey; married Alison Margaret Summers (a theater director), March 16, 1985; children: Sam, Charley. *Education:* Attended Monash University, 1961.

■ Addresses

Home—New York, NY. *Agent*—Amanda Urban, International Creative Management, 40 West 57th St., New York, NY 10019.

■ Career

Writer. Worked part-time in advertising in Australia from 1962 to 1988; also worked as a writing instructor at New York University, Columbia Univeristy, and Princeton University.

■ Awards, Honors

New South Wales Premier's Literary Award, 1980, for *War Crimes;* Miles Franklin Award, 1981, New South Wales Premier's Literary Award, and National Book Council Award, both 1982, all for *Bliss;* AWGIE Award and awards for best film and best screenplay from the Australian Film Institute, all 1985, all for *Bliss; The Age* Book of the Year Award and nomination for Booker Prize, both 1985, and Victorian Premier's Literary Award and National Book Council Award, both 1986, all for *Illywhacker;* Booker Prize, 1988, for *Oscar and Lucinda;* Litt.D., University of Queensland, Australia, 1989; *The Age* Book of the Year Award, 1995, for *The Unusual Life of Tristan Smith;* Honour Book, Australian

Children's Book of the Year Award, Children's Book Council of Australia, 1996, for *The Big Bazoohley.*

■ Writings

FOR CHILDREN

The Big Bazoohley, Holt (New York City), 1995, University of Queensland Press (St. Lucia, Queensland, Australia), 1995.

SHORT FICTION; FOR ADULTS

The Fat Man in History (includes "Crabs," "Peeling," "She Wakes," "Life and Death in the South Side Pavilion," "Room No. 5 (Escribo)," "Happy Story," "A Windmill in the West," "Withdrawal," "Report on the Shadow Industry," "Conversations with Unicorns," "American Dreams," and "The Fat Man in History"; also see below), University of Queensland Press, 1974.

War Crimes (includes "The Journey of a Lifetime," "Do You Love Me?" "The Uses of Williamson Wood," "The Last Days of a Famous Mime," "A Schoolboy Prank," "The Chance," "Fragrance of Roses," "The Puzzling Nature of Blue," "Ultra-violet Light," "Kristu-Du," "He Found Her in Late Summer," "Exotic Pleasures," and "War Crimes"; also see below), University of Queensland Press, 1979.

The Fat Man in History, and Other Stories (contains selections from *The Fat Man in History* and *War Crimes,* including "The Fat Man in History," "Peeling," "Do You Love Me?" "The Chance," "The Puzzling Nature of Blue," "Exotic Pleasures," "The Last Days of a Famous Mime," "A Windmill in the West," "American Dreams," and "War Crimes"), Random House (New York City), 1980, also published as *Exotic Pleasures,* Picador Books, 1981.

Collected Stories (includes "Do You Love Me?," "The Last Days of a Famous Mime," "Kristu-Du," "Crabs," "Life and Death in the South Side Pavilion," "Room No. 5," "Happy Story," "A Million Dollars Worth of Amphetamines," "Peeling," "A Windmill in the West," "Concerning the Greek

Tyrant," and "Withdrawal"), University of Queensland Press, 1994.

NOVELS

Bliss, University of Queensland Press, 1981, Harper
    (New York City), 1982 (also see below).
Illywhacker, Harper, 1985.
Oscar and Lucinda, Harper, 1988.
The Tax Inspector, Faber & Faber (London), 1991,
    Knopf (New York City), 1992.
The Unusual Life of Tristan Smith, Knopf, 1995.

OTHER

(With Ray Lawrence) *Bliss* (screenplay; adapted from
    Carey's novel of the same title), Faber, 1986.
A Letter to Our Son, University of Queensland Press,
    1994.

Work represented in anthologies, including *The Most
Beautiful Lies,* Angus & Robertson.

■ Sidelights

Peter Carey is an Australian writer noted for his quirky,
inventive fiction. In his first short story collection
written for adults, *The Fat Man in History,* published in
1974, he presented a matter-of-fact perspective on
bizarre and occasionally grotesque subjects. Included in
this book are "Conversations With Unicorns," in which
the narrator recalls his various encounters with the
extraordinary creatures, and "American Dreams,"
where a clerk succumbs to madness and isolates himself
from his community. Upon his death, townspeople
discover that in seclusion he constructed a model of
their village. More gruesome are "Peeling," in which a
character's quirky obsession results in a surreal mutila-
tion, and "Withdrawal," in which the protagonist is a
necrophile dealer of corpses and severed limbs. Among
the curious figures in this tale is a pig who becomes
dependent on narcotics after consuming an addict's
excrement.

The publication of *The Fat Man in History* quickly
established Carey as an important new figure in Australian literature. Bruce Bennett declared in *World Literature Written in English* that Carey's first collection of
stories "stamps him as the major talent among ... new
writers." Bennett found similarities between Carey's
work and that of Kurt Vonnegut and Evelyn Waugh, but
he added that "the shaping imagination is Carey's own."
Bennett called Carey "a true fabulator ... whose
inventive, witty fictions both delight and instruct."
Similarly, David Gilbey wrote in *Southerly* that *The Fat
Man in History* is an "impressive volume," one that
"dramatizes some of the dark myths beneath uncertainty and anxiety in contemporary life and does so with
deadly, though not humourless, seriousness." Gilbey
added that Carey's work is "intricately and surreally
resonant and stands out markedly amongst contemporary Australian writing."

Equally unique is *War Crimes,* Carey's second collection of stories. The volume includes such vividly bizarre

accounts as "The Chance," where a man vainly attempts
to dissuade his lover from entering a lottery in which the
major prize is a repulsive body. In the similarly disturbing title piece, a hippie-turned-businessman kills people
threatening his profits from frozen food sales. Like
Carey's first collection, *War Crimes* was immensely
popular in Australia and received the New South Wales
Premier's Literary Award in 1979.

Stories from both *The Fat Man in History* and *War
Crimes* comprise Carey's third collection, *The Fat Man
in History, and Other Stories.* This 1980 compilation
brought Carey's unusual sensibility to American and
British readers, many of whom readily acknowledged
him as a unique and masterful storyteller. In his *Times
Literary Supplement* review of the compilation, Peter
Lewis called Carey an "outstanding writer" and praised
his ability to write in a low-key but nonetheless compelling manner. "This naturalizing of the fantastic is

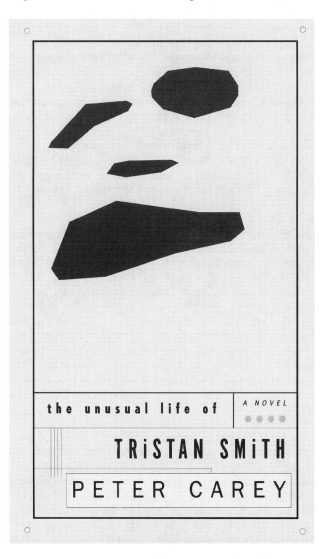

**Told through the eyes of a narrator whose deformity
sends him on a search for self-identity, Carey's novel
relates the similar struggle of the imaginary nation of
Efica to retain its own culture after being colonized by a
huge world power. (Cover illustration by Chip Kidd.)**

probably Carey's most distinctive characteristic," Lewis wrote. "But he is also notable for his supposedly old-fashioned ability to hold the reader's attention." Similarly, *Saturday Review* critic Sandra Katz, who described Carey's work as "somewhere between science fiction and surrealism," declared that "the stories in [*The Fat Man in History*] are as brilliant as they are bizarre."

In 1981 Carey published his first novel, *Bliss*. Like his short stories, *Bliss* is fairly surreal, rendering the bizarre as if it is the norm. The novel's protagonist is Harry Joy, an overworked advertising executive who suffers a near-fatal heart attack. Upon recovering from the heart attack and equally life-threatening open-heart surgery, Joy believes that he is in Hell. He discovers that his wife is compromising him with a close friend and that his seemingly lethargic son is actually a freewheeling drug dealer who forces his sister—Joy's daughter—to commit incest in return for drugs. Joy eventually forsakes his family for Honey Barbara, a worldly nature lover who regularly supports herself as a drug dealer and prostitute. Around the time that he befriends the charge-card accommodating prostitute, Joy also discovers that his advertising company maintains a map indicating cancer density for the area, with accountability traced to the company's clients. Aghast, Joy renounces his work and grows further remote from his family. Eventually, his wife has him committed to a mental institution, where he once again meets Honey Barbara, who has also been incarcerated. Together they escape to her home in a rain forest, where Joy finally finds happiness and fulfillment before meeting an unfortunate demise.

With *Bliss,* Carey gained further acclaim from American and British reviewers. In *British Book News,* Neil Philip referred to *Bliss* as "a rich, rewarding novel: crisply written, daringly conceived, brilliantly achieved," and in the *Washington Post Book World,* Judith Chettle wrote that Carey's novel possessed "all the virtues of a modern fable." For Chettle, Carey was "a writer of power and imagination." Even more impressed was *Spectator* critic Francis King. "In both the breadth of his vision of human life," wrote King, "in all its misery and happiness, and in the profundity of his insight into moral dilemmas, Mr. Carey makes the work of most of our 'promising' young and not so young novelists seem tinselly and trivial."

In 1985 Carey also published his second novel, *Illywhacker,* a wide-ranging comic work about Herbert Badgery, a 139-year-old trickster and liar. Badgery's life, which parallels the development of Australia following its independence from England, is full of odd adventures, including stints as a pilot, car salesman, and snakehandler. His accounts of his escapades, however, are not entirely reliable, and over the course of the novel's 600 pages Badgery often revels in tomfoolery and good-natured treachery. But he is hardly the novel's only unusual figure: Molly MaGrath maintains her sanity by periodically shocking herself with an "invigorator belt"; Emma, Badgery's daughter-in-law, lives in a lizard's cage; and an entire village proves gullible

enough to cooperate with Badgery in his hastily organized plan to build an Australian airplane. By novel's end, Badgery has recounted many more mad schemes and regaled the reader with recollections of seemingly countless eccentrics.

Illywhacker, like Carey's previous works, impressed many critics. In *Encounter,* D. J. Taylor called *Illywhacker* "a dazzling and hilarious book" and described the narrative as "a vast, diffuse plot chock-full of luminous characters and incident." Curt Suplee, who reviewed *Illywhacker* in the *Washington Post Book World,* recommended the novel as "huge and hugely rewarding" and added that it was a "rare and valuable" work. Howard Jacobson, writing in the *New York Times Book Review,* considered *Illywhacker* "a big, garrulous, funny novel, touching, farcical, and passionately bad-tempered." Jacobson also found *Illywhacker* a uniquely Australian work and contended that the experience of reading it was nearly the equivalent of visiting Australia. After noting occasional excesses in the narrative, Jacobson added: "Yet reading *Illywhacker* is not unlike spending a week in the company of the best kind of Australian. The stories keep coming, told with deceptive guilelessness and innocence. The talk is bawdy, the jokes are throwaways and rank, the sex is avid but democratic. Withal there is that haunting nostalgia and desolation that seems to be the immutable condition of the country. If you haven't been to Australia, read *Illywhacker.* It will give you the feeling of it like nothing else I know."

Carey's third novel, *Oscar and Lucinda,* is an extraordinary tale of two compulsive gamblers. The work begins in Victorian England, where the child Oscar endures life under the rigid rule of his intimidating father, a preacher. Later, Oscar breaks from his father and joins the conventional Anglican church, which he serves as a clergyman. Lucinda, meanwhile, has been raised in Australia by her mother, an intellectual who maintains the farm inherited from her late husband. Upon her mother's death, Lucinda inherits funds from the farm's sale. She also becomes owner of a glassworks and consequently devises construction of a glass cathedral. Eventually, Oscar and Lucinda meet on a ship, where Lucinda reveals her own obsession with gambling. Together, Oscar and Lucinda commence an extensive gambling excursion through Australia while simultaneously attempting to spread Christianity throughout the still wild country. When Oscar discovers Lucinda's glass cathedral, he wagers with Lucinda that he can deliver the model to a faraway clergyman with whom he mistakenly believes she is in love. His sea voyage, in which he is accompanied by a memorably colorful crew, constitutes a crisis of faith and self-awareness.

Oscar and Lucinda resulted in still further praise for Carey and received the 1988 Booker Prize. Beryl Bainbridge, writing in the *New York Times Book Review,* was particularly impressed with those portions devoted to Oscar's traumatic childhood, though adding that the remaining episodes were "racy with characters, teeming with invention and expressed in superlative

To save his family, Sam's got to find . . .

Nine-year-old Sam is determined to come up with "The Big Bazoohley"—as his father calls the jackpot—to help his troubled family in this Carey comedy. (Cover illustration by Michael Chesworth.)

language." Bainbridge also declared that Carey shared with Thomas Wolfe "that magnificent vitality, that ebullient delight in character, detail and language that turns a novel into an important book." Even more enthusiastic was *Los Angeles Times Book Review* contributor Carolyn See, who wrote: "There's so much richness here. The sweetness of the star-crossed lovers. The goodness within the stifled English clergyman. The perfect irrationality of human behavior as it plays itself out in minor characters." See contended, "We have a great novelist living on the planet with us, and his name is Peter Carey."

Carey returned to writing about modern-day life with his fourth novel, *The Tax Inspector,* which describes four apocalyptic days in the life of the Catchprice family, proprietors of a crumbling auto dealership in a slummy suburb of Sydney, Australia. "Light-years beyond the merely dysfunctional, they're the Beverly Hillbillies on bad acid," stated Francine Prose in the *New York Times Book Review.* "The Catchprices are the sort of people you'd rather read about than spend time with." Granny Frieda Catchprice is a tough, half-senile widow who carries explosives in her pocketbook; her

middle-aged daughter Cathy still dreams of leaving the family business to become a country-western singer; Cathy's brother Mort seems mild-mannered and harmless but has cruelly abused his two sons, as he himself was abused by Granny's late husband. One of Mort's children, 16-year-old Benny, listens religiously to "self-actualization" tapes until he comes to believe that he is an angel. Suspecting that her children are about to put her in a nursing home, Granny reports them to the Australian Taxation Office, which sends Maria Takis—an unmarried, pregnant tax collector—to investigate. Maria's sympathy for Granny draws her into the Catchprices' malevolent vortex. "To summarize the novel's characters or its twisted plot is to risk making the book sound simply cartoonish, quirky and grotesque," warned Prose. "In fact, there's something extremely likable about all this, and especially about the way Mr. Carey gives the combative Catchprices great complexity and depth." Prose asserted that eventually, "the black hole these people call home" is transformed into "a dark mirror for the larger world outside." Edmund White, reviewing for the *Times Literary Supplement,* also found much merit in the way the author made even his most unpleasant characters seem human. "Carey's triumph is that he doesn't ever turn his eccentrics into grotesques. We experience everything so intimately from several points of view that we scarcely judge anyone at all, any more than we ordinarily judge ourselves in the usual moments of just being. This suspension of moral discrimination is brought to our appalled attention only at the end of the book; the climax makes us recognize that we've dangerously misplaced our sympathies."

Carey's next novel, *The Unusual Life of Tristan Smith,* is a sprawling tale, set in the imaginary country of Efica—a tiny island nation colonized and exploited by Voorstand, a huge world power. Carey supplies a rich background for Efica, including a glossary of Efican dialect. The plot is typically convoluted, involving the Eficans' struggle to retain their own cultural identity. The Voorstanders attack that identity with a high-tech, semi-religious entertainment spectacle known as the Sirkus. The featured players in the Sirkus—Broder Mouse, Oncle Duck, and Hairy Man—bear more than a passing resemblance to three icons of the Walt Disney empire, Mickey Mouse, Donald Duck, and Goofy. The story is narrated by Tristan Smith, whose mother belongs to a radical theater group determined to resist the influence of the Sirkus. Hideously deformed at birth, Tristan finally finds love and acceptance after disguising himself in an electronic Broder Mouse costume.

Writing in the *Chicago Tribune,* Douglas Glover found *Tristan Smith* "at once bizarre, comic and nauseating . . . a deeply melancholy book about the Australia of the human heart . . . . Disturbing, wildly original and terribly sad, *The Unusual Life of Tristan Smith* is a book about the place where nation, myth and the personal intersect." Remarking on the novel's themes and relation to contemporary society, Michael Heyward, writing in the *New Republic,* stated: "If all the world is not a stage now but a themepark, we really are destined to become the residents of Voorstand and Efica. Could there be anything worse, Carey seems to be asking, than a situation in which practically everyone espoused the values of mass culture, especially in societies that did not create them?" The novel's driving force, Heyward continued, is "the savage irony of the provincial who has learned that the metropolis is merely a larger and more powerful province than his own." *Washington Post Book World* contributor Carolyn See was also enthusiastic, declaring that "Peter Carey has attempted to do about 100 things in this very ambitious novel and—if I'm correct—has about a 90 percent success rate. This, combined with his always magical, absolutely lovable narrative voice, makes *The Unusual Life of Tristan Smith* an important contribution to contemporary fiction."

Carey's unique, imaginative style and clever wit is also evident in his first story for children, *The Big Bazoohley*. In this tale, young Sam Kellow travels with his parents to Toronto, where a millionaire art collector has reserved one of Sam's mother's artistic miniatures. The family claim a room at a posh hotel, but fail to complete the big-money transaction when they cannot find an entrance in the mansion to which they've been directed. Sam seeks to help his parents by himself coming up with the big jackpot that his father always dreams about. Slipping away from their hotel, he is ultimately kidnapped by an eccentric couple who want him as a replacement for their sick child in the "Perfecto Kiddo" contest, which awards ten thousand dollars to the parents of a kid who, among other things, can eat a plate of spaghetti without splashing. Sam, of course, has his own ideas about the contest and the grand prize money. "By turns predictable and magical, this engaging little gem exhibits a delicately unfettered imagination that revels in small slices of enchantment among the everyday," enthused a *Kirkus Reviews* commentator. A *Publishers Weekly* reviewer also offered high praise for the "outlandish world" sketched by Carey in his children's book debut, asserting that in *The Big Bazoohley* the author "combines daring exaggeration with cozily wrought details for an exquisitely balanced comedy."

■ Works Cited

Bainbridge, Beryl, review of *Oscar and Lucinda, New York Times Book Review*, May 29, 1988, p. 1.

Bennett, Bruce, review of *The Fat Man in History, World Literature Written in English*, November, 1976.

Review of *The Big Bazoohley, Kirkus Reviews*, September 1, 1995, p. 1278.

Review of *The Big Bazoohley, Publishers Weekly*, September 18, 1995, p. 134.

Chettle, Judith, review of *Bliss, Washington Post Book World*, May 2, 1982, p. 8.

Gilbey, David, review of *The Fat Man in History, Southerly*, December, 1977.

Glover, Douglas, review of *The Unusual Life of Tristan Smith, Tribune Books*, February 19, 1995, p. 5.

Heyward, Michael, review of *The Unusual Life of Tristan Smith, New Republic*, April 10, 1995, p. 38.

Jacobson, Howard, review of *Illywhacker, New York Times Book Review*, November 17, 1985, p. 15.

Katz, Sandra, review of *The Fat Man in History, Saturday Review*, August, 1980, p. 65.

King, Francis, review of *Bliss, Spectator*, December 12, 1981, p. 21.

Lewis, Peter, review of *The Fat Man in History, and Other Stories, Times Literary Supplement*, October 31, 1980, p. 1240.

Philip, Neil, review of *Bliss, British Book News*, May, 1982, p. 320.

Prose, Francine, review of *The Tax Inspector, New York Times Book Review*, January 12, 1992, p. 1.

See, Carolyn, review of *Oscar and Lucinda, Los Angeles Times Book Review*, June 11, 1989, p. 12.

See, Carolyn, review of *The Unusual Life of Tristan Smith, Washington Post Book World*, February 17, 1995, p. 2.

Suplee, Curt, review of *Illywhacker, Washington Post Book World*, August 18, 1985, p. 1.

Taylor, D. J., review of *Illywhacker, Encounter*, September, 1985, p. 52.

White, Edmund, review of *The Tax Inspector*, August 30, 1991, p. 21.

■ For More Information See

BOOKS

Contemporary Literary Criticism, Gale, Volume 40, 1986; Volume 55, 1989.

Hassall, Anthony J., *Dancing on Hot Macadam: Peter Carey's Fiction*, University of Queensland Press, 1994.

Krassnitzer, Hermine, *Aspects of Narration in Peter Carey's Novels: Deconstructing Colonialism*, E. Mellen Press, 1995.

Woodcock, Bruce, *Shadow Maker: The Novels and Stories of Peter Carey*, Manchester University Press, 1996.

PERIODICALS

Australian Book Review, October, 1995, pp. 57-58.

Bulletin of the Center for Children's Books, December, 1995, p. 121.

Christian Science Monitor, February 9, 1989, p. 12.

Magpies, September, 1995, p. 32.

Newsweek, January 27, 1992, p. 60.

New York Review of Books, June 25, 1992, p. 35-6.

New York Times Book Review, November 12, 1995, p. 30.

School Library Journal, October, 1995, p. 132.

* * *

CARON, Romi
See CARON-KYSELKOVA', Romana

ROMANA CARON-KYSELKOVA'

CARON-KYSELKOVA', Romana 1967-
(Romi Caron)

■ Personal

Born April 1, 1967, in Brno, Czechoslovakia (now Czech Republic); came to Canada, 1990; daughter of Mojmi'r (an architect) and Jitka (an art teacher; maiden name, Podivi'nska') Kyselkova'; married Harris Caron, January 27, 1990; children: Samuel, Jonathan. *Education:* Attended College of Applied Arts, Brno, Czech Republic, 1981-85, and University of Applied Arts, Prague, Czech Republic, 1985-90. *Religion:* Roman Catholic.

■ Addresses

Home and office—Okapia Services, 15 de l'Equinoxe, Hull, PQ, Canada J9A 2X3. *Electronic mail*—Romi@ infonet.ca.

■ Career

Hinton Animation Studio, Ottawa, Ontario, assistant animator, 1990-91; graphic designer and illustrator at an advertising studio, Hull, Quebec, 1991-93; freelance illustrator, 1993—.

■ Awards, Honors

Little Wonders and *Time to Eat* were "Our Choice" selections, Canadian Children's Book Centre.

■ Illustrator

UNDER NAME ROMI CARON

Danielle Rochette, *La semeuse cannibale: roman,* Editions Pierre Tisseyre (St. Laurent, Quebec, Canada), 1995.

Daniele Gallichand, *La fete de meme Angeline,* Editions du Vermillon (Ottawa, Ontario, Canada), 1996.

"AMAZING THINGS ANIMALS DO" SERIES; UNDER NAME ROMI CARON

Marilyn Baillie, *Little Wonders: Animal Babies and Their Families,* Owl Books (Toronto, Ontario, Canada), 1995.

Baillie, *Time to Eat: Animals Who Hide and Save Their Food,* Owl Books, 1995.

Baillie, *Wild Talk: How Animals Talk to Each Other,* Owl Books, 1996.

Baillie, *Side by Side,* Owl Books, 1997.

■ For More Information See

PERIODICALS

School Library Journal, December, 1995, p. 94.

*   *   *

CASANOVA, Mary 1957-

■ Personal

Born February 2, 1957, in Duluth, MN; daughter of Eugene (a business manager) and Joyce (a homemaker; maiden name, Anderson) Gazelka; married Charles Casanova (an insurance agent), July 1, 1978; children: Katie, Eric. *Education:* University of Minnesota, B.A., 1981. *Religion:* Judeo-Christian/Lutheran. *Hobbies and other interests:* Reading, writing, cross-country and downhill skiing, camping, canoeing, hiking, running, horseback riding, and playing the piano.

■ Addresses

Agent—Kendra Marcus, Bookstop Literary Agency, 67 Meadow View Road, Orinda, CA 94563.

■ Career

Author, lecturer, and writing instructor. Eslinger Sled-dog Races, International Falls, MN, volunteer; Voyageurs National Park, Artist in Residency Program, selection judge, 1996; Junior High Youth Group leader.

Has taught writing workshops at colleges, universities, and for the Institute of Children's Literature, West Redding, CT.

Also worked variously as an immigrations clerk, horticultural worker, piano player, real estate agent, nursing home aid, ski-bum, maid, and English Department assistant. *Member:* Society of Children's Book Writers and Illustrators, The Loft (a national writing organization), Toastmasters.

MARY CASANOVA

■ Awards, Honors

Emily Johnson Award, Children's Literature Conference, 1990, for short story "Father's Boots"; Career Development Grant, Minnesota State Arts Board, 1992; Career Opportunity Grants, Arrowhead Regional Arts Council, 1992-94; Fellowship in Literature, Arrowhead Regional Arts Council/Mcknight Foundation, 1995; *Moose Tracks* was selected as a Children's Book of the Month, 1995, and nominated for the Northeastern Book Award, 1995, the North Dakota Library Association Flicker Tale Children's Book Award, 1997, the Iowa Readers' Choice Book Award, 1998, and the Indian Paintbrush Book Award, 1998; *Riot* was nominated for the Minnesota Book Award for Young Adults, 1996, and the Northeastern Book Award, 1997, and was named a Junior Library Guild selection, 1996.

■ Writings

The Golden Retriever (nonfiction), Crestwood House/ Macmillan, 1990.
Moose Tracks (middle-grade novel), Hyperion, 1995.
Riot (middle-grade novel), Hyperion, 1996.
Wolf Shadows (middle-grade novel, sequel to *Moose Tracks*), Hyperion, 1997.
Stealing Thunder (middle-grade novel), Hyperion, 1998.
One Dog Canoe (picture book), illustrated by Carter Goodrich, Dorling Kindersley, in press.

Contributor of short stories and articles to *Cricket, Highlights,* and *Once upon a Time.*

■ Sidelights

Mary Casanova told *SATA:* "When I set out to write for children, I had two main goals: to write books that kids couldn't put down and to write books that matter. Coming from a family of ten children—seven boys and three girls—I was always active: riding horses, playing tag off the pontoon boat in the summer and ice-hockey with our own 'team' in the winter. I was also a reluctant reader. I loved being outside, and if a book was going to hold my attention it had to be a fast-paced story. *Moose Tracks,* my first novel, hooks the kind of reader I was.

"I love to throw my character in the midst of issues, issues I can't quite get my arms around. *Riot* is that kind of story. After living through a two-year labor dispute that erupted into violence in my small northern town in 1989, I knew I'd have to write about it and somehow make sense of it. The result is the fictionalized account of a riot through 12-year-old Bryan Grant's eyes; his father is increasingly involved in the fervor, protesting the work he doesn't get at the paper mill. Bryan's mother, on the other hand, is a union member and teacher who desires a peaceable solution to the dispute." "Casanova has created an exciting, realistic novel," Cheryl Cufari commented in a *School Library Journal* review of *Riot.* Although Elizabeth Bush complained in a review in *Bulletin of the Center for Children's Books* that "good guy/bad guy treatment of the labor action grossly oversimplifies the issues," Lauren Peterson concluded in a review in *Booklist* that "this fast-paced story poses challenging questions that have no easy answers."

Casanova fulfills her intention to write fast-paced stories centered on issues that make her young-adult readers think hard about important questions. In Casanova's sequel to *Moose Tracks, Wolf Shadows,* Matt illegally shoots a wolf, causing a nearly insurmountable rift in his longtime friendship with Seth who vehemently opposes poaching. In *Kirkus Reviews* a critic wrote that "the attention-grabbing action and emotional struggles of the hero [in *Moose Tracks*] will hook reluctant readers." Centered on twelve-year-old Seth, who kills a rabbit in a protected wilderness area without his warden stepfather's permission, the novel stages a coming-of-age story in which Seth comes to question ideas he had formerly held about himself and his family. *School Library Journal* reviewer Todd Morning said that "Casanova's precise and evocative descriptions" add depth to the adventure story that culminates when Seth orchestrates the capture of poachers and confesses to his own misdeed.

■ Works Cited

Bush, Elizabeth, review of *Riot, Bulletin of the Center for Children's Books,* January, 1997, p. 165.

Cufari, Cheryl, review of *Riot, School Library Journal,* October, 1996, p. 120.

Review of *Moose Tracks, Kirkus Reviews,* May 15, 1995, p. 708.

Morning, Todd, review of *Moose Tracks, School Library Journal,* June, 1995, p. 108.

Peterson, Lauren, review of *Riot, Booklist,* November 1, 1996, p. 497.

■ For More Information See

PERIODICALS

Los Angeles Times, Novemeber 24, 1996, p. 1328.
Pioneer (Bemidji, Minnesota), May 14, 1997, p. 6.
Publishers Weekly, June 19, 1995, p. 60.
Star Tribune, October 22, 1995, p. F13.

*   *   *

CHAPMAN, Lynne F(erguson) 1963-

■ Personal

Born March 14, 1963, in Los Angeles, CA; daughter of James (a professor of English) and Lorice (a library assistant and teacher; maiden name, Mittry) Ferguson; married Paul Chapman (a neuroscientist), June 21, 1986; children: Thomas, Samuel. *Education:* DePauw University, B.A., 1985. *Hobbies and other interests:* Reading, watching films, cooking, playing games, drawing and graphic design, travel.

■ Addresses

Home and office—7 Westbourne Rd., Cardiff CF4 2BP, Wales.

■ Career

Mayfield Publishing, Mountain View, CA, editorial assistant, 1985-87; Windsor Publications, Northridge, CA, photography editor, 1987-88; Dushkin Publishing, Guilford, CT, annual editions editor, 1988-89; freelance editor and writer, 1989—. *Member:* National Childbirth Trust, Eglwys Newydd Primary School and Parents Association (secretary, 1996—).

■ Writings

Sylvia Plath, photographs by Benno Friedman, Creative Company (Mankato, MN), 1994.
Leo Tolstoy, Creative Company, 1997.

■ Work in Progress

Jane Austen and *The Bronte Sisters,* both for Creative Company.

■ Sidelights

Lynne F. Chapman told *SATA:* "Because both of my parents taught English, it was probably inevitable that I, after a proper period of teenage rebelliousness, would want to have a lot to do with books. Publishing seemed an obvious career choice, so I spent several years after college moving from one small publishing company to another as my husband pursued his academic career at various universities. Then I decided to take up freelance editing, not coincidentally before the birth of my first child, and I have worked at home ever since. While living in Minnesota, I was asked to try writing for a small, upmarket publisher of beautiful educational books. I wrote my first book with equal parts nervousness and delight, and three more followed. Now we have settled overseas, in Cardiff, Wales, and as my children get older, I hope to have more time for writing—although those nerves just won't go away!"

*   *   *

CHOYCE, Lesley 1951-

■ Personal

Born March 21, 1951, in Riverside, NJ; son of George (a mechanic) and Norma (a homemaker; maiden name, Willis) Choyce; married Terry Paul (a teacher); children: Sunyata, Pamela. *Education:* Rutgers University, B.A., 1972; Montclair State College, M.A. in American literature, 1974; City University of New York, M.A. in English literature, 1983.

■ Addresses

Home—83 Leslie Rd., East Lawrencetown, Nova Scotia, B2Z 1P8, Canada. *Office*—English Department, Dalhousie University, Halifax, Nova Scotia, B3H 3J5, Canada.

■ Career

Writer, publisher, professor, television show host, music performer, surfer. Referrals Workshop, Denville, NJ, rehabilitation counselor, 1973-74; Bloomfield College, Bloomfield, NJ, coordinator of writing tutorial program, 1974; Montclair State College, Upper Montclair, NJ, instructor in English, 1974-78; Alternate Energy Consultants, Halifax, Nova Scotia, writer and consultant to Energy, Mines and Resources Canada, 1979-80; Dalhousie University, Halifax, 1981—, began as instructor, became professor of English. Founder of Pottersfield Press. Creative writing instructor, City of Halifax continuing education program, 1978-83; instructor at St. Mary's University, 1978-82, Nova Scotia College of Art and Design, 1981, and Mount St. Vincent University, 1982. Participant in creative writing workshops; public reader and lecturer; freelance broadcaster, 1972—; host of television talk show "Choyce Words," beginning 1985. *Member:* International PEN, Atlantic Publishers Association, Canadian Periodical Publishers Association, Association of Canadian Publishers, Literary Press

Group, Canadian Poetry Association, Writers' Union of Canada, Writers Federation of Nova Scotia.

■ Awards, Honors

Canadian Science Fiction and Fantasy Award finalist, 1981; recipient, Order of St. John Award of Merit, 1986; Dartmouth Book Award, 1990, 1995, shortlist, 1991-93; *Event* magazine Creative Nonfiction winner, 1990; Ann Connor Brimer Award for Children's Literature, 1994; Manitoba Young Reader's Choice Award finalist, 1994; Authors Award, Foundation for the Advancement of Canadian Letters, co-winner, 1995.

■ Writings

FOR YOUNG ADULTS

Skateboard Shakedown, Formac Publishing, 1989.
Hungry Lizards, Collier-Macmillan (Toronto), 1990.
Wave Watch, Formac Publishing, 1990.
Some Kind of Hero, Maxwell-Macmillan, 1991.
Wrong Time, Wrong Place, Formac Publishing, 1991.
Clearcut Danger, Formac Publishing, 1992.
Full Tilt, Maxwell-Macmillan, 1993.
Good Idea Gone Bad, Formac Publishing, 1993.
Dark End of Dream Street, Formac Publishing, 1994.
Big Burn, Thistledown, 1995.
Falling through the Cracks, Formac Publishing, 1996.

FOR ADULTS

Eastern Sure, Nimbus Publishing, 1981.
Billy Botzweiler's Last Dance (stories), Blewointment Press, 1984.
Downwind, Creative Publishers, 1984.
Conventional Emotions (stories), Creative Publishers, 1985.
Coming up for Air, Creative Publishers, 1988.
The Second Season of Jonas MacPherson, Thistledown, 1989.
Magnificent Obsessions (photo-novel), Quarry Press, 1991.
The Ecstasy Conspiracy, Nuage Editions, 1992.
Margin of Error (stories), Borealis Press, 1992.
The Republic of Nothing, Goose Lane Editions, 1994.
Dance the Rocks Ashore, Goose Lane Editions, 1997.

SCIENCE FICTION

The Dream Auditor, Ragweed Press, 1986.
The Trap Door to Heaven, Quarry Press, 1996.

NONFICTION

Edible Wild Plants of the Maritimes, Wooden Anchor Press, 1977.
An Avalanche of Ocean (autobiography), Goose Lane Editions, 1987.
December Six/The Halifax Solution, Pottersfield Press, 1988.
Transcendental Anarchy (autobiography), Quarry Press, 1993.
Nova Scotia: Shaped by the Sea, Penguin (Toronto), 1996.

LESLEY CHOYCE

POETRY

Reinventing the Wheel, Fiddle Head Poetry Books, 1980.
Fast Living, Fiddle Head Poetry Books, 1982.
The End of Ice, Fiddle Head Poetry Books, 1982.
The Top of the Heart, Thistledown Press, 1986.
The Man Who Borrowed the Bay of Fundy, Brandon University, 1988.
The Coastline of Forgetting, Pottersfield Press, 1995.

EDITOR

The Pottersfield Portfolio, Volumes 1-7, Pottersfield Press, 1971-1985.
Alternating Current: Renewable Energy for Atlantic Canada, Wooden Anchor Press, 1977.
Chezzetocook (fiction and poetry), Wooden Anchor Press, 1977.
(With Phil Thompson) *ACCESS,* Pottersfield Press, 1979.
(With John Bell) *Visions from the Edge,* Pottersfield Press, 1981.
The Cape Breton Collection, Pottersfield Press, 1984, 1989.
(With Andy Wainwright) Charles Bruce, *The Mulgrave Road,* Pottersfield Press, 1985.
Ark of Ice: Canadian Futurefiction, Pottersfield Press, 1985.
(With Rita Joe) *The Milkmaq Anthology,* Pottersfield Press, 1997.

OTHER

Go for It, Carrie (for children), Formac, 1997.

Contributor to more than one hundred magazines and anthologies.

■ Work in Progress

Cold Clear Morning, a novel.

■ Sidelights

American-born Canadian author and editor Lesley Choyce, who has written numerous works of fiction (for both adults and young adults), nonfiction, science fiction, and poetry, shows no signs of slowing down. Though he has experience in many genres, Choyce told *SATA* that it was writing his autobiography that really opened a new door to his fiction: "I decided to be a writer with high hopes that it would allow me to avoid work. When writing turned out to be work as well as fun, I stuck with it anyway, simply because it seemed too late to turn back. I stuck mostly to fiction, where it seemed that the facts need not get in the way of the truth, but then as time went on I found that some of the facts of my own life were more revealing than the fictional truths I create. This came as a surprise and a shock to me.

"As a kid, I had a fairly minute ego—no one within earshot was ready to persuade me that my opinions and insights were of much value in the world I lived in. So later, when I grew into my skin as a writer, I pretended for awhile that *what I had to say* really was of importance. After a time, I started believing in the myth, and this convinced me to abandon fiction for awhile and get autobiographical.

"Since my life story would be exceedingly boring, I was forced to edit my personal history ruthlessly until there was something left worth sharing. My first fragmented history of the self came out as *An Avalanche of Ocean,* and I almost thought that I was done with autobiography. What more could I possibly say once I'd written about winter surfing, transcendental wood-splitting, and getting strip-searched for cod tongues in a Labrador airport?

"But then something happened to me that I can't quite explain. *Avalanche* had set off something in me—a kind of manic, magical couple of years where I felt like I was living on the edge of some important breakthrough. It was a time of greater compressed euphoria and despair than I'd ever felt before. Stuff was happening to me, images of the past were flooding through the doors, and I needed to get it all down. Some of it was funny, some of it was not. Dead writers were hovering over my shoulder, saying, 'Dig deep; follow it through. Don't let any of it go.' And I didn't.

"So again I have the audacity to say that these things that happened to me are worth your attention. Like Wordsworth, I am a man 'pleased with my own voli-

tions.' Like Whitman, I find myself saying to readers, 'to you, endless announcements.'

"As I write this, I am bumping into forty-five and I need to share the discoveries of the last ten years. For me it was a time of great battles. I fought the construction of street lights in the wilderness, the tedium of organizations, and the relentless, well-intentioned blundering of government and science.

"In *Transcendental Anarchy* I celebrated the uncompromising passages of a midthirties male, admitting that I would never be an astronaut or a president, and instead finding satisfaction in building with wood, arguing a good cause, or even undergoing a successful vasectomy.

"Write about what makes you feel the most uncomfortable, a voice in my head told me. So I tackled fear and my own male anger and my biggest failures. And, even more dangerous, I tried writing about the most ordinary of things: a morning in Woolco, an unexceptional day, the thread of things that keeps a life together."

Choyce has worked some of his many passions—including nature and the environment, surfing, windsurfing, skateboarding, and music—into several novels for young adults. In his first effort, *Skateboard Shakedown* (1989), a skateboarder, his girlfriend, and a group of friends take on a corrupt mayor who wants to turn their favorite skateboard site into a shopping mall. Writing in *Quill & Quire,* reviewer Norene Smiley said that "this fast-paced novel marks the entrance of a new and refreshing voice for young readers."

In *Hungry Lizards* (1990), a sixteen-year-old rock band leader finds that the advantages of winning a performing contract at a local club can be outweighed by the realities of the entertainment business, the conflicting time demands of school and work, and the temptations of a questionable lifestyle. The book is designed for reluctant teen readers, and reviewer Kenneth Oppel concluded in *Quill & Quire* that the book's "tempered view of teenage street life and the rock 'n' roll underworld should appeal to young readers."

Wrong Time, Wrong Place (1991) explores racial tensions and social injustice through the story of Corey, a young man with one parent who is black and one who is white. Corey first becomes aware of his different status as a biracial youth when he is branded as a troublemaker and rebel and begins to notice how both students and faculty treat lighter-skinned students differently. Through his Uncle Larry's good example and Larry's stories of a black community in Halifax called Africville, Corey comes to identify with his black forebears. As described by *Canadian Children's Literature* reviewer Heidi Petersen, Corey "realises that he must face injustices himself, and embraces a form of social activism which begins by keeping the past, the truth, alive."

In *Clearcut Danger* (1992), as in *Skateboard Shakedown,* two teenage protagonists take on adult greed, this time in the form of a joint government-business project to build a pollution-prone pulp and paper mill in a job-starved town. Praising Choyce's "strong and interesting" characterization and "good, strong story," reviewer Patty Lawlor concluded in *Quill & Quire* that "booksellers, teachers, and librarians should talk this one up."

In *Dark End of Dream Street* (1994), Choyce takes up the problem of homeless youth in the person of Tara, who always thought her friend Janet was the one with problems until Tara's own life starts to spin out of control. *Quill & Quire* reviewer Fred Boer found the author's subplots—about Tara's friendship with an elderly woman, and both Tara's and Janet's problems with their boyfriends—somewhat distracting, and the absence of swearing oddly cautious. Boer nevertheless praised the book for being "entertaining and readable."

While most of Choyce's young adult novels are in the high interest/low vocabulary category, *Big Burn* appeals to a more sophisticated audience. Nevertheless, the main plot—two teens against a new incinerator that threatens to poison the atmosphere—is familiar Choyce terrain. In *Quill & Quire,* reviewer Maureen Garvie especially praised the "infectious" quality of the "outrage the author and his characters feel." Other strengths include the portrayal of John's "adolescent darknesses" and the death of a parent.

About his writing, Choyce further told *SATA:* "Throughout it all, there is, I hope, a record of a search for love and meaning fraught with failure and recovery. Maybe I've developed a basic mistrust of the rational, logical conclusions. I've only had the briefest glimpses beyond the surface, but I've seen enough to know that sometimes facts are not enough. There are times to make the leap, to get metaphysical, and suppose that we all live larger lives than appearances would suggest."

■ Works Cited

Boer, Fred, review of *Dark End of Dream Street, Quill & Quire,* March, 1995, p. 79.

Garvie, Maureen, review of *Big Burn, Quill & Quire,* May, 1995, pp. 46-47.

Lawlor, Patty, review of *Clearcut Danger, Quill & Quire,* May, 1993, pp. 33-34.

Oppel, Kenneth, review of *The Hungry Lizards, Quill and Quire,* August, 1990, p. 15.

Petersen, Heidi, review of *Wrong Time, Wrong Place, Canadian Children's Literature,* Number 76, 1994, pp. 72-6.

Smiley, Norene, review of *Skateboard Shakedown, Quill & Quire,* March, 1990, p. 22.

■ For More Information See

PERIODICALS

Books in Canada, October, 1995, pp. 49-50.

Canadian Children's Literature, Number 62, 1991, pp. 86-88.

Canadian Materials, January, 1991, p. 34; May, 1992, p. 165.

Maclean's, August 15, 1994, p. 44.

Quill & Quire, April, 1991, p. 18.

* * *

CLAYTON, Elaine 1961-

■ Personal

Born September 17, 1961, in Texas; daughter of Robert (a doctor) and Bonnie (a homemaker) Clayton; married Simon Boughton (a publisher), September 14, 1996. *Education:* Atlanta College of Art, B.F.A., 1984; attended Georgia State University, 1986, School of Visual Arts, New York City, M.F.A., 1996. *Hobbies and other interests:* "Riding horses, western and English style, in-line skating, playing with my dog Ah Wing, traveling, learning to speak Italian."

■ Addresses

Home and office—65 Sussex St., Jersey City, NJ 07302. *Agent*—William Reiss, John Hawkins and Associates, Inc., 71 West 23rd St., Suite 1600, New York, NY 10010.

■ Career

Illustrator and author. Cesar Chavez Migrant Camp, Mobile, AL, head start teacher, 1980; High Museum of Art, Atlanta, GA, gallery instructor, 1980-85; St. Anthony's Summer Camp, Atlanta, art instructor, 1983; Woodruff Memorial Arts Center Gallery, Atlanta, gallery manager, 1984; Paideia School, Atlanta, assistant

ELAINE CLAYTON

teacher and artist in residence, 1985-89; Mary Lin Elementary School, Atlanta, artist-in-residence, 1985; Atrium School, Watertown, MA, elementary teacher, 1990-94. Volunteer with Glen Mary Missionary. *Exhibitions:* Has presented work at exhibitions at Woodruff Memorial Arts Center, Atlanta, GA, 1984; The Visual Club, New York City, 1995; Art Directors Club, New York City, 1996; and The New York Women's Foundation, New York City, 1996.

■ Writings

(Self-illustrated) *Pup in School,* Crown, 1993.
(Self-illustrated) *Ella's Trip to the Museum,* Crown, 1996.
Gregory Maguire, *Six Haunted Hairdos,* Clarion, 1997

Editor, "Puzzle Gallery Books," Crown, 1997. Contributor of reviews and illustrations to magazines and newspapers, including *Drawing, Raygun, Curio, Drawing Instructor, Southline,* and *New York Times.*

■ Work in Progress

Picture books.

■ Sidelights

Elaine Clayton told *SATA:* "I grew up in a big family and learned the importance of lively conversation and storytelling. As I grew up, my private world was one involving characters I drew, whole families of people with stories I made up. Before and while studying art in college, I worked with children—never doing art without being at times surrounded by children to even out the intensity of painting and drawing, and never working with children without bringing my creative process (and theirs) to the forefront.

"Eventually, children asked that I put my stories on paper, not disposable marker boards or chalk boards where they disappear when story time is over. I had to do as they asked since, as a teacher, I expected stories from them on paper! This is when I began pursuing publication of my work, and I have loved the entire process. I make stories involving the same types of characters I made up as a child, always meeting new ones in real life along the way. I want more than anything to encourage children to delight in their view of the world and, through art and stories, change the world by showing us what they see."

■ For More Information See

PERIODICALS

New York Times Book Review, May 19, 1996, p. 28.
Publishers Weekly, June 28, 1993, p. 75; June 3, 1996, p. 82.
School Library Journal, October, 1993, p. 97; June, 1996, p. 99.*

CLEMENTS, Bruce 1931-

■ Personal

Born November 25, 1931, in New York, NY; son of Paul Eugene (a salesman) and Ruth (an editor; maiden name, Hall) Clements; married Hanna Charlotte Margarete Kiep (a community worker), January 30, 1954; children: Mark, Ruth, Martha, Hanna. *Education:* Columbia University, A.B., 1954; Union Theological Seminary, B.D., 1956; State University of New York at Albany, M.A., 1962. *Politics:* Democrat. *Religion:* Protestant.

■ Addresses

Office—Department of English, Eastern Connecticut State College, Willimantic, CT 06226.

■ Career

Ordained minister of United Church of Christ; pastor in Schenectady, NY, 1957-64; Union College, Schenectady, NY, instructor, 1964-67; Eastern Connecticut State College, Willimantic, CT, professor of English and department chairman, 1967—.

■ Awards, Honors

National Book Award finalist, American Academy and Institute of Arts and Letters, 1975, and "Best of the Best, 1966-1978," *School Library Journal,* 1979, both for *I Tell a Lie Every So Often.*

■ Writings

FICTION; FOR CHILDREN

Two against the Tide, Farrar, Straus, 1967.
The Face of Abraham Candle, Farrar, Strauss, 1969.
I Tell a Lie Every So Often, Farrar, Strauss, 1974.
Prison Window, Jerusalem Blue, Farrar, Strauss, 1977.
Anywhere Else But Here, Farrar, Strauss, 1980.
Coming About, Farrar, Strauss, 1984.
The Treasure of Plunderell Manor, Farrar, Strauss, 1987.
Tom Loves Anna Loves Tom, Farrar, Strauss, 1990.

NONFICTION; FOR CHILDREN

From Ice Set Free: The Story of Otto Kiep, Farrar, Strauss, 1972.
(With wife, Hanna Clements) *Coming Home to a Place You've Never Been Before,* Farrar, Strauss, 1975.

OTHER

Author of plays for radio and theatre.

■ Sidelights

The author of several well-received books for young people, Bruce Clements began writing in the late 1960s. His novels, which include *I Tell a Lie Every So Often, Anywhere Else But Here,* and *The Treasure of Plunderell Manor,* focus on the importance of caring for one's fellow man and, by extension, our society's need to be tolerant and supportive of other cultures. Mary Lystad remarked of Clements in *Twentieth-Century Young Adult Writers:* "His writing style is crisp and clear; in a few words and phrases Clements conjures up vivid images of people, places, and times in conflict." Lystad further noted that Clements's books are products of his extensive research, with carefully detailed historical and geographical settings. "Clements is not easy reading, but he is worth the effort," Lystad continued. "His stories are powerful, with strong characters facing basic human choices."

Clements was born in New York City in 1931, and was writing plays with Hank, a boyhood friend, before he had entered high school. "Our idea was to start a radio station that would broadcast a one-hour play every night," he explained in *Fifth Book of Junior Authors and Illustrators.* "We thought we'd write half of them, use old plays for the other half, and get our friends and other people to act in them. It was a great idea, but we found out that it was impossible to produce a play every other day."

The Treasure of Plunderell Manor

Bruce Clements

All is not as it should be at Plunderell Manor

Fourteen-year-old Laurel, maidservant to Alice Plunderell, uncovers a scheme designed to rob her young mistress of the family fortune in Bruce Clements's adventure story set in Victorian England. (Cover illustration by Ted Lewin.)

While Clements dreamed of becoming a writer—as a way to become rich and famous, he admits—he later realized that "that *heaven of successful artists* doesn't exist"; as an adult, he studied theology and became a pastor instead. However, the writing bug never quite let go, and "after many years of writing plays, in 1965 I wrote a novel," he explained. "It was so awful that I still blush when I think about it. Writing it, however, taught me a lot about how to do something that long, and in 1966, I tried a second novel."

In 1967 Clements joined the English department of Eastern Connecticut State College, where he has since been a professor of English. His entry into the world of academia coincided with the publication of his second novel, *Two against the Tide.* Set on an island off the rocky coast of Maine, the story concerns a community of nearly fifty residents who have been able to stop the aging process through the use of a drug discovered by a local doctor and nurse more than a century earlier. When a young brother and sister are gently "kidnapped" by their aunt in order to rejuvenate this island utopia, they are faced with the choice of arresting their development and remaining children forever or returning to society and confronting the attendant joys and sorrows of growing up and growing older. A *Booklist* reviewer called Clements's debut novel "a thought-provoking, sometimes frightening and suspenseful story," while *Horn Book* reviewer Mary Silva Cosgrave praised *Two against the Tide* as a "highly original first book for children."

The Face of Abraham Candle, Clements's second novel, began "with some odd stories that I liked a lot," the author once told *SATA.* "I started to wonder who might have told such stories and who might have listened to them. The storyteller, I came to see, was John Candle, and he told them to his son Abraham. Then Abraham, with the stories in his head, began his adventure, and I followed along, writing down what he said and did."

The Face of Abraham Candle takes place in Colorado during that state's heyday—the silvermining era of the early 1890s. Bored, a young orphaned teen—the Abraham Candle of the title—decides to join two men in their exploration of caves on the Mesa Verde in search of ancient Native American artifacts. Undertaking the trip as a means of gaining experience of life and perhaps gaining wealth as well, Abraham grows in understanding and maturity through his eventual realization of the importance of preserving the ancient ruins.

One of Clements's most highly praised novels for young adults is *I Tell a Lie Every So Often,* published in 1974. A finalist for the National Book Award, the story is based on the 1850 diary of one Thaddeus Culbertson, who Clements fictionalizes as a fourteen-year-old cooper's apprentice named Henry Desant. Almost a decade after his young cousin has mysteriously disappeared, Henry claims to have heard of a young woman resembling her living with a tribe of Native Americans in the Dakota Territory. This fib fuels older-brother Clayton's desire to find his cousin, and the two boys set out on a

BRUCE CLEMENTS

Tom Loves Anna Loves Tom

aerial fiction

Clements's novel explores two weeks in which Tom and Anna fall in love while they grapple with several challenges. (Cover illustration by Elaine Norman.)

thousand-mile trek into the North American wilderness, traveling by steamboat, wagon, and horseback. Noting that Clayton's pomposity provides most of the book's humor, Zena Sutherland of the *Bulletin of the Center for Children's Books* asserted that "there's considerable humor and wit in other characters and they are all involved in dashing action."

The Treasure of Plunderell Manor is the adventure story that Clements always wanted to write. Taking place in Victorian England, it features a fourteen-year-old serving girl named Laurel Bybank. Orphaned, she finds work with Lord and Lady Stayne, who, motivated by greed, have confined their wealthy teenage niece, Alice Plunderell, to the tower room of their large home. Ordered by the couple to convince Alice to reveal the whereabouts of the treasure hidden by her deceased parents, Laurel befriends the young woman instead, thwarting the couple's evil plans. Ilene Cooper praised *The Treasure of Plunderell Manor* in *Booklist,* calling it a "Dickensian romp [that] is loads of fun, though Clements walks a thin line as he slyly parodies a familiar

genre." *School Library Journal* contributor Michael Cart called Clements "a talented and convincing story-teller with a rich gift for characterization."

Published in 1990, *Tom Loves Anna Loves Tom* is "an honest and direct, modern-day love affair," according to Lystad. Narrated by Tom, Clements's novel relates the two emotionally intense weeks that teens Tom and Anna share while Anna comes from out of town to visit her dying Aunt Barbara. "The question is not whether Tom and Anna will fall in love," noted Betsy Hearne of the *Bulletin of the Center for Children's Books.* "The question is how they will sustain each other through self-disclosures and mutual experiences." Commenting on the author's skillful pacing, Ilene Cooper noted in *Booklist* that "so much is embraced in that [two weeks] time—love, fear, regret, longing, death—that in many ways it does seem as if a lifetime has passed."

In addition to fiction, Clements has also written several works of nonfiction for younger readers. *From Ice Set Free: The Story of Otto Kiep,* published in 1972, is the biographical account of Clements's father-in-law, a German-born Scot who returned to the country of his birth to serve in the German Army during World War I. A successful lawyer and diplomat by the dawn of the Second World War, Kiep courageously spoke out against Adolf Hitler until his execution at the hands of the Nazis as an enemy of the Third Reich in 1944. Written in tandem with his wife, Hanna, Clements's *Coming Home to a Place You've Never Been Before* is a documentary account of a twenty-four-hour period in Perception House, a local half-way house for troubled young people where the authors have worked. "Essentially, it is a book about change," Clements noted, "and the slow attempts of change through interaction with others who have been in trouble."

"I write because I want to say to young people that life can be put together," Clements once explained, "that you can make sense out of yourself and the world around you, that you don't have to be a victim. The characters I write about are sometimes frightened and uncertain, but they don't give up. They make decisions and stick to them and survive."

■ Works Cited

Cart, Michael, review of *The Treasure of Plunderell Manor, School Library Journal,* March, 1988, p. 212.

Clements, Bruce, autobiographical essay in *Fifth Book of Junior Authors and Illustrators,* edited by Sally Holmes Holtze, H. W. Wilson, 1983, pp. 71-72.

Cooper, Ilene, review of *The Treasure of Plunderell Manor, Booklist,* January 15, 1988, p. 861.

Cooper, Ilene, review of *Tom Loves Anna Loves Tom, Booklist,* October 1, 1990, p. 330.

Cosgrave, Mary Silva, review of *Two against the Tide, Horn Book,* October, 1967, pp. 587-88.

Hearne, Betsy, review of *Tom Loves Anna Loves Tom, Bulletin of the Center for Children's Books,* December, 1990, p. 81.

Lystad, Mary, "Bruce Clements," *Twentieth-Century Young Adult Writers,* St. James Press, 1994, p. 136.

Sutherland, Zena, review of *I Tell a Lie Every So Often, Bulletin of the Center for Children's Books,* November, 1974, p. 39.

Review of *Two against the Tide, Booklist,* January 1, 1968, p. 542.

■ **For More Information See**

PERIODICALS

Bulletin of the Center for Children's Books, February, 1970, pp. 93-94; November, 1980, p. 49; December, 1990, p. 81.

Booklist, June 15, 1972, p. 902; October 15, 1977, p. 373; June 1, 1980, p. 1422.

Horn Book, April, 1974, pp. 151-52; April, 1978, p. 169.

Kirkus Reviews, August 15, 1967, p. 966; April 1, 1972, p. 412.

Publishers Weekly, November 24, 1969, p. 42; March 25, 1974, p. 57; July 13, 1990, p. 56.

School Library Journal, September, 1984, p. 126.

Voice of Youth Advocates, February, 1985, p. 323; April, 1988, pp. 21-22; April, 1991, p. 28.

* * *

COALSON, Glo 1946-

■ **Personal**

Born March 19, 1946, in Abilene, TX; daughter of Bill L. (a teacher) and LaVerne (an elementary school teacher; maiden name, Bowles) Coalson. *Education:* Abilene Christian University, B.A., 1968; also attended University of Colorado, University of Texas, and Columbia Teachers College. *Hobbies and other interests:* Camping, sailing, snorkeling, "all watery things done on top of the water."

■ **Addresses**

Home—Route 5, Box 860, Abilene, TX 79605.

■ **Career**

Writer and illustrator. Ed Triggs/Al Boyd—Graphic Designers, Austin, TX, graphic designer, 1969; artist in Kotzebue, AK, 1969-70; freelance illustrator in New York City, 1971-78, and Dallas, TX, 1978-80.

■ **Awards, Honors**

Friends of American Writers award for illustration, 1974, for *The Long Hungry Night.*

■ **Writings**

FOR CHILDREN

(Self-illustrated) *Three Stone Woman,* Atheneum, 1971.

ILLUSTRATOR

Ann Herbert Scott, *On Mother's Lap,* McGraw, 1972, revised edition, Clarion, 1992.

E. C. Foster and Slim Williams, *The Long Hungry Night,* Atheneum, 1973.

Arnold Griese, *At the Mouth of the Luckiest River,* Crowell, 1973.

Clyde Robert Bulla, *Dexter,* Crowell, 1973.

Jonathan Gathorne-Hardy, *Operation Peeg,* Lippincott, 1974.

Phyllis LaFarge, *Abby Takes Over,* Lippincott, 1974.

Helen S. Rodgers, *Morris and His Brave Lion,* McGraw, 1975.

Tom Robinson, *An Eskimo Birthday,* Dodd, 1975.

Hila Coleman, *That's the Way It Is, Amigo,* Crowell, 1975.

Gloria Skurzynski, *In a Bottle with a Cork on Top,* Dodd, 1976.

Gathorne-Hardy, *The Airship Lady Ship Adventure,* Lippincott, 1977.

Valentina P. Wasson, *The Chosen Baby,* Lippincott, 1977.

Griese, *The Wind Is Not a River,* Crowell, 1978.

Patricia C. Hass, *Windsong Summer,* Dodd, 1978.

Jay Leech and Zane Spencer, *Bright Fawn and Me,* Crowell, 1979.

Lee Bennett Hopkins, *By Myself,* Crowell, 1980.

Arnold Adoff, *Today We Are Brother and Sister,* Crowell, 1981.

Scott, *Hi!,* Philomel/Putnam, 1994.

Gina Willner-Pardo, *Daphne Eloise Slater, Who's Tall for Her Age,* Houghton, 1996.

Scott, *Brave as a Mountain Lion,* Clarion, 1996.

Jan Slepian, *Emily Just in Time,* Philomel, 1997.

■ **Sidelights**

Illustrator and author Glo Coalson grew up with a love of art and of the out-of-doors. It wasn't until she was almost ready to graduate from college that she decided to begin a career as a children's book illustrator and author. Since writing and illustrating *Three Stone Woman* in 1971, Coalson has used her talent with ink, watercolor, and oil pastels to illustrate numerous picture books and poetry collections for children.

When Coalson was four years old, she and her family moved to Abilene, Texas. "My sparse and rather isolated new neighborhood soon yielded to me one special girlfriend and a whole slew of boys," Coalson recalled to *SATA.* "To my eternal delight, there was also an inexhaustible supply of innumerable cats! There were lots of cousins who came to visit. My friends and my cousins and I built forts, camps, and playhouses—in mesquite trees, inside cardboard boxes, under grandmother's quilts, beside the barnyard fence ... anyplace where there was a nook or cranny or some such piece of magic."

On the occasions when she wasn't busy with friends, Coalson would go fishing. "On our farm outside Abilene there were several stock tanks or ponds," she explained. "We spent endless summer days fishing there. Patiently

"It feels good," said Michael.

Glo Coalson captures the warmth of a mother's love in her illustrations for Ann Herbert Scott's *On Mother's Lap*.

making ourselves places to sit on the hard, cattle-hoofed mud banks and impatiently waiting and watching for our corks to bob under." Coalson's grandmother was devoted to fishing during her later years, and Coalson recalls the many hours she spent sitting on the bank beside the elderly woman, rod in hand: "Such rich and sensual memories! Being so immersed with her in a mud-watery world of 'silversides' and stink-bait, sun bonnets and rusty minnow buckets. Granny stretched my imagination and splashed me with color."

Coalson demonstrated creativity throughout her childhood—"All my life I've been making things—sculpture and pottery—and drawing things"—but never considered channelling her talents into illustration until 1968. "I was sitting in a college figure drawing class, about to graduate that spring with a B.A. in art," she told *SATA*, adding that "to me [that] was the equivalent of stepping off the edge of the earth!" A classmate's enthusiastic comment, "You should illustrate books!" helped to determine the young artist's future. Two years later, while Coalson was visiting Alaska, one of her favorite parts of the United States, she collected some Eskimo folktales and designed several book proposals around them. In 1971, her first book, *Three Stone Woman,* was released by the New York City publishing house of Atheneum.

In *Three Stone Woman,* Coalson relates a folktale about a widowed woman, Ana, whose difficult circumstances force her to beg for food for her children from her brother and her sister-in-law, Tula. But instead of filling Ana's sack with food, the miserly Tula fills it with three stones. Fortunately, Ana eventually is helped by two strangers, who give her a magic sealskin pouch, which provides her and her family with more than enough food, and the entire village is well fed during the long winter months. Needless to say, when her brother comes to visit Ana the following spring and discovers his wife's deception, he abandons Tula and resolves to help support his sister and her family. *Library Journal* reviewer Marilyn McCulloch called *Three Stone Woman,* which Coalson illustrated with graphic black ink-and-brush, "an excellent choice for story hours and for units on Eskimo life."

Coalson has also garnered recognition for her work with author Ann Herbert Scott, publishing such books as *On Mother's Lap, Hi!,* and *Brave as a Mountain Lion.* First published in 1972, *On Mother's Lap* was reprinted twenty years later with new pastel illustrations replacing the original black ink drawings. The story follows a young Inuit boy as he discovers that his mother's lap, as well as his mother's heart, has room enough for both him and his new baby sister. Calling the book a "classic, re-illustrated with finesse," *Booklist* reviewer Carolyn Phelan remarks that children reading the book for the first time will enjoy the story as much as a "rocking chair ride on a mother's lap." Writing in *School Library Journal,* Mollie Bynum claims that Coalson's new artwork "improves upon a fine original work," going on to say that they give the book "revitalized energy to reach a new generation of youngsters."

Friendly Margarita is ignored by everyone in the post office queue until her determination wins her a new friend. (From *Hi!,* written by Ann Herbert Scott and illustrated by Coalson.)

In another collaboration with Scott, the two have produced *Hi!,* a story about young Margarita as she attempts to make contact with people waiting in line at the post office. Initially shouting a cheerful "hi" to everyone she sees, Margarita becomes less confident as no one returns her greetings. Finally, after whispering one last "hi," Margarita finds a happy recipient when the postal clerk responds with a smile and "hi" of her own. In *School Library Journal,* Anna Biagioni Hart wrote that Coalson's drawings capture "exactly what it is like to feel small and unnoticed." Describing Coalson's watercolors as "true-to-life," a reviewer in *Publishers Weekly* praised her illustrations which "affectionately portray a diverse, multiracial cast."

In addition, Coalson and Scott have also teamed up on the 1996 work *Brave as a Mountain Lion.* When a young Shoshone boy is asked to participate in a spelling bee, Spider must find a way to fight his performance anxiety. After receiving advice from each member of his family, Spider decides to take strength from his namesake, the spider, and enter the contest. In a *Booklist* review of *Brave as a Mountain Lion,* Shelley Townsend-Hudson noted that Coalson's "subtle watercolor illustrations effectively evoke ... the warmth of [a] family's love." Praising Coalson's subdued watercolor and pastel illustrations, Susan Hepler, writing in *School Library Journal,* suggested that the book would be useful for teachers looking to depict modern Native American families in their classrooms.

"In my book art, I try always to do things that people can identify with, the typical human experience," Coalson once explained. "I like to pack energy into my drawings, as much as is appropriate for each manuscript. In my personal art I keep exploring, playing off ever-accumulating life experiences, hoping for the satisfaction that comes with learning how to express more

about myself in a visual way." Coalson sees expanding her own experiences as a way of advancing her skill as an artist. In addition to maintaining a strong attachment to Alaska, she has retained ties to Manhattan, where she lived for seven years. "I try to spend a few weeks there each year," she told *SATA:* "It's a revitalization process."

■ Works Cited

Bynum, Mollie, review of *On Mother's Lap, School Library Journal,* May, 1992, p. 93.

Hart, Anna Biagioni, review of *Hi!, School Library Journal,* July, 1994, p. 89.

Hepler, Susan, review of *Brave as a Mountain Lion, School Library Journal,* April, 1996, p. 118.

Review of *Hi!, Publishers Weekly,* May 30, 1994, p. 56.

McCulloch, Marilyn, review of *Three Stone Woman, Library Journal,* October 15, 1971, p. 3457.

Phelan, Carolyn, review of *On Mother's Lap, Booklist,* April 1, 1992, p. 1458.

Townsend-Hudson, Shelley, review of *Brave as a Mountain Lion, Booklist,* March 15, 1996, p. 1269.

■ For More Information See

PERIODICALS

Booklist, May 15, 1994, p. 1684.

Horn Book, July/August, 1994, p. 445.

Kirkus Reviews, August 1, 1971, p. 801.

Publishers Weekly, May 30, 1994, p. 56; January 22, 1996, p. 73.

School Library Journal, May, 1992; July, 1994, p. 89; April 1996, p. 118.*

COHEN, Sholom 1951-

■ Personal

Born May 23, 1951, in Kansas City, MO; son of Eugene Joseph (a typographer) and Clara (Stillman) Cohen; married Bryna Chorner (a school administrator), August 21, 1978; children: Avraham, Chaim, Menachem Mendel, Yisroel, Nechama Dina, Sara Leah, Mushkie. *Education:* Massachusetts Institute of Technology, B.S., 1973; University of Michigan, M.L.S., 1974; attended University of Western Ontario, 1976-78; Columbia University, M.S., 1981. *Religion:* Jewish.

■ Addresses

Home—6383 Douglas St., Pittsburgh, PA 15217. *Office*—Software Engineering Institute, Carnegie-Mellon University, Pittsburgh, PA 15213. *Electronic mail*—sgc@sei.cmu.edu.

■ Career

University of Western Ontario, London, Canada, music librarian, 1974-78; Columbia University, New York City, systems librarian, 1979-81; McDonnell Douglas Corp., St. Louis, MO, software engineer, 1982-88; Carnegie-Mellon University, Pittsburgh, PA, software consultant, 1988—.

SHOLOM COHEN

■ Writings

"YITZ BERG FROM PITTSBURGH" SERIES

Yitzy and the G.O.L.E.M., HaChai Publications (Brooklyn, NY), 1992.
The Lopsided Yarmulke, HaChai Publications, 1995.

■ Work in Progress

Additional books in the "Yitz Berg from Pittsburgh" series.

■ Sidelights

Sholom Cohen told *SATA:* "It had never occurred to me to write fiction, let alone a children's novel, until about six years ago. At that time, I hadn't written anything of a fictional nature in over twenty years, since high school. (That's apart from the technical reports I do for government sponsors, which might be considered fiction in some quarters.)

"My actual inspiration was the lack of appropriate fiction for my children. There is a void of meaningful fiction for and about Jewish kids in the preteen years. As a Chassidic Jew, I wanted something that was, in a sense, for and about religiously observant Jewish children growing up in contemporary America. At the same time, I wanted to avoid the stereotypical religious themes of some Jewish children's literature and provide something that would appeal to a non-Jewish audience as well. I have tried to develop characters and tell stories that are clearly about the Jewish experience, but that also explore the universal themes of friendship, trust, and honesty.

"I also wanted to use Pittsburgh as a setting. The urban locale offers so many opportunities for plot development, and I've tried to make the city a character in some ways. The exploration of Pittsburgh has given me the chance to share some of the city's unique features with readers.

"Over the past six years of writing for children, I've had the greatest pleasure in hearing from readers of my books. I never tire of the best question of all: 'When's the next book coming out?'"

* * *

COOK, Jean Thor 1930-

■ Personal

Born March 10, 1930, in Little Falls, MN; daughter of Melvin H. (a construction company executive) and Florence (a teacher and homemaker; maiden name, Bohman) Thor; married Alan F. Cook (an automotive executive), August 5, 1950; children: Siri Cook Everett, Jodi Cook Nelson, Terry, Jill Cook Jensen, Jon. *Education:* Macalester College, B.S., 1951; University of Missouri, M.A., 1979. *Politics:* "Independent voter."

Religion: Lutheran. *Hobbies and other interests:* Travel, literature, sailing, relationships.

■ Addresses

Home—325 Jack Boot Rd., Monument, CO 80132.

■ Career

Writer. St. Mary College, Kansas City, KS, publicity director for an inner-city adult baccalaureate program, 1978-80.

■ Writings

Hugs for Our New Baby, illustrated by Michelle Dorenkamp, Concordia Publishing House (St. Louis, MO), 1987.
Butterflies for Grandpa, R.A.D.A.R., 1990.
Audrey and the Nighttime Skies, Concordia Publishing House, 1994.
Sam, the Terror of Westbrook Elementary, Concordia Publishing House, 1994.
Jesus Calms the Storm, Concordia Publishing House, 1994.
Room for a Stepdaddy, illustrated by Martine Gourbault, Albert Whitman (Morton Grove, IL), 1995.

■ Work in Progress

Who's Under My Bed?; Calhoun Becomes a Service Dog; Libby and Her Stepmommy; The Lopez Family Posada; Mrs. Pip's Wacky Tea Party; Where's Mama?; Molly's Wedding.

■ Sidelights

Jean Thor Cook told *SATA:* "My great love in writing is the picture book. I compare it to my son-in-law's creation of a fine French sauce. He begins with a variety of ingredients in a big kettle, simmered and stirred over several days until only a small amount of the original is left, then strained. Spices are added and *voila!* The broth becomes a superb, exquisite sauce to be savored with an entree.

"So it is with picture books as I write pages and pages, adding experiences, information, power words, the problems children experience, the things they like, the things they don't, relationship needs, a bit of the spiritual side of life, a pinch of how one can give something back to the world, and a big shake of humor. Then I put on my editing hat and start the torturous process of deciding what to keep. When my story is stripped down to bare bones, I add more words, better ones this time around, I hope, all the time reading the story aloud. Next I divide it into pages, making sure I have fruitful grist for an illustrator's imagination. Throughout this process I do my best not to be didactic, to keep the story entertaining, to find a dynamite beginning and a satisfying ending—all of this in less than a thousand words! Next I put the story aside for a few weeks, so I can have a fresh eye for the finishing

Jean Thor Cook with her husband, Alan.

touches before sending it on to the publishing companies. It's a challenge, but a process that I enjoy, just as my son-in-law does his French cuisine.

"My writing began when I took care of my elderly parents, folks in a health crisis. I had just finished a master's degree in adult education with an emphasis in counseling and was polishing my resume when I learned my life was going on a different highway. I wrote a manuscript about my experience, hoping that it would help others in the 'sandwich generation.' Then the road branched again as my husband took an early retirement. At this point we hoisted backpacks to travel extensively here and abroad, purchased a boat to sail in the Puget Sound and ultimately to Alaska, and pursued our hobbies, families, and friends.

"Then I discovered the picture book, and writing became a perfect accompaniment to this lifestyle, especially when grandchildren became the authentic spice for my stories. I wrote *Jesus Calms the Storm* off the shores of Canada when the wind blew up knee-knocking 'lumpy' seas, as the sailors call them. *Room for a Stepdaddy* came as a suggestion from a Minnesota bookstore employee whose life was in trauma. A Seattle grandchild was featured in *Audrey and the Nighttime Skies. Butterflies for Grandpa* was about my father's death. For one who has always done extensive community work, these stories have become my avenue to helping others. It's a wonderful way to mix pleasure and work. Have briefcase, will travel."

■ For More Information See

PERIODICALS

School Library Journal, January, 1996, p. 77.

CRAIG, Helen 1934-

■ Personal

Born August 30, 1934, in London, England; daughter of Edward (a writer and designer for theater and films) and Helen (maiden name, Godfrey) Craig; children: Ben Norland. *Education:* Attended King Alfred's School, London, England. *Hobbies and other interests:* Collecting children's books, etching, working with ceramic sculpture and in her garden.

■ Addresses

Home—Vine Cottage, Harroell, Long Crendon, Aylesbury, Buckinghamshire HP18 9AQ, England.

■ Career

Gee & Watson (commercial photographers), London, England, apprentice, 1950-56; owner and operator of photographic studio in Hampstead, London, 1956-63; sculptor and artist in southern Spain, 1964-66; freelance potter and photographer in London, 1967-69; began illustrating children's books, 1969—; Garland Compton (advertising agency), London, photographer, 1969-72; freelance photographer, potter, and Chinese wallpaper restorer, 1972-74; OXFAM, England, photographer, 1975-77.

■ Awards, Honors

Award from Society of Illustrators (United States), 1977, for *The Mouse House ABC* foldout concertina; Kentucky Blue Grass Award, 1985, for *Angelina Ballerina;* Smarties Book Prize shortlist, 1992, for *The Town Mouse and the Country Mouse.* Three of Craig's books have been chosen for the British Book Design and Production exhibitions, of which *Angelina's Birthday* won a category award in 1990.

■ Writings

SELF-ILLUSTRATED CHILDREN'S BOOKS

A Number of Mice, Aurum Press, 1978.
The Little Mouse Learning House: ABC, Simon & Schuster, 1983. *The Little Mouse Learning House: 123,* Simon & Schuster, 1983.
Susie and Alfred in the Knight, the Princess, and the Dragon, Knopf, 1985.
Susie and Alfred in the Night of the Paper Bag Monsters, Knopf, 1985.
Susie and Alfred in A Welcome for Annie, Walker, 1986.
Susie and Alfred in a Busy Day at Town, Walker, 1986.
The Town Mouse and the Country Mouse, Walker, 1992, Candlewick, 1992.
I See the Moon and the Moon Sees Me: Helen Craig's Book of Nursery Rhymes, Harper, 1992.
Charlie and Tyler at the Seashore, Candlewick, 1995, published in England as *Charlie and Tyler at the Seaside,* Walker, 1995.

HELEN CRAIG

"THE MOUSE HOUSE" SERIES; FOLDOUT CONCERTINA BOOKS

The Mouse House ABC, Random House, 1978. *The Mouse House 123,* Random House, 1980.
The Mouse House Months of the Year, Random House, 1981.
The Mouse House The Days of the Week, Random House, 1982.

ILLUSTRATOR

Robert Nye, *Wishing Gold,* Macmillan, 1970.
Tanith Lee, *Animal Castle,* Farrar, Straus, 1972.
Lee, *Princess Hynchatti and Some Other Surprises,* Macmillan, 1972.
Katharine Holabird, *Angelina Ballerina,* C. N. Potter, 1983.
Holabird, *Angelina and the Princess,* C. N. Potter, 1984.
Holabird, *Angelina Goes to the Fair,* C. N. Potter, 1985.
Holabird, *Angelina's Christmas,* C. N. Potter, 1985.
Margaret Mahy, *JAM: A True Story,* Atlantic Monthly Press, 1985.
Sarah Hayes, *This Is the Bear,* Candlewick, 1986.
Judy Corbalis, *The Wrestling Princess,* Deutsch, 1986.
Holabird, *Angelina on Stage,* C. N. Potter, 1986.
Nigel Gray, *The One and Only Robin Hood,* Little, Brown, 1987.
Blake Morrison, *The Yellow House,* Harcourt, 1987.

Holabird, *Angelina and Alice,* C. N. Potter, 1987.

Hayes, *This Is the Bear & the Picnic Lunch,* Candlewick, 1988.

Corbalis, *Porcellus the Flying Pig,* Dial, 1988.

Holabird, *Alexander and the Dragon,* C. N. Potter, 1988.

Holabird, *Angelina's Birthday,* Aurum Press, 1989, published as *Angelina's Birthday Surprise,* C. N. Potter, 1989.

Hayes, *Crumbling Castle,* Candlewick, 1989.

Hayes, *Mary Mary,* McElderry, 1989.

Mahy, *The Pumpkin Man and the Crafty Creeper,* Lothrop, 1990.

Holabird, *Alexander and the Magic Boat,* C. N. Potter, 1990.

Hayes, *This Is the Bear and the Scary Night,* Candlewick, 1991.

Holabird, *Angelina's Baby Sister,* C. N. Potter, 1991.

Jenny Nimmo, *The Stone Mouse,* C. N. Potter, 1993.

Holabird, *Angelina Ice Skates,* C. N. Potter, 1993.

Hayes, *This Is the Bear and the Bad Little Girl,* Candlewick, 1995.

Phyllis Root, *One Windy Wednesday,* Candlewick, 1996.

Martin Waddell, *My Aunty Sal and the Mega-Sized Moose,* Candlewick, 1996.

Mara Bergman, *Bears Bears, Everywhere,* Orchard, 1997.

Also contributed illustrations to *Stories for a Prince,* Hamish Hamilton, 1983, to *The Children's Book,* in aid of Save the Children, Walker, 1985, and to *The Tail Feathers of Mother Goose,* Walker, 1988.

■ Work in Progress

Illustrations for a new publication of Charlotte Zolotov's *The Bunny Who Found Easter,* for Houghton Mifflin; illustrations for *Turnover Tuesday,* by Phyllis Root, for Candlewick.

■ Sidelights

Helen Craig is an English illustrator of children's books best known for her "Angelina Mouse" character, written by Katharine Holabird. She has also teamed up with Sarah Hayes on "This Is the Bear" series in which she has created a lovable, cuddly stuffed bear. In addition, Craig has produced her own popular "Susie and Alfred" series of picture books which feature a pair of porcine pals, and her "Charlie and Tyler" series about a country mouse and a town mouse. In fact, Craig has made a cottage industry out of mice and piggies and bears—quite literally—for she lives and works in a three hundred-year-old cottage in Buckinghamshire. She has been writer-illustrator or illustrator of over fifty books for children, and "can be compared favorably to all of the other great artists of anthropomorphic mice," according to Jean Hammond Zimmerman writing in *School Library Journal.*

Craig was no stranger to the world of art as a child. In fact, she come from a long line of theater people—both actors and designer-writers. Her great-grandmother was Dame Ellen Terry, the famous actress, and her grandfather, Terry's son, was Edward Gordon Craig, the revolutionary theatrical designer and producer who was also a brilliant and innovative wood engraver. Craig's father is a writer and designer for theater and films, and her brother is an artist. "I felt rather overwhelmed by this wealth of talent around me," Craig once told *Something about the Author* (*SATA*). Craig grew up in a remote part of Essex in England, living in a tiny thatched cottage with neither electricity or running water. At sixteen she became a photographer's apprentice, then ran her own photography studio in London. It

Craig employed a modified version of the comic strip format when illustrating *The Town Mouse and the Country Mouse,* her retelling of Aesop's fable about two mice who long for the familiarity of home when visiting one another.

It gave him a peck.

Tyler was furious
and drew his sword.

"Take that!"
he shouted.
"Ow!" squawked
the chick.

Various adventures ensue when Charlie, the cautious country mouse, and Tyler, the extroverted city mouse, visit the seacoast. (From *Charlie and Tyler at the Seashore,* written and illustrated by Craig.)

was only later, during a three-year sojourn in Spain, that Craig finally began drawing seriously and also making ceramics. Back in England, she continued to try to find her true medium. As she told *SATA,* "It had always been my ambition that one day I would be a creative artist of some sort." Craig began illustrating children's books while raising her son as a single mother. "I bought Maurice Sendak's book, *Where the Wild Things Are,* for my small son, and that really gave me direction," she told *SATA.* "As a child I had been strongly impressed by the books I looked at and read, and I can still recall those feelings and try to remember them when working."

Craig first illustrated for books by Tanith Lee, but by the late 1970s she had developed her own series of

foldout concertina books called "The Mouse House." These first picture books taught alphabet and number skills, as well as months of the year and days of the week. In 1983 she teamed up with Katharine Holabird for *Angelina Ballerina,* the first of a series of Angelina books that has proven popular enough to support eight further titles as well as spin-offs such as the Angelina Doll (which Craig designed) and miniature Angelina books. In these books, such childhood themes as jealousy, shyness, birthday happiness, dedication, wonderment, and even despair are explored in a light format centering around the adventures of the balletic mouse, Angelina. *Angelina and the Princess,* for example, is the story of Angelina's ballet class which has been chosen to dance for Her Royal Highness. Angelina works so hard she becomes ill and does poorly in tryouts, but comes through on the final night with a marvelous dance. Anita Silvey, writing in *Horn Book,* felt that though the story was "predictable," Craig's illustrations were "extraordinary." Silvey noted Craig's "ever so slight a line" which "magnificently delineates character" in pictures "alive with movement, vitality, and humor." *School Library Journal*'s Zimmerman commented that "Craig's pastel colored ink drawings ... steal the show," and *Publishers Weekly* concluded that "Craig's gently humorous pastel pictures will appeal to little ones." Another title in the ongoing series is *Angelina's Christmas,* in which she enlists a lonely postman to become the school Santa. *Kirkus Reviews* commented that Craig's "cheerful pastel scenes are delicate but not sentimental." Peggy Forehand, reviewing the book in *School Library Journal,* noted that the character of Angelina "has charmed readers with her sensitivity and tenderness without melodrama," and that her art reveals "unusual attention to tone and detail." She concludes that the author and illustrator have again provided "simple lessons that create a real celebration." In *Angelina on Stage,* the little mouse must overcome jealousy toward her younger cousin who wins a part in the adult ballet she is participating in, and in *Angelina and Alice,* she applies her talents to gymnastics, in a book in which "Craig steals the show," according to *Horn Book*'s Silvey. Silvey noted also the "marvelous things [Craig] accomplishes with the arc of a mouse tail." Angelina is happily surprised by a new red bicycle in *Angelina's Birthday Surprise,* another team effort in which "Text and illustrations work together beautifully," according to Jane Gardner Connor in *School Library Journal.* Craig has also partnered with Holabird on two non-mouse books, *Alexander and the Dragon* and *Alexander and the Magic Boat.*

Craig reports that she loves her work and considers herself lucky to be able to work at it for a living. "But it is not always easy," as she told *SATA.* "Many times it is a great struggle to produce one's best work. When I illustrate a book, I will first of all read through the story a number or times to really get the feel of it. Then, once I know how many pages will be in the final book, I go through the story marking passages where I feel a picture will complement or extend the story in some way." Craig then makes small page mock-ups to be able to see the balance of picture and words on the page, using very sketchy drawings. Next comes the full-sized dummy of the book in which she draws print and picture as close to the size of the published work as possible. These pictures she will show to the art director and writer, after which she starts the final pictures. Two or three roughs precede putting the final rough onto watercolor paper with a very light pencil. "I work in the basic design with a very fine pen and ink," Craig explained to *SATA,* "then I will work into this with the watercolour. After this, I will go back and work up some of the pen lines to get more contrast. This can go on for a long time, alternating colour with line until I am satisfied. This is only one method. *The Yellow House* was illustrated by doing etchings with aquatint; the color was added on the back of the etching using a light box, thereby ensuring a perfect registration and clean colour, as the colour plates had no admix of black in them. I have been experimenting with opaque colours such as gouache and I am hoping to experiment with other techniques later on."

Craig has also teamed up extensively with the writer Sarah Hayes, especially with *This Is the Bear* and its sequels. Intended as read-alouds, the books are written with chanting rhyme and follow the adventures of a little boy, his stuffed bear, and the dog who, although jealous of the bear, quite often comes to his rescue. The first title in the series sets the tone for the rest: Bear is mistakenly put into a garbage bin and ends up at the

Craig's animated drawings have enlivened Katharine Holabird's tales of the well-loved balletic mouse, Angelina. (From *Angelina Ice Skates.*)

dump where the boy and his dog eventually save him. Judith Glover in *School Library Journal* noted that "Bear's face is wonderfully expressive," and Barbara Elleman, writing in *Booklist,* commented that "The softly colored economical drawings are framed in thin, coordinated borders.... Sure to be a winner with the toddler crowd." More adventures follow in *This Is the Bear and the Picnic Lunch,* in which Craig's delicate and expressive artwork "nicely counterpoint the rollicking text," according to *Kirkus Reviews.* Bear is carelessly left out in the park overnight in *This Is the Bear and the Scary Night,* a "spare story" with just the correct "sequencing," according to Trev Jones in *School Library Journal.* Jones went on to comment that all "the action takes place in Craig's pictures." Martha V. Parravano, reviewing the fourth title in the series, *This Is the Bear and the Bad Little Girl,* concluded that Hayes's "chantable, mock-cumulative text" is well-matched by Craig's "humorous, airy" illustrations and "droll" speech balloons. Craig and Hayes have also teamed up on *Crumbling Castles,* three stories about a wizard named Zeb, and *Mary Mary,* a contrary girl who befriends a lonely giant.

Craig's solo efforts as author-illustrator have thus far been highlighted by the "Susie and Alfred" books and the town mouse and country mouse duet of picture books. The mischievous piglet neighbors who "dress, live and behave like middle-class human children of fifty years ago," as described by a reviewer writing in *The Junior Bookshelf,* experience a variety of adventures in the series, from a fancy dress party to welcoming a new neighbor. *Susie and Alfred in the Night of the Paper Bag Monsters,* for example, has the duo preparing for a party. When Alfred spills green paint all over Susie's fancy dress clothes, they must come up with alternative dress. Margery Fisher, writing in *Growing Point,* noted that this small glimpse into neighborhood life is borne out by appropriate "humanisation in the dress, posture and facial expressions" of the two featured piglets. With *The Town Mouse and the Country Mouse,* however, Craig went back to her beloved mice and to an interesting format for the retelling of the familiar fable by Aesop. "I have always liked comic books where the action is shown in a sequence of pictures," Craig told *SATA.* "I looked to the work of Windsor McKay, whom I really admire, for inspiration when designing the sequence of image and type." The resulting book was well received, shortlisted for England's prestigious Smarties Prize in 1992. Kathryn Jennings in *Bulletin of the Center for Children's Books* dubbed it a "cozy version" of the traditional tale. "The pen-and-wash illustrations have a comic-book-format appeal and a bucolic air."

"I enjoyed the two mice characters so much," Craig told *SATA,* "that I followed it up with another adventure using the same 'comic book' style layout." *Charlie and Tyler at the Seaside* tells the tale of Tyler, the town mouse, and Charlie from the country, who spend a day together at the seashore. They are flown there by Mrs. Pigeon, and immediately find themselves in adventures galore. They are nearly washed out to sea in a tiny boat,

become members of a toy theater company, and narrowly avoid becoming dinner for a predator. Finally they are flown back home, exhausted, by Mrs. Pigeon. Cynthia Anthony, writing in *Magpies,* concluded that "Craig's cosy illustrations and her depiction of two very different mice, jaunty Tyler and the more cautious Charlie, are sure to please."

"I was exploring many relationships and contrasts in these books," Craig explained to *SATA.* "Not only the 'child-giant' theme—here represented by the 'mouse-human,' but also the small secret 'unknown' fantastical world of the mice existing within the giant 'known' world of humans with which every child is familiar. Also the relationship of the swaggering Tyler Townmouse contrasting with the retiring quality of the timid Charlie Country Mouse. At the same time, one double-page spread has, in a sense, two contrasting time scales. The dining table where Tyler invites Charlie to eat shows the whole table as one picture but is also divided into little moments in time in which Charlie is being offered a new tasty treat."

"Recently," Craig continued, "I have been experimenting with a new technique which I used for *One Windy Night* written by Phyllis Root. The original pictures were drawn in fine line on a very small scale and then enlarged a number of times on a photocopier. This gave them a very bold quality—they were then coloured. I hope to use this more often." It is this spirit of innovation and creative endeavor that comes through in Craig's illustrations and that has made her a favorite with young readers.

■ Works Cited

Review of *Angelina and the Princess, Publishers Weekly,* November 30, 1984, p. 89.

Review of *Angelina's Christmas, Kirkus Reviews,* January, 1986, pp. 86-7.

Anthony, Cynthia, review of *Charlie and Tyler at the Seaside, Magpies,* September, 1995, pp. 27-8.

Connor, Jane Gardner, review of *Angelina's Birthday Surprise, School Library Journal,* December, 1989, p. 82.

Elleman, Barbara, review of *This Is the Bear, Booklist,* April 1, 1986, p. 1141.

Fisher, Margery, review of *Susie and Alfred in the Night of the Paper Bag Monsters, Growing Point,* September, 1988, p. 5041.

Forehand, Peggy, review of *Angelina's Christmas, School Library Journal,* October, 1985, p. 190.

Glover, Judith, review of *This Is the Bear, School Library Journal,* September, 1986, p. 122.

Jennings, Kathryn, review of *The Town Mouse and the Country Mouse, Bulletin of the Center for Children's Books,* January, 1993, pp. 138-9.

Jones, Trev, review of *This Is the Bear and the Scary Night, School Library Journal,* April, 1992, p. 92.

Parravano, Martha V., review of *This Is the Bear and the Bad Little Girl, Horn Book,* November-December, 1995, p. 760.

Silvey, Anita, review of *Angelina and the Princess, Horn Book,* January-February, 1985, p. 46.

Silvey, Anita, review of *Angelina and Alice, Horn Book,* March-April, 1988, pp. 192-3.

Review of *Susie and Alfred in the Night of the Paper Bag Monsters, The Junior Bookshelf,* October, 1985, p. 211.

Review of *This Is the Bear and the Picnic Lunch, Kirkus Reviews,* April 15, 1989, p. 624.

Zimmerman, Jean Hammond, review of *Angelina and the Princess, School Library Journal,* January, 1985, p. 65.

■ For More Information See

PERIODICALS

Bulletin of the Center for Children's Books, January, 1985, p. 87; September, 1985, p. 5; January, 1986, pp. 86-7; June, 1986. p. 183; February, 1987, p. 108.

Horn Book, January, 1985, p. 46; March, 1987, p. 202; January/February, 1989, p. 54; November/December, 1989, p. 760; September/October, 1992, pp. 575-6; January, 1993, p. 103.

Junior Bookshelf, August, 1986, pp. 146-7; February, 1987, p. 20; April, 1993, p. 63.

Los Angeles Times Book Review, February 17, 1985, p. 7; April 19, 1987, p. 4.

New York Times Book Review, November 11, 1984, p. 55.

Times Educational Supplement, June 21, 1985, p. 25; February 14, 1992, p. 27; July 7, 1995, p. R2.

—Sketch by J. Sydney Jones

*   *   *

CREECH, Sharon 1945-

■ Personal

Also writes under name Sharon Rigg; born July 29, 1945, in Cleveland, OH; divorced once; married Lyle D. Rigg (headmaster at TASIS England American School, Thorpe, Surrey), 1981; children: Rob, Karin. *Education:* Hiram College, B.A.; George Mason University, M.A.

■ Addresses

Home—c/o TASIS England, Coldharbour Lane, Thorpe, Surrey, England; and Chautauqua, NY. *Agent*—Carol Smith, and Jonathan Dolger.

■ Career

Federal Theater Project Archives, Fairfax, VA; editorial assistant, *Congressional Quarterly,* Washington, DC; teacher of American and British literature, TASIS England American School, Surrey, England, 1979-82, and 1984-, and TASIS (The American School in Switzerland), Lugano, Switzerland, 1983-85.

SHARON CREECH

■ Awards, Honors

Billee Murray Denny Poetry Award, Lincoln College, IL, 1988, for "Cleansing"; Best Books, *School Library Journal,* 1994, Notable Children's Books, American Library Association, 1995, Newbery Medal, American Library Association, 1995, and Young Readers Award, Virginia State Reading Association, 1997, all for *Walk Two Moons.*

■ Writings

FOR YOUNG PEOPLE

Absolutely Normal Chaos, Macmillan (England), 1990, HarperCollins, 1995.

Walk Two Moons, HarperCollins, 1994.

Pleasing the Ghost, illustrated by Stacey Schuett, HarperCollins, 1996, published in England as *The Ghost of Uncle Arvie,* illustrated by Simon Cooper, Macmillan, 1996.

Chasing Redbird, HarperCollins, 1997.

OTHER

The Center of the Universe: Waiting for the Girl (play), produced in New York City, 1992.

Also author, under name Sharon Rigg, of *The Recital,* published in England, 1990, and *Nickel Malley.*

■ Sidelights

"On February 6th, [1995]" recalled Sharon Creech in comments reprinted in *Horn Book,* "I was home alone in England and had been wrestling all morning with a manuscript. Feeling ornery and frustrated, I fled to our back yard to vent one of my muffled screams (muffled because I am a headmaster's wife and it isn't seemly for me to scream too loudly). In the midst of that scream, the phone rang.

"A ringing telephone in a headmaster's house often signals a crisis," she continues, "and when it rings, I'm well-trained; I grab pencil and paper.... That afternoon, I scribbled: American Library Association and Newbery Med..."

"The writing trails off there."

Walk Two Moons, the 1995 Newbery Medal winner, brought Creech instant celebrity in the United States, where her first novel for young adults, *Absolutely Normal Chaos,* had not yet been published. "I still don't know how I feel about it," she confessed to Judy Hendershot and Jackie Peck in *Reading Teacher.* "It's like someone has given me this beautiful suit of Armani clothes. They look nice and everyone admires them, but I'm a little uncomfortable in them. I like to wear them for brief periods of time and then change back to my blue jeans."

Despite her years living and working in England, Sharon Creech is an American citizen. She was born and raised in Cleveland, Ohio, part of "a big, noisy family ... with hordes of relatives telling stories around the kitchen table," she explained in the *Seventh Book of Junior Authors & Illustrators.* "Here I learned to exaggerate and embellish, because if you didn't, your story was drowned out by someone else's more exciting one." She was an enthusiastic writer throughout grade school and high school, and she was often captivated by the "instruments of writing: paper, pens, pencils, books. I hoarded them." She was an equally enthusiastic reader. "I don't remember the titles of books I read as a child, but I do remember the *experience* of reading—of drifting into the pages and living in someone else's world." "I loved myths—American Indian myths, Greek myths, and the King Arthur legends," she concluded, "—and I remember the lightning jolt of exhilaration when I read *Ivanhoe* as a teenager."

After receiving her bachelor's degree from Hiram College, Creech went on to George Mason University in Washington, D.C., for her master's. "During graduate school," she stated in the *Seventh Book of Junior Authors & Illustrators,* "I worked at the Federal Theater Project Archives and longed to write plays. Next I worked at *Congressional Quarterly,* as an editorial assistant, but this was not pleasant work for me, for it was all politics and facts." Nonetheless, Creech remained in Washington for several years. She married, had two children, and was divorced. In 1979, she persuaded the headmaster of TASIS (The American School in Switzerland) England School, a grade school for the children of expatriate Americans in Thorpe, England, to hire her as a teacher of literature. "Before receiving an offer of employment, however," noted Creech's husband, Lyle D. Rigg, in *Horn Book,* "Sharon

had to convince the headmaster that she, a single parent with two young children, could handle the considerable demands of teaching in an international day/boarding school in the suburbs of London. Although I have never read Sharon's letter to that headmaster, I have heard that it was a masterpiece of persuasion and was instrumental in getting her hired."

Sharon Creech and Lyle D. Rigg were married about three years after they met. "I think it was a combination of our Buckeye roots and ice cubes that drew us together," Rigg recalled. "We met on our first day in England, when Sharon borrowed some ice—that rare commodity in Europe—from me." Rigg had been hired as assistant headmaster—the British equivalent of a school principal—and soon after he and Creech were married, they were transferred to the TASIS branch in Switzerland. In 1984, Rigg returned to Thorpe as headmaster of the English branch, and he and Creech have been there ever since (although they spend their summers in a cabin in Chautauqua, New York). "As a teacher of American and British literature to American and international teenagers," Rigg added, "Sharon has shared her love both of literature and of writing. She'd

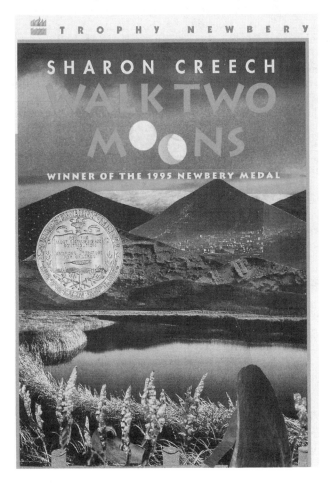

In Creech's Newbery Medal-winning novel of growth and self-recognition, thirteen-year-old Salamanca Tree Hiddle comes to terms with her mother's death and her own sense of desertion and loss. (Cover illustration by Lisa Desimini.)

open up Chaucer's world in *The Canterbury Tales* and then head off to Canterbury with her students so that they could make the pilgrimage themselves. She'd offer *Hamlet,* and then off they would all go to Stratford-upon-Avon."

For many years Creech devoted her time almost exclusively to her teaching and her family. "In 1980, when my children and I had been in England for nine months," she recalled in *Horn Book,* "my father had a stroke. Although he lived for six more years, the stroke left him paralyzed and unable to speak.... Think of all those words locked up for six years...." Creech started her first novel a month after her father's death in 1986, "and when I finished it," she continued, "I wrote another, and another, and another. The words rushed out."

Absolutely Normal Chaos, Creech's first book for young readers, was published in England in 1990. "When I wrote *Absolutely Normal Chaos,*" Creech told Hendershot and Peck, "I didn't know it was a children's book." *Absolutely Normal Chaos* deals with a variety of themes, some specific to adolescence (first love, growing up, schoolwork), and others that can apply to any period in life (dealing with relatives and friends, learning compassion and understanding). The book is the journal of one summer in the life of thirteen-year-old Mary Lou Finney of Easton, Ohio. At the beginning of the book Mary Lou begs her English teacher not to read the remainder of the story. Her summer, it becomes apparent, has been more bizarre than usual. "Her life is disrupted in more ways than one by the arrival of a gangling, uncommunicative cousin, Carl Ray, from West Virginia, by his curious relationship with Charlie Furtz, the genial neighbour from across the road, who subsequently dies of a heart attack, and by her own budding romance with Alex Cheevey," explained Joan Zahnleiter in *Magpies.* These circumstances force Mary Lou to confront issues in her own life and to come to terms with her own family and its functionings. Throughout her summer, Mary Lou learns to confront such diverse issues as classic literature, death, questionable legitimacy, and family life. "Mary Lou is a typical teen whose acquaintance with the sadder parts of life is cushioned by a warm and energetic family," stated Cindy Darling Codell in her *School Library Journal* review. "Her entertaining musings on Homer, Shakespeare, and Robert Frost are drawn in nifty parallels to what is happening in her own life." Nancy Vasilakis of *Horn Book* added: "Her own hilarious brush with culture shock occurs when she accompanies Carl Ray on a trip to his home. This visit also provides Mary Lou with some insights into what her cousin has had to endure at her house. Mary Lou grows in a number of important ways throughout the summer, and the metaphors she now recognizes in the *Odyssey* could, she realizes, very well apply to her own life."

The same themes of growth and self-recognition appear in Creech's second novel (the first published in the United States), *Walk Two Moons.* In this story, Salamanca Tree Hiddle, another 13-year-old girl like Mary

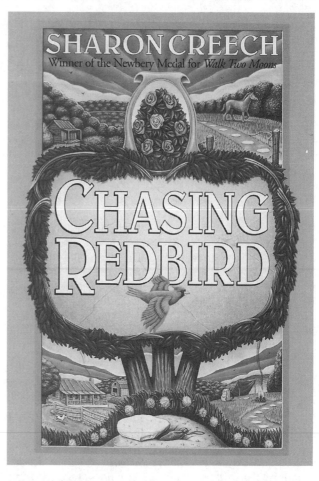

Thirteen-year-old Zinnia Taylor embarks upon a journey of self-discovery when she begins clearing an overgrown trail that starts at her family's farm. (Cover illustration by Marc Burckhardt.)

Lou, relates the plight of her friend Phoebe, whose mother has left home. What makes Phoebe's story particularly relevant to Sal is the fact that Sal's mother Sugar also left home and never returned. Sal is on a trip to Idaho with her grandparents to visit her mother. "Sal finds that recounting Phoebe's story helps her understand the desertion of her own mother," explained Deborah Stevenson in the *Bulletin of the Center for Children's Books.* "Creech skillfully keeps these layers separate but makes their interrelationship clear, and the plot moves along amid all this contemplation with the aid of a mysterious noteleaver, a local 'lunatic,' an eccentric English teacher, and Sal's budding romance."

Some of the elements of *Walk Two Moons* came from Creech's own experiences. "In every book I've done," she told Hendershot and Peck, "the characters are combinations of people. I do draw very much from my family, and so I've speculated that Salamanca and her mother are very much me and my own daughter combined." Creech explained that the idea that originally inspired the writing of *Walk Two Moons* came from a message she found in a fortune cookie: "Don't judge a man until you've walked two moons in his moccasins." The framework of the story was based on Creech's trip to Lewiston, Idaho with her family at the age of twelve. Sal's Native American ancestry was also inspired by the author's childhood experiences. "I inhaled Indian myths, and among my favorites were those which involved stories of reincarnation," she commented in her Newbery acceptance speech. "How magnificent and mysterious to be Estsanatlehi, 'the woman who never dies. She grows from baby to mother to old woman and then turns into a baby again, and on and on she goes, living a thousand, thousand lives.' I wanted to be that Navajo woman."

Sal's full name, Salamanca Tree, also evokes Creech's fondness for the outdoors. "I think I spent half my childhood up a tree," she recalled in *Horn Book*. "You could climb and climb, and you could reach a place where there was only you and the tree and the birds and the sky. And maybe the appeal of trees also lay in the sense that they live 'a thousand, thousand lives,' appearing to die each autumn." "The Indianness is one of the best things about this book," asserted *New York Times Book Review* contributor Hazel Rochman, "casual, contemporary and mythic, not an exotic thing apart. Sal is only a small part Indian, and she knows her parents gave her what they thought was the tribe's name but got it wrong. Still, the heritage is a part of her identity. She loves the Indian stories her mother told her, and they get mixed in with Genesis and Pandora's box and Longfellow and with family stories and, above all, with a celebration of the sweeping natural world and our connectedness with it." "For once in a children's book," Rochman concluded, "Indians are people, not reverential figures in a museum diorama. Sal's Indian heritage is a natural part of her finding herself in America."

One of the most dramatic themes common to both *Absolutely Normal Chaos* and *Walk Two Moons* is that of death, examined in relation to subsequent feelings of grief and loss. Mary Lou and Carl Ray have to come to terms with the loss of Charlie Furtz. Sal has to deal with death and her own sense of desertion and loss. These themes are also linked to Creech's life. "When I read Salamanca's story now, with some distance," the author revealed in *Horn Book*, "I hear such longing in her voice—for her mother, for her father, for the land—and I know that her longing is also my longing ... for my children, my larger family, and for my own country."

Creech's next story, *Pleasing the Ghost,* directed to a somewhat younger audience, also deals with death and loss, but with a lighter touch. Nine-year-old Dennis is visited in his bedroom by a parade of ghosts—"but never the one I want." Hoping to encounter his late father, Dennis instead meets up with his Uncle Arvie, who wants the boy to help Arvie's widow, Dennis's Aunt Julia, find gifts and money he has left hidden for her. Mystery blends with comedy in Creech's tale as Dennis must first decipher his uncle's messages, jumbled due to a speech impairment caused by a stroke Arvie suffered before his death. "The book has several mythical elements: three wishes, magic, ghosts, a lonely young boy whose father has died, a quest and a satisfactory conclusion," asserted *School Librarian* contributor Ann

Jenkin. A *Publishers Weekly* reviewer observed: "Arvie's earnest affection for Julia and Dennis make him a role model as well as a clown, and Creech's attention to nuances of feeling grounds this light tale in emotional truth." *Booklist* reviewer Michael Cart called *Pleasing the Ghost* an "engaging story that manages to deal lightheartedly with emotional loss by offering [Creech's] readers the enduring promise of hope."

Creech returns to the hills of Kentucky, the setting for the opening of *Walk Two Moons,* for *Chasing Redbird,* another well-received story of grief, loss, and discovery. Thirteen-year-old Zinnia Taylor, the third of seven siblings, enjoys escaping to the "Quiet Zone" of her neighboring aunt and uncle's home. The death of Zinny's aunt, however, causes her despondent uncle to engage in increasingly eccentric behavior as he succumbs to unrelenting grief, leaving Zinny to find solace elsewhere. The teenager soon becomes obsessed with her discovery of a long, winding trail near her home—a trail once used by trappers and Indians. As Zinny works to clear the trail, occasionally interrupted by the attentions of an older boy, she unearths markers and other indications of her ancestors' presence in the region. "Creech has written a striking novel, notable for its emotional honesty," declared Ethel L. Heins in a *Horn Book* review of *Chasing Redbird*. "In her Newbery Medal acceptance speech," Heins added, "the author spoke of her predilection for mystery and for metaphorical journeys; she has worked both into the novel and, in addition, once again bridges the gap between the generations and binds them together." A *Kirkus Reviews* commentator also had high praise for the book, maintaining: "Creech crams her novel full of wonderful characters, proficient dialogue, bracing descriptions, and a merry use of language." A *Publishers Weekly* reviewer called *Chasing Redbird* "Creech's best yet," while Deborah Stevenson of the *Bulletin of the Center for Children's Books* concluded: "Creech again demonstrates her expertise at evoking physical and emotional landscapes and the connections between the two as Zinny blazes her way down literal and spiritual paths."

■ Works Cited

Cart, Michael, review of *Pleasing the Ghost, Booklist,* September 1, 1996, p. 125.

Review of *Chasing Redbird, Kirkus Reviews,* February 1, 1997, p. 220.

Review of *Chasing Redbird, Publishers Weekly,* January 20, 1997, p. 403.

Codell, Cindy Darling, review of *Absolutely Normal Chaos, School Library Journal,* November, 1995, p. 119.

Creech, Sharon, "Newbery Medal Acceptance," *Horn Book,* July/August, 1995, pp. 418-25.

Creech, Sharon, essay in *Seventh Book of Junior Authors and Illustrators,* edited by Sally Holmes Holtze, H. W. Wilson, 1996, pp. 67-69.

Heins, Ethel L., review of *Chasing Redbird, Horn Book,* May-June, 1997, pp. 316-17.

Hendershot, Judy, and Jackie Peck, "An Interview with Sharon Creech, 1995 Newbery Medal Winner," *Reading Teacher,* February, 1996, pp. 380-82.

Jenkin, Ann, review of *The Ghost of Uncle Arvie, School Librarian,* February, 1997, p. 23.

Review of *Pleasing the Ghost, Publishers Weekly,* July 22, 1996, p. 242.

Rigg, Lyle D., "Sharon Creech," *Horn Book,* July/August, 1995, pp. 426-29.

Rochman, Hazel, "Salamanca's Journey," *New York Times Book Review,* May 21, 1995, p. 24.

Stevenson, Deborah, review of *Chasing Redbird, Bulletin of the Center for Children's Books,* March, 1997, p. 243.

Stevenson, Deborah, review of *Walk Two Moons, Bulletin of the Center for Children's Books,* November 15, 1994, p. 590.

Vasilakis, Nancy, review of *Absolutely Normal Chaos, Horn Book,* March/April, 1996, pp. 204-05.

Zahnleiter, Joan, review of *Absolutely Normal Chaos, Magpies,* September, 1991, p. 32.

■ For More Information See

BOOKS

Children's Literature Review, Volume 42, Gale, 1997.

PERIODICALS

Booklist, November 15, 1994, p. 590.
Bulletin of the Center for Children's Books, January, 1995, p. 162; November, 1995, p. 87.
Carousel, summer, 1997, p. 25.
Detroit Free Press, February 7, 1995, pp. 1C, 3C.
Fiction, May/June, 1996, pp. 34-35.
Kirkus Reviews, June 15, 1994, p. 832.
New York Times Book Review, May 21, 1995, p. 34.
Publishers Weekly, February 13, 1995, p. 16; March 20, 1995, pp. 24-25.
Teaching PreK-8, May, 1996, pp. 48-49.
Top of the News, spring, 1995, pp. 313-14.
Voice of Youth Advocates, February, 1995, pp. 337-38; June, 1996, p. 94.*

D

JOHN DANAKAS

DANAKAS, John 1963-

■ Personal

Born September 26, 1963, in Winnipeg, Manitoba, Canada; son of Constadinos (a restaurateur) and Maria (a restaurateur; maiden name, Stamatakos) Danakas; married Sophia Aggelopoulos (a sales clerk), June 16, 1990; children: Costa. *Education:* University of Manitoba, B.A., 1986, M.A., 1994.

■ Addresses

Home—7 Stanford Bay, Winnipeg, Manitoba R3P 0T5, Canada.

Office—Public Affairs Office, University of Manitoba, 423 University Cres., Winnipeg, Manitoba R3T 2N2, Canada.

■ Career

Winnipeg Sun, Winnipeg, Manitoba, journalist, 1986-91; University of Manitoba, Winnipeg, media relations officer, 1996—. Dal's Restaurant, restaurateur.

■ Writings

Curve Ball, James Lorimer (Toronto, Ontario), 1993.
Lizzie's Soccer Showdown, James Lorimer, 1994.
Hockey Night in Transcona, James Lorimer, 1995.

■ Work in Progress

The Case of the Missing Spirit Pipe; sequel to *Hockey Night in Transcona.*

■ Sidelights

John Danakas told *SATA:* "I love people, meeting them, getting to know them, finding out their personal stories. My writing is an attempt to communicate to others what I have learned about the people I have known, about what is important to them and why, about how they deal with the ordinary and extraordinary occurrences in their lives. Writing for young people is particularly rewarding because they are such appreciative readers. One of the best things about having published books for young readers is being able to visit schools and meet with many of my readers. They never fail to remind me just how intelligent, clever, and perceptive they are and that, if I want to ensure that my writing meets their standards, I should be prepared to work extra hard.

"I came to writing through reading. After reading a good book, I'd want to take a crack myself at telling a story through words on paper. Some of the writers whose books generated such a desire in me include William Saroyan, Harlan Ellison, Harry Mark Petrakis, Raymond Souster, Walter Dean Myers, Jack Schaefer, John O'Hara, and Daphne Du Maurier, to name only a few.

"I believe in young people and their dreams. I also believe that the best thing adults can do for young people—beyond ensuring their health and safety—is to let them be young—in body, mind, and soul—as long as possible."

■ For More Information See

PERIODICALS

Books in Canada, April, 1995, p. 58.
Canadian Materials, September, 1994, p. 124.
Quill & Quire, January, 1994, p. 38; January, 1995, pp. 40-41; January, 1996, p. 44.*

* * *

DAVIS, Tim(othy N.) 1957-

■ Personal

Born October 17, 1957, in Medina, NY; son of Everett (a pastor) and Linda (a homemaker; maiden name, Childs) Davis; married Rebecca Henry (a writer and editor), December 15, 1984; children: Katie, Stephen, Christiana, Joshua. *Education:* Attended Cedarville College, 1976-78; Bob Jones University, B.A. (cum laude), 1982. *Politics:* Conservative Republican. *Religion:* "Bible-believing Christian." *Hobbies and other interests:* Writing, inventing games.

■ Addresses

Home—60 Main St., Germantown, NY 12526.

■ Career

Bob Jones University Press, Greenville, SC, staff illustrator, 1982-91, elementary art director, 1986-91, advertising art director, 1989-91; freelance children's illustrator and writer, 1990—. Elementary school speaker, 1994—; pastoral intern, 1996-97.

■ Awards, Honors

Mice of the Seven Seas was named a C. S. Lewis Noteworthy Book by the Christian School Children/Youth Book Awards in 1995.

■ Writings

SELF-ILLUSTRATED CHILDREN'S BOOKS; ALL PUBLISHED BY BOB JONES UNIVERSITY PRESS (GREENVILLE, SC)

Mice of the Herring Bone, 1992.
Mice of the Nine Lives, 1994.

Tim Davis with his family.

Mice of the Seven Seas, 1995.
Tales from Dust River Gulch, 1996.

Contributor of stories to elementary reading textbooks.

ILLUSTRATOR

Dawn L. Watkins, *The Cranky Blue Crab: A Tale in Verse,* Bob Jones University Press, 1990.
Abigail Nunn, *The Land of Tuppitry,* 2nd edition, Victory Press (Monterey, CA), 1991.
Marjorie Hodgson Parker, *Jellyfish Can't Swim, and Other Secrets from the Animal World,* Chariot Books (Elgin, IL), 1991.
John Menken, *Grandpa's Gizmos,* Bob Jones University Press, 1992.
Dawn L. Watkins, *Pocket Change: Five Small Fables,* Bob Jones University Press, 1992.
Connie Williams, *Right-Hand Man,* Bob Jones University Press, 1992.
Anna Turner and Beth Kitching, *El Pato Paco: A First Look at Spanish,* Bob Jones University Press, 1993.
Dawn L. Watkins, *Once in Blueberry Dell,* Bob Jones University Press, 1995.

Illustrator of the "Darcy Doyle" book series, Zondervan (Grand Rapids, MI) and *Tony Salerno's Good News Express.* Contributor of illustrations to magazines, including *Children's Playmate* and *Highlights for Children.*

■ Sidelights

Tim Davis told *SATA:* "I've always been an illustrator. For as long as I can remember, I've been drawing imaginary characters and scenes. Writing came much later, after graduating from Bob Jones University. My wife-to-be was a professional writer when we met. She challenged me to write a children's story. I did—and it was published! Since then I've tried to write when I can. My children are a constant source of inspiration, as well as a ready test audience for my stories.

"Growing up in a pastor's home, and now doing pastoral work myself, I've always had a strong sense of right and wrong. I believe this foundation underlies everything I write—though my stories are far from pedantic. I love fun and adventure too much! I write fanciful fiction of faraway places, but I try to make my heroes exhibit real character in what they do and say."

*   *   *

DAY, Shirley 1962-

■ Personal

Born June 15, 1962, in Manila, Philippines; daughter of Salvador Dipasupil (a civil engineer) and Eden Miraflores (an accountant). *Education:* Attended University of Houston, 1980-84; University of South Florida, B.S., 1987.

■ Addresses

Home—Tampa, FL.

■ Career

St. Petersburg Times, St. Petersburg, FL, marketing coordinator, 1990-93, senior copywriter, 1993-96; Staff Leasing, Bradenton, FL, marketing communications manager, 1996; Danka (office equipment distributor), manager of employee relations and community affairs, 1996-97.

■ Awards, Honors

First place award, Southern Circulation Managers Association, 1991, for a newspaper carrier recognition campaign; first place awards, International Circulation Managers Association, 1992, for a quality control advertisement and for the advertisement "Real People, Real Stories," and 1993, for a t-shirt design; Gold ADDY Award, 1992, for a radio spot; Gold Award, Southern Classified Advertising Managers Association, 1993, for a "Yellow Pages" campaign; first place award, promotion/market development awards competition, Newspaper Association of America, 1994, for a "Santa Tracking" sales campaign.

■ Writings

Luna and the Big Blur: A Story for Children Who Wear Glasses, illustrated by Don Morris, Magination Press (New York City), 1995.

■ Work in Progress

A children's story about a little girl from the Philippines.

■ Sidelights

Shirley Day told *SATA:* "My children's book *Luna and the Big Blur* sits on a local bookshelf because of one reason: swim season. A few years ago, swim season, which runs from August through November, kept my former husband away from home nearly every day. After working full-time as a high school teacher, he would head directly to the pool to coach the school's swim team. It was during one of his extended absences that I decided to write a book.

"At the time, I worked for a newspaper, where I was able to seek advice from published authors and from Don Morris, an artist who had illustrated children's books. I attended local writing conferences, researched the process, from writing an effective query letter to selecting publishers, and made frequent visits to the children's section in bookstores.

"I sent queries only to receive rejection letters. 'It could take decades,' I thought. It didn't matter, as long as I was trying. The drive to continue stemmed from my business marketing background. I found it challenging.

"The call from Magination Press, a psychotherapy publishing house, caught me by surprise. Apparently my timing was perfect. They were in search of a more mainstream story for four- to eight-year-old children. I was elated that *Luna* fit that slot. Magination also reviewed Don Morris's artwork and quickly agreed to let him illustrate the book. It was truly an exciting time."

■ For More Information See

PERIODICALS

School Library Journal, January, 1996.

*   *   *

DECHAUSAY, Sonia E.

■ Personal

Born in Curacao, Netherland Antilles; daughter of Joseph Gabriel (a merchant) and Seraphine Marie (a merchant) Dechausay; children: Colette Sarah. *Education:* Concordia University, Montreal, Quebec, B.A., 1992.

■ Addresses

Home—Winnipeg, Manitoba, Canada.

■ Career

Goodwill Junior High School, Commonwealth of Dominica, West Indies, kindergarten and primary schoolteacher, 1969-73; Dominica Banana Growers' Association, West Indies, assistant secretary, 1973-77; Protestant School Board of Greater Montreal, Montreal, Quebec, director's assistant and school coordinator, 1982-84, kindergarten extension educator, 1984-95, director of kindergarten extension and day care services, 1993-95. Quebec Board of Black Educators, Inc., member, 1982—, executive member, 1992-96, Adult Literacy program coordinator, 1995–96; City of Montreal, member of the Division of Intercultural Affaires Round Table planning committee, 1996. *Member:* Federation of English Language Writers of Quebec, Montreal Association of Early Childhood Educators (member of board of directors, 1993), Concordia University Alumni Association (member of board of directors, 1996).

■ Writings

What's a Memory? (juvenile), illustrated by Daryl Anderson, Winston-Derek (Nashville, TN), 1995.

Member of editorial staff, *Kola.*

■ Work in Progress

Jason's Red Box; Steven Is Not Hurryuping; The Best Storyteller in the World.

■ Sidelights

Sonia E. Dechausay told *SATA:* "I've always loved books. Both of my parents were avid readers who encouraged us, their children, to read. My mother and maternal grandmother were great storytellers. My brothers and sisters would listen for hours as my mom told us the stories her mother had told her, as well as stories she made up herself. Sometimes our friends would join us in the dining room of our house to listen to our mom.

"I enjoyed writing short stories. One day, my mom showed a customer my stories. That customer was a writer and was also the owner and editor of a local newspaper. Her name was Mrs. Phyllis Sand-Allfrey. One of her books, *The Black Orchid,* I believe, was developed into a movie. She published a few of my short stories in her newspaper and encouraged me to continue writing. I was thrilled when my first book *What's a Memory?* was published by Winston-Derek, making me the first Canadian author to sign with them. This was a dream come true."

DOLAN, Edward F(rancis), Jr. 1924-

■ Personal

Born February 10, 1924, in Oakland, CA; son of an engineer. *Education:* Attended University of Southern California, San Francisco State College, and University of San Francisco. *Hobbies and other interests:* Travel, the theater.

■ Career

Has worked as a freelance radio and television writer, teacher of communications, reporter, and director of publications.

■ Awards, Honors

Children's Books of the Year, Child Study Association of America (CSAA), 1965, for *The Camera,* 1979, for *Kyle Rote, Jr.: American-Born Soccer Star,* 1980, for *The Bermuda Triangle and Other Mysteries of Nature,* 1984, for *Great Mysteries of the Air,* 1986, for *Anti-Semitism,* 1992, for *Our Poisoned Sky,* and 1996, for both *The American Revolution: How We Fought the War of Independence,* and *Your Privacy: Protecting It in a Nosy World;* Best Books for Young Adults, American Library Association (ALA), 1977, for *How to Leave Home—And Make Everybody Like It,* and 1981, for *Adolph Hitler: A Portrait of Tyranny.*

■ Writings

Pasteur and the Invisible Giants, Dodd, 1958.
Green Universe: The Story of Alexander von Humboldt, Dodd, 1959.
Jenner and the Miracle of Vaccine, Dodd, 1960.
White Background: The Conquest of the Arctic, Dodd, 1961.
Vanquishing Yellow Fever: Dr. Walter Reed, Britannica Press, 1962.
Adventure with a Microscope: A Story of Robert Koch, Dodd, 1964.
The Camera, Messner, 1965.
Disaster 1906: The San Francisco Earthquake and Fire, Messner, 1967.
(With H.T. Silver) *William Crawford Gorgas: Warrior in White,* Dodd, 1968.
Explorers of the Arctic and Antarctic, Crowell Collier, 1968.
The Explorers: Adventures in Courage, Reilly & Lee, 1970.
Inventors for Medicine, Crown, 1971.
Engines Work Like This, McGraw, 1971.
Legal Action: A Layman's Guide, Regnery, 1972.
(With Frederick J. Hass) *What You Can Do About Your Headaches,* Regnery, 1973.
(With Frederick J. Hass) *The Foot Book,* Regnery, 1973.
A Lion in the Sun: A Background Book for Young People on the Rise and Fall of the British Empire, Parents Magazine Press, 1973.
The Complete Beginner's Guide to Bowling, Doubleday, 1974.

The Complete Beginner's Guide to Ice Skating, Double-day, 1974.

Starting Soccer: A Handbook for Boys and Girls, illustrated with photographs by Jameson C. Goldner, Harper, 1976.

Basic Football Strategy: An Introduction for Young Players, foreword by Duffy Daugherty, Doubleday, 1976.

Amnesty: The American Puzzle, F. Watts, 1976, revised edition, 1977.

The Complete Beginner's Guide to Making and Flying Kites, Doubleday, 1977.

The Complete Beginner's Guide to Magic, Doubleday, 1977.

How to Leave Home—And Make Everybody Like It, Dodd, 1977.

(With Richard B. Lyttle) *Archie Griffin,* Doubleday, 1977.

(With Lyttle) *Bobby Clarke,* Doubleday, 1977.

(With Lyttle) *Martina Navratilova,* Doubleday, 1977.

(With Lyttle) *Scott May: Basketball Champion,* Doubleday, 1978.

(With Lyttle) *Fred Lynn: The Hero from Boston,* Doubleday, 1978.

(With Lyttle) *Janet Guthrie: First Woman Driver at Indianapolis,* Doubleday, 1978.

Gun Control: A Decision for Americans, F. Watts, 1978, revised edition, 1982.

(With Richard B. Lyttle) *Dorothy Hamill: Olympic Skating Champion,* Doubleday, 1979.

(With Lyttle) *Jimmy Young: Heavyweight Challenger,* Doubleday, 1979.

(With Lyttle) *Kyle Rote, Jr.: American-Born Soccer Star,* Doubleday, 1979.

Matthew Henson, Black Explorer, Dodd, 1979.

Child Abuse, F. Watts, 1980, revised edition, 1992.

The Complete Beginner's Guide to Gymnastics, illustrated with photographs by James Stewart, Doubleday, 1980.

The Bermuda Triangle, and Other Mysteries of Nature, F. Watts, 1980.

Let's Make Magic, Doubleday, 1980.

Adolf Hitler: A Portrait in Tyranny, Dodd, 1981.

Calling the Play: A Beginner's Guide to Amateur Sports Officiating, Atheneum, 1981.

It Sounds Like Fun: How to Use and Enjoy Your Tape Recorder and Stereo, Simon & Schuster, 1981.

Great Moments in the World Series, F. Watts, 1982.

Great Moments in the Indy 500, F. Watts, 1982.

Great Moments in the Super Bowl, F. Watts, 1982.

Great Moments in the NBA Championships, F. Watts, 1982.

Bicycle Touring and Camping, Simon & Schuster, 1982.

Matters of Life and Death, F. Watts, 1982.

Protect Your Legal Rights: A Handbook for Teenagers, Simon & Schuster, 1983.

Great Mysteries of the Air, Dodd, 1983.

History of the Movies, Bison, 1983.

(With Shan Finney) *The New Japan,* F. Watts, 1983.

(With Shan Finney) *Youth Gangs,* Simon & Schuster, 1984.

Great Mysteries of the Sea, Dodd, 1984.

The Insanity Plea, F. Watts, 1984.

The Simon & Schuster Sports Question and Answer Book, Simon & Schuster, 1984.

Be Your Own Man, Prentice-Hall, 1984.

International Drug Traffic, F. Watts, 1985.

Anti-Semitism, F. Watts, 1985.

Great Mysteries of the Ice and Snow, Dodd, 1985.

Hollywood Goes to War, Bison, 1985.

Money Talk, Messner, 1986.

Animal Rights, F. Watts, 1986.

Drugs in Sports, F. Watts, 1986. Revised edition, 1992.

Famous Builders of California, Dodd, 1987.

(With Margaret M. Scariano) *Cuba and the United States: Troubled Neighbors,* F. Watts, 1987.

(With Margaret M. Scariano) *The Police in American Society,* F. Watts, 1988.

The Old Farmer's Almanac Book of Weather Lore: The Fact and Fancy behind Weather Predictions, Superstitions, Old-Time Sayings, and Traditions (foreword by Willard Scott), Yankee Books, 1988.

Victory in Europe: The Fall of Hitler's Germany, F. Watts, 1988.

Missing in Action: A Vietnam Drama, F. Watts, 1989.

Famous Firsts in Space, Dutton, 1989.

Edward F. Dolan's study draws upon current research into compulsive gambling, revealing its genesis in people with little self-esteem and its horrendous impact on the individual, the family, and society.

America After Vietnam: Legacies of a Hated War, F. Watts, 1989.

(With Margaret M. Scariano) *Nuclear Waste: The 10,000-Year Challenge*, F. Watts, 1990.

Our Poisoned Sky, Cobblehill Books, 1990.

Panama and the United States: Their Canal, Their Stormy Years, F. Watts, 1990.

Drought: The Past, Present, and Future Enemy, F. Watts, 1990.

America in World War II: 1941, Millbrook, 1991.

Animal Folklore: From Black Cats to White Horses, Ivy Books, 1992.

America in World War II: 1943, Millbrook, 1992.

The American Wilderness and its Future: Conservation versus Use, F. Watts, 1992.

Folk Medicine Cures and Curiosities, Ivy Books, 1993.

Teenagers and Compulsive Gambling, F. Watts, 1994.

America in World War II: 1945, Millbrook, 1994.

(With Margaret M. Scariano) *Guns in the United States*, F. Watts, 1994.

(With Margaret M. Scariano) *Illiteracy in America*, F. Watts, 1995.

The American Revolution: How We Fought the War of Independence, Millbrook Press, 1995.

Your Privacy: Protecting It in a Nosy World, Cobblehill, 1995.

In Sports, Money Talks, Twenty-First Century Books, 1996.

America in World War I, Millbrook Press, 1996.

(With Margaret M. Scariano) *Shaping U.S. Foreign Policy: Profiles of Twelve Secretaries of State*, F. Watts, 1996.

Our Poisoned Waters, Cobblehill, 1997.

■ Sidelights

Edward F. Dolan started writing at the age of twelve, and by age sixteen he had published his first story. In the years since 1958, the date of his first published book, Dolan has written over seventy books of nonfiction and co-authored nearly twenty more—a remarkable number that ranks him among the most prolific authors of nonfiction for children. While many of his titles have dealt with sports or science, he has also written widely on topics in history, social studies, the environment, health, law, and on contemporary problems like drugs, gun control, and compulsive gambling.

Dolan's first published book was *Pasteur and the Invisible Giants*, but his first title to receive special note was *The Camera* in 1965, which was praised by the Child Study Association as an "exciting history." Dolan's next book, *Disaster 1906: The San Francisco Earthquake and Fire* was a selection of the Junior Library Guild. Marion Marx, writing in *Horn Book*, concluded that the book will "appeal to the science-oriented child as well as to the child with an interest in the human drama and tragedy resulting from natural disasters."

The Complete Beginner's Guide to Bowling was the first of many books Dolan has written or co-authored in the field of sports. Praised in *Booklist* as perhaps "the next

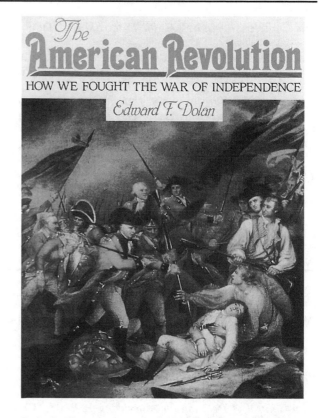

Dolan's history of the American Revolution highlights major figures on both sides and the key factors that brought about an unexpected victory for the colonists.

best thing to private lessons," the book was also singled out by *Kirkus Reviews* for its "attention to fundamentals" and "detailed instruction." Dolan has written similar how-to books on ice-skating, soccer, football, kitemaking, gymnastics, and officiating. *The Complete Beginner's Guide to Gymnastics* was recommended in *Booklist* as a "valuable primary resource" for beginning gymnasts. Dolan has won equal attention for his series (co-authored with R. B. Lyttle) on sports heroes in sports ranging from tennis to baseball, racing car driving, soccer, ice skating, and boxing. The Child Study Association singled out *Kyle Rote, Jr.: American-Born Soccer Star* in particular as a "lively biography" with "action-packed photographs." Dolan has also written several titles in the general category of sports-related information books. *The Simon & Schuster Sports Question and Answer Book* was cited by a *Bulletin of the Center for Children's Books* reviewer for its "good job" in answering questions about twelve different sports.

Dolan's tackling of contemporary problems in his books dates from 1977, when he published *Amnesty: The American Puzzle*, described in *Booklist* as a "straightforward examination" of Vietnam-era war evaders or deserters. After summarizing the history of amnesty in the United States, Dolan examines the arguments for and against amnesty. *Booklist* found the book "useful for students of American history and government." That same year, Dolan received his first major recognition when the American Library Association named *How to Leave Home—And Make Everybody Like It* a

Notable Book selection for young adults. The book is a guide to leaving home and living independently, including how to tell one's family, find a job, and handle finances. The author also discusses the pros and cons of running away. In *Gun Control: A Decision For Americans,* Dolan explores the background and conflicting viewpoints on this controversial subject, analyzing present gun control laws and surveying public opinion. The book was described as "thorough and objective" by Zena Sutherland of the *Bulletin of the Center for Children's Books.* In *Child Abuse,* Dolan discusses the various manifestations of this problem, its psychological causes, and the sources of help that are available for victims and abusers. *School Library Journal* contributor Linda Rombough commended the book for the "firm, straightforward" manner and "honesty and sensitivity" with which it handles a difficult topic. Zena Sutherland of the *Bulletin of the Center for Children's Books* also noted the book's "serious but not heavy" writing and "objective tone." The revised edition was praised in *Booklist* by Carolyn Phelan as a "good resource," and in *School Library Journal* contributor Libby K. White commented, "The author writes clearly, putting the problem of abuse in proper perspective.... He aims to inform, not to frighten."

Nolan's interest in history, especially that of the World War II era, blossomed in *Adolph Hitler: A Portrait in Tyranny,* which garnered the author's second ALA Notable Book honor. The book was praised by Ethel R. Twichell in *Horn Book* as a "solid and well-researched biography" written in "sober and workmanlike style." While finding fault with the author's occasionally "tortured" writing style and inferior organization, Lorraine Douglas, writing in *School Library Journal,* nevertheless found the book an "absorbing and graphic description of Hitler." A decade later, Dolan followed up his interest in World War II with the first in a series of books, each devoted to one year in the conflict. The first, *America in World War II: 1941,* was commended by Eldon Younce in *School Library Journal* as a "readable introduction" with "well-written" text, "well-chosen" photographs and an "attractive overview" of the period. The same reviewer also praised the "clear and concise writing" of the third book in the series, covering the year 1943. In a similar vein, Ilene Cooper, reviewing *America in World War II: 1941* in *Booklist,* noted Dolan's "straightforward" approach and "accessible text." Extending this same historical treatment to World War I, Dolan's *America in World War I* was singled out by reviewer David A. Lindsey in *School Library Journal* as a "concise introductory survey" marked by the author's "taut and seemingly effortless" prose. The work was also praised by reviewer Susan Dove Lempke in *Booklist* as "fine work" which proceeds in an "understandable, orderly fashion."

Dolan applied a more thematic approach to a broad subject in *Anti-Semitism,* dividing the topic into three forms: personal prejudice, discrimination, and persecution. *School Library Journal* contributor Ruth Horowitz found this approach too "abstract," while a *Bulletin of the Center for Children's Books* commentator com-

plained that the book "lacks personality." Nevertheless, the latter reviewer also noted the advantage of its "objective tone" in dealing with sensitive issues like Black anti-Semitism in the United States, and the Child Study Committee gave the work one of its Children's Books of the Year citations in 1986.

In general, Dolan has been praised for the balanced point of view he takes toward controversial topics, ranging from the police (*The Police in American Society*) to guns in the United States (*Gun Control: A Decision for Americans*) to issues of privacy (*Your Privacy: Protecting It in a Nosy World*). In other works like *Animal Rights,* however, the author has taken a strong advocacy position—in this case, in favor of more humane treatment. On the whole, Dolan's large body of work has won an impressive number of favorable assessments for its breadth and conciseness.

■ Works Cited

Review of *Amnesty: The American Puzzle, Booklist,* May 15, 1976, pp. 1329-30.

Review of *Anti-Semitism, Bulletin of the Center for Children's Books,* March, 1986, p. 125.

Review of *Anti-Semitism, Children's Books of the Year,* Child Study Children's Book Committee, 1986.

Review of *The Camera, Children's Books of the Year,* Child Study Association of America, 1967.

Review of *The Complete Beginner's Guide to Bowling, Booklist,* September 1, 1974, p. 39.

Review of *The Complete Beginner's Guide to Bowling, Kirkus Reviews,* March 1, 1974, p. 255.

Review of *The Complete Beginner's Guide to Gymnastics, Booklist,* March 1, 1980, p. 935.

Cooper, Ilene, review of *America in World War II: 1941, Booklist,* October 10, 1991, p. 319.

Review of *Disaster 1906: The San Francisco Earthquake and Fire, Kirkus Reviews,* September 1, 1967, p. 1061.

Douglas, Lorraine, review of *Adolph Hitler: A Portrait in Tyranny, School Library Journal,* October, 1981, p. 119.

Horowitz, Ruth, review of *Anti-Semitism, School Library Journal,* February, 1986, p. 94.

Review of *Kyle Rote, Jr.: American-Born Soccer Star,* Child Study Children's Book Committee, 1979.

Lempke, Susan Dove, review of *America in World War I, Booklist,* June 1, 1996, p. 1708.

Lindsey, David A., review of *America in World War I, School Library Journal,* May 5, 1996, p. 137.

Marx, Marion, review of *Disaster 1906: The San Francisco Earthquake and Fire, Horn Book,* April, 1968, pp. 191-92.

Phelan, Carolyn, review of *Child Abuse, Booklist,* January 1, 1993, p. 888.

Rombough, Linda, review of *Child Abuse, School Library Journal,* September, 1980, p. 82.

Review of *The Simon & Schuster Sports Question and Answer Book, Bulletin of the Center for Children's Books,* April, 1985, p. 145.

Sutherland, Zena, review of *Gun Control: A Decision for Americans, Bulletin of the Center for Children's Books,* March, 1979, p. 113.

Sutherland, Zena, review of *Child Abuse, Bulletin of the Center for Children's Books,* November, 1980, pp. 50-51.

Twichell, Ethel R., review of *Adolph Hitler: A Portrait in Tyranny, Horn Book,* February, 1982, p. 63.

White, Libby K., review of *Child Abuse, School Library Journal,* January, 1993, p. 136.

Younce, Eldon, review of *America in World War II: 1941, School Library Journal,* September, 1991, p. 268.

Younce, Eldon, review of *America in World War II: 1943, School Library Journal,* May, 1992, p. 121.

■ **For More Information See**

PERIODICALS

Booklist, October 15, 1986, p. 342.
Bulletin of the Center for Children's Books, April, 1997, p. 280.
Kirkus Reviews, April 1, 1997, p. 553.
School Library Journal, February, 1981, p. 64; January, 1987, p. 82.
Voice of Youth Advocates, February, 1983, pp. 48-49; April, 1986, p. 45; June, 1989, p. 122; October, 1995, p. 245.
Wilson Library Bulletin, June, 1987, p. 65.*

*   *   *

DORRIS, Michael A(nthony) 1945-1997

OBITUARY NOTICE—See index for *SATA* sketch: Born January 30, 1945, in Louisville, KY; died following an apparent suicide, April 11, 1997, in Concord, NH. Author, essayist, and educator. Dorris's award-winning 1989 book, *The Broken Cord: A Father's Story,* which detailed his adopted son's battle with fetal alcohol syndrome, brought international attention to the problem and led to new alcohol labeling laws. But the highly regarded author who worked to improve the lives of others apparently took his own life in a New Hampshire motel. His estranged wife, author Louise Erdrich, told the *New York Times* that Dorris had a problem with depression and had attempted suicide before. Dorris was educated at Georgetown and Yale University and founded Dartmouth College's Native American Studies Program. He was also a professor and department chairman at Dartmouth. Dorris was of mixed Native American, Irish, and French ancestry and his first two books—*Native Americans: Five Hundred Years After* (1977) and (along with Arlene Hirschfelder and Mary Byler) *A Guide to Research on North American Indians* (1983)—dealt with the subject of his studies and teaching. His first novel, *A Yellow Raft in Blue Water,* was published in 1987. But his breakthrough book, *The Broken Cord: A Father's Story,* was a nonfiction work of a personal nature—his adopted son's lifelong struggle of living with brain damage brought on by his mother's drinking. It won the National Book Award, among

others, and inspired Congress to draft legislation requiring warning labels on alcoholic beverages. Dorris and his wife also found literary success together with their co-written books *Route Two and Back* and *The Crown of Columbus,* both published in 1991. For young adults, Dorris wrote *Morning Girl* (1992) and *Guests* (1995). His other works include *Rooms in the House of Stone, Working Men* (both in 1993), and *Paper Trail: Collected Essays, 1967-1992* (1994). He had been working on a follow-up to *Broken Cord* entitled *Matter of Conscience.* Besides his teaching and writing career, Dorris also served on the U.S. Advisory Committee on Infant Mortality, was a member of the National Indian Education Association, the American Association for the Advancement of Science, and was a board member of the Save the Children Foundation. He was also a consultant to the National Endowment for the Humanities. *Broken Cord* was made into a television movie and Dorris appeared on numerous radio and television programs. His first work for young people, *Morning Girl,* received a Scott O'Dell Award for Historical Fiction from the American Library Association in 1992, and was named to best books lists by *Publishers Weekly, Horn Book, Booklist, School Library Journal,* and the *New York Times Book Review.*

OBITUARIES AND OTHER SOURCES:

BOOKS

Authors and Artists for Young Adults, Vol. 20, Gale Research, 1997.
Seventh Book of Junior Authors and Illustrators, edited by Sally Holmes Holtze, H. W. Wilson, 1996, pp. 86-87.

PERIODICALS

Los Angeles Times, April 15, 1997, p. A18.
New York Times, April 15, 1997, p. B11; April 16, 1997, p. A12; April 18, 1997, p. A14.

*   *   *

DOUGLAS, Garry
See KILWORTH, Garry (D.)

*   *   *

DOYLE, Charlotte (Lackner) 1937-

■ **Personal**

Born June 25, 1937, in Vienna, Austria; immigrated to the United States, 1939; daughter of George (a restaurant worker) and Mary (a poet and homemaker; maiden name, Meisel) Lackner; married Jim Doyle (a playwright), 1959. *Education:* Temple University, B.A., 1959; University of Michigan, M.A., 1961, Ph.D., 1965. *Hobbies and other interests:* Camping in national and state parks, travelling to new places, reading, watching public television, playing with the computer.

CHARLOTTE DOYLE

■ Addresses

Office—Department of Psychology, Sarah Lawrence College, Bronxville, NY 10708-5999. *Electronic mail*—cdoyle@mail.slc.edu. *Agent*—Liza Pulitzer Voges, Kirchoff/Wohlberg, 866 United Nation Plaza, New York, NY 10017.

■ Career

Sarah Lawrence College, Bronxville, NY, professor of psychology and children's literature. *Member:* American Psychological Association (member of executive committee, Division on Psychology and the Arts), Society for Children's Book Writers and Illustrators, American Association for the Advancement of Science.

■ Writings

CHILDREN'S BOOKS

Hello Baby, illustrated by Kees de Kiefte, Random House (New York City), 1989.
Freddie's Spaghetti, illustrated by Nicholas Reilly, Random House, 1991.
Where's Bunny's Mommy?, illustrated by Rick Brown, Simon & Schuster (New York City), 1995.
You Can't Catch Me, illustrated by Roseanne Litziger, HarperCollins (New York City), 1997.

OTHER

(With W. J. McKeachie) *Psychology* (textbook), Addison-Wesley (Reading, MA), 1966.
(With W. J. McKeachie) *Psychology: The Short Course* (textbook), Addison-Wesley, 1972.

Explorations in Psychology (textbook), Brooks/Cole (Monterey, CA), 1987.

Contributor to periodicals, including *Creativity Research Journal.*

■ Work in Progress

Little Flower, the First Potter, an imaginary account of how a young girl discovered the secret of making pots out of clay.

■ Sidelights

Charlotte Doyle told *SATA:* "I never expected to be writing children's books. I was a college professor, an author of psychology texts and articles, and a researcher into the creative process. Then, one day, I sat down to write a letter to a child, and the letter turned into a children's story. I read it to the children at Sarah Lawrence's Early Childhood Center. The children were so responsive and it was so much fun that I began to hang out there.

"Again and again, being with children has inspired me. I watched some children be loving about having new baby brothers and sisters and others be resentful, and that gave me *Hello Baby.* A child, so happy to be eating spaghetti that it seemed life couldn't get any better, gave me *Freddie's Spaghetti.* Watching very young children happy to be in school, but stopping every once in a while to look around, puzzled, and asking 'Where's Mommy?' inspired *Where's Bunny's Mommy?* Seeing the pleasures of chasing and being chased on the playground led to *You Can't Catch Me.*

"When I write, I try to enter the world of young children, to see the world as a child does. My greatest pleasure is when children recognize the world created by my books as their world, as giving voice to their fears and hopes and joys, and so say to me, 'Read it again.'"

■ For More Information See

PERIODICALS

Booklist, April 1, 1995, p. 1424.
New York Times, November 4, 1990.
School Library Journal, June, 1990, p. 98; July, 1995, p. 61.

*　　*　　*

DUGGLEBY, John 1952-

■ Personal

Born January 1, 1952, in Muscatine, IA; children: Katie. *Education:* University of Iowa, B.A., 1973.

JOHN DUGGLEBY

■ Addresses

Home and office—Duggleby Communications, 5322 Norma Rd., McFarland, WI 53558-9479. *Electronic mail*—duggleby@mailbag.com.

■ Career

Allstate Insurance, Northbrook, IL, magazine editor, 1976-78; American Telephone & Telegraph, Chigaco, IL, member of corporate communications staff, 1978-81; Burson-Marsteller Public Relations, Chicago, member of creative staff, 1981-84; Duggleby Communications, McFarland, WI, owner, 1984—. *Member:* Society of Children's Book Writers and Illustrators, Wisconsin Public Relations Forum, Wisconsin Communicators Council.

■ Awards, Honors

Awards from Illinois Press Association and International Association of Business Communicators, as well as a Children's Crown nomination from the National Association of Christian Schools.

■ Writings

The Sabertooth Cat, Crestwood House/Macmillan, 1989.
Pesticides, Crestwood House/Macmillan, 1990.
Doomed Expeditions, illustrated by Robert Andrew Parker, Crestwood House/Macmillan, 1990.
Impossible Quests, illustrated by Allan Eitzen, Crestwood House/Macmillan, 1990.
Artist in Overalls: The Life of Grant Wood, Chronicle Books (San Francisco, CA), 1996.

Contributor of numerous articles and poems to periodicals, including *Business Week Careers, Country Living, Home, Mature Outlook, Redbook,* and *WaldenBooks Kid's Club.*

■ Sidelights

John Duggleby told *SATA:* "I was the first baby born in Muscatine, Iowa, on New Year's Day in 1952. I was raised in the eastern Iowa Mississippi River town of Clinton, in the same general area of rolling hills and fields that Grant Wood painted. Interestingly, *American Gothic* began to re-emerge as a cultural icon while I was growing up, so Wood became sort of an Iowa hero. Though I grew up in town, several people in my family were, or had been, farmers. My grandfather, Red Harter, gave me accounts of farming in the 'old days' that were remarkably similar to those of Wood, which I uncovered in researching *Artist in Overalls: The Life of Grant Wood.*

"I went to the University of Iowa, where Wood first sneaked into art classes, and I graduated with a degree in journalism. I went through a series of jobs in my younger days, ranging from selling sporting goods to spending a summer lobster fishing in Long Island Sound, but I have made my living as a writer for the past twenty years. I began in newspaper work, was on the staff of a travel magazine, and did creative and public relations work before creating my own company, Duggleby Communications, in 1984.

"I now live just outside Madison, Wisconsin, in a little town called McFarland. It looks much like the Wood landscapes where I grew up, except there are more lakes and Holsteins. I am a single parent with a very cool daughter, Katie.

"Although I grew up among the Wood landscapes, I was no more than mildly interested in the artist until the mid-1980s. That's when a major retrospective of his work toured the country and stopped at Chicago, where I was living. His work absolutely bowled me over, and I wanted to know more about this relative unknown who painted what is arguably the most-recognized American artwork.

"As I learned more about this unique artist and the way his childhood so profoundly shaped his work, I thought he would make an excellent subject for a children's book. Wood's approach is very populist, and his work is very approachable. Wood himself was very childlike his whole life, and was interested in turning kids and other 'typical' people on to art. He believed art is for everyone, not just for a cultural elite and that art should be fun.

"I've witnessed the truth of these assertions firsthand, because, since the book was published, I've been a frequent guest of schools and libraries doing presentations on Wood's life and work. At the end of each program we all draw a live chicken—my co-star, Henrietta—and we definitely have lots of fun!"

■ For More Information See

PERIODICALS

Booklist, April 15, 1996, p. 1435.
Kirkus Reviews, March 1, 1996, p. 372.
Publishers Weekly, April 1, 1996, p. 77.
School Library Journal, February, 1991, p. 87; May, 1996, p. 121.

DURRELL, Julie 1955-

■ Personal

Born June 28, 1955, in Springfield, MA; daughter of James F. (a landlord; also in sales) and Ernestine B. (a music teacher) Durrell. *Education:* Pratt Institute, B.A. *Hobbies and other interests:* Playing the cello.

■ Addresses

Home—Cambridge, MA. *Agent*—Paige Gillies, Publisher's Graphics, 251 Greenwood Ave., Bethel, CT 06801.

■ Career

Writer and illustrator.

■ Writings

FOR CHILDREN; SELF-ILLUSTRATED

Mouse Tails, Crown (New York City), 1985.
Tickety-Tock, What Time Is It?, Golden Books (Racine, WI), 1990.
It's My Birthday!, Grosset (New York City), 1990.
The Colorful Mouse: A Story about Colors, Golden Books, 1991.

ILLUSTRATOR

The Pudgy Book of Toys (picture book), Grosset, 1983.
The Pudgy Book of Farm Animals (picture book), Grosset, 1984.
The Little Red Hen and Other Stories to Color, Happy House Group (New York City), 1985.
Joan Ryder, *The Evening Walk,* Golden Books, 1985.
Carolyn Haywood, *Summer Fun,* Morrow (New York City), 1986.
Haywood, *Merry Christmas from Eddie,* Morrow, 1986.

JULIE DURRELL

Durrell provided carefully detailed illustrations for Linda Taylor's story of Rabbit the mail carrier, who has trouble remembering where he is supposed to deliver a special birthday note. (From *The Lettuce Leaf Birthday Letter.*)

Donna R. Parnell, adaptor, *Chicken Licken,* Lady Bird Books (Loughborough, England), 1987.

Haywood, *Hello Star,* Morrow, 1987.

Fran Manushkin, *Ketchup, Catch Up!,* Golden Books, 1987.

Stephanie Calmenson, *The Toy Book,* Golden Books, 1987.

Christmas Carols: A Coloring Book, Happy House Group, 1988.

Cory Nash, reteller, *My Gingerbread Fairy Tale House,* four volumes, Warner Books (New York City), 1988.

Michael Pellowski, *Professor Possum's Great Adventure,* Troll (Mahwah, NJ), 1989.

Jean Harmon, *My Jesus Pocketbook of Let's Pretend,* David Cook (Elgin, IL), 1991.

Vivian L. Werner, *Dolls: An Inside Look at Dolls from Raggedy Ann to Barbie,* Avon Books, 1991.

Harmon, *My Jesus Pocketbook of Prayer,* David Cook, 1992.

Anne Benjamin, *Young Helen Keller: Woman of Courage,* Troll, 1992.

Judith Bauer Stamper, *Easter Holiday Grab Bag,* Troll, 1993.

Melissa Getzoff, *Let's Tell Time,* Troll, 1995.

Cynthia Alvarez, *Reindeer Baby,* Random House (New York City), 1995.

Linda Taylor, *The Lettuce Leaf Birthday Letter,* Dial (New York City), 1995.

Doris Orgel, *The Spaghetti Party,* Bantam (New York City), 1995.

Mary Packard, *I Am a Firefighter,* Scholastic Inc. (New York City), 1995.

Melissa Getzoff, *Let's Tell Time,* Troll, 1996.

Patricia Reilly Giff, *Dance with Rosie,* Viking, 1996.

Giff, *Rosie's Nutcracker Dreams,* Viking, 1996.

Pamela Jane, *The Scariest Place,* Delacorte, 1997.

"LAURA LEE" SERIES; WRITTEN BY ALICE SULLIVAN FINLAY

Laura Lee and the Monster Sea, Zondervan, 1994.
A Victory for Laura Lee, Zondervan, 1994.
Laura Lee and the Little Pine Tree, Zondervan, 1994.
A Gift from the Sea for Laura Lee, Zondervan, 1994.

■ Sidelights

Julie Durrell has commented: "Ever since early childhood I wanted to be an artist. A deep devotion and love for animals limited my artistic vocabulary. All I ever wanted to draw were animals, mostly horses. My mother informed me that a professional artist would have to know how to draw all kinds of things. She was right and I did!"

Durrell's love of animals is evident in her illustrations both for her own children's stories and those of a number of other authors. Her *Mouse Tails,* for instance, features a series of four-line verses in which a mouse describes tails of other animals and asks the reader to name the animal. "The illustrations are stylized yet detailed and done in bright colors," noted *School Library Journal* contributor Margaret C. Howell. A *Publishers Weekly* commentator called *Mouse Tails* "a dandy game and fun to explore," adding that Durrell's pictures "gleam with color and inventive extras."

In *The Lettuce Leaf Birthday Letter,* written by Linda Taylor, Duck sends Goose birthday greetings in the form of a painting on a lettuce leaf. The mail Rabbit, however, becomes confused and visits a number of animals with the gift before finally getting the now-wilted leaf to Goose. "Brilliantly colored and spilling over with comical particulars, Durrell's buoyant pictures deserve top billing here," enthused a *Publishers Weekly* critic. A *Kirkus Reviews* commentator also praised Durrell's "snappy, daffy artwork," while *School Library Journal* contributor Lisa S. Murphy added: "The full-color art is vibrant and whimsical, and observant readers will enjoy picking up the distinctive characteristics of each animal's house."

■ Works Cited

Howell, Margaret C., review of *Mouse Tails, School Library Journal,* October, 1985, p. 151.

Review of *The Lettuce Leaf Birthday Letter, Kirkus Reviews,* February 15, 1995, p. 234.

Review of *The Lettuce Leaf Birthday Letter, Publishers Weekly,* March 27, 1995, p. 84.

Review of *Mouse Tails, Publishers Weekly,* June 14, 1985, p. 72.

Murphy, Linda S., review of *The Lettuce Leaf Birthday Letter, School Library Journal,* April, 1995, p. 118.

■ For More Information See

PERIODICALS

Booklist, May 1, 1995, p. 1581.*

E–F

MARYANN EASLEY

EASLEY, MaryAnn
(MaryAnn Black)

■ Personal

Born November 8, in Los Angeles, CA; daughter of Wendell C. (an educator) and Sarah M. (a homemaker) Black; married Robert A. Knox (marriage ended); married Richard L. Easley (a teacher); children: (first marriage) Robert, Sherry Erickson, John, Tracy. *Education:* University of Redlands, B.A.; Chapman University, M.A. *Politics:* Democrat. *Religion:* Christian.

■ Addresses

Home—Oceanside, CA. *Office*—300 Carlsbad Village Dr., Suite 108A-355, Carlsbad, CA 92008.

■ Career

Fallbrook Union Elementary School District, Camp Pendleton Marine Base, CA, elementary school teacher. Also worked as a teacher in California and Alaska. Worked as an editor, typesetter, and circulation manager for a regional magazine. Fished commercially for salmon along the Pacific Northwest, 1976-82. *Member:* Society of Children's Book Writers and Illustrators, PEN, National Writers Association, National Education Association, Publishers Marketing Association, California Teachers Association.

■ Awards, Honors

I Am the Ice Worm was an American Library Association Best Book and a Junior Library Guild selection, both 1997.

■ Writings

I Am the Ice Worm, Boyds Mill Press, 1996.

Also author of audio cassette learning programs for Achievement Dynamics, including *Miss Mary's Super-Phonics, SuperPhonics Plus, The New Verbal Advantage, Verbal Advantage Plus,* and *Verbal Advantage: Student Edition.* Contributor to national and regional magazines and newspapers, sometimes under the name MaryAnn Black.

■ Work in Progress

Several young adult novels.

■ Sidelights

MaryAnn Easley told *SATA:* "I am concentrating most of my writing efforts at present for the ten-to-fourteen age group. The stories I write feature a fourteen-year-old heroine actively involved in her own survival. My stories deal with truths. As my heroine encounters one ordeal after another, she learns about the world and about herself. It is this journey that takes her one step closer to maturity. In *I Am the Ice Worm,* when the tiny bush plane carrying my heroine to her mother in the Arctic crashes and the pilot is killed, Allison's real journey begins. She encounters a strange new world and learns the true meaning of love and home.

"I have written for as long as I can remember, before I owned a typewriter and before computers existed. I have written everything from poetry to magazine articles to learning programs, but what I like best is writing novels for the young adult."

■ For More Information See

PERIODICALS

Booklist, October 15, 1996, p. 420.
Kirkus Reviews, August 1, 1996, p. 1152.

*   *   *

ELLIS, Anyon
    See ROWLAND-ENTWISTLE, (Arthur) Theodore (Henry)

*   *   *

ERDRICH, Louise 1954-

■ Personal

Has also written under joint pseudonyms Heidi Louise and Milou North; born Karen Louise Erdrich June 7, 1954, in Little Falls, MN; daughter of Ralph Louis (a teacher with the Bureau of Indian Affairs) and Rita Joanne (affiliated with the Bureau of Indian Affairs; maiden name, Gourneau) Erdrich; married Michael Anthony Dorris (a writer and professor of Native American studies), October 10, 1981 (died, 1997); children: Abel, Jeffrey, Sava, Madeline, Persia, Pallas, Aza. *Education:* Dartmouth College, B.A., 1976; Johns Hopkins University, M.A., 1979. *Politics:* Democrat. *Religion:* "Anti-religion." *Hobbies and other interests:* Quilling, running, drawing, "playing chess with daughters and losing, playing piano badly, speaking terrible French, studying Ojibwa."

■ Career

Writer. North Dakota State Arts Council, visiting poet and teacher, 1977-78; Boston Indian Council, Boston, MA, communications director and editor of *Circle,* 1979-80; Charles-Merrill Co., textbook writer, 1980. Previously employed as a beet weeder in Wahpeton,

LOUISE ERDRICH

ND; waitress in Wahpeton, Boston, and Syracuse, NY; psychiatric aide in a Vermont hospital; poetry teacher at prisons; lifeguard; and construction flag signaler. Has judged writing contests. *Member:* International Writers, PEN (member of executive board, 1985-88), Authors Guild, Authors League of America.

■ Awards, Honors

Johns Hopkins University teaching fellow, 1979; Mac-Dowell Colony fellow, 1980; Yaddo Colony fellow, 1981; Dartmouth College visiting fellow, 1981; First Prize, *Chicago* magazine's Nelson Algren fiction competition, 1982, for "The World's Greatest Fisherman"; Pushcart Prize, 1983; National Magazine Fiction awards, 1983 and 1987; *Love Medicine* received the National Book Critics Circle Award for best work of fiction, and the Virginia McCormick Scully Prize for best book of the year, both 1984; *Love Medicine* received the *Los Angeles Times* Award for best novel, the best first fiction award from the American Academy and Institute of Arts and Letters, the Sue Kaufman Prize, and was named one of the best eleven books of 1985 by the *New York Times Book Review;* Guggenheim fellow, 1985-86; *The Beet Queen* was named one of *Publishers Weekly*'s best books, 1986; First Prize, O. Henry awards, 1987; National Book Critics Circle Award nomination.

■ Writings

FOR CHILDREN

Grandmother's Pigeon, illustrated by Jim LaMarche, Hyperion, 1996.

NOVELS; FOR ADULTS

Love Medicine, Holt, 1984.
The Beet Queen, Holt, 1986.
Tracks, Harper, 1988.
(With husband, Michael Dorris) *The Crown of Columbus,* HarperCollins, 1991.
The Bingo Palace, HarperCollins, 1994.
Tales of Burning Love, HarperCollins, 1996.

POETRY

Jacklight, Holt, 1984.
Baptism of Desire, Harper, 1989.

NONFICTION

The Blue Jay's Dance: A Birth Year, HarperCollins, 1995.

OTHER

Imagination (textbook), C. E. Merrill, 1980.
(Author of preface) Michael Dorris, *The Broken Cord: A Family's Ongoing Struggle with Fetal Alcohol Syndrome,* Harper, 1989.
(Author of preface) Desmond Hogan, *A Link with the River,* Farrar, Straus, 1989.
(Author of introduction) John Tanner, *The Falcon: A Narrative of the Captivity and Adventures of John Tanner,* Penguin, 1994.

Author of short story, "The World's Greatest Fisherman"; contributor to anthologies, including the *Norton Anthology of Poetry; Best American Short Stories* of 1981-83, 1983, and 1988; and *Prize Stories: The O. Henry Awards,* in 1985 and 1987; contributor of stories, poems, essays, and book reviews to periodicals, including *New Yorker, New England Review, Chicago, American Indian Quarterly, Frontiers, Atlantic, Kenyon Review, North American Review, New York Times Book Review, Ms.* magazine, *Redbook* (with her sister Heidi, under the joint pseudonym Heidi Louise), and *Woman* magazine (with Dorris, under the joint pseudonym Milou North).

■ Sidelights

Louise Erdrich published her first two books—*Jacklight,* a volume of poetry, and *Love Medicine,* a novel—at the age of thirty. The daughter of a Chippewa Indian mother and a German-American father, Erdrich explores Native American themes in her works, with major characters representing both sides of her heritage. *Love Medicine,* which traces two Native American families from 1934 to 1984 in a unique multi-narrator format, was extremely well-received, earning Erdrich the National Book Critics Circle Award in 1984. Since then, she has gone on to publish *The Beet Queen, Tracks,* and *The Bingo Palace*—three more novels exploring the roots of *Love Medicine's* characters, as

well as those of their white neighbors. These novels, which are related through recurring characters and themes, have all been well-received, and in 1989 the author completed a second volume of poetry, titled *Baptism of Desire.*

Although Erdrich's name is the only one appearing on the covers of these books, her work often included the input of her late husband, Michael Dorris, an educator who was also part Native American. Erdrich and Dorris co-wrote the novel *Crown of Columbus,* which explores the meaning of Columbus's voyage for both Native Americans and white people today. While *Tracks* and *Crown of Columbus* are political in nature, examining the exploitation of Native Americans by those of European descent, the majority of Erdrich's works concern relationships and the human condition. The Native American folklore and myths form a backdrop for stories of individuals struggling against fate and circumstances of birth. While *Love Medicine* is solely concerned with American Indians, *The Beet Queen* expands the focus to include whites and those who—like Erdrich—are of mixed descent.

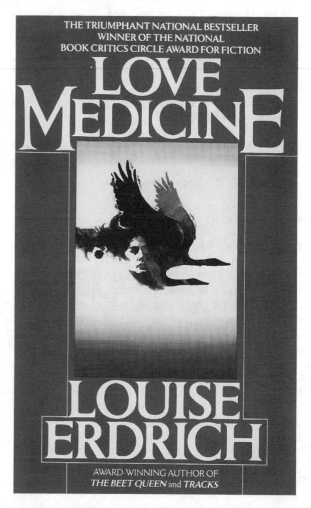

THE TRIUMPHANT NATIONAL BESTSELLER
WINNER OF THE NATIONAL
BOOK CRITICS CIRCLE AWARD FOR FICTION

LOVE MEDICINE

LOUISE ERDRICH

AWARD-WINNING AUTHOR OF
THE BEET QUEEN and *TRACKS*

Erdrich's award-winning novel traces three generations of two Chippewa families by relating fourteen stories in an unusual seven-narrator format. (Cover illustration by Glenn Harrington.)

Erdrich's interest in writing can be traced to her childhood and her heritage. She told *Writer's Digest* contributor Michael Schumacher, "People in [Native American] families make everything into a story.... People just sit and the stories start coming, one after another. I suppose that when you grow up constantly hearing the stories rise, break, and fall, it gets into you somehow." The oldest in a family of seven children, Erdrich was raised in Wahpeton, North Dakota. Her Chippewa grandfather had been the tribal chair of the nearby Turtle Mountain Reservation, and her parents worked at the Bureau of Indian Falls boarding school. Erdrich once commented of the way in which her parents encouraged her writing: "My father used to give me a nickel for every story I wrote, and my mother wove strips of construction paper together and stapled them into book covers. So at an early age I felt myself to be a published author earning substantial royalties."

But Erdrich would not feel ready to write about her ethnic heritage until adulthood. In fact, the author stated in an interview with *Publishers Weekly* contributor Miriam Berkley that as she was growing up, she "never thought about what was Native American and what wasn't. I think that's the way a lot of people who are of mixed descent regard their lives—you're just a combination of different backgrounds." It was during her adolescent years that Erdrich first began to think of herself as a writer; her interests included keeping journals and reading poems. As a creative writing major at Dartmouth University—where she won awards for her poetry and fiction—Erdrich decided to pursue writing as a career.

Erdrich's first year of college—1972—was the year that Dartmouth began admitting women, as well as the year the Native American studies department was established. The author's future husband and collaborator, anthropologist Michael Dorris, was hired to chair the department. In his class, Erdrich began the exploration of her own ancestry that would eventually inspire her novels. Intent on balancing her academic training with a broad range of practical knowledge, Erdrich told Berkley, "I ended up taking some really crazy jobs, and I'm glad I did. They turned out to have been very useful experiences, although I never would have believed it at the time." In addition to working as a lifeguard, waitress, poetry teacher at prisons, and construction flag signaler, Erdrich became an editor for the Circle, a Boston Indian Council newspaper. She told Schumacher, "Settling into that job and becoming comfortable with an urban community—which is very different from the reservation community—gave me another reference point. There were lots of people with mixed blood, lots of people who had their own confusions. I realized that this was part of my life—it wasn't something that I was making up—and that it was something I wanted to write about." In 1978, the author enrolled in an M.A. program at Johns Hopkins University, where she wrote poems and stories incorporating her heritage, many of which would later become part of her books. She also began sending her work to publishers, most of whom sent back rejection slips.

The second title in a planned four-part series, *The Beet Queen* explores the history of several characters from Erdrich's *Love Medicine.* (Cover illustration by Wendel Minor.)

After receiving her master's degree, Erdrich returned to Dartmouth as a writer-in-residence. Dorris—with whom she had remained in touch—attended a reading of Erdrich's poetry there, and was impressed. A writer himself—Dorris would later publish the best-selling novel *A Yellow Raft in Blue Water* and receive the 1989 National Book Critics Circle Award for his nonfiction work *The Broken Cord*—he decided then that he was interested in working with Erdrich and getting to know her better. When he left for New Zealand to do field research and Erdrich went to Boston to work on a textbook, the two began sending their poetry and fiction back and forth with their letters, laying a groundwork for a literary relationship. Dorris returned to New Hampshire in 1980, and Erdrich moved back there as well. The two began collaborating on short stories, including one titled "The World's Greatest Fisherman." When this story won five thousand dollars in the Nelson Algren fiction competition, Erdrich and Dorris decided to expand it into a novel—*Love Medicine.* At the same time, their literary relationship led to a deeply romantic one. In 1981 they were married.

Dorris had previously adopted three children, and the couple had three more. Erdrich's days became a flurry of babies and manuscripts. She and her husband were building a family of novels alongside their family of children. Erdrich told Berkley, "*The Beet Queen* was written while either rocking, feeding, or changing," and she adds that her two consecutive pregnancies inspired the many birth scenes in the work. In the couple's interview with Schumacher, Dorris drew a parallel between their children and the characters they have created: "The fictional characters belong to both of us, regardless of who's trotting them out at any given time." Erdrich also spoke of their dual partnership: "Marriage is a process of coming to trust the other person over the years, and it's the same thing with our writing."

Erdrich's first major work, *Jacklight,* is a volume of poetry closely associated with the author's mixed heritage. Some of the selections deal with tribal myth and express anger at white people's treatment of Native Americans. The series of poems "The Butcher's Wife" is derived from Erdrich's German roots and tells the story of an immigrant community. *Jacklight* established the author's gift for language, and reviewers also noted the use of character and setting that foreshadowed her ability as a novelist.

Erdrich's novels *Love Medicine, The Beet Queen, Tracks,* and *The Bingo Palace* encompass the stories of three interrelated families living in and around a reservation in the fictional town of Argus, North Dakota, from 1912 through the 1990s. The novels have been compared to those of William Faulkner—one of Erdrich's favorite authors—because of Faulkner's fictional county of Yoknapatawpa, as well as the multi-voice narration and nonchronological storytelling which he employed in works such as *As I Lay Dying.* Erdrich's works, linked by recurring characters who are victims of fate and the patterns set by their elders, are structured like intricate puzzles in which bits of information about individuals and their relations to one another are slowly released in a seemingly random order, until three-dimensional characters—with a future and a past—are revealed. As one moves through the novels, one repeatedly discovers surprising connections between the characters in the three books. For example, a character in the third novel, *Tracks,* turns out to be the mother of a woman who, in the first novel, *Love Medicine,* was a grandmother; we also discover in *Tracks* that a pair of lovers in *Love Medicine* are committing incest. Through her characters' antics, Erdrich explores universal family life cycles while also communicating a sense of the changes and loss involved in the twentieth-century Native American experience.

Erdrich continued to explore the dual nature of her spiritual heritage in *Baptism of Desire,* her 1989 collection of poems. Many of the selections were composed late at night when Erdrich's pregnancy gave her insomnia, and these works capture both the ordinary and the inspirational in her nightly experience. In the poem "Hydra," Erdrich explores female sexuality, birthing, and mothering, historically and in various cultures. Comparing herself to both Mary and Eve, the poet addresses her unborn child, as well as the mythical serpent, in the lines, "Blessed one, beating your tail across heaven, / uncoiling through the length of my life." The final selection deals with gardening, childrearing, and marriage. Erdrich explored the subject of childbearing again more fully in her first full-length nonfiction study, *The Blue Jay's Dance: A Birth Year,* which a *Kirkus Reviews* critic described as "astute, poetic reflections on the powerful mother-daughter relationship from conception through the baby's first year."

Erdrich and Dorris's jointly-authored novel, *The Crown of Columbus,* explores Native American issues from the standpoint of the authors' current experience, rather than the world of their ancestors. Marking the quincentennial anniversary of Spanish explorer Christopher Columbus's voyage in a not-so-celebratory fashion,

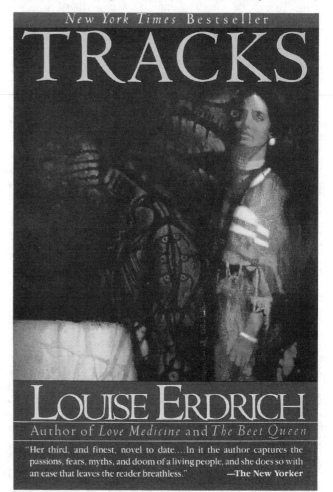

New York Times Bestseller

TRACKS

LOUISE ERDRICH
Author of *Love Medicine* and *The Beet Queen*

"Her third, and finest, novel to date....In it the author captures the passions, fears, myths, and doom of a living people, and she does so with an ease that leaves the reader breathless." —The New Yorker

The third book in Erdrich's best-selling series about families living in or near a reservation in North Dakota, *Tracks* examines the tension between the Native Americans' ancient beliefs and the Christian tenets of the Europeans. (Cover illustration by Glenn Harrington.)

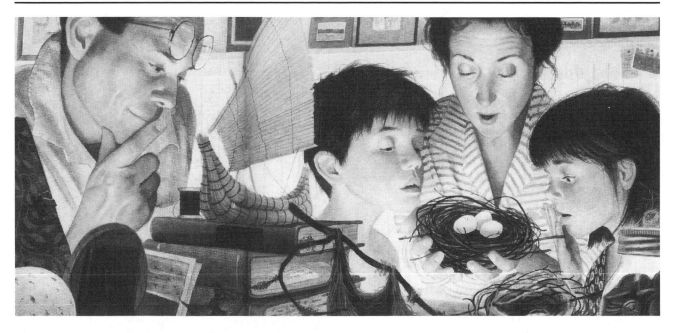

Eccentric Grandmother abandons her family in the middle of their vacation and hops on a porpoise for a journey to Greenland, leaving quite a surprise for her grandchildren to discover at home. (From *Grandmother's Pigeon,* written by Erdrich and illustrated by Jim LaMarche.)

Erdrich and Dorris raise important questions about the meaning of that voyage for both Europeans and Native Americans today. The story is narrated by the two central characters, both Dartmouth professors involved in projects concerning Columbus. Vivian Twostar is a Native American single mother with eclectic tastes and a teenage son, Nash. Vivian is asked to write an academic article on Columbus from a Native American perspective and is researching Columbus's diaries. Roger Williams, a stuffy New England Protestant poet, is writing an epic work about the explorer's voyage. Vivian and Roger become lovers—parenting a girl named Violet—but have little in common. Vivian judges Roger an unfit father and sends him away, but when he learns to appreciate some of her opinions, she forgives him and takes him back. In her research, Vivian then discovers what appear to be two pages from Columbus's lost diary. She believes the remainder of the diary to be in the possession of a businessman living on a Caribbean island. Roger dismisses her findings, but agrees to accompany Vivian, Violet, and Nash to the Bahamas to discover the truth about Columbus.

During their trip, Vivian and Roger struggle to find a common ground in their relationship and have a series of adventures. First Violet is set adrift alone on a raft, and then Roger must battle a shark before becoming trapped in a cave full of bats. Meanwhile, the businessman they have come to see desperately craves the two pages Vivian has found, which may contain directions to the jeweled crown Columbus once buried on the island. The man takes Vivian out in his sailboat, ties her to a bucket of sand, and attempts to throw her overboard. But all is well in the end, as Vivian and Roger rediscover themselves as they rediscover America. Acknowledging the destructive impact of Columbus's voyage on the Native American people, Vivian and

Roger vow to redress the political wrongs symbolically by changing the power structure in their relationship. Some reviewers found *The Crown of Columbus* unbelievable and inconsistent, and considered it less praiseworthy than the individual authors' earlier works. However, *New York Times Book Review* contributor Robert Houston appreciated the work's timely political relevance. He also stated, "There are moments of genuine humor and compassion, of real insight and sound satire."

Erdrich made her picture book debut with *Grandmother's Pigeon,* a well-received fantasy that *School Library Journal* contributor Harriett Fargnoli described as "a small gem, a bit of a puzzle, and a delight to pore over and ponder." In the story, Grandmother abandons her family in the middle of their vacation and hops on a porpoise for a journey to Greenland. After avoiding the inevitable for a year, the family finally determines to clean out Grandmother's room—and find among a host of odd treasures a nest with three eggs, just beginning to hatch. Baby passenger pigeons—an extinct species—emerge, and the family home is the center of a media circus until the narrator/granddaughter and her brother come up with an intriguing idea about how they might contact grandmother. "Erdrich makes every word count in her bewitching debut children's story," enthused a *Publishers Weekly* reviewer. Ilene Cooper of *Booklist* also offered high praise for *Grandmother's Pigeon.* "Besides the sense of the unexpected that permeates every page is the freshness of the language," Cooper wrote. "The sentence structure is elegant, and since one quality of elegance is simplicity, the writing is never over children's heads." *New York Times Book Review* contributor Nancy Caldwell Sorel asserted: "We know Louise Erdrich as a writer of luminous poetry and fiction and a perceptive observer of the natural world, so we expect *Grandmother's Pigeon* to excel both in style and story. In fact, it soars."

■ **Works Cited**

Berkley, Miriam, "Louise Erdrich," *Publishers Weekly,* August 15, 1986, p. 58-59.

Review of *The Blue Jay's Dance: A Birth Year,* Kirkus Reviews, February 15, 1995, p. 195.

Cooper, Ilene, review of *Grandmother's Pigeon, Booklist,* May 1, 1996, p. 1502.

Fargnoli, Harriett, review of *Grandmother's Pigeon, School Library Journal,* July, 1996, p. 59.

Review of *Grandmother's Pigeon, Publishers Weekly,* April 22, 1996, p. 71.

Houston, Robert, review of *The Crown of Columbus, New York Times Book Review,* April 28, 1991, p. 10.

Schumacher, Michael, "Louise Erdrich and Michael Dorris: A Marriage of Minds," *Writer's Digest,* June, 1991, pp. 28-31.

Sorel, Nancy Caldwell, review of *Grandmother's Pigeon, New York Times Book Review,* November 10, 1996, p. 49.

■ **For More Information See**

PERIODICALS

Bulletin of the Center for Children's Books, July-August, 1996, p. 369.

Kirkus Reviews, April 15, 1996, p. 600.

People, June 10, 1991, p. 26-27.

*   *   *

EYRE, Dorothy
  See McGUIRE, Leslie (Sarah)

*   *   *

FLEMING, Candace 1962-

■ **Personal**

Born May 24, 1962; daughter of Charles (a superintendent) and Carol (a homemaker; maiden name, Price) Groth; married Scott Fleming (in commercial real estate), November 9, 1985; children: Scott, Michael. *Education:* Eastern Illinois University, B.A., 1985. *Religion:* Lutheran. *Hobbies and other interests:* Reading, collecting antiquarian books, camping, hiking, travel.

■ **Addresses**

Office—415 East Golf Rd., Arlington Heights, IL 60005.

■ **Career**

Writer, 1990—. Junior Great Books coordinator, 1995-97; Adjunct professor, Liberal Arts Department, Harper College, Palatine, IL, 1997—. *Member:* Society of Children's Book Writers and Illustrators.

CANDACE FLEMING

■ **Awards, Honors**

Highlights for Children History Feature of the Year, 1995; *Highlights for Children* Patriotic Feature of the Year, 1996; award from Chicago Women in Publishing, 1996, for *Women of the Lights.*

■ **Writings**

Professor Fergus Fahrenheit and His Wonderful Weather Machine, illustrated by Don Weller, Simon & Schuster, 1994.

Women of the Lights, illustrated by James Watling, Albert Whitman (Morton Grove, IL), 1996.

Madame LaGrande and Her So High, to the Sky, Uproarious Pompadour, illustrated by S. D. Schindler, Knopf, 1996.

Gabriella's Song, illustrated by Giselle Potter, Atheneum, 1997.

Westward Ho, Carlotta!, illustrated by David Catrow, Atheneum, 1998.

The Hatmaker's Sign, illustrated by Robert Andrew Parker, Orchard Books, 1998.

Contributor to magazines, including *Boys' Life* and *American Baby.*

■ **Work in Progress**

When Agnes Caws, for Atheneum; *A Big Cheese for the White: A True Tale of a Tremendous Cheddar;* research on eighteenth-century New England life.

■ Sidelights

Candace Fleming told *SATA:* "I remember the day I discovered the music and magic of words. It was the day my second-grade teacher, Miss Johnson, held up a horn-shaped basket filled with papier-mache pumpkins and asked the class to repeat the word 'cornucopia.' It sounded good. I said it again, and again, and I decided I loved that word. I loved its rhythm and cadence. I loved the way it felt on my tongue and fell on my ears. I skipped all the way home from school that day chanting 'Cornucopia! Cornucopia!' From then on, I really began listening to words—to the sounds they made, and the way they were used, and how they made me feel. I longed to put them together in ways that were beautiful, and yet told a story.

"Now, my family and close friends will tell you that I have always made up stories. My mother loves to tell of the time I regaled our next-door neighbor with tales of our family trip to Paris, France. So vivid were my descriptions of that romantic city that my neighbor believed every word I said. I can only imagine his chagrin when he learned I had never been beyond my home state of Indiana.

"I told many stories like this. My classmates heard the saga of my three-legged dog Tiger. My Sunday school teacher listened, wide-eyed, as I told the tale of the ghost in our attic. Lots of people heard my tall tales. Lots of people believed them.

"Technically, I suppose you could call this lying. Fortunately, I had parents who understood the difference between imagination and lies. They encouraged me to make up stories, but they strongly suggested that I not claim these stories as truth. Eventually, I took their advice.

"The result? My love of language and my need to tell a good story merged, and I became a writer. I filled notebook after notebook with my stories, poems, and plays. I couldn't stop the flow of words and ideas that rushed from my pencil, and I didn't try. Often, I arrived home from school, closed my bedroom door, and wrote for hours on end. When I wasn't writing, I was reading, and if something I read sparked my imagination, I would start writing all over again.

"I still have many of those notebooks today. I cherish them. They are a record of my writing life, from second grade to the present. In them I can see my struggle to tell a good and believable story. I can see my struggle to use musical language. I can't help but recognize that these are the same struggles I have as a writer today. They are also my goals. I want to tell you a good story. I want to tell it in a believable way. And I want to tell it with language that opens your ears to the music and magic of words."

■ For More Information See

PERIODICALS

Booklist, October 15, 1994, p. 434; March 15, 1996, p. 1258; July, 1996, p. 1829.
Kirkus Reviews, May 1, 1996, p. 687.
Publishers Weekly, October 3, 1994, p. 68; June 24, 1996, p. 59.
School Library Journal, January, 1995, p. 86; April, 1996, p. 144; July, 1996, p. 59.
Smartkid, May, 1996, pp. 20, 45.

*   *   *

FRANK, Lucy 1947-

■ Personal

Born March 22, 1947, in New York, NY; daughter of Sidney (a dentist) and Viola (a teacher and photographer; maiden name, Sobol) Kantrowitz; married Peter C. Frank (a film editor), September 30, 1978; children: Michael. *Education:* Barnard College, A.B., 1968. *Hobbies and other interests:* Reading, gardening, nature study.

■ Addresses

Home—New York, NY. *Electronic Mail*—Lucy_frank @msn.com.

LUCY FRANK

■ Career

Author of books for young adults. Assistant portfolio manager and marketing manager for a major mutual fund company, New York City, 1986-96; placement counselor for a temporary employment service, New York City, 1996—. *Member:* Society of Children's Book Writers and Illustrators, Authors Guild.

■ Writings

I Am an Artichoke, Holiday House, 1995.
Will You Be My Brussels Sprout?, Holiday House, 1996.

■ Work in Progress

Additional young adult novels.

■ Sidelights

Lucy Frank is considered a promising new young adult author whose tales of adolescent angst center on intelligent and funny characters going through realistic problems. Frank, whose own son was in early adolescence while she was writing her first published book, *I Am an Artichoke,* relied not only on her son's input ("I figured if he laughed we were OK," Frank told Bella Stander in a *Publishers Weekly* interview), but on her observations of people she saw on the street and on buses in her hometown of Manhattan. "Part of getting the voice right is listening to kids," Frank told Stander, "and part of it is just letting my imagination rip." The draw of writing for young adults is that "the teenage point is where a lot is changing fast and emotions are running high," Frank continued. "Kids have a highly developed sense of the ridiculous or weird, which appeals to me."

In *I Am an Artichoke,* fifteen-year-old Sarah is bored with her dull suburban existence and decides that working in Manhattan as a mother's helper over the summer will be just what she needs. Thus begins her association with the dysfunctional Friedman family. Florence Friedman, a flamboyant magazine writer—"presented with a vividness that has a fingernail-across-the-chalk board effect on the reader," according to Dolores J. Sarafinski in *Voice of Youth Advocates*—hires Sarah in the hope that she will be able to cure twelve-year-old Emily's anorexia, an agenda that becomes painfully obvious only after Sarah accepts the job. "As the story evolves," noted Elizabeth S. Watson in *Horn Book,* "it becomes clear that, while Sarah can make a difference, she will not cure Emily or the myriad problems in the family."

"This accomplished first novel sparkles with deliciously wry humor," enthused a reviewer in *Publishers Weekly* about *I Am an Artichoke.* The novel was warmly received by other critics as well, who praised the author for consistent characterization, solid pacing, and thoughtful treatment of issues such as self-esteem, family, and friendship—all without losing track of her

sense of humor. Susan Dove Lempke concluded her review in *Bulletin of the Center for Children's Books* with the following summation: "Tart, witty narration, strong characterization, and well-paced, realistic plot development make this writer's initial entry into fiction bode well for her future work."

The first example of Frank's "future work" was *Will You Be My Brussels Sprout?,* the sequel to *I Am an Artichoke* in which Sarah meets and falls in love with Emily's older brother David on one of her weekly trips to Manhattan to take cello lessons at the New York Conservatory of Music. Frank's account of first love is "punctuated with humor and witty dialogue and filled with all the angst any teen could ever want," remarked Lauren Peterson in *Booklist.* Some other reviewers were less enthusiastic, however, complaining, like Alice Casey Smith in *School Library Journal,* that the conclusion is "disappointingly open-ended." And, although reviewers generally commended the author's treatment of sex as responsible and age-appropriate, a critic for *Kirkus Reviews* concluded that Sarah's inability to break up with David, who pressures her for sex and undermines her musical ambitions, may leave some readers with the feeling that "all the sexual stereotypes they've been taught to recognize and resist have just been reinforced—in spades." Nevertheless, like *I Am an Artichoke, Will You Be My Brussels Sprout* garnered praise as a "well-paced [novel] with fresh characters and an appealing plot," from *Voice of Youth Advocates* reviewer Judy Sasges.

■ Works Cited

Review of *I Am an Artichoke, Publishers Weekly,* March 27, 1995, p. 86.

Lempke, Susan Dove, review of *I Am an Artichoke, Bulletin of the Center for Children's Books,* June, 1995, pp. 342-43.

Peterson, Lauren, review of *Will You Be My Brussels Sprout?, Booklist,* April 15, 1996, p. 1433.

Sarafinski, Dolores J., review of *I Am an Artichoke, Voice of Youth Advocates,* August, 1995, p. 158.

Sasges, Judy, review of *Will You Be My Brussels Sprout?, Voice of Youth Advocates,* October, 1996, pp. 208-209.

Smith, Alice Casey, review of *Will You Be My Brussels Sprout?, School Library Journal,* April, 1996, p. 154.

Stander, Bella, "Flying Starts," *Publishers Weekly,* July 3, 1995, pp. 31-32.

Watson, Elizabeth S., review of *I Am an Artichoke, Horn Book,* September, 1995, p. 609.

Review of *Will You Be My Brussels Sprout?, Kirkus Reviews,* January 15, 1996, p. 133.

■ For More Information See

PERIODICALS

Booklist, February 1, 1995, p. 999.
Publishers Weekly, April 15, 1996, p. 70.
School Library Journal, March, 1995, p. 222.*

G

GABRIEL, Adriana
See ROJANY, Lisa

* * *

GERINGER, Laura 1948-

■ **Personal**

Born February 23, 1948, in New York, NY; daughter of Benjamin and Ann Geringer. *Education:* Barnard College, B.A., 1968; Yale University, M.F.A., 1975.

■ **Career**

Author of books for children and young adults. Also worked as an editor of children's books, Harper and Row Publishers, Inc., New York City, beginning in 1980. *Member:* Women's National Book Association, New York Critics Circle.

■ **Writings**

PICTURE BOOKS

Seven True Bear Stories, illustrated by Carol Maisto, Hastings, 1978.
A Three Hat Day, illustrated by Arnold Lobel, Harper and Row, 1985.
Molly's New Washing Machine, illustrated by Petra Mathers, Harper and Row, 1986.
The Cow Is Mooing Anyhow: A Scrambled Alphabet Book to Be Read at Breakfast, illustrated by Dirk Zimmer, HarperCollins, 1991.
Look Out, Look Out, It's Coming, illustrated by Sue Truesdell, HarperCollins, 1992.
Yours 'til the Ice Cracks: A Book of Valentines, illustrated by Andrea Baruffi, HarperCollins, 1992.
(Reteller) Jacob and Wilhelm Grimm, *The Seven Ravens,* illustrated by Edward S. Gazsi, HarperCollins, 1994.
(Reteller) *The Pomegranate Seeds: A Classic Greek Myth,* illustrated by Leonid Gore, Houghton Mifflin, 1995.

"MYTH MEN" SERIES

Hercules, the Strong Man, Scholastic, 1996.
Perseus, the Boy with Super Powers, Scholastic, 1996.
Ulysses, Scholastic, 1996.
Guardian, Scholastic, 1997.

OTHER

Silverpoint (young adult novel), HarperCollins, 1991.

Contributor of book reviews to periodicals, including *Saturday Review* and *Newsweek.*

■ **Sidelights**

Laura Geringer is the author of several original picture books for children and one novel for young adults, as well as a number of retellings of classic myths and folktales. In reviews of her works, critics have commented favorably on her rich use of language and her ability to entertain readers with zany details.

Like many of Geringer's picture books, *Molly's New Washing Machine,* published in 1986, features an unusual premise and raucous action. One day, two burly brown rabbits unexpectedly deliver a washing machine to a human named Molly. Soon three of her animal friends—a dog named Bongo, a fox named Click, and a mole named Pocket—show up to do their laundry. When they turn the machine on, it begins to make funny, rhythmic noises that compel the friends to dance around the suds-filled kitchen with abandon until they finally collapse from exhaustion. Later, the two rabbits show up to reclaim the washing machine, explaining that they delivered it to Molly by mistake. Denise M. Wilms, writing in *Booklist,* called *Molly's New Washing Machine* "an odd tale with an originality that is beguiling," while a *Publishers Weekly* reviewer added that the book "is sure to have both adults and children laughing with delight."

Another offbeat Geringer picture book, *A Three Hat Day,* features the somewhat quirky Pottle clan, in particular R. R. Pottle the Third and his wife Isabel, who indulge their love of hats in comic fashion.

Adapted from the Greek myth which explains the origin of the seasons, Laura Geringer's retelling *The Pomegranate Seeds* portrays Persephone as an outspoken, modern young woman who becomes the focus of Hades's and Demeter's jealous rivalry. (Illustrated by Leonid Gore.)

"Although the characters are adult right up to the last page, they share the compelling urge to collect, which seems instinctive to most children," noted a reviewer for the *Bulletin of the Center for Children's Books. School Library Journal* contributor Judith Gloyer offered a favorable assessment of the "fun-filled story," praising the "richness and rhythm of the language." Other uniquely Geringer picture-book offerings include *The Cow is Mooing Anyhow: A Scrambled Alphabet Book to Be Read at Breakfast,* featuring letters that are *not* in alphabetical order, and *Yours 'til the Ice Cracks: A Book of Valentines,* with whimsical professions of love that the accompanying illustrations reveal to be not quite so enduring as they sound.

Silverpoint, Geringer's novel for middle graders, was dubbed "an unusually fine first novel" by a *Kirkus Reviews* critic. *Silverpoint* focuses on twelve-year-old Cora, abandoned at an early age by her father. Cora and her best friend Charley, similarly distressed by his own father's death, search for information about Cora's father while masking their loneliness in a world of games, rituals, and fantasy. "The events are sparse in this carefully constructed, beautifully written story, but Cora's inner life is fascinating, rich with interconnected leitmotifs," added the *Kirkus Reviews* commentator. In another favorable assessment, Maeve Visser Knoth of *Horn Book* praised Geringer's "intricately drawn, sym-

pathetic characters," adding: "Geringer's prose is filled with imagery, and Cora's dream and fantasy lives are as strong and rich as her everyday life.... Her impressive first novel is remarkable for its restrained storytelling and deft characterization."

For her 1995 book *The Pomegranate Seeds,* Geringer retold and updated the classic Greek myth that explains the origin of the four seasons of the year. In Geringer's version, Persephone becomes an outspoken, modern young woman who is kidnapped by her uncle, Hades, not to become his bride, but merely to provide him with company in his lonely underworld kingdom. Persephone's overprotective mother, Demeter, is so distressed by her daughter's disappearance that she uses her powers to make the earth barren. Zeus finally intervenes to offer a compromise to the gods of the earth and the underworld. Persephone will be returned to her mother on the earth's surface, but since she has been tricked into eating three pomegranate seeds by Hades, she will be required to spend three months of each year with her uncle in the underworld. Thus the earth is barren for three months in winter, then blooms in joyous spring when Persephone returns to the surface, and eventually begins to wither as the time nears for her to rejoin Hades in fall. A *Publishers Weekly* reviewer commented that "despite the updating, [Geringer] captures the timeless, bittersweet atmosphere of the ancient tale." Jennifer Fleming, writing in *School Library Journal,* called *The Pomegranate Seeds* "a moving, evocative retelling ... that is at once contemporarily relevant and solidly classic."

■ Works Cited

Fleming, Jennifer, review of *The Pomegranate Seeds, School Library Journal,* March, 1996, p. 208.

Gloyer, Judith, review of *A Three Hat Day, School Library Journal,* November, 1985, p. 70.

Knoth, Maeve Visser, review of *Silverpoint, Horn Book,* January-February, 1992, pp. 69-70.

Review of *Molly's New Washing Machine, Publishers Weekly,* July 25, 1986, p. 186.

Review of *The Pomegranate Seeds, Publishers Weekly,* November 13, 1995, p. 61.

Review of *Silverpoint, Kirkus Reviews,* September 1, 1991, p. 1160.

Review of *A Three Hat Day, Bulletin of the Center for Children's Books,* January, 1986, pp. 85-86.

Wilms, Denise M., review of *Molly's New Washing Machine, Booklist,* September 15, 1986, p. 128.

■ For More Information See

PERIODICALS

Booklist, September 1, 1994, p. 45.

Bulletin of the Center for Children's Books, October, 1991, p. 37; October, 1994, p. 48.

Kirkus Reviews, February 1, 1991, p. 182; December 15, 1991, p. 1590.

Publishers Weekly, April 30, 1979, p. 114; March 8, 1991, p. 74; July 25, 1994, p. 55.

School Library Journal, December, 1986, p. 86; January, 1992, p. 102.

* * *

GLASER, Isabel Joshlin 1929-

■ Personal

Born June 7, 1929, in Birmingham, AL; daughter of Notreab (a farmer) and Kathleen (a homemaker; maiden name, Sigler) Joshlin; married Melvin William Glaser (an educator), November 7, 1953 (died, 1966); children: Susan Elaine, Stephen Philip. *Education:* Attended Randolph-Macon Woman's College, 1947-49; George Peabody College for Teachers, Vanderbilt University, B.A., 1951; also attended Baldwin-Wallace College, Ohio University, Kent State University, and Memphis State University. *Religion:* Methodist.

■ Addresses

Home and office—5383 Mason Rd., Memphis, TN 38120-1707.

■ Career

High school teacher of English and Spanish in Tennessee, 1951-53; elementary school teacher in Ohio, 1953-66; elementary school teacher in Memphis, TN, 1979-87. Writer, 1968—. *Member:* Society of Children's Book Writers and Illustrators, Jane Austen Society of North America, Tennessee Writers Alliance.

■ Awards, Honors

Golden Owl Award, state chapter of National League of Pen Women, 1974; named poet laureate by the Poetry Society of Tennessee, 1990-91; finalist, Children's Books of Distinction, *Hungry Mind Review,* 1996, for *Dreams of Glory.*

■ Writings

Old Visions ... New Dreams, Old Hickory Press (Jackson, TN), 1977.

(Compiler and contributor) *Dreams of Glory: Poems Starring Girls,* illustrated by Pat Lowery Collins, Atheneum, 1995.

Work represented in anthologies, including *Extra Innings,* Harcourt Brace, 1993; *Weather,* HarperCollins, 1994; and *Hand in Hand,* Simon & Schuster, 1994. Contributor to textbooks, including *Celebrate Reading!,* Scott, Foresman, 1995; *Reading and Writing: Teaching for the Connections,* Harcourt, 1995; and *Literature Works,* Silver Burdett Ginn, 1997. Contributor to magazines, including *Cricket, Spider, School Magazine,* and *Instructor.*

■ Work in Progress

Poetry and prose projects.

ISABEL JOSHLIN GLASER

■ Sidelights

Isabel Joshlin Glaser told *SATA:* "I grew up in southwest Tennessee. Both of my parents were tremendous storytellers and were never at a loss for anecdotes that stretched the boundaries of imagination with their humor, folkishness, wildness, and so on.

"One way or another, my three siblings and I were surrounded by books, and I read a great deal. My early (and continuing) favorites were brief, gentle animal stories, which I brought home from the Cossitt Library in Memphis. We owned—and I memorized from cover to cover—*A Child's Garden of Verses* by Robert Louis Stevenson and *Mother Goose.* One of the small novels that I liked best was about a cuckoo clock, another was about a lost doll. Strangely, I have forgotten the titles.

"In elementary school, I read through the Nancy Drew books in my spare time and went on to the boring Bobbsey twins. Mother built a bookcase for our books and hers. I read her books with particular affection, everything from *Poor Miss Finch* to *Oliver Twist* and *Beltane the Smith,* a romance written poetically in a form replete with inversions.

"At some point, Mother decided that reading fiction was a time-waster. She liked it when I read books on geography, though. I had never been to any of the places, and they seemed fictional to me. After a while, I became very knowledgeable about the geography and explorations of the Americas, the Arctic regions, and Antarctica . . . .

"William Cowper, William Blake, William Wordsworth, John Keats, Jane Austen, Charles Dickens, and Flannery O'Connor are all writers from the past who have influenced me as a writer—the poets with the beauty of their work and the authors of fiction with their use of humor, wisdom, attention to detail, and engrossing plots.

"As a writer, I have found the following advice helpful. Read the work of today's successful writers. Study books and journals focusing on the creative and business aspects of writing and publishing. Rewrite, rewrite, rewrite, and still be open to suggested revisions. Keep journals of ideas, names, possible titles, and so on. Support the work of others through subscriptions and purchases. Recognize the element of luck involved in attracting and maintaining the interest of an editor. Excellence is no guarantee that work will be published, but it helps. Finally, be stubborn, persist, and bounce back regardless of obstacles."

■ For More Information See

PERIODICALS

Booklist, November 15, 1995, p. 551.
Horn Book, March, 1996, p. 214.
Kirkus Reviews, November 1, 1995.
School Library Journal, December, 1995, p. 116.

* * *

GOLDBERG, Jacob 1943-
(Jake Goldberg)

■ Personal

Born November 7, 1943, in Brooklyn, NY; son of Norman (a commercial artist) and Florence (maiden name, Frankenstein) Goldberg. *Education:* Harpur College, B.A., 1966. *Hobbies and other interests:* Flying, fencing, chess, wilderness travel, progressive politics.

■ Addresses

Home—423 11th St., Brooklyn, NY 11215.

■ Career

Crown Publishers, Inc., New York City, senior editor, 1970-90; Chelsea House Publishers, New York City, senior editor, 1990-96.

JACOB GOLDBERG

■ Writings

Rachel Carson: Biologist and Author (children's book), Chelsea House, 1993.
Miguel Cervantes (young adult), Chelsea House, 1994.
Economics and the Environment (young adult), Chelsea House, 1994.
The Disappearing American Farm (young adult), F. Watts, 1995.
Albert Einstein: The Rebel behind Relativity (young adult), F. Watts, 1995.
Food (young adult), F. Watts, 1997.
Hawaii (children's book), Marshall Cavendish, 1997.

■ Sidelights

Jake Goldberg told *SATA:* "I have wide-ranging interests, and I view the writing experience as an opportunity to research subjects I'd like to learn more about. I like to write for younger readers because I am forced to clearly explain all the components of my argument and carefully test my understanding of ideas I might otherwise have taken for granted."

Goldberg is the author of several nonfiction books for older elementary-school students and young adults. Critics praise Goldberg for presenting even the most controversial topics with clarity and objectivity. In his first book, a biography of Rachel Carson, *Bulletin of the Center for Children's Books* reviewer Zena Sutherland wrote that "Goldberg's tone is impartial" as he conveys Carson's apocalyptic theories about the damage being done to the environment by the pesticides commonly in use on America's farms. Goldberg also describes the strong resistance with which those theories were met by some.

Like critics of *Rachel Carson: Biologist and Author,* Kathleen Beck, who reviewed Goldberg's *Economics and the Environment* in *Voice of Youth Advocates,* praised the author for his "clear and provocative" narrative. In this book, the author "raises important questions, ones which are seldom addressed on a young adult level," Beck continued, though she questioned the author's objectivity on such issues as the effect of international banking on economic development in the Third World.

Goldberg attempted to provide a concise history of farming, with particular emphasis on federal subsidies of American farms, in his book *The Disappearing American Farm,* which received mixed reviews. A *Kirkus Reviews* critic felt that Goldberg's approach to his complicated topic lacked focus, and thus "does little to clarify the issues" raised. However, Eldon Younce wrote in *School Library Journal* that Goldberg does "an exceptional job" of recounting the history of his subject and objectively presents arguments both for and against federal subsidies.

■ Works Cited

Beck, Kathleen, review of *Economics and the Environment, Voice of Youth Advocates,* June, 1993, p. 111.
Review of *The Disappearing American Farm, Kirkus Reviews,* April 15, 1996, p. 601.
Sutherland, Zena, review of *Rachel Carson, Bulletin of the Center for Children's Books,* July, 1991, p. 262.
Younce, Eldon, review of *The Disappearing American Farm, School Library Journal,* June, 1996, p. 156.

* * *

GOLDBERG, Jake
    See GOLDBERG, Jacob

* * *

GOODMAN, Joan Elizabeth 1950-

■ Personal

Born June 18, 1950, in Fairfield, CT; daughter of Milton Joel (an architectural engineer) and Fayalene (a psychiatric social worker; maiden name, Decker) Goodman; married Keith A. Goldsmith, September 12, 1987; children: a son and daughter. *Education:* Attended L'Accademia di Belle Arti, Rome, 1969-70; Pratt Institute, B.F.A., 1973. *Hobbies and other interests:* Tennis, bridge, medieval history.

■ Addresses

Home—684 Washington St., 1-B, New York, NY 10014. *Agent*—Robin Rue, Anita Diamant Agency, 310 Madison Ave., New York, NY 10017.

JOAN ELIZABETH GOODMAN

■ Career

Writer and illustrator. *Village Voice,* New York City, type specker, 1968-69; Hallmark Cards, Kansas City, MO, greeting card artist, 1974-76.

■ Writings

FOR CHILDREN; SELF-ILLUSTRATED, EXCEPT WHERE NOTED

Teddy Bear, Teddy Bear, Grosset, 1979.
Bear and His Book, Simon & Schuster, 1982.
Right's Animal Farm, Western Publishing, 1983.
Amanda's First Day of School, Western Publishing, 1985.
The Secret Life of Walter Kitty, Western Publishing, 1986.
Good Night, Pippin, Western Publishing, 1986.
The Bunnies' Get Well Soup, Western Publishing, 1987.
Edward Hopper's Great Find, Western Publishing, 1987.
Hillary Squeak's Dreadful Dragon, Western Publishing, 1987.
The Bears' New Baby, Western Publishing, 1988.
Time for Bed, Western Publishing, 1989.
(Adaptor) *Hush Little Darling: A Christmas Song,* Scholastic, 1992.
Bernard's Bath, illustrated by Dominic Catalano, Boyds Mills, 1996.

NOVELS

(Self-illustrated) *Songs from Home,* Harcourt Brace, 1994.
The Winter Hare, Houghton Mifflin, 1996.
Hope's Crossing, Houghton Mifflin, 1998.

ILLUSTRATOR

David Cutts, reteller, *The Gingerbread Boy,* Troll, 1979.
Olive Blake, *The Grape Jelly Mystery,* Troll, 1979.

Ruben Tanner, *The Teddy Bear's Picnic: A Counting Book,* Dutton, 1979.

Carol Beach York, *Johnny Appleseed,* Troll, 1980.

Judith Grey, *Yummy, Yummy,* Troll, 1981.

Rose Greydanus, *Hocus Pocus, Magic Show!,* Troll, 1981.

Robyn Supraner, *The Case of the Missing Rattles,* Troll, 1982.

Eileen Curran, *Easter Parade,* Troll, 1985.

Supraner, *The Cat Who Wanted to Fly,* Troll, 1986.

■ Work in Progress

Woodland Lullabies, a self-illustrated series of poems about animal parents singing to their babies.

■ Sidelights

Joan Elizabeth Goodman has gone from being a successful author and illustrator of picture books for young children to writing novels for older readers. Combining her love of history with her talent for art, Goodman has entertained countless young people with her whimsical illustrations and her imaginative stories.

Goodman was born and raised in Fairfield, Connecticut, in a household full of artists. "My father was an architectural engineer," she once told *SATA.* "My mother was a very talented painter, but she kept that hidden until her early seventies when she began doing beautiful impressionistic oils. My older brother is a very fine artist. His work appears regularly in *Scientific American.* My grandmother lived with us and she, too, was an artist. Being surrounded by artists it seemed inevitable that I should be drawn to art." From an early age Goodman knew the answer to that most important of questions: What do you want to be when you grow up? "I feel lucky that I found out very early on what I loved doing and I've just stuck with it," she noted.

Her grandmother introduced Goodman to the medium of oils "as soon as she could trust me not to eat them," the illustrator recalled. "They *did* look delicious but I traded off the need to taste them for the greater need to keep on painting." After graduating from high school, she enrolled at Pratt Institute, a prestigious art school in New York City, "because being an art major was not enough. I wanted to be surrounded by ART and to live in a community of ARTISTS." During her freshman year at Pratt, Goodman worked part-time for the *Village Voice* as a type specker, and she quickly advanced to doing advertising design and layout. During her sophomore year, she decided to go to Italy to tour the museums there and study art at L'Accademia di Belle Arti in Rome; "It was *fantastico!,*" she later recalled. Returning to New York City in 1971, she worked for designer, Leslie Tillett, on a number of design projects, which included film strips, jewelry designs, and craft kits. Although Goodman also tried her hand at designing patterns for woven textiles, she found such work wasn't her strength.

Meanwhile, at Pratt, Goodman was inspired by a design course taught by Werner Pfeiffer. "We had to design, illustrate, print and bind our own books," she remembered. "Well, that was *it* for me ... I decided then on a career as a children's book illustrator." However, she was quick to add: "Deciding on a career and having it are two separate things." While refocusing her art on a career in book illustration, Goodman took on many assignments, including designing greeting cards for Hallmark Cards in Kansas City, Missouri, and even working in local bookstores. Despite the hard work, she remained committed to her goal. "It made great sense. I have always loved books: *Babar* by Jean de Brunhoff, first of all, *Mary Poppins* by P. L. Travers, the 'Narnia' books by C. S. Lewis, and many, many others. Books have enlightened me, comforted me, and taught me the value of humor." And books would become her life's work.

Goodman's first published work as an illustrator would be author David Cutt's version of the classic story *The Gingerbread Boy,* which appeared in 1979. Many illustration projects would follow, including *Yummy, Yummy* by Judith Grey, and *The Cat Who Wanted to Fly,* a picture book by author Robyn Supraner. In addition to providing the artwork for others' stories, Goodman knew that she wanted to write as well. "I had early delusions about BEING A WRITER, but my initial attempts at fiction were too pitiful to pursue," she admitted. "However, I had a fine teacher in the ninth grade, Mrs. Demers, who got me started keeping a journal, which I'm still keeping. Even though I was writing drivel, at least I was in the habit of writing. And I read copiously and enthusiastically.

"As soon as I began focusing on a future as an illustrator, I began trying to write my own children's books," Goodman explained to *SATA.* "Trying does *not* mean succeeding. But I did keep trying." In the early 1980s she began attending a writers' workshop run by Margret Gabel at New York City's New School for Social Research. The writers who gathered there— "some of the best writers of children's literature currently being published" by Goodman's standards—were both helpful and inspiring. "By paying attention to what they do, and taking to heart their sensitive and sensible editorial direction, I have been learning to write," she maintained.

During the 1980s, in addition to continuing to illustrate the works of other writers, Goodman began composing stories of her own. In *Good Night, Pippin,* a not-so-sleepy young bear and his mother share an adventurous tale of make-believe at bedtime. Pippin wants a story about what things were like when he was a baby, and Mama weaves tales of pirates and wizards and aliens with freeze beams into an imaginative saga that finds the baby Pippin safe at home at the end. "Goodman's watercolor illustrations of the bear at home are warmly reassuring, as is the gentle dialogue," noted Genevieve Stuttaford in *Publishers Weekly.* And in *Bernard's Bath,* an elephant's dislike of a good soaking won't get him into the bathtub, despite the lure of lots of bubbles and

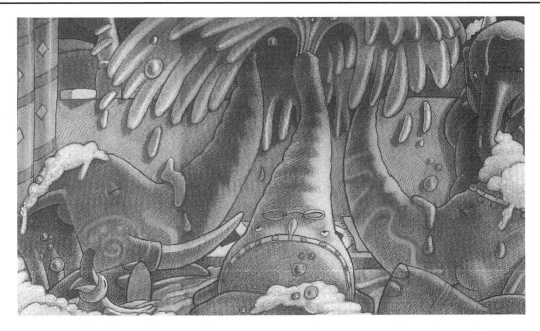

The whole family revels in the bathtub to show reluctant Bernard how much fun he is missing. (From *Bernard's Bath*, written by Goodman and illustrated by Dominic Catalano.)

bath toys. Finally, Papa, Mama, and even Grandma climb in the tub, just to show Bernard how much fun getting clean can be. In *Kirkus Reviews,* a critic praised Goodman's technique of having parents practice what they preach, noting that *Bernard's Bath* is exemplary for its omittance of the "pandering found in some books targeted at balkers." And Patricia Pearl Dole added in *School Library Journal* that "The humorous, lively, yet simple text reads aloud well."

In later years, Goodman's career would move from illustrator to writer as she became increasingly interested in writing fiction for older readers. Part of the change was due to getting married and beginning a family. "I've been able to pursue my interests in history and enjoy the more leisurely pace of writing a novel," she explained to *SATA.* "Now that I have two children—a daughter and son—the writing career is easier to maintain than the illustrating. A sentence can be interrupted by a baby's cry without much damage done, but an interrupted watercolor can be ruined."

Goodman's first full-length work of juvenile fiction, *Songs from Home,* was published in 1994. In the story, eleven-year-old Anna Hopkins has lived in Europe with her widower father for most of her life, traveling from place to place. Tired of living such a Bohemian existence, she gradually comes to understand the reason for her father's refusal to return to the United States and tries to help him to come to terms with their future, the family left behind in the States, and his wife's tragic death. While several critics noted that the characters were not quite believable, they praised the author's vivid descriptions of life in Italy. "Young readers will enjoy the local color of [the novel's] Roman setting and Anna's exotic and glamorously shabby existence," maintained Deborah Stevenson in the *Bulletin of the Center for Children's Books.* And Beth E. Anderson called

Songs from Home "a sweet tale gently told of the child-as-parent" in her review of Goodman's first novel in *Voice of Youth Advocates.*

In *The Winter Hare,* which takes place in twelfth-century Britain, Goodman tells the story of twelve-year-old Will Belet as he aspires to become a knight worthy of the legendary round table of King Arthur. Dubbed "little rabbit" due to his shortness, Will eventually finds himself involved in court intrigue and several battles between rival factions supporting King Stephen and his rival, the Empress Matilda. Praising the novel, a contributor to *Kirkus Reviews* noted that Goodman has created a "riveting plot that culminates in an escape scene worthy of translation into film."

Goodman believes that those writers who chose to create books for children must have a special way of looking at the world and remembering. "I don't particularly remember details about the past," she once commented. "Neither do I always remember the sense of a past situation. My past, my childhood, is a jumble of oddly assorted sounds, scents, and images, sometimes vague and sometimes crystal clear. What I *do* remember with extreme clarity are the *feelings* of childhood.

"When I write a picture book text or a 'young' novel, I reach back to that emotional grab bag for my material. My aim is to convey that emotional truth, whether I'm writing about bunnies, duckies, or bears."

■ Works Cited

Anderson, Beth E., review of *Songs from Home, Voice of Youth Advocates,* December 1994, p. 273.
Review of *Bernard's Bath, Kirkus Reviews,* December 15, 1995, p. 1770.

Dole, Patricia Pearl, review of *Bernard's Bath, School Library Journal,* March 1996, p. 174.

Stevenson, Deborah, review of *Songs from Home, Bulletin of the Center for Children's Books,* December 1994, p. 128.

Stuttaford, Genevieve, review of *Good Night, Pippin, Publishers Weekly,* August 22, 1986, p. 94.

Review of *The Winter Hare, Kirkus Reviews,* October 1, 1996, p. 1466.

■ **For More Information See**

PERIODICALS

Booklist, September 1, 1994, p. 41; February 1, 1996, p. 938.

Kirkus Reviews, November 15, 1994, p. 1529.

Publishers Weekly, September 7, 1992, p. 70; January 15, 1996, p. 461.

H

HADDIX, Margaret Peterson 1964-

■ Personal

Born April 9, 1964, in Washington Court House, OH; daughter of John Albert (a farmer) and Marilee Grace (a nurse; maiden name, Greshel) Peterson; married Doug Haddix (a newspaper editor), October 3, 1987; children: Meredith, Connor. *Education:* Miami University, B.A. (summa cum laude with university honors and honors in English), 1986. *Religion:* Presbyterian. *Hobbies and other interests:* Travel.

■ Addresses

Home—615 Timber Lane, Clarks Summit, PA 18411. *Agent*—Renee Cho, McIntosh & Otis, 310 Madison Ave., New York, NY 10020.

■ Career

Fort Wayne Journal-Gazette, Fort Wayne, IN, copy editor, 1986-87; *Indianapolis News,* Indianapolis, IN, reporter, 1987-91; Danville Area Community College, Danville, IL, adjunct faculty, 1991-93; freelance writer, 1991-94. *Member:* Phi Beta Kappa, Society of Children's Book Writers and Illustrators.

■ Awards, Honors

Honorable mention, *Seventeen* magazine fiction contest, 1983; fiction contest award, National Society of Arts and Letters, 1988; Junior Library Guild selection, *American Bestseller* Pick of the Lists selection, nominee for Mystery Writers of America's Edgar Allen Poe award, listed as a Quick Pick for Reluctant Young Adult Readers and as a 1997 Best Book for Young Adults by the Young Adult Library Services Association, and listed as a Notable Children's Trade Books in the Field of Social Studies for 1996 by the National Council for Social Studies and the Children's Book Council, all for *Running Out of Time;* Children's Book Award (older reader category), International Reading Association, 1997, and listed as a Quick Pick for Reluctant Young

MARGARET PETERSON HADDIX

Adult Readers and as a 1997 Best Book for Young Adults by the Young Adult Library Services Association, all for *Don't You Dare Read This, Mrs. Dunphrey.*

■ Writings

Running Out of Time, Simon & Schuster, 1995.
Don't You Dare Read This, Mrs. Dunphrey, Simon & Schuster, 1996.
Leaving Fishers, Simon & Schuster, 1997.
Among the Hidden, Simon & Schuster, 1998.

Short stories published in *Indiannual* and *The Luxury of Tears* (National Society of Arts and Letters, 1989).

■ Work in Progress

A young adult novel.

■ Sidelights

Margaret Peterson Haddix told *SATA:* "I grew up on lots of stories, both from books and in my family. My father in particular was always telling tales to my brothers and sister and me—about one of our ancestors who was kidnapped, about some friends who survived lying on a railroad bridge while a train went over the top of them, about the kid who brought possum meat to the school cafeteria when my father was a boy. So I always thought that becoming a storyteller would be the grandest thing in the world. But I didn't want to just tell stories. I wanted to write them down.

"For a long time, I tried to write two different kinds of stories: real and imaginary. In college I majored in both journalism and creative writing (and history, just because I liked it). After college, I got jobs at newspapers, first as a copy editor in Fort Wayne, then as a reporter in Indianapolis. It was a lot of fun, especially getting to meet and talk to people from all walks of life, from homeless women to congressmen. And in the evenings and on weekends, I tried to write down the made-up stories that were accumulating in my head. But this was frustrating, because there was never enough time. So, in 1991, when my husband got a new job in Danville, Illinois, I took a radical step: I quit newspapers. I took a series of temporary and part-time jobs, such as teaching at a community college, and used the extra time to write.

"The first book I wrote was *Running Out of Time.* I'd gotten the idea when I was doing a newspaper story about a restored historical village. I kept wondering what it would be like if there was a historical village where all the tourists were hidden and the kids, at least, didn't know what year it really was.

"I wrote my second book, *Don't You Dare Read This, Mrs. Dunphrey,* when I was eight months pregnant with my first child, and feeling a little bored. The story should have been very difficult to write, because I had a happy childhood and wonderful parents, and should have had nothing in common with the main character—tough-talking, big-haired Tish, whose parents abandoned her. But I'd once worked on a newspaper series where I talked to more than a dozen abused and neglected kids, and their stories haunted me for years. So writing *Don't You Dare* was almost like an exorcism—I did feel possessed by Tish's spirit. Actually, in a way, everything I've written has felt like that, like being possessed. When I'm writing, I feel like I *must* write.

"I have two kids now, Meredith and Connor, and I'm amused that I felt like I didn't have enough time to write before they were born. It's much harder now. But I think I've found a balance. I write intensely when my kids are at play groups and preschool or taking naps. And a lot of times when I'm doing the ordinary things that go along with having two kids, a husband, and a house—cooking, playing chauffeur, running to Wal-Mart for diapers—I'm listening to a voice in my head insisting, 'Write about me!' or suggesting things like, 'What if Dorry's dad confronts her before she goes to the mall?' Now, I'll be the first to admit that it sounds a little weird to have voices talking in my head, but I wouldn't have it any other way."

Haddix's novels for young adults are built upon stories and scenarios she learned about while working as a newspaper reporter. While her books share little in terms of plot, setting, or theme, critics have commended the author's ability to involve even reluctant readers in the lives of her characters. In *Running Out of Time,* thirteen-year-old Jessie Keyser lives with her family in a frontier village in 1840, but when the town's children are stricken with diphtheria, Jessie's mother reveals that it is actually the 1990s, and the village is a tourist exhibit and scientific experiment gone awry. "The action moves swiftly, with plenty of suspense" as Jessie attempts to make her way through the modern world, looking for help for her family and friends, Lisa Dennis noted in *School Library Journal. Voice of Youth Advocates* critic Ann Welton, however, complained that Jessie's adjustment to the drastic shift in time "is far too smooth, resulting in a lack of narrative tension." In his review of *Running Out of Time, Bulletin of the Center for Children's Books* critic Roger Sutton concluded that "many kids ... will be gripped by the concept, and the book, readable throughout, [is] exciting in spots."

Critics noted that Haddix relies on a much more familiar set-up when she places Tish Bonner, the main character in her second novel, *Don't You Dare Read This, Mrs. Dunphrey,* in an English class where she is required to keep a journal, giving the reader an insiders' view of her troubles. Since Tish has no one but her journal to confide in as she deals with an absent father, a depressed mother unable to care for her or her younger brother, and a part-time job where the manager subjects her to sexual harassment, "the tone here shifts only in terms of varying shades of anger," a reviewer observed in *Publishers Weekly.* "Tish's journal entries have an authentic ring in phrasing and tone and will keep readers involved," Carol Schene claimed in *School Library Journal.* The result, according to Jean Franklin in *Booklist,* is "a brief, gritty documentary novel, ... a natural for reluctant readers."

■ Works Cited

Dennis, Lisa, review of *Running Out of Time, School Library Journal,* October, 1995, p. 133.

Review of *Don't You Dare Read This, Mrs. Dunphrey, Publishers Weekly,* August 12, 1996, p. 85.

Franklin, Jean, review of *Don't You Dare Read This, Mrs. Dunphrey, Booklist,* October 15, 1996, p. 413.

Schene, Carol, review of *Don't You Dare Read This, Mrs. Dunphrey, School Library Journal,* October, 1996, p. 147.

Sutton, Roger, review of *Running Out of Time, Bulletin of the Center for Children's Books,* November, 1995, p. 91.

Welton, Ann, review of *Running Out of Time, Voice of Youth Advocates,* December, 1995, p. 302.

* * *

HALL-CLARKE, James
See ROWLAND-ENTWISTLE, (Arthur) Theodore (Henry)

* * *

HAMILTON, Carol (Jean Barber) 1935-

■ Personal

Born August 23, 1935, in Enid, OK; daughter of Clarence DeWitt (an electrical engineer) and Ruby (a teacher of English and writing; maiden name, Settles) Barber; married J. Jefferson Hamilton (a legislator), August 25, 1956 (marriage ended June 29, 1994); children: Debra Susan Hamilton Havenar, Christopher David, Stephen Anthony. *Education:* Phillips University, B.S., 1956; University of Central Oklahoma, M.A., 1978; also attended University of Oklahoma, Hiram College, University of Colorado, Rose State College, and Academia Hispano Americano. *Politics:* Democrat. *Religion:* "Christian Church (Disciples of Christ)."

■ Addresses

Home—9608 Sonata Ct., Midwest City, OK 73130. *Office*—Creative Studies, Box 184, University of Central Oklahoma, 73034-0184.

■ Career

Elementary schoolteacher in North Haven, CT, 1957-60, Indianapolis, IN, 1970-71, and Tinker Air Force Base, OK, 1971-82; Academic Center for Enrichment, Pleasant Hill, OK, teacher of elementary gifted education, 1982-93. Rose State College, Midwest City, OK, adjunct professor of English, 1988-96; University of Central Oklahoma, adjunct professor, 1996—. Freelance writer and storyteller at camps, churches, libraries, and schools. Olympics of the Mind, local, regional, and state judge, 1985—. Artist in residence at Contemporary Arts Foundation and Warehouse Theater. Interpreter and teacher at medical missions in Mexico, Bolivia, Dominican Republic, and Oklahoma City, OK. *Member:* Association of Classroom Teachers (member of executive board, 1980-85), League of American Pen Women (state chairperson, 1988—; literary chairperson of Oklahoma City branch), Oklahoma Writers Federation (member of board of directors), Poetry Society of Oklahoma (president, 1984), Individual Artists of Oklahoma, Mid-Oklahoma Writers (past president).

CAROL HAMILTON

■ Awards, Honors

Southwest Book Award and Pegasus Award, both 1988, both for *The Dawn Seekers;* Oklahoma Book Award and Pegasus Award, both 1992, both for *Once the Dust;* grand prize, Poetry Society of Oklahoma contest, 1994; Cherubim Award, 1995, for *The Mystery of Black Mesa;* named poet laureate, State of Oklahoma, 1995.

■ Writings

Deserts, Dry Places, and Other Aridities (poems), University of Central Oklahoma (Edmond, OK), 1978.
Daring the Wind, Broncho Press (Edmond, OK), 1985.
The Dawn Seekers (juvenile novel), illustrated by Jeremy Guitar, Albert Whitman (Morton Grove, IL), 1987.
Once the Dust, Broncho Press, 1992.
Legends of Poland, illustrated by Toni Britt, Central European Refugee Committee and Kirkpatrick Foundation, 1992.
Mystery of Black Mesa (juvenile novel), illustrated by John Roberts, Bob Jones University Press (Greenville, SC), 1995.

Contributor of more than three thousand articles, poems, and stories to periodicals, including *Christian Science Monitor, New York Quarterly, South Dakota Review, Astronomy, Revista Interamericana, Oklahoma Today, Voices International, Chiron Review, Arizona Quarterly,* and *Humpty Dumpty.*

■ Work in Progress

When the Wolf Comes, a historical novel for young people; a poetry manuscript.

■ Sidelights

Carol Hamilton told *SATA:* "Writing began for me when I was a child and wrote scary stories to frighten my friends. My stories, unfortunately, scared me so much that I lay awake at night expecting them to come true. That habit has helped me over the years, for I've always written early in the mornings while the rest of the world is still sleeping.

"I began my writing and publishing career with articles and short stories. My first published piece in a national magazine, in 1965, was called 'Winnie the Pooh as Existentialist.' I never dreamed of writing poetry or children's literature, but these two fields have given me the most success and satisfaction over the years. Today, I still rise at five o'clock in the morning to write in various fields. I feel constantly challenged to shape words and experience into poetry and to create worlds of adventure and enchantment that children, and I count myself as one of them, will want to enter again and again."

■ For More Information See

PERIODICALS

Booklist, May 15, 1987, p. 1446.
Kirkus Reviews, January 1, 1987, p. 56.
School Library Journal, March, 1987, p. 160.

* * *

HASS, Robert 1941-

■ Personal

Surname rhymes with "grass"; born March 1, 1941, in San Francisco, CA; son of Fred (in business) and Helen Louise (Dahling) Hass; married Earlene Leif (a psychotherapist), September 1, 1962 (divorced, 1990); married Brenda Hillman (a writer), July 23, 1994; children: (first marriage) Leif, Kristin, Luke. *Education:* St. Mary's College of California, B.A., 1963; Stanford University, M.A., 1965, Ph.D., 1974. *Politics:* Democrat.

■ Addresses

Home—Box 807, Inverness, CA 94937. *Office*—Department of English, University of California at Berkeley, Berkeley, CA 94720. *Agent*—Steven Barclay Agency, 321 Pleasant St., Petaluma, CA 94952.

■ Career

State University of New York at Buffalo, assistant professor, 1967-71; St. Mary's College of California, Moraga, professor of English, 1971-74, 1975-87; University of California, Berkeley, professor of English,

1987—. Visiting lecturer at University of Virginia, 1974, Goddard College, 1976, and Columbia University, 1982. Poet in residence, The Frost Place, Franconia, NH, 1978.

■ Awards, Honors

Woodrow Wilson fellow, 1963-64; Danforth fellow, 1963-67; Yale Series of Younger Poets Award from Yale University Press, 1972, for *Field Guide;* United States-Great Britain Bicentennial Exchange Fellow in the Arts, 1976-77; William Carlos Williams Award, 1979, for *Praise;* Guggenheim fellow, 1980; National Book Critics Circle Award in criticism, 1984, and Belles Lettres Award, Bay Area Book Reviewers Association, 1986, for *Twentieth Century Pleasures: Prose on Poetry;* award of merit, American Academy of Arts and Letters, 1984; MacArthur Foundation grant, 1984; United States Poet Laureate, 1995-97.

■ Writings

POETRY

Field Guide, Yale University Press (New Haven, CT), 1973.
Winter Morning in Charlottesville, Sceptre Press, 1977.
Praise, Ecco Press (Hopewell, NJ), 1979.
The Apple Trees at Olema, Ecco Press, 1989.
Human Wishes, Ecco Press, 1989.
Sun Under Wood, Ecco Press, 1996.

Contributor of poetry to various anthologies, including *The Young American Poets,* edited by Paul Carroll, Follett (New York City), 1968, and *Five American Poets,* Carcanet (Manchester, England), 1979.

TRANSLATOR

(With Robert Pinsky) Czeslaw Milosz, *The Separate Notebooks,* Ecco Press, 1983.
(With Milosz) Milosz, *Unattainable Earth,* Ecco Press, 1986.
(With Louis Iribarne and Peter Scott) Milosz, *Collected Poems, 1931-1987,* Ecco Press, 1988.
(With Milosz) Milosz, *Provinces,* Ecco Press, 1993.
(And editor and author of introduction) *The Essential Haiku: Versions of Basho, Buson, and Issa,* Ecco Press, 1994.

OTHER

Twentieth Century Pleasures: Prose on Poetry, Ecco Press, 1984.
(Editor) *Rock and Hawk: A Selection of Shorter Poems by Robinson Jeffers,* Random House (New York City), 1987.
(Co-editor with Bill Henderson and Jorie Graham) *The Pushcart Prize XII,* Pushcart (Wainscott, NY), 1987.
(Editor with Charles Simic) Tomaz Salamun, *Selected Poems* (translations from the Slovene), Ecco Press, 1988.
(Editor) May Swenson and others, translators, *Selected Poems of Tomas Transtroemer, 1954-1986,* Ecco Press, 1989.

(Editor with Stephen Mitchell) *Into the Garden: A Wedding Anthology, Poetry and Prose on Love and Marriage,* HarperCollins (New York City), 1993.

■ Sidelights

American Poet Laureate Robert Hass pays tribute to some of his non-Western mentors in *The Essential Haiku: Versions of Basho, Buson, and Issa,* translations of short works by the most famous seventeenth-and eighteenth-century masters of the short Japanese poem. According to Mark Ford in the *New Republic,* the verse form known as *haiku* was developed in the nineteenth century from an older form named *hokku. Hokku* in turn was only part of a larger verse form known as *haikai,* which was practiced as a sort of game by several collaborating poets. Each of the three *haiku* masters (Basho, Buson, and Issa) used the short verse form to record commonplace images in an uncommon way. "Hass's language is unflashy, his interpretations sensible and his pacing effective," Ford declared. The three chosen writers in Hass's book "demonstrate the ways in which great art may intensify and illuminate our engagements with the real, the experience of art."

Hass told *SATA:* "The book of mine that is, perhaps, appealing to young people is *The Essential Haiku,* a volume of translations of the three great masters in the haiku tradition.

"I am a poet by trade and I came upon these wonderful small poems in my reading. I loved the freshness of the way they saw the world and also the intensity and humor and originality of their vision. So I began to study Japanese and the practice of Zen Buddhism to learn more about them. Over the years—as a kind of peaceful and centering work, done when I had a little spare time—I made my own versions of some of the poems, several hundred as it turned out.

"I loved doing it and kept feeling I was learning to see more clearly and to experience the world more vividly."

■ Works Cited

Ford, Mark, review of *The Essential Haiku, New Republic,* October 31, 1994, pp. 48-51.

■ For More Information See

PERIODICALS

Publishers Weekly, October 28, 1996, p. 51.
Time, May 22, 1995, p. 27.*

*   *   *

HAYNES, Betsy 1937-
(James Betts)

■ Personal

Born October 20, 1937, in Benton, IL; daughter of Paul DeWitte (a musician) and Marounah Lee (a secretary;

BETSY HAYNES

maiden name, Phillips) Shadle; married James Monroe Haynes (a manager for General Telephone and Electronics, Corp.), October 8, 1960; children: Craig Johansen, Stephanie Jo. *Education:* Attended University of Illinois, 1955-57; Southern Illinois University, B.J., 1962.

■ Career

Writer, 1967—. Has worked as a clerk, switchboard operator, insurance claims examiner, classified advertising manager for a newspaper, and secretary. *Member:* Authors Guild, Authors League of America, Society of Children's Book Writers, Children's Reading Round Table.

■ Awards, Honors

Book for Brotherhood Award, National Conference of Christians and Jews, 1974, for *Cowslip;* Journalism Alumnus Award, Southern Illinois University School of Journalism, 1978; Children's Choice designation, Children's Book Council/International Reading Association, 1985, for *Taffy Sinclair Strikes Again.*

■ Writings

Cowslip, T. Nelson (Toronto), 1973, published as *Slave Girl,* Scholastic, Inc. (New York City), 1973.
Spies on the Devil's Belt, T. Nelson (Toronto), 1974.
The Ghost of the Gravestone Hearth, T. Nelson, 1977.
The Shadows of Jeremy Pimm, Beaufort Books, 1981.
The Power (part of "Twilight" Series), Dell (New York City), 1982.

(With husband, James Haynes, under pseudonym James Betts) *Demon Wheels,* Dell, 1983.

The Great Mom Swap, Bantam (Toronto), 1986.

Faking It, New American Library (New York City), 1986.

The Great Boyfriend Trap, Bantam, 1987.

The Great Dad Disaster, Bantam, 1994.

Deadly Deception, Delacorte (New York City), 1994.

"TAFFY SINCLAIR" SERIES

The Against Taffy Sinclair Club, T. Nelson, 1976.

Taffy Sinclair Strikes Again, Bantam, 1984.

Taffy Sinclair, Queen of the Soaps, Bantam, 1985.

Taffy Sinclair and the Romance Machine Disaster, Bantam, 1987.

Taffy Sinclair and the Secret Admirer Epidemic, Bantam, 1988.

The Truth about Taffy Sinclair, Bantam, 1988.

Taffy Sinclair Goes to Hollywood, Bantam, 1990.

"FABULOUS FIVE" SERIES

Seventh-grade Rumors, Bantam, 1988.

The Popularity Trap, Bantam, 1988.

The Trouble with Flirting. Bantam, 1988.

The Kissing Disaster, Bantam, 1989.

Katie's Dating Tips, Bantam, 1989.

Grade Me, Bantam, 1989.

The Fabulous Five in Trouble, Bantam, 1990.

The Scapegoat, Bantam, 1991.

Melanie Edwards, Bantam, 1992.

Class Trip Calamity, Bantam, 1992.

"BONE CHILLERS" SERIES

Little Pet Shop of Horrors, HarperCollins (New York City), 1994.

Back to School, HarperCollins, 1994.

Frankenturkey, HarperCollins, 1994.

Welcome to Alien Inn, HarperCollins, 1995.

Strange Brew, HarperCollins, 1995.

Slime Time, HarperCollins, 1995.

Toilet Terror, HarperCollins, 1995.

Teacher Creature, HarperCollins, 1995.

Frankenturkey II, HarperCollins, 1995.

Attack of the Killer Ants, HarperCollins, 1996.

Night of the Living Clay, HarperCollins, 1996.

Terminal Case of the Uglies, HarperCollins, 1997.

"BOY TALK" SERIES

Sneaking Around, Random House (New York City), 1995.

Double Dumped, Random House, 1995.

Crazy in Love, Random House, 1995.

Tongue-Tied, Random House, 1995.

Too Blue, Random House, 1996.

OTHER

Contributor of stories and articles to periodicals, including *Wee Wisdom, Weekly Reader, News Explorer, Five/Six, Junior Challenge, Ideals, Grit,* and *New York Times.*

Cowslip has been translated into French and German. *Spies on the Devil's Belt* has been translated into French.

■ Sidelights

Beginning her career as an author of historical fiction for middle school readers, Betsy Haynes has gone on to create several series of popular books for young teens. The "Fabulous Five" series revolves around a group of middle school-aged girls, vividly portraying their sometimes misguided efforts to fit in, their budding interest in boys, and their consuming jealousy with a popular classmate named Taffy Sinclair. Other Haynes' series, including "Boy Talk," "Taffy Sinclair," and "Bone Chillers," also feature the array of concerns most common to Haynes's young teen readers: clothes, boys, popularity, boys, being accepted by the "in" group, and, of course, boys.

Haynes's sense of humor is evident in novels like *The Great Mom Swap, The Great Boyfriend Trap,* and *The Great Dad Disaster.* In the first book, Haynes sets up a scenario that could well be the envy of many adolescents: being able to trade away their parents for a time. Middle school friends Lorna and Scotti use the excuse of practicing to become foreign exchange students to con their mothers into letting them switch families for a few weeks, then quickly coming to regret their plotting. *The Great Boyfriend Trap* finds Lorna and Scotti once again thinking up clever ways to get what they want—this time, boyfriends named Fletcher and Skip, respectively. The two teens help each other manipulate circumstances to put them side-by-side with their love-interests. Haynes's "lively dialogue and breezy style capture the energy, excitement, and craziness of first love," according to Phyllis Graves in *School Library Journal.* And in *The Great Dad Disaster,* described as a "lighthearted and fun" book by *School Library Journal* contributor Lynn Cockett, widely divergent fathering styles cause the two girls to contemplate yet another parent swap. Lorna, faced with an aggressive boyfriend, wishes that her easygoing dad would step in so that she won't have to be the one to say "No" and risk losing her beau, while Scotti's father keeps her and her date under closer scrutiny than she would like.

The machinations of modern teens like Lorna and Scotti have provided Haynes with her most successful subject matter. In the many books she has written in her various series, the concerns, attitudes, and actions of pre-teen and middle school-aged girls and boys are portrayed in a realistic and entertaining manner. Mark Twain Elementary and Wakeman "Wacko" Junior High provide the five girls in the "Fabulous Five" club with enough social dilemmas to fuel two of the series: Jana Morgan and her four close friends—Melanie, Beth, Katie, and Christie—not only act as a team in their clique, but in the "Taffy Sinclair" series they do social battle with the most beautiful, most popular, most fortunate girl in their entire grade. In *The Against Taffy Sinclair Club,* the "Five," who have been preoccupied with their popular classmate throughout fourth grade to the point that they have actually had meetings at which notes about Taffy were taken, become doubly jealous when Taffy returns to school in the fall of fifth grade with a budding bustline. The club members' efforts to compete with their rival in the physical attribute department—they collectively purchase a Milo Venus Bustline Developer in the hopes of speeding up Mother Nature—eventually become public after Taffy's mother finds out what has been going on. "What may appeal most to readers is the believable relationships and hostilities among the group of fifth-graders," commented Zena Sutherland of the *Bulletin of the Center for Children's Books.* Balancing her readers' perspective, Haynes has also written *The Truth about Taffy Sinclair,* as Taffy's own concerns over losing her diary show her to be as vulnerable to the gossip of her fellow sixth graders as the Fabulous Five has been to her popularity. Taffy's side of things is further explored in *Taffy Sinclair Goes to Hollywood,* as an acting assignment about a popular girl who is hated by her schoolmates mirrors Taffy's own circumstances, both with the Fabulous Five, and with a jealous fellow actress on the movie set.

The "Fabulous Five" series takes place when the five girls, and their arch rival, reach middle school. In *The Popularity Trap,* Jana and her fellow "Fives" encourage

Scotti Wheeler and Lorna Markham, best friends who swap mothers in a previous Haynes title, contemplate yet another parent exchange with the realization that different fathering styles might improve each girl's relationship with her boyfriend. (Cover illustration by Andy Bacchus.)

clubmember Christie to run for seventh-grade class president, only to find stiff competition for the post from a member of a rival clique, the "Fantastic Four." Boy-crazy Melanie studies how-to-get-boys tips in a teen magazine in *The Trouble with Flirting,* only to end up with more attention than she can handle.

Boy-girl relationships like Melanie's are the overriding concern in another of Haynes's series: the "Boy Talk" novels. With titles like *Sneaking Around, Crazy in Love,* and *Double Dumped,* the series features Joni, Crystal, and Su Su, three seventh grade friends who set up a phone-in advice line called "Boy Talk" that enables them to eavesdrop on classmates' private problems and concerns. In addition to nosiness, their overriding hope is that they will discover if their boyfriends are loyal or not. Comparing the first volume in the series, *Sneaking Around,* to other series novels for young teens, Kenneth E. Kowen maintained in *School Library Journal* that "parents are noticeably absent" from events that would realistically involve them, and also expressed his concern over the "ethics of the situations involved." Also reviewing *Sneaking Around,* a *Publishers Weekly* commentator concluded: "At its best, this book is a giddy quasi-fantasy; at its worst, it encourages high jinks that are irresponsible."

While Haynes had been writing imaginative stories since she was eight years old, she credits her fifth grade experiences as the basis for her series. "In fifth grade I had an enemy," the author once admitted to *SATA.* "Her name was Mary Beth, and she had long blond hair and big blue eyes and was the most beautiful girl in our school. Of course, she had a rotten personality while I, on the other hand, had a fabulous personality. Mary Beth and I were rivals for everything, and our dislike for each other grew so intense that we actually had clubs against each other. Our relationship never really improved, but as we grew up and went on to live our separate lives, I forgot about Mary Beth. Following the dream of my childhood I became a writer, publishing short stories and two historical novels.

"Then one day my daughter, Stephanie, who just happened to be in fifth grade, began coming home with stories about her enemy, Laura. 'Mom, you should have seen Laura today,' she would begin and then launch into a story that, except for the date and setting, could have been one of my experiences with Mary Beth. It wasn't long until I began to realize that while times do change, we all must face many of the same growing up experiences, and that perhaps I had something to share with young readers about relationships, both good and bad. And so I wrote *The Against Taffy Sinclair Club.* I was asked to turn the book into a series by Bantam. The second book, *Taffy Sinclair Strikes Again,* was again based upon an incident from my childhood. My best friends and I had foolishly agreed that in the name of self-improvement we should level with each other and tell each other her worst fault. It had been a disaster in real life, and it became an even bigger disaster for my fictional characters. My series was off and running, and in 1985, *Taffy Sinclair, Queen of the Soaps* was published, followed by *Taffy Sinclair and the Romance Machine Disaster.*"

Haynes has received many letters from teen readers that have shown her that her own experiences were not that unusual. "They have convinced me of the value of my original premise, that there is someone in each of our lives who dangles like the carrot in front of our nose, always prettier, always getting what we want, be it boyfriends or promotions, and that we must learn first to cope and then to deal with this person. If I could I would thank Mary Beth. I would thank her first for helping me to learn valuable things about life and relationships, and then I would thank her for being such a strong presence as to keep the agonies and joys of that stage of childhood vivid enough in my mind so that I can translate them for my readers."

In addition to her series novels focusing on the everyday social lives of modern teens, Haynes has also written several historical and mystery novels, and has published short fiction in several periodicals. "As a writer of historical fiction for young people in these days of rapid advance and transition, I believe that it is important to help children see themselves as a part of the whole historical perspective, not just the future but the past as well," she once commented. In her first novel, 1973's *Cowslip*, Haynes portrays the horrors of slavery through her thirteen-year-old protagonist who works for the owner of a cotton plantation in the pre-Civil War South. Sold to her current owner at an auction, Cowslip experiences the humiliations of slavery first-hand, yearns for freedom, and finds solace and support through her new close-knit African-American plantation community.

Set during the American Revolution, *Spies on the Devil's Belt* finds fourteen-year-old Jonathan Barlowe freshly recruited into a Continental Army regiment assigned to raid a Tory outpost across Long Island Sound—the "Devil's Belt" of the title. Sent on what he considers to be routine errands—delivering bread to his regiment from a local tavern—because of his youth, Jonathan slowly begins to realize that his friend is a spy for the British, and that he himself has been unknowingly transporting messages hidden within the baked goods he has been delivering. *The Ghost of the Gravestone Hearth* also takes readers back to the eighteenth century, as modern-day teen Charlie helps Aaron, a sixteen-year-old ghost, locate a treasure that had been buried near Charlie's vacation house in 1712. Drowned at sea centuries before while in the service of ocean-going pirates, the spectral Aaron eventually locates his buried chest, only to discover that the gold he left in it was removed by another pirate. Zena Sutherland of the *Bulletin of the Center for Children's Books* charged that the novel lacked character development and that "The ghost ... is a little too cute to be believable." However, in a *Booklist* review, Barbara Elleman called *The Ghost of the Gravestone Hearth* "a glibly told tale with wide appeal."

Haynes is also the author of the young adult novels *Deadly Deception, The Power,* and *The Shadows of Jeremy Pimm,* which combine teen concerns with mystery, murder, and the supernatural. In *Jeremy Pimm,* published in 1981, an abandoned New England mansion is haunted with the angry spirit of a rebellious youth who committed suicide one hundred and fifty years ago but continues to overpower living teens who have problems relating to their parents. *Deadly Deception* finds seventeen-year-old Ashley Brennen embroiled in a murder mystery after her drug-abusing boyfriend becomes implicated in the death of a high school counselor. And in *The Power,* a young high schooler realizes that what she at first thought were harmless pranks may actually be the affects of spells cast by someone capable of harming her.

■ Works Cited

Cockett, Lynn, review of *The Great Dad Disaster, School Library Journal,* August, 1994, p. 156.

Elleman, Barbara, review of *The Ghost of the Gravestone Hearth, Booklist,* September 1, 1977, p. 41.

Graves, Phyllis, review of *The Great Boyfriend Trap, School Library Journal,* May, 1988, p. 109.

Kowen, Kenneth E., review of *Sneaking Around, School Library Journal,* August, 1995, p. 140.

Review of *Sneaking Around, Publishers Weekly,* May 22, 1995, p. 60.

Sutherland, Zena, review of *The Against Taffy Sinclair Club, Bulletin of the Center for Children's Books,* March, 1977, p. 107.

Sutherland, Zena, review of *The Ghost of the Gravestone Hearth, Bulletin of the Center for Children's Books,* December, 1977, p. 60.

■ For More Information See

PERIODICALS

Booklist, September 15, 1986, p. 136; February 15, 1989, p. 1008; October 1, 1990, p. 344; May 15, 1994, p. 1674; June 7, 1994, p. 1803.

Bulletin of the Center for Children's Books, January, 1974, pp. 79-80; September, 1975, p. 11; April, 1994, p. 260.

Horn Book, March/April, 1985, p. 213.

Junior Bookshelf, October, 1989, p. 238.

Kirkus Reviews, March 15, 1973, p. 316; August 15, 1974, p. 877; October 15, 1976, p. 1136.

Publishers Weekly, June 27, 1986, p. 92; June 10, 1988, p. 82; September 30, 1988, p. 70; July 27, 1990, p. 234.

School Library Journal, April, 1983, pp. 120-21; February, 1989, p. 81.

Voice of Youth Advocates, October, 1981, p. 33; April, 1983, p. 37; April, 1989, p. 34; June, 1994, p. 82.*

*   *   *

HENRY, T. E.
See ROWLAND-ENTWISTLE, (Arthur) Theodore (Henry)

HEO, Yumi

■ Personal

Born in Korea. *Education:* Graduated from the New York School of Visual Arts.

■ Addresses

Home—New York, NY.

■ Career

Author and illustrator of children's books.

■ Writings

SELF-ILLUSTRATED

One Afternoon, Orchard, 1994.
Father's Rubber Shoes, Orchard, 1995.
(Reteller) *The Green Frogs: A Korean Folktale,* Houghton Mifflin, 1996.

ILLUSTRATOR

Suzanne Crowder Han, reteller, *The Rabbit's Judgment,* Holt, 1994.
Han, reteller, *The Rabbit's Escape,* Holt, 1995.
Verna Aardema, reteller, *The Lonely Lioness and the Ostrich Chicks: A Masai Tale,* Knopf, 1996.
Cynthia Chin-Lee, *A Is for Asia,* Orchard, 1997.

■ Sidelights

Yumi Heo's distinctive artwork, which appears in her own picture books as well as some written by others, has garnered enthusiastic responses from critics impressed with her eccentric use of perspective, her energetic use of color, and her unique blend of primitive and sophisti- cated styles. The illustrator described her excitement at getting the assignment for her first book, Suzanne Crowder Han's retelling of a Korean folktale entitled *The Rabbit's Judgment,* to Sally Lodge in a *Publishers Weekly* interview. "This was a tale I had known since I was a child in Korea, and I felt a real connection with it," Heo said. "I was very comfortable with it from the start," she remarked of the artistic process that culmi- nated in the illustrations for Han's text. "I would say that this art came from inside of me."

The story of *The Rabbit's Judgment* tells of a man lured into rescuing a tiger from a pit; though the tiger promises not to attack the man, once he is freed from the pit he changes his mind. The man looks first to a pine tree, then to an ox, and finally to a rabbit for a judgment that will rescue him; the first two are unsym- pathetic, but the rabbit slyly tricks the tiger back into the pit, and the man goes on his way. "The text ... highlights amusingly eloquent interchanges" between the characters, noted a *Publishers Weekly* contributor, "while arrestingly skewed illustrations in a rich, natural palette illuminate the story's childlike wisdom." Other reviewers similarly highlighted Heo's winning addition to Han's well-told story; a *Kirkus Reviews* critic charac- terized the artist's style as "a pleasing blend of sophisti- cated design, ethnic reference, and visual storytelling."

Heo paired up with Han for another adaptation of a Korean folktale in *The Rabbit's Escape,* in which a rabbit is tricked into visiting the Dragon King of the East Sea, who wants to eat the rabbit's liver in order to cure his own illness. The fast-talking rabbit assures the king that he keeps his liver in a safe place and manages to escape when given permission to return to land to retrieve it. "Yumi Heo's original, quirky illustrations, with their Klee-like seas of floating figures, contribute significantly to the book's appeal," averred Nancy

Yumi Heo retells a Korean pourquoi tale in which the actions of two disobedient little frogs are used to explain why frogs sing when it rains. (From *The Green Frogs,* illustrated by Heo.)

This Masai folktale about an ostrich who rescues her abducted offspring from a lonely lioness is illustrated by Heo with her characteristic blending of primitive and sophisticated styles. (From *The Lonely Lioness and the Ostrich Chicks,* retold by Verna Aardema and illustrated by Heo.)

Vasilakis in *Horn Book.* The judgment was echoed by other reviewers, who, as with the duo's earlier collaborative effort, commented on the happy synergy between author and artist. Lisa S. Murphy, a contributor to *School Library Journal,* concluded: "Whimsical details [in the illustrations] reveal themselves with each new look, and this folktale is engaging enough to warrant many such readings!"

Equally successful are Heo's collaborations with other writers, including Verna Aardema, who adapted *The Lonely Lioness and the Ostrich Chicks,* and Cynthia Chin-Lee, whose alphabet book, *A Is for Asia,* provides information about the languages, people, and customs of the countries of Asia. As in her collaborations with Suzanne Han, Heo's illustrations for *The Lonely Lioness and the Ostrich Chicks* combine several art forms, including pencil, paper collage, and oil paints, and a style that characteristically tosses details or smaller elements in an almost wallpaper-like manner across the

background. "Unique compositions and perspectives, combined with a subdued palette ... challenge existing geometric notions of African art," remarked a *Kirkus Reviews* critic. Heo's artwork for *A Is for Asia* experiments in both traditional and tradition-breaking styles, according to a *Publishers Weekly* reviewer who concluded, "Heo's illustrations make turning every page an adventure into contemporary and historical Asia."

Heo's own picture books combine her signature illustrations with a variety of stories. In her first effort, *One Afternoon,* "the kinetic energy of life in the big city motors this zippy picture book right along," according to a *Publishers Weekly* critic. The story of a little boy who spends his day running errands with his mother, *One Afternoon* emphasizes the loud noises the pair encounter everywhere they go, noises which appear as words within the illustrations. In addition, the illustrator presents each destination from the child's viewpoint; "perspective, comparative size, and realistic details are forgotten" in the process, explained Nancy Seiner in *School Library Journal*, who feared that Heo's "extraordinary arrangements of details" in her pictures might captivate some children, but would confound others. Nancy Vasilakis reveled in the author-artist's "free-wheeling style," and concluded that the "vibrant look at bustling city life ... offers ample opportunity for creative applications in group story sessions."

Father's Rubber Shoes, Heo's second self-illustrated picture book, tells the story of a young boy whose family has just moved to the United States from Korea. Yungsu is understandably lonely at his new school, but his father tells the story of the poverty he endured as a child in Korea—carrying his precious rubber shoes instead of wearing them—and explains that they came to America so that Yungsu would have an easier childhood. "Heo's innovative compositions—flat, kinetic paintings incorporating many patterns and details—reflect Yungsu's changing feelings," observed Martha V. Parravano in *Horn Book.* While some critics found "the understated story too elusive for young children," as did *Booklist* reviewer Hazel Rochman, Heo's illustrations, which John Philbrook described in his review for *School Library Journal* as "primitive and appealing in [their] simplicity," were almost universally admired.

Heo tried her hand at retelling a Korean folktale in her third self-illustrated picture book, *The Green Frogs: A Korean Folktale,* a pourquoi tale that explains why green frogs sing when it rains. The story of two naughty little frogs who love to disobey their mother comes to its "gleefully fatalistic" ending, according to a *Kirkus Reviews* critic, when their dying mother tries to trick them into burying her on a sunny hill by requesting that they bury her by the side of the stream. For once the frogs obey their mother's wish and thus, every time it rains, they sit by the side of the stream and cry, afraid that the rain will wash her grave away. "This is a quirkier pourquoi tale than most," *Horn Book* critic Nancy Vasilakis observed, "but it's too mischievous to be morbid." Others concurred, some pointing to what a critic for *Kirkus Reviews* called Heo's "magnificently eccentric illustrations" as the most successful element in the book. A reviewer for *Publishers Weekly* enthusiastically enjoined, "This Korean folktale is so beguilingly retold and visualized with such individuality that it deserves a wide audience."

■ Works Cited

Review of *A Is for Asia, Publishers Weekly,* February 3, 1997, p. 106.
Review of *The Green Frogs: A Korean Folktale, Kirkus Reviews,* June 1, 1996, p. 823.
Review of *The Green Frogs: A Korean Folktale, Publishers Weekly,* August 26, 1996, pp. 96-97.
Lodge, Sally, "Flying Starts," *Publishers Weekly,* July 4, 1994, p. 39.
Review of *The Lonely Lioness and the Ostrich Chicks, Kirkus Reviews,* September 1, 1996, p. 1318.

Murphy, Lisa S., review of *The Rabbit's Escape, School Library Journal,* June, 1995, pp. 101-102.
Review of *One Afternoon, Publishers Weekly,* July 11, 1994, p. 77.
Parravano, Martha V., review of *Father's Rubber Shoes, Horn Book,* November, 1995, p. 733.
Philbrook, John, review of *Father's Rubber Shoes, School Library Journal,* November, 1995, p. 74.
Review of *The Rabbit's Judgment, Kirkus Reviews,* March 1, 1994, p. 305.
Review of *The Rabbit's Judgment, Publishers Weekly,* March 7, 1994, pp. 70-71.
Rochman, Hazel, review of *Father's Rubber Shoes, Booklist,* September, 15, 1995, p. 175.
Seiner, Nancy, review of *One Afternoon, School Library Journal,* November, 1994, pp. 81-82.
Vasilakis, Nancy, review of *One Afternoon, Horn Book,* November, 1994, pp. 719-20.
Vasilakis, Nancy, review of *The Rabbit's Escape, Horn Book,* September, 1995, p. 613.
Vasilakis, Nancy, review of *The Green Frogs: A Korean Folktale, Horn Book,* November, 1996, pp. 748-49.

■ For More Information See

PERIODICALS

Booklist, June 1, 1994, p. 1825; August, 1994, p. 2048; November 15, 1996, p. 589.
Bulletin of the Center for Children's Books, February, 1997, p. 198.
Kirkus Reviews, March 15, 1997, p. 459.
Publishers Weekly, April 3, 1995, p. 62; October 7, 1996, p. 73.
School Library Journal, June, 1994, p. 119.*

*   *   *

HIGH, Linda Oatman 1958-

■ Personal

Born April 28, 1958, in Ephrata, PA; daughter of Robert (a miner and bus driver) and Mary Myrna Millard (an office worker) Haas; married John High (a recycler); children: J.D. High (stepson), Justin Oatman, Kala High (stepdaughter), Zachary High. *Religion:* Christian.

■ Addresses

Home and office—1209 Reading Rd., Narvon, PA 17555.

■ Career

News reporter and feature writer; contributor of a weekly column, "Jake's View," to local newspapers. *Member:* Society of Children's Book Writers and Illustrators; Pennwriters.

■ Awards, Honors

Recipient, John Crane Memorial Scholarship, Highlights Foundation, 1993; winner, work in progress grant,

Society of Children's Book Writers and Illustrators, 1994.

■ Writings

Maizie (young adult novel), Holiday House, 1995.
Hound Heaven (young adult novel), Holiday House, 1995.
The Summer of the Great Divide (young adult novel), Holiday House, 1996.
A Stone's Throw from Paradise (novel), William B. Eerdmans, 1997.
A Christmas Star (picture book), illustrated by Ronald Himler, Holiday House, 1997.

■ Work in Progress

Picture books *The Barn Savers,* illustrated by Ted Lewin, *Winter Shoes for Shadow Horse,* illustrated by Lewin, and *The Beekeepers,* illustrated by Doug Chayka, all for Boyds Mills Press; picture books *The Horse Carvers,* illustrated by Floyd Cooper, and *Under New York,* both for Holiday House; *Last of the Diving Horses,* set on the Atlantic City Boardwalk in 1977; research on Atlantic City, New Jersey.

■ Sidelights

Linda Oatman High told *SATA:* "I was born and raised in Lancaster County, Pennsylvania, living in the boondocks on Swamp Road. Swamp Road was just a road like any other country road, with no swamp in sight. There were woods and trails and trees and creeks and relatives for neighbors. And there was me, wondering

LINDA OATMAN HIGH

why in the world somebody named it Swamp Road when there was no swamp in sight. That wondering was probably one of the first signs that I'd be a writer. We writers spend lots of time thinking about titles and names and words and why people call things something they're not.

"So there I was, growing up on Swamp Road with two parents, one brother, and an assortment of pets. We had many pets: a nervous Chihuahua named Vester, who trembled whenever we looked his way; a yellow canary named Tweety-Bird, who threw birdseed all over my bedroom; an aquarium full of fish; a strawberry roan pony, Pedro the Burro; a sheep named Lambchop, who thought she was a dog; and Whitey, a fluffy Samoyed dog I loved with all my heart. It was my memory of the love I felt for Whitey which formed the backbone of *Hound Heaven.* In the book, twelve-year-old Silver Nickles longs for a dog to love, to maybe make up for the hurt she's felt since her family died in a car wreck. Silver covers her ceiling with pictures of dogs from the *Sunday News* adoption column, an idea which came to me when my son Justin began clipping pictures of dogs and saving them as a sort of dream dog collection.

"I was a child who believed in everything: angels, fairies, ghosts, UFOs, Santa Claus, the Easter Bunny. Once, I swore I saw Rudolph the Red-Nosed Reindeer through my bedroom window, and it wasn't anywhere near Christmas. Mom said that I had a crazy imagination, and Dad said I ate too many bananas before bed. You need a crazy imagination to write, but you don't necessarily need bananas.

"For first grade, I was lucky enough to attend California School. California School was a one-room school with a hill for sledding and the best spring water ever and a creek out back where I threw my bologna sandwiches. The teacher said that was why I was so skinny, but he never could explain why California School was on California Road, smack-dab in the center of Pennsylvania.

"My year in first grade—1964—was the last year of California School. The next year, I went to a brand-new school in a nearby town called Churchtown, which of course had lots of churches. The new school had unscratched desks, fresh paint, a cafeteria, a gym, and a black macadam playground with hoops and nets and hopscotch squares. The brand-new school had lots of rooms, but no creek for bologna sandwiches. No hill for sledding. No spring water. No coal stoves in the corners or creaking wooden floors. I thought they should have built another church instead.

"Speaking of churches, they seem to pop up in most of the novels I write. My characters attend church, probably because I began going to church when I was twelve years old. I wrote a poem about that fact, titled 'Faith':

Never heard much of Heaven
or faith,
till I went to California Church on California Road

with Aunt Julia and Uncle Dave
one day.
Sunday.
Twelve years old,
didn't know Matthew from Mark
or Luke from John,
but I went anyway,
with Aunt Julia and Uncle Dave on Sunday.
Little white church
with a bell and an organ and pews full of relatives,
the ones who were still living.
And,
after I went to California Church that day,
I finally figured out
where
the ones who were dead
went.

"As a child, I had an obsessive fear of death, until I found faith in California Church that day. In *Hound Heaven*, Silver Nickles is dealing with the death of her mama and daddy and baby sister, and faith plays a large part in the novel.

"When I was in the tenth grade, I wrote an essay about the Fireman's Fair in a nearby town. I wrote about the greasy French fries and the hillbilly music and the spinning roulette wheels that steal your money away. I wrote the essay for a creative writing class taught by Mrs. Severs (who we secretly called by her first name, Susie). Mrs. Severs—*Susie*—loved my essay and hung it on the bulletin board for everybody to see. She raved and raved about my writing and said that I should be a writer. From that moment on, I was. That's all I needed: to hear the words out loud.

"I wasn't officially published until 1984, after my first child was born. I had quit my job as a secretary and wanted to stay home with my baby, while still bringing in some money. Writing fit in my plans perfectly, and I wrote feature articles for local newspapers until 1987, when I decided that I wanted to write from my heart and not my head, as I'd been doing with newspaper reporting.

"In 1987, Justin was four years old, and I was reading a lot of picture books to him, becoming very interested in children's literature in the process. That's when I began writing for magazines, selling some stories to *Highlights for Children, Hopscotch,* and *Children's Digest.* I loved writing fiction for magazines, but I had a dream. My dream was to write *books*—picture books, novels, chapter books. So I wrote and I wrote and I wrote, creating and submitting and collecting rejection slips as I acquired three more children: my stepchildren J.D. and Kala, then Zachary.

"There were times when I almost gave up, because it was hard. The writing was hard, the waiting was hard, the competition was tough. I had lots of kids and little time for writing. I almost gave up, but not quite.

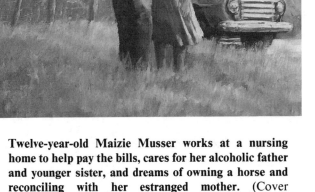

Twelve-year-old Maizie Musser works at a nursing home to help pay the bills, cares for her alcoholic father and younger sister, and dreams of owning a horse and reconciling with her estranged mother. (Cover illustration by Ronald Himler.)

"In 1990, right after my son Zachary was born, I wrote a novel called *Maizie,* published by Holiday House in April of 1995. It was my first published book, and *Hound Heaven* was to follow on the fall list of Holiday House, then *The Summer of the Great Divide,* in the spring.

"My dream has come true, with a bit of faith, a dash of determination, and lots of hard work. In *Hound Heaven,* Silver Nickles never gives up. She has faith and determination, and she works hard toward her goal. I try to instill all my fictional characters with these very real attributes ... they can make dreams come true! In giving advice to aspiring writers, I would quote Ben Franklin: 'Never, ever, ever, ever, ever give up.'"

Linda Oatman High's novels for young adults feature spunky heroines whose unwillingness to give up their dreams, even in the face of unpleasant realities, helps ease the passage from childhood to adolescence. In *Maizie,* High's twelve-year-old central character has taken care of her alcoholic father and her four-year-old sister since her mother ran off with a vacuum-cleaner

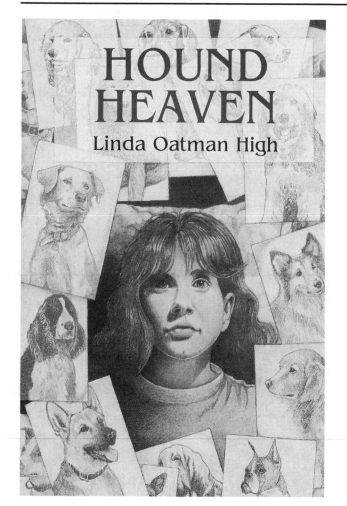

HOUND HEAVEN
Linda Oatman High

Living with her grandfather in desperate circumstances since the death of her parents, Silver Nickles wishes for a dog and determines to obtain her goal by working in a kennel. (Cover illustration by Stephen Marchesi.)

salesman. Maizie and Grace, her little sister, keep their dreams alive by making "wish" books from pictures cut out of magazines. Maizie's most ardent wishes are for a horse and to see her mother again. In pursuit of her dreams, she takes a job at a nursing home to raise money to buy a horse, and writes to her mother.

"The characters [in *Maizie*] are fresh, and their dialogue is natural, with just a hint of mountain flavor," observed Elizabeth S. Watson in the *Horn Book*. Several reviewers noted Maizie's ability to keep her spirits up, even when faced with seemingly insurmountable troubles. This feature of High's narrative "keeps the book from being dreary but makes [*Maizie*] unrealistically plucky," complained Susan Dove Lempke in the *Bulletin of the Center for Children's Books,* though she admitted, that "overall, readers will find Maizie both likable and admirable." "Maizie is a character readers will not soon forget," Carrie Eldridge asserted in *Voice of Youth Advocates,* adding that High's first effort deserves comparison to Vera Cleaver's classic tale about Mary Call, the strong female protagonist of *Where the Lilies Bloom.*

Like Maizie, Silver Nickles, the main character in *Hound Heaven,* lives in rural poverty on a mountain in the eastern United States. Silver has lived with her grandfather since the death of her parents and little sister in a car crash and only wishes she could have a dog to love, a thing she feels will soothe her aching sadness. "High creates a rich and at times humorous cast of characters around Silver," Jeanne M. McGlinn remarked in *Voice of Youth Advocates* about High's second novel for young adults. Others found the plot of *Hound Heaven,* which includes a one-sided schoolboy crush with overtones of stalking and a beauty pageant, strains the story's credibility. But, according to a critic for *Kirkus Reviews,* "this quirky novel is satisfying despite its odd detachment from reality." *Bulletin of the Center for Children's Books* contributor Deborah Stevenson credited the ultimate success of *Hound Heaven* to Silver's first-person narration, which "is touching in its yearning and appealing in its gentle humor."

Also told in the first-person is *The Summer of the Great Divide,* High's third novel for young adults. Set in the turbulent 1960s, this novel finds High's heroine spending the summer on her aunt and uncle's farm while her parents decide whether they should divorce. There, thirteen-year-old Wheezie is confronted by strange and arduous tasks connected with life on a farm, as well as making peace with a retarded cousin, the onset of puberty, and the ongoing war in Vietnam. *Summer of the Great Divide* failed to maintain the standard of characterization found in High's earlier novels, some reviewers observed, particularly in the book's secondary characters, who were faulted as sketchy. But readers are likely to sympathize with Wheezie's problems, according to Leone McDermott in *Booklist,* and "the 1960s time frame gives an interesting twist to a familiar theme."

■ Works Cited

Eldridge, Carrie, review of *Maizie, Voice of Youth Advocates,* October, 1995, p. 220.

Review of *Hound Heaven, Kirkus Reviews,* October 15, 1995, p. 1493.

Lempke, Susan Dove, review of *Maizie, Bulletin of the Center for Children's Books,* April, 1995, p. 277.

McDermott, Leone, review of *Summer of the Great Divide, Booklist,* June 1 & 15, 1996, p. 1718.

McGlinn, Jeanne M., review of *Hound Heaven, Voice of Youth Advocates,* February, 1996, p. 372.

Stevenson, Deborah, review of *Hound Heaven, Bulletin of the Center for Children's Books,* December, 1995, p. 129.

Watson, Elizabeth S., review of *Maizie, Horn Book,* May, 1995, p. 332.

■ For More Information See

PERIODICALS

Booklist, April 15, 1995, p. 1500.

School Library Journal, April, 1995, p. 132; April, 1996, p. 134.

HIMMELMAN, John C. 1959-

■ Personal

Born October 3, 1959, in Kittery, ME; son of John A. (manager, New York Stock Exchange) and Pauline (a receptionist; maiden name, Nault) Himmelman; married Elizabeth Shanahan (an art teacher), September 6, 1982; children: Jeffrey Carl, Elizabeth Ann. *Education:* School of Visual Arts, B.F.A., 1981. *Politics:* Independent. *Religion:* Christian. *Hobbies and other interests:* Nature photography, backpacking, travel.

■ Addresses

Home and office—67 Schnoor Road, Killingworth, CT 06419. *Electronic mail*—jhimmel @ connix.com.

■ Career

Writer and illustrator, 1981—. Teacher of children's book writing and illustration, lecturer on nature topics. *Member:* Society of Children's Book Writers and Illustrators, The Lepidopterists Society, Connecticut Butterfly Association (co-founder and director), Connecticut Botanical Society, Connecticut Entomological Society, Connecticut Ornithological Society, New Haven Bird Club (director and past president), Killingworth Land Trust (director).

■ Awards, Honors

A Book Can Develop Empathy Award, New York State Humane Association, 1991, for *Ibis, A True Whale Story.*

■ Writings

SELF-ILLUSTRATED

Talester the Lizard, Dial, 1982.
Amanda and the Witch Switch, Viking, 1985.
Amanda and the Magic Garden, Viking, 1986.
The Talking Tree, or, Don't Believe Everything You Hear, Viking, 1986.
Montigue on the High Seas, Viking, 1988.
The Ups and Downs of Simpson Snail, Dutton, 1989.
The Day-Off Machine, Silver Burdett, 1990.
Ellen and the Goldfish, Harper, 1990.
The Great Leaf Blast-Off, Silver Burdett, 1990.
Ibis, A True Whale Story, Scholastic, 1990.
The Clover County Carrot Contest, Silver Burdett, 1991.
A Guest Is a Guest, Dutton, 1991.
The Super Camper Caper, Silver Burdett, 1991.
Simpson Snail Sings, Dutton, 1992.
Wanted: Perfect Parents, Troll, 1993.
I'm Not Scared! A Book of Scary Poems, Scholastic, 1994.
Lights Out!, Troll, 1995.
J.J. Versus the Babysitter, Troll, 1996.
Honest Tulio, Troll, 1997.

JOHN C. HIMMELMAN

ILLUSTRATOR

Barbara Ware Holmes, *Charlotte Cheetham, Master of Disaster,* Harper, 1985.
Marjorie Sharmat, *Go to Sleep, Nicholas Joe,* Harper, 1986.
Michele Stepto, *Snuggle Piggy and the Magic Blanket,* Dutton, 1986.
Holmes, *Charlotte the Starlet,* HarperCollins, 1988.
Holmes, *Charlotte Shakespeare and Annie the Great,* HarperCollins, 1989.
Marcia Leonard, *Rainboots for Breakfast,* Silver Burdett, 1989.
Leonard, *Shopping for Snowflakes,* Silver Burdett, 1989.
Julia Hoban, *Buzby,* HarperCollins, 1990.
Leonard, *What Next?,* Silver Burdett, 1990.
Eric Carpenter, *Young Christopher Columbus: Discoverer of New Worlds,* Troll, 1992.
Andrew Woods, *Young George Washington: America's First President,* Troll, 1992.
Leslie Kimmelman, *Hanukkah Lights, Hanukkah Nights,* HarperCollins, 1992.
Hoban, *Buzby to the Rescue,* HarperCollins, 1993.
Wendy Lewison, *Let's Count,* Joshua Morris, 1995.
Carolyn Graham, *The Story of Myrtle Marie,* Harcourt, 1995.
Graham, *The Story of the Fisherman and the Turtle Princess,* Harcourt, 1995.
Claire Nemes, *Young Thomas Edison: Great Inventor,* Troll, 1995.
Leslie Kimmelman, *Hooray, It's Passover!,* HarperCollins, 1996.
Kimmelman, *Uncle Jake Blows the Shofar,* HarperCollins, 1998.

OTHER

Also author of *Ben's Birthday Wish* and *Sarah and the Terns,* published by Harcourt; illustrator of *Animal Countdown* and *The Christmas Star,* published by Joshua Morris, and *The Myrtle Marie Chant Book,* published by Harcourt; illustrator of *Ugrashimataro* (a children's animated video), ALC Press. Contributor of articles to *Birdwatcher's Digest* and illustrations to *Wildlife Conservation Magazine.*

■ Work in Progress

Eight books for the "Nature Up-Close" series for Grolier, each of which will feature an insect, plant, or animal as it goes through the cycle of life; *Animal Rescue Club,* for Harper, about a group of children who rescue and rehabilitate injured and orphaned wildlife.

■ Sidelights

Author-illustrator John C. Himmelman was born in Kittery, Maine, but moved to Long Island, New York, at the age of two. "Growing up, my main interests revolved around watching and collecting insects. In fact, the first book I ever wrote (in third grade) was about this subject. I wanted to be an entomologist and I was eager to learn as much as I could about the little crawly things that surround us," he told *SATA.* "As time went on, my interests broadened, but still remained in the field of natural science. Throughout my high school years, my plan was to become a veterinarian. However, writing and art were also a very big part of my life. I wrote stories just for the fun of it, and painting and drawing took up a good amount of my spare time."

Because he loved both animals and art, Himmelman had a difficult time deciding which field to study. "When it came time to choose a college, and subsequently a career, it came down to becoming an artist or a veterinarian," he explained to *SATA.* "One night, after weeks of deliberation, I went for a walk. I told my parents that I wasn't coming back until I had made a decision. I walked for hours, mulling over my choices. I decided that being a veterinarian would leave me little time for being an artist; however, if I pursued art, there would be other avenues open to me in which I could work with animals, such as wildlife rehabilitation."

Himmelman's choice led him to enroll at the School of Visual Arts in 1977, but again he faced a difficult career decision. He took courses in cartooning, advertising, and creative writing, but found that "the prospect of making a living in these fields was frightening!" as he recalled to *SATA.* "By the last half of my fourth and last year of college, I still had no idea of how I was going to make a living as an artist. Then, for the fun of it, I took a course in writing and illustrating children's books. It was taught by Dale Payson. One of the assignments was to write and illustrate your own book. (This was close to the end of the course.) I did a story about a lizard named Talester. My teacher liked it and showed it to her editor at Dial Publishers, and *Talester the Lizard* became my first published book! I now knew what I wanted to do."

After earning his bachelor of fine arts degree in 1981, Himmelman used the proceeds from his first book to buy a car and travel across the country. In 1982, he moved to East Haven, Connecticut, and married Elizabeth (Betsy) Shanahan, who was then studying to be an art teacher. "I paid the bills by working as a cook and then a carpenter, while at night I worked on my books. It took about six years before I could make a full-time living in children's books," Himmelman told *SATA.* "Betsy and I spent many years building a house on an abandoned pig farm which was once run by her grandparents. The house was surrounded by acres of woods and I got to pursue my love of nature. In time, birds and butterflies became my main focus of interest, and they still are." In fact, Himmelman served as president of the New Haven Bird Club for two years and created a survey on the number and types of birds that visited bird feeders throughout the county. He also helped found the Connecticut Butterfly Association and spent time rehabilitating orphaned and injured wildlife with The Nature Connection.

In 1991, Himmelman and his family moved from East Haven, which they felt was "building up too fast," to Killingworth, Connecticut. "Our new home is in a peaceful, rural part of the state, and that suits us nicely," he explained to *SATA.* Himmelman noted that his two children, Jeffrey and Elizabeth, share many of his interests—including reading, writing, and drawing— while his wife, Betsy, provides valuable help with his work. "Not a drawing, painting, or manuscript goes off to an editor or art director without input from my wife, Betsy. Being married to an art teacher has helped to ease that uncomfortable feeling of wondering how a piece of art will look to someone else. I will never forget the time while I was white-knuckledly working on a very frustrating illustration for *Wanted: Perfect Parents,* and she

Gregory raises havoc with one of the 117 pets he imagines "perfect" parents would allow him to own. (From *Wanted: Perfect Parents,* written and illustrated by Himmelman.)

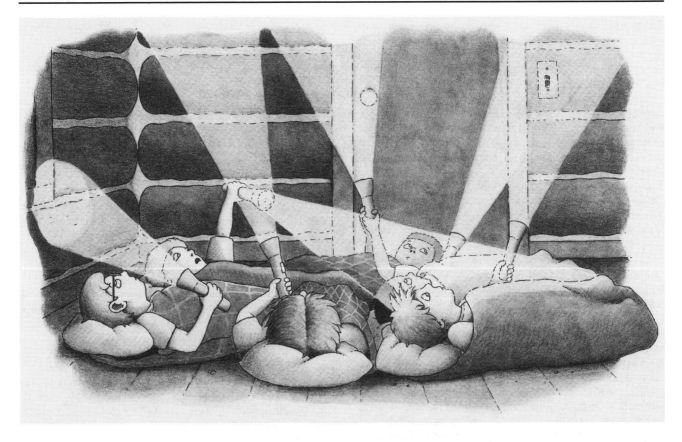

The Camp Badger Scouts keep finding reasons for Counselor Jim to illuminate their dark cabin in Himmelman's humorous picturebook. (From *Lights Out!,* illustrated by Himmelman.)

quietly walked up behind me. After I briefly railed at everyone in the whole world who was responsible for the difficulties I was having—the art director, the paintbrush company, the sun, my dog noisily passing gas in the next room—Betsy very calmly said, 'Stop fighting the watercolors.' It was that simple. I knew what she meant. My knuckles regained their healthy glow and I approached the illustration, and all the ones following, with a whole new outlook."

Over the course of his career, Himmelman has written or illustrated more than forty books. A reviewer for *Publishers Weekly* noted that Himmelman's first self-illustrated work, *Talester the Lizard,* was "sure to please tots and beginning readers." *Talester* tells the story of a pop-eyed green lizard who lives inside a curled-up leaf that hangs over a pond. Every day, he peeks out of his house to see his reflection in the water below, which he thinks is another lizard. Although his friend never speaks, Talester finds him a sympathetic listener and enjoys his company. But one day, the pond dries up and his friend disappears. Talester then sets out on a comic adventure in search of his missing friend, but is unable to find him. He returns home in a rainstorm, and the next morning he is amazed to find that his friend has reappeared. "Pastel pictures, spare in composition, make it clear that Talester sees his reflection," stated Zena Sutherland of the *Bulletin of the Center for Children's Books,* "and children can enjoy the superiority of knowing that."

Another of Himmelman's early successes came with his "Amanda" books, *Amanda and the Witch Switch* and *Amanda and the Magic Garden.* Both stories center around a well-meaning witch who encounters trouble despite her best efforts. In the first book, Amanda walks through the woods using her magic for good things, like making the flowers bloom and teaching the trees to sing. Then she meets a toad and grants his wish to become a witch. But the toad uses his powers badly, turning Amanda into a toad, transforming rocks into marshmallows, and making a bee become the size of a bear. Finally, after the bee attacks him, the toad asks Amanda to restore him to his old self. She makes everything right again except the giant marshmallows, which she shares with the animals of the forest. A reviewer for *Publishers Weekly* called the story "entrancing, graced by witty, almost speaking pictures in brilliant hues."

In the second book, Amanda plants magic seeds that grow giant vegetables, only to find that any animals eating the vegetables become huge as well. She finally finds another spell that undoes the damage: she grows tiny vegetables that restore the animals to their original size. Although Barbara Peklo of *School Library Journal* called the story "strained," Denise M. Wilms of *Booklist* commented that "the changing proportions add a comical element that will appeal to children."

Himmelman's self-illustrated book, *Wanted: Perfect Parents,* tells the story of a young boy named Gregory who posts a "help wanted" sign on his bedroom door.

When his parents ask him about it, he provides them with a detailed description of the qualities that he felt would make up ideal parents. Perfect parents would never make their children clean their rooms, for example, but would allow them to make snowballs out of ice cream, paint all over the walls of the house, and purchase 117 pets. Gregory's descriptions become more and more outrageous until finally he comes up with the most important requirement: perfect parents would tuck their children into bed, wish them sweet dreams, and check under the bed for monsters. His own parents are happy to comply with this request. Writing in *Booklist,* Deborah Abbott stated that "the read-aloud crowd will love the fantasies of this 'perfect' world, made thoroughly enticing by Himmelman's whimsical color drawings."

In addition to writing and illustrating his own books, Himmelman has helped other people to become published authors. Along with an author-illustrator friend, Kay Kudlinski, he established a "traveling school" known as Storycraft Studios for this purpose. "Over the years, several of our students have gotten published, which is as exciting to me as getting one of my own books published," he related to *SATA.* Himmelman also visits schools and libraries to teach children the basics of creating stories and to present slide shows about birds, butterflies, moths, and amphibians. He also enjoys watching and photographing animals, particularly the annual migration of birds along the coast of Connecticut. "So many natural events," Himmelman concluded, "so many stories to be inspired by them."

■ Works Cited

Abbott, Deborah, review of *Wanted: Perfect Parents, Booklist,* October 15, 1993.
Review of *Amanda and the Witch Switch, Publishers Weekly,* June 28, 1985, p. 75.
Peklo, Barbara, review of *Amanda and the Magic Garden, School Library Journal,* August, 1987, p. 69.
Sutherland, Zena, review of *Talester the Lizard, Bulletin of the Center for Children's Books,* June, 1982, p. 188.
Review of *Talester the Lizard, Publishers Weekly,* February 5, 1982, p. 387.
Wilms, Denise M., review of *Amanda and the Magic Garden, Booklist,* March 1, 1987, p. 1013.

■ For More Information See

PERIODICALS

Booklist, March 15, 1988, p. 1258; December 1, 1989, p. 751; June 1, 1991, p. 1883.
Bulletin of the Center for Children's Books, January, 1986, p. 87; February, 1988, p. 118.
Kirkus Reviews, January 1, 1988, p. 54; August 1, 1989, p. 1158; November 1, 1989, p. 1602; August 15, 1990, p. 1176; June 1, 1991, p. 736; January 1, 1997, p. 59.
Publishers Weekly, December 11, 1987, p. 64; January 15, 1988, p. 97; June 29, 1990, p. 101; March 8, 1991, p. 74; September 7, 1992, p. 62; May 1, 1995, p. 58.
School Library Journal, October, 1985, p. 155; December, 1988, p. 87; January, 1991, p. 86; March, 1991, p. 173; October, 1992, p. 42; May, 1996, p. 92.

* * *

HO, Minfong 1951-

■ Personal

Born January 7, 1951, in Rangoon, Burma; daughter of Rih-Hwa (an economist) and Lienfung (a chemist and writer; maiden name, Li) Ho; married John Value Dennis, Jr. (a soil scientist), December 20, 1976; children: Danfung, MeiMei, Christopher. *Education:* Attended Tunghai University, Taichung, Taiwan, 1968-69; Cornell University, B.A. (honors) in history and economics, 1973; M.F.A. in creative writing, 1980. *Religion:* Agnostic. *Hobbies and other interests:* Swimming, hiking, growing things.

■ Addresses

Home—893 Cayuga Heights Rd., Ithaca, NY, 14850. *Agent*—Renee Cho, McIntosh and Otis, Inc., 310 Madison Ave., New York, NY 10017.

■ Career

Writer. *Straits Times* newspaper, Singapore, journalist, 1974-75; Chiengmai University, Chiengmai, Thailand, lecturer in English, 1975-76; Cornell University, Ithaca, NY, English literature teaching assistant, 1978-80; Catholic Relief Services, Thai-Cambodian border, nutritionist and relief worker, 1980; Singapore University, writer-in-residence, 1983. Also presenter of various writing

MINFONG HO

workshops in middle schools and high schools in Ithaca, NY, and international schools in Switzerland, Indonesia, Thailand, and Malaysia, 1990-96. *Member:* Authors Guild, PEN America.

■ Awards, Honors

First prize from Council of Interracial Books for Children, 1975, for *Sing to the Dawn;* first prize, Annual Short Story Contest of Singapore, Ministry of Culture, Singapore, 1982, and first prize, Annual Short Story Contest, *AsiaWeek Magazine,* Hong Kong, 1983, both for *Tanjong Rhu;* second place, prose section, Commonwealth Book Awards, Commonwealth Book Council, 1987, first prize, National Book Development Council of Singapore, 1988, Parents Choice Award, 1990, and Best Books for Young Adults, American Library Association (ALA), Editor's Choice, *Booklist,* and Books for the Teen Age selection, New York Public Library, all 1991, and all for *Rice without Rain;* National Council on Social Studies/Children's Book Council (NCSS-CBC) Notable Children's Book in the Field of Social Studies and Best Books selection, *Parents Magazine,* both 1991, "Pick of the Lists," American Booksellers Association (ABA), Notable Children's Trade Books in the Language Arts, and Children's Book of Distinction, Hungry Mind Review, all 1992, all for *The Clay Marble;* Southeast-Asian Write Award, conferred by the Crown Prince of Thailand, 1996; *Horn Book* Fanfare, Notable Book designation, ALA, Children's Book of Distinction, *Hungry Mind Review,* and Caldecott Honor, all 1997, all for *Hush!: A Thai Lullaby;* Notable Book designation, ALA, Best Books selection, New York Public Library, and Children's Book of Distinction, *Hungry Mind Review,* all 1997, all for *Maples in the Mist: Children's Poems from the Tang Dynasty;* "Pick of the Lists," ABA, 1997, for *Brother Rabbit: A Folktale from Cambodia.*

■ Writings

Sing to the Dawn, illustrated by Kwoncjan Ho, Lothrop, Lee and Shepard (New York), 1975.

Tanjong Rhu and Other Stories, Federal Press (Singapore), 1986.

Rice without Rain, Andre Deutsch (London), 1986, Lothrop, Lee and Shepard, 1990.

The Clay Marble, Farrar, Straus and Giroux, 1991.

(With Saphan Ros) *The Two Brothers,* illustrated by Jean Tseng and Mou-sien Tseng, Lothrop, Lee and Shepard, 1995.

Hush!: A Thai Lullaby, illustrated by Holly Meade, Orchard Books, 1996.

(Translator and compiler) *Maples in the Mist: Children's Poems from the Tang Dynasty,* illustrated by Jean and Mou-Sien Tseng, Lothrop, Lee and Shepard, 1996.

(With Saphan Ros) *Brother Rabbit: A Cambodian Tale,* illustrated by Jennifer Hewitson, Lothrop, Lee and Shepard, 1997.

Ho's work has been anthologized in *Starwalk,* Silver, Burdett and Ginn, 1989; *Prizewinning Stories: Asian Fiction,* Times Edition, 1991; *Ripples: Short Stories,*

RICE WITHOUT RAIN
MINFONG HO

Seventeen-year-old Jinda questions the traditional ways of her Thai village when outsiders seem to offer hope to her starving family. (Cover illustration by Susan Bonners.)

EPB Publishers, 1992; *Tapestry: Selected Short Stories from Singapore,* Heinemann, 1992; *Join In: An Anthology of Multicultural Short Stories,* Dell, 1994; and *Battling Dragons,* Heinemann, 1995. Ho's work has also been translated into Thai, Chinese, Japanese, Tagalog, and French.

■ Adaptations

Sing to the Dawn was adapted as a musical in 1996 for the Singapore Arts Festival. Ho co-wrote the libretto with Stephen Clark, music by Dick Lee, performed by the Singapore Repertory Theatre, and published by Times Edition, 1996.

■ Work in Progress

Motherless Malik, for Lothrop, Lee and Shepard; "Turning Thirty," for the anthology *More Than Half the Sky,* Times Publishing Group, Singapore; *Jataka Tales: A Selection of Buddha's Birth Stories; Surviving the Peace,* a non-fiction book about the children born after 1975 now living in Vietnam, Laos, and Cambodia, for Lothrop, Lee and Shepard; *Mosaic: An Anthology of*

Short Stories from Southeast Asia; Duty Free, a novel of Singapore in the 1840s; *The Great Pond,* a translation from the Thai novel by Thepsiri.

■ Sidelights

Minfong Ho, in award-winning novels such as *Sing to the Dawn, Rice without Rain,* and *The Clay Marble,* presents realistic depictions of her native Southeast Asia, avoiding the romanticism of many writers on the subject. Characteristically focusing on strong female protagonists who interact with their families and friends against the backdrop of real events, she is often recognized for the sensitivity and understanding with which she treats the feelings of her characters as well as for her depiction of Asian life and locale. Her books include stories for young adult readers and middle graders as well as picture books for younger children. In all of these works, Ho does not back off from harsher elements such as poverty and violent death, but she also weaves the theme of the stabilizing influence of family throughout her work.

Will Dara survive in war-torn Cambodia?

Incorporating experiences she had as a relief worker at the refugee camps along the Thai-Cambodian border, Ho relates the tale of twelve-year-old Dara, whose courage is tested when she is separated from her family. (Cover illustration by Susan Bonners.)

Ho's own life reflects an ability to interpret the East to the West, to adapt to new and sometimes confusing and troubling circumstances. Born in Burma in what might be called privileged circumstances, Ho grew up in both Singapore and Thailand. She also did most of her studying in English, so that she is fluent in three languages. More than that, each language rules a separate part of her, as she noted in a biographical sketch for *Seventh Book of Junior Authors and Illustrators.* Chinese, Ho's first language, is the language of her "heart," while Thai, her workaday language, is that of her "hands." English, the language of study, is the language of her "head." The resulting fragmentation, or "linguistic schizophrenia" as she terms it, has never been resolved for Ho. Though she writes in English, she feels that she has never been able to bridge the languages of her life; having lived in the United States for two decades, she notes that "even now, when I cry, I cry in Chinese."

In part it is this very fragmentation—linguistic as well as cultural—that led Ho into writing stories. Educated at Bangkok's Patana School and the International School as well as at Taiwan's Tunghai University, Ho came to Cornell University in Ithaca, New York, to complete her undergraduate degree. At Cornell, she began a short story that later became her first novel, *Sing to the Dawn.* "When I wrote *Sing to the Dawn,* it was in moments of homesickness during the thick of winter in upstate New York, when Thailand seemed incredibly far away," Ho once told *Something about the Author* (*SATA*). "Writing about the dappled sunlight and school children of home brought them closer to me; it aired on paper that part of me which couldn't find any place in America. That story was not meant to be read—it was only one hand clapping." But Ho found another hand, a reader, in the Council for Interracial Books for Children to whom she submitted the work for their annual short story contest. The original story describes how Dawan, a schoolgirl from a rural Thai village, encounters resistance from her father and brother when she wins a scholarship to the city high school. Ho won the award for the Asian American Division of unpublished Third World Authors, and she was then encouraged to enlarge the story into a novel. "The manuscript was later published (through no effort of mine)," Ho recalled for *SATA.* "Suddenly a whole new dimension of writing opened to me: it became a communicative rather than a cathartic activity. I had always written, but now I would have readers!"

Ho also began to see the writing process as one that was inherently "a political expression," as she once wrote in *Interracial Books for Children Bulletin.* "I had never enjoyed reading stories of Asia in my own childhood.... Children's books about Thailand, China, Burma, etc. were invariably about princes and emperors and/or their elephants, peacocks and tigers. The few about village life portrayed it as idyllic and easy-going, full of kites and candles and festivals at the temples. This was not the Asia I knew, and I had resented the writers—usually white—who out of condescension and ignorance misrepresented these countries." With *Sing to*

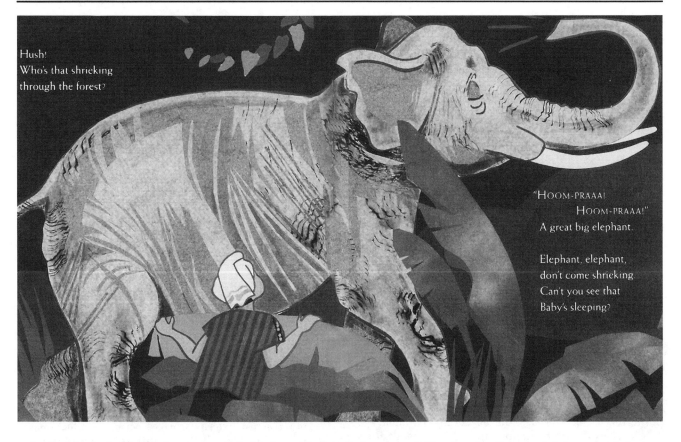

Hush!
Who's that shrieking
through the forest?

"HOOM-PRAAA!
    HOOM-PRAAA!"
A great big elephant.

Elephant, elephant,
don't come shrieking.
Can't you see that
Baby's sleeping?

A colorful parade of animals are admonished to be quiet when their noisy activities threaten the peaceful sleep of an infant.
(From *Hush!: A Thai Lullaby,* written by Ho and illustrated by Holly Meade.)

the Dawn, Ho attempted to avoid these pitfalls and created a realistic story of one girl's struggles to get an education. Dawan has won a government exam for a high school scholarship, an exam in which her younger brother has come in second. But her real fight comes after the test: now she must convince her father and her brother that she—the girl of the family—should be allowed to go to the city and study. She enlists the aid of her timid mother, of a Buddhist monk, and of a cousin who has lived in the city. Support also comes from her grandmother and from a flower girl named Bao. Dawan learns an important lesson along the way—that she must struggle to become free. Finally she convinces her brother to give his blessing and she leaves for school, her father still resistant. "The author's love of her native countryside is evident in her vivid descriptions," commented Cynthia T. Seybolt in a *School Library Journal* review of the book. Seybolt also noted that Dawan's story "provides a perspective on women's liberation far removed and much more important than breaking into the local Little League." Though many reviewers noted that this first novel was slow in parts because of frequent descriptive passages, a *Kirkus Reviews* critic maintained that, "underneath the delicate lotus imagery, this small, understated story is infused with passion and determination," such that Dawan confronts her battle for freedom and equality with a "rage so powerful" that it makes "this otherwise modest narrative vibrate." The book was illustrated by Ho's younger brother, Kwoncjan, and proceeds from its sales were used to help set up a nursing scholarship for village girls in Thailand.

Meanwhile, Ho had graduated from Cornell and returned to Asia, working as a journalist on the Singapore *Straits Times* and then as a lecturer at Chiengmai University in Thailand. While in Thailand, she observed firsthand the military coup of October 6, 1976. During these post-college years, Ho worked in "prisons and plywood factories," as she told *SATA.* "I have transplanted rice seedlings and helped a peasant woman give birth; I have attended trade union meetings in stuffy attics and international conferences in plush hotels. There is so much, so much beauty and so much pain in the world around me which I want to write about—because I want to share it." But it would be another decade before she wrote her second book, using much of this material. Married in 1976 to a soil scientist she had met during her Cornell years, Ho returned to the United States and settled in Ithaca, New York. She finished an M.F.A. in creative writing at Cornell while working as a teaching assistant. She also spent some time in relief work along the Thai-Cambodian border in 1980, gaining experience that would inform yet another novel.

In 1986, after starting a family, Ho returned to writing fiction, publishing *Rice without Rain,* a book which retells the experiences of another village girl in Thailand. This time, however, the stakes are higher than in *Sing to the Dawn.* Jinda is seventeen the summer when young intellectuals arrive in her remote village from Bangkok. Two years of drought have brought deprivations to the village: Jinda's sister has no milk and her baby starves to death. Still, the villagers greet these outsiders with suspicion, especially when they encourage the men to form a rent resistance movement. Slowly the villagers, including Jinda's father, the headman, take up the rallying cry, and slowly too does Jinda fall in love with Ned, the leader of the student radicals. When Jinda's father is arrested, she follows Ned to Bangkok where he organizes a demonstration that might help free Jinda's father. However, the military put down the demonstrators in a bloody massacre. Returning to her village, Jinda discovers that her father has died in prison. Ned and she part ways, he to join communist guerrillas fighting the government, and she to "grow things and be happy" in her village. The title, taken from a Thai folk ballad, points to the fundamental importance of rice—of agriculture—in the life of the common people. Caught up in the larger ideologies of the college students, the villagers have become pawns. Jinda chooses the simpler path in life, the eternal way. Hazel Rochman, writing in *Booklist,* maintained that though the book has violent and sometimes gritty passages, "The violence is quietly told, never exploited." *School Library Journal* contributor John Philbrook, despite finding some of the characters too "predictable," felt on the whole that Ho's novel "gives an interesting and at times absorbing glimpse of class struggle in the Thailand of the 1970s.... Not a masterpiece, but a novel from an author to watch." A *Kirkus Reviews* commentator called *Rice without Rain* "a valuable, memorable portrait of a little-known country."

Ho stayed with the land of her childhood for her third novel, incorporating experiences she had gleaned while serving as a relief worker along the Thai-Cambodia border. But with *The Clay Marble,* Ho created a book for middle grade readers rather than strictly young adults. Twelve-year-old Dara, with her mother and older brother Sarun, journeys to the Thai border in search of food after the fall of Cambodia's Khmer Rouge. At a refugee camp, Dara meets another Cambodian family and becomes fast friends with Jantu, while Jantu's sister falls in love with Sarun. Jantu gives Dara a clay marble which Dara believes has magical properties. When fighting breaks out between rival guerrilla factions, Dara and Jantu are cut off from their families. Surviving several adventures, the two are finally reunited with their families, but Jantu is mistakenly shot and killed by Sarun—overly zealous on watch duty. Dara, in the end, convinces Sarun not to go off with the army, but to return home with his family. Once again, Ho presents a strong female protagonist and employs the theme of family unity in the face of adversity. Though some reviewers felt that Ho's characters lacked depth and that her language was at times too sophisticated for a twelve-year-old protagonist, most found, as does Maeve Visser Knoth in *Horn Book,* that Ho's story was "moving." Knoth noted that the book depicted a "people who have rarely had a voice in children's literature." A *Kirkus Reviews* critic commented that Ho "shapes her story to dramatize political and humanitarian issues," and concluded that the book was "touching, authentic," and "carefully wrought."

Little Pine

My little pine tree is just a few feet tall.
It doesn't even have a trunk yet.
I keep measuring myself against it
But the more I watch it, the slower it grows.
—Wang Jian

Ho translated sixteen unrhymed poems from the Tang Dynasty (618-907 A.D.) in this collection of verse traditionally used to teach Chinese children to read. (From *Maples in the Mist,* written by Ho and illustrated by Jean and Mou-sien Tseng.)

A change of pace for Ho came with her third child and next few books. *The Two Brothers,* a picture book for young readers, was co-written with Saphan Ros. The orphaned brothers Kem and Sem have grown up in a monastery. Leaving the monastery for the big world, Kem takes the abbot's parting words of advice to heart and prospers, while Sem at first ignores the words of advice and leads the life of a peasant. Only after Sem remembers the abbot's words does his life turn around; he eventually becomes the king of Cambodia. "This entertaining picture book provides its own lively interpretation of one dramatic folktale from Cambodia," wrote Carolyn Phelan in a *Booklist* review of *The Two Brothers.* Margaret A. Chang, writing in *School Library Journal,* concluded that it was a book "to value for its authentic setting, engaging story, and portrayal of one culture's take on the balance between choice and destiny." Ho again teamed up with Ros on 1997's *Brother Rabbit,* a story about a crocodile, two elephants and an old woman who prove to be no match for a mischievous rabbit. Other picture books by Ho include *Maples in the Mist,* her translations of sixteen short Tang Dynasty unrhymed poems, and *Hush!: A Thai Lullaby,* a bedtime tale that requests various animals including a lizard and monkey to be quiet and not disturb a sleeping baby. *Kirkus Reviews* dubbed *Hush!* a "charming, repetitive rhyme," and John Philbrook in *School Library Journal* concluded that it is a "delightful, reassuring bedtime book with a unique setting." Reviewing *Maples in the Mist,* a writer in *Five Owls* noted that Ho's "translations are as clear and bright as the paintings" in this book that is "a successful example of contemporary picture book design." Karen L. MacDonald, writing in *School Library Journal,* called the book a "beautiful anthology." Commenting on *Brother Rabbit, Horn Book* reviewer Nancy Vasilakis asserted that "the back and forth between deceiver and deceived invests the tale with an unpredictability and kinetic edge that suits its theme well."

Ho continues to write novels for young people, and is presently at work on a story set in eighteenth century Nantucket Island, focusing on its links with the Far East through its China Trade. Infusing all of her work is her emphasis on sharing her cross-cultural experiences with others, sometimes in the guise of fiction, sometimes in retellings of folktales or poems. "I have grown up in Thailand and Singapore, and lived in Taiwan, Laos and the United States—and yes, sometimes it's been a bit of a stretch, to try to absorb and adapt to the different cultures, but it's been very enriching as well," Ho told *SATA.* "If my writing has helped other children become more 'elastic' in their appreciation of Southeast Asian cultures, then my stretching would have been truly worthwhile!"

■ Works Cited

Chang, Margaret A., review of *The Two Brothers, School Library Journal,* June, 1995, p. 102.

Review of *The Clay Marble, Kirkus Reviews,* October 1, 1991, p. 1287.

Ho, Minfong, "Writing the Sound of One Hand Clapping," *Interracial Books for Children Bulletin,* Volume 8, No. 7, 1977, pp. 5, 21.

Ho, Minfong, *Rice without Rain,* Lothrop, Lee and Shepard, 1990.

Ho, Minfong, autobiographical essay in *Seventh Book of Junior Authors and Illustrators,* edited by Sally Holmes Holtze, H. W. Wilson, 1996, pp. 131-33.

Review of *Hush!: A Thai Lullaby, Kirkus Reviews,* February 1, 1996, p. 227.

Knoth, Maeve Visser, review of *The Clay Marble, Horn Book,* January-February, 1992, p. 71.

MacDonald, Karen L., review of *Maples in the Mist: Children's Poems from the Tang Dynasty, School Library Journal,* September, 1996.

Review of *Maples in the Mist: Children's Poems from the Tang Dynasty, Five Owls,* January-February, 1997, p. 57.

Phelan, Carolyn, review of *The Two Brothers, Booklist,* March 1, 1995, p. 1244.

Philbrook, John, review of *Rice without Rain, School Library Journal,* September, 1990, p. 250.

Philbrook, John, review of *Hush!, School Library Journal,* March, 1996, p. 175.

Review of *Rice without Rain, Kirkus Reviews,* May 1, 1991, p. 649.

Rochman, Hazel, review of *Rice without Rain, Booklist,* July, 1990, p. 2083.

Seybolt, Cynthia T., review of *Sing to the Dawn, School Library Journal,* March, 1976, p. 104.

Review of *Sing to the Dawn, Kirkus Reviews,* June 1, 1975, p. 604.

Vasilakis, Nancy, review of *Brother Rabbit: A Cambodian Tale, Horn Book,* May-June, 1997, pp. 333-34.

■ For More Information See

BOOKS

Children's Literature Review, Volume 28, Gale, 1992, pp. 131-34.

Twentieth-Century Young Adult Writers, St. James Press, 1994, pp. 292-93.

PERIODICALS

Bulletin of the Center for Children's Books, November, 1975, p. 46; June, 1990, p. 241; December, 1991, p. 92; April, 1996, p. 266; May, 1997, p. 324.

Horn Book, November, 1990, p. 749; July, 1995, p. 471.

New York Times Book Review, October 7, 1990, p. 30; April 26, 1992, p. 25; August 13, 1995, p. 23.

Publishers Weekly, March 25, 1996, p. 82; April 14, 1997, p. 75.

Straits Times, September 26, 1996, p. 4.

Times Educational Supplement, February 13, 1987, p. 44; September 22, 1989, p. 30.

Voice of Youth Advocates, December, 1995, p. 302.

—*Sketch by J. Sydney Jones*

*　　*　　*

HOESTLANDT, Jo(celyne) 1948-

■ Personal

Born May 13, 1948, in Le Pecq, Yvelines, France; daughter of Daniel (a mushroom producer) and Evelyne (a mushroom producer; maiden name, Gooden) Ravary; married Dominique Hoestlandt (an executive vice president), 1970; children: Maud, Bertrand, Olivier. *Education:* B.A., University of Sorbonne. *Politics:* "I don't like parties. I want to avoid being biased. Every day I meet children and work for acknowledgment of each other." *Religion:* Catholic.

■ Addresses

Home—5 rue Felix Faure, 92500 Rueil Malmaison, France.

■ Career

Teacher in Paris, France, 1969-72; writer. Organizer of reading and writing animations for children in art centers and schools.

■ Awards, Honors

Sydney Taylor Book Award and Das Rote Tuch Award, 1996, both for *Star of Fear, Star of Hope.*

■ Writings

Le petit Pousse, Ecole des Loisirs, 1980.

JO HOESTLANDT

Le Moulin a paroles: Abecedaire (title means "The Word Mill: An ABC"), illustrated by Frederic Stehr, Ecole des Loisirs, 1980.

La rentree de mamans, Bayard Presse, 1990, translation published as *Back to School with Mom: A Story,* illustrated by Claude and Denise Millet, Child's World (Mankato, MN), 1992.

La grande peur sous les etoiles, Syros, translation by Mark Polizzotti published as *Star of Fear, Star of Hope,* illustrated by Johanna Kang, Walker (New York City), 1995.

Les passants de Noel, Syros, 1996.

Les amoureue de Leonie, Casterman, 1996.

Other books in French include *Emile bille de clown,* published by Bayard Presse, and *Peurs,* published by Syros.

■ Work in Progress

Six books, including a book of poems for children and an Easter book.

■ Sidelights

While the works of children's author Jo Hoestlandt are primarily in French, a few of them have been translated into English. One such work, described by Maria W. Posner in *School Library Journal* as an "extraordinarily moving picture book ... [with] spare prose and appropriately stark illustrations," is *Star of Fear, Star of Hope.*

The story begins with the narrator, an aging woman named Helen, taking the reader back to Nazi-occupied France in 1942 on the eve of her ninth birthday. Her best friend Lydia, who is Jewish, spends the night at Helen's apartment. During the night, however, Lydia wants to go home after being frightened by strangers outside Helen's home. As Lydia leaves, Helen tells her that she is no longer her friend. Helen soon realizes her mistake and she tries to find Lydia the next day. But she is too late—Lydia and her family have disappeared. By telling her story to the world, Helen hopes that she and Lydia will meet again one day. "Fluidly written and centered in events a child can comprehend, the book is an ideal starting point for serious discussions about the Holocaust," noted a reviewer in *Publishers Weekly.* Similarly, *Horn Book* commentator Mary M. Burns appreciated how "the book translates history into a form accessible to young audiences."

Hoestlandt told *SATA:* "I think words hide secrets, and stories tell secrets more or less hidden by the words.

"The most important book of my career is *Star of Fear, Star of Hope.* None of my family who lived during World War II suffered deportation, though my grandfather was a political prisoner. When I was very young, however, I understood that many children died just because they were Jewish, and I felt concerned just because I was alive.

"When I was a child, I decided I was a dancer-writer, because I liked to dance and to write. Later, I understood I have found exactly the same thing in writing and in dancing. I stood on tiptoe, or I was poised at the end of the pen, just as on a leg, light and grave, high and low together, touching earth and sky at the same moment.

"I always try to write unaffectedly, sincerely, with words so simple that they can touch hearts and minds just like sunlight or darkness or dancing snow. People say that all of my books tell love or friend stories. Maybe all that we need to learn during life is actually included in our love and friend stories."

■ Works Cited

Burns, Mary M., review of *Star of Fear, Star of Hope, Horn Book,* September-October, 1995, pp. 588-89.

Posner, Marcia W., review of *Star of Fear, Star of Hope, School Library Journal,* August, 1995, p. 124.

Review of *Star of Fear, Star of Hope, Publishers Weekly,* June 5, 1995, pp. 63-64.

■ For More Information See

PERIODICALS

Booklist, February 15, 1985, p. 850; May 1, 1995, p. 1573; March 15, 1996, p. 1289.

Bulletin of the Center for Children's Books, June, 1995, p. 347.

Kirkus Reviews, May 15, 1995, p. 711.

Tribune Books, September 10, 1995, p. 396.

HOOKS, William H(arris) 1921-

■ Personal

Born November 14, 1921, in Whiteville, NC; son of Ulysses G. (a farmer) and Thetis (Rushing) Hooks. *Education:* University of North Carolina at Chapel Hill, B.A., 1948, M.A., 1950; also attended American Theatre Wing, New School for Social Research, and Bank Street College.

■ Addresses

Home—718 E. Franklin St., Chapel Hill, NC 27514.

■ Career

High school teacher of history and social studies in Chapel Hill, NC, 1949; Hampton Institute, Hampton, VA, instructor in history and dance, 1950; Brooklyn College of the City University of New York, Brooklyn, NY, choreographer at Opera Workshop, 1955-64; owner of a dance studio in New York City, 1965-70; Bank Street College, New York City, member of staff in Publications Division, 1970-72, chairperson of division, 1972-91, managing editor of "Bank Street Readers," revised edition, "Discoveries: An Individualized Approach to Reading," "Tempo Series," and "Education Before Five." Ballet Concepts, Inc., vice-president; choreographer for New Jersey Opera Guild, Paramount Pictures, outdoor dramas, and off-Broadway productions, and for his own dance company; educational consultant to Columbia Broadcasting System (CBS), National Broadcasting Co. (NBC), and American Broadcasting Co. (ABC). *Military service:* U.S. Army, Medical Corps, 1942-46; became technical sergeant. *Member:* Phi Beta Kappa, Society of Children's Book Writers and Illustrators.

■ Writings

FOR CHILDREN

The Seventeen Gerbils of Class 4A, illustrated by Joel Schick, Coward (New York City), 1976.

Maria's Cave, illustrated by Victor Juhasz, Coward, 1977.

Doug Meets the Nutcracker, illustrated by Jim Spanfeller, F. Warne (New York City), 1977.

The Mystery on Bleecker Street, illustrated by Susanna Natti, Knopf (New York City), 1980.

Mean Jake and the Devils, illustrated by Dirk Zimmer, Dial (New York City), 1981.

The Mystery on Liberty Street, illustrated by Susan Detrich, Knopf, 1982.

Three Rounds With Rabbit, illustrated by Lissa McLaughlin, Lothrop (New York City), 1984.

(With Seymour V. Reit and Betty D. Boegehold) *When Small Is Tall, and Other Read-Together Tales,* illustrated by Lynn Munsinger, Random House (New York City), 1985.

(With Betty D. Boegehold and Joanne Oppenheim) *Read-a-Rebus: Tales and Rhymes in Words and*

WILLIAM H. HOOKS

Pictures, illustrated by Munsinger, Random House, 1986.

Moss Gown, illustrated by Donald Carrick, Clarion (New York City), 1987.

(Co-author) *Barron's Book of Fun and Learning: Preschool Learning Activities,* illustrated by Joel Schick, Barron's (New York City), 1987.

The Legend of the White Doe, illustrated by Dennis Nolan, Macmillan (New York City), 1988.

Pioneer Cat, illustrated by Charles Robinson, Random House, 1988.

(With Barbara Brenner) *Lion and Lamb,* illustrated by Bruce Degen, Bantam (New York City), 1989.

Mr. Bubble Gum, illustrated by Paul Meisel, Bantam, 1989.

The Three Little Pigs and the Fox, illustrated by S. D. Schindler, Macmillan, 1989.

The Ballad of Belle Dorcas, illustrated by J. Brian Pinkney, Knopf, 1990.

Mr. Monster, illustrated by Paul Meisel, Bantam, 1990.

A Dozen Dizzy Dogs, illustrated by Gary Baseman, Bantam, 1990.

(With Barbara Brenner) *Lion and Lamb Step Out,* illustrated by Degen, Bantam, 1990.

The Gruff Brothers, illustrated by Pierre Cornuel, Bantam, 1990.

Lo-Jack and the Pirates, illustrated by Tricia Tusa, Bantam, 1991.

Where's Lulu? illustrated by Robert W. Alley, Bantam, 1991.

(With Barbara Brenner) *Ups and Downs With Lion and Lamb,* illustrated by Bruce Degen, Bantam, 1991.

Mr. Baseball, illustrated by Paul Meisel, Bantam, 1991.

(With Barbara Brenner and Joanne Oppenheim) *No Way, Slippery Slick! A Child's First Book About Drugs,* illustrated by Joan Auclair, HarperCollins (New York City), 1991.

(With Betty Boegehold) *The Rainbow Ribbon: A Bank Street Book About Values,* illustrated by Lynn Munsinger, Viking (New York City), 1991.

Peach Boy, illustrated by June Otani, Bantam, 1992.

(With Barbara Brenner and Joanne Oppenheim) *How Do You Make a Bubble?* illustrated by Doug Cushman, Bantam, 1992.

Little Poss and Horrible Hound, illustrated by Carol Newsom, Bantam, 1992.

Rough, Tough, Rowdy: A Bank Street Book About Values, illustrated by Lynn Munsinger, Viking, 1992.

The Monster From the Sea, illustrated by Angela Trotta Thomas, Bantam, 1992.

(Reteller) *Feed Me! An Aesop Fable,* illustrated by Doug Cushman, Bantam, 1992.

The Mighty Santa Fe, illustrated by Angela Trotta Thomas, Macmillan, 1993.

Mr. Dinosaur, illustrated by Paul Meisel, Bantam, 1994.

Snowbear Whittington: An Appalachian Beauty and the Beast, illustrated by Victoria Lisi, Macmillan, 1994.

The Girl Who Could Fly, illustrated by Kees de Kiefte, Macmillan, 1995.

Freedom's Fruit, illustrated by James Ransome, Knopf, 1996.

Mr. Garbage, illustrated by Kate Duke, Bantam, 1996.

The Mystery of the Missing Tooth, illustrated by Nancy Poydar, Bantam, 1997.

Also author of *Come Out,* for Macmillan, *What Color Is This?, You Come, Too,* and *Open It.*

YOUNG ADULT NOVELS

Crossing the Line, Knopf, 1978.
Circle of Fire, Atheneum, 1982.
A Flight of Dazzle Angels, Macmillan, 1988.

OTHER

(With Ellen Galinsky) *The New Extended Family: Day Care That Works,* illustrated with photographs by Galinsky, Houghton (Boston, MA), 1977.

Scriptwriter for the television series *Captain Kangaroo.* Associate editor, "U.S.R.D. Readers" and "Bank Street Unit Readers." Contributor to magazines, including *Dance Digest.*

■ Sidelights

Born in the small town of Whiteville, North Carolina, William H. Hooks has made broad use of the stories and settings of the rural south in his many books for children and young adults. With writings ranging from American folktales crafted in the idiom of his native North Carolina to stories of friendship that overcome the barriers of race and age, Hooks has become a well-regarded figure in the genre of children's literature. In addition, his young adult novels, including *Crossing the Line* (1978) and *Circle of Fire* (1982), represent his in-depth look at the depression-era south told from the perspective of a adolescent boy.

Hooks did not begin writing full-time for children until he had reached his fifties. Instead, his early life was spent developing a long and varied career in education and in dance choreography. Throughout this period, however, the concerns of children and young adults remained one of the constants in his life. In 1949, while completing work toward his master's degree at the University of Carolina, Hooks was employed as a high school teacher specializing in history and social studies. The following year he became an instructor of dance and history at the Hampton Institute in Virginia. His relocation to New York City in the 1950s offered new opportunities as a choreographer at Brooklyn's Opera Workshop and as the owner of his own dance studio. In 1970 Hooks found employment with Bank Street College; he soon became managing editor of the "Bank Street Reader" series and has since written works for the series, including his *Mr. Dinosaur* in 1994.

Accompanying the growth of his editorial responsibilities with Bank Street in the 1970s, Hooks also put his talents to work in children's television. He was involved as a consultant for the ABC-TV "Afterschool Specials" and wrote scripts for CBS's *Captain Kangaroo.* Hooks also began to focus his attention on the writing of children's books in the 1970s. His first published work for young people, *The Seventeen Gerbils of Class 4A,* was heralded as "ingenious" by a critic in *Publishers Weekly.* This educational story follows Josh, Chris, and Rogue as they attempt to solve the dilemma of distributing two adult gerbils and their fifteen babies between the three of them.

Hooks continued his focus on education in his next story, *Maria's Cave.* This time the subject is anthropology and history. Set in 1879, the story is one of many historical fictions penned by Hooks. Its heroine, Maria Sautuola, discovers rare stone age cave paintings at Altimira, Spain. Despite the aid of her father, however, the scientific community fails to acknowledge the value of her findings for several decades. Nevertheless, Maria's perseverance assures that the paintings eventually receive worldwide recognition. Reviews of the work praised its simplicity of style and vocabulary.

Crossing the Line, Hooks's first book for young adults, introduces Harrison Hawkins, a twelve-year-old white boy who encounters hatred and racial prejudice in his North Carolina town during the 1930s. Harrison befriends an elderly African-American woman named Little Hattie and later learns that the two are related through her nephew, Horatio. In the course of the narrative Horatio is shot and killed by a bigot and Harrison learns that his own cousin is the murderer. Zena Sutherland of the *Bulletin of the Center for Children's Books* praised Hooks's ability to "evoke setting and the sense of intricacy of community relations" in *Crossing the Line.*

Circle of Fire, the prequel to *Crossing the Line,* appeared in 1982. In this story, set in 1936, eleven-year-old Harrison and his two friends, Kitty and Scrap, both of whom are black, become frightened when the activities of the Ku Klux Klan begin to invade their hometown. Harrison's fears grow as he begins to suspect that his father might be involved with the Klan. Fortunately his suspicions are proven incorrect and the bigoted attacks of the Klan on innocent people are thwarted. Nancy Sheridan of *Horn Book* characterized *Circle of Fire* as "an exciting story filled with vivid characters and mounting tension," adding that "it is, even more, a powerful lingering tale of shattered innocence and changing relationships."

Hooks's third novel for young adults, *A Flight of Dazzle Angels,* is somewhat of a departure from his first two such works. In this southern romance set in the summer of 1908, fifteen-year-old Annie Earle Roland finds herself beset with numerous family problems. Her mother has yet to recover from her father's death, her brother suffers from severe epilepsy, and her wicked Aunt Kat has plans to institutionalize her mother and seize the family fortune. Hope for Annie Earle comes in the form of Achilles McPherson, who arrives kicking up flecks of August sunlight like a "flight of dazzle angels." Her affection for Achilles propels events to a happy conclusion in this story that a *Publishers Weekly* reviewer called "a beautiful look at coming-of-age in a time and place now past."

By the late 1980s, Hooks had once again turned his attention to books for younger children. His successful retellings of local tales and folk legends from the

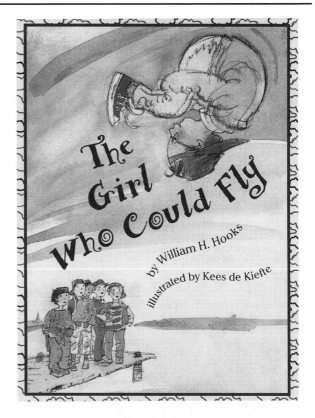

Tomasina Jones seems like the ideal coach for Adam Lee's baseball team because of her magical gifts. (Cover illustration by Kees de Kiefte.)

Carolina region, such as *Moss Gown* and *The Legend of White Doe,* foreshadowed his so-called "conjure stories," the first of which was *The Ballad of Belle Dorcas* in 1990. Ethel L. Heins of *Horn Book* called *The Ballad of Belle Dorcas* an "eerie tale of cruelty, tragedy, transfiguration, and steadfast love." The story recreates the nineteenth-century slaves' tales of conjuring and witchcraft, originally devised as a means of confronting the atrocities of their white oppressors. Belle Dorcas, the daughter of a white plantation-owner and his black mistress, is born "free issue" and thus has her freedom. Yet she falls in love with Joshua, a slave who will be sold by his master and removed to another plantation. In order to resolve this situation Belle calls upon the aid of Granny Lizard. The old conjure woman casts a spell that transforms Joshua into a cedar tree during the day and back to his human form for a few hours each night. When the tree is chopped down to build a smokehouse, Belle nearly succumbs to madness. She maintains her sanity, however, and at her death the smokehouse disappears, magically replaced by two cedar trees standing side by side. Christine Behrmann, writing for the *School Library Journal,* called Hooks's story "smooth and powerful," and praised the author's ability to "[limn] the events of the plot with incisively concrete language."

In *The Ballad of Belle Dorcas*, Hooks's retelling of a nineteenth-century conjure story, Belle elicits the help of an old woman who uses witchcraft to help Belle's lover trick his master. (Illustrated by Brian Pinkney.)

Hooks's second conjure tale, *Freedom's Fruit,* presents a theme similar to that of *The Ballad of Belle Dorcas.* In *Freedom's Fruit* a conjure woman named Mama Marina outwits her greedy master and earns freedom for her

In another retelling of a conjure tale he heard as a boy, Hooks describes how Mama Marina outwits a slave owner and helps two lovers buy their freedom. (From *Freedom's Fruit,* illustrated by James Ransome.)

daughter, Sheba. When the plantation owner tells her to use her magic to prevent the other slaves from eating his wine grapes, Marina casts a potent curse on the vines. Recognizing her power, no one dares touch the grapes until Marina asks her daughter and Joe Nathan, with whom Sheba is in love, to eat several. They do and soon begin to weaken and grow old like the grapevines in winter. Because they are no longer valuable to the master, Marina then cheaply buys freedom for the pair, who regain their youth and strength the following spring. In his introduction to the book, Hooks notes that he heard the tale while a youth in North Carolina's low country and has endeavored to make it accessible to new generations. *Horn Book* reviewer Maeve Visser Knoth asserted that in *Freedom's Fruit* Hooks "weaves a hopeful, poetic story about the ability of the oppressed to outwit those with power." A *Publishers Weekly* critic also offered a favorable assessment of Hooks's retelling, commending his "rich descriptive passages and flowing dialogue."

Among William Hooks's other stories are several retellings of well-known fairy tales within an Appalachian setting, including *The Three Little Pigs and the Fox* and *Snowbear Whittington: An Appalachian Beauty and the Beast.* He has also written several books that emphasize the importance of love and understanding between family members. In *The Mighty Santa Fe,* this love becomes magical when a young boy discovers that his grandmother shares his affection for model trains and the two take an enchanted midnight train ride in the attic on Christmas eve. A *Publishers Weekly* reviewer dubbed *The Mighty Santa Fe* "an inventive holiday tale," and praised Hooks for "triumphantly meshing the realistic and the magical" in this work.

■ Works Cited

Behrmann, Christine, review of *The Ballad of Belle Dorcas, School Library Journal,* October, 1990, p. 116.

Review of *A Flight of Dazzle Angels, Publishers Weekly,* October 14, 1988, pp. 78-79.

Review of *Freedom's Fruit, Publishers Weekly,* December 4, 1995, p. 62.

Heins, Ethel L., review of *The Ballad of Belle Dorcas, Horn Book,* March-April, 1991, pp. 208-09.

Knoth, Maeve Visser, review of *Freedom's Fruit, Horn Book,* May-June, 1996, p. 325.

A review of *The Mighty Santa Fe, Publishers Weekly,* November 1, 1993, p. 79.

Review of *The Seventeen Gerbils of Class 4A, Publishers Weekly,* May 31, 1976, p. 198.

Sheridan, Nancy, review of *Circle of Fire, Horn Book,* October, 1982, p. 517.

Sutherland, Zena, review of *Crossing the Line, Bulletin of the Center for Children's Books,* April, 1979, pp. 138-39.

■ For More Information See

PERIODICALS

Booklist, February 1, 1992, p. 1042; November 15, 1993, p. 632; April 1, 1994, p. 1466; October 15, 1994, p. 431; August, 1995, p. 1946; February 15, 1996, p. 1020.

Bulletin of the Center for Children's Books, March, 1987, p. 127; July-August, 1995, p. 385.

New York Times Book Review, November 12, 1989, p. 27.

Publishers Weekly, September 28, 1990, p. 102.

School Library Journal, November, 1994, p. 98; July, 1995, p. 64; February, 1996, p. 84.

—Sketch by Sean McCready

*   *   *

HOWARTH, Lesley 1952-

■ Personal

Born in Bournemouth, England, 1952; married Phil Howarth (a civil engineer); children: Sadie, Georgia, Bonnie. *Education:* Studied at Bournemouth College of Art; Croydon College of Art.

■ Addresses

Home—Callington, Cornwall, England.

■ Career

Writer, 1993—.

■ Awards, Honors

Shortlisted, Whitbread Award for a Children's Novel, 1993, and shortlisted, *Guardian* Children's Fiction Award, 1994, both for *The Flower King;* highly commended list, Carnegie Medal, 1995, for *MapHead.*

■ Writings

The Flower King, Walker, 1993.
MapHead, Walker, 1994, Candlewick, 1994.
Weather Eye, Walker, 1995, Candlewick, 1995.
The Pits, Walker, 1996, Candlewick, 1996.
Fort Biscuit, illustrated by Ann Kronheimer, Walker, 1997.
MapHead: The Return, Candlewick, 1997.

■ Sidelights

With her first young adult novel, *The Flower King,* British author Lesley Howarth made it to several shortlists for fiction awards. With her second book, *MapHead,* she served up a fictional brew that "one only occasionally happens upon," according to Robyn Sheahan in a cover story in *Magpies.* Sheahan went on to note that Howarth writes the sort of book that "is respectful of its readers' imaginative and intellectual capabilities, and which offers real insights into the difficult business of growing up." Howarth herself was coming of age as a writer with these first published books and has since broadened her fictional universe to encompass not only a turn-of-the-century world filled with flowers and a modern country town with alien visitors in its midst, but also a wind farm in the near future in *Weather Eye,* and the chilly world of prehistory in *The Pits,* a story of an ice-age man told by a chatty ghost. These are all parts of Howarth and are indicative of the varied life she herself has led.

Born in Bournemouth, England, she attended grammar school there and at the Bournemouth School for Girls. A self-confessed lazy student, she commented in an interview with Stephanie Nettell for *Magpies* that she puts her lack of success in school down to stubbornness and a "fierce strain of individualism: the more people told me to buckle down the less likely I was to do it." But she did develop a love for story at an early age; as an only child

Twelve-year-old alien Boothe Powers, known as MapHead, visits earth to meet his human mother for the first time in this Carnegie Medal-commended science fiction novel by Lesley Howarth. (Cover illustration by Rob Day.)

she created a rich interior life. "I'd live in a story, in its atmosphere, for days," she told Nettell, "and spent long hours plonking out stories on my Dad's typewriter." Growing up in the Westbourne district of Bournemouth, she was also in close proximity to the house where Robert Louis Stevenson lived while writing *Dr. Jekyll and Mr Hyde* and *Kidnapped.* Howarth would sit in the garden of the house where Stevenson created those classics and marvel at how close the past was to her. Stevenson continues to be a major influence in her own writing—especially his sense of adventure and his ability to use "just the right word every time," as she explained to Nettell.

Upon graduation, Howarth attended the Bournemouth College of Art for a time, but soon met her future husband, Phil. Married at age eighteen and off to London where Phil had a job, Howarth attended the Croydon College of Art for three years. Quite by accident, she became involved in fashion designing, a course of study that did her little good when returning to the country with her husband for a new job. Instead, in the country Howarth worked various casual labor jobs, including gardening and assisting in a retirement home. Her days spent in the flower beds and the tomato hothouses stood her in good stead with material when later she took up writing. Together with her husband, Howarth built the family house in Cornwall. One night while soaking in the bath after a particularly strenuous day of building, she suddenly felt she was "burning to write all these rather quirky stories," as she said in her interview with Nettell.

Howarth proceeded to write short stories and short screenplays which were submitted for a BBC video project. Though the films were not accepted, the process of writing them spurred Howarth into taking evening classes in creative writing. Soon her stories were expanding, turning into novels, and the voice she consistently wrote in was one directed at children. Finally, with three novels under her belt—none of them accepted by a publisher—she was able to place her fourth with the British publisher, Walker Books. This was "only the second unsolicited novel published by Walker," according to Kevin Steinberger in *Reading Time.* As Steinberger goes on to point out, Howarth's varied background in work and family all play a large part in her fiction. This first young adult novel, *The Flower King,* is a "gentle turn-of-the century story," according to *Magpies,* and some of the characters that she worked with in the retirement home find their way into the novel, as well as Howarth's experiences working in flower gardens. Shortlisted for both the Whitbread and *Guardian* children's fiction prizes, *The Flower King* won Howarth recognition and an agent. The novel has not been published in the United States.

For her second published novel, *MapHead,* Howarth adopted a science fiction format. Alien beings from the Subtle World, twelve-year-old MapHead and his father, Ran, come to Earth to search for the boy's mother, Kay. Before MapHead's birth, Ran saved the Earthling woman from death by a lightning bolt, and she returned

Thirteen-year-old Telly Craven resolves to alter the human destructiveness responsible for the severe weather which is threatening twenty-first century earth in Howarth's futuristic novel. (Cover illustration by Fletcher Sibthorp.)

with him to the Subtle World where they had a baby. But pining for her home, Kay returned to Earth with no memory of her encounter with Ran nor of her son. Now MapHead—so-called because of his ability to project a map of the terrain on his face and bald head—needs to find his mother before he can enjoy the Dawn of Power. Under the names of Boothe and Powers, the son and father take up residence in a tomato glasshouse on Earth, and Boothe enrolls in the local school where he meets the boy who is his half-brother and will take him to find his mother. In the process, he and his half-brother, Kenny, become friends, and MapHead begins to fit in and know what it means to be loved. Meeting his mother, he experiences an internal integration that gives him power equal to his father's, but the actual process of his search has led him to this self-integration.

Told with humor and attention to detail, *MapHead* "is a sweet, tender, coming-of-age story ... a marvelous read," according to Dorothy M. Broderick in *Voice of Youth Advocates,* and a "deliciously grotesque tale," according to John Peters in *School Library Journal.* Merri Monks in *Booklist* noted that "Howarth skillfully

evokes the internal landscapes of a young man's emotions and imagination," while *Magpies'* Sheahan praised the novel's "felicitous turns of phrase," noting that it was "brimful with lyrical, luscious language; written with an intensity, a distillation of the senses...." Though MapHead eventually leaves Earth without his mother, he has most definitely found himself: "Don't you know?" he asks toward the end of the book. "Can't you see? I'm not a little kid anymore. No one's got me, because I've got myself." In *Junior Bookshelf* a reviewer concluded that "Lesley Howarth has mixed the imaginary and the real ingredients with great skill." Howarth has returned to MapHead and his adventures in a 1997 sequel, *MapHead: The Return,* in which MapHead finds himself alone without his father for the first time and must return to Earth to find his destiny.

With increased recognition came the working hours of a full-time novelist. Howarth begins work at nine—once her children are off to school—and works until two, after which she takes a walk to clear her head and work out plot twists for the next day's writing. "I'm not interested in oral storytelling," Howarth told Steinberger for his *Reading Time* article. "For me the whole buzz is the word—the word making an effect on the page; that's what interests me." Normally Howarth does not begin her novels with a grand plan, but once in the story, she relishes in doing research and gathering more information than she'll ever need. "Then I let the stuff percolate for a long time," she told Steinberger. "You have to edge up to a story.... The whole essence of storywriting is to be excited. Once I get bored or find it a slog I decide to let it go."

Howarth's third novel is sometimes typified as an environmental story, though the author herself rejects the notion that she begins with a theme. For her, story is paramount and meaning follows story. With *Weather Eye,* Howarth was influenced both by an article about a near-death experience and by an apocalyptic feeling engendered in the novel by changing weather patterns. Thirteen-year-old Telly lives with her parents on a weather farm in Cornwall in 1999, just before the millennium. She helps her parents on this farm which generates electricity with huge windmills. All around the world unseasonal weather patterns are causing immense damage to property and life; in Cornwall strong winds have been blowing for days, and Telly is almost killed when struck on the head by a damaged turbine blade from one of the giant windmills. Telly feels she is imbued with special powers after this close scrape with death and resolves to do something to alter the human destructiveness responsible for the severe weather. Networking with youths around the world via computers, Telly, the Weather Eye, hopes to save the planet by redirecting energies. After many adventures and much hard work, a new turbine is brought on line at the climax of the novel, just in time for the new millennium. Telly describes it, "wheeling into the twenty-first century. Dad has the right idea: 'Next century belongs to you lot.... I've a feeling you'll all make the best of it.'"

When an archaeologist unearths the body of an iceman, his daughter wonders about everyday life in the Stone Age until a 9000-year-old ghost appears to fill in the details. (Cover illustration by Fletcher Sibthorp.)

In a *Magpies* review of the novel, Steinberger noted that *Weather Eye* "may be read as a very reassuring 'environmental' novel but it is immediately a humorous, suspenseful, thoughtful narration.... It is a story for, and of, our times, but in Howarth's inimitable style." Other critics, including Maeve Visser Knoth in *Horn Book,* also commented on Howarth's humor: "The author ... has written an unusual novel that will appeal to readers with its empowering theme and its strong element of humor." In *Junior Bookshelf,* a critic also remarked on Howarth's use of humor, saying "[Howarth's] vision of the world is essentially comic as well as profoundly moral." The reviewer went on to conclude that young readers "will read her book with joy and satisfaction because her children are drawn clearly and with humour as well as understanding."

Steinberger, in his *Reading Time* article on Howarth, noted that her use of idiom for both comic effects and depth of story set her apart from other writers. In *The Pits* she uses idiom to heightened effects. The book was inspired by news reports of the discovery of an iceman in the west of Austria and also by an article relating the discovery of an Ice-Age pine chewing gum. This started

Howarth looking for parallels between that time and ours and ended up with "a *West Side Story*-like gang rivalry set in Ice Age coastal Britain," according to Steinberger. The archaeologist Needcliff discovers Arf, the Iceman, a relic of a distant age, but his daughter, with him for the summer, wonders all the time what really made the Iceman tick. Such particulars are supplied by an adolescent ghost, Broddy Bronson, who was a pal of Arf's. Broddy has been drifting around for some 9,000 years, picking up the speech and experiences of each succeeding age, and it is his voice—entered into the archaeologist's computer—that relates the story of Arf, and of Broddy. It is Broddy's distinctive idiom that gives life to the tale. There are parallels between Broddy's time and ours, especially the gang fighting and turf wars. There is also "much humor," according to a reviewer in *Magpies,* who went on to conclude that "*The Pits* is a great read. It rollicks along ... and rejoices in telling an original story in an original way." Janice M. Del Negro, writing in the *Bulletin of the Center for Children's Books,* echoed this opinion of originality and commented that "what is most unusual about this book is that it works, and works remarkably well. Howarth creates a prehistoric world that is eminently credible, peopled by individuals with complex personalities."

Howarth, who complains that she is easily bored, has created in a short span of time, a most original group of works, full of adventure, humor, and meaning. As she concluded in her interview with Nettell, she feels that writing children's books is essentially fun. She sets out both to provide it and receive it. "Adult novelists could learn a thing or two about plotting and pace from children's fiction," Howarth said. "It's a world of the imagination I particularly enjoy roaming around in.... It's the best job ever."

■ Works Cited

Broderick, Dorothy M., review of *MapHead, Voice of Youth Advocates,* February, 1995, p. 348.

Del Negro, Janice M., review of *The Pits, Bulletin of the Center for Children's Books,* December, 1996, pp. 138-9.

Howarth, Lesley, *MapHead,* Walker Books, 1994.

Howarth, Lesley, *Weather Eye,* Walker Books, 1995.

Knoth, Maeve Visser, review of *Weather Eye, Horn Book,* March-April, 1996, pp. 208-09.

Review of *MapHead, Junior Bookshelf,* August, 1994, p. 145.

Monks, Merri, review of *MapHead, Booklist,* October 1, 1994, p. 319.

Nettell, Stephanie, "Know the Author: Lesley Howarth," *Magpies,* May, 1996, pp. 18-21.

Peters, John, review of *MapHead, School Library Journal,* October, 1994, p. 124.

Review of *The Pits, Magpies,* May, 1996. p. 21.

Sheahan, Robyn, review of *MapHead, Magpies,* July, 1994, p. 4.

Steinberger, Kevin, review of *Weather Eye, Magpies,* July, 1995, p. 25.

Steinberger, Kevin, "Lesley Howarth," *Reading Time,* May, 1996, p. 12.

Review of *Weather Eye, Junior Bookshelf,* June, 1995, p. 108.

■ For More Information See

PERIODICALS

Books for Keeps, November, 1993, p. 14; July, 1994, pp. 6, 28; July, 1995, p. 12; January, 1996, p. 11.
Bulletin of the Center for Children's Books, November, 1995, p. 93.
Horn Book Guide, spring, 1995, p. 78; spring, 1996, p. 73.
Magpies, May, 1994, p. 24.
Publishers Weekly, November 14, 1994, p. 69.
Times Educational Supplement, November 12, 1993, p. R12; December 24, 1993, p. 8.
U.S. News & World Report, December 5, 1994, p. 97.*

—*Sketch by J. Sydney Jones*

* * *

HURD, (John) Thacher 1949-

■ Personal

Born March 6, 1949, in Burlington, VT; son of Clement G. (an illustrator of children's books) and Edith (an author of children's books; maiden name, Thacher) Hurd; married Olivia Scott (co-owner with husband of Peaceable Kingdom Press), June 12, 1976; children: Manton, Nicholas. *Education:* Attended University of California, Berkeley, 1967-68; California College of Arts and Crafts, B.F.A., 1972.

■ Addresses

Home—188 Tamalpais Rd., Berkeley, CA 94708. *Agent*—Marilyn Marlow, Curtis Brown Ltd., 10 Astor Pl., New York, NY 10003.

■ Career

Writer and illustrator of children's books. Grabhorn-Hoyem Press (now Arion Press), apprentice printer, 1967, 1969; self-employed builder, designer, and cabinetmaker, 1972-78; teacher of writing and illustrating children's books at California College of Arts and Crafts and Dominican College, 1981-1986; co-owner with wife, Olivia Hurd, of Peaceable Kingdom Press (a children's greeting card publishing company), 1983—. Artist with group show at California College of Arts and Crafts, 1972; one-man show in Monkton, VT, 1973. Lecturer and guest speaker at seminars, conferences, and schools. *Member:* Society of Children's Book Writers and Illustrators.

■ Awards, Honors

Boston Globe-Horn Book award for illustration, 1985, for *Mama Don't Allow.*

THACHER HURD

■ Writings

(With mother, Edith Hurd) *Little Dog Dreaming* (juvenile), illustrated by father, Clement G. Hurd, Harper, 1965.

SELF-ILLUSTRATED JUVENILE BOOKS

The Old Chair, Greenwillow, 1978.
The Quiet Evening, Greenwillow, 1978, reissued, 1992.
Hobo Dog, Scholastic Book Services, 1980.
Axle the Freeway Cat, Harper, 1981.
Mystery on the Docks, Harper, 1983.
Hobo Dog's Christmas Tree, Scholastic Inc., 1983.
Mama Don't Allow, Harper, 1984.
Hobo Dog in the Ghost Town, Scholastic Inc., 1985.
Pea Patch Jig, Crown, 1986, published with cassette, Random House/McGraw Hill, 1988, HarperCollins, 1995.
A Night in the Swamp (pop-up book), Harper, 1987.
Blackberry Ramble, Crown, 1989, HarperCollins, 1995.
Little Mouse's Big Valentine, Harper, 1990.
Tomato Soup, Crown, 1991.
Little Mouse's Birthday Cake, HarperCollins, 1992.
Art Dog, HarperCollins, 1996.
Zoom City (board book), HarperCollins, 1998.

ILLUSTRATOR

Ida Luttrell, *Mattie and the Chicken Thief,* Dodd, 1988.
Dayle Ann Dodds, *Wheel Away!,* Harper, 1989.
Carolyn Otto, *Dinosaur Chase,* HarperCollins, 1991.
Komaiko, Leah, *Fritzi Fox Flew in from Florida,* HarperCollins, 1995.

OTHER

Hurd is also co-author, with John Cassidy, of *Watercolor for the Artistically Undiscovered*, Klutz Press, 1992.

■ Adaptations

Mystery on the Docks was adapted for television and broadcast on *Reading Rainbow,* Public Broadcasting Service (PBS-TV), 1984. *Mama Don't Allow* was adapted for television and broadcast on *Reading Rainbow,* PBS-TV, 1984, and on *CBS Storybreak,* Columbia Broadcasting System, Inc. (CBS-TV), 1986; was adapted for videocassette, Random House, 1988; and was adapted for a children's opera, *Muskrat Lullaby,* performed by the Los Angeles City Opera, October 6, 1989.

■ Sidelights

Author-illustrator Thacher Hurd combines a love of music, indefatigable tongue-in-cheek humor, and vibrantly bright colors to create children's books that provide lessons and chuckles. In titles such as *Hobo Dog* and its sequels, in *Mama Don't Allow, Peach Patch Jig, Blackberry Ramble,* and the "Little Mouse" books, Hurd serves up simple stories with cartoon-like artwork that make for excellent read-aloud books.

Born in Burlington, Vermont, Hurd grew up in rural North Ferrisburg, Vermont, son of the children's book illustrator, Clement Hurd, and the children's book author, Edith Thacher Hurd. Hurd's parents both collaborated on books and worked with others. "On the hill above our house in Vermont my father had a studio filled with his paintings and drawings and the children's books he was working on," Hurd once told *Something about the Author* (*SATA*). "I loved to just sit and watch him work and be in the atmosphere of paint smells, color, and creativity. I think this was how I learned about children's books from my parents when I was growing up. My father never sat me down and said 'Learn this' or 'This is how you must draw.' I took everything at my own pace, and when the time was right I started to do my own books." At age sixteen, Hurd collaborated with his mother on *Little Dog Dreaming,* illustrated by his father. An enviable apprenticeship.

Hurd attended the California College of Arts and Crafts, where he later taught writing and illustrating for children. But initially, once out of art school, he set on a course to become a serious artist. "Children's books were the furthest thing from my mind then and I drew mostly classical stuff," Hurd once commented. Finally, however, he discovered that he had no real love for still lifes, landscapes or figure drawing, which seemed like "empty exercises." Slowly he came to see that "the little doodles and fanciful drawings I was doing on the side were really expressing some deeper part of me." It was then he realized that children's books could be an outlet for his true feelings. At first, his mother, Edith Thacher Hurd, consulted with him on story lines, instructing him on how stories flow and to make them strong enough to support the pictures. Other artists and writers figured in his development: Maurice Sendak and his *Where the*

Because he thinks his friends have forgotten his birthday, Little Mouse goes skiing—and nearly misses out on his own surprise party. (From *Little Mouse's Birthday Cake,* written and illustrated by Hurd.)

Wild Things Are; Don Freeman and his *Pet of the Met;* Margaret Wise Brown and her *Sailor Dog;* Taro Yashima and his *Crow Boy;* and William Steig. "I love picture books that are real adventures, full of daring and danger," Hurd once said. Though raised a country boy, Hurd possesses an urban sensibility. "I try to create characters in my books who are part of the tough, fast world of the city," Hurd told *SATA,* "but who are still able to make their own cozy lives within that world."

One of Hurd's first solo efforts, *The Quiet Evening,* was a bedtime book describing the sounds and sights of a day drawing to a close. A child lies in bed "thinking quiet thoughts," including not only thoughts of home but of distant places made safe by the security felt at home. "The simple text" has accompanying illustrations rendered in "clear, dark colors..." noted a reviewer for *Horn Book.* Martha Davis Beck, writing in *Hungry Mind Review,* commented that Hurd "splendidly makes the link between the worlds inside and outside a house at night. His illustrations are gorgeous, but also friendly."

"I find myself drawn to characters on the fringes of life: drifters, hoboes, short-order cooks, gangsters, litter collectors," Hurd told *SATA.* "Music also seems to play an important part in my books. The rhythms of music spark the rhythms of a picture book and music always seems to creep into my books." Hurd was a budding trombonist in his school orchestra, then gave it up in high school for the guitar. Folk music was his forte for a time, then came an electronic guitar and membership in a band called The New Tokaloma Swamp Band—a name which later found a home in *Mama Don't Allow.* Hurd still plays music, but of a more subdued variety now on the piano. And music does find its way into many of his books: the protagonist of *Axle the Freeway Cat* plays a harmonica; Ralph in *Mystery on the Docks* sings opera; and Miles plays the saxophone in *Mama Don't Allow,* the title and concept of which are based on the traditional jazz song of the same name.

His interest in hoboes led Hurd to three picture books about the adventures of a Hobo Dog: *Hobo Dog, Hobo Dog's Christmas Tree,* and *Hobo Dog in the Ghost Town.* A lonely, harmonica-playing cat meets a new friend in a traffic jam in *Axle the Freeway Cat.* Sometimes Hurd begins a book with a mood rather than a favorite fringe character. Such was the case with *Mystery on the Docks,* in which Ralph, a short-order cook, rescues a kidnapped opera singer from Big Al and his gang of rats. Yet this story began with "a foggy night, a dark pier and some nasty rats," Hurd explained to *SATA.* "The book grew out of those feelings and they were the basis for the plot and action of the story. My characters seem to be innocents in search of adventure in the big world and a place to call home."

Hurd's award-winning *Mama Don't Allow* was inspired by the theme music for a show on a local radio station. The old jazz song of that name "sounded like the most raucous, wonderful thing I had ever heard and I couldn't stop thinking about it," Hurd noted in *Harper Highlights.* The lyrics to the song sounded like a natural for a

SMUSH!

George fell into the onions and rotten tomatoes and potato peelings in the pigs' trough. The pigs were amazed. Poor George.

A baby mouse uses numerous tricks to get out of taking her medicine in Hurd's self-illustrated *Tomato Soup.*

children's book: "Mama don't allow no music playin' round here, now we don't care what Mama don't allow, we're gonna play that music anyhow!" The inspiration was slow in percolating, and several years passed before the story of Miles, the saxophone-playing possum, was published. This "engaging and nonsensical romp," according to *Bulletin of the Center for Children's Books,* tells the story of Miles Possum who receives a saxophone as a birthday present from his uncle. Miles drives his parents and neighbors crazy with his loud practicing, and soon forms a combo with three other animals called the Swamp Band. The alligators seem to be the only true connoisseurs of music, and invite the band to perform at their party aboard a riverboat. Not only are they a success, but they are also intended to be the alligators' main course. The band manages to escape, however, by playing a lullaby that sends the alligators off to dreamland with empty stomachs. The reviewer for *Bulletin of the Center for Children's Books* concluded that the story was "Ebullient, fast-paced, and funny . . . "

Swamps also figure in Hurd's pop-up book, *A Night in the Swamp,* which represents the activities of swamp animals between sundown and sunrise. Yvonne A. Frey in *School Library Journal* noted that the book was "exceptionally well engineered and nicely illustrated," with flaps that reveal animals underneath or a wheel on one page which, when turned, makes a catfish family swim and fireflies flicker on the following page. "This is a delightful book for children of any age," Frey concluded. Writing in *Publishers Weekly,* a reviewer concluded that Hurd's "delightful" pop-up creation supplied plenty of tabs to lift or pull, which provided "a fun lesson" on animals of the night, at the same time "fancifully capturing night's many moods."

"I think that I like to write the books that I would have liked to have read when I was a child—books with strong characters and a sense of mystery," Hurd once noted about his own work. "Children often identify so completely with the characters they read about in books that they live through these characters and see themselves as the characters. So I feel that the main character in a picture book should be strong and full of energy with a spirit of adventure and a sense of his own power to solve whatever comes his way." A family of such characters are presented in *Pea Patch Jig* and its sequels, *Blackberry Ramble* and *Tomato Soup.* Father Mouse, Mother Mouse, and Baby Mouse, who is a born troublemaker, live near Farmer Clem's garden. In the first of the books, the family is involved in a trio of adventures involving lettuce, tomatoes, and a pea shooter employed by the precocious Baby Mouse in scaring off a fox. The colors are brilliant primaries and the text simple. Music is again in attendance, with a rendition of "The Pea Patch Jig" concluding the capers. "Energy pulsates throughout the whole book," noted Ann A. Flowers in *Horn Book,* going on to describe the story as "A festive salad of a book, filled with snap, crackle, and crunch." Roger Sutton, in *Bulletin of the Center for Children's Books,* commented that "Bright, jazzy shapes and colors complement this sprightly ode to vegetables," while a critic in *Publishers Weekly*

Arthur, the quiet guard at the Dogopolis Museum of Art, has a secret life as a flamboyant masked painter in this lighthearted picturebook. (From *Art Dog,* written and illustrated by Hurd.)

concluded that Hurd's "kaleidoscopic colors and mischievous sense of humor make this book ripe for picking." In *Blackberry Ramble,* Baby Mouse is once again troublesome, celebrating the arrival of spring by bothering Farmer Clem's animals, in particular, Becky the Cow. Mary Lou Budd, writing in *School Library Journal,* concluded that the "vibrant watercolor illustrations ... are the attraction here," while Sutton in *Bulletin of the Center for Children's Books* felt that though Baby Mouse's antics were "amusing," the book lacked "the vibrancy of the first." Baby Mouse makes a return visit in *Tomato Soup,* in which the little rodent is sick in bed upstairs while its parents are out planting. The doctor is called, but Baby Mouse is no friend of doctors and escapes, only to be pursued by George the cat. *Booklist*'s Ilene Cooper commented that "A bright, witty text meets its match in good-size colorful pencil illustrations."

Hurd's penchant for mice carried him through two further books: *Little Mouse's Big Valentine* and *Little Mouse's Birthday Cake.* Little Mouse makes a big valentine in the first of these, but has trouble finding the right recipient until Gloria the Mouse comes along. However, the two finally figure out an even better solution: They cut up the giant valentine into many smaller ones and distribute them to everybody. Cooper dubbed this easy-to-read book "Simple yet sweet," and a critic in *Kirkus Reviews* commented that "This beguiling fable is both told and illustrated with disarming simplicity." In the second Little Mouse adventure, it seems that his friends have forgotten his birthday and so he goes off skiing by himself. Lost for a time, he is found by his three friends who have a surprise party waiting for him. *School Library Journal*'s Budd noted that young readers would feel "the warmth and kindness of friendship through the sweeping watercolor illustrations and anticipatory text." Karen Hutt of *Booklist* conclud-

ed that "With a minimum of detail, Hurd conveys the beauty of solitude and the warmth of friendship."

With his 1996 *Art Dog,* Hurd left the world of mice for a time, creating a superhero dog who solves problems and finds happiness through art. When the famous Mona Woofa painting is stolen from the Dogopolis Museum of Art, Arthur Dog—known simply as Art Dog—goes in search of the thieves. Famous artists in the museum include Vincent Van Dog and Henri Muttisse, all joining forces with Art Dog to create an adventure that "has a camp, cartoonish Batman zaniness to it that kids will sink their canines into," according to Deborah Stevenson, writing in *Bulletin of the Center for Children's Books.* Virginia Golodetz in *School Library Journal* noted that "Hurd infuses every page of this book with dramatic watercolors," and a contributor to *Kirkus Reviews* concluded that "Art Dog is a superhero for all times." Hurd has also illustrated books for other authors, most recently Leah Komaiko's *Fritzi Fox Flew in from Florida.* Patricia Pearl Dole in *School Library Journal* commented that the text of the book was "enhanced by Hurd's bold, watercolor cartoons."

Hurd's ambitions for his children's books are straightforward, as Hurd himself explained to *SATA.* "To make a book exciting, to make the pages turn, to make a child laugh, to bring out a child's sense of wonder: these are what I am aiming at in my books. I believe that children's books should be for children, and not for the coffee tables of educators and librarians. I remember I loved to read as a child, and I think I try to write ... something that could draw me into another world: an alive, vibrant wold of energy and wild, bursting color."

■ Works Cited

Review of *Art Dog, Kirkus Reviews,* November 15, 1995.

Beck, Martha Davis, review of *The Quiet Evening, Hungry Mind Review,* Summer, 1993, p. C-16.

Budd, May Lou, review of *Blackberry Ramble, School Library Journal,* November, 1989, p. 84.

Budd, May Lou, review of *Little Mouse's Birthday Cake, School Library Journal,* February, 1992, p. 74.

Cooper, Ilene, review of *Little Mouse's Big Valentine, Booklist,* January 1, 1990, p. 916.

Cooper, Ilene, review of *Tomato Soup, Booklist,* May 1, 1992, p. 1608.

Dole, Patricia Pearl, review of *Fritzi Fox Flew in from Florida, School Library Journal,* March, 1995, p. 182.

Flowers, Ann A., review of *The Pea Patch Jig, Horn Book,* November-December, 1986, p. 735.

Frey, Yvonne A., review of *A Night in the Swamp, School Library Journal,* April, 1987, p. 84.

Golodetz, Virginia, review of *Art Dog, School Library Journal,* February, 1996, pp. 85-6.

Hurd, Thacher, *The Quiet Evening,* Greenwillow, 1978.

Hurd, Thacher, *Mama Don't Allow,* Harper, 1984.

Hurd, Thacher, author comments included in *Harper Highlights,* promotional brochure, HarperCollins, 1996.

Hutt, Karen, review of *Little Mouse's Birthday Cake, Booklist,* November 15, 1991, p. 630.

Review of *Little Mouse's Big Valentine, Kirkus Reviews,* January 1, 1990, p. 46.

Review of *Mama Don't Allow, Bulletin of the Center for Children's Books,* October, 1984, p. 28.

Review of *A Night in the Swamp, Publishers Weekly,* January 16, 1987, p. 72.

Review of *The Pea Patch Jig, Publishers Weekly,* June 27, 1986, p. 86.

Review of *The Quiet Evening, Horn Book,* November-December, 1992, p. 741.

Stevenson, Deborah, review of *Art Dog, Bulletin of the Center for Children's Books,* February, 1996, p. 191.

Sutton, Roger, review of *The Pea Patch Jig, Bulletin of the Center for Children's Books,* October, 1986, p. 28.

Sutton, Roger, review of *Blackberry Ramble, Bulletin of the Center for Children's Books,* January, 1990, pp. 110-11.

■ **For More Information See**

PERIODICALS

Booklist, January 1 & 15, 1996, p. 845.

Horn Book, January, 1985, p. 72; January/February, 1990, p. 89; March, 1992, p. 219.

Kirkus Review, January 15, 1987, p. 131; July 1, 1989, p. 991; December 1, 1991, p. 1541; May 15, 1992, p. 671.

Los Angeles Times Book Review, May 29, 1994, p. 13.

New York Times Book Review, February 15, 1987, p. 41.

Publishers Weekly, August 11, 1989, p. 457; December 8, 1989, p. 53; November 29, 1991, p. 51; December 20, 1991, p. 83; May 11, 1992, p. 71; January 9, 1995, p. 63; December 18, 1995, p. 53.

—Sketch by J. Sydney Jones

J–K

JINKS, Catherine 1963-

■ Personal

Born November 17, 1963; daughter of Brian and Rhonda (Dickings) Jinks; married Peter Dockrill (November 22, 1992); children: one child. *Education:* University of Sydney, B.A. (with honors), 1986. *Politics:* "Left."

■ Addresses

Agent—Margaret Connolly, 16 Winton St., Warrawee, Sydney, NSW 2074, Australia.

■ Career

Westpac Banking Corp., Sydney, Australia, journalist, 1986-93.

■ Awards, Honors

Australian Children's Book of the Year Award shortlist, Children's Book Council of Australia, 1993, for *Pagan's Crusade,* and 1997, for *Pagan's Scribe;* Victorian Premier's Award shortlist, 1993, for *Pagan's Crusade;* Australian Children's Book of the Year Award (Older Readers category), Children's Book Council of Australia, and Adelaide Festival Award shortlist, both 1996, both for *Pagan's Vows.*

■ Writings

This Way Out, Omnibus, 1991.
Pagan's Crusade, Hodder & Stoughton, 1992.
The Future Trap, Omnibus, 1993.
Pagan in Exile, Omnibus, 1994.
Witch Bank, Penguin, 1995.
Pagan's Vows, Omnibus, 1995.
Pagan's Scribe, Omnibus, 1996.
An Evening with the Messiah (adult novel), Penguin, 1996.
Eye to Eye, Penguin, 1997.
Little White Secrets (adult novel), Penguin, 1997.

The Secret of Hermitage Isle (cartoon book), ABC Books, 1997.

■ Work in Progress

Piggy in the Middle.

■ Sidelights

Catherine Jinks told *SATA:* "In Australia I'm best known for my medieval historical series, the 'Pagan' books—*Pagan's Crusade, Pagan in Exile, Pagan's Vows,* and *Pagan's Scribe.* So far only *Pagan's Crusade* has made a low-key appearance outside this country—in the United Kingdom and Canada. They are humorous books, written in present tense/first person. My interest in medieval history was fuelled by my study of it in university; it's an abiding interest, and will probably result in more medieval books.

"I've always wanted to produce books, and sent my first 'novel' off to a publisher when I was twelve. I feel shocking if I'm not working on a book and have no problem applying myself to their creation—no writer's block for me. I love creating stories; if I didn't, I wouldn't be doing it. It's the best job in the world (I just wish it paid more!).

"P.S. I grew up in Papua New Guinea and spent eighteen months in Nova Scotia from 1993 to 1994 (being married to a Canadian). Canada will be the subject of my next published adult book."

When *Pagan's Vows* won the Australian Children's Book of the Year Award for the older readers category from the Children's Book Council of Australia, Jinks remarked in her acceptance speech: "In a funny sort of way I see the award as more of a tribute to Pagan than to me.... He's been through a lot, yet he's kept his humour and his courage and his loving heart. More than any other character I've created ... he's the one who deserves, and has the strength, to live on a bit—instead of disappearing into the black hole of the remainders

CATHERINE JINKS

bin. So I'd like to express my gratitude on Pagan's behalf."

Catherine Jinks's first book for young adults, *This Way Out,* is unique in her body of published work. This novel is a contemporary story that focuses on a fifteen-year-old girl's dissatisfaction with her life and her search for a job that will pay for the photographs that she hopes will begin her modeling career. "*This Way Out* reveals the author's awareness of some of the frustrations and longings of youth," remarked Cathryn Crowe in *Magpies.*

The author is better known for creating a twelfth-century ragamuffin character named Pagan Kidrouk, squire to Lord Roland during the last days of the Crusades. *Pagan's Crusade,* Jinks's first installment in what has become a series of novels, is "a curious, and curiously fascinating, novel," commented Marcus Crouch in *Junior Bookshelf.* Critics have noted the author's unusual choice of modern vernacular speech for her medieval characters, a choice that yields "a style

which is elliptical and abrupt and, at times, wildly funny," according to a reviewer for *Magpies.*

The focus of *Pagan's Crusade* is the relationship that develops between Pagan, a boy from the streets, and Lord Roland, who is the epitome of upper-class strength and valor. "The interplay between these two strong characters, each of which supplies a need in the other, underpins the whole fabric of the book," remarked Joan Zahnleiter in *Magpies.* "The aristocratic Templar [Roland] and his scruffy squire make an unlikely partnership and it is a measure of the success of Ms. Jinks' story that we accept the mutual respect that grows up between the partners under the stress of violent action," continued Marcus Crouch in *Junior Bookshelf.* In the first sequel, *Pagan in Exile,* Lord Roland takes Pagan back to his estate in France, where he becomes involved in the domestic wars among the twelfth-century landed aristocracy. Both books are noted for Pagan's humorous first-person narration. "Though the time and setting may not sound conducive to hilarity," Karen Jameyson admitted in her review of *Pagan's Crusade* in *Horn*

Book, "the book certainly has elements of the hysterical historical." Indeed, echoed the reviewer in *Magpies,* Jinks's sense of humor enables her to "present the historical novel in an accessible style for today's readers."

■ Works Cited

Crouch, Marcus, review of *Pagan's Crusade, Junior Bookshelf,* December, 1993, pp. 246-47.

Crowe, Cathryn, review of *This Way Out, Magpies,* March, 1993, p. 32.

Jameyson, Karen, review of *Pagan's Crusade, Horn Book,* July, 1993, p. 498.

Jinks, Catherine, acceptance speech for Australian Children's Book of the Year Award, *Reading Time,* November, 1996, pp. 7-8.

Review of *Pagan in Exile, Magpies,* July, 1995, p. 24.

Review of *Pagan's Crusade, Magpies,* November, 1992, p. 14.

Zahnleiter, Joan, review of *Pagan's Crusade, Magpies,* May, 1993, p. 24.

* * *

KANOZA, Muriel Canfield 1935-
(Muriel Canfield)

■ Personal

Born May 14, 1935, in Oak Park, IL; daughter of Donald (a roofing contractor) and Audrey (a homemaker; maiden name, Hinden) Hansen; married Eugene D. Canfield (a civil engineer), September 21, 1956 (died July 3, 1989); married Daniel J. Kanoza (a manager and industrial engineer); children: (first marriage) Donald, Deborah Canfield Morgan, Douglas. *Education:* Miami University, B.S. (summa cum laude), 1978. *Politics:* Conservative. *Religion:* Christian. *Hobbies and other interests:* Walking, investing, reading, art, traveling, Bible study.

■ Addresses

Home—4043 Resolute Circle, Cincinnati, OH 45252. *Agent*—Joyce Hart, 123 Queenstown Dr., Pittsburgh, PA 15235.

■ Career

Real estate agent in Cincinnati, OH, 1968-76; free-lance writer, Cincinnati, 1981—. Alcoholics Victorious, Cincinnati organizer; Welcome Wagon, local vice-president; co-facilitator of a support group for battered women; volunteer at a nursing home and a battered women's shelter; court advocate for battered women.

■ Writings

UNDER NAME MURIEL CANFIELD

I Wish I Could Say I Love You (autobiography), Bethany House (Minneapolis, MN), 1983.

MURIEL CANFIELD KANOZA

Anne (young adult novel), Bethany House, 1984, revised edition, 1994.

A Victorian Marriage (historical novel), Bethany House, 1986.

Contributor to Christian magazines.

■ Work in Progress

Nowhere to Run, concerning domestic violence; *College Girl's Conflict,* a young adult romance novel; *The Failing Mind,* an adult novel about Alzheimer's disease.

■ Sidelights

Muriel Canfield Kanoza told *SATA:* "I was not praised for my writing as a child, nor did I desire to be a writer. I wanted to travel and see the world. I didn't consider a career in writing until I was an adult. I had returned to college to complete a degree in English education, and my professors informed me that I had writing ability. After graduation, my first project was a book, the story of my alcoholism and search for love. It was quite an undertaking. Seven drafts later, the book was finished and accepted for publication. While writing all those drafts, I read well-written books and compared my work. I analyzed, why does this writer's sentence or this paragraph work so well? I also studied grammar books. In fact, one day while waiting for outpatient surgery, I was studiously reading grammar tips.

"Although I have written nonfiction, I prefer to write fiction, either for young adults or adults. In fiction one creates something from nothing. The world with which one starts has no landscape, no people, and no action. It's like when I was a child and played with Sally, an imaginary friend. Sally and I had a world of our own that I created. We had adventures I never had in my everyday life. It's the same with writing books; I have wonderful experiences at my computer.

"Despite loving to live in my imagination, I research carefully for each book to provide authenticity. For *The Failing Mind,* a novel I'm writing about a family coping with Alzheimer's disease, I volunteer in an Alzheimer's ward and interview professionals and family members who care for Alzheimer's patients. I keep a journal about the experiences of a friend who has Alzheimer's disease. Although I start a book with a blank world, I want this world to become as realistic as possible.

"I am now hooked on writing, and I hope to continue this work for a long time."

*　　*　　*

KELLER, Debra 1958-

■ Personal

Born September 25, 1958, in New York, NY; daughter of Herbert B. (a mathematician) and Loretta (an artist) Keller; married James Muldavin (an executive director), July 11, 1991; children: Noah, Elana. *Education:* Attended University of California, San Diego; California State University, Long Beach, B.A. *Hobbies and other interests:* Hiking, biking, gardening.

■ Addresses

Office—1220 H St., No. 102, Sacramento, CA 95814.

■ Career

Advertising copywriter in Los Angeles and San Francisco, CA, 1984-90; freelance copywriter, Sacramento, CA, 1990—. *Member:* Society of Children's Book Writers and Illustrators.

■ Awards, Honors

The Trouble with Mister was an *American Booksellers Association* "Pick of the List," 1995, and a Junior Library Guild selection, 1996.

■ Writings

The Trouble with Mister, illustrated by Shannon McNeill, Chronicle Books (San Francisco, CA), 1995.

■ Work in Progress

A mystery picture book.

DEBRA KELLER

■ Sidelights

Debra Keller told *SATA:* "I've always loved to write. I wrote my first (unpublished) children's book when I was nine years old. My teacher read it to the class, and no one laughed when he (or she) was supposed to. I wrote my second (unpublished) children's book in college. My professor, who was also a freelance editor, said she would help me revise the text and submit the manuscript, but I didn't believe her.

"I went on to become an advertising copywriter at a big Los Angeles agency. My first job was to write dog food coupons. My first (published) children's book was about a dog.

"Although I only have one book out, I write stories all the time. When I write, I begin with something I want to say. *The Trouble with Mister* began with my wanting to tell children, 'You're safe. You're okay. Use your imagination, and your world will be just right.'

"My favorite picture book authors are William Steig and Peggy Rathmann, which is funny because they were both illustrators first. Although their books are very different, they each speak to my heart in an honest, warm manner, which is what I think the best children's books do.

"My advice to aspiring authors is just to do it. If you have never written, but want to, just try it. No one has to read a word you write, and it's really very safe. If you have written a little, but want to write more, just do. As I once learned at a writer's conference, you can't fail unless you stop trying."

In her first children's book, *The Trouble with Mister,* Keller writes about a young boy who desperately wants a dog. When his parents refuse, Alex paints himself a picture of a dog, complete with long purple hair and bright yellow socks. One evening, his dream dog Mister comes alive, and the two play together all night. The next morning Mister runs away, and Alex is afraid his dog is gone forever until he receives a mysterious envelope with his original painting of Mister inside. Writing in *School Library Journal,* reviewer Jody McCoy praised Keller's well constructed text and claimed the book was "a treat for the eye, the ear, the imagination, and the heart." Ilene Cooper remarked in *Booklist* that children should enjoy the picture book, "especially the frisky Mister." A reviewer in *Kirkus Reviews* praised the "winning combination" of Keller's story with Shannon McNeill's illustrations, going on to describe *The Trouble with Mister* as "a colorful, bouncy romp."

■ Works Cited

Cooper, Ilene, review of *The Trouble with Mister, Booklist,* January 1, 1996, p. 846.
McCoy, Jody, review of *The Trouble with Mister, School Library Journal,* February, 1996, p. 86.
Review of *The Trouble with Mister, Kirkus Reviews,* October 1, 1995, p. 1431.

■ For More Information See

PERIODICALS

Boston Book Review, November, 1995, p. 28.
Family Fun, November, 1995, p. 152.
Publishers Weekly, October 16, 1995, p. 60.
Working Mother, April, 1996, p. 68.

* * *

KENDALL, Gordon
See SHWARTZ, Susan (Martha)

* * *

KEYSER, Sarah
See McGUIRE, Leslie (Sarah)

* * *

KILWORTH, Garry (D.) 1941-
(Garry Douglas, F. K. Salwood)

■ Personal

Born July 5, 1941, in York, England; son of George (a Royal Air Force sergeant) and Joan (a bookkeeper;

maiden name, Hodges) Kilworth; married Annette Bailey (a therapist and social worker); children: Richard, Chantelle. *Education:* King's College, London University, honors degree in English literature, 1985. *Religion:* Quaker.

■ Addresses

Agent—Maggie Noach, 21 Redan St., London; Ralph Vicinanza, 111 8th Ave., New York, NY 10011.

■ Career

Writer, 1977—. Cable and Wireless, London, executive, 1974-82. *Military Service:* Royal Air Force, 1956-74, worked on making and breaking codes in Singapore, Maldives, Germany, Aden, Bahrain, Kenya, Malta, and Cyprus; Sergeant Cryptographer.

■ Awards, Honors

Winner of the Gollancz/*Sunday Times* Best SF Prize for a short story, 1974, for "Let's Go to Golgotha!"; winner of World Fantasy Award for the best novella, 1992, British Science Fiction Association Award and *Interzone Magazine* readers' Short Fiction Poll, both 1994, and all for *The Ragthorn* (written with Robert Holdstock); winner of *Interzone Magazine* readers' Short Story Poll, 1992, for "The Sculptor"; British Library

GARRY KILWORTH

Association's Carnegie Medal Commendation, 1992, for *The Drowners;* Children's Book of the Year Award, Lancashire County Library/National Westminster Bank, 1995, for *The Electric Kid.* Many of Kilworth's other short stories, short story collections, and novels have been shortlisted for various British literary awards, including the Carnegie Medal and the World Fantasy Award.

■ Writings

FOR CHILDREN AND YOUNG ADULTS

The Wizard of Woodworld, Collins, 1987.
The Voyage of the Vigilance, Collins, 1988.
The Rain Ghost, Scholastic, 1989.
Dark Hills, Hollow Clocks (short story collection), Methuen, 1990.
The Third Dragon, Scholastic, 1991.
The Drowners, Methuen, 1991.
Billy Pink's Private Detective Agency, Methuen, 1993.
The Phantom Piper, Methuen, 1994.
The Electric Kid, Bantam, 1994.
The Bronte Girls, Methuen, 1995.
Cybercats, Bantam, 1996.
The Raiders, Mammoth Books, 1996.
The Gargoyle, Heinemann, 1997.

FOR ADULTS; NOVELS

In Solitary, Faber and Faber, 1977.
The Night of Kadar, Faber and Faber, 1978.
Split Second, Faber and Faber, 1979.
Gemini God, Faber and Faber, 1981.
A Theatre of Timesmiths, Gollancz, 1984.
Witchwater Country, Bodley Head, 1986.
Spiral Winds, Bodley Head, 1987.
Cloudrock, Unwin Hyman, 1988.
Abandonati, Unwin Hyman, 1988.
Hunter's Moon, Unwin Hyman, 1989.
Midnight's Sun, Unwin Hyman, 1990.
Standing on Shamsan, HarperCollins, 1992.
Frost Dancers, HarperCollins, 1992.
Angel, Gollancz, 1993.
Archangel, Gollancz, 1994.
House of Tribes, Bantam, 1995.
The Roof of Voyaging (part one of *The Navigator Kings* trilogy), Little, Brown, 1996.
A Midsummer's Nightmare, Bantam, 1996.
The Princely Flower (part two of *The Navigator Kings* trilogy), Little, Brown, 1997.

ADULT NOVELS; AS GARRY DOUGLAS

Highlander (novelization of SF film), Grafton Books, 1986.
The Street, Grafton Books, 1988.
The Devil's Own (historical novel), HarperCollins, 1997.

ADULT NOVELS; AS F. K. SALWOOD

The Oystercatcher's Cry, Headline Books, 1993.
The Saffron Fields, Headline Books, 1994.
The Ragged School, Headline Books, 1995.

SHORT STORY COLLECTIONS FOR ADULTS

The Songbirds of Pain, Gollancz, 1984.

In the Hollow of the Deep-Sea Wave, Bodley Head, 1989.
In the Country of Tattooed Men, HarperCollins, 1993.
Hogfoot Right and Bird-Hands, Edgewood Press, 1993.

Kilworth has published short stories in *Fantasy and Science Fiction Magazine, Interzone Magazine, Ad Astra Magazine,* and *Ambit Magazine,* among others, and his short stories have also been anthologized in various collections. His works have been translated into fifteen languages.

■ Adaptations

The Drowners was adapted for a cassette tape by Chivers, 1993; *Billy Pink's Private Detective Agency* was adapted for broadcast on the BBC's "Jackanory" program.

■ Sidelights

Garry Kilworth is a man of many professions. He joined the Royal Air Force as a young man, serving around the world until he was thirty-three. Thereafter, he took a business course and became a senior executive at an international telecommunications company. By age forty-one he had left that position to become a full-time writer, and his writing has been as varied as the rest of his life. Beginning as a writer for adults, he published science fiction, mystery, fantasy, horror, and family sagas before turning his hand to young adult fare with his 1987 publication, *The Wizard of Woodworld.* Since that time, he has written a dozen more YA titles on subjects from ghosts to street children to the Bronte sisters. Meanwhile, he has continued a prodigious publishing schedule of adult titles.

Kilworth was born in 1941, as he told *Something about the Author* (*SATA*), "to itinerant low-income parents, themselves from trawler fishing/farm labourer stock." With his father a sergeant in the Royal Air Force, Kilworth was raised and educated on the go. He attended over twenty schools and was raised partly in south Arabia. Some of his earliest childhood memories are of family adventures and near-tragedies. He and his family came close to being swept away in the floods of 1953 in southeastern England; neighbors just across the road were drowned. The Kilworths were rescued by launch seven hours after their house was totally inundated. Another such adventure took place in Arabia where he and a school friend were lost in the Hadrahmaut Desert without water for two days. They were finally located by an RAF rescue team.

Kilworth left public school at age fifteen to attend the Royal Air Force Training School, then joined the RAF at eighteen as a Senior Aircraft Telegraphist. Fifteen years later he left the RAF as a Sergeant Cryptographer, having served in Europe, Africa, the Middle East, and finally the Maldives, where he spent "a lonely year on a coral island looking after an outpost for the RAF," as he told *SATA.* During those years he also served as an RAF corporal "for the bloody withdrawal of British troops" from Aden in 1966-67, and found himself fighting against former Arab schoolmates. It was, Kilworth explained, "a very disturbing and unhappy experience which still haunts me."

Out of the RAF, Kilworth attended the Southwest London Polytechnic, where he took a diploma in business studies, then joined Cable and Wireless as an executive, travelling frequently to the U.S. and the Caribbean during the eight years he was with the company. But during all these busy years, Kilworth was also working on his writing. He was twenty when he wrote his first full-length novel, a children's book that has never been published. But he kept working at the craft, and in 1974 a science fiction short story won a prestigious British prize, and his career was partly launched. Three years later his first novel, *In Solitary,* was published by Faber and Faber. He stayed with science fiction for adults through his first few titles, but as he told *SATA,* "my natural bent took me towards the retelling of old mythologies and the inventing of new." Among these are animal fantasies, Polynesian tales, and a reworking of Shakespeare's *Midsummer Night's Dream.* Kilworth's military background has also come to the fore in historical war novels, such as *The Devil's Own,* set during the Crimean War. A resident of two acres of lovely Essex land for the past twenty years, Kilworth also writes what he calls "County Sagas," under the name F. K. Salwood, his grandmother's maiden name.

It was not until late in his career, however, that Kilworth returned to his dream of writing children's and young adult books. As the author noted in *Books for Keeps,* he worked his way into the genre by asking a friend if he could submit a piece for an anthology of children's stories. The attempt was a success, and Kilworth was off and running with a new field of writing endeavor. "I believe writing for children to be more important than writing for adults," Kilworth wrote in his *Books for Keeps* article. "The formative years are a long, heady period in anyone's life, and writers who deal in them must do so with care ... without appearing to preach or demand." Kilworth was, as a child, heavily influenced by the writing of British author Richmal Crompton, herself an author of over forty books for adults, but forever remembered in England for her William Brown books, about the mid-century adventures of an adolescent boy. Kipling and Twain were other childhood favorites of Kilworth and instilled in him a lasting love for wit, adventure, and the well-turned phrase.

One of Kilworth's early YA novels, *The Rain Ghost,* uses the frame of a traditional ghost story to tell a story of alienation, peer pressure, and old-fashioned romance. Steve Winston, a teenager, is lost in the mountains on a school outing. While hunkering down in the bog to await rescue, Steve discovers an ornate antique dagger in the heather. But strange feelings after his rescue lead him to research the dagger, and this brings him to the realization that he pulled the knife from the mummified fingers of one of an ancient tribe of Rain Warriors slaughtered on the mountain. That long dead warrior is now haunting him. Susan R. Farber, writing in *Voice of Youth Advocates,* noted that the book was "a nice horror story which has plenty of suspense but is not too terrifying."

A collection of ten tales for YA readers, *Dark Hills, Hollow Clocks,* ranges from dragons to ghosts to wizards, to changelings and even animate scarecrows. The tales include "The Goblin Jag," "Warrior Wizards," "The Sleeping Giants," "The Hungry Ghosts," and "The Orkney Trows," among others, and are "told with exceptional imagination and verve," according to *Junior Bookshelf.* Margery Fisher in *Growing Point* concluded that the "almost conversational tone of the stories makes for pleasurable reading while inventive plots and the constant reminiscences of true folk-tale give to this sparkling collection a certain justification...."

Kilworth's 1992 *The Drowners* won him a Carnegie Medal Commendation. It is another tale full of adventure and somewhat arcane knowledge, this time of a historical sort. "A fascinating byway of history," according to *Junior Bookshelf,* the novel is set in the English

Two adolescents support themselves in a city dump in the year 2061 using their talent for reconditioning electronic equipment, until their unique skills draw the unwanted attention of a crime syndicate with its own ideas. (Cover illustration by Greg Couch.)

county of Hampshire in the first half of the nineteenth century. The drowners of the title were actually early irrigation engineers, who found that they could use a complicated system of sluices and channels to release the waters of a local river, flood the land in a controlled manner, and provide just the right conditions to promote the most feed for their cattle and thus get them to market early for the best prices. Tim, the youthful apprentice to the Master Drowner, is himself drowned attempting to save a lady from the waters. Other complications follow: the absentee landlord is jealous of the other men's cattle and sends a tough to set matters right in Hampshire. Before the Master Drowner can teach Jem, the new apprentice, the complicated craft of "drowning," he also dies. But Tim's ghost comes back to help the local farmers and to teach Jem how to control the flooding. The reviewer for *Junior Bookshelf* concluded: "This is a splendidly gripping story."

One of Kilworth's strengths as a writer is creating the unexpected, giving voice to the little known. His tales always feature an element of adventure, a holdover from the sort of book he enjoyed reading as a youth. In *The Phantom Piper*, Kilworth turns *Lord of the Flies* on its head, and has the adults of the Scottish Highland village of Canlish answer the call of a phantom piper to take to the hills, leaving the children behind to run the village and their own lives. Four centuries earlier, the village had been wiped out in the tribal fighting of the sixteenth century, the efforts of a local piper to raise the alarm going unheeded. But now the adults have finally answered the call, and for a time the children of the village do quite well on their own. Then comes the arrival of two travellers, Tyler and McFee, who have been trapped in the snow. Their arrival also brings evil into the village, and now the children are on a desperate search for the music which will recall their parents and rid them of the two interlopers. A reviewer for *Junior Bookshelf* dubbed *The Phantom Piper* "a tense and frightening suspense story," with "fully rounded" characters and a theme that is an "affirmation of the human spirit."

"You may wonder why I should wish to spend part of my time writing stories and novels for kids when I can earn five times as much in advances for those who've reached maturity," Kilworth wrote in *Books for Keeps.* "Well, the truth is ... it's not about money. I've been hooked on children's books since ... the age of 11 .... My love of children's books has never left me. I write them for that reason and because a special purity of vision is needed when telling the tale." *The Electric Kid* is a novel full of a certain type of vision, one that was inspired by what Kilworth himself saw on the rubbish heaps of Manila, where homeless children fight for who will take first grab at the new trash. It is a harsh world, and one that Kilworth tried to deal with in a metaphoric way in this science fiction tale set in the year 2061 when two such adolescents learn to support themselves in a city dump. Blindboy and Hotwire team up to survive the harsh world of the twenty-first century. Blindboy has compensatory hearing; he can hear so acutely as to pick up electronic impulses under mountains of trash. Hot-

wire is a girl who is something of an electronic genius, expert at re-wiring discarded electronic ware for resale. But what are survival skills for the two kids become a hot commodity for a crime syndicate who kidnap the pair and force them to use their skills to aid them in crime. "It's a thriller, a survival story, and science fiction all rolled into one tightly developed adventure," commented Heather McCammond-Watts in *Bulletin of the Center for Children's Books.* "Hotwire and Blindboy are meaty characters with plenty of humor, sarcasm, and attitude to spare." Sarah Guille, writing in *Horn Book,* noted that this "action-filled tale, dripping with atmosphere, will please fans of sci-fi and detective stories alike," and Jill Western, writing in *Voice of Youth Advocates,* dubbed *The Electric Kid* a "fast-paced and exciting book ... a great read-aloud or a good choice for reluctant readers." An award-winning title in England as well as a break-through book for Kilworth in the U.S., *The Electric Kid* was followed up with a sequel, *Cybercats,* detailing more adventures of Hotwire and Blindboy.

Kilworth's theory that there is little difference in style and technique between writing for adults and young adults was proved with his 1995 book, *The Bronte Girls.* Kilworth blended his interest in history and fantasy to come up with this tale of the three Bronte sisters— Emily, Anne, and Charlotte—inhabiting a farm in the twentieth century. But past and present soon collide and ultimately force the reader to decide which of the two times and societies is best. Kilworth originally planned the book as an adult title, but could not place it because it did not fit tidily into a genre box, so he subsequently sold it as a YA title, writing it exactly as if it were intended for the adult market. *Books for Keeps,* in its review of the novel, called it a "thought-provoking reality."

For Kilworth, it is this very lack of genre importance which is a saving grace of YA literature. With adult titles, genre is everything, Kilworth contends. But with children's books there are "no tags needed, no explanations required," Kilworth wrote in *Books for Keeps.* "The young readers will either love it or hate it, or remain indifferent to it." Kilworth maintains that the hard and fast lines of genre and categories in adult fiction have ruined individuality in many writers, whereas the writer of children's literature is free simply to tell a story however he or she feels it should be told. Thus far, the smaller world of children's books has allowed for more autonomy. "Long may it remain uncontaminated," Kilworth concluded in *Books for Keeps.*

■ Works Cited

Review of *The Bronte Girls, Books for Keeps,* January, 1996, p. 11.

Review of *Dark Hills, Hollow Clocks, Junior Bookshelf,* December, 1990, p. 297.

Review of *The Drowners, Junior Bookshelf,* December, 1991, p. 264.

Farber, Susan R., review of *The Rain Ghost, Voice of Youth Advocates,* October, 1990, p. 229.

Fisher, Margery, "Tradition in Perpetuity," *Growing Point,* January, 1991, pp. 5442-46.

Guille, Sarah, review of *The Electric Kid, Horn Book,* May-June, 1996, p. 336.

Kilworth, Garry, "My Pal William Brown," *Books for Keeps,* September, 1996, pp. 6-7.

McCammond-Watts, Heather, review of *The Electric Kid, Bulletin of the Center for Children's Books,* November, 1995, p. 95.

Review of *The Phantom Piper, Junior Bookshelf,* December, 1994, pp. 228-29.

Western, Jill, review of *The Electric Kid, Voice of Youth Advocates,* December, 1995, p. 316.

■ For More Information See

PERIODICALS

Booklist, March 15, 1994, p. 1385.
Books for Keeps, November, 1994, pp. 5, 12, 15; March, 1996, p. 12.
Kirkus Reviews, July 15, 1995, p. 1026.
School Librarian, November, 1994, pp. 165-66.
School Library Journal, October, 1995, p. 134.
Times Educational Supplement, November 9, 1990, p. R12; January 17, 1992, p. 28.

—Sketch by J. Sydney Jones

* * *

KNEELAND, Linda Clarke 1947-

■ Personal

Born May 29, 1947, in Baltimore, MD; daughter of Julian Sangston (in sales) and Beatrice (a homemaker; maiden name, Cookling) Clarke; married Chase E. Kneeland (a psychotherapist), December 16, 1972; children: Stephanie, Katie. *Education:* Ursinus College, B.A., 1970; Chestnut Hill College, M.S., 1991. *Religion:* Protestant. *Hobbies and other interests:* Botanical illustration, choir, gardening, developing friendships.

■ Addresses

Home and office—2021 Berks Rd., Lancaster, PA 19446. *Electronic mail*—LindaCKnee @ aol.com.

■ Career

Northwestern Corp., Philadelphia, PA, group therapist, 1991-93; writer, 1993—. *Member:* American Association of University Women, Pennsylvania Horticulture Society, Down Syndrome Interest Group.

■ Writings

Cookie, illustrated by Todd Fargo, Jason & Nordic (Hollidaysburg, PA), 1989.

■ Sidelights

Linda Clarke Kneeland told *SATA:* "I was brought into writing by the publishers at Jason & Nordic because I had written for a local newspaper and was the parent of a five-year-old daughter with Down Syndrome. There is a lack of reading material for children with disabilities, and the mission of the publisher was to provide such books in a story context relevant to these kids.

"The book I wrote was based on our actual experience of having difficulty communicating with my daughter and both her frustrations and our frustrations with that. With the help of a speech therapist who introduced a visual/sensory approach to communication (children's sign language) we were finally, delightedly, able to understand one another.

"I am so grateful to those people who were able to help us, and I was delighted to contribute our story in a way that might help others."

* * *

KONIGSBURG, E(laine) L(obl) 1930-

■ Personal

Born February 10, 1930, in New York, NY; daughter of Adolph (a businessman) and Beulah (maiden name, Klein) Lobl; married David Konigsburg (a psychologist), July 6, 1952; children: Paul, Laurie, Ross. *Education:* Carnegie Mellon University, B.S., 1952; graduate study, University of Pittsburgh, 1952-54. *Religion:* Jewish.

■ Addresses

Office—c/o Atheneum Books for Young Readers, 1230 Avenue of the Americas, New York, NY 10020.

■ Career

Writer. Shenango Valley Provision Co., Sharon, PA, bookkeeper, 1947-48; Bartram School, Jacksonville, FL, science teacher, 1954-55, 1960-62. Worked as manager of a dormitory laundry, playground instructor, waitress, and library page while in college; research assistant in tissue culture lab while in graduate school at the University of Pittsburgh.

■ Awards, Honors

Honor book, *Book Week,* Children's Spring Book Fair, 1967, and Newbery Honor Book, American Library Association (ALA), 1968, both for *Jennifer, Hecate, Macbeth, William McKinley, and Me, Elizabeth;* Newbery Medal, ALA, 1968, and William Allen White Award, 1970, both for *From the Mixed-up Files of Mrs. Basil E. Frankweiler;* Carnegie Mellon Merit Award, 1971; Notable Children's Book, ALA, and National Book Award nomination, both 1974, both for *A Proud Taste for Scarlet and Miniver;* Best Books for Young

Adults, ALA, for *The Second Mrs. Giaconda* and *Father's Arcane Daughter;* Notable Children's Book, ALA, and American Book Award nomination, both 1980, both for *Throwing Shadows; Jennifer, Hecate, Macbeth, William McKinley, and Me, Elizabeth, About the B'nai Bagels, A Proud Taste for Scarlet and Miniver,* and *Journey to an 800 Number* were all chosen Children's Books of the Year by the Child Study Association of America; Notable Children's Book, ALA, Parents' Choice Award for Literature, and NCTE Notable Children's Trade book for the Language Arts, all 1987, all for *Up from Jericho Tel;* Special Recognition Award, Cultural Council of Greater Jacksonville, FL, 1997; Newbery Medal, ALA, 1997, for *The View From Saturday.*

■ Writings

FOR YOUNG PEOPLE; SELF-ILLUSTRATED

Jennifer, Hecate, Macbeth, William McKinley, and Me, Elizabeth, Atheneum, 1967, published in England as *Jennifer, Hecate, MacBeth, and Me,* Macmillan, 1968.
From the Mixed-up Files of Mrs. Basil E. Frankweiler, Atheneum, 1967.
About the B'nai Bagels, Atheneum, 1969.
(George), Atheneum, 1970, published in England as *Benjamin Dickenson Carr and His (George),* Penguin, 1974.
A Proud Taste for Scarlet and Miniver, Atheneum, 1973.
The Dragon in the Ghetto Caper, Atheneum, 1974.
Samuel Todd's Book of Great Colors, Macmillan, 1990.
Samuel Todd's Book of Great Inventions, Atheneum, 1991.
Amy Elizabeth Explores Bloomingdale's, Atheneum, 1992.

FOR YOUNG PEOPLE

Altogether, One at a Time (short stories), illustrated by Gail E. Haley, Mercer Meyer, Gary Parker, and Laurel Schindelman, Atheneum, 1971, 2nd edition, Macmillan, 1989.
The Second Mrs. Giaconda, illustrated with museum plates, Atheneum, 1975.
Father's Arcane Daughter, Atheneum, 1976.
Throwing Shadows (short stories), Atheneum, 1979.
Journey to an 800 Number, Atheneum, 1982, published in England as *Journey by First Class Camel,* Hamish Hamilton, 1983.
Up from Jericho Tel, Atheneum, 1986.
T-Backs, T-Shirts, COAT, and Suit, Atheneum, 1993.
The View From Saturday, Atheneum, 1996.

FOR ADULTS; NONFICTION

The Mask Beneath the Face: Reading about and With, Writing about and For Children, Library of Congress, 1990.
TalkTalk: A Children's Book Author Speaks to Grown-Ups, Atheneum, 1995.

OTHER

Also author of promotional pamphlets for Atheneum and contributor to the Braille anthology, *Expectations 1980,* Braille Institute, 1980.

■ Adaptations

From the Mixed-up Files of Mrs. Basil E. Frankweiler was adapted for a record and cassette, Miller-Brody/Random House, 1969, and Listening Library, 1996; a motion picture, starring Ingrid Bergman, Cinema 5, 1973, released as *The Hideaways,* Bing Crosby Productions, 1974; and a television movie, starring Lauren Bacall, 1995; *Jennifer, Hecate, Macbeth, William McKinley, and Me, Elizabeth* was adapted for a television movie titled *Jennifer and Me,* NBC-TV, 1973, and for a cassette, Listening Library, 1986; *The Second Mrs. Giaconda* was adapted for a play, first produced in Jacksonville, FL, 1976. *Father's Arcane Daughter* was adapted for television as *Caroline?,* for the Hallmark Hall of Fame, 1990.

About the B'nai Bagels and *From the Mixed-up Files of Mrs. Basil E. Frankweiler* are available as Talking Books. *From the Mixed-up Files of Mrs. Basil E. Frankweiler* is also available in Braille.

Collections of E. L. Konigsburg's manuscripts and original art are held at the University of Pittsburgh, Pennsylvania.

■ Sidelights

An impressive figure in children's literature, E. L. Konigsburg is the only author to have had two books on the Newbery list at the same time. *From the Mixed-up Files of Mrs. Basil E. Frankweiler* won the 1968 Newbery Medal and *Jennifer, Hecate, Macbeth, William McKinley, and Me, Elizabeth* was a runner-up for the title in the same year. Konigsburg has also won not one but two of the coveted Newbery Medals, capturing the 1997 award for *The View From Saturday.* Known for her witty and often self-illustrated works for young people, Konigsburg has carved out a unique niche with her score of published books, generally writing out of personal experience, but sometimes also verging far afield to the medieval world and the Renaissance. As Perry Nodelman noted in *Dictionary of Literary Biography,* Konigsburg is an innovator and tireless experimenter, "a creator of interesting messes." The term "messes" is for Nodelman hardly pejorative; rather it is an indication of a truly artistic temperament at work.

Konigsburg did not set her sights on writing as a career until later in life. Born in New York City in 1930, she was the middle of three daughters. She grew up in small towns in Pennsylvania, not only absorbing books such as *The Secret Garden* and *Mary Poppins,* but also much unabashed "trash along the lines of *True Confessions,*" as she once reported in *Saturday Review.* "I have no objection to trash. I've read a lot of it and firmly believe it helped me hone my taste." Konigsburg also mentioned that as a child she did much of her reading in the

E. L. KONIGSBURG (Courtesy of *The Florida Times-Union.*)

bathroom because "it was the only room in our house that had a lock on the door." She also drew often as a child and was a good student in school, graduating valedictorian of her class. Yet for a young person growing up in small mill towns in Pennsylvania as Konigsburg did, college was not necessarily the next step. There were advantages to such an upbringing, however. As Konigsburg has commented, "Growing up in a small town gives you two things: a sense of place and a feeling of self-consciousness—self-consciousness about one's education and exposure, both of which tend to be limited. On the other hand, limited possibilities also means creating your own options. A small town allows you to grow in your own direction, without a bombardment of outside stimulation."

And that is precisely what Konigsburg did—she grew in her own way, and decided to head for college. Completely ignorant of such things as scholarships, she devised a plan whereby she would alternate working for a year with a year of school. The first year out of high school she took a bookkeeping job at a local meat plant where she met the brother of one of the owners—the man who would become her husband, David Konigsburg. The following year, Konigsburg enrolled in Carnegie Mellon University in Pittsburgh, choosing a chemistry major. She survived not a few laboratory accidents to eventually take her degree in chemistry. Early in her college career, however, a helpful instructor directed her to scholarships and work-study assistance, so that she was able to continue her studies without break. Konigsburg noted that college was "a crucial 'opening up'" period.

"I worked hard and did well. However, the artistic side of me was essentially dormant." She graduated with honors, married David Konigsburg, and went on for graduate study at the University of Pittsburgh. Meanwhile, her husband was also studying, preparing himself for a career in industrial psychology. When her husband won a post in Jacksonville, Florida, Konigsburg picked up and moved with him, working for several years as a science teacher in an all-girls school. The teaching experience opened up a new world for Konigsburg, giving her insight into the lives of these young girls whom she expected to be terribly spoiled. But she quickly learned that economic ease did nothing to ease inner problems.

Konigsburg left teaching in 1955 after the birth of her first child, Paul. A year later a daughter, Laurie, was born, and in 1959 a third child, Ross. Konigsburg became a full-time mom, taking some time out, however, to pursue painting. She returned to teaching from 1960-1962 until her husband's work required a move to New York. With all the children in school, Konigsburg then started her writing career. She employed themes and events close to her family life for her books. She also used her children as her first audience, reading them her morning's work when they came home for lunch. Laughter would encourage her to continue in the same vein; glum faces prompted revision and rewrites. Konigsburg commented that she had noticed that her kids were growing up very differently from the way she did, but that their growing up "was related to this middle-class kind of child I had seen when I had taught at the private girls' school. I recognized that I wanted to write something that reflected their kind of growing up, something that addressed the problems that come about even though you don't have to worry if you wear out your shoes whether your parents can buy you a new pair, something that tackles the basic problems of who am I? What makes me the same as everyone else? What makes me different?"

Such questions led Konigsburg to her first two books, *Jennifer, Hecate, Macbeth, William McKinley, and Me, Elizabeth,* inspired by her daughter's experience making friends in their new home in Port Chester, New York, and *From the Mixed-up Files of Mrs. Basil E. Frankweiler,* which was inspired by the finicky manner in which her kids behaved on a picnic. Konigsburg also illustrated both these books, as she has many of her titles, using her children as models. The first novel tells the story of Elizabeth, new in town, and her attempts at finding friendship. It doesn't help that she is small for her age, and Cynthia, the cool kid in school, is quick to dismiss her. But then Elizabeth meets Jennifer, another classic outsider who styles herself as a witch. Elizabeth soon becomes her apprentice, and suddenly life is full of adventures. Jennifer is a source of mystery for Eliza-

beth: she never lets the new girl know where or how she lives, and this is just fine for Elizabeth, smitten by Jennifer to the point of declaring that even if she "discovered that Jennifer lived in an ordinary house and did ordinary things, I would know it was a disguise."

Nodelman, writing in *Dictionary of Literary Biography,* noted that, baldly told, the story sounds like a "typical wish-fulfillment novel.... [But] as its title suggests this is no ordinary novel. It is too witty." As Nodelman pointed out, Elizabeth comes face to face with the important issue of what it means to be "normal," and decides not to worry about that. "The idea that it is better to be yourself than to be 'normal' and accepted by others transcends the cheap egocentricity of most wish-fulfillment fantasies," according to Nodelman. It is this extra dimension of story-telling that has set Konigsburg apart from other children's writers from the outset of her career. She eschews the easy solution and turns cliches on their head. Critical reception for this first book was quite positive. Ruth P. Bull in *Booklist* called it "a fresh, lively story, skillfully expressed," and a contributor in *Publishers Weekly* warned against allowing a too-cute title to scare readers away from "one of

Amy Elizabeth visits her grandmother in New York City, where the two enjoy many interesting diversions as they make their daily rescheduled trips to shop at Bloomingdale's. (From *Amy Elizabeth Explores Bloomingdale's,* written and illustrated by Konigsburg.)

the freshest, funniest books of the season." This same reviewer went on presciently to say that the reader will have "the smug pleasure" of saying in later years—when the author would surely make a name for herself—that he or she had read Konigsburg when she was just beginning. Writing in *Horn Book,* Ruth Hill Viguers also praised the book, noting that the story "is full of humor and of situations completely in tune with the imaginations of ten-year-old girls."

Konigsburg's second novel, *From the Mixed-up Files of Mrs. Basil E. Frankweiler,* was published shortly after her first. Following a family picnic in Yellowstone Park in which Konigsburg's children complained of the insects and the warm milk and the general lack of civilization, Konigsburg came to the realization that if they should ever run away from home, they would surely carry with them all the stuffy suburban ways that were so inbred in them. This started her thinking of a pair of children who run away from home to the Metropolitan Museum of Art, a safe sort of imitation of far-away places. Claudia, tired of being taken for granted at home, plans to run away and takes her younger brother Jamie—the one with a sense for finances—with her on this safe adventure. Together they elude guards at the Met, sleep on royal beds, bathe in the cafeteria pool, and hang about lecture tours during the day. Their arrival at the museum coincides with the showing of a recent museum acquisition, a marble angel believed to have been sculpted by Michelangelo. Soon they are under the spell of the angel and want to know the identity of the carver, and this brings them to the statue's former owner, Mrs. Frankweiler. The story is narrated in the form of a letter from Mrs. Frankweiler to her lawyer, and it is she who confronts Claudia with the truth about herself. "Returning with a secret is what she really wants," says Mrs. Frankweiler. "Claudia doesn't want adventure. She likes baths and feeling comfortable too much for that kind of thing. Secrets are the kind of adventure she needs. Secrets are safe, and they do much to make you different. On the inside, where it counts."

Booklist reviewer Ruth Bull concluded that this second novel was "fresh and crisply written" with "uncommonly real and likable characters," and Bull praised the humor and dialogue as well. Viguers, writing in *Horn Book,* noted that the novel violated every rule of writing for children, yet was still "one of the most original stories of many years." A critic in *Kirkus Reviews* commented that whereas Konigsburg's first title was a "dilly," this one was a "dandy—just as fast and fresh and funny, but less spoofing, more penetrating." Plaudits continued from Alice Fleming in the *New York Times Book Review,* who noted that Konigsburg "is a lively, amusing and painlessly educational storyteller," and from Polly Goodwin writing in *Washington Post Book World,* who commented that the book is "an exceptional story, notable for superlative writing, fresh humor, an original theme, clear-eyed understanding of children, and two young protagonists whom readers will find funny, real and unforgettable." Award committees agreed with the reviewers, and for the first time in its

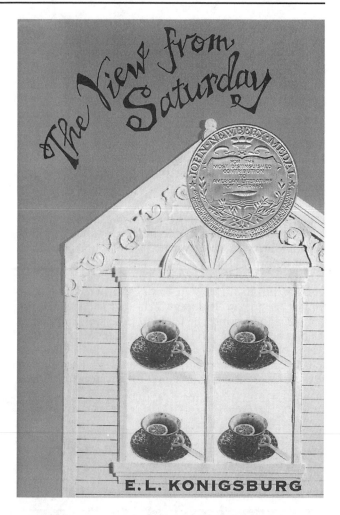

Konigsburg's Newbery Medal-winning novel portrays the growing bond between four sensitive, gifted members of a sixth-grade championship quiz bowl team and their paraplegic teacher. (Cover illustration by the author.)

history, the Newbery list contained two titles by the same author.

In Konigsburg's acceptance speech for her first Newbery, she talked about her overriding feeling of owing kids a good story. "[I try to] let the telling be like fudge-ripple ice cream. You keep licking the vanilla, but every now and then you come to something richer and deeper and with a stronger flavor." Her books all explore this richer and deeper territory, while employing humor in large doses. However, instant success is a hard act to follow, and her third book, *About the B'nai Bagels,* a Little League baseball story with a Jewish Mother twist, was not as well received as the first two. A further suburban tale is *(George),* Konigsburg's "most unusual, messiest, and most interesting book," according to Nodelman in *Dictionary of Literary Biography.* Ben is a twelve-year-old with an inner voice he calls George who acts as a sort of higher intelligence and conscience for the boy. When Ben, who is a bright student, is placed in a high school chemistry class, George starts acting out, causing a crisis of identity.

A fascination for medieval times led Konigsburg to a major departure from suburban themes with her *A Proud Taste for Scarlet and Miniver,* a historical fantasy—told from the participants' points of view in heaven—about the life of Eleanor of Aquitaine. Though some critics found the book to be too modern for the subject, Zena Sutherland in *Bulletin of the Center for Children's Books* called it "one of the most fresh, imaginative, and deft biographies to come along in a long, long time." Paul Heins, writing in *Horn Book,* also noted that Konigsburg's drawings "are skillfully as well as appropriately modelled upon medieval manuscript illuminations and add their share of joy to the book." Following in this historical vein is *The Second Mrs. Giaconda,* the story of Leonardo da Vinci's middle years. Konigsburg posits a solution to the riddle of the Mona Lisa and serves up a "unique bit of creative historical interpretation" with a glimpse of Renaissance culture she has "artfully and authentically illumined," according to Shirley M. Wilton in *School Library Journal.* Another more experimental novel—though in theme rather than period—is *Father's Arcane Daughter,* a mystery. The novel tells of the return of Caroline after having been kidnapped and presumed dead seventeen years earlier. The story focuses on the effects of Caroline's reappearance on her father, his new wife, and their children in a "haunting, marvelously developed plot," according to a reviewer in *Publishers Weekly.*

Konigsburg returned to more familiar ground with *The Dragon in the Ghetto Caper* and *Throwing Shadows,* the latter a group of short stories nominated for an American Book Award. Both *Journey to an 800 Number* and *Amy Elizabeth Explores Bloomingdale's* are vintage Konigsburg, the second of which tells the story of a girl and her grandmother trying to find the time to see Bloomingdale's. *Up from Jericho Tel* relates the encounter between the ghost of a dead actress and two children, who are turned invisible and sent out with a group of street performers to search for a missing necklace. "A witty, fast-paced story," is how a reviewer in *Publishers Weekly* characterized the novel. *Bulletin of the Center for Children's Books,* in its review, provided a summation of Konigsburg's distinctive gift to children's literature: "Whether she is writing a realistic or a fanciful story, Konigsburg always provides fresh ideas, tart wit and humor, and memorable characters."

With *T-Backs, T-Shirts, COAT, and Suit,* Konigsburg proved that she not only still had the knack for a weird title but also for telling a story. Young Chloe spends the summer in Florida with her stepfather's sister, who runs a meals-on-wheels van and becomes involved in a controversy over T-back swimming suits. Rachel Axelrod, reviewing the book in *Voice of Youth Advocates,* concluded that Konigsburg "has produced another winner!"

The View From Saturday tells the story of four members of a championship quiz bowl team and the paraplegic teacher who coaches them. A series of first-person narratives from the students display links between their lives in a story that is "glowing with humor and dusted with magic," according to a critic in *Publishers Weekly.* Julie Cummins in *School Library Journal* concluded that "brilliant writing melds with crystalline characterizations in this sparkling story that is a jewel in the author's crown of outstanding work." Konigsburg won the 1997 Newbery Medal for this novel, her second in three decades of writing. Commenting on *The View From Saturday* in relation to Konigsburg's previous medal winner, *The Mixed-up Files of Mrs. Basil E. Frankweiler,* the author's daughter, Laurie Konigsburg Todd, commented in *Horn Book:* "Although the inspiration for these Newbery books was as disparate as the three decades which separate their publication, their theme is the same. In fact, every one of E. L. Konigsburg's fourteen novels are about children who seek, find, and ultimately enjoy who they are. Despite this common denominator, [her] writing is the antithesis of the formula book. Her characters are one-of-a-kind."

Some of Konigsburg's characters, such as Jennifer, Elizabeth, and Claudia, have become not only best friends to readers, but also telegraphic symbols of complex emotions and adolescent conditions. "The strong demands Konigsburg makes of her characters and the fine moral intelligence she gives them imply much respect for children, a respect she has continued to express in all of her books," asserted Nodelman. A writer who takes her craft seriously yet manages to avoid heavy-handed thematic writing, Konigsburg views children's books as "the primary vehicle for keeping alive the means of linear learning," as she wrote in *TalkTalk: A Children's Book Author Speaks to Grown-Ups.* "[Children's books] are the key to the accumulated wisdom, wit, gossip, truth, myth, history, philosophy, and recipes for salting potatoes during the past 6,000 years of civilization. Children's books are the Rosetta Stone to the hearts and minds of writers from Moses to Mao. And that is the last measure in the growth of children's literature as I've witnessed it—a growing necessity." It is a necessity that Konigsburg has elegantly served.

■ Works Cited

Axelrod, Rachel, review of *T-Backs, T-Shirts, COAT and Suit, Voice of Youth Advocates,* December, 1993, p. 254.

Bull, Ruth P., review of *Jennifer, Hecate, Macbeth, William McKinley, and Me, Elizabeth, Booklist,* June 1, 1967, p. 1048.

Bull Ruth P., review of *From the Mixed-up Files of Mrs. Basil E. Frankweiler, Booklist,* October 1, 1967, p. 199.

Cummins, Julie, review of *The View From Saturday, School Library Journal,* September, 1996, p. 204.

Review of *Father's Arcane Daughter, Publishers Weekly,* July 19, 1976, p. 132.

Fleming, Alice, review of *From the Mixed-up Files of Mrs. Basil E. Frankweiler, New York Times Book Review,* November 5, 1967, p. 44.

Review of *From the Mixed-up Files of Mrs. Basil E. Frankweiler, Kirkus Reviews,* July 1, 1967, p. 740.

Goodwin, Polly, review of *From the Mixed-up Files of Mrs. Basil E. Frankweiler, Washington Post Book World,* November 5, 1967, p. 22.

Heins, Paul, review of *A Proud Taste for Scarlet and Miniver, Horn Book,* October, 1973, pp. 466-67.

Review of *Jennifer, Hecate, Macbeth, William McKinley, and Me, Elizabeth, Publishers Weekly,* April 10, 1967, p. 80.

Konigsburg, E. L., "A Book is a Private Thing," *Saturday Review,* November 9, 1968, pp. 45-46.

Konigsburg, E. L., *From the Mixed-up Files of Mrs. Basil E. Frankweiler,* Atheneum, 1967.

Konigsburg. E. L., *Jennifer, Hecate, Macbeth, William McKinley, and Me, Elizabeth,* Atheneum, 1967.

Konigsburg, E. L., "Newbery Award Acceptance," *Horn Book,* August, 1968, pp. 391-95.

Konigsburg, E. L., *TalkTalk: A Children's Book Author Speaks to Grown-Ups,* Atheneum, 1995.

Nodelman, Perry, "E. L. Konigsburg," *Dictionary of Literary Biography, Volume 52: American Writers for Children from 1960, Fiction,* Gale, 1986, pp. 214-27.

Sutherland, Zena, review of *A Proud Taste for Scarlet and Miniver, Bulletin of the Center for Children's Books,* September, 1973, pp. 10-11.

Todd, Laurie Konigsburg, "E. L. Konigsburg," *Horn Book,* July-August, 1997, pp. 415-17.

Review of *Up from Jericho Tel, Bulletin of the Center for Children's Books,* March, 1986, p. 131.

Review of *Up from Jericho Tel, Publishers Weekly,* April 25, 1986, p. 80.

Review of *The View From Saturday, Publishers Weekly,* July 22, 1996, p. 242.

Viguers, Ruth Hill, review of *Jennifer, Hecate, Macbeth, William McKinley, and Me, Elizabeth, Horn Book,* April, 1967, pp. 206-07.

Viguers, Ruth Hill, review of *From the Mixed-up Files of Mrs. Basil E. Frankweiler, Horn Book,* October, 1967, p. 595.

Wilton, Shirley M., review of *The Second Mrs. Giaconda, School Library Journal,* September, 1975, p. 121.

■ For More Information See

BOOKS

Hanks, Dorrel Thomas, *E. L. Konigsburg,* Twayne, 1992.

Schwartz, Narda, *Articles on Women Writers,* Volume 2, ABC-Clio, 1986.

Twentieth-Century Children's Writers, Fourth Edition, St. James Press, 1995.

PERIODICALS

Booklist, May 1, 1986, p. 1313.

Bulletin of the Center for Children's Books, June, 1967, p. 155; February, 1971, p. 94; September, 1971, pp. 10-11; January, 1976, p. 80; September, 1976, p. 12; September, 1979, p. 10; March, 1982, p. 133; May, 1990, p. 216; September, 1992, p. 16; November, 1993, p. 88.

Growing Point, November, 1983, pp. 4161-64.

Horn Book, June, 1969, p. 307; October, 1975, pp. 470-71; June, 1982, pp. 289-90; May/June, 1986, p. 327; July-August, 1997, pp. 404-14.

Kirkus Reviews, July 1, 1973, p. 685; February 1, 1986, p. 209.

New York Times Book Review, March 30, 1969, p. 29; June 8, 1969, p. 44; October 20, 1974, p. 10; November 7, 1976, p. 44; July 5, 1980, p. 19; May 25, 1986, p. 25; April 10, 1994, p. 35; November 10, 1996, p. 49.

Publishers Weekly, September 28, 1970, pp. 78-79.

School Library Journal, September, 1979, p. 141; May, 1982, p. 72; April, 1983, p. 122; May, 1986, p. 93; March, 1990, p. 208; October, 1991, p. 98; September, 1992, p. 206; October, 1993, p. 124; December, 1993, p. 26; February, 1996, p. 42.

Teaching and Learning Literature, May/June, 1997, p. 75.

Voice of Youth Advocates, December, 1986, p. 219; December, 1995, p. 335.

—*Sketch by J. Sydney Jones*

*   *   *

KRESH, Paul 1919-1997

OBITUARY NOTICE—See index for *SATA* sketch: Born December 3, 1919, in New York, NY; died of Parkinson's disease, January 12, 1997, in New York, NY. Publicist, broadcaster, record producer, critic, author. Kresh was a prolific writer who dabbled in various forms of the craft throughout his career. He is remembered for his work with spoken-word recordings, which captured readings by famous writers such as E. E. Cummings, Allen Ginsberg, and Gertrude Stein, among others. Kresh worked as a publicist for various firms throughout his career, including the National Jewish Welfare Board, United Jewish Appeal, American Organization for Rehabilitation through Training, and Richard Cohen Associates. In addition to handling publicity for the Union of American Hebrew Congregations, he also edited the organization's *American Judaism* magazine from 1959 to 1967. He served as vice president of Spoken Arts, Inc. until 1970, then joined Caedmon Records for two years. He began work as a consultant in 1981, operating Paul Kresh Communications, Inc. Author of a monthly column for several periodicals, he was also a music critic. His articles appeared in publications such as *Stereo Review, High Fidelity, Audiofile, Victorian, Jewish Week,* and *Classical Music.* He wrote scripts for television programs, including *Trial in Heaven,* and he wrote the screenplay for *The Day the Doors Closed.* His books include *Tales Out of Congress, Isaac Bashevis Singer: The Story of a Storyteller,* and *An American Rhapsody: The Story of George Gershwin.* He received numerous honors for his work, including an Emmy Award in 1980.

OBITUARIES AND OTHER SOURCES:

PERIODICALS

New York Times, January 16, 1997, p. D25.

KUBINYI, Laszlo 1937-

■ Personal

Born December 20, 1937, in Cleveland, OH; son of professional artists; married to Suzanne Kubinyi (a special education teacher). *Education:* Attended School of the Museum of Fine Arts in Boston, and School of Visual Arts and the Art Students League in New York City.

■ Addresses

Home and office—115 Evergreen Pl., Teaneck, NJ 07666-4920.

■ Career

Author and illustrator of children's books; illustrator for editorial, advertising, and medical fields. Has traveled throughout the world, and played a *dumbek* (a Middle-Eastern drum) in Armenian, Turkish, and Arabic musical groups.

■ Awards, Honors

Grammy Award nomination, National Academy of Recording Arts and Sciences, 1967, for "best album cover"; Canadian Library Association award, 1969, for *And Tomorrow the Stars: The Story of John Cabot* by Kay Hill; American Library Association Notable Book and New York Times Notable Book, both 1972, both for *The Haunted Mountain* by Maureen Mollie Hunter McIlwraith; Children's Book Showcase award, 1974, for *Peter the Revolutionary Tsar*, by Peter Brock Putnam; Fifty Books of the Year, AIGA, 1974, for *Our Fathers Had Powerful Songs*, edited by Natalia Maree Belting; "Certicficate of Excellence," AIGA, 1977, for *The Town Cats and Other Tales*, written by Lloyd Alexander; Andy Award of Merit, 1979.

■ Writings

SELF-ILLUSTRATED

The Cat and the Flying Machine, Simon & Schuster, 1970.

Zeki and the Talking Cat Shukru, Simon & Schuster, 1970.

ILLUSTRATOR

Paul Anderson, *The Fox, the Dog, and the Griffin*, Doubleday, 1966.

Cristoforo Columbo, *Across the Ocean Sea: A Journal of Columbus's Voyage*, edited by George Sanderlin, Harper, 1966.

William C. Harrison, *Dr. William Harvey and the Discovery of Circulation*, Macmillan, 1967.

Kay Hill, *And Tomorrow the Stars: The Story of John Cabot*, Dodd, 1968.

Coralie Howard, *What Do You Want to Know?*, Simon & Schuster, 1968.

Martin Gardner, *Perplexing Puzzles and Tantalizing Teasers*, Simon & Schuster, 1969.

Robert Froman, *Science, Art, and Visual Illusions*, Simon & Schuster, 1969.

Jeanne B. Hardendorff, *Witches, Wit, and a Werewolf*, Lippincott, 1971.

Betty Jean Lifton, *The Silver Crane*, Seabury, 1971.

Adrien Stoutenburg, *Haran's Journey*, Dial, 1971.

Tony Hillerman, *The Boy Who Made Dragonfly: A Zuni Myth*, Harper, 1972.

Maureen Mollie Hunter McIlwraith, *The Haunted Mountain*, Harper, 1972.

F. N. Monjo, *Slater's Mill*, Simon & Schuster, 1972.

Morton Friend, *The Vanishing Tungus: The Story of a Remarkable Reindeer People*, Dial, 1972.

David C. Knight, *Poltergeists: Hauntings and the Haunted*, Lippincott, 1972.

Arthur S. Gregor, *Witchcraft and Magic: The Supernatural World*, Scribner, 1972.

Peter Brock Putnam, *Peter the Revolutionary Tsar*, Harper, 1973.

Felice Holman, *I Hear You Smiling, and Other Poems*, Scribner, 1973.

Maia Wojciechowska, *Winter Tales from Poland*, Doubleday, 1973.

Natalia Maree Belting, editor, *Our Fathers Had Powerful Songs*, Dutton, 1974.

Lloyd Alexander, *The Wizard in the Tree*, Dutton, 1975.

Margaret Greaves, *The Dagger and the Bird: A Story of Suspense*, Harper, 1975.

Ellen Pugh, *The Adventures of Yoo-Lah-Teen: A Legend of the Salish Coastal Indians*, Dial, 1975.

Miriam Anne Bourne, *Patsy Jefferson's Diary*, Coward, 1975.

Martin Gardner, *More Perplexing Puzzles and Tantalizing Teasers*, Archway, 1977.

Lloyd Alexander, *The Town Cats and Other Tales*, Dutton, 1977.

Brigid Clark and Christopher Noel, *The Gingham Dog and the Calico Cat: Season of Harmony*, Rabbit Ears Books, 1990.

Tom Roberts, adaptor, *Goldilocks*, Rabbit Ears Books, 1990.

Tom Roberts, adaptor, *Red Riding Hood*, Rabbit Ears Books, 1991.

Nomi Joval, *Room of Mirrors*, Wonder Well, 1991.

Mary Blount Christian, *Who'd Believe John Colter?*, Macmillan, 1993.

Nomi Joval, *Color of Light*, Wonder Well, 1993.

Nomi Joval, *Power of Glass*, Wonder Well, 1993.

Mihai Spariosu and Dezso Benedek, retellers, *Ghosts, Vampires, and Werewolves: Eerie Tales from Transylvania*, Orchard, 1994.

Roy Edwin Thomas, compiler, *Come Go with Me: Old-Timer Stories from the Southern Mountains*, Farrar, Straus & Giroux, 1994.

Roger B. Swain, *Earthly Pleasures: Tales from a Biologist's Garden*, Lyons & Burford, 1994.

Sea of Cortes, Copper Canyon (travel guide), Secretaria de Turismo, Mexico, 1994.

Kelly Trumble, *Cat Mummies*, Clarion, 1996.

Goldilocks and *Red Riding Hood*, narrated by Meg Ryan and containing over two hundred illustrations by Kubinyi, and *The Gingham Dog and the Calico Cat: Season of Harmony,* narrated by Amy Grant with illustrations also by Kubinyi, were originally produced as vidoetapes.

■ Sidelights

Laszlo Kubinyi believes children are influenced by the literature they read and that he, as a children's book illustrator, must be careful not to convey racism, sexism, or unnecessary violence in his work. Kubinyi's self-illustrated storybooks for children include *The Cat and the Flying Machine* and *Zeki and the Talking Cat Shukru.* Although the latter title was not widely reviewed, *The Cat and the Flying Machine* was noted for its far-fetched, whimsical story. This picture book centers on the adventures of Shukru, a talking cat who gets involved in a revolution while trying to rescue an alchemist from the dungeon of an evil Count. Kubinyi's illustrations are "soft-toned and pleasant," according to a reviewer in *New York Times Book Review.*

Kubinyi, who is primarily an illustrator, has contributed to numerous picture books, some of which, like his own stories, feature cats as main characters. Notable among these is *Cat Mummies,* by Kelly Trumble, a nonfiction exploration of the role of cats in the lives of the ancient Egyptians. In a laudatory review in *Booklist,* Ilene Cooper singled out Kubinyi's illustrations as an "enormous help" to the author who has to introduce unfamiliar terms and an ancient, foreign culture without losing her audience. "The delightful watercolors not only visually expand the text," Cooper contended, "but also have an easy, inviting quality to them that draws readers right in."

While the reviewer of *Cat Mummies* for *Kirkus Reviews* failed to echo Cooper's high estimation of the author's abilities, it was stated that "Kubinyi's highly detailed, softly colored drawings bring immediacy to ancient events and objects." Likewise, other critics view Kubinyi's illustrations as enhancements to the text. Thus, though a critic in *Kirkus Reviews* complained that Mary Blount Christian's text in *Who'd Believe John Colter?* contains the author's conjectures about the inner thoughts and feelings of historical figures, the critic stated that Kubinyi's drawings, "recalling 19th-century engravings, contribute nicely to an inviting format." Well-regarded works, such as *Come Go with Me: Old-Timer Stories from the Southern Mountains,* Roy Edwin Thomas's collection of tales about life among mountain people in the late part of the nineteenth century, are similarly considered to be augmented by what *Bulletin of the Center for Children's Books* reviewer Betsy Hearne referred to as Kubinyi's "incisive pen-and-ink crosshatch drawings."

■ Works Cited

Review of *The Cat and the Flying Machine, New York Times Book Review,* February 21, 1971, p. 22.

Review of *Cat Mummies, Kirkus Reviews,* July 15, 1996, p. 1057.

Cooper, Ilene, review of *Cat Mummies, Booklist,* September 15, 1996, p. 236.

Hearne, Betsy, review of *Come Go with Me: Old-Timer Stories from the Southern Mountains, Bulletin of the Center for Children's Books,* March, 1994, pp. 235-36.

Review of *Who'd Believe John Colter?, Kirkus Reviews,* June 1, 1993, p. 717.

■ For More Information See

PERIODICALS

Bulletin of the Center for Children's Books, November, 1969, p. 46; November, 1973, p. 50.

Kirkus Reviews, July 1, 1968, p. 701; October 15, 1970, p. 1148; May 1, 1994, pp. 637-38.

Publishers Weekly, May 31, 1993, p. 55; February 21, 1994, p. 256.

School Library Journal, August, 1993, p. 170; October, 1994, p. 140.

L

ELAINE LANDAU

LANDAU, Elaine 1948-

■ Personal

Born February 15, 1948, in Lakewood, NJ; daughter of James and May (a department store manager; maiden name, Tudor) Garmiza; married Edward William Landau (an electrical engineer), December 16, 1968; children: Michael Brent. *Education:* New York University, B.A., 1970; Pratt Institute, M.L.S., 1975. *Religion:* Jewish. *Hobbies and other interests:* Botany.

■ Addresses

Home—15720 Southwest 72nd Street, Suite 301, Miami, FL 33193.

■ Career

Reporter on community newspaper in New York City, 1970-72; Simon & Schuster, New York City, editor, 1972-73; Tuckahoe Public Library, Tuckahoe, NY, director, 1975-79. *Member:* National Organization for Women, Women's Equity Action League, American Library Association.

■ Awards, Honors

New Jersey Institute of Technology awards, 1977, for both *Death: Everyone's Heritage* and *Hidden Heroines: Women in American History,* 1981, for both *Occult Visions: A Mystical Gaze into the Future* and *The Teen Guide to Dating,* and 1989, for both *Alzheimer's Disease* and *Surrogate Mothers.*

■ Writings

(With Jesse Jackson) *Black in America: A Fight for Freedom,* Messner, 1973.
Woman, Woman! Feminism in America, Messner, 1974.
Hidden Heroines: Women in American History, Messner, 1975.
Death: Everyone's Heritage, Messner, 1976.
Yoga for You, Messner, 1977.
Occult Visions: A Mystical Gaze into the Future, illustrated by Carol Gjertsen, Messner, 1979.
The Teen Guide to Dating, Messner, 1980.
The Smart Spending Guide for Teens, Messner, 1982.
Why Are They Starving Themselves?: Understanding Anorexia Nervosa and Bulimia, Messner, 1983.
Child Abuse: An American Epidemic, Messner, 1984, second edition, 1990.
Growing Old in America, Messner, 1985.

Different Drummer: Homosexuality in America, Messner, 1986.

Sexually Transmitted Diseases, Enslow, 1986.

Alzheimer's Disease, Franklin Watts, 1987.

The Homeless, Messner, 1987.

On the Streets: The Lives of Adolescent Prostitutes, Messner, 1987.

Surrogate Mothers, Franklin Watts, 1988.

Teenagers Talk about School—and Open Their Hearts about Their Closest Concerns, Messner, 1988.

The Sioux, Franklin Watts, 1989.

Black Market Adoption and the Sale of Children, Franklin Watts, 1990.

Cowboys, Franklin Watts, 1990.

Teenage Violence, Messner, 1990.

Tropical Rain Forests around the World, Franklin Watts, 1990.

Nazi War Criminals, Franklin Watts, 1990.

Lyme Disease, Franklin Watts, 1990.

We Have AIDS, Franklin Watts, 1990.

Weight: A Teenage Concern, Lodestar, 1991.

Wildflowers around the World, Franklin Watts, 1991.

We Survived the Holocaust, Franklin Watts, 1991.

Armed America: The Status of Gun Control, Messner, 1991.

Dyslexia, Franklin Watts, 1991.

Mars, Franklin Watts, 1991.

Chemical and Biological Warfare, Lodestar, 1991.

Interesting Invertebrates: A Look at Some Animals without Backbones, Franklin Watts, 1991.

Colin Powell: Four-Star General, Franklin Watts, 1991.

Jupiter, Franklin Watts, 1991.

Robert Fulton, Franklin Watts, 1991.

Saturn, Franklin Watts, 1991.

Neptune, Franklin Watts, 1991.

Endangered Plants, Franklin Watts, 1992.

The Warsaw Ghetto Uprising, New Discovery, 1992.

Terrorism: America's Growing Threat, Lodestar, 1992.

Big Brother Is Watching: Secret Police and Intelligence Services, Walker, 1992.

Teens and the Death Penalty, Enslow, 1992.

The Cherokees, Franklin Watts, 1992.

State Birds: Including the Commonwealth of Puerto Rico, Franklin Watts, 1992.

State Flowers: Including the Commonwealth of Puerto Rico, Franklin Watts, 1992.

Bill Clinton, Franklin Watts, 1993.

Sexual Harassment, Walker, 1993.

Yeti: Abominable Snowman of the Himalayas, Millbrook Press, 1993.

The White Power Movement: America's Racist Hate Groups, Millbrook Press, 1993.

Sasquatch: Wild Man of the Woods, Millbrook Press, 1993.

The Loch Ness Monster, Millbrook Press, 1993.

Rabies, Lodestar, 1993.

The Right to Die, Franklin Watts, 1993.

Interracial Dating and Marriage, Messner, 1993.

Environmental Groups: The Earth Savers, Enslow, 1993.

Allergies, Twenty-first Century Books, 1994.

Epilepsy, Twenty-first Century Books, 1994.

Deafness, Twenty-first Century Books, 1994.

Teenage Drinking, Enslow, 1994.

The Chilulas, Franklin Watts, 1994.

Blindness, Twenty-first Century Books, 1994.

The Beauty Trap, New Discovery, 1994.

Sibling Rivalry: Brothers and Sisters at Odds, Millbrook Press, 1994.

Diabetes, Twenty-first Century Books, 1994.

The Pomo, Franklin Watts, 1994.

Cancer, Twenty-first Century Books, 1994.

The Hopi, Franklin Watts, 1994.

Breast Cancer, Franklin Watts, 1995.

Your Legal Rights: From Custody Battles to School Searches, the Headline-making Cases that Affect Your Life, Walker, 1995.

Hooked: Talking about Addiction, Millbrook Press, 1995.

Ghosts, Millbrook Press, 1995.

Tuberculosis, Franklin Watts, 1995.

The Abenaki, Franklin Watts, 1996.

Temperate Forest Mammals, Children's Press, 1996.

Tropical Forest Mammals, Children's Press, 1996.

ESP, Millbrook Press, 1996.

UFO's, Millbrook Press, 1996.

Mountain Mammals, Children's Press, 1996.

Stalking, Franklin Watts, 1996.

The Ottawas, Franklin Watts, 1996.

Fortune Telling, Millbrook Press, 1996.

Foretelling the Future, Millbrook Press, 1996.

Grassland Mammals, Children's Press, 1996.

Desert Mammals, Children's Press, 1996.

Ocean Mammals, Children's Press, 1996.

Near-Death Experiences, Millbrook Press, 1996.

The Shawnee, Franklin Watts, 1996.

The Curse of Tutankhamen, Millbrook Press, 1996.

Bill Clinton and His Presidency, Franklin Watts, 1997.

Joined at Birth: The Lives of Conjoined Twins, Franklin Watts, 1997.

Short Stature: From Folklore to Fact, Franklin Watts, 1997.

Standing Tall: Unusually Tall People, Franklin Watts, 1997.

The Sumerians, Millbrook Press, 1997.

Contributor of reviews to *New York Times Book Review*.

■ Work in Progress

A series of books for young readers on dinosaurs.

■ Sidelights

A prolific author of nonfiction for younger readers, Elaine Landau has been praised by reviewers for her well-researched and well-written books. In topics ranging from the legendary Loch Ness Monster to the presidency of Bill Clinton, and from UFO's and ESP to up-to-the minute advances in Alzheimer's Disease research, Landau presents factual information often highlighted by case studies, interviews, and other information that provides readers with added insight into the topic at hand.

Many of Landau's books have been of particular interest to modern teens facing a far different world than that of previous generations, a fact that makes older nonfiction books irrelevant. Eating disorders are dealt with in detail in *Why Are They Starving Themselves? Understanding Anorexia Nervosa and Bulimia,* which contains interviews with several women and teens, as well as a list of resources on where to get help for both anorexics and their families. Landau's related work, *Weight: A Teenage Concern,* published in 1991, examines the social pressures on young women to be thin, and the prejudice that overweight teens often face. "Readers will enjoy the testimonials of teens and appreciate the author's nonjudgmental tone," according to *Voice of Youth Advocates* reviewer Joyce Hamilton. *The Beauty Trap,* which Landau published in 1994, focuses on the root cause of eating disorders: society's obsession with physical beauty and how that obsession is internalized and acted upon by women. Providing basic information on the consequences of falling into the beauty trap in four chapters, the book also includes a list of organizations that offers readers more information on ways to break the cycle. "Landau's insightful and disturbing examination" of modern culture's obsession with the physical appearance of women and girls "should be required reading for all young girls, their parents, and their teachers," according to Jeanne Triner in *Booklist.*

Landau scrutinizes the fashion and beauty industries along with the media and their often damaging influences on young women's self-perceptions. (Cover photo by Rick Mastelli.)

Other books of interest to teen readers have concerned topics of equal seriousness. *Teenage Drinking,* published in 1994, involves readers in the personal life of teens whose lives are controlled by the out-of-control drinking of either themselves or someone close to them. Praised for her ability to "reveal the impact and danger of alcoholism much more clearly and compellingly than the typical statistics and charts" by *Voice of Youth Advocates* reviewer Joanne Eglash, Landau combines stories of young alcoholics with information and advice to family members and friends. Similarly, in *Hooked: Talking about Addiction,* the author divides her discussion into causes of addiction, its effect, and the steps that must be taken in the recovery process. *Teenagers Talk about School—and Open Their Hearts about Their Concerns,* which features interviews with a wide variety of students across the United States, encompasses many of the topics covered in more detail in Landau's other books. "Teens will surely recognize themselves and their friends in Landau's bittersweet mosaic of the American teen social environment," according to Libby K. White, reviewing the 1989 work for *School Library Journal.*

Sexuality figures prominently in teen life, and Landau has written several books dealing with various aspects of human sexual relationships, from dating to marriage. *Interracial Dating and Marriage* covers everything from the history of cross-race relationships between men and women to interviews with those involved with partners of a different race. White praised the book in *School Library Journal,* calling Landau's approach "warmly supportive of those who find love outside their own group," adding that "there is no attempt to minimize potential difficulties." Concerns over the medical hazards associated with sexual intercourse are covered in 1987's *Sexually Transmitted Diseases* and *We Have AIDS,* a 1990 work that "will surely help to dispel the notion among teenagers that, 'it can't happen to me,'" according to *Appraisal* reviewer Tippin McDaniel. Landau speaks with nine young adults that have contracted the deadly disease, illustrating the fact that AIDS does strike across racial, cultural, and economic boundaries. The AIDS epidemic also serves as one of Landau's topics in her *Different Drummer: Homosexuality in America.* Examining homosexuality as it currently exists throughout the American social fabric—from same-sex parenting to homophobia—the author "aims to foster a better understanding of homosexuality rather than to offer direct support to those who are questioning their sexual orientation," in the words of Stephanie Zvirin in *Booklist.*

In addition to such broader topics as Native American tribal history, wildlife studies, and medicine, social issues such as child abuse, sexual harassment, homelessness, and surrogate parenting have also come under scrutiny in several of Landau's books. *The Homeless,* published in 1988, features several interviews that illustrate the serious plight of Americans with no permanent place to live. Landau's "writing is sober, the text carefully organized, the topic important," noted Zena Sutherland in *Bulletin of the Center for Children's Books.* In *Surrogate Mothers,* the author discusses the

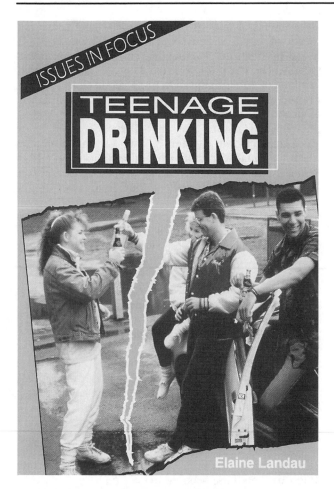

ISSUES IN FOCUS

TEENAGE DRINKING

Elaine Landau

In this study of adolescent alcoholism, Landau spotlights the experiences of teens whose lives have been profoundly impacted by their obsession with drinking or by the addiction of someone close to them. (Cover illustration by J. Greenberg.)

various causes of infertility, and the ethics involved in some of the solutions to this problem. In addition to providing an in-depth examination of the "Baby M" case, Landau also includes several other case studies involving couples who wished to have children but, for various reasons, were unable to either bear children of their own or adopt. "The clarity of the writing and the organization of the material work together to capture and hold the reader's interest," commented Leonard J. Garigliano in *Appraisal.*

Born in New Jersey in 1948, Landau had written her first book by the time she was nine years old, composing it "in the children's room of my local library," as she once recalled to *SATA.* "I spent a lot of time in that room, reading and growing, while remaining safely hidden from a mother, older sister, and aunt who assured me that to dream of becoming an author was an unrealistic career aspiration." But Landau was not to be discouraged by the advice of her family. "The relative hasn't been born who can dampen the magic of a well-spun story," she declared. "Besides, I was a very determined little girl. So determined that by the time I

was fifteen, I had written over two dozen books—the longest of which was a full nine pages!

When Landau was in her mid-twenties and living in New York City, she published the first of her many books. "Although being a 'real' author is often a very lonely occupation (you can't entertain friends while completing a chapter), it is also my greatest joy," she once explained. "I've always loved the idea of reaching out to share my thoughts and feelings with others, and I still can't think of a better way to do so."

Writing nonfiction remains her chosen occupation. "Being a nonfiction writer is like taking an unending voyage in a sea of fascinating facts," Landau recently explained to *SATA.* "Through extensive research and travel, I've learned about desert camels, dolphin intelligence, UFO's, the Loch Ness Monster, and some very deadly diseases. The best part of the experience is sharing the information with young people across America. Even though I may never meet all my readers, I feel as though I'm talking to them whenever they open one of my books."

■ Works Cited

Eglash, Joanne, review of *Teenage Drinking, Voice of Youth Advocates,* December, 1994, p. 300.

Garigliano, Leonard J., review of *Surrogate Mothers, Appraisal,* winter, 1989, pp. 44-45.

Hamilton, Joyce, review of *Weight: A Teenage Concern, Voice of Youth Advocates,* June, 1991, p. 126.

McDaniel, Tippin, review of *We Have AIDS, Appraisal,* summer, 1990, pp. 31-32.

Sutherland, Zena, review of *The Homeless, Bulletin of the Center for Children's Books,* January, 1988, pp. 94-95.

Triner, Jeanne, review of *The Beauty Trap, Booklist,* March 15, 1994, p. 1340.

White, Libby K., review of *Teenagers Talk about School—and Open Their Hearts about Their Closest Concerns, School Library Journal,* January, 1989, p. 100.

White, Libby K., review of *Interracial Dating and Marriage, School Library Journal,* September, 1993, p. 257.

Zvirin, Stephanie, *Different Drummer: Homosexuality in America, Booklist,* March 15, 1986, p. 1074.

■ For More Information See

PERIODICALS

Appraisal, winter, 1991, p. 35; winter, 1994, pp. 55-56; winter, 1995, pp. 118-19; summer, 1996, p. 54.

Booklist, November 1, 1979, p. 450; December 15, 1987, p. 710; February 1, 1989, p. 932; May 1, 1993, p. 1586.

Bulletin of the Center for Children's Books, December, 1976, pp. 59-60; October, 1983, p. 31; June, 1986, pp. 187-88; November, 1988, p. 76; June, 1991, p. 242; September, 1993, p. 15; February, 1994, pp. 191-92.

Kirkus Reviews, November 15, 1975, p. 1292; December
15, 1982, p. 1339; May 1, 1986, p. 722; October 15,
1991, p. 1345.
School Library Journal, February, 1976, p. 46; March,
1980, p. 134; February, 1981; September, 1983, p.
131; November, 1987, p. 110; January, 1994, p.
138; March, 1994, p. 243; January, 1996, p. 134.
Voice of Youth Advocates, April, 1981, p. 45; December,
1987, pp. 46-47; April, 1989, p. 60; August, 1990, p.
177; December, 1991, p. 337; August, 1993, p. 179;
February, 1994, p. 397; February, 1995, p. 360.

* * *

LAWRENCE, J. T.
See ROWLAND-ENTWISTLE, (Arthur) Theodore (Henry)

* * *

LESLIE, Sarah
See McGUIRE, Leslie (Sarah)

* * *

LINDBLOM, Steven (Winther) 1946-

■ Personal

Born March 29, 1946, in Minneapolis, MN; son of
Charles Edward (a professor of political science and
writer) and Rose Catherine Lindblom; married True
Kelley (a writer and illustrator); children: Jada Winter.
Education: Attended St. John's College, Annapolis, MD,
1964-65; Rhode Island School of Design, B.F.A., 1972.
Hobbies and other interests: Old bicycles and machinery,
flying, diving.

■ Addresses

Home—Old Denny Hill, Warner, NH 03278.

■ Career

Freelance illustrator and writer. Pilot.

■ Awards, Honors

Best Books selection, Bank Street College of Education,
1985, for *How to Build A Robot.*

■ Writings

FOR CHILDREN

(With wife, True Kelley) *The Mouse's Terrible Christmas,* illustrated by Kelley, Lothrop (New York),
1978.
(With Kelley) *The Mouse's Terrible Halloween,* illustrated by Kelley, Lothrop, 1980.
Let's Give Kitty a Bath!, illustrated by Kelley, Addison-
Wesley (Reading, MA), 1982.

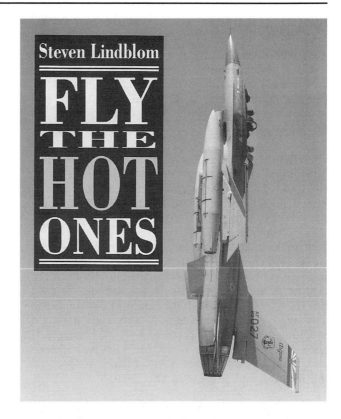

Pilot Steven Lindblom details the capabilities and
differences of seven types of aircraft in this high-flying
book. (Cover photo by George Hall.)

Let's Go Shopping, illustrated by Kathy Allert, Western
Publishing (New York), 1988.
Tiny Dinosaurs, illustrated by Gino D'Achille, Western
Publishing, 1988.
Snakes and Reptiles, Western Publishing, 1989, pub-
lished as *The Golden Book of Snakes and Other
Reptiles,* illustrated by James Spence, Golden Books
(New York), 1990.
Airplanes and Other Things That Fly, Western Publish-
ing, 1990.
Flying Dinosaurs, illustrated by Christopher Santoro,
Western Publishing, 1990.

SELF-ILLUSTRATED; FOR CHILDREN

The Fantastic Bicycles Book, Houghton (Boston), 1979.
How to Build a Robot, Crowell (New York), 1985.
Fly the Hot Ones, Houghton, 1991.

ILLUSTRATOR

Bernie Zubrowski, *Messing Around with Water Pumps
and Siphons: A Children's Museum Activity Book,*
Little, Brown (Boston), 1981.
Ross R. Olney, *The Internal Combustion Engine,* Lip-
pincott (Philadelphia), 1982.
Seymour Simon, *Computer Sense, Computer Nonsense,*
Lippincott, 1984.
(With Kelley) Niles Eldredge, Gregory Eldredge, and
Douglas Eldredge, *The Fossil Factory: A Kid's Guide
to Digging Up Dinosaurs, Exploring Evolution, and
Finding Fossils,* Addison-Wesley, 1989.

■ Adaptations

Let's Give Kitty a Bath! was produced by Gary Templeton and Susan Osborn as both a motion picture and videocassette recording of the same title, Phoenix/BFA Films & Video (New York), 1986.

■ Sidelights

"Nonfiction writing is my first love," author and illustrator Steven Lindblom once told *SATA.* "There are two things good children's nonfiction can do: encourage kids to get out and do things for themselves and reduce the world around them to manageable terms."

One of Lindblom's earliest self-illustrated nonfiction works, *The Fantastic Bicycles Book,* provides specific instructions for creating customized bicycles from recycled or unwanted parts. It "is not a book for casual tinkerers," observed Richard Luzer in *School Library Journal.* Written in an "almost conversational style," according to *Horn Book* reviewer Kate M. Flanagan, the book "includes sensible advice on when and where to seek adult or professional help." Flanagan added that the illustrations "are useful and detailed."

How to Build a Robot provides "a lucid and interesting discussion" of the many factors involved in creating a robot, commented Margaret Bush in *Appraisal.* Alfred B. Bortz, also writing in *Appraisal,* maintained that *How to Build a Robot* "is strong in both its literary and technological aspects," and added that Lindblom's "drawings are clear and have a touch of humor, as does his prose." *School Library Journal* contributor Jeffrey A. French wrote, "In a readable and clear style, Lindblom distinguishes among robots, computers and automatons," thereby offering "an enjoyable rudimentary introduction to the topic."

For *Fly the Hot Ones,* Lindblom flew seven different types of aircraft—including a glider, Piper Cub, and biplane—to research their capabilities and differences. The book also includes discussion of an F-14 Tomcat fighter jet, although the author did not pilot that particular plane. Carolyn Phelan commented of Lindblom's work in *Booklist:* "The immediacy of his experiences promises to involve readers who aren't flight fanatics and mesmerize those who are." Lola H. Teubert observed in *Voice of Youth Advocates* that the author's experience as a pilot is "obvious ... as he writes about his subject with an abundance of knowledge and enthusiasm." While Teubert found some of the vocabulary "too complex" for those readers unfamiliar with piloting, she nevertheless concluded, "Teen flying enthusiasts and would-be future pilots will find the book entertaining and informative."

Lindblom has also written well-received fiction for children. In *Let's Give Kitty a Bath!,* Lindblom and his wife, illustrator True Kelley, depict the antics of a brother and sister attempting to give their wily cat a bath. A *Publishers Weekly* reviewer noted that the "mad suspense and fun are perfectly clear in Kelley's ineffable

ink drawings." The reviewer continued that both "author and illustrator ... deserve high marks" for their efforts. Margaret L. Chatham described the story in *School Library Journal* as a "cheerful book even a preschooler will be able to read the second time through." Lindblom again teamed with Kelley to illustrate *The Fossil Factory: A Kid's Guide to Digging Up Dinosaurs, Exploring Evolution, and Finding Fossils.* Cathryn A. Camper remarked in *School Library Journal* that the pair's "cartoon drawings work well with the playfulness of the text."

■ Works Cited

Bartz, Alfred B., review of *How to Build a Robot, Appraisal,* fall, 1986, p. 63.

Bush, Margaret, review of *How to Build a Robot, Appraisal,* fall, 1986, p. 63.

Camper, Cathryn A., review of *The Fossil Factory: A Kid's Guide to Digging Up Dinosaurs, Exploring Evolution, and Finding Fossils, School Library Journal,* May, 1990, p. 115.

Chatham, Margaret L., review of *Let's Give Kitty a Bath!, School Library Journal,* August, 1982, p. 101.

Flanagan, Kate M., review of *The Fantastic Bicycles Book, Horn Book,* December, 1979, p. 679.

French, Jeffrey A., review of *How to Build a Robot, School Library Journal,* January, 1986, p. 69.

Review of *Let's Give Kitty a Bath!, Publishers Weekly,* February 12, 1982, p. 99.

Luzer, Richard, review of *The Fantastic Bicycles Book, School Library Journal,* March, 1980, p. 142.

Phelan, Carolyn, review of *Fly the Hot Ones, Booklist,* July, 1991, p. 2044.

Teubert, Lola A., review of *Fly the Hot Ones, Voice of Youth Advocates,* October, 1991, p. 263.*

*   *   *

LISANDRELLI, Elaine Slivinski 1951-

■ Personal

Born July 11, 1951, in Pittston, PA; daughter of Leo J. (a retired postal employee) and Gabriella A. (a retired registered nurse; maiden name, Sharek) Slivinski; married Carl A. Lisandrelli (a history teacher), June 20, 1980. *Education:* Marywood University, B.A., 1973, M.S., 1976; further graduate study at Marywood University, Indiana University—Bloomington, and Villanova University. *Hobbies and other interests:* "Exercise; research; visiting libraries; spending time with my husband, family, friends and animals (especially dogs); watching movies and documentaries; listening to music (especially Broadway tunes and love songs), lending a helping hand to others whenever I can."

■ Addresses

Home—Moosic, PA. *Office*—North Pocono Middle School, Church St., Moscow, PA 18444.

▪ Career

North Pocono Middle School, Moscow, PA, English teacher, 1973—; Marywood University, Scranton, PA, adjunct faculty member, 1986—. Member of Pennsylvania Writing Assessment Committee, Pennsylvania Department of Education, 1989. International Correspondence School, proofreader, summer, 1991; educational consultant. *Member:* Society of Children's Book Writers and Illustrators, National Council of Teachers of English, Kosciuszko Foundation, Polish Arts and Culture Foundation, Humane Society of the United States, La Plume (writer's group), Kappa Gamma Pi, Lambda Iota Tau.

▪ Writings

FOR YOUNG PEOPLE

Maya Angelou: More Than a Poet, Enslow Publishers, 1996.
Bob Dole: Legendary Senator, Enslow Publishers, 1997.

OTHER

(Co-author) *Easywriter,* Levels G and H, ERA/CCR, Inc., 1987.
(With Susan Campbell Bartoletti) *The Study Skills Workout,* Scott, Foresman, 1988.

Contributor to magazines, including *Pockets* and *Cobblestone.*

▪ Work in Progress

A biography of Ignacy Jan Paderewski, publication by Morgan Reynolds expected in 1998; a biography of Ida B. Wells-Barnett and a biography of Jack London, both for Enslow Publishers.

▪ Sidelights

Elaine Slivinski Lisandrelli told *SATA:* "I've always loved history. In grade school, I wanted to look up a different historical time, person, or place every night. Biographies are important to me because they bring people, events, and times past back to life.

"My parents, my older brother Dennis, and my teachers encouraged me to read on my own, and they also read to me. I found a fascinating world in books. Books taught me so much and still do. I try to instill this love for

ELAINE SLIVINSKI LISANDRELLI

reading in my students. I hope my writing will touch my readers in a special way and make them hungry to learn more. I believe in the words of Frederick Douglass: 'Education means emancipation; it means light and liberty.'

"I've been fortunate to belong to a writer's group whose members have helped me to grow as a writer. Their feedback is invaluable, and their support and encouragement gives me hope."

▪ For More Information See

PERIODICALS

Booklist, September 1, 1996, pp. 116, 118.
School Library Journal, June, 1996, p. 160.
Voice of Youth Advocates, October, 1996, p. 234.

M

MacDONALD, Margaret Read 1940-

■ Personal

Born January 21, 1940, in Seymour, IN; daughter of Murray Ernest (a carpenter and builder) and Mildred (a homemaker; maiden name, Amick) Read; married James Bruce MacDonald (an auditor), August 20, 1965; children: Jennifer Skye, Julie Liana. *Education:* Indiana University, A.B., 1962, Ph.D., 1979; University of Washington, M.L.S., 1964; University of Hawaii, M.Ed.Ec., 1969.

■ Addresses

Home—11507 Northeast 104th St., Kirkland, WA 98033. *Office*—Bothell Regional Library, King County Library System, 18215 98th Ave. N.E., Bothell, WA 98011. *Electronic mail*—margmacd @ rain.kcls.org.

■ Career

Hawaii State Library, Honolulu, bookmobile librarian, 1966-68; Mountain Valley Library System, Sacramento, CA, children's consultant, 1969-70; Montgomery County Library System, White Oak, MO, children's librarian, 1970-72; University of Washington, Seattle, visiting lecturer in librarianship, 1975-79; King County Library System, Seattle, children's librarian, 1979—. Professional storyteller, including national festivals in Japan, Australia, and New Zealand, 1992—. Washington State Folklife Council, member of board of directors, 1986-90, president, 1989-90; Youth Theatre Northwest, member of board of directors, 1988-91, president, 1989-90. *Member:* International Board on Books for Young People, National Storytelling Association (member of board of directors, 1992-95), American Folklore Society (president of Children's Folklore Section, 1993-94), American Library Association, Association for Library Service to Children, Society of Children's Book Writers and Illustrators, Children's Literature Association, Washington Library Media Association, Washington Library Association.

MARGARET READ MacDONALD

■ Awards, Honors

RTSD Outstanding Reference Source, American Library Association, 1982, for *The Storyteller's Sourcebook;* Notable Children's Trade Book in the Field of Social Studies, National Council for the Social Studies and Children's Book Council (NCSS/CBC), 1992, for *Peace Tales; Storytelling World* Award, 1995, for the story "The Lion's Whisker," and 1996, for *The Old Woman Who Lived in a Vinegar Bottle;* Storytelling Information Winner, *Storytelling World* Awards, 1995, for *The Storyteller's Start-Up Book;* Fulbright scholar, Mahasarakham University, Thailand, 1995-97.

■ Writings

FOR CHILDREN

The Skit Book: 101 Skits from Kids, illustrated by Marie-Louise Scull, Linnet Books (Hamden, CT), 1989.

Peace Tales: World Folktales to Talk About, illustrated by Zobra Anasazi, Linnet Books, 1992.

(Editor) Supaporn Vathanaprida, *Thai Tales: Folktales of Thailand,* illustrated by Boonsong Rohitasuke, Libraries Unlimited (Englewood, CO), 1994.

The Old Woman Who Lived in a Vinegar Bottle: A British Fairy Tale, illustrated by Nancy Dunaway Fowlkes, August House (Little Rock, AR), 1995.

Tuck-Me-In Tales: Bedtime Stories from Around the World, illustrated by Yvonne LeBrun Davis, August House, 1996.

The Girl Who Wore Too Much: A Pu-Thai Folktale, illustrated by Yvonne LeBrun Davis, August House, 1997.

(With Vathanaprida) *The Peacock and the Crow and Other Thai Animal Tales,* illustrated by Wilas Nirumsunsiri, Fulcrum (Golden, CO), 1997.

Pickin' Peas, illustrated by Pat Cummings, HarperCollins, 1997.

(With Winifred Jaeger) *The Round Book,* illustrated by Yvonne LeBrun Davis, Linnet Books, 1997.

Slop! A Welsh Folktale, illustrated by Yvonne LeBrun Davis, Fulcrum, 1997.

FOR ADULTS

The Storyteller's Sourcebook: A Subject, Title, and Motif-Index to Folklore Collections for Children, Gale Research, 1982.

Twenty Tellable Tales: Audience Participation Folktales for the Beginning Storyteller, H. W. Wilson, 1986.

Booksharing: 101 Programs to Use with Preschoolers, illustrations by Julie Liana MacDonald, Shoe String (North Haven, CT), 1988.

When the Lights Go Out: Twenty Scary Tales to Tell, illustrated by Roxane Murphy Smith, H. W. Wilson, 1988.

Scipio, Indiana: Threads from the Past, Ye Galleon (Fairfield, WV), 1988.

(Editor) *The Folklore of World Holidays,* Gale, 1992.

Look Back and See: Twenty Lively Tales for Gentle Tellers, illustrations by R. M. Smith, H. W. Wilson, 1991.

Tom Thumb, illustrated by Joanne Caroselli, Oryx, 1993.

The Storyteller's Start-Up Book: Finding, Learning, Performing, and Using Folktales, Including Twelve Tellable Tales, August House, 1993.

Bookplay: 101 Creative Themes to Share with Young Children, illustrations by Julia L. MacDonald, Library Professional Publications (North Haven), 1995.

Celebrate the World: Twenty Tellable Folktales for Multicultural Festivals, illustrations by R. M. Smith, H. W. Wilson, 1994.

Ghost Stories from the Pacific Northwest, August House, 1995.

The Parent's Guide to Storytelling: How to Make up New Stories and Retell Old Favorites, illustrations by Mark T. Smith, HarperCollins, 1995.

Scipio Storytelling: Talk in a Southern Indiana Community, University Press of America (Lanham, MD), 1996.

Contributor to books, including *Once upon a Folktale: Capturing the Folklore Process with Children,* edited by Gloria T. Blatt, Teachers College Press (New York City), 1993, and *The Storyteller's Guide: Storytellers Share Advice,* by Bill Mooney and David Holt, August House, 1996.

■ Adaptations

Peace Tales was adapted for a videotape titled *Folktales of Peace,* which received a CINE Golden Eagle Award from the Council on International Nontheatrical Events in 1996; *Tuck-Me-In Tales* was released on audiocassette with music by Richard Scholtz, August House, 1997.

■ Work in Progress

Editing *Traditional Storytelling Today: An International Encyclopedia,* for Fitzroy Dearborn (Chicago); *The Tale-Finder: A Motif, Subject, and Title Index to Popular Folktale Collections,* with Brian Sturm, H. W. Wilson; *Earth Tales: World Folktales to Talk About,* for Linnet Books.

■ Sidelights

A children's librarian and professional storyteller, Margaret Read MacDonald is best known for her books associated with folktales and the art of storytelling. While some of MacDonald's works focus on individual tales, such as her picture books, others contain a collection of tales usually centered around a particular theme or country. In many cases the author added detailed notes for beginning storytellers on how to tell the folktale to an audience. Appreciated for her thorough research and vast knowledge of folklore, MacDonald is also credited for her "gift of making stories easy to tell without sacrificing quality," noted *School Library Journal* reviewer Donna L. Scanlon.

Among MacDonald's notable picture book tales is her first one, *The Old Woman Who Lived in a Vinegar Bottle: A British Fairy Tale.* This British version of *The Fisherman and His Wife* features an old woman who is discontent living in a vinegar bottle and a kind fairy who offers her better living quarters. Although the woman is happy with her new home, she soon demands more and more from the fairy. Eventually, the fairy sends the ungrateful woman back to the vinegar bottle, concluding that the woman will never be satisfied. *Booklist* contributor Susan Dove Lempke enjoyed MacDonald's version, which "is so rhythmic and conversational even a first-time storyteller will be successful."

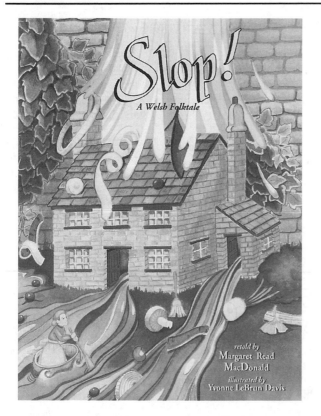

An old man and woman unknowingly throw their dinner leftovers onto the miniature home of a tiny man and his wife in MacDonald's retelling of a Welsh folktale. (Illustration by Yvonne LeBrun Davis.)

Similarly, a contributor in *Kirkus Reviews* appreciated the way MacDonald delivered the tale "in a rapid, comic style."

Peace Tales: World Folktales to Talk About and *Thai Tales: Folktales of Thailand* are examples of MacDonald's folktale collections organized by theme or country. *When the Lights Go Out: Twenty Scary Tales to Tell* contains tales "that will absorb and chill primary and preschool audiences," noted *Booklist* reviewer Barbara Elleman. To aid beginning storytellers in this work, MacDonald included after each tale a detailed list of sources, a further information section on tale origins and variants, and tips on how to tell the story to an audience. *School Library Journal* reviewer Patricia Manning noted that while not everyone can be transformed into excellent tellers, this book "may help them find confidence to get started." Other books MacDonald has written for novice storytellers include *Twenty Tellable Tales: Audience Participation Folktales for the Beginning Storyteller* and *The Storyteller's Start-Up Book: Finding, Learning, Performing, and Using Folktales, Including Twelve Tellable Tales.*

MacDonald told *SATA:* "I was born and bred in southern Indiana. When I was young we didn't have many books in my home, but my mother still read to me a lot. My favorites were poems by James Whitcomb Riley, which she would read over and over. Those rhythms are still in my head. We also had some *National Geographic* magazines, and they were such a treat. I would pore over them again and again. I decided I wanted to be a missionary when I grew up and travel to wonderful places. Later I decided I wanted to be an anthropologist. Later still I decided to become an anthropological librarian. Then in my last summer of college, I took a class in storytelling. I *loved* it! That changed everything, and I became a children's librarian. I still got to travel, though. I have worked as a librarian in Hawaii, Singapore, Argentina, and Thailand, and I have traveled as a storyteller to New Zealand, Malaysia, Indonesia, Japan, Germany, France, and other exciting spots.

"When I was working on a bookmobile in Hawaii, I told stories six or seven times every day. Each time the bookmobile stopped, I would throw some beach mats under a tree, plop down on a folding stool, and start telling stories. The way to become a really good storyteller is to get lots of practice. I became fairly good at telling stories, but I had trouble finding enough stories to tell. I decided to go to Indiana University and study folklore, and I started working on an index to folktale collections, so that I (and other storytellers) could find the stories we wanted more easily.

"Soon I started retelling in print some of the folktales I had discovered. I retold them in a format that folklorists call 'ethnopoetic,' because it makes the words look almost like poetry. That way of writing tells the person reading aloud when to take a breath. It makes the story flow more naturally, as if it were being spoken, not just written. My books *Twenty Tellable Tales* and *Look Back and See* are in that format.

"Sometimes I write adult books, using my doctoral folklore background on topics like the folklore of world holidays or ghost stories from the Pacific Northwest. Other times I use my children's librarian background and write for other children's librarians. Sometimes I combine the two and write a book like *The Skit Book.* Camp skits are really the folklore of kids, so I collected them from my friends who were kids.

"Recently I decided that some of the stories I tell would be enjoyable if they were illustrated and published as picture books. Then many more folks could enjoy these great stories. They wouldn't have to wait for a storyteller to learn them and tell them. Parents and teachers could read them to children, and older kids could read them for themselves. I wrote lots of letters to publishers and finally sold a few of these stories. *The Old Woman Who Lived in a Vinegar Bottle* was my first picture book, and I was really happy when I heard someone reading it aloud. They were reading just the way I had hoped they would! That means I did my work right.

"All my life I have tried to remember what a minister once told me. I was wondering what I should be when I grew up. 'Margaret,' he said, 'Where your talents and the needs of the world meet ... that is where you should make your contribution.' I remind myself of that now and then. I try to tackle writing projects which only I would or could do. I sometimes get myself into hot water, with projects like *The Storyteller's Sourcebook,* which took eleven years to complete, or my current project, a storytelling encyclopedia for which I need to collect articles from scholars all around the world.

"Sometimes I wonder if I should write picture books, since there seem to be so many already. Then someone tells me how much fun they have sharing them, and I go ahead and try to sell some more. There are so many stories I want to share: the one about the greedy cat, the one about the thieving little pot, and that creepy one about the sasquatch, and...."

■ Works Cited

Elleman, Barbara, review of *When the Lights Go Out: Twenty Scary Tales to Tell, Booklist,* October 1, 1988, p. 331.

Lempke, Susan Dove, review of *The Old Woman Who Lived in a Vinegar Bottle: A British Fairy Tale, Booklist,* October 1, 1995, p. 323.

Manning, Patricia, review of *When the Lights Go Out: Twenty Scary Tales to Tell, School Library Journal,* August, 1989, p. 88.

Review of *The Old Woman Who Lived in a Vinegar Bottle: A British Fairy Tale, Kirkus Reviews,* September 1, 1995, p. 1283.

Scanlon, Donna L., review of *The Old Woman Who Lived in a Vinegar Bottle: A British Fairy Tale, School Library Journal,* January, 1996, pp. 102-103.

■ For More Information See

PERIODICALS

Booklist, July, 1986, p. 1620; April 1, 1988, p. 1356; May 15, 1990, p. 1811; April 15, 1992, p. 1550; July, 1993, pp. 1928, 1981; October 1, 1996, p. 355.

Books for the Young, October 1, 1995, p. 323.

Bulletin of the Center for Children's Books, December, 1995, p. 147.

Children's Book Watch, July, 1993, p. 5.

Journal of Youth Services in Libraries, summer, 1988, p. 464; winter, 1992, p. 48; summer, 1993, p. 425; fall, 1993, p. 93; winter, 1995, p. 210.

Kirkus Reviews, July 1, 1992, p. 858.

Library Journal, March 1, 1992, p. 82; July, 1993, p. 81.

Publishers Weekly, June 22, 1992, p. 63.

School Library Journal, April, 1987, p. 50; August, 1988, p. 48; June, 1990, pp. 132-133; November, 1991, pp. 30, 58; October, 1992, p. 132; November, 1993, p. 42; December, 1995, p. 38; November, 1996, p. 99.

Wilson Library Bulletin, October, 1988, p. 114; May, 1992, p. 124; December, 1992, p. 33; June, 1993, p. 102.

*   *   *

MATHIEU, Joe
See MATHIEU, Joseph P.

MATHIEU, Joseph P. 1949-
(Joe Mathieu)

■ Personal

Born January 23, 1949, in Springfield, VT; son of Joseph A. (a car dealer) and Patricia (Biner) Mathieu; married Melanie Gerardi, September 7, 1970; children: Kristen, Joey. *Education:* Rhode Island School of Design, B.F.A., 1971. *Hobbies and other interests:* Bicycling (especially touring the New England states), jazz and ragtime.

■ Addresses

Home—64 Pheasant Lane, Brooklyn, CT 06234.

■ Career

Author and illustrator of books for children. Designer of album covers for Stomp Off records.

■ Awards, Honors

Best Books selection, American Institute of Graphic Arts, 1973, for *The Magic Word Book, Starring Marko the Magician!;* Children's Choice selection, International Reading Association, 1982, for *Ernie's Big Mess.*

JOSEPH P. MATHIEU

■ Writings

SELF-ILLUSTRATED; UNDER NAME JOE MATHIEU

The Amazing Adventures of Silent "E" Man, Random House, 1973.
The Magic Word Book, Starring Marko the Magician! Random House, 1973.
Big Joe's Trailer Truck, Random House, 1974.
I Am a Monster (a "Sesame Street" book), Golden Press, 1976.
The Grover Sticker Book, Western Publishing, 1976.
The Count's Coloring Book, Western Publishing, 1976.
The Sesame Street Mix or Match Storybook: Over Two Hundred Thousand Funny Combinations, Random House, 1977.
Who's Who on Sesame Street, Western Publishing, 1977.
Busy City (nonfiction), Random House, 1978.
The Olden Days (nonfiction), Random House, 1981.
Bathtime on Sesame Street, edited by Jane Schulman, Random House, 1983.
Big Bird Visits the Dodos, Random House, 1985.
Fire Trucks, Random House, 1988.
Trucks in Your Neighborhood, Random House, 1988.
Sesame Street 123: A Counting Book from 1 to 100, Random House, 1991.

ILLUSTRATOR; UNDER NAME JOE MATHIEU

Ossie Davis, *Purlie Victorious,* Houghton, 1973.
Scott Corbett, *Dr. Merlin's Magic Shop,* Little, Brown, 1973.
Genevieve Gray, *Casey's Camper,* McGraw, 1973.
Byron Preiss, *The Electric Company: The Silent "E's" from Outer Space,* Western Publishing, 1973.
Scott Corbett, *The Great Custard Pie Panic,* Little, Brown, 1974.
Suzanne W. Bladow, *The Midnight Flight of Moose, Mops, and Marvin,* McGraw, 1975.
Howard Liss, *The Giant Book of Strange But True Sports Stories,* Random House, 1976.
Hedda Nussbaum, *Plants Do Amazing Things* (nonfiction), Random House, 1977.
Katy Hall and Lisa Eisenberg, *A Gallery of Monsters,* Random House, 1981.
Cindy West, *The Superkids and the Singing Dog,* Random House, 1982.
Harold Woods and Geraldine Woods, *The Book of the Unknown* (nonfiction), Random House, 1982.
Howard Liss, *The Giant Book of More Strange But True Sports Stories,* Random House, 1983.
Deborah Kovacs, *Brewster's Courage,* Simon & Schuster, 1992.
Leslie McGuire, *Big Dan's Moving Van,* Random House, 1993.
Laura Joffe Numeroff, *Dogs Don't Wear Sneakers,* Simon & Schuster, 1993.
Laura Joffe Numeroff, *Chimps Don't Wear Glasses,* Simon & Schuster, 1995.
Leslie McGuire, *Big Frank's Fire Truck,* Random House, 1995.

ILLUSTRATOR; UNDER NAME JOE MATHIEU; "SESAME STREET" SERIES

Matt Robinson, *Matt Robinson's Gordon of Sesame Street Storybook,* Random House, 1972.
Emily Perl Kingsley and others, *The Sesame Street 1,2,3 Storybook,* Random House, 1973.
Norman Stiles and Daniel Wilcox, *Grover and the Everything in the Whole Wide World Museum: Featuring Lovable, Furry Old Grover,* Random House, 1974.
Jeffrey Moss, Norman Stiles, and Daniel Wilcox, *The Sesame Street ABC Storybook,* Random House, 1974.
Anna Jane Hays, *See No Evil, Hear No Evil, Smell No Evil,* Western Publishing, 1975.
E. P. Kingsley, David Korr, and Jeffrey Moss, *The Sesame Street Book of Fairy Tales,* Random House, 1975.
Norman Stiles, *Grover's Little Red Riding Hood,* Western Publishing, 1976.
Norman Stiles, *The Ernie and Bert Book,* Western Publishing, 1977.
Patricia Thackray, *What Ernie and Bert Did on Their Summer Vacation,* Western Publishing, 1977.
E. P. Kingsley, *The Exciting Adventures of Super-Grover,* Golden Press, 1978.
Sharon Lerner, *Big Bird's Look and Listen Book,* Random House, 1978.
Patricia Thackray, *Grover Visits His Granny,* Random House, 1978.
Daniel Korr, *Cookie Monster and the Cookie Tree,* Western Publishing, 1979.
Valjean McLenigham, *Ernie's Work of Art,* Western Publishing, 1979.
Linda Hayward, *The Sesame Street Dictionary,* Random House, 1980.
Sarah Roberts, *Ernie's Big Mess,* Random House, 1981.
Jon Stone and Joe Bailey, *Christmas Eve on Sesame Street* (based on the television special "Christmas Eve on Sesame Street"), Random House, 1981.
Sarah Roberts, *Nobody Cares about Me!,* Random House, 1982.
Dan Elliott, *Ernie's Little Lie,* Random House, 1983.
Dan Elliott, *A Visit to the Sesame Street Firehouse,* Random House, 1983.
Sarah Roberts, *Bert and the Missing Mop Mix-Up,* Random House, 1983.
Norman Stiles, *I'll Miss You, Mr. Hooper,* Random House, 1984.
Dan Elliott, *Two Wheels for Grover,* Random House, 1984.
Sharon Lerner, *Big Bird's Copycat Day,* Random House, 1984.
Dan Elliott, *My Doll Is Lost,* Random House, 1984.
Sarah Roberts, *The Adventures of Big Bird in Dinosaur Days,* Random House, 1984.
Sarah Roberts, *I Want to Go Home,* Random House, 1985.
Deborah Hautzig, *A Visit to the Sesame Street Hospital,* Random House, 1985.
Sharon Lerner, *Big Bird Says,* Random House, 1985.

Brewster, a shy ferret from South Dakota, becomes enchanted with the zydeco music of Louisiana's bayou country, but when he travels there he finds he must prove himself to the unfriendly residents of Moustafaya Swamp. (From *Brewster's Courage,* written by Deborah Kovacs and illustrated by Mathieu.)

Deborah Hautzig, *A Visit to the Sesame Street Library,* 1986.

Judy Freudberg and Tony Geiss, *Susan and Gordon Adopt a Baby,* Random House, 1986.

Liza Alexander, *A Visit to the Sesame Street Museum,* Random House, 1987.

Molly Cross, *Wait for Me,* Random House, 1987.

Deborah Hautzig, *It's Easy,* Random House, 1988.

Virginia Holt, *A My Name Is Alice,* Random House, 1989.

Deborah Hautzig, *Get Well, Granny Bird,* Random House, 1989.

Deborah Hautzig, *Grover's Bad Dream,* Random House, 1990.

Lisa Alexander, *How to Get to Sesame Street,* Western Publishing, 1990.

Deborah Hautzig, *Ernie and Bert's New Kitten,* Random House, 1990.

Deborah Hautzig, *Big Bird Plays the Violin,* Random House, 1991.

Liza Alexander, *Bird Watching with Bert,* Western Publishing, 1991.

Bobbi Jane Kates, *We're Different, We're the Same,* Random House, 1992.

Elizabeth Rivlin, *Elmo's Little Glowworm,* Random House, 1994.

Anna Ross, *Elmo's Big Lift-and-Look Book,* Random House, 1994.

Norman Stiles, *Around the Corner on Sesame Street,* Random House, 1994.

Lou Berger, *Sesame Street Stays up Late,* Random House, 1995.

Annie Cobb, *B Is for Books,* Random House, 1996.

Anna Ross, *Elmo's Lift-and-Peek around the Corner Book,* Random House, 1996.

■ Sidelights

Joe Mathieu once told *SATA:* "I became addicted to drawing pictures at about three years old. I was never interested in drawing completely straight. It's almost impossible for me to avoid humor, caricature and lots of action.

"I don't feel that an artist has to be particularly encouraged to draw. I think he'll draw no matter what. The same with a writer or a musician for that matter.

"As a youngster, I became enamored of Jim Henson and the Muppets long before they were really famous. I would beg permission to miss the bus if they were going to appear on the 'Dave Garroway Show' or I'd get special permission to stay up late if they were scheduled for Jack Parr.

"When Random House and CTW (Children's Television Workshop) started looking for illustrators to interpret the Muppet characters from 'Sesame Street,' I just fell into it and I love drawing them. The 'Sesame Street' characters are my favorites of all the many Muppet characters."

Joe Mathieu has made a career illustrating many of the numerous books for children that feature Jim Henson's Muppets from the award-winning children's program, *Sesame Street.* Although he began his career illustrating books he had also written, such as *The Magic Word Book, Starring Marko the Magician!* and *The Amazing Adventures of Silent "E" Man,* the majority of his work has appeared in books written by others. Among these are *Elmo's Lift-and-Peek around the Corner Book,* in which numbers, opposites, and matching concepts are taught with the aid of Mathieu's "loudly colored, chaotic-looking pages," in the estimation of a *Publishers Weekly* reviewer.

Other *Sesame Street* tie-in books illustrated by Mathieu include *We're Different, We're the Same,* in which Mathieu's drawings of the Muppets "cavort cheerfully with people of all sizes, shapes and ethnicities," according to a *Publishers Weekly* critic. In *A Visit to the Sesame Street Hospital,* Grover is given a tour of the hospital where he will stay during a tonsillectomy operation. In *Get Well, Granny Bird,* Big Bird visits his grandmother when she gets a cold, and though his attempts to help out generally fail he learns that just his being there is a treat to Granny Bird. Mathieu's illustrations "are typical" of the *Sesame Street* books, that is, "realistically drawn and in full color," Sharron McElmeel observed in *School Library Journal.*

Mathieu has also illustrated a number of books outside the *Sesame Street* tie-in industry. A *Publishers Weekly* critic praised the "exuberant art" in Laura Numeroff's *Dogs Don't Wear Sneakers,* in which pictures of animals in implausible situations accompany the author's nonsensical rhymes. Indeed, according to Lori A. Janick of *School Library Journal,* "It's Mathieu's wacky and inventive illustrations that really carry the show." The book's sequel, *Chimps Don't Wear Glasses,* was deemed less successful by a *Kirkus Reviews* critic, who nonetheless noted Mathieu's "busy, literal cartoons." Deborah Kovacs's picture book, *Brewster's Courage,* features a ferret who travels to Louisiana to enjoy the zydeco music and learns how to make friends in a new situation. It also bears Mathieu's "amusing drawings," which accompany "a story with appeal for anyone who has ever felt like an outsider," according to a *Kirkus Reviews* commentator.

■ Works Cited

Review of *Brewster's Courage, Kirkus Reviews,* June 15, 1992, p. 780.

Review of *Chimps Don't Wear Glasses, Kirkus Reviews,* August 1, 1995, p. 1115.

Review of *Dogs Don't Wear Sneakers, Publishers Weekly,* August 19, 1996, p. 69.

Review of *Elmo's Lift-and-Peek around the Corner Book, Publishers Weekly,* January 29, 1996, p. 99.

Janick, Lori A., review of *Dogs Don't Wear Sneakers, School Library Journal,* January, 1994, p. 96.

McElmeel, Sharron, review of *Get Well, Granny Bird, School Library Journal,* August, 1989, p. 122.

Review of *We're Different, We're the Same, Publishers Weekly,* November 23, 1992, p. 61.

■ **For More Information See**

PERIODICALS

Booklist, September 1, 1995, p. 89.
School Library Journal, September, 1992. p. 254.

* * *

**McDEVITT, Jack
  See McDEVITT, John Charles**

* * *

**McDEVITT, John Charles 1935-
  (Jack McDevitt)**

■ **Personal**

Born April 14, 1935, in Philadelphia, PA; son of John A. (a refinery worker) and Elizabeth (a homemaker; maiden name, Norman) McDevitt; married Maureen McAdams (a teacher's aid), March 18, 1967; children: one daughter and two sons. *Education:* LaSalle College, B.A. 1957; Wesleyan University, M.A.L.S., 1971. *Religion:* "No affiliation." *Hobbies and other interests:* Chess, astronomy, history, theater.

■ **Addresses**

Home and office—Cryptic Inc., 57 Sunset Blvd., Brunswick, GA, 31525. *Agent*—Ralph Vicinanza, 111 Eighth Ave., Suite 1501, New York, NY 10011.

■ **Career**

Woodrow Wilson High School, Levittown, PA, instructor in English, history, and theatre director, 1963-68; Mount St. Charles Academy, Woonsocket, RI, instructor in English, history, and theatre, 1968-71; Newfound Memorial High School, Bristol, NH, English department chair, 1971-73; U.S. Customs Service, customs inspector in Pembina, ND, 1975-82, regional training officer in Chicago, IL, 1982-85, and supervisor and management trainer specializing in motivational techniques and leadership at the Federal Law Enforcement Training Center in Glynco, GA, 1985-95; full-time writer, 1995—. *Military service:* U.S. Navy, 1958-62, as commissioned officer. *Member:* U.S. Chess Federation, Science Fiction Writers of America.

■ **Awards, Honors**

Nebula award nomination for best short story, 1984, for "Cryptic"; Locus Award and Philip K. Dick Award special award, 1987, for *The Hercules Text;* Hugo Award and Nebula Award nominations for best short story, 1988, for "The Fort Moxie Branch," and for best novella, 1996, for "Time Travelers Never Die"; UPC Awards, 1992, for novella "Ships in the Night," and

JOHN CHARLES McDEVITT

1994, for "Time Travelers Never Die"; Homer Award, best novella, 1996, for "Time Travelers Never Die"; Arthur C. Clarke Award nomination, Science Fiction Foundation, University of Liverpool Library, 1996, for *The Engines of God.*

■ **Writings**

SCIENCE-FICTION NOVELS, UNDER NAME JACK McDEVITT

The Hercules Text, Ace (New York City), 1986.
A Talent for War, Ace, 1989.
The Engines of God, Ace, 1994.
Ancient Shores, HarperPrism (New York City), 1996.
Standard Candles (short story collection), Tachyon Publications (San Francisco), 1996.
Eternity Road, HarperPrism, 1997.

OTHER

Contributor of short stories to magazines, including *Isaac Asimov's Science Fiction Magazine, Fantasy and Science Fiction, Twilight Zone,* and *Full Spectrum.*

■ **Sidelights**

Although one of his childhood ambitions was to become a science fiction writer, John Charles McDevitt did not realize his dream until he was in his forties. Prompted by his wife, Maureen, McDevitt wrote a short story, "The Emerson Effect," which was purchased by *Twilight Zone* magazine. Since then, McDevitt has been writing under his nickname "Jack," and has produced five novels, a short story collection, as well as numerous story contributions to periodicals; until 1995, McDevitt did this while working full-time for the United States Customs Service, in the small town of Pembina, North Dakota. In fact, his job with Customs revived his interest in science fiction—indirectly, as the author explained to *SATA:* "It became so routine at one point that I began writing as a diversion." A town with a population of just six hundred, Pembina appears as Fort Moxie in several of McDevitt's short stories and in his novel, *Ancient Shores.*

McDevitt is considered a "humanist" science fiction writer, as his stories typically pose an ordinary person in unusual, sometimes threatening situations which often result from encounters with intellectually superior aliens or powerful governments. As McDevitt has commented: "I don't use antagonists (in the sense of villainous characters) in my writing. Each character thinks he/she is doing the right thing. The conflicts arise from differences in perception." McDevitt also makes occasional use of religious themes in his fiction, exposing his characters to circumstances that challenge their belief systems. Said McDevitt: "I have no [religious] affiliation, but I enjoy creating situations in which characters must confront what they say they believe."

McDevitt's first novel, *The Hercules Text,* finds protagonist Harry Carmichael involved in a race with cold war Russian scientists to decode information transmitted by extra-galactic aliens from a source in the Hercules constellation. Speculation that the transmission's data could have military applications has caused each government to scramble for the answers. Among the individuals assisting Carmichael in the processing of the information is a scientist and Catholic priest whose involvement with science may have cost him his faith. In McDevitt's second novel, *A Talent for War,* which is set thousands of years in the future, a young man searches for the truth about an idolized war hero, and an understanding of how a ship supposedly destroyed in that hero's military engagement turned up orbiting a distant world some two centuries later. *Voice of Youth Advocates* contributor Lisa Lane praised *A Talent for War* as "a thought-provoking book that will capture the imagination," while *Booklist* reviewer Roland Green asserted that the novel "features excellent pacing, a wonderfully lived-in world, superior characterizations, and a rare quality of ethical concern." McDevitt's third book, *The Engines of God,* similarly revolves around a people's search for understanding of seemingly inexplicable events, this time the discovery of a mysterious formation on a moon of a world in space. "With plenty of startling plot twists, a heavy dose of intrigue, and an unusual amount of character development for science fiction, McDevitt holds us fast right through to a thrilling finish," maintained *Booklist*'s Carl Hays in a review of *The Engines of God.* A *Kirkus Reviews* critic similarly asserted: "McDevitt is at his best award-winning style in this intelligent and wide-ranging novel."

McDevitt's 1996 novel, *Ancient Shores,* is set in motion by an ordinary man's discovery of a quite remarkable artifact. In the story, a North Dakota wheat farmer, while clearing a field, unearths a sea vessel in perfect condition. Scientific tests reveal that the boat has been constructed of unknown materials that will never decompose—with tremendous implications for the global economy, which relies heavily on obsolescence. "A large cast of colorful characters, a wry overview of society's extreme behavior in the face of the unknown, and a surprise ending make this irresistibly compelling reading," asserted *Booklist* reviewer Carl Hays. McDevitt also published a short story collection, *Standard Candles,* in 1996, followed by his novel *Eternity Road,* the story of an archaeologist's quest to locate a site that no one believes exists. Only upon his death is it revealed that he had indeed made his discovery—all the while keeping it secret from everyone close to him.

Commenting on the human and spiritual elements of his stories, McDevitt told *Locus* magazine: "Anything that's intelligent almost by definition is going to want to explain its existence. That gets you into the area of myth, into religious cycles. I would expect that if you could go back far enough with any intelligent species, assuming there are others, you'd find religious systems. The real question might be, what becomes of the religious systems, in time? Maybe you toss those over the side. If science is the new religion, science fiction is maybe the new mythology. I think science fiction is a more noble effort at resolving some of these issues than religion ever was anyhow." Summarizing his attraction to his chosen genre, McDevitt has commented: "I've always enjoyed a good mystery. Science Fiction allows considerable space for this technique, not the classic whodunit, but rather a what-could-possibly-have-happened-here?"

■ Works Cited

Review of *The Engines of God, Kirkus Reviews,* August 1, 1994, p. 1032.

Green, Roland, review of *A Talent for War, Booklist,* February 15, 1989, p. 977.

Hays, Carl, review of *Ancient Shores, Booklist,* April 15, 1996, p. 1425.

Hays, Carl, review of *The Engines of God, Booklist,* September 15, 1994, p. 118.

Lane, Lisa, review of *A Talent for War, Voice of Youth Advocates,* August, 1989, p. 166.

McDevitt, John Charles, comments in *Locus,* February, 1995, pp. 4-5, 74-75.

■ For More Information See

BOOKS

Twentieth-Century Science Fiction Writers, St. James Press, 1991.

PERIODICALS

Kirkus Reviews, March 1, 1996, p. 342.

Locus, December, 1994, p. 65.

Science Fiction Chronicle, June, 1997.

Voice of Youth Advocates, December, 1994, p. 288.

McGUIRE, Leslie (Sarah) 1945-
(Louisa Britton, Leslie Burton, Dorothy Eyre, Sarah Keyser, Sarah Leslie, Shari Robinson, David Strong, pseudonyms)

■ **Personal**

Born January 18, 1945, in New York, NY; daughter of Timothy Strong and Virginia Wenderoth (Hastings) McGuire; married Daniel Max, April 10, 1971; children: David. *Education:* Barnard College, A.B., 1966. *Politics:* Democrat. *Religion:* Episcopalian.

■ **Career**

Writer and illustrator. Guild for the Blind, New York City, public relations assistant, 1966-67; Public School #165, New York City, special reading teacher, 1967-69; Platt & Munk Publishers, New York City, editor, 1969-77.

■ **Awards, Honors**

Children's Books of the Year, Child Study Association of America, 1986, for *The Poky Little Puppy and the Lost Bone.*

■ **Writings**

FOR CHILDREN

Farm Animals, Platt, 1970.
Birds, Platt, 1970.
Forest Animals, Platt, 1970.
Fish, Platt, 1970.
Wild Animals, Platt, 1970.
Water Life, Platt, 1970.
You: How Your Body Works, Platt, 1974, revised edition published as *Susan Perl's Human Body Book,* 1977.
Pebbles and Bamm-Bamm: The Little Helpers, Tuffy Books, 1980.
Dino's Happy and Sad Book, Tuffy Books, 1980.
Fred Flintstone's Counting Book, Tuffy Books, 1980.
Yogi Bear's Animal Friends, Tuffy Books, 1980.
Huckleberry Hound Takes a Trip, Tuffy Books, 1980.
Barney's Picnic, Tuffy Books, 1980.
(Self-illustrated) *This Farm Is a Mess,* Parents' Magazine Press, 1981.
Miss Mopp's Lucky Day, illustrated by Jody Silver, Parents' Magazine Press, 1981.
Scooter Computer and Mr. Chips: The Computer in the Candy Store, illustrated by John Costanza, Golden Books, 1984.
Rainbow Brite and the Big Color Mix-Up, Western Publications, 1984.
Bialosky's Christmas (created by Peggy and Alan Bialosky), illustrated by Jerry Joyner, Golden Books, 1984.
Bialosky's Special Picnic (created by Peggy and Alan Bialosky), Golden Books, 1985.
My Pop-up Farm, Golden Books, 1985.
My Pop-up Zoo, Golden Books, 1985.
My Pop-up Mother Goose, Golden Books, 1985.

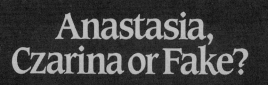

Leslie McGuire's entry in Greenhaven Press's "Great Mysteries: Opposing Viewpoints" series investigates the possibility that Princess Anastasia may have escaped execution when the Bolsheviks murdered her parents, the last czar and czarina of Russia.

Catherine the Great, Chelsea House, 1986.
Napoleon, Chelsea House, 1986.
Bialosky's Best Behavior: A Book of Manners (created by Peggy and Alan Bialosky), illustrated by Tom Cooke, Golden Books, 1986.
Garfield and the Space Cat (created by Jim Davis), Golden Books, 1988.
Lions, photographs by Leonard Lee Rue III and Len Rue, Jr., Atheneum, 1989.
Anastasia, Czarina or Fake? Opposing Viewpoints, Greenhaven Press, 1989.
Baby Night Owl, illustrated by Mary Szilagyi, Random House, 1989.
Who Will Play with Little Dinosaur?, illustrated by Norman Gorbaty, Random House, 1989.
Barbie: A Picnic Surprise, illustrated by Art and Kim Ellis, Western Publications, 1990.
(With Norma Simone and Jack C. Harris) *Garfield Stories* (created by Jim Davis), illustrated by Mike Fentz, Western Publications, 1990.
Is There Life After Sixth Grade?, illustrated by Paul Henry, Troll Associates, 1990.
The Cleanup, illustrated by Sue DiCiccio, Western Publications, 1990.

Minnie and Daisy Go to the Mall: A Book of Opposites, illustrated by Darrel Baker, Golden Books, 1990.
Suicide, Rourke Corporation, 1990.
Death and Illness, Rourke Corporation, 1990.
Victims, Rourke Corporation, 1991.
Magellan Saves the Day, illustrated by Tom Brannon, Western Publications, 1991.
I Know How to Dress, Little & Woods Press, 1991.
I Know My Animals, Little & Woods Press, 1991.
I Know My Colors, Little & Woods Press, 1991.
I Know My Foods, Little & Woods Press, 1991.
I Know My Numbers, Little & Woods Press, 1991.
I Know the Time, Little & Woods Press, 1991.
(Reteller) *The Three Bears,* illustrated by Carolyn Bracken, Little & Woods Press, 1991.
(Reteller) *Cinderella,* illustrated by Bracken, Little & Woods Press, 1991.
(Editor) *Mother Goose,* illustrated by Hitomi Kuroki, Little & Woods Press, 1991.
Big Bug, Little Bug, illustrated by Jill Dubin, Little & Woods Press, 1991.
Farm, illustrated by Yoko Kawasaki, Little & Woods Press, 1991.
Zoo, illustrated by Nanako Murabayashi, Little & Woods Press, 1991.
Find the Kittens, 1 to 10, illustrated by Dubin, Little & Woods Press, 1991.
Where Are My Toys?, illustrated by Dubin, Little & Woods Press, 1991.
Who Will Play with Me?, illustrated by Dubin, Little & Woods Press, 1991.
Fred and the Pet Show Panic, illustrated by Dave Henderson, Fawcett Columbine, 1991.
Fred in Charge, illustrated by Henderson, Fawcett Columbine, 1991.
Fred Saves the Day, illustrated by Henderson, Fawcett Columbine, 1991.
Fred to the Rescue, illustrated by Henderson, Fawcett Columbine, 1991.
The Terrible Truth about Third Grade, illustrated by Henderson, Troll Associates, 1992.
Big Dan's Moving Van, illustrated by Joe Mathieu, Random House, 1993.
(Adapter) Liz Farrington, *Nightmares in the Mist,* illustrated by Brian McGovern, Enchante Publishing, 1994.
Time for Bed?: An Action Pop-up Book, illustrated by Jean Pidgeon, Reader's Digest Association, 1994.
Big Frank's Fire Truck, illustrated by Joe Mathieu, Random House, 1995.
Bobby's World: I'm Not a Baby, designed by Jim Deesing, illustrated by Adrienne Brown and Floyd Norman, Bedrock Press, 1995.
Bobby's World: Things that Go Bump, designed by Deesing, illustrated by Brown and Norman, Bedrock Press, 1995.
(Adapter) Sherri Stoner and Deanna Oliver, *Casper: The Movie Storybook,* Price Stern Sloan, 1995.
(Adapter) Charles Edward Pogue, *Dragonheart: The Movie Storybook,* Price Stern Sloan, 1996.

UNDER PSEUDONYM SARAH KEYSER

(Editor) James Kruess, *The Zoo That Grew,* Platt, 1970.

Numbers Are Things, Platt, 1971.
Up, Down, All Around, Platt, 1971.
Pop up Circus Book, Platt, 1973.
Pop up Construction Book, Platt, 1973.
Who Lives Here?, Platt, 1973.
Gregg Finds an Egg, Platt, 1973.

UNDER PSEUDONYM LESLIE BURTON

Growing Up in Nature, Platt, 1971.
Parade of Seasons, Platt, 1971.
Nature's Helpers, Platt, 1971.
Children Here, Children There, Platt, 1971.

UNDER PSEUDONYM DOROTHY EYRE

Petrouchka: From an Old Russian Legend, Platt, 1971.
Rainbow Bright Saves Spring, illustrated by Roy Wilson, Golden Books, 1985.

UNDER NAME SARAH LESLIE

Who Invented It and What Makes It Work?, Platt, 1976.
Seasons, Platt, 1977.
The Curious Little Kitten Plays Hide-and-Seek, illustrated by Maggie Swanson, Golden Books, 1985.
The Poky Little Puppy and the Lost Bone, illustrated by Jean Chandler, Golden Books, 1985.
The Saggy Baggy Elephant and the New Dance, illustrated by Frank Rehkiewicz, Golden Books, 1985.

OTHER

(With Beatrice Lewis) *Making Mosaics* (adult), Drake, 1973.
(Under pseudonym Louisa Britton) *The Bible Story Picture Book: Stories from the Old and New Testaments,* Platt, 1975.
(Under pseudonym Shari Robinson) *Numbers, Signs, and Pictures: A First Number Book,* Platt, 1975, published as *A First Number Book,* illustrated by Sal Murdocca, Grosset, 1981.
(Under pseudonym David Strong) *The Magic Book,* Platt, 1977.
(Illustrator) Nancy Cocola, *These Little Piggies,* Warner Juvenile Books, 1991.

Also author, under pseudonym David Strong, of *Magic Tricks,* Platt.

■ Sidelights

A prolific author and illustrator of books for children, Leslie McGuire has created board books and pop-up books for young children, chapter books for middle grade readers, and books dealing with modern and historical issues for teenagers. An example of the author's versatility, *Anastasia: Czarina or Fake?,* McGuire's entry in Greenhaven Press's "Great Mysteries: Opposing Viewpoints" series for adolescents, offers an engaging exploration of the princess's unresolved disappearance. "The text in Anastasia is involving, and does introduce a segment of Russian history," noted *School Library Journal* contributor Marilyn Long Graham.

■ Works Cited

Graham, Marilyn Long, review of *Anastasia: Czarina or Fake? School Library Journal,* May, 1990, p. 129.

■ For More Information See

PERIODICALS

Booklist, December 15, 1989, p. 830; March 1, 1990, p. 1337.
Publishers Weekly, March 11, 1996, p. 62.
School Library Journal, May, 1990, p. 129; September, 1990, p. 230; February, 1992, p. 94.*

* * *

McMOREY, James L.
See MOYER, Terry J.

* * *

MEAD, Alice 1952-

■ Personal

Born January 11, 1952, in Portchester, NY; daughter of Richard (a teacher) and Jeanne (a secretary) Weber; married Larry Mead (a recreation director), November, 1983; children: Jeffrey O'Hara, Michael O'Hara. *Education:* Bryn Mawr College, B.A., 1973; Southern Connecticut State University, M.Ed., 1975; University of Southern Maine, B.A. (in art education), 1985. *Politics:* Democrat. *Religion:* Quaker. *Hobbies and other interests:* Flute, gardening, painting-nature, photography, video.

■ Career

Has worked as an art teacher in Connecticut and Maine, 1974-92, and as a preschool teacher in Maine, 1980-83. Board member for Project Co-Step for developmentally delayed preschoolers; active in efforts to aid children in Kosovo, Serbia. Flutist. *Member:* Maine Writers and Publishers Alliance, Maine Art Education Association.

■ Writings

Crossing the Starlight Bridge, Bradbury, 1994.
Walking the Edge, Albert Whitman, 1995.
Junebug, Farrar, Straus, 1995.
Journey to Kosovo, Loose Cannon Press, 1995.
(Editor with Arnold Neptune) *Giants of the Dawnland: Ancient Wabanaki Tales,* Loose Cannon Press, 1996.
Adem's Cross, Farrar, Straus, 1996.
Junebug 2, Farrar, Straus, 1997.

■ Work in Progress

Research on Scotland in 1606, the end of the Scottish clan system, and MacBeth.

ALICE MEAD

■ Sidelights

Alice Mead's novels for young adults and middle graders often feature young people coping with dire circumstances, who with ingenuity, determination, and the aid of helpful adults make positive, if small, changes in their own lives and the lives of those around them. In *Crossing the Starlight Bridge,* Mead's first work, nine-year-old Rayanne's artistic abilities help smooth the transition when she and her mother move in with her grandmother, forcing Rayanne to adjust all at once to living in the city, making friends at a new school, and dealing with the break-up of her parents' marriage. Scott, the main character in *Walking the Edge,* Mead's next story, is also suffering the effects of his parents' broken marriage. In *Junebug,* Mead depicts life in the housing projects, with its ever-present drug dealers and gang warfare, and the efforts of one African American family not to be defeated by these circumstances. *Adem's Cross* takes place in the Eastern European country formerly known as Yugoslavia, where twelve-year-old Adem witnesses the death of his sister at the hands of soldiers, and must flee for his life as a consequence. Mead told *SATA:* "I have always been interested in writing about children who—for some reason—live on the edge of the mainstream society. I feel that authors and artists should travel to these edges, to widen the circle of inclusion through empathy and art.

"For many years I was an art teacher working with low-income children," Mead explained. "In America, wealth abounds yet a large proportion of American children are poor. Everyone tells poor kids to have hopes, to dream—but how do you go about it? We have a society that sees children in very negative ways. I like to celebrate the intensity and steadfastness of kids, their creativity and fresh energy."

Rayanne, the central character in *Crossing the Starlight Bridge,* is a member of the Penobscot tribe of Native Americans. She and her parents have always lived on their island reservation but now her father, who is unable to find work there, decides to leave. "Mead deftly establishes a child's point of view with simple and unpretentious language," observed Deborah Stevenson in the *Bulletin of the Center for Children's Books,* noting that Rayanne's misery over her father's absence is deepened when she realizes that she and her mother must leave the island, and her pet rabbit, behind. References to traditional Penobscot lore arise in the character of the grandmother, with whom Rayanne and her mother go to live, "a strong, contemporary, optimistic woman whose warmth and encouragement are restorative," Susan Scheps asserted in *School Library Journal.* Though Scheps found the novel's ending a little too abrupt, a *Kirkus Reviews* critic called *Crossing the Starlight Bridge* "a believable and compelling portrayal of a Native American family coexisting with white society while retaining its own traditions."

Like Rayanne and other Mead protagonists, Scott, the main character in *Walking the Edge,* looks to something positive outside of himself to give him strength to endure the poverty and unhappiness of his life. Set in Maine and based on real events, the novel describes Scott's involvement in a science project that aims to restock the local bay with clams. *School Library Journal* contributor Connie Tyrrell Burns, commenting favorably on Mead's realistic depiction of the turbulent emotions of her adolescent hero, maintained that "Scott's amazement at the delicate and relentless process of life will be shared by readers."

Reeve McClain, known as Junebug, reluctantly approaches his tenth birthday in Mead's novel *Junebug,* knowing that he will then be recruited to join one of the gangs that terrorizes his housing project. Junebug develops an idea he hopes will help him realize his dream of learning to sail and captaining his own boat. He collects and cleans fifty glass bottles and seals in each a piece of paper describing his dream, then sets the bottles free on a boat trip around the harbor in New Haven, Connecticut. "The novel is a hopeful one," Maeve Visser Knoth commented in *Horn Book,* "in spite of the vivid portrait of the housing project's grim realities." Elizabeth Bush, on the other hand, writing in *Bulletin of the Center for Children's Books,* called *Junebug*'s happy ending "soothing but decidedly too easy," though her conclusion echoed that of a critic in *Kirkus Reviews,* who wrote that "readers will be rooting for Junebug and his dreams all the way." Mead commented to *SATA:* "I grew up near the water and have always loved boats. I wanted to be either a sea captain or a lighthouse keeper and live on an island. Writing a book is a lot like putting a message in a bottle and tossing it overboard—you never know who will read it! Or where!"

In *Adem's Cross,* Mead sets her story in Kosovo, a province of the former Yugoslavia which has been taken over by Serbian soldiers bent on "cleansing" the population of Albanians, descendants of the land's ancient

Adem, an Albanian youth living in the former Yugoslavia, witnesses the death of his sister at the hands of Serbian soldiers and now must run for his life. (Cover illustration by Ed Young.)

conquerors. Twelve-year-old Adem and his family have been waiting for the Serb troops to leave their hometown for four years when Adem's older sister takes the bold stance of participating in a peaceful demonstration against the invaders. She is subsequently killed by Serb soldiers, and Adem, enraged at his family's passivity, rebels by going out alone one night. He is caught by three soldiers who break his hand and carve a Serbian symbol, a Cyrillic cross, into his chest with a knife. He decides to leave Kosovo and is aided in his flight by a Serb and a gypsy. "Mead preps readers with a quick, efficient sketch of Yugoslavia's recent history before jumping into this disturbing society," observed Marilyn Payne Phillips in her review in *School Library Journal.* Critics noted that Mead does not take sides in the real-life deadly conflict. Instead, she "writes powerfully and eloquently about Adem's attempt to understand why people mistreat each other," Susan Dove Lempke remarked in *Booklist.*

Mead continued: "For the past two years, I have been traveling to Eastern Europe. When I was little I was told that these countries lay behind the Iron Curtain, a place Americans didn't go. Since the collapse of communism,

I have traveled there twice a year to document the conditions of children's lives. My novel, *Adem's Cross,* is about the cleansing of Albanian children in southern Serbia. I have brought nine teenagers to the U.S. to study in high schools in Maine. In addition, a group of schools got together and sent a truckload of toys to Kosovo, Serbia."

■ Works Cited

Burns, Connie Tyrrell, review of *Walking the Edge, School Library Journal,* December, 1995, p. 106.

Bush, Elizabeth, review of *Junebug, Bulletin of the Center for Children's Books,* December, 1995, pp. 133-34.

Review of *Crossing the Starlight Bridge, Kirkus Reviews,* May 1, 1994, p. 634.

Review of *Junebug, Kirkus Reviews,* September 1, 1995, p. 1284.

Knoth, Maeve Visser, review of *Junebug, Horn Book,* March, 1996, p. 198.

Lempke, Susan Dove, review of *Adem's Cross, Booklist,* November 15, 1996, pp. 579, 581.

Phillips, Marilyn Payne, review of *Adem's Cross, School Library Journal,* November, 1996, p. 109.

Scheps, Susan, review of *Crossing the Starlight Bridge, School Library Journal,* June, 1994, pp. 132-33.

Stevenson, Deborah, review of *Crossing the Starlight Bridge, Bulletin of the Center for Children's Books,* June, 1994, p. 329.

■ For More Information See

PERIODICALS

Booklist, June 1, 1994, p. 1811.
Children's Book Review Service, July, 1994, p. 155.
Children's Book Watch, January, 1996, p. 5.
Five Owls, January, 1996, p. 65.
Horn Book, September, 1994, p. 589.
Instructor, April, 1996, p. 58.
Kirkus Reviews, May 1, 1994, p. 634; September 1, 1995, p. 1284; October 15, 1996, p. 1535.
New York Times Book Review, January 14, 1996, pp. 23, 66.
Parents, December, 1995, p. 232.
Publishers Weekly, April 18, 1994, p. 64; October 21, 1996, p. 84.
School Library Journal, December, 1995, p. 106.
Voice of Youth Advocates, February, 1996, p. 374.

*   *   *

MOLONEY, James 1954-

■ Personal

Born September 20, 1954, in Sydney, Australia; son of Frank (a manager of truck manufacturing) and Betty (a teacher; maiden name, Wilkinson) Moloney; married Kate Hickey (a teacher and librarian), April 4, 1983; children: Siobhan, Julia, Bede. *Education:* Griffith University, Diploma in Primary Teaching, 1975; Queensland University of Technology, Graduate Diplomas in

JAMES MOLONEY

Computer Education, 1988, and Teacher Librarianship, 1979; University of Queensland, B.E.S., 1981. *Religion:* Roman Catholic. *Hobbies and other interests:* Reading, family activities, travel.

■ Addresses

Home and office—142 Buena Vista Ave., Coorparoo, Queensland 4151, Australia. *Electronic mail*—mcap @ ozemail.com.au.

■ Career

Marist College Ashgrove, Brisbane, Australia, teacher and librarian at primary school, 1983-93, 1995-96; writer, 1994—.

■ Awards, Honors

Family Award, Relationships Australia, 1992, for *Crossfire,* and 1993, for *Dougy;* Children's Book of the Year Honour Book, Children's Book Council of Australia (CBCA), 1994, for *Dougy,* and 1995, for *Gracey;* Multicultural Award, Australian Department of Multicultural Affairs, 1995, for *Gracey;* Children's Book of the Year, CBCA, 1996, for *Swashbuckler;* Shortlist, Children's Book of the Year, CBCA, 1996, for *The House on River Terrace,* and 1997, for *A Bridge to Wiseman's Cove.*

■ Writings

Crossfire, University of Queensland Press (St. Lucia, Australia), 1992.
Dougy, University of Queensland Press, 1993.
Gracey, University of Queensland Press, 1994.
Swashbuckler, University of Queensland Press, 1995.
The House on River Terrace, University of Queensland Press, 1995.
A Bridge to Wiseman's Cove, University of Queensland Press, 1996.
The Pipe, Lothian, 1996.

■ Work in Progress

Buzzard Breath and Brains, a sequel to *Swashbuckler.*

■ Sidelights

James Moloney told *SATA:* "The question I am most often asked in letters from my readers is 'Are you an Aborigine?' This is because my second and third books, *Dougy* and *Gracey,* tell the story of an Aboriginal family in outback Australia. Both are written in the first person, and I suppose my readers are wondering how much of the story is autobiographical.

"In fact, I am not an Australian Aborigine, though I feel a deep empathy for the traditional owners of this land. As a young man, I was posted to the small town of Cunnamulla to teach in the school there. Cunnamulla has a large Aboriginal population, and it was here that I became troubled by the latent racism hidden under the surface of otherwise cordial relations between white and black. I felt that the slightest spark could burn away the superficial tolerance, revealing the ugliness beneath. This is precisely the scenario I created in *Dougy.* I was also disturbed by the ease with which newcomers to the town would slide into the mind-set of prejudice. I highlighted this through the character of Trent Foster in *Gracey.*

"I have heard many authors say that their stories begin with a character, while others point to a particular setting. For me, stories usually begin with a big idea, some philosophical or political conundrum which niggles at me for weeks or months, or even years, until I feel compelled to express my feelings in a story. Gradually the issues at hand become less important as my interest turns to the characters I have invented. In fact, I use this transition to judge my literary progress, for only when the characters mean more to me than their predicaments do I know I am on the right track.

"There was much from my time in Cunnamulla to occupy my mind in this way. The first time this compulsion led to publication, the story was not concerned with racial relations, but with violence and the 'gun culture' so beloved of Australian, and I suspect American, men. The novel was *Crossfire. Dougy* followed quickly but, by the time I was plotting *Gracey,* I found that my growing family was taking more of my time in the evenings. I began rising at four o'clock in the morning and working until it was time to get ready for work. This has been a feature of my writing routine ever since, and it is likely to remain so until I become a full-time writer.

"*Swashbuckler* was my first attempt at a younger audience. Its success has encouraged me to focus more on this eight- to twelve-year-old age group. The wider critical acclaim for my work also prompted people to point out that all of my stories tend to explore the child's alienation from family, particularly son from father. This reaches its extreme in my novel *A Bridge to Wiseman's Cove.* The strange thing is that, having discovered this theme in my work, I now feel the urge to turn away from it."

■ For More Information See

PERIODICALS

Australian Book Review, February, 1992, p. 58; July, 1994, p. 65; June, 1995, p. 61; August, 1995, p. 60; February, 1996, p. 57.
Bookbird, summer, 1994, p. 54.
Horn Book, March-April, 1995, pp. 237-39.
Magpies, November, 1992, p. 33.
Reading Time, February, 1997, p. 30.

* * *

MOYER, Terry J. 1937-
(James L. McMorey)

■ Personal

Born January 27, 1937, in Idaho Falls, ID; son of Hushul B. and Verna Mary (Metcalf) Moyer; married Donna Mae Schipper (a teacher); children: Cynthia Anne Moyer Manning, Vikki Vreni Moyer Bolich, Adrian C. *Education:* Brigham Young University, B.A., 1960; University of Southern California, M.S.Ed., 1964; attended California State University, Northridge, 1965-68. *Politics:* Conservative Republican. *Religion:* Church of Jesus Christ of Latter-day Saints (Mormon). *Hobbies and other interests:* Mountain climbing, genealogical research, the Civil War, gardening, hiking.

■ Addresses

Home—3202 Sagebrush Circle, Salt Lake City, UT 84121. *Office*—50 East North Temple St., 21st Floor, Salt Lake City, UT 84150.

■ Career

High school teacher in Simi Valley, CA, 1961-75; Latter-day Saints Social Services, Salt Lake City, UT, administrator of program development, 1975-90; Latter-day Saints Translation, Salt Lake City, translation supervisor and linguist, 1991—. State coordinator for Civil War database project, U.S. National Parks. Has held various leadership positions within Church of Jesus Christ of Latter-day Saints (LDS). *Military service:*

Army National Guard, 1960-66; became staff sergeant.
Member: National Right to Life Organization.

■ Writings

Crescendo (young adult novel), Horizon Publishers,
1995.
Have I Got a Story for You! (inspirational stories),
Horizon Publishers, 1996.

Some writings appear under the pseudonym James L.
McMorey.

■ Work in Progress

Ritter, a young adult novel; *Remembering Brigham
Young University; The Defector,* a Latter-day Saints
novel.

■ Adaptations

Movie rights to *Crescendo* have been sold.

* * *

MUNSINGER, Lynn 1951-

■ Personal

Born December 24, 1951, in Greenfield, MA; daughter
of Robert William and Jeanne (Currey) Munsinger;
married Dan Lace (a sales manager), November 27,
1981. *Education:* Tufts University, B.A., 1974; Rhode
Island School of Design, B.F.A., 1977.

■ Addresses

Home—Arlington, MA, 02174.

■ Career

Freelance illustrator, 1977—.

■ Awards, Honors

Volunteer State award, 1984, for *Howliday Inn* by
James Howe; *New York Times Notable Book* selection,
1986, for *Hugh Pine and the Good Place* by Janwillem
Van de Wetering; Emphasis on Reading award (Grades
2-3), 1987-88, for *My Mother Never Listens to Me* by
Marjorie Weinman Sharmat; Little Archer award, 1989,
for *Underwear!* by Mary Monsell; Colorado Children's
Book Award, 1990, California Young Reader (Primary),
1991, and Golden Sower award (K-3), 1991, all for
Tacky the Penguin by Helen Lester.

■ Illustrator

Margret Elbow, *The Rootomom Tree,* Houghton, 1978.
William Cole, editor, *An Arkful of Animals: Poems for
the Very Young,* Houghton, 1978.
Jane Sutton, *What Should a Hippo Wear,* Houghton,
1979.

When postman Mr. McTosh discusses his plans for a
trip to New York, Hugh Pine invites himself along in
this installment of Janwillem van de Wetering's
humorous stories featuring the elderly porcupine.
(From *Hugh Pine and Something Else,* illustrated by
Munsinger.)

Nancy Robison, *The Lizard Hunt,* Lothrop, 1979.
Gloria Skurzynski, *Martin by Himself,* Houghton, 1979.
Elaine M. Willoughby, *Boris and the Monsters,* Hough-
ton, 1980.
Janwillem van de Wetering, *Hugh Pine,* Houghton,
1980.
Karen J. Gounaud, *A Very Mice Joke Book,* Houghton,
1981.
Sandol Stoddard, *Bedtime Mouse,* Houghton, 1981.
James Howe, *Howliday Inn,* Atheneum, 1982.
Judy Delton, *A Pet for Duck and Bear,* edited by Ann
Fay, A. Whitman, 1982.
Galway Kinnell, *How the Alligator Missed Breakfast,*
Houghton, 1982.
Phyllis Rose Eisenberg, *Don't Tell Me a Ghost Story,*
Harcourt, 1982.
Helen Lester, *The Wizard, the Fairy, and the Magic
Chicken,* Houghton, 1983.
Judy Delton, *Duck Goes Fishing,* A. Whitman, 1983.
Joseph Slate, *The Mean, Clean, Giant Canoe Machine,*
Crowell, 1983.

Lynn Munsinger's endearing illustrations spotlight Zachary Zebra and Orfo Orangutan, who try to convince surly Bismark Buffalo that there is great enjoyment in wearing zany underwear. (From *Underwear!,* written by Mary Elise Monsell.)

Caroline Levine, *Silly School Riddles and Other Classroom Crack-Ups,* A. Whitman, 1984.

Judy Delton, *Bear and Duck on the Run,* A. Whitman, 1984.

Richard Latta, *This Little Pig Had a Riddle,* A. Whitman, 1984.

Ann Tompert, *Nothing Sticks Like a Shadow,* Houghton, 1984.

Eve Bunting, *Monkey in the Middle,* Harcourt, 1984.

Marjorie Weinman Sharmat, *My Mother Never Listens to Me,* A. Whitman, 1984.

Virginia Mueller, *A Playhouse for Monster,* A. Whitman, 1985.

Mueller, *Monster and the Baby,* A. Whitman, 1985.

Seymour Reit and others, *When Small Is Tall and Other Read-together Tales,* Random House, 1985.

Helen Lester, *It Wasn't My Fault,* Houghton, 1985.

Judy Delton, *The Elephant in Duck's Garden,* A. Whitman, 1985.

Helen Lester, *A Porcupine Named Fluffy,* Houghton, 1986.

Joan Phillips, *My New Boy,* Random House, 1986.

Virginia Mueller, *Monster Can't Sleep,* A. Whitman, 1986.

Judy Delton, *Rabbit Goes to Night School,* A. Whitman, 1986.

Janwillem van de Wetering, *Hugh Pine and the Good Place,* Houghton, 1986.

William H. Hooks and others, *Read-a-Rebus: Tales and Rhymes in Words and Pictures,* Random House, 1986.

Virginia Mueller, *A Halloween Mask for Monster,* A. Whitman, 1986.

Helen Lester, *Pookins Gets Her Way,* Houghton, 1987.

Barbara Bottner, *Zoo Song,* Scholastic, Inc., 1987.

Joanna Cole, *Norma Jean, Jumping Bean,* Random House, 1987.

Helen Lester, *Tacky the Penguin,* Houghton, 1988.

Gloria Whelan, *A Week of Raccoons,* Knopf, 1988.

Linda Hayward, *Hello, House!,* Random House, 1988.

Mary Ada Schwartz, *Spiffen, a Tale of a Tidy Pig,* A. Whitman, 1988.

Sandol Stoddard, *Bedtime for Bear,* Houghton, 1988.

Mary Elise Monsell, *Underwear!,* A. Whitman, 1988.

Susan Heyboer O'Keefe, *One Hungry Monster: A Counting Book in Rhyme,* Little, Brown, 1989.

Janwillem van de Wetering, *Hugh Pine and Something Else,* Houghton, 1989.

William J. Smith, *Ho for a Hat!,* Little, Brown, 1989.

Pat Lowery Collins, *Tomorrow, Up and Away,* Houghton, 1990.

Maryann Macdonald, *Hedgehog Bakes a Cake,* Gareth Stevens, 1990.

Joanna Cole, *Don't Call Me Names,* Random House, 1990.

Helen Lester, *The Revenge of the Magic Chicken,* Houghton, 1990.

Virginia Mueller, *Monster's Birthday Hiccups,* A. Whitman, 1991.

Mueller, *Monster Goes to School,* A. Whitman, 1991.

Maryann Macdonald, *Rabbit's Birthday Kite,* Bantam, 1991.

Joanne Oppenheim, *Rooter Remembers: A Bank Street Book about Values,* Viking, 1991.

William Cole, selector, *A Zooful of Animals,* Houghton, 1992.

Helen Lester, *Me First,* Houghton, 1992.

William H. Hooks, *Rough, Tough, Rowdy: A Bank Street Book about Values,* Viking, 1992.

Barbara Brenner, *Group Soup: A Bank Street Book about Values,* Viking, 1992.

Ann Tompert, *Just a Little Bit,* Houghton, 1993.

Valiska Gregory, *Babysitting for Benjamin,* Little, Brown, 1993.

Helen Lester, *Three Cheers for Tacky,* Houghton, 1994.

William H. Hooks and Betty Boegehold, *The Rainbow Ribbon: A Bank Street Book about Values,* Puffin, 1994.

Abby Levine, *Ollie Knows Everything,* A. Whitman, 1994.

Helen Lester, *Lin's Backpack,* Addison-Wesley, 1994, translated as *La Mochila de Lin,* 1995.

Sandol Stoddard, *Turtle Time: A Bedtime Story,* Houghton, 1995.

Stephen Krensky, *The Three Blind Mice Mystery,* Dell, 1995.

Ogden Nash, *The Tale of Custard the Dragon,* Little, Brown, 1995.

Helen Lester, *Listen, Buddy,* Houghton, 1995.

Joanna Cole and Stephanie Calmenson, *Gator Girls,* Morrow, 1995.

Helen Lester, *Princess Penelope's Parrot,* Houghton, 1996.

Ogden Nash, *Custard the Dragon and the Wicked Knight,* Little, Brown, 1996.

A. M. Monson, *Wanted—Best Friend,* Dial, 1997.

Stephanie Calmenson and Joanna Cole, *Rockin' Reptiles,* Morrow, 1997.

Kay Winters, *The Teeny Tiny Ghost,* HarperCollins, 1998.

Illustrator of textbooks and greeting cards. Contributor of illustrations to *Cricket.*

■ Sidelights

The whimsical animal characters created by illustrator Lynn Munsinger have decorated the pages of numerous children's books by a wide variety of authors. From Ogden Nash's early twentieth-century classic, *The Tale of Custard the Dragon,* to works by such contemporary authors as Joanna Cole, Helen Lester, and Virginia Mueller, Munsinger has brought her creative talent and imagination to bear. "I ... feel very fortunate to be an illustrator," Munsinger once told *SATA.* "I really enjoy my work and cannot conceive of doing anything else."

Born in Greenfield, Massachusetts, in 1951, Munsinger knew she wanted to be an artist since she was a young girl. After graduating from high school, she attended Tufts University, moving on to Rhode Island School of Design (RISDI) after earning her B.A. in 1974. Munsinger obtained her B.F.A. degree from RISDI in 1977, and immediately began looking for freelance assignments. Her first illustration job, Margret Elbow's *The Rootomom Tree,* was published a year later. Many more

In their second book about Tacky the Penguin, author Helen Lester and illustrator Munsinger follow Tacky's awkward attempts to help his team win the Penguin Cheering Contest. (From *Three Cheers for Tacky.*)

book illustration projects would follow in the coming years, meeting with critical praise. Of Munsinger's work for Mary Elise Monsell's *Underwear!,* for instance, a *Booklist* reviewer called the "zany," "perky-colored" illustrations "a perfect foil for the text," while Lori A. Janick maintained in *School Library Journal* that "what could have been an unbelievable moralistic tale ... is saved by Munsinger's delightful illustrations." And reviewing Judy Delton's *Rabbit Goes to Night School, Booklist*'s Denise M. Wilms stated that "Munsinger's deft pen-and-ink drawings ... lend a good deal of personality to the story."

While Munsinger has illustrated books for numerous authors, including Delton, Marjorie Weinman Sharmat, Galway Kinnell, and Ann Tompert, she has developed multi-book working relationships with several popular children's book writers. Dutch-immigrant author Janwillem van de Wetering's three-book series featuring a large, elderly porcupine named Hugh Pine benefit from Munsinger's pen-and-ink renderings. In *Hugh Pine,* the first book in the series, the wise porcupine learns to walk upright and mimic a small human being in order to avoid getting hit by passing cars, and then finds ways to help his younger, more inexperienced friends cross busy roads in safety. In *Hugh Pine and the Good Place,* the clever old porcupine longs to move out to the deserted island he can see from his home in a tree growing on the Maine coast, but changes his mind after a few days of loneliness. "Munsinger provides sprightly line drawings with just the right elan to give this porcupine person believability," commented Barbara Elleman in *Booklist.* And in *Hugh Pine and Something Else,* Munsinger captures Hugh as he accompanies his friend, Postman McTosh, to New York City, meeting a host of sophisticated city-dwelling animals before returning to his comfortable woodland home in Maine.

The humorous "Monster" stories of Virginia Mueller are also enhanced by Munsinger's artwork. In full-color illustrations, Munsinger portrays green-furred, toothsome young Monster in a variety of childlike situations but makes the setting particularly monster-like—the Monster family has carnivorous Venus fly-traps instead of regular houseplants, and their antimacassars are made of spider webs! In *Monster and the Baby* he tries to quiet his baby sister with building blocks, but finds she's only happy when the buildings crash to the ground. And in *A Playhouse for Monster,* the young creature thrills to having a place all his own, until he realizes that sharing his new playhouse with his friends is far more fun. *A Halloween Mask for Monster* finds the furry green creature donning fearsome masks that look like human children—and scaring everyone in his family—until he decides that they're *too* scary and his own face will do just fine. A *Publishers Weekly* reviewer praised the story, noting that it is "made more agreeable because of Munsinger's good-natured pictures." Other Monster stories illustrated by Munsinger include *Monster Can't Sleep, Monster's Birthday Hiccups,* and *Monster Goes to School.*

Spoiled Princess Penelope loses her chance to impress a handsome young prince when her parrot echoes all the princess's rude comments. (From *Princess Penelope's Parrot,* written by Helen Lester and illustrated by Munsinger.)

Munsinger's most prolific working relationship has been with author Helen Lester. Beginning with Lester's 1983 book *The Wizard, the Fairy, and the Magic Chicken,* the two have joined forces on numerous stories filled with zany humor. Beginning their collaboration with the story of a competition between three sorcerers, Lester and Munsinger produced a sequel, *The Revenge of the Magic Chicken,* which reunites the Chicken with his friends the Wizard and the Fairy. "The text's humor gets the full treatment in Munsinger's raucous art," noted Ilene Cooper, reviewing the appealing picture book for *Booklist.*

Two books featuring a penguin named Tacky have also been produced by the creative Munsinger-Lester duo. While most penguins try hard to fit in with their formally attired fellows in *Tacky the Penguin,* Tacky is a free spirit. Unlike the properly bow-tied Angel, Goodly, Lovely, and friends, Tacky wears gaudy, rumpled Hawaiian-print shirts, making him a stand-out around the Arctic Circle. When Tacky encounters a band of penguin-snatching hunters, his crazy antics flabbergast them so much that they question whether these birds are penguins after all. And in *Three Cheers for Tacky,* the nonconformist penguin makes a muddle of his team's routine for the Penguin Cheering Contest, only to find his efforts the highlight of what would otherwise be a boring competition. *Booklist* reviewer Kathryn Broderick praises Munsinger for her "slyly humorous watercolors" and calls *Three Cheers for Tacky* "a funny, funny picture book."

Lester and Munsinger have also worked together on several other picture books for young children, many of which feature animal characters. In *A Porcupine Named Fluffy,* a young prickly porcupine ends up with the name

"Fluffy," a name that his sharp quills just won't let him live up to. Only after he meets a young rhinoceros with an equally silly name—Hippo—does he begin to think of his name as a source of fun. "Munsinger's expressively drawn pictures ... wring out every funny nuance," noted Ilene Cooper in *Booklist*. In *Me First*, youngsters watch Pinkerton Pig learn a lesson about being pushy through Munsinger's series of brightly colored watercolor washes. And *Listen, Buddy* features a hare with his head in the clouds instead of on what people are telling him. Mistaking his father's request for a pen, Buddy brings a hen, signaling even more silliness to come.

Although animals figure most prominently in Munsinger's drawings, human children take center stage in several books written by Lester. In *It Wasn't My Fault*, published in 1985, a young boy is always quick to blame something else for his own actions. A spoiled girl who makes a foolish wish to be turned into a flower is featured in *Pookins Gets Her Way*, a book that features illustrations that are "full of mischief," according to a *Publishers Weekly* critic. And *Princess Penelope's Parrot* features another spoiled child, this time a princess whose nasty words come back to haunt her during her birthday party, when a parrot who refused to speak to her suddenly begins mimicking the Princess's words—"Gimme, Gimme, Gimme"—in earshot of the wealthy Prince Percival, whom Penelope was hoping to impress. The author's "spoiled-brat princess is perfectly embodied in Munsinger's ... illustration," asserted Janice M. Del Negro in a review of *Princess Penelope's Parrot* for *Bulletin of the Center for Children's Books.*

While Munsinger has concentrated mainly upon illustrating picture books for young children, she has also done artwork for children's textbooks, greeting cards, and *Cricket* magazine. Her media continue to be Indian ink and crow quill pens, to which she often adds watercolor washes. "The aspect of illustration that most interests me is development of the characters," Munsinger once explained to *SATA*. "I feel humor and expression add to a character's appeal and aid in telling a story. I especially like anthropomorphic animals but enjoy all sorts of characters."

■ Works Cited

Broderick, Kathryn, review of *Three Cheers for Tacky, Booklist,* February 15, 1994, pp. 1092-93.

Cooper, Ilene, review of *A Porcupine Named Fluffy, Booklist,* April 15, 1986, pp. 1223-24.

Cooper, Ilene, review of *The Revenge of the Magic Chicken, Booklist,* March 1, 1990, p. 1344.

Del Negro, Janice M., review of *Princess Penelope's Parrot, Bulletin of the Center for Children's Books,* January, 1997, p. 179.

Elleman, Barbara, review of *Hugh Pine and the Good Place, Booklist,* December 1, 1986, p. 582.

Review of *A Halloween Mask for Monster, Publishers Weekly,* August 22, 1986, p. 93.

Janick, Lori A., review of *Underwear!, School Library Journal,* March, 1988, p. 172.

Review of *Pookins Gets Her Way, Publishers Weekly,* February 27, 1987, p. 163.

Review of *Underwear!, Booklist,* April 1, 1988, p. 1352.

Wilms, Denise M., review of *Rabbit Goes to Night School, Booklist,* February 1, 1987, p. 842.

■ For More Information See

PERIODICALS

Booklist, March 1, 1983, p. 907; October 15, 1985, pp. 339-40; September 1, 1986, p. 66; October 1, 1992, p. 336; October 15, 1995, p. 412.

Bulletin of the Center for Children's Books, June, 1985, p. 188; April, 1988, p. 159; March, 1990, pp. 168-9; April, 1996, p. 273.

Horn Book, March-April, 1987, p. 214; May-June, 1987, pp. 328-29; November-December, 1992, pp. 716-7; July-August, 1995, p. 485.

Junior Bookshelf, October, 1987, p. 218.

Kirkus Reviews, September 15, 1986, p. 1452; December 15, 1986, p. 1861.

Publishers Weekly, September 19, 1980, p. 161; May 27, 1983, p. 68; April 25, 1986, p. 73; May 8, 1995, p. 295.

School Library Journal, December, 1985, pp. 109-10; August, 1987, p. 70; April, 1988, p. 82; October, 1992, p. 91; May, 1994, p. 98.*

O–P

OESTERLE, Virginia Rorby
See RORBY, Ginny

* * *

PARTON, Dolly (Rebecca) 1946-

■ Personal

Born January 19, 1946, in Locus Ridge, Sevier County, TN; daughter of Robert Lee (a farmer) and Avie Lee (Owens) Parton; married Carl Dean (a contractor), May 30, 1966.

■ Addresses

Agent—Creative Artists Agency, Inc., 1888 Century Park East, Suite 1400, Los Angeles, CA 90067.

■ Career

Singer and songwriter, 1956—. Singer on the *Cass Walker Program,* Knoxville, TN, 1956; appeared at the Grand Ole Opry, 1958; costar of *The Porter Wagoner Show,* 1967-74; solo artist, 1974—. Formed and headed "Dolly Parton and the Traveling Family Band," c. 1970-77; star of the musical variety show *Dolly,* ABC-TV, 1987. Actor in feature films, including *Nine to Five,* 1980; *The Best Little Whorehouse in Texas,* 1982; *Rhinestone,* 1984; *Steel Magnolias,* 1989; *Straight Talk,* 1991; and *The Beverly Hillbillies,* 1994. Television guest on *The Bill Anderson Show, The Wilburn Brothers Show,* and *The Barbara Mandrell Show;* host or featured performer on *Kenny, Dolly, and Willie: Something Inside So Strong, A Tennessee Mountain Thanksgiving, A Smoky Mountain Christmas,* and *Wild Texas Wind.* Owner of the theme park Dollywood, Sevier County, TN, 1985—. Partner, with Sandy Gallin, of Sandollar Productions.

■ Awards, Honors

Dolly Parton Day proclaimed in Sevier County, TN, on October 7, 1967, and in Los Angeles, CA, September 20,

DOLLY PARTON

1979; vocal group of the year citation (with Porter Wagoner), 1968; vocal duet of the year citation, All Country Music Association, 1970 and 1971; named female vocalist of the year, Academy of Country Music, 1975, 1976, and 1980; named country star of the year, Sullivan Productions, 1977; Grammy Award, National Academy of Recording Arts and Sciences, 1978, for *Here You Come Again;* named entertainer of the year, Country Music Association, 1978; Nashville Metronome award, 1979; recipient of People's Choice awards, 1980 and 1988; Academy Award nomination, Academy of Motion Picture Arts and Sciences, and Golden Globe nomination, Hollywood Foreign Press Association, both 1981, both for song "Nine to Five"; American Music

Award for best duo performance (with Kenny Rogers), 1984; album of the year award (with Emmylou Harris and Linda Ronstadt), Academy of Country Music, 1987, for *Trio;* Grammy Award, 1988, for *Trio;* named to Small Town of America Hall of Fame, and East Tennessee Hall of Fame, both 1988.

■ Writings

FOR CHILDREN

Coat of Many Colors, illustrated by Judith Sutton, HarperCollins, 1994.

OTHER

Just the Way I Am: Poetic Selections on "Reasons to Live, Reasons to Love and Reasons to Smile" from the Songs of Dolly Parton, Blue Mountain Press (Boulder, CO), 1979.
Dolly: My Life and Other Unfinished Business (autobiography), HarperCollins (New York), 1994.

RECORDINGS

Just Because I'm a Woman, RCA (New York), 1968.
In the Good Old Days, RCA, 1969.
My Blue Ridge Mountain Boy, RCA, 1969.
Fairest of Them All, RCA, 1970.
A Real Live Dolly, RCA, 1970.
Hello, I'm Dolly, Monument (Nashville, TN), 1970.
Best of Dolly Parton, RCA, 1970.
Golden Streets of Glory, RCA, 1971.
Joshua, RCA, 1971.
As Long As I Have Love, Monument, 1971.
Coat of Many Colors, RCA, 1971.
Touch Your Woman, RCA, 1972.
My Favorite Songwriter: Porter Wagoner, RCA, 1972.
Just the Way I Am, Camden, 1973.
My Tennessee Mountain Home, RCA, 1973.
Mine, RCA, 1973.
Real Live Bubbling Over, RCA, 1974.
Love Is Like a Butterfly, RCA, 1974.
Jolene, RCA, 1974.
Best of Dolly Parton, RCA, 1975.
All I Can Do, RCA, 1976.
New Harvest ... First Gathering, RCA, 1977.
Here You Come Again, RCA, 1977.
Heartbreaker, RCA, 1978.
Great Balls of Fire, RCA, 1979.
Dolly Dolly Dolly, RCA, 1980.
9 to 5 and Odd Jobs, RCA, 1980.
Heartbreak Express, RCA, 1982.
The Best Little Whorehouse in Texas, RCA, 1982.
(With Kris Kristofferson, Willie Nelson, and Brenda Lee) *Kris, Willie, Dolly, and Brenda: The Winning Hand,* Monument, 1982.
Burlap and Satin, RCA, 1983.
The Great Pretender, RCA, 1984.
Collector's Series, RCA, 1985.
Portrait, RCA, 1986.
Think about Love, RCA, 1986.
The Best of Dolly Parton, Volume 3, RCA, 1987.
The Best There Is, RCA, 1987.
(With Emmylou Harris and Linda Ronstadt) *Trio,* Warner Bros. (Burbank, CA), 1987.

Rainbow, Columbia (New York), 1988.
White Limozeen, Columbia, 1989.
Home for Christmas, Columbia, 1990.
Eagle When She Flies, Columbia, 1991.
Straight Talk, Hollywood Records (Buena Vista, CA), 1992.
(With Loretta Lynn and Tammy Wynette) *Honky Tonk Angels: Loretta, Dolly, Tammy,* Sony (New York), 1993.
The Essential Dolly Parton, RCA, 1995.

■ Sidelights

The fourth of twelve children born to Robert Lee and Avie Lee Parton in rural East Tennessee, famed performing artist Dolly Parton grew up in grinding poverty. She began a career in country music when she was only ten, singing on the radio, and performed at the Grand Ole Opry at the age of thirteen. By her mid-twenties Parton was a recording star, featured on television with singer-songwriter Porter Wagoner and on her way to becoming an international celebrity. Parton has since received honors and acclaim for her accomplishments in a number of different arenas: in addition to her decades-long prominence as a country music vocalist and songwriter, she has written three books, including her autobiography and a picture book for children, and has starred in a number of popular films and television programs.

Parton's on-stage presence and her appearances in films such as *Nine to Five, The Best Little Whorehouse in Texas,* and *Rhinestone* have contributed greatly to her celebrity status, but her success in country music is due primarily to her skillful songwriting. "As a singer," declares *Women's Review of Books* commentator Emily Toth in a review of Parton's autobiography, "she's less naturally gifted than Patsy Cline, who could sing and be heard without a microphone; Parton's voice is high and thin. But she's a fine performer and a superb songwriter." "Dolly's still making a killing off material she penned eons ago," noted *Washington Post* contributor Dave McKenna. "Whitney Houston's version of a Parton tune, 'I Will Always Love You,' now stands as one of the most popular singles of all time."

Parton tells her own story in her 1994 autobiography *Dolly: My Life and Other Unfinished Business.* "Parton tells of being one of a handful of trailblazing female artists who did more than merely sing some of the biggest tunes to come out of Nashville in the mid-1960s. They wrote them," stated McKenna. Toth praised Parton's account for its down-home humor, calling it "hilarious, reminiscent of [Rita Mae Brown's] *Rubyfruit Jungle* and [Fannie Flagg's] *Fried Green Tomatoes* in its irreverence and exaggeration." Toth added: "The book's a page-turner, not because it's suspenseful—we know Dolly will be a star—but because it's so earthy and engaging, entirely suited to Dolly Parton's cheery image." *Booklist* reviewer Ray Olson called *Dolly* "an entertaining country music rags-to-riches story, full of just enough humor and heart to thoroughly charm the fans."

Mama sewed the rags together,
she sewed every stitch with love,
and made my coat of many colors
that I was so proud of.

This picture book, based on one of Parton's popular songs, relates the tale of a little girl who, despite being taunted by her schoolmates because she wears a coat made of rags, treasures the coat because of the love her mother expressed in making it. (From *Coat of Many Colors,* written by Parton and illustrated by Judith Sutton.)

Parton is also the author of *Coat of Many Colors,* a children's picture book based on one of her songs. The story tells of a young girl whose family is too poor to afford a new dress for her, so her mother sews her a coat made from rags and scraps of different colors. Roger Sutton of the *Bulletin of the Center for Children's Books* found the original song "a fine, lilting tune," but lamented that "Parton's lyrics *sans* melody do not dance comfortably from the mouth." *School Library Journal* contributor Kathy Piehl also noted that "at some points reading aloud turns bumpy." In a more favorable assessment of *Coat of Many Colors,* a *Publishers Weekly* reviewer praised Parton's "appetizingly sweet first foray into picture books," asserting that "the heartfelt verses are imbued with the same genuine, infectiously likable spirit Parton herself projects."

■ Works Cited

Review of *Coat of Many Colors, Publishers Weekly,* July 4, 1994, p. 60.

McKenna, Dave, review of *Dolly: My Life and Other Unfinished Business, Washington Post,* October 24, 1994, p. B2.

Olson, Ray, review of *Dolly: My Life and Other Unfinished Business, Booklist,* October 15, 1994, p. 371.

Piehl, Kathy, review of *Coat of Many Colors, School Library Journal,* September, 1994, pp. 191-92.

Sutton, Roger, review of *Coat of Many Colors, Bulletin of the Center for Children's Books,* September, 1994, pp. 22-23.

Toth, Emily, "Country Queens," *Women's Review of Books,* March, 1995, pp. 24-25.

■ For More Information See

BOOKS

Berman, Connie, *The Official Dolly Parton Scrapbook,* Grosset and Dunlap, 1978.

Busnar, Gene, *Superstars of Country Music,* J. Messner, 1984.

Caraeff, Ed, *Dolly: Close Up/Up Close,* Delilah Communications, 1983.

Contemporary Musicians, Volume 2, Gale, 1990.

James, Otis, *Dolly Parton,* Quick Fox, 1978.

Keely, Scott, *Dolly Parton,* Creative Education, 1979.

Krishef, Robert K., *Dolly Parton,* Lerner Publications Co., 1980.

Nash, Alanna, *Dolly Parton,* Reed Books, 1976.

Saunders, Susan, *Dolly Parton, Country Goin' to Town,* Viking Kestrel, 1985.

Simon, George T., *The Best of the Music Makers,* Doubleday, 1971.

Willadeene, *In the Shadow of a Song: The Story of the Parton Family,* Bantam (Toronto), 1985.

PERIODICALS

Kirkus Reviews, July 15, 1994, p. 993.*

* * *

PETRY, Ann (Lane) 1908-1997

OBITUARY NOTICE—See index for *SATA* sketch: Born October 12, 1908, in Old Saybrook, CT; died April 28, 1997, near Old Saybrook, CT. Pharmacist, journalist, educator, and author. Petry is best known for her work as a novelist, particularly for her 1946 work, *The Street,* which described life in Harlem. The daughter of a pharmacist, Petry grew up in the resort town of Old Saybrook, Connecticut, being among the few black families to live in the predominantly white town. She attended the University of Connecticut, receiving her degree in pharmacology, and later attended Columbia University. From 1931 to 1938 she worked at James' Pharmacy. In 1938, after a move to New York City, she began writing and selling ads for the *Amsterdam News.* From 1941 to 1944, she served as reporter and editor of the *People's Voice* women's page. In the mid-1970s she taught English at the University of Hawaii. She also worked with New York City's American Negro Theatre as a teacher and actress. Her novel *The Street* was written after she moved with her husband, George Petry, to Harlem. She penned the novel, which became a critical and popular success, while her husband was serving in the military during World War II. Petry also wrote other novels, such as *The Narrows* and *Country Place,* and penned stories and biographies for children and young adult readers, including *Harriet Tubman:*

Conductor on the Underground Railroad, The Drugstore Cat, and *Tituba of Salem Village.* Petry received a distinguished writer award in 1994 and was inducted into the Connecticut Women's Hall of Fame that same year.

OBITUARIES AND OTHER SOURCES:

BOOKS

Twentieth-Century Children's Writers, Fourth Edition, St. James Press, 1995, pp. 754-55.

PERIODICALS

New York Times, April 30, 1997, p. B9.

* * *

POE, Ty (Christopher) 1975-

■ Personal

Born October 6, 1975, in Crescent City, CA; son of William J. (a non-commissioned army officer) and Kay D. (a homemaker) Poe. *Education:* Student at Clark University. *Religion:* Southern Baptist.

■ Addresses

Home—1217 College Park, Fairmont, WV 26554. *Electronic mail*—wpoe @ avalon.imagixx.net (internet); and tpoe@vax.clarku.edu (internet).

■ Illustrator

Geraldine M. Bennett, *Katrina Tells Jamie about John's Invisible Lesson,* New Dawn Publishing, 1994.

Bennett, *Katrina and Elishia Teach about the Aura,* New Dawn Publishing, 1994.

Bennett, *Rebecca Tells of a Miracle of Life: A Special Belief in the Healing Power of Love,* New Dawn Publishing, 1994.

Bennett, *Katrina and Elishia Learn about Ouija Boards,* New Dawn Publishing, 1994.

Bennett, *Katrina Tells about Bee Stings,* New Dawn Publishing, 1995.

Bennett, *Katrina Tells about Healing a Kitten,* New Dawn Publishing, 1995.

Bennett, *Katrina Helps a Friend Through a Time of Depression,* New Dawn Publishing, 1995.

TY POE

Bennett, *Katrina and Her Friends Learn about Self-Esteem,* New Dawn Publishing, 1995.

Bennett, *Katrina Learns How to Meditate,* New Dawn Publishing, 1995.

Bennett, *Jonchen, Son of Cara,* New Dawn Publishing, 1995.

Bennett, *Mickey and Honor,* New Dawn Publishing, 1995.

John D. Blacke, *Herman the Hamster: Beware of Ignoring Me,* New Dawn Publishing, 1995.

■ Sidelights

Ty Poe told *SATA:* "I am a college student attending Clark University. I was given an incredible opportunity, while still a teenager, to illustrate a series of children's books. My whole life had been devoted to art, but this was the first time that art was actually my job. I loved doing the books for children because I believe children are the most underrated artists out there. Their work is wonderful. I hope that my art will influence some child to go for his dreams the way that I am going for mine."

R

RATHMANN, Peggy (Margaret Crosby) 1953-

■ Personal

Born March 4, 1953, in St. Paul, MN; married John Wick. *Education:* University of Minnesota, B.A. in psychology; attended American Academy, Chicago, IL, Atelier Lack, Minneapolis, MN, and Otis Parson's School of Design, Los Angeles, CA.

■ Addresses

Office—c/o Putnam/Berkeley Publicity Department, 200 Madison Ave., New York, NY 10016.

■ Career

Children's book writer and illustrator, 1991—.

■ Awards, Honors

"Most promising new author" mention, Cuffies Awards, *Publishers Weekly,* 1991, for *Ruby the Copycat;* Notable Children's Book, American Library Association (ALA), 1994, for *Good Night, Gorilla;* Chicago Public Library, Best Books of the Year list, 1995, *School Library Journal*'s Best Books of 1995 list, and Caldecott Medal, 1996, all for *Officer Buckle and Gloria.*

■ Writings

WRITTEN AND ILLUSTRATED BY RATHMANN, UNLESS OTHERWISE NOTED

Ruby the Copycat, Scholastic, 1991.
(Illustrator) Barbara Bottner, *Bootsie Barker Bites,* G.P. Putnam's Sons, 1992.
Good Night, Gorilla, Putnam, 1994.
Officer Buckle and Gloria, Putnam, 1995.

■ Sidelights

Peggy Rathmann pulled a hat trick with her first children's book, *Ruby the Copycat,* turning an embar-

PEGGY RATHMANN

rassing personal incident into a well-received story and earning the "most promising new author" distinction in the 1991 Cuffies Awards. Her second self-illustrated book, *Good Night, Gorilla,* was an ALA Notable Children's Book. And with her third title, *Officer Buckle and Gloria,* Rathmann walked off with the Caldecott Medal in 1996. Not bad for someone who got into children's books only to curry favor with her nieces.

In her Caldecott acceptance speech, as reported in *Horn Book,* Rathmann explained the genesis of her writing/illustrating career. "Ten summers ago," Rathmann recalled, "I was vacationing with my two nieces. The girls were three and five years old, and as far as I could tell, they didn't like me nearly enough." One day on a car trip the nieces both wanted to sit in front next to another aunt. "Now, this aunt cannot help that she is extremely attractive, intelligent, and pleasant to be around. *I* wanted to sit next to her, too." But there was only room for one, so the younger niece was sent howling to the back seat with Rathmann. "She glowered at me; I was the booby prize." In desperation, Rathmann pulled out her sketch pad and began drawing a story "that starred my niece and me as extremely attractive people with good personalities and high IQs. It worked." It was also the start of an award-winning career. According to Diane Roback and Shannon Maughan in *Publishers Weekly,* Rathmann creates "characters with built-in kid appeal: a copycat, a girl who bites, a young gorilla who slips the keys away from the zookeeper." Roback and Maughan also noted that while Rathmann's books may be "spare in text," they are "long on action, much of it related through her cleverly expressive pictures."

Peggy Rathmann was born in St. Paul, Minnesota in 1953, one of five children. She grew up in the suburbs of St. Paul and started her illustrating career in the seventh grade, with campaign posters for her older brother's successful bid for student council. After graduation from Mounds View High School in New Brighton, Minnesota, Rathmann attended several colleges before settling down at the University of Minnesota where she took a degree in psychology. Rathmann once said that she "wanted to teach sign language to gorillas, but after taking a class in signing, I realized what I'd rather do

was draw pictures of gorillas." There followed various career plans from commercial artist to fine artist, but meanwhile she continued to work on the picture book she had begun with her nieces, a book that became "endless," as she described it in her Caldecott acceptance speech. "A whopping 150 pink-and-purple pages.... The book had everything—except conflict and a plot."

A publisher's rejection and a subsequent tip from a published writer sent Rathmann back to school, this time to a children's book-writing and illustration class. It was there that Rathmann began an assignment on an embarrassing incident in her life that led to her first published book. The teacher of this class suggested the students develop a story idea from the worst or most embarrassing thing they knew about themselves. At first Rathmann was unsuccessful, but as her classmates began presenting *their* stories, she developed the "overwhelming compulsion to swipe" the embarrassing incidents of other students, as she confessed in her Caldecott acceptance speech. Eventually she decided that this very tendency toward copying was the shameful thing she could use for the assignment which eventually turned into the book, *Ruby the Copycat.* "Since then, all of my books have been based on embarrassing secrets," Rathmann said in her Caldecott speech.

Ruby the Copycat, a book that *Kirkus Reviews* dubbed "a solid debut," tells the story of a new girl in class named Ruby who tries to act just like the popular girl, Angela. Ruby's poem is almost exactly like Angela's; Ruby was a flower girl in a wedding, just like Angela. Initially, the popular girl finds such adulation flattering, but ultimately it is flat out irritating. Ruby even copies the painted nails of the teacher, Miss Hart, who finally takes Ruby in hand and lets her know it is okay to be

Using her illustrations to tell the story, Rathmann composed *Good Night, Gorilla,* the tale of a zookeeper who bids the animals goodnight while a mischievous gorilla who has stolen the keeper's keys unlocks the cages so the menagerie can follow him home.

In this Caldecott Medal-winning book, Officer Buckle's safety lectures are suddenly in great demand when the new police dog, Gloria, begins performing acrobatics behind the unsuspecting patrolman's back. (From *Officer Buckle and Gloria,* written and illustrated by Rathmann.)

herself. In fact, the kindly teacher advises her that is the only way she will really fit in and win friends. So Ruby shows off her hopping ability, and the other kids soon are copying her. This feat even wins Angela's friendship.

Martha Topol, reviewing *Ruby the Copycat* in *School Library Journal*, noted that this was a "book with a strong story and complementary illustrations that addresses the philosophical question of individuality vs. conformity." Topol concluded the book "a small gem." Other critics noted the originality of Rathmann's artwork and how integrally it fitted in and helped develop the story. Ilene Cooper in *Booklist* commented that Rathmann's "colorful artwork adds new bits of humor to the text," and a *Publishers Weekly* reviewer asserted

that her "expressively illustrated, quirky and individualistic first book" inspired confidence in children and taught them "not to take skills ... for granted."

Rathmann followed up this success with the illustrations for Barbara Bottner's *Bootsie Barker Bites,* and then with her own story, *Good Night, Gorilla,* inspired by another classroom assignment and aided by a childhood memory. The writing and illustrating, however, were not the matter of a quick study session. The initial draft of the manuscript had value, but everyone concurred that the ending was problematic. It took two years and ten more endings to put together the final manuscript for *Good Night, Gorilla,* which went on to win an ALA Notable Book citation in 1994. This book relies heavily on pictures to convey story; words are limited to a bubbled "Good night," as the keeper of a zoo makes his rounds, tucking in the various animals he cares for. There is a gorilla, a lion, a giraffe, an armadillo, a hyena, and even a non-zoo mouse. But little does the zookeeper know that the gorilla in the first cage has lifted his keys and is setting free the animals in back of him, and that they are all following him home to the cozy security of a surrogate 'parent.' The zookeeper's wife finally takes the menagerie back to their proper places—all except the gorilla and the mouse who in the end snuggle down next to the zookeeper and his wife.

Deborah Stevenson of the *Bulletin of the Center for Children's Books* noted both the story and pictorial value of the book in her review. Indicating that it was a "livelier bedtime story" than *Good Night, Moon*, Stevenson went on to comment on Rathmann's lines, "rounder here than in her previous work," on the animals, which "have a cheerful simplicity of mien," and the palate, which "relies on a twilit glow of pink and green that lends a gentle circus flavor to the proceedings." *Booklist*'s Ilene Cooper noted that Rathmann's "Jaunty four-color artwork carries the story and offers more with every look," while *Kirkus Reviews* dubbed the book "delightful" and *Horn Book*'s Ann A. Flowers called it "an outstanding picture book." Considering the effect of both picture and story, Jan Shepherd Ross in *School Library Journal* concluded that *Good Night, Gorilla* is "a clever, comforting bedtime story."

"There's a funny thing that happens between words and pictures," Rathmann said in her interview with Roback and Maughan for *Publishers Weekly*. Rathmann learned the symbiotic nature of the two in her classes at Otis Parsons. She also learned that neither could exist without the other. In fact, it was yet another class assignment that led to her Caldecott Medal with *Officer Buckle and Gloria.* "The assignment was to write and illustrate a story which could not be understood by reading the text alone," she related in her Caldecott acceptance speech. "I did it because the teacher told us to, but in the process I discovered that this challenge was the very definition of a picture book. Officer Buckle was the words, Gloria was the pictures, and neither could entertain or enlighten without the other." Employing the acrobatic and clowning talents of her own family dog, Rathmann wrote and illustrated a story about a school safety officer and the dog who makes him fabulously popular for a time. Officer Buckle knows more about safety than just about anybody in the town of Napville, but he is a tremendous bore when he gives assemblies to impart his safety tips. One day, though, the Napville Police Department buys a police dog with the improbable name of Gloria. Buckle begins taking Gloria with him to his demonstrations and, behind his back, the jolly dog performs a series of skillful acrobatic tricks, much to the amazement and amusement of the audience. Suddenly, Officer Buckle is much in demand, and things go along wonderfully until the policeman sees a video of his performance on the television news and understands that the cheers have been for Gloria, and not for him. Outraged, Officer Buckle refuses to visit

any more schools, and when Gloria goes on her own, she is a bomb. In fact, the two need each other, and when they return to the stage, they present a final safety tip: "Always stick with your buddy."

Deborah Stevenson in *Bulletin of the Center for Children's Books* noted that "This is at heart the old story of the importance of friendship, but the safety tips ... and the rest of the plot devices give it a fresh twist." Indeed, Rathmann spent much time and money on the 101 safety tips which are posted throughout the book and on the endpapers. With deadlines approaching and more tips needed, Rathmann offered her nieces and nephews $25 apiece for any safety tips that made it past her editor. "The response was very expensive," Rathmann recalled in her Caldecott acceptance speech. Though many such tips are quite humorous, Stevenson went on to note in her review that the illustrations are "the lifeblood" of the book: "scratchy-edged watercolors in a luminous palette." Carolyn Phelan, writing in *Booklist*, commented that "the deadpan humor of the text and slapstick wit of the illustrations make a terrific combination." Kathie Krieger Cerra in *The Five Owls* noted especially how Rathmann's illustrations "move beyond the story and enrich it," and concluded that *Officer Buckle and Gloria* "is a book that children return to repeatedly, for there is much to be discovered in the illustrations and the language." A *Publishers Weekly* reviewer asserted that Rathmann "brings a lighter-than-air comic touch to this outstanding, solid-as-a-brick picture book," and *Horn Book*'s Ann A. Flowers called it "a glorious picture book." Lisa S. Murphy in *School Library Journal* summed up critical opinion in the conclusion of her review: "A five-star performance."

Hard at work on further picture books, Rathmann is still tongue-in-cheek about her achievements. As she said in her *Publishers Weekly* interview with Roback and Maughan, "To be frank, I like making these books so I can crack myself up." And at last report, her nieces seem to like her a lot better now.

■ Works Cited

Cerra, Kathie Krieger, review of *Officer Buckle and Gloria, The Five Owls,* March-April, 1996, pp. 85-6.

Cooper, Ilene, review of *Ruby the Copycat, Booklist,* November 15, 1991, p. 631.

Cooper, Ilene, review of *Good Night, Gorilla, Booklist,* July, 1994, p. 1956.

Flowers, Ann A., review of *Good Night, Gorilla, Horn Book,* July-August, 1994, pp. 443-44.

Flowers, Ann A., review of *Officer Buckle and Gloria, Horn Book,* November-December, 1995, pp. 736-37.

Review of *Good Night, Gorilla, Kirkus Reviews,* April 15, 1994, p. 562.

Murphy, Lisa S., review of *Officer Buckle and Gloria, School Library Journal,* September, 1995, p. 185.

Review of *Officer Buckle and Gloria, Publishers Weekly,* July 17, 1995, p. 229.

Phelan, Carolyn, review of *Officer Buckle and Gloria, Booklist,* November 1, 1995, p. 471.

Rathmann, Peggy, *Officer Buckle and Gloria,* Putnam, 1995.

Rathmann, Peggy, "Caldecott Medal Acceptance," *Horn Book,* July-August, 1996, pp. 424-27.

Roback, Diane, and Shannon Maughan, "About Our Cover Artist," *Publishers Weekly,* February 20, 1995, p. 125.

Ross, Jan Shepherd, review of *Good Night, Gorilla, School Library Journal,* July, 1994, p. 87.

Review of *Ruby the Copycat, Kirkus Reviews,* November 15, 1991, p. 1474.

Review of *Ruby the Copycat, Publishers Weekly,* November 8, 1991, p. 64.

Stevenson, Deborah, review of *Good Night, Gorilla, Bulletin of the Center for Children's Books,* May, 1994, p. 299.

Stevenson, Deborah, review of *Officer Buckle and Gloria, Bulletin of the Center for Children's Books,* October, 1995, p. 66.

Topol, Martha, review of *Ruby the Copycat, School Library Journal,* January, 1992, p. 96.

■ For More Information See

PERIODICALS

Kirkus Reviews, August 15, 1995, p. 1193.
Los Angeles Times Book Review, February 25, 1996, p. 11.
Publishers Weekly, March 14, 1994, p. 71.
Wilson Library Bulletin, February, 1995, p. 94.

—*Sketch by J. Sydney Jones*

* * *

RAU, Dana Meachen 1971-

■ Personal

Born October 15, 1971, in Connecticut; married Christopher Rau (a teacher), July 2, 1994. *Education:* Trinity College, Hartford, CT, B.A., 1993. *Hobbies and other interests:* Reading, watching movies, and eating pizza.

■ Addresses

Home—621 Courtland Ave., Bridgeport, CT 06605.

■ Career

Children's book writer and editor. *Member:* Society of Children's Book Writers and Illustrators, Phi Beta Kappa.

■ Awards, Honors

Trumbull Arts Festival Literary Competition, first place award, 1993, for the story "The Date," honorable mentions, 1996, for the stories "The Traveler" and "Delusions of Grandeur."

■ Writings

FOR CHILDREN

Robin at Hickory Street, illustrated by Joel Snyder, Soundprints, 1995.
One Giant Leap: The First Moon Landing, illustrated by Thomas Buchs, Soundprints, 1996.
A Box Can Be Many Things, illustrated by Paige Billin-Frye, Children's Press, 1997.
Undersea City: A Story of a Caribbean Coral Reef, illustrated by Katie Lee, Soundprints, 1997.
Arctic Adventure: Inuit Life in the 1800s, illustrated by Peg Magovern, Soundprints, 1997.

OTHER

Wall (play), first produced by Company One Theater in Hartford, CT, 1993.

Also author of short stories for adults.

■ Work in Progress

Thomas Edison (tentative title), Soundprints, 1997; *The Secret Code,* for Children's Press.

■ Sidelights

Dana Meachen Rau told *SATA:* "Currently, my career can be defined as writer and editor. I have been a children's book editor for the past four years, working on both fiction and nonfiction. I coordinate the entire book process and collaborate with a diverse group of authors and illustrators. In my free time, I have been writing fiction for all ages.

"I have always thought that one of the most important things an author can have is an active imagination. When I was little, my brother and I always used our imaginations. We pretended our beds were pirate ships, and the hallway was a bowling alley. The best creation of all was setting up the boxes in the basement to look like a palace!

"Now that I am an adult, I find that I am still always using my imagination. I pretend that driving my car is a roller coaster ride. I pretend that a walk in the woods is a safari adventure. When I look around my small apartment, I still pretend that I live in a palace!"

■ For More Information See

PERIODICALS

Booklist, October 15, 1996, p. 419.*

* * *

ROBBINS, Ken

■ Personal

Education: Cornell University.

■ Addresses

Home—East Hampton, NY.

■ Career

Editor, photographer, and author of nonfiction books for children.

■ Awards, Honors

Best Illustrated Children's Books, *New York Times,* 1983, and inclusion in the American Institute of Graphic Arts Book Show, 1984, both for *Tools.*

■ Writings

FOR CHILDREN; SELF-ILLUSTRATED WITH PHOTOGRAPHS

Trucks of Every Sort, Crown (New York), 1981.
Tools, Four Winds Press (New York), 1983.
Building a House, Four Winds Press, 1984.
City/Country: A Car Trip in Photographs, Viking Kestrel (New York), 1985.
Beach Days, Viking Kestrel, 1987.
At the Ballpark, Viking Kestrel, 1988.
Boats, Scholastic (New York), 1989.
A Flower Grows, Dial (New York), 1990.
Bridges, Dial, 1991.
Make Me a Peanut Butter Sandwich and a Glass of Milk, Scholastic, 1992.
Power Machines, Henry Holt, 1993.
Water, Holt, 1994.
Earth: The Elements, Holt, 1995.

Air, Holt, 1995.
Fire: The Elements, Holt, 1996.
Rodeo, Holt, 1996.

OTHER

(Editor with Bill Strachan) *Springs: A Celebration,* Springs Improvement Society (East Hampton, NY), 1984.
(Contributor of photographs) Lynn Sonberg, *A Horse Named Paris,* Bradbury (Scarsdale, NY), 1986.
(With Stephen Taylor; contributor of photographs) *A Place of Your Own Making: How to Build a One-Room Cabin, Studio, Shack, or Shed,* H. Holt, 1988.

■ Sidelights

Much of Ken Robbins's work for young people focuses on descriptive picture books. In such books as *Trucks of Every Sort, Tools, A Flower Grows,* and *Make Me a Peanut Butter Sandwich and a Glass of Milk,* Robbins supplements generally brief text with his own photographs to depict everyday life. He hand-colors his black-and-white photographic prints to produce illustrations "reminiscent ... of 1940's picture postcards," according to a *Kirkus Reviews* critic. A *Publishers Weekly* reviewer asserted that "Robbins has become a master of well-crafted nonfiction books featuring hand-tinted photographs."

Robbins's works cover a broad spectrum of human endeavor and natural wonders and have generally been well-received. *Trucks of Every Sort,* according to *Horn Book* contributor Karen M. Klockner, "is a well-designed and carefully photographed book." Denise M. Wilms in *Booklist* labeled *Tools* "simple" and "straightforward," while a *Bulletin of the Center for Children's Books* reviewer found the book "unusual in the simplicity and tasteful layout of the pages." Ann A. Flowers observed in *Horn Book* that the tools "as artistic forms are successful, even excellent, examples of the beauty to be found in homely objects." *Building a House,* both written and photographed by Robbins, is "a fine photographic documentary," according to Ethel R. Twichell of *Horn Book.* A reviewer for the *Bulletin of the Center for Children's Books* hailed *Building a House* as "one of the best books on construction that has appeared." Robbins's *City/Country: A Car Trip in Photographs* is a "feast for the eyes," raved Anna Biagioni Hart in *School Library Journal.* She especially remarked upon the "compelling" photographs in this "outstanding book." A *Bulletin of the Center for Children's Books* critic described the hand-tinted photographic illustrations as "never strident but often dramatic." In *Horn Book,* Elizabeth S. Watson commented on the text for *City/Country,* asserting that it has the "almost pounding, jagged rhythm of tires on the New York State thruway."

In *Beach Days,* "a myriad of photos and a minimal text ... celebrate the manifold joys of the summer shore," explained Patricia Dooley in *School Library Journal.* She suggested that readers will be "beguiled" by this book. A *Kirkus Reviews* critic remarked that photographs evoke the "simple joys of a visit to the beach,"

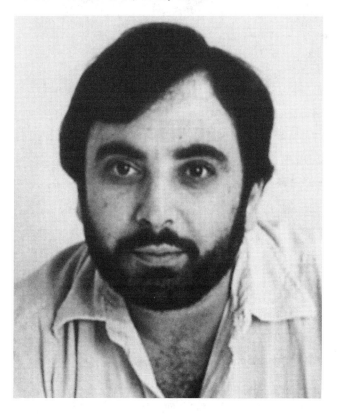

KEN ROBBINS

noting, however, that the hand-tinting "may delight some, but be off-putting to others." *Horn Book* reviewer Margaret A. Bush found the book "lovingly rendered," and added: "Robbins's use of hand-tinted photographs is particularly felicitous in conveying the sandy, shimmery haze of many beach days." *A Flower Grows* employs the same hand-coloring of black-and-white photos found in the author's previous work. Kathleen Odean stated in *School Library Journal* that the illustrations have the "unusual, still quality characteristic of Robbins's work." An *Appraisal* reviewer commented, "The highlight of this book is its art—beautiful, elegant, hand-tinted photographs which show every detail of the amaryllis' growth." Carolyn K. Jenks claimed in *Horn Book:* "Reading this book is almost like watching a real flower grow."

In *Bridges,* Robbins turns his attention once again to man-made wonders, exploring numerous kinds of bridges, from a simple log to complicated suspension, truss, and draw bridges. Nancy E. Curran observed in *School Library Journal* that the author's "unusual illustrative technique combines the detail of a photograph with the soft hues of a painting." According to Roger Sutton in the *Bulletin of the Center for Children's*

Books, the coloration gives a "nostalgic look" to the photographs, but because "many of the color juxtapositions are just the other side of likely," the result is also "postmodern" in appearance. *Make Me a Peanut Butter Sandwich and a Glass of Milk* traces the basic ingredients—peanuts, wheat, and milk—of this typical children's meal from nature to grocery store. While several critics commented on the inherent beauty of the hand-tinted photos, they felt the sepia tones detracted from this particular subject matter. Eunice Weech remarked in *School Library Journal* that Robbins's photography, which provided some of his earlier works with "a mystical, poetic quality," is a "less than appetizing technique when used on food." In the *Bulletin of the Center for Children's Books,* Deborah Stevenson concluded the general effect of photographs, type font, and brown tones "stodgy." Karen Hutt of *Booklist,* however, commented that "the large photos and minimal text make the book an outstanding read-aloud."

Robbins's "Elements" series looks at water, earth, air, and fire using his trademark hand-tinted photographs as a departure from the traditional science book format. *Water* examines the three states of water and its myriad uses, from survival to entertainment. Sutton writes in

By hand-tinting his photographs, Robbins creates distinctive illustrations for nonfiction works such as *Make Me a Peanut Butter Sandwich and a Glass of Milk,* in which he explains the processes necessary for the production of milk, bread, and peanut butter.

Robbins's *Rodeo* traces some historical elements of the modern rodeo and explains many of the events in which cowboys compete. (Photographs by Robbins.)

the *Bulletin of the Center for Children's Books* that, though "beautiful" with its "nostalgic wash to waterfalls, seascapes, and even ice cubes ... the text is often bumpy." About the illustrations, Patricia Manning noted in *School Library Journal,* "The colors are delicate and restrained, providing viewers with an open window into the artist's perception of his world." Frank Truesdale observed in *Appraisal* that this "coffee-table quality volume ... beautifully blends science and art, and blurs boundaries between juvenile and adult literature," adding that the text is "informative, accurate and often poetic." *Earth: The Elements* focuses on solids and their uses. In a review of *Earth,* again in *School Library Journal,* Manning commented that the author's "conversational tone is pleasingly affable" as he confides his thoughts "in a voice both eloquent and clear." Applauding the author's multidisciplinary approach to science in *Earth, Booklist*'s Mary Harris Veeder opines, "This is truly science for poets." The third book in the series, *Air,* treats topics from kites and parachutes to seed dispersion to weather. A *School Library Journal* critic remarked, "As in the previous volumes, the author's personal musings are richer than the factual material report writers crave." April Judge, writing in *Booklist,* labeled *Air* a "visual gem." She further described it as "a memorable, evocative, and powerful photo-essay." In

Horn Book, Daniel J. Brabander finds *Air* "graced with imaginative, thought-provoking" photography and "eloquent descriptions" of the numerous aspects of air and atmosphere. In *Fire: The Elements,* the final book of the quartet, Robbins "reflects on the usefulness, beauty, and danger of combustion," stated *School Library Journal* contributor Patricia Manning. As fire differs from the other elements in that it is a process rather than a substance, Robbins explores all facets of fire, from the "Big Bang" theory of the creation of the universe to fireworks. Manning further commented on the book's appeal to readers who "find personal satisfaction in thinking about things." Susan Dove Lempke observed in *Booklist* that "each photograph is in itself a work of art, carefully composed and nicely hand-labeled."

■ Works Cited

Review of *Air, School Library Journal,* January, 1996, pp. 124-25.

Review of *Beach Days, Kirkus Reviews,* May 1, 1987, p. 724.

Brabander, Daniel A., review of *Air, Horn Book,* May-June, 1996, p. 358.

Review of *Bridges, Publishers Weekly,* May 31, 1991, p. 75.

Review of *Building a House, Bulletin of the Center for Children's Books,* April, 1984, pp. 153-54.

Bush, Margaret A., review of *Beach Days, Horn Book,* September-October, 1987, p. 602.

Review of *City-Country: A Car Trip in Photographs, Bulletin of the Center for Children's Books,* October, 1985, p. 36.

Curran, Nancy E., review of *Bridges, School Library Journal,* June, 1991, p. 119.

Dooley, Patricia, review of *Beach Days, School Library Journal,* June-July, 1987, p. 88.

Review of *A Flower Grows, Appraisal,* spring, 1991, pp. 42-43.

Flowers, Ann A., review of *Tools, Horn Book,* December, 1983, p. 703.

Hart, Anna Biagioni, review of *City-Country: A Car Trip in Photographs, School Library Journal,* October, 1985, p. 159.

Hutt, Karen, review of *Make Me a Peanut Butter Sandwich and a Glass of Milk, Booklist,* September 1, 1992, p. 63.

Jenks, Carolyn K., review of *A Flower Grows, Horn Book,* July-August, 1990, pp. 470-71.

Judge, April, review of *Air, Booklist,* October 1, 1995, p. 311.

Klockner, Karen M., review of *Trucks of Every Sort, Horn Book,* February, 1982, p. 66.

Lempke, Susan Dove, review of *Fire: The Elements, Booklist,* May 1, 1996, p. 1504.

Manning, Patricia, review of *Water, School Library Journal,* December, 1994, p. 126.

Manning, Patricia, review of *Earth: The Elements, School Library Journal,* May, 1995, p. 115.

Manning, Patricia, review of *Fire: The Elements, School Library Journal,* June, 1996, p. 147.

Odean, Kathleen, review of *A Flower Grows, School Library Journal,* May, 1990, p. 100.

Stevenson, Deborah, review of *Make Me a Peanut Butter Sandwich and a Glass of Milk, Bulletin of the Center for Children's Books,* October, 1992, p. 52.

Sutton, Roger, review of *Bridges, Bulletin of the Center for Children's Books,* June, 1991, p. 248.

Sutton, Roger, review of *Water, Bulletin of the Center for Children's Books,* December, 1994, p. 143.

Review of *Tools, Bulletin of the Center for Children's Books,* October, 1983, p. 36.

Truesdale, Frank, review of *Water, Appraisal,* winter, 1995, pp. 58-59.

Twichell, Ethel R., review of *Building a House, Horn Book,* June, 1984, pp. 350-51.

Veeder, Mary Harris, review of *Earth: The Elements, Booklist,* April 15, 1995, p. 1496.

Watson, Elizabeth S., review of *City-Country: A Car Trip in Photographs, Horn Book,* January-February, 1986, p. 51.

Weech, Eunice, review of *Make Me a Peanut Butter Sandwich and a Glass of Milk, School Library Journal,* October, 1992, p. 108.

Wilms, Denise M., review of *Tools, Booklist,* September 1, 1983, p. 91.

■ For More Information See

PERIODICALS

Appraisal, summer, 1986, p. 58.

Booklist, September 15, 1989, p. 189.

Kirkus Reviews, August 15, 1989, p. 1256; July 15, 1992, p. 930.

New York Times Book Review, November 10, 1996, p. 42.

Publishers Weekly, June 7, 1993, p. 70.

School Library Journal, March, 1982, p. 139; May, 1988, p. 92; October, 1996, pp. 116-17.*

*   *   *

ROBINSON, Shari
See McGUIRE, Leslie (Sarah)

*   *   *

ROJANY, Lisa
(Adriana Gabriel)

■ Personal

Born on February 14, in Los Angeles, CA; daughter of Avi Rojany and Mary Marks. *Education:* University of California, Los Angeles, B.A. (magna cum laude), 1986; Sorbonne, Universite de Paris, and Alliance Francaise,

LISA ROJANY

Translation Certificate and Diplome des Hautes Etudes en Francais, 1987; Brown University, M.A., 1989.

■ Addresses

Office—Gateway Learning Corp., c/o Rosewood Capital, 1 Maritime Plaza, San Francisco, CA 94111. *Electronic mail*—lrojany@aol.com (America Online).

■ Career

Triangle Publications, Los Angeles, CA, writer and editor for *TV Guide*, 1987-88; Brown Daily Herald Newspaper Services, Providence, RI, staff editor, 1989; Ligature, Inc., Boston, MA, textbook editor, 1989-90; Intervisual Books, Inc., Santa Monica, CA, senior editor, 1991-93; Price Stern Sloan, Inc., Los Angeles, editorial director, 1993-97; Gateway Learning Corp., San Francisco, CA, editorial director, 1997—. Also works as a freelance writer and editor, including ghostwriter for other authors; public speaker. *Member:* International Women's Writing Guild, PEN Center USA West, Society of Children's Book Writers and Illustrators, Women's National Book Association (Los Angeles chapter), National Writers Club (Los Angeles chapter), Book Publicists Club of Southern California, Phi Beta Kappa.

■ Awards, Honors

King Arthur's Camelot was a Book-of-the-Month Club selection; *Exploring the Human Body* was named among "Ten Best New Parenting Books," *Child*, 1993; *Giant Animal Fold-Outs* books were included in *American Bookseller* "Pick of the List," 1995.

■ Writings

The Hands-On Book of Big Machines, illustrated by Joel Snyder, Little, Brown, 1992.

(With Stacie Strong) *Exploring the Human Body*, illustrated by Linda Hill Griffith, Barron's, 1992.

(Adapter) *King Arthur's Camelot*, four volumes, illustrated by Laszlo Batki, Dutton, 1993.

The Story of Hanukkah, illustrated by Holly Jones, Hyperion, 1993.

Where's That Pig? illustrated by John Wallner, Price Stern Sloan, 1993.

Santa's New Suit, illustrated by Mike Lester, Price Stern Sloan, 1993.

Jake and Jenny on the Town, illustrated by Barney Saltzberg, Price Stern Sloan, 1993.

Mr. Bump, illustrated by Adam Hargreaves, Price Stern Sloan, 1993.

Mr. Funny, illustrated by Adam Hargreaves, Price Stern Sloan, 1993.

Mr. Silly, illustrated by Adam Hargreaves, Price Stern Sloan, 1993.

Walt Disney's Alice in Wonderland: Down the Rabbit Hole, illustrated by Robbin Cuddy, Disney Press, 1994.

Token of Love, illustrated with antique changing pictures by Ernest Nister, Philomel, 1994.

Spring Gardens, illustrated with antique changing pictures by Ernest Nister, Philomel, 1994.

Mickey Mouse: Where's the Picnic?, Mouse Works, 1994.

Winnie the Pooh: The Surprise Party, Mouse Works, 1994.

(With Craig Walker) *Make Your Own Valentines*, illustrated by Wendy All, Price Stern Sloan, 1994.

(Compiler) *Birthday Celebrations*, illustrated by Kathy Hendrickson, Andrews & McMeel, 1994.

(Compiler) *Cats: Those Wonderful Creatures*, illustrated by Kathy Mitchell, Andrews & McMeel, 1994.

(Compiler) *Flowers for My Friend*, illustrated by Karen Lidbeck, Andrews & McMeel, 1994.

(Compiler) *Friendship: What You Mean to Me*, illustrated by Kathy Mitchell, Andrews & McMeel, 1994.

(Compiler) *Thoughts for a Sunny Day*, illustrated by Kathy Mitchell, Andrews & McMeel, 1994.

(Compiler) *Wedding Sentiments*, illustrated by Gwen Connelly, Andrews & McMeel, 1994.

Melvin Martian, illustrated by David Crossley, Price Stern Sloan, 1995.

Dena Dinosaur, illustrated by David Crossley, Price Stern Sloan, 1995.

Morty Monster, illustrated by David Crossley, Price Stern Sloan, 1995.

Wanda Witch, illustrated by David Crossley, Price Stern Sloan, 1995.

Casper: The Junior Novelization (based on the screenplay by Sherri Stoner and Deanna Oliver), Price Stern Sloan, 1995.

Dumbo's Circus Train: A Rolling Wheels Book, Mouse Works, 1995.

Cinderella's Coach: A Rolling Wheels Book, Mouse Works, 1995.

Kangaroo and Company (Giant Animal Fold-Outs), illustrated by Cristina Mesturini and Michele Tranquillini, Price Stern Sloan, 1995.

Hippo and Pals (Giant Animal Fold-Outs), illustrated by Michele Tranquillini, Gianni Ronco, and Elena Rozzo, Price Stern Sloan, 1995.

(Reteller) *The Magic Feather: A Jamaican Legend*, illustrated by Philip Kuznicki, Troll Associates, 1995.

Tell Me About When I Was a Baby, illustrated by K. A. Bickle, Price Stern Sloan, 1996.

Gold Diggers: The Secret of Bear Mountain (based on the screenplay by Barry Glasser), Price Stern Sloan, 1996.

(Under pseudonym Adriana Gabriel) *Dragonheart: The Junior Novelization*, Price Stern Sloan, 1996.

Giant Animal Fold-Outs: Big Trucks and Bigger Diggers, Price Stern Sloan, 1996.

Giant Animal Fold-Outs: Giant Giants and Magic Mermaids, Price Stern Sloan, 1996.

Leave It to Beaver: The Novelization (based on the screenplay by Brian Levant and Lon Diamond), Price Stern Sloan, 1997.

Author of two books in the series "Code Blue: In the Emergency Room," HarperCollins, 1996; author of *Making the Grade*, 1997. Author of *Pandora's Box* and

Over in the Meadow, CD-ROM books for children, Rose Studios, 1995. *Center: Publication of PEN Center USA West,* editor in chief, 1992-95, then member of editorial board; member of editorial staff, *Clerestory: Brown/RISD Journal of the Arts* and *Hwaet! Graduate Journal of Medieval Studies,* 1989; founding editor, *Together,* 1985-86.

■ Work in Progress

She-Pirate, the first title for a proposed adventure series for girls.

■ Sidelights

Lisa Rojany told *SATA:* "I was born and grew up in Los Angeles. After college, where I wrote for newspapers and a women's news magazine, I spent three years in New England going to graduate school at Brown. There I freelanced at various publishing houses in Boston and embarked upon my children's book writing and editorial career.

"I have had over thirty children's books published, both fiction and nonfiction. My favorite projects are the ones for which I have conceived paper engineering/interactive elements as well as text, such as *The Hands-On Book of Big Machines, The Story of Hanukkah,* and *Tell Me About When I Was a Baby.* I have also written quote books, pop-up books, books about animals and machines, board books, original YA novels, movie tie-in novelizations—you name it, I'm willing to try it.

"The most impressive-*looking* book that I wrote was an Intervisual Books package called *King Arthur's Camelot.* The artist for this project—an oversized book with a huge pop-up castle and four storybooks based on the King Arthur legend—was Hungarian and, although we had trouble understanding one another, we communicated so well that, with the help of the designer, the end result was something very exciting.

"I also wrote two interactive CD-ROM titles for children, *Over in the Meadow* and *Pandora's Box.* Because the story lines are nonlinear, I had to relearn what it means to tell a story, while helping the animators and 'techies' learn how a story must be a larger total than the sum of its parts. Writing animation sequences is the zaniest experience, because the writer gets to translate visual humor and drama into words and then watch them transmogrify back into moving visual images. For somcone who has a facility with words but absolutely no hands-on artistic talent, that's quite an experience.

"What I like most about writing for children is that there are very few *real* boundaries. Kids don't see limitations like we do, and I love being in the imaginative place where children live, a place where anything is possible. The world becomes a place with an infinite amount of adventure just waiting to happen."

■ For More Information See

PERIODICALS

Horn Book Guide, spring, 1995, p. 53.
Learning, March, 1995, p. 43.
Publishers Weekly, September 20, 1993, p. 32.

* * *

ROOT, Phyllis 1949-

■ Personal

Born February 14, 1949, in Fort Wayne, IN; daughter of John Howard and Esther (Traut) Root; married James Elliot Hansa (a mason); children: Amelia Christin, Ellen Rose. *Education:* Valparaiso University, B.A., 1971.

■ Addresses

Home—3842 Bloomington Ave. S., Minneapolis, MN 55407.

■ Career

Writer. Has worked as architectural drafter, costume seamstress, bicycle repair person, and administrative assistant. *Member:* Society of Children's Book Writers and Illustrators.

■ Awards, Honors

Children's Books of the Year citation, Child Study Association of America, and Bologna International Children's Book Fair selection, both 1985, both for *Moon Tiger;* Minnesota Picture Book Award, 1997, for *Aunt Nancy and Old Man Trouble. Moon Tiger* and *Soup for Supper* were both Junior Library Guild selections.

■ Writings

Hidden Places, illustrated by Daniel San Souci, Carnival Press, 1983.
(With Carol A. Marron) *Gretchen's Grandma,* illustrated by Deborah K. Ray, Carnival Press, 1983.
(With Marron) *Just One of the Family,* illustrated by George Karn, Carnival Press, 1984.
(With Marron) *No Place for a Pig,* illustrated by Nathan Y. Jarvis, Carnival Press, 1984.
My Cousin Charlie, illustrated by Pia Marella, Carnival Press, 1984.
Moon Tiger, illustrated by Ed Young, Holt, 1985.
Soup for Supper, illustrated by Sue Truesdell, Harper, 1986.
Galapagos, Carnival/Crestwood, 1988.
Great Basin, Carnival/Crestwood, 1988.
Glacier, Carnival/Crestwood, 1989.
The Old Red Rocking Chair, illustrated by John Sanford, Arcade, 1991.
The Listening Silence, illustrated by Dennis McDermott, Harper, 1992.

Coyote and the Magic Words, illustrated by Sandra Speidel, Lothrop, 1993.

Sam Who Was Swallowed by a Shark, illustrated by Axel Scheffler, Candlewick, 1994.

Aunt Nancy and Old Man Trouble, illustrated by David Parkins, Candlewick, 1996.

Mrs. Potter's Pig, illustrated by Russell Ayto, Candlewick, 1996.

Contrary Bear, illustrated by Laura Cornell, HarperCollins/Geringer, 1996.

One Windy Wednesday, illustrated by Helen Craig, Candlewick, 1996.

Rosie's Fiddle, illustrated by Kevin O'Malley and Margot Apple, Lothrop, 1997.

The Hungry Monster, illustrated by Sue Heap, Candlewick, 1997.

■ **Adaptations**

Just One of the Family was recorded on cassette, Raintree, 1985.

■ **Work in Progress**

All For the New-Born Baby; One Duck Stuck; What Baby Wants; Aunt Nancy and Cousin Lazybones; Aunt Nancy and Old Woeful.

■ **Sidelights**

Phyllis Root has been writing for as long as she can remember. "I made up stories, poems, and songs," she once told *SATA.* "In first grade I wrote a poem about love and a dove, and in second grade I won a class essay contest for my four-sentence story about the Sahara desert. In fifth grade I had a remarkable and wonderful teacher, Mrs. Keller, who encouraged me to write. It was in her class that I decided I would by an 'authoress' when I grew up."

Indeed, Root has written many well-regarded and award-winning children's books during her career as an "authoress." One of her earliest books was *Gretchen's Grandma,* published in 1983, and cowritten with colleague Carol A. Marron. It tells the story of Gretchen and her Oma, or grandmother, who is visiting from Germany. At the beginning of the visit, the language barrier seems troublesome, but is eventually overcome by pantomime and love. Ilene Cooper, writing for *Booklist,* describes the tale as "a gentle story that could be used as [a] starting point for some preschool discussion."

Root's award-winning title *Moon Tiger,* published in 1985, has been described by a *Bulletin of the Center for Children's Books* writer as "the stuff of which dreams are made," and by *School Library Journal* contributor Nancy Schmidtmann as a "heavenly treat." The story delves into a young girl's imagination and weaves her fantasy of being carried away by a magical tiger, who rescues her from having to care for her younger brother. Yet when the tiger offers to eat the boy, the sister

declines, admitting that she might actually miss her brother after all.

The idea for Root's next book, *Soup for Supper,* published in 1986, came to her during a thunderstorm, as she once told *SATA.* "I had gotten up to comfort my daughter Amelia, and remembered how, when I was a child, my sister and I had sat on the bed with our parents, watching the lightning and rain. 'Don't let the thunder scare you,' they reassured us. 'It's just the noise potatoes make spilling out of the giant's cart.' Listening to the thunder with my own daughter, I suddenly saw the giant with his cart of vegetables and a wee small woman chasing after him. The next morning I wrote down the first draft of *Soup for Supper.*" The result is "an original story with a folkloric ring," as described by a *Bulletin of the Center for Children's Books* writer, which is "dandy [for] reading aloud because of the simple rhymes, name-calling, and sound effects." The wee small woman of Root's tale vigorously defends her garden against the Giant Rumbleton's attempts to plunder it. After an energetic confrontation, the two enemies discover a common culinary goal, and become friends as together they make vegetable soup. Root even includes music for the giant's song at the end of the book.

In 1988 and 1989, Root wrote three books for a series based on natural wonders and National Parks, aimed at middle and upper elementary students. Root's contributions were *Galapagos, Great Basin,* and *Glacier,* each containing maps, large color pictures, and clear text written as an introduction to young armchair travelers.

In *The Old Red Rocking Chair,* published in 1991, a discarded rocking chair is rescued time and time again from the garbage by various eagle-eyed dump-pickers. Each new owner takes from the chair different pieces and discards the remains, until what was once a chair evolves into a blue footstool which is sold to its original oblivious owner at a garage sale. A *Publishers Weekly* critic writes that "while the premise is hardly new ... Root's cheerfulness and lucid logic propel the story."

Root's 1992 novel *The Listening Silence* draws on Native American traditions, with a "strong, believable" heroine at the center of the action, according to Ruth S. Vose in *School Library Journal.* Kiri is a young orphaned girl who is raised in a tribe where a healer recognizes Kiri's ability to send her spirit inside of other people and animals. Reluctant to use her power, Kiri goes on a vision quest to discover her true calling, and eventually uses her gift to heal a young man she encounters. Vose praised the "smooth, lyrical, language" of the tale, while a *Kirkus Reviews* writer similarly hailed the "spare, carefully honed narration." Much like J. R. R. Tolkien did in his classic *Lord of the Rings,* Root invents names for the woodland plants and animals, creating what Kathryn Pierson Jennings described in *Bulletin of the Center for Children's Books* as "a fantasy culture ... [which] is orderly and compelling and may inspire young creative writing students who need a more modest fantasy world than Tolkien."

Root's next book also employs elements of folklore, including the use of a coyote as the trickster, a common character in Native American lore, and her character, the Maker-of-all-things, based on the Pueblo Thinking Woman. Root described *Coyote and the Magic Words* as "a story about storytelling, about how to create worlds with nothing more than our words." In the book, the Maker-of-all-things uses words to speak her creation into existence, and grants her creatures the power to meet their own needs simply by speaking into existence what they want. But the Coyote grows bored with this easy way of life and begins to incite mischief using the magic words. To punish him, the Maker-of-all-things takes away the magic of the words, except the ones Coyote uses in storytelling. Karen Hutt, writing for *Booklist,* characterized the tale as "simple but satisfy-

ing," and a *Kirkus Reviews* critic observed that "Root's Coyote is appropriately childlike; her lively narration is well-honed and agreeably informal, just right for oral sharing."

Sam Who Was Swallowed by a Shark is Root's story of a rat who is determined to build a boat and sail the sea, despite the naysaying of his rat neighbors. When he finally accomplishes his goal and leaves, the neighbors assume the worst when they don't hear from him, although Sam is actually having the time of his life. A *Publishers Weekly* critic hailed Root's "understated prose" and "chipper dialogue" and noted that "the even pacing underlines [Sam's] quiet persistence and progress."

The coyote creates mischief using the magic words given to all creatures by the Maker-of-all-things in Phyllis Root's retelling of a Southwestern Native American folktale. (From *Coyote and the Magic Words,* illustrated by Sandra Speidel.)

A little girl blames her obstinate behavior on her favorite toy teddy bear in Root's *Contrary Bear*, illustrated by Laura Cornell.

The "Aunt Nancy" of *Aunt Nancy and Old Man Trouble,* published in 1996, does not refer to the Aunt Nancy of the "Anansi" storytelling tradition; however Root's story, like many others she written, has a folklore flair to it. Using a down-home dialect, Root describes Aunt Nancy and the way she outsmarts Old Man Trouble when he dries up her well. When he shows up at her door and causes more mischief, Aunt Nancy just tells him it doesn't bother her because "I just knowed it was my lucky day when I saw the spring dried up this morning. No more mud tracking up my floor. No more dampness aching in my bones." Old Man Trouble falls for it and restores the well before he leaves in one more attempt to squash Aunt Nancy's good spirits, not realizing he has been had. Deborah Stevenson of the *Bulletin of the Center for Children's Books* commented that this story of the "victory of the underestimated" is a "kid-pleasing version with some bite to it."

A *Publishers Weekly* writer called Root's 1996 book *Mrs. Potter's Pig* a "cheery tale of compromise." The story features Mrs. Potter, a neat freak who learns to appreciate the joy of mud when she has to rescue her dirt-loving daughter from a pigpen. After that, although Mrs. Potter still keeps a spotless house, she and her daughter enjoy regular romps in the pigpen. The premise of *Contrary Bear,* a toy which is blamed for its owner's obstinate behavior, is described in another *Publishers Weekly* review as made "fresh all over again" by Root's "knowing wit." Contrary Bear takes the rap for making loud train whistles during naptime and wanting a bigger piece of cake, but the last straw for Dad is when Contrary Bear splashes water all over the bathroom. Contrary Bear is relegated to the clothesline to dry and his penitent owner promises to help Contrary Bear "try harder to be good tomorrow."

Root's ten-year-old daughter assisted with the text of *One Windy Wednesday,* a tale about a day so windy it blew the sound right out of the farm animals and into others. The lamb starts quacking, the ducks start mooing, and the cow starts oinking until Bonnie Bumble fixes everything by hitching the right animal to the right sound. Hazel Rochman, writing in *Booklist,* describes *One Windy Wednesday* as a "simple, funny story."

Rosie's Fiddle is a "reworking of [an] American folktale [which] bursts with vitality and spunk," according to *Kirkus Reviews.* Root's 1997 story features the devil himself in a fiddling contest with Rosie after he hears of her stellar fiddling reputation. After three rounds, Rosie fiddles the devil into a puff of smoke, wins his golden instrument, and saves her own soul from the devil's hands. A *Publishers Weekly* critic commented that "the folksy prose and stormy spreads convey the tale's intensity—the only thing missing is a bluegrass soundtrack." Janice M. Del Negro of the *Bulletin of the Center for Children's Books* also offered a favorable estimation of *Rosie's Fiddle,* asserting: "Root's adaptation of this traditional motif has a fine readaloud rhythm and a thoroughly satisfying progression as the devil gets his musical due." Also in 1997, Root published *The Hungry Monster,* a picture book directed to the preschool set. When a hungry monsters lands on Earth, his hunger cannot be satisfied until a little girl offers him a banana, peel and all. A *Kirkus Reviews* writer praised "this silly story that includes a dash of suspense," concluding that the author's economy of words makes it "a just-right read-aloud for board-book graduates."

Root recalled for *SATA:* "When I was thirty, I took my first writing class with Marion Dane Bauer, a gifted writer and teacher, who gave me the tools I needed to write. I have been writing ever since, through lean years and good years. Some stories come to me unbidden, out

Rosie tucked her fiddle under her chin, tuned a string, and started to
play, sweet and high.
Along came a soft little breeze. It tickled the roses out of their buds,
shook out the laundry and folded it up, then gathered the chickens and
shooed them home.

**Rosie's talent with the fiddle causes the devil to challenge her to a musical contest for her soul in this picture book based on
a classic American folktale.** (From *Rosie's Fiddle*, written by Root and illustrated by Kevin O'Malley and Margot
Apple.)

of wherever stories come from, and I feel blessed by
these gifts. Some come only after endless rewrites.
Through it all, my hope is to keep writing and to keep
having stories to tell."

■ **Works Cited**

Review of *Contrary Bear, Publishers Weekly,* May 13,
1996, p. 75.
Cooper, Ilene, review of *Gretchen's Grandma, Booklist,*
January 1, 1984, p. 684.
Review of *Coyote and the Magic Words, Kirkus Reviews,*
September 1, 1993, p. 1151.
Del Negro, Janice M., review of *Rosie's Fiddle, Bulletin
of the Center for Children's Books,* April, 1997, p.
293.
Review of *The Hungry Monster, Kirkus Reviews,* Janu-
ary 1, 1997, p. 63.
Hutt, Karen, review of *Coyote and the Magic Words,
Booklist,* November 15, 1993, p. 633.
Jennings, Kathryn Pierson, review of *The Listening
Silence, Bulletin of the Center for Children's Books,*
March, 1992, p. 191.
Review of *The Listening Silence, Kirkus Reviews,* May
1, 1992, p. 616.
Review of *Moon Tiger, Bulletin of the Center for
Children's Books,* January, 1986, p. 95.
Review of *Mrs. Potter's Pig, Publishers Weekly,* June 10,
1996, p. 99.

Review of *The Old Red Rocking Chair, Publishers
Weekly,* May 18, 1992, p. 68.
Rochman, Hazel, review of *One Windy Wednesday,
Booklist,* October 15, 1996, p. 437.
Review of *Rosie's Fiddle, Kirkus Reviews,* February 1,
1997, p. 227.
Review of *Rosie's Fiddle, Publishers Weekly,* January
13, 1997, pp. 75-76.
Review of *Sam Who Was Swallowed by a Shark,
Publisher's Weekly,* May 30, 1994, pp. 55-56.
Review of *Soup for Supper, Bulletin of the Center for
Children's Books,* July-August, 1986, p. 216.
Schmidtmann, Nancy, review of *Moon Tiger, School
Library Journal,* December, 1985, p. 81.
Stevenson, Deborah, review of *Aunt Nancy and Old
Man Trouble, Bulletin of the Center for Children's
Books,* March, 1996, p. 240.
Vose, Ruth S., review of *The Listening Silence, School
Library Journal,* June, 1992, p. 125.

■ **For More Information See**

PERIODICALS

Booklist, July, 1986, p. 1616.
Horn Book, September-October, 1996, pp. 585-87.
Kirkus Reviews, May 15, 1996, p. 749.
Publishers Weekly, November 4, 1996, p. 74.
School Library Journal, May, 1986, p. 84; January,
1994, p. 97.

—Sketch by Maria Sheler Edwards

* * *

RORBY, Ginny 1944-
(Oesterle, Virginia Rorby)

■ Personal

Born August 9, 1944, in Washington, DC; adopted daughter of Noel (in sales) and Kathryn (a homemaker; maiden name, Loonan) Rorby; married Stan Clarke, August 29, 1964 (marriage ended, December 29, 1965); married Douglas Oesterle (an accountant), May 22, 1971 (separated, 1980); stepchildren: Robert A., Mark W. *Education:* University of Miami, FL, A.B. (biology and English), 1985; Florida International University, M.F.A. (creative writing), 1991. *Politics:* Democrat. *Hobbies and other interests:* Wildlife photography, kayaking, canoeing, travel.

■ Addresses

Home and office—Fort Bragg, CA. *Agent*—Barbara Kouts, P.O. Box 558, Bellport, NY 11713.

■ Career

National Airlines (later Pan American Airways), Miami, FL, flight attendant, 1966-89; writer. Chairperson, Glass Beach Access Committee; member, Leadership Mendocino. *Member:* National Audubon Society (president, Mendocino Coast chapter), Phi Kappa Phi.

■ Awards, Honors

Keystone to Reading Book Award nomination, Keystone State Reading Association, 1997, for *Dolphin Sky.*

■ Writings

Dolphin Sky (juvenile novel), Putnam, 1996.

■ Work in Progress

At Home in the Dark, a fictionalized memoir; *Without Voices,* a young adult novel; a natural history of the Mendocino coast.

■ Sidelights

Ginny Rorby told *SATA:* "I was born in the Florence Crittenton Home for unwed mothers in Washington, D.C. My birth mother was forced to care for me for about three months, throughout the adoption process. I was adopted by Kathryn and Noel Rorby, who lived in Detroit at the time. When I was two, we moved to Maitland, Florida. I have always loved animals. Before we left Detroit, I got my head stuck between the bars of the lions' cage at the Detroit Zoo.

"I lived the next twenty years in central Florida, first in Maitland in the house that is now the headquarters of

GINNY RORBY

the Florida Audubon Society, then in Winter Park. By the time I was four, it was discovered that I had a weak muscle in my right eye, which caused it to turn inward when I was tired. The doctors tried a patch, then glasses. All through school, my greatest fear was being called on to read aloud in class. I barely got out of high school.

"I excelled at nothing as a youngster. I was a moderately good swimmer, singer, and painter, but I started smoking when I was fifteen, ruining my chances at two out of three, and I lost interest in painting. I attended a junior college in Orlando, where I was admitted on academic probation. I took remedial English three times before I finally received a 'D.' I still can't diagram a sentence.

"In 1964 I married to get away from home. The marriage lasted eleven months, and only that long because I felt guilty about the wedding gifts. In 1966 I was hired by National Airlines as a 'stewardess.' Pan American Airways bought the company in 1980. I flew for twenty-three years. It was a wonderful life for about the first fifteen, then I began to feel trapped. In 1977, when I went back to school, it was with the intention of someday becoming a veterinarian. As it worked out, it took me eight years to get my undergraduate degree. By the time I graduated, I had begun to write.

"That I am now a writer was an accident. Until August, 1982, I had only written a couple of searing letters, one to a store owner in Orlando who had fired a former co-

GINNY RORBY
Dolphin Sky

Dyslexic, boyish Buddy Martin is timid around jeering schoolmates and her critical father, but her love of animals forces her to take brave action when the dolphins she treasures are cruelly mistreated. (Cover illustration by Ted Lewin.)

worker with breast cancer, and one to an eye doctor who went to a patient's deathbed to collect his fee. Some time in 1981, a friend of mine (who did become a vet) found a starving dog. Maggots were already consuming its flesh. When I came home from a trip, she had gained its trust. We collected every sleeping pill and valium that we had between us, drugged the dog, took it to a vet, and had it put to sleep. The first thing I ever wrote, aside from those letters, was about that dog.

"A year later, I found the 'story' stuffed in the side pocket of my uniform purse. It made my heart hurt all over again, so I typed it and took it to the smaller of our two Miami newspapers. They published 'We Found Your Dog' in 1982. An editor called me at home and said, 'If you can write like that, we will publish anything you write.' Of course, I couldn't. It would be years before I found my way back to writing about what knots my guts. In the interim, I started taking writing courses and ended up with an M.F.A. in creative writing. In 1991 I moved to the north coast of California. *Dolphin Sky* was sold five days before my fiftieth birthday."

Dolphin Sky tells the story of twelve-year-old Buddy, who empathizes with the mistreated dolphins she sees in

a cut-rate tourist show near her Florida home. Buddy herself feels neglected by her single father and confused and "dumb" in school. She has the love and respect of her elderly grandfather, however, and with his help and that of a new biologist friend, she grows in self-esteem. She learns that she is not stupid but has a learning disability, and she comes up with a plan to free her mistreated dolphin friends. Buddy's boating trips with her grandfather "bring suspense, and the theme of our inhumane treatment of other mammals adds substance and tenderness," Susan DeRonne noted in *Booklist*. While *School Library Journal* contributor Susan Oliver found some of the events implausible, she praised Rorby's "sensitively drawn" characters and her "provocatively and emotionally discussed" treatment of animal rights. As a *Publishers Weekly* reviewer concluded, "convincingly portrayed relationships, a deeply moving plot" and interesting detail on the Florida Everglades "combine to make this debut a real winner."

■ Works Cited

DeRonne, Susan, review of *Dolphin Sky, Booklist,* March 1, 1996, p. 1184.

Review of *Dolphin Sky, Publishers Weekly,* March 25, 1996, p. 85.

Oliver, Susan, review of *Dolphin Sky, School Library Journal,* April, 1996, p. 140.

* * *

ROWLAND-ENTWISTLE, (Arthur) Theodore (Henry) 1925- (John Briquebec, Anyon Ellis, James Hall-Clarke, T.E. Henry, J.T. Lawrence)

■ Personal

Born July 30, 1925, in Clayton-le-Moors, Lancashire, England; son of Arthur (an author and journalist) and Sylvia Morton (a teacher; maiden name, Clarke) Rowland-Entwistle; married Jean Isobel Esther Cooke (a writer and editor), March 18, 1968 (died, 1994). *Education:* Downsend School, Leatherhead; Open University, B.A. (Hons). *Religion:* Church of England. *Hobbies and other interests:* Earth sciences, history, geography, natural history.

■ Addresses

Agent—Rupert Crew Ltd., King's Mews, London, WC1N 2JA, England.

■ Career

Daily Mail, Manchester and London, England, sub-editor, 1944-45; *TV Times,* London, chief sub-editor, 1955-56, production editor, 1956-61; *World Book Encyclopedia,* London, senior editor, 1961-67; Leander Associates Ltd. (an editorial agency), director, 1967-68; First Features Ltd. (a newspaper features agency), director, 1970-75; Hastings Talking Newspaper (for the Blind)

Association, president. *Member:* Royal Geographical Society (fellow), Zoological Society of London (fellow).

■ Writings

Teach Yourself Violin, English Universities Press, 1967, published as *Violin,* McKay, 1974.

(Editor) Paddy Hopkirk, *The Longest Drive of All: Paddy Hopkirk's Story of the London-Sydney Motor Rally,* illustrated by John C. Smith, Geoffrey Chapman, 1969.

(As John Briquebec) *Winston Churchill,* McGraw, 1972.

Napoleon, Hart-Davis, 1973.

Facts and Records Book of Animals, Purnell, 1975.

The World You Never See: Insect Life, Rand McNally, 1976.

Our Earth, World Distributor, 1977.

The Restless Earth, edited by Trisha Pike, Purnell, 1977.

Exploring Animal Homes, illustrated by Graham Allen and others, Watts, 1978, revised expanded edition published as *Animal Homes,* Kingfisher, 1987.

Exploring Animal Journeys, illustrated by Graham Allen and others, Watts, 1978, revised expanded edition published as *Animal Journeys,* Kingfisher, 1987.

Let's Look at Wild Animals, edited by Jennifer Justice, illustrated by Mike Atkinson, Ward Lock, 1978.

Habits and Habitats: Insects, World Distributor, 1979.

Natural Wonders of the World, Octopus, 1980.

The Illustrated Atlas of the Bible Lands, Longman, 1981.

Ancient World, Galley Press, 1981.

Illustrated Facts and Records Book of Animals, Arco, 1981.

(As John Briquebec) *Animals and Man,* Purnell, 1982.

(As Anyon Ellis) *Wild Animals,* Granada, 1982, abridged edition, Carnival, 1989.

(As John Briquebec) *Trees,* illustrated by David Salariya, Granada, 1982.

(As J. T. Lawrence) *Fossils,* Granada, 1982.

Insects, illustrated by Rachel Birkett, Granada, 1983.

(As T. E. Henry) *The Seashore,* Granada, 1983.

(As James Hall-Clarke) *Fishes,* illustrated by Rod Sutterby, Granada, 1983.

Heraldry, illustrated by Jim Dugdale and Charlotte Styles, Granada, 1984.

Confucius and Ancient China, illustrated by Gerry Wood, Wayland, 1986.

Inventors, Franklin Watts, 1986.

Kings and Queens, Franklin Watts, 1986.

Architects, Franklin Watts, 1986.

Reformers, Franklin Watts, 1986.

Focus on Rubber, Wayland, 1986.

Rivers and Lakes, Wayland, 1986, Silver Burdett Press, 1987.

Stamps, Wayland, 1986.

Nebuchadnezzar and the Babylonians, illustrated by Gerry Wood, Wayland, 1986.

The Royal Marines, Wayland, 1987.

The Secret Service, Wayland, 1987.

The Special Air Service, Wayland, 1987.

Flags, Wayland, 1987.

Focus on Coal, Wayland, 1987.

Jungles and Rainforests, Wayland, 1987.

Focus on Silk, Wayland, 1988.

Thomas Edison, illustrated by Tony Morris, Marshall Cavendish, 1988.

Wilbur and Orville Wright, illustrated by W. Francis Phillipps, Marshall Cavendish, 1988.

Guns, Wayland, 1988.

A Three-Dimensional Atlas of the World, Simon & Schuster, 1988.

The Pop-up Atlas of the World, illustrated by Philip Jacobs and Mike Peterkin, Simon & Schuster, 1988.

(As John Briquebec) *The Middle Ages: Barbarian Invasions, Empires around the World and Medieval Europe,* Warwick Press (New York), 1990.

The First Empires, Watts, 1990.

Prehistoric Life, Belitha, 1990, adapted by Robert Brown as *The Prehistoric World,* Gareth Stevens Children's Books, 1990.

(As John Briquebec) *The Ancient World: From the Earliest Civilizations to the Roman Empire,* Warwick Press, 1990, published as *Ancient World: From the Earliest Civilizations to the Roman Empire, 30,000 BC - AD 456,* Kingfisher, 1991.

Weather and Climate, Belitha, 1991.

(As John Briquebec, with Simon Adams and Ann Kramer) *Illustrated Atlas of World History,* Kingfisher, 1991, Random House, 1992.

(Editor) R. Tucker Abbott, *Seashells of Great Britain and Europe,* Dragon's World, 1993, Thunder Bay Press, 1994.

(As Anyon Ellis, with Tom Mariner) *The Cherrytree Book of the Earth,* Cherrytree (Bath, England), 1993, Dillon Press (New York), 1994.

(Editor) Michael O'Donoghue, *Rocks and Minerals of the World,* Dragon's World, 1993, Thunder Bay Press, 1994.

(With Ann Kramer) *The Dorling Kindersley Question and Answer Quiz Book,* Dorling Kindersley, 1994.

Eureka!: A Puzzle Book of Inventions, illustrated by Hemesh Alles, Templar, 1995.

(Compiler) *World Events and Dates,* illustrated by Peter Rutherford, Henderson, 1995.

More Errata: Another Book of Historical Errors, illustrated by Hemesh Alles, Simon & Schuster, 1995.

The Paras: The Story of the Parachute Regiment, Parragon, 1997.

"FUN FAX" HISTORY OF BRITAIN SERIES

The Invaders, illustrated by David Marshall, Henderson, 1994.

Middle Ages, illustrated by Bob Moulder, Henderson, 1994.

Tudor Times, illustrated by Shaun Campbell, Henderson, 1994.

Cavaliers and Roundheads, illustrated by Mike Taylor, Henderson, 1994.

Revolution and Change, illustrated by Peter Rutherford, Henderson, 1994.

The Victorians, illustrated by Sean Duggan, Henderson, 1994.

WITH JEAN COOKE

Animal Worlds, illustrated by Bernard Robinson and others, Sampson Low, 1974, Watts, 1976.

Famous Composers, David & Charles, 1974.

Famous Explorers, David & Charles, 1974.

Famous Kings and Emperors, David & Charles, 1976, reissued as *Great Rulers of History,* Barnes & Noble, 1995.

(And with Ann Kramer) *World of History,* illustrated by Brian Dear and Constance Dear, Hamlyn, 1977.

(Editors) *The Junior General Knowledge Encyclopedia,* foreword by Magnus Magnusson, Octopus, 1978.

(Editors) *Purnell's Concise Encyclopedia of the Arts,* Purnell, 1979.

(Editors) *Purnell's Pictorial Encyclopedia,* Purnell, 1979.

(Editors) *Purnell's Pictorial Encyclopedia of Nature,* Purnell, 1980.

(And with Peter Robson) *The Book of Great Escapes: Based on True Life Stories!,* Purnell, 1980.

(And with Ann Kramer) *History's Timeline: A 40,000-Year Chronology of World Civilization,* Crescent Books, 1981.

(And with Kramer) *History Fact-finder,* illustrated by Brian Dear and Constance Dear, Ward Lock, 1981.

(Compilers) *The World Almanac Infopedia: A Visual Encyclopedia for Students,* World Almanac, 1990.

(Compilers) *Fact Finder,* Kingfisher, 1992, updated edition published as *The Kingfisher Fact Finder,* Kingfisher, 1993.

OTHER

Contributor of articles and consultant to encyclopedias, including *New Junior World Encyclopedia, Encyclopedia of Wild Life, Apollo Encyclopedia, Modern Century Illustrated Encyclopedia, Encyclopedia of Africa, Encyclopedia of Inventions, Concise Encyclopedia of Geography, Concise Encyclopedia of History, Rainbow Encyclopedia, Millennium Encyclopedia, Peoples of Africa,* and *Pictorial Encyclopedia of History.* Contributor of articles and consultant to atlases, including *St. Michael Atlas of World Geography* and *My First Picture Atlas.*

Editor, *Hastings Talking Newspaper for the Blind,* 1981-93. Contributor of articles to periodicals, including *Mind Alive* and *The Woodworker.* Contributor of crossword puzzles to periodicals. Contributor of questions to television programs, including *It's Your Word,* BBC, 1971, and *Brainchild,* BBC, 1972.

■ Work in Progress

Various books and contributions to encyclopedias.

■ Sidelights

Theodore Rowland-Entwistle told *SATA:* "I always wanted to be a writer. I began by writing verses, and had the great advantage of being trained in poetry writing by my father, himself a poet. Contrary to popular belief, writing poetry is like music: you need training to produce decent results. Only three of my poems have ever been published.

"My career got off to a good start by landing a job (helped by my father) with a great national newspaper; it was wartime, journalists (and even potential ones) were in short supply, and I had been rejected for military service because of severe chronic asthma, the effects of which have handicapped me all my life. From there I was seconded to help start a programme paper for the new independent television channel. All this time I was editing but rarely having a chance to write.

"A real break-through came when I joined the staff of *World Book Encyclopedia,* which was about to produce an international edition. There I was able to do some writing, and in my leisure time produced my first book, *Teach Yourself the Violin.* When the encyclopedia job came to an end I became a freelance writer and editor, working with my wife Jean Cooke, a former studio manager with the British Broadcasting Corporation, until her early death in 1994. Between us we wrote over seventy books, and contributed to a great many more.

"I enjoy my writing, and am glad to be able to continue with it when most other people would expect to have retired—and no doubt have died of boredom."

Rowland-Entwistle is an exceptionally prolific writer, compiler, and editor of science and history books for young people. With his wife, Jean Cooke, as well as other co-authors, and under a variety of pseudonyms, he has produced works as varied as *The World You Never See: Insect Life, Confucius and Ancient China,* and *Illustrated Facts and Records Book of Animals.* Given the audience for the majority of Rowland-Entwistle's works, the challenge, as reviewers have often noted, is to present clearly the most relevant information on a subject about which vast stores of knowledge may be available in other formats. Thus, clarity of prose and such criteria as organization and presentation are of primary importance to the reviewers who evaluate Rowland-Entwistle's efforts. Along these lines, Stephanie Zvirin remarked in *Booklist* of *Illustrated Facts and Records Book of Animals* that "The text is concise, informal, and fairly basic in nature," qualities which make it "a useful, approachable overview" of the animal kingdom, suitable for students. Similarly, *The World You Never See: Insect Life* garnered praise from *Science Books and Films* contributor B. J. R. Philogene for its "clearly written and concise text." Philogene maintained that "this book will appeal to a large audience and particularly to teachers."

Among Rowland-Entwistle's contributions that increase children's access to information on the natural world are *Rivers and Lakes* and *Jungles and Rainforests,* both for the "Our World" series from Silver Burdett press, of which a *Booklist* commentator concluded: "These up-to-date, fact-filled volumes with an emphasis on the need for making wise use of our geographical heritage will provide useful resource materials." Deirdre R. Murray echoed these sentiments in her *School Library Journal* review of Rowland-Entwistle's *Rivers and Lakes* and *Jungles and Rainforests,* noting that these works "are so attractive and well designed that they will also be picked up just for interesting reading." Rowland-Entwistle has also contributed to Wayland's "Focus On" series of books on natural resources.

In the realm of history and human society, Rowland-Entwistle's efforts, including *Guns, Flags, Confucius and Ancient China, Fact Finder,* and *Illustrated Atlas of World History,* have been reviewed in much the same manner as his contributions to the field of natural history. Of the *Illustrated Atlas of World History,* the reviewer for *Booklist* concluded: "Presenting an inclusive introduction to world cultures in one inexpensive volume is a laudatory goal, and this atlas provides a first view of a holistic world." Rowland-Entwistle has also published a number of studies for young people on noteworthy historical figures, including *Winston Churchill, Napoleon, Thomas Edison,* and *Wilbur and Orville Wright.*

■ Works Cited

Review of *Illustrated Atlas of World History, Booklist,* April 15, 1992, p. 1551.
Review of *Jungles and Rainforests* and *Rivers and Lakes, Booklist,* February 1, 1988, pp. 935-36.

Murray, Deirdre R., review of *Jungles and Rainforests* and *Rivers and Lakes, School Library Journal,* April, 1988, p. 110.
Philogene, B. J. R., review of *The World You Never See: Insect Life, Science Books and Films,* September, 1977, p. 84.
Zvirin, Stephanie, review of *Illustrated Facts and Records Book of Animals, Booklist,* July, 1983, p. 1397.

■ For More Information See

PERIODICALS

Appraisal, Spring, 1988, p. 49; Summer, 1988, pp. 60-61; Spring, 1991, pp. 82-84.
Booklist, August, 1993, p. 2088.
Bulletin of the Center for Children's Books, October, 1988, p. 45; January 1, 1989, p. 785.
School Library Journal, February, 1979, p. 57; May, 1984, p. 24; August, 1987, p. 84; May, 1993, p. 139.

S

SAGAN, Carl 1934-1996

OBITUARY NOTICE—See index for *SATA* sketch: Born November 9, 1934, in New York, NY; died of pneumonia, December 20, 1996, in Seattle, WA. Scientist and author. Through books, television and lectures, Sagan made the world of scientific research and astronomy understandable and fascinating to the public. He was best known as the author of the 1980 book *Cosmos* and host of the public television (PBS) series of the same name. Born to a working-class family in Brooklyn, Sagan left New York to study at the University of Chicago, where he earned bachelor's, master's and doctorate degrees in physics, astronomy and astro-physics, the latter in 1960. Sagan served as a fellow at the University of California, Berkeley, and assistant professor of astronomy at Harvard University before moving to Cornell University, where he became a professor in 1971. In his 20s, Sagan deduced that radio emissions from Venus were caused by high surface temperatures and atmospheric pressure. He also correctly interpreted the changing colors of Mars, which some thought were from plant life. Sagan maintained they were caused by dust kicked up by wind storms. The Mariner spacecraft proved him right. He took his ivory tower knowledge to the public, popularizing astronomy through books and television and getting the public to support scientific research. While the television appearances, especially talk shows, irked some of his conservative colleagues, none of them could question Sagan's knowledge or methods because he was first and foremost a scientist. He wrote dozens of books and hundreds of scientific papers and articles in popular magazines. Sagan's first book (with W. W. Kellogg) was 1961's *The Atmospheres of Mars and Venus*. He was also instrumental in giving scientific legitimacy to the search for extraterrestrial life and, with I. S. Shklovskii, wrote one of the first serious scientific books on the subject in 1978, *Intelligent Life in the Universe*. In 1980, he hosted a 13-part series on PBS called *Cosmos* and wrote a best-selling book of the same name to accompany it. He won numerous awards, including the Pulitzer Prize for Literature in 1978 for his book *The Dragons of Eden: Speculations on the Evolution of Human Intelligence*. Sagan's *Cosmos* re-ceived Best Books for Young Adults recognition from the American Library Association in 1980, and his *Broca's Brain* and *Murmurs of Earth* were both selected Books for the Teen Age by the New York Public Library that same year. Besides writing, Sagan was also instrumental in developing the Mariner 9 mission to Mars, the Viking 1 and Viking 2 landings on Mars and the Pioneer and Voyager missions to the outer planets. Sagan was also active in more earthly affairs such as foreign policy and nuclear arms reduction. He served on the Council on Foreign Relations and, with Richard Turco, wrote *A Path Where No Man Thought: Nuclear Winter and the End of the Arms Race* in 1989. His last best-seller was *Pale Blue Dot* in 1994.

OBITUARIES AND OTHER SOURCES:

PERIODICALS

Chicago Tribune, December 21, 1996, sec. 1, p. 21.
Christian Science Monitor, December 24, 1996, p. 15.
Los Angeles Times, December 21, 1996, p. A1.
New York Times, December 21, 1996, p. 26.
Times (London), December 21, 1996, p. 19.
USA Today, December 23, 1996, p. D4.
Washington Post, December 21, 1996, pp. A12, B1, B3.

* * *

SALWOOD, F. K.
See KILWORTH, Garry (D.)

* * *

SANDIN, Joan 1942-

■ Personal

Born April 30, 1942, in Watertown, WI; daughter of Robert L. (a teacher) and Frances K. (an interviewer; maiden name, Somers) Sandin; married Sigfrid Leijonhufvud (a journalist), April 30, 1971 (divorced, 1986); children: Jonas and Jenny. *Education:* University of Arizona, B.F.A., 1964.

■ Addresses

Home—Tucson, AZ.

■ Career

Illustrator, author, and translator of children's books. *Exhibitions:* Solo shows in Sweden and the United States of illustrations for *The Long Way to a New Land.* Art represented in The Kerlan Collection. *Member:* FST, The Swedish Society of Illustrators.

■ Awards, Honors

Best Children's Books, American Institute of Graphic Artists, 1970, for *Crocodile and Hen;* travel and work grants from Forfattarfonden (The Swedish Writers' Fund); exhibition grant from Bildkonstnarsfonden (The Swedish Artists' Fund); Notable Children's Trade Books in the Field of Social Studies, National Council for the Social Studies and Children's Book Council (NCSS/ CBC), for *Hill of Fire,* 1971, *The Lemming Condition,* 1976, *The Long Way to a New Land,* 1981, and *Time for Uncle Joe,* 1981; Georgia Children's Award, 1973, for *"Hey, What's Wrong with This One?";* Outstanding Science Trade Book for Children, National Science Teachers Association (NSTA) and Children's Book Council, 1974, for *Woodchuck;* nominee, Edgar Allan Poe Award, Mystery Writers of America, 1975, for *The Mysterious Red Tape Gang;* Notable Book, American Library Association, 1981, for *The Long Way to a New Land,* and 1988, for translation of Christina Bjork's *Linnea's Windowsill Garden.*

■ Writings

SELF-ILLUSTRATED

The Long Way to a New Land, Harper & Row, 1981.
The Long Way Westward, Harper & Row, 1989.
Pioneer Bear: Based on a True Story, Random House, 1995.

ILLUSTRATOR

Carol Beach York, *The Blue Umbrella,* Watts, 1968.
Randolph Stow, *Midnite: The Story of a Wild Colonial Boy,* Prentice-Hall, 1968.
Harold Felton, *True Tall Tales of Stormalong: Sailor of the Seven Seas,* Prentice-Hall, 1968.
Edith Brecht, *The Little Fox,* Lippincott, 1968.
Eleanor Hull, *A Trainful of Strangers,* Atheneum, 1968.
Ellen Pugh, *Tales from the Welsh Hills,* Dodd, 1968.
Maia Wojciechowska, *"Hey, What's Wrong with This One?",* Harper, 1969.
Joan Lexau, *Crocodile and Hen,* Harper, 1969.
Jan M. Robinson, *The December Dog,* Lippincott, 1969.
Constantine Georgiou, *Rani, Queen of the Jungle,* Prentice-Hall, 1970.
Joan Lexau, *It All Began with a Drip, Drip, Drip,* McCall/Dutton, 1970.
Jean Little, *Look through My Window,* Harper, 1970.
Joanna Cole, *The Secret Box,* Morrow, 1971.
Thomas P. Lewis, *Hill of Fire,* Harper, 1971.

Barbara Brenner, *A Year in the Life of Rosie Bernard,* Harper, 1971.
Ellen Pugh, *More Tales from the Welsh Hills,* Dodd, 1971.
Jean Little, *From Anna,* Harper, 1972.
Nathaniel Benchley, *Small Wolf,* Harper, 1972.
Edna Mitchell Preston, *Ickle Bickle Robin,* Watts, 1973.
Alison Morgan, *A Boy Called Fish,* Harper, 1973.
Joan L. Nixon, *The Mysterious Red Tape Gang,* Putnam, 1974.
Hans Eric Hellberg, translated by Patricia Crampton, *Grandpa's Maria,* Morrow, 1974.
Faith McNulty, *Woodchuck,* Harper, 1974.
Kathryn Ewing, *A Private Matter,* Harcourt Brace Jovanovich, 1975.
Liesel Skorpen, *Michael,* Harper, 1975.
Liesel Skorpen, *Bird,* Harper, 1976.
Sandra Love, *But What about Me?,* Harcourt Brace Jovanovich, 1976.
Alan Arkin, *The Lemming Condition,* Harper, 1976.
Thomas P. Lewis, *Clipper Ship,* Harper & Row, 1978.
Clyde Robert Bulla, *Daniel's Duck,* Harper & Row, 1979.
Nancy Jewell, *Time for Uncle Joe,* Harper & Row, 1981.
Eleanor Coerr, *The Bell Ringer and the Pirates,* Harper & Row, 1983.
Doreen Rappaport, *Trouble at the Mines,* Crowell, 1987.
Aileen Fisher, *The House of a Mouse: Poems,* Harper & Row, 1988.
Aileen Fisher, *Always Wondering: Some Favorite Poems of Aileen Fisher,* HarperCollins, 1991.
Nancy Smiler Levinson, *Snowshoe Thompson,* Harper Collins, 1992.
Elaine Marie Alphin, *A Bear for Miguel,* HarperCollins, 1996.

TRANSLATOR

Gunilla Bergstrom, *Who's Scaring Alfie Atkins?,* Farrar, Straus & Giroux, 1987.
Christina Bjork, *Elliot's Extraordinary Cookbook,* Farrar, Straus & Giroux, 1991.
Christina Bjork, *The Other Alice: The Story of Alice Liddell and Alice in Wonderland,* R & S Books/ Farrar, 1993.
Christina Bjork, *Big Bear's Book: By Himself,* Farrar, Straus & Giroux, 1994.
Olof Landstrom, *Boo and Baa in a Party Mood,* Farrar, Straus & Giroux, 1996.
Olof Landstrom, *Boo and Baa in Windy Weather,* Farrar, Straus & Giroux, 1996.

■ Sidelights

Joan Sandin once told *SATA:* "I most enjoy working with folk tales and books demanding research and/or travel." Sandin lived in Sweden for more than a decade before returning to the United States in the mid-1980s. Her extensive travels in Europe and Mexico as well as the U.S. have inspired her work. A prolific illustrator, Sandin is also a skilled translator and a storyteller in her own right.

Among the many books Sandin has illustrated is *A Bear for Miguel*, by Elaine Maria Alphin, an unusual story for early readers, according to reviewers, but one that is effectively done and sensitively rendered in pictures and words. When Maria brings her stuffed toy bear, Paco, along to the market with her father, she has no intention of trading him. However, her realization of what the ongoing war in their country of El Salvador has meant for her father's ability to find work, and her understanding that a little boy injured in the war would love to have Paco, impels Maria to trade the toy for food for her family. "Sandin's watercolors add to the emotional impact ... and do an effective job of setting the scene," remarked Gale W. Sherman in *School Library Journal*.

Sandin has translated several books from Swedish into English. Among those for children is *Boo and Baa in a Party Mood* and *Boo and Baa in Windy Weather*, two picture books written by Olof and Lea Landstrom featuring a couple of hapless lambs. In *Boo and Baa in a Party Mood*, the two prepare for a birthday party by practicing their dance steps, but things get sticky when they try to wrap the present. In *Boo and Baa in Windy Weather*, the two go to the grocery store, but dragging home a sled laden with their purchases through a snow storm presents a problem. *Big Bear's Book*, according to *School Library Journal* contributor Marilyn Taniguchi, is not a picture book but "a whimsical reminiscence of childhood" best suited to sentimental adults. Written by Christina Bjork, *Big Bear's Book* tells the story of a toy bear's relationship to his owner, from childhood, through a sojourn in the attic, to a place in the child's adult life and a career in the movies. Sandin is also the translator of Bjork's tribute to the children's classic, *Alice in Wonderland*. In *The Other Alice*, Bjork describes the model for Lewis Carroll's main character, Alice Liddell, and explains some of the games and other trivia associated with the book. The result is "a unique pleasure," Ann A. Flowers maintained in *Horn Book*.

Sandin's own background—her ancestors immigrated to the United States from Sweden in the nineteenth century—inspired the research that went into *The Long Way to a New Land* and *The Long Way Westward*, two self-illustrated early readers that tell the story of an immigrant family's journey from Sweden to the United States in the 1860s. Told from the perspective of Carl Erik, the family's older son, *The Long Way to a New Land* describes a drought that forces Erik's family to sell their farm and try to make a fresh start in America, and the trip by boat to the United States, where bad weather, bad smells, and crowding mean long days of discomfort before they reach their destination. Critics noted that Sandin utilizes her illustrations effectively to augment a necessarily spare text intended for beginning readers. "It isn't always easy to make history comprehensible to younger children," remarked Zena Sutherland of the *Bulletin of the Center for Children's Books*, "[but] Sandin does a nice job of it." Similarly praised as "an interesting, well-researched slice of history" by a critic for *Kirkus Reviews*, *The Long Way Westward* completes the story of the Erik family's journey as they travel from

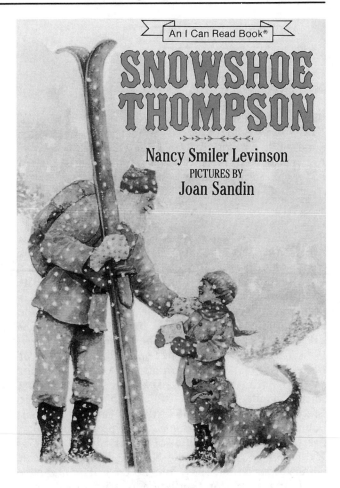

Joan Sandin illustrates Nancy Smiler Levinson's story of the pioneering skier John Thompson, who completed a ninety-mile trek across the Sierra Nevada in winter to plot a trail for the passage of people and mail.

New York by railroad to Minnesota to live among their relatives.

Also set in the nineteenth century, *Pioneer Bear* tells the story of John Lacy, a photographer who has heard that young Andrew Irwin has taught a bear to dance. Lacy travels thirty miles to the Irwin farm to photograph the bear; but when he arrives Bearly the Bear is nowhere to be found, and Sandin provides a visual survey of pioneer life on a farm as the family goes from room to room, from barn to outhouse, in search of the cub. "Pioneer activities such as washing laundry in tubs ... and smoking meats are realistically presented in warm watercolor illustrations," Mary Ann Bursk observed in *School Library Journal*. Reviewers also noted Sandin's sly infusion of humor into the story through her illustrations. "Primary schoolers will enjoy sighting Bearly ... as he peeks from behind outbuildings and foliage," remarked Elizabeth Bush in *Bulletin of the Center for Children's Books*.

■ Works Cited

Bursk, Mary Ann, review of *Pioneer Bear*, *School Library Journal*, October, 1995, p. 117.

Bush, Elizabeth, review of *Pioneer Bear, Bulletin of the Center for Children's Books,* July, 1995, p. 397.

Flowers, Ann A., review of *The Other Alice, Horn Book,* March, 1994, p. 215.

Review of *The Long Way Westward, Kirkus Reviews,* August 15, 1989, p. 1250.

Sherman, Gale W., review of *A Bear for Miguel, School Library Journal,* June, 1996, p. 92.

Sutherland, Zena, review of *The Long Way to a New Land, Bulletin of the Center for Children's Books,* March, 1982, p. 138.

Taniguchi, Marilyn, review of *Big Bear's Book, School Library Journal,* April, 1995, p. 130.

■ For More Information See

PERIODICALS

Booklist, November 1, 1996, pp. 507-08.

Horn Book, February, 1982, p. 39; May, 1996, pp. 331-32.

Kirkus Reviews, November 15, 1981, pp. 1406-07.

Publishers Weekly, August 25, 1989, p. 63; August 5, 1996, p. 440.

* * *

SCHMIDT, Karen Lee 1953-

■ Personal

Born August 28, 1953, in Albuquerque, NM; daughter of Norman (an air force test pilot) and Marie (a teacher; maiden name, Gavin) Schmidt. *Education:* Attended University of California (one year), Santa Barbara Art Institute (two years), Art Students' League (two years), School of Visual Arts (two years); Oregon College of Art/ Oregon State College, B.A.

■ Addresses

Home—361 West 22nd St. #2, New York, NY 10011.

■ Career

Illustrator. Visiting speaker at schools; also conducts workshops and interactive drawing demonstrations.

■ Illustrator

Thomas M. Disch, *The Brave Little Toaster: A Bedtime Story for Small Appliances,* Doubleday & Company, 1986.

My First Book of Baby Animals, Platt & Munk, 1986.

Down by the Station, Bantam, 1987.

Marcia Leonard, *Little Fox's Best Friend,* Bantam, 1987.

Marcia Leonard, *Little Kitten Sleeps Over,* Bantam, 1987.

Eve Merriam, *You Be Good and I'll Be Night: Jump-on-the-Bed Poems,* Morrow, 1988.

Mary Pope Osborne, comp., *Bears, Bears, Bears: A Treasury of Stories, Songs, and Poems about Bears,* Silver Press, 1990.

KAREN LEE SCHMIDT

Joanne Barkan, *Whiskerville Bake Shop,* Grosset & Dunlap, 1990.

Barkan, *Whiskerville Firehouse,* Grosset & Dunlap, 1990.

Barkan, *Whiskerville School,* Grosset & Dunlap, 1990.

Barkan, *Whiskerville Theater,* Grosset & Dunlap, 1991.

Barkan, *Whiskerville Toy Shop,* Grosset & Dunlap, 1991.

Barkan, *Whiskerville Train Station,* Grosset & Dunlap, 1991.

Barkan, *Whiskerville Grocery,* Grosset & Dunlap, 1991.

Elizabeth Lee O'Donnell, *The Twelve Days of Summer,* Morrow, 1991.

Iris Hiskey, *Hannah the Hippo's No Mud Day,* Simon & Schuster, 1991.

Pat Upton, *Who Lives in the Woods,* Bell Books, 1991.

Diane Patenaude, *The Monster Counting Book,* Doubleday, 1992.

Alan Benjamin, *A Nickel Buys a Rhyme,* Morrow Junior Books, 1993.

Linda Glaser, *Stop That Garbage Truck,* A. Whitman, 1993.

Maxine Meltzer, *Pups Speak Up,* Bradbury Press, 1994.

Pollita Tita (Chicken Little), Putnam, 1995.

Tom Paxton, *Going to the Zoo,* Morrow, 1996.

Joanna Cole, *Monster & Muffin,* Putnam, 1996.

Peter Cottontail, Putnam, 1996.

Wee Puppy, Putnam, 1996.

■ Work in Progress

Illustrations for *The Jungle Baseball Game,* by Tom Paxton, for Morrow Junior Books, and *One Was Gone,* by Caron Lee Cohen, for Dutton Children's Books.

■ Sidelights

Karen Lee Schmidt told *SATA:* "When I was growing up, my father named the spiders in our house Sam, Herman, and Henry and told us their detailed family histories so that we, his five children, would not be inclined to stomp on them! There were also many occasions when he stopped the car to give an assist to slow-moving snakes and turtles trying to make their way across the highway. Like our visiting spiders, they too had families to go home to. We also had Vertigo, an old palomino parade horse, and Charlie, a Labrador retriever. We lived in the Mojave Desert, in California, when there were few houses and no fences so our yard played host to a wide variety of desert animals. Two large turtles took up residence in our cactus garden. Roadrunners and jackrabbits ventured into and out of the yard. There were legions of lizards and herds of horned toads, not to mention snakes and tarantulas.

"My illustrations are populated by as wide a variety of animals as my youth was. The animals in my books, like those I imagined as a child, have human characteristics and find themselves in situations usually reserved for humans. I attribute my inclination to anthropomorphize to my animal-filled childhood and to my humorous father, with his tendency to create complicated lives and thoughts for even the most common insects.

"My inspiration also comes from my childhood reading list, which included *Black Beauty, Call of the Wild, The Wind in the Willows, Stuart Little, Doctor Dolittle, Charlotte's Web,* and the works of Dr. Seuss, among many others.

"I loved to draw as a child and was always encouraged by my parents. They kept me well stocked with art supplies, and, when my father's career as an air force pilot took our family to Taiwan for two years, they arranged for me to study with a Chinese brush-painting master.

"My mother, a first-grade teacher, was keenly appreciative of the importance of art and creativity in her students' lives. She enlisted me early on to create drawings for her classrooms and to help with art projects. Her encouragement and my 'career' as a classroom art decorator greatly contributed to my goal of becoming an illustrator. It gave me the confidence to keep trying, to go to college as an art major, and finally to move to New York—a forbidding city to someone from the deserts of California—to continue my studies. It was in New York that I discovered my calling as a children's book illustrator.

"Fifteen years and twenty-seven books later, I still live in New York City, in a small apartment with my grouchy cat, Larry, who does not allow me to have any other animals (although an occasional spider does sneak into our lives). I have come to love and appreciate New York City, but I do try to escape in the summer and for holidays to Bozeman, Montana, our new family home. There I hike and ski and seek new inspiration.

MAMA'S IN THE KITCHEN

Mama's in the kitchen
bakin' pies.
Daddy's on the back porch
swattin' flies.
Sister's with her boyfriend
sighin' sighs.
Brother's on the corner
tellin' lies.

From *A Nickle Buys a Rhyme,* a collection of poems written by Alan Benjamin and illustrated by Karen Lee Schmidt.

Illustrated by Schmidt, *Going to the Zoo* leads readers on a bouncy journey through the animal kingdom in this picture book based on the 1961 song by Tom Paxton.

"Children's books address universal themes—love, friendship, jealousy, loss, joy, sadness—often in poetic, humorous, or profound ways. As an artist I am able to give my own voice to these themes by playing off the words and building on them from page to page. I am currently working on two very different books. One is suspenseful and sad, the other, rollicking and funny. It is that variety I love—that, and being able to integrate my artistic training with themes that have occupied me since childhood."

Schmidt's illustrations have been warmly received for the colorful and humorous addition they have made to numerous story books for young children. The drawings for *You Be Good and I'll Be Night,* by Eve Merriam, received praise as enthusiastic as that bestowed on the book's award-winning author. A collection of nearly thirty poems with "rollicking rhymes" full of the author's "signature humor and playfulness," according to *New York Times Book Review* contributor Laurel Graeber, *You Be Good and I'll Be Night* "allows the illustrator . . . to show off her talents to best advantage." Schmidt's "bouncy watercolor scenes" accompany each poem, observed Betsy Hearne in the *Bulletin of the Center for Children's Books,* "often including comically incongruous animals." Indeed, echoed Graeber, "[Schmidt's] sprightly pictures of creatures ranging from jigging pigs to cuddling crocodiles are the visual equivalents of the poems, right down to the hidden joke: carved fish on a bear's bed, for instance."

Another collection of rhyming poems, Alan Benjamin's *A Nickel Buys a Rhyme,* features Schmidt's "exuberant" and "dapper" interpretations of "silly and sweet, modern Mother Goose-style rhymes," according to Annie Ayres of *Booklist.* "Contagiously rhythmic and deliciously funny," Benjamin's poems are accompanied by "Schmidt's lively, good-natured illustrations," making this "an inviting book to share," asserted the critic for *Kirkus Reviews.* Tom Paxton's *Going to the Zoo,* in which Schmidt's "energetic illustrations" appear on double-page spreads that highlight her "exaggerated yet still somewhat realistic" illustrations, was likewise recommended for reading aloud by Lauren Peterson in *Booklist.* Based on a song from 1961, the book features additional lyrics as well as musical notation; with the illustrations, these features, according to Peterson, make *Going to the Zoo* ideal for use in classroom settings or during story hour.

A veteran of more than a decade of work with children's books, Schmidt frequently visits elementary schools, speaking on her life and work as an illustrator. She also conducts workshops and interactive drawing demonstrations.

■ Works Cited

Ayres, Annie, review of *A Nickel Buys a Rhyme, Booklist,* July, 1993, pp. 1968-69.

Graeber, Laurel, review of *You Be Good and I'll Be Night,* New York Times Book Review, March 26, 1989, p. 19.

Hearne, Betsy, review of *You Be Good and I'll Be Night,* Bulletin of the Center for Children's Books, October, 1988, p. 48.

Review of *A Nickel Buys a Rhyme,* Kirkus Reviews, March 1, 1993, p. 297.

Peterson, Lauren, review of *Going to the Zoo,* Booklist, June 1, 1996, p. 1728.

■ For More Information See

PERIODICALS

Booklist, March 1, 1991, p. 1394.
Kirkus Reviews, March 1, 1991, p. 327.
Publishers Weekly, March 29, 1993, p. 56.
School Library Journal, April, 1987, p. 78; August, 1991, p. 152; June, 1993, p. 95; March, 1996, p. 191.

*   *   *

SCOTT, Ann Herbert 1926-

■ Personal

Born November 19, 1926, in Germantown, Philadelphia, PA; daughter of Henry Laux (a newspaperman) and Gladys (a homemaker, singer and painter; maiden name, Howe) Herbert; married William Taussig Scott (a professor of physics) September 29, 1961; children: Peter Herbert, Katherine Howe; (stepchildren) Jennifer, Christopher (deceased), Stephanie, Melanie. *Education:* University of Pennsylvania, B.A., 1948, graduate student, 1948-49; Yale University, M.A., 1958. *Politics:* Democrat. *Religion:* Society of Friends.

■ Career

Editor, writer, and lecturer. Rider College, Trenton, NJ, teacher of English, 1949-59; New Haven State Teachers College (now Southern Connecticut State College), New Haven, part-time teacher of English, 1956-58; Wider City Parish, New Haven, coordinator of volunteer work, 1958-61; American Friends Service Committee, Northern California Office, member of Reno area committee, 1966-84; co-founder and member, Children's Literature Interest Group, 1980—; director, All the Colors of the Race, Nevada Humanities Committee Conference on Ethnic Children's Literature, 1983; founder and chairperson, SIERRA Interfaith Action for Peace, 1986. *Member:* Society of Children's Book Writers and Illustrators, National Association for the Advancement of Colored People, Phi Beta Kappa, Mortar Board, Sphinx and Key.

■ Awards, Honors

American Institute of Graphics Arts Children's Books, 1967-68, and Notable Book, American Library Association (ALA), 1967, for *Sam;* Children's Books of the Year, Child Study Association of America (CSAA),

ANN HERBERT SCOTT

1968, for *Not Just One,* 1972, for *On Mother's Lap,* 1993, for *A Brand Is Forever* and *Cowboy Country,* and 1996, for *Brave as a Mountain Lion;* Nevada State Council on the Arts Grant, 1987; Best Books, *School Library Journal,* 1993, for *Cowboy Country;* Notable Books, ALA, 1995, for *Hi.*

■ Writings

Big Cowboy Western, illustrated by Richard W. Lewis, Lothrop, 1965.

Let's Catch a Monster, illustrated by H. Tom Hall, Lothrop, 1967.

Sam, illustrated by Symeon Shimin, McGraw, 1967.

Not Just One, illustrated by Yaroslava, Lothrop, 1968.

Census, U.S.A.: Fact Finding for the American People, 1790-1970 (young adult), Seabury, 1968.

On Mother's Lap, illustrated by Glo Coalson, McGraw, 1972.

Someday Rider, illustrated by Ronald Himler, Clarion, 1989.

One Good Horse: A Cowpuncher's Counting Book, illustrated by Lynn Sweat, Greenwillow, 1990.

Grandmother's Chair, illustrated by Meg Kelleher Aubrey, Clarion, 1990.

A Brand is Forever, illustrated by Ronald Himler, Clarion, 1993.

Cowboy Country, illustrated by Ted Lewin, Clarion, 1993.

Hi, illustrated by Glo Coalson, Philomel/Putnam, 1994.

Brave as a Mountain Lion, illustrated by Glo Coalson, Clarion, 1996.

OTHER

Contributor to periodicals, including *Reno Gazette-Journal* and *Nevada Highways.*

■ Adaptations

"Books about Real Things" (based on *Sam,* along with discussion of author's work; filmstrip and cassette), Pied Piper, 1982; "On Mother's Lap" (based on book of same name; sound recording), 1994.

■ Sidelights

Over the last three decades, Ann Herbert Scott has published many stories for younger readers that share a simple narrative format and realistic dialogue and description. Through these stories, she evokes such universal themes as, in her own words, "the security of a mother's love, the yearning to be big and important, the courage to deal with fear or jealousy."

"I can hardly remember a time when I wasn't 'writing,'" Scott commented in the *Fourth Book of Junior Authors & Illustrators.* "The only child of overly appreciative parents, I early discovered the good feel of words. When I was tiny, my mother began collecting my stories and poems in a scrapbook, and for many years she saved anything that was published in our little school magazine."

Both in high school and in college Scott edited the newspaper, worked on the yearbook, and participated in the theater. In her teens and twenties, she also worked with inner-city children. As the author once told *SATA:* "When I worked in New Haven in the 1950s, I was appalled by the lack of children's books picturing either urban neighborhoods or dark-skinned families. I initiated and directed LINK, a program designed 'to give inner-city children between the ages of eight and twelve the chance to become friends with a caring adult and, through an ongoing relationship, to widen their horizons and raise their aspirations.' I dreamed that someday I would write true-to-life stories that would be set in the housing project where I worked, stories in which my New Haven friends could find themselves. However, it was not until I had moved to Nevada that *Big Cowboy Western* evolved."

Big Cowboy Western is about an inner-city boy who gets a cowboy outfit for his fifth birthday but feels unimportant because he has nobody to play with—until an understanding fruit peddler gives him a job watching his horse. The book was praised by Zena Sutherland of the *Bulletin of the Center for Children's Books* for its "excellent" depiction of relationships and the value of its "particular urban setting."

"I believe the pull toward children's writing comes from something childlike within me," Scott has written. "I've always enjoyed being around little children, and wherever we've lived—farm, city, housing development—there have been a few small children who have been among my closest friends. The sense of delight and wonder little children bring to the here and now seems to awaken something deep in me. In contrast to writing for adults, which is often dreary and difficult for me, writing for children is often fun; it springs up unexpectedly in familiar places with some of the same spontaneous independence as forgotten daffodils in a leaf-covered bed.

"In general I work over material for some time, usually simplifying and resimplifying, often cutting out favorite phrases because they are not necessary to the thrust of the story. When there is something I am unsure about, six-year-old children's ideas about monsters, for example, I do a lot of talking with children. Otherwise I work from memory and imagination. I always *see* picture books as I write them; the sense of the graphics helps the development of the manuscript."

The author's conversations with children about monsters led to 1967's *Let's Catch a Monster,* in which a small boy on Halloween tracks down a monster that turns out to be a cat. The story was described as an "appealing anecdote" by a *Publishers Weekly* reviewer. That same year, Scott's *Sam* appeared, which was an exception to the author's general rule of spending a lot of time on her stories. "It came as I was scrubbing out the bathtub after a visit from a particularly experimental young neighbor. I wrote it in a few minutes, made some minor changes the next day, and sent it off." *Sam*

Set on a contemporary Shoshone reservation, *Brave as a Mountain Lion* is the tale of Spider, a young boy whose family helps him find the courage to compete in a spelling bee. (Written by Scott and illustrated by Glo Coalson.)

I was helping my dad round up cattle
when I was a lot younger than you are now,
watching my uncles break wild horses,
listening to the stories of rustlers
and mean old bulls and wrecks in rodeo rides,
when we camped beside the cattle
out there in the sagebrush
where the wind sings to the coyotes
and the coyotes sing to the moon.

Based on Scott's interviews with Nevada buckaroos, *Cowboy Country* is the story of a boy who spends the night on the range with an old-timer who teaches him about the work and lore of the cowboy. (Illustrated by Ted Lewin.)

is the story of a small African-American child whose parents and older siblings are all too busy to pay attention to him. The story was widely praised. What one reviewer writing in *Booklist* called a "touching family story" was described by a later *Booklist* critic as "perceptively interpreted in expressive drawings," referring to the work of artist Symeon Shimin.

"As a writer who specializes in picture books for young children, my work has peculiar aesthetic concerns. Although I am not an artist, I continually work with images in mind, leaving much of the telling to the skill of the illustrator. My work is often described as 'simple,' and so it is. However, it is the simplicity of discovering the organic shape of an idea, eliminating all that is unessential, depicting the large in the small. My manuscripts often go through twenty to thirty revisions."

On Mother's Lap and *Grandmother's Chair* both illustrate this 'make-it-simple' ideal. In the first story an Eskimo boy happily snuggles with his mother, gradually adding his favorite toys until he is sure there is no room for his baby sister, and yet there is. "The simplicity and familiarity of the situation are universal," said Zena Sutherland in the *Bulletin of the Center for Children's Books*. In *Grandmother's Chair*, children learn concepts of relationships and family trees from the story of a family heirloom that has been handed down through three generations. "Scott's text is plain and clear," wrote *Booklist* reviewer Leone McDermott. "Its understated

warmth comes from the sense of continuity as the chair passes from one little girl to the next."

Scott once commented to *SATA* that she had become "drawn to new themes and ideas linked to the life of remote Nevada, the buckaroos and ranchers, the Paiute and Shoshone people. The book ideas evoked by these themes are not just for children but the sort of picture book one critic called the 'Everybody Book.' An opportunity to interview a number of old buckaroos was provided by a Nevada State Council on the Arts grant in 1986-87, inspiring a number of partly finished stories and a book entitled *Someday Rider*."

In *Someday Rider*, Kenny wants to join his dad and the cowboys on their western ranch, but his parents have put off teaching him to ride. After Kenny practices riding a goose, a sheep, and a calf, his mother finally shows him the basics, and the two then both join the roundup. "Would-be cowpokes should hanker to read this coming-of-age story," concluded reviewer Charlene Strickland. A *Kirkus Reviews* critic praised Scott for the "warmth" of the story. Mining the same western lode, Scott next wrote *One Good Horse: A Cowpuncher's Counting Book*. Writing in *Horn Book*, reviewer Elizabeth S. Watson noted that the book's theme would surely gain "warm reception" from the "spurs-and-six-gun set."

In her four most recent books, *A Brand is Forever, Cowboy Country, Hi,* and *Brave as a Mountain Lion,*

Scott has continued to explore mostly western subject matter and universal themes, using the same pared-down approach. The author has also not been afraid to deal head-on with a topic like branding that might not be considered suitable in an age of political correctness but that nevertheless exists in the real world. *A Brand is Forever* is basically "a warm family story" and "a good yarn" about a girl on a ranch and her pet calf, according to *Horn Book* reviewer Elizabeth S. Watson. Critic Roger Sutton praised "Scott's quiet but plain-speaking tone." But isn't branding a cruel practice, and isn't Annie's mistress-pet relationship behind the times? the reader may ask. Reviewer Ilene Cooper tackled these questions in an extended essay-review in *Booklist* and reached several conclusions. On one hand, "it's a bit disconcerting to see the pleasures of ownership celebrated quite so blatantly, especially when the item being owned is a living animal," contended Cooper. At the same time, Cooper added, "Scott makes a good case for the practical reasons behind branding, and readers with some knowledge of branding are likely to agree ... that the procedure is necessary." For Cooper, the bottom line is that "the book should be judged on [its] merits, not on how well it fits the attitudinal climate of the times."

Drawing on her research and interviews with old Nevada buckaroos, Scott's next book, *Cowboy Country*, shows an old-timer guiding a young greenhorn in both the work and the lore of the cowboy, contrasting present practices with earlier methods. "Youngsters swept up by space-opera technomyths may rediscover the wonders of the West with this book," maintained *Bulletin of the Center for Children's Books* reviewer Deborah Stevenson. Elizabeth S. Watson of *Horn Book* found that "the strength of the book is the atmosphere created."

In *Hi,* Scott returns to the theme of persistence that she first treated in *Sam.* Margarita and her mother are waiting in line at the post office. The toddler calls out "Hi" to each person in the line, but when she gets no response her greeting becomes progressively weaker. Finally the "post-office lady" to whom she gives her package responds warmly, and Margarita's confidence is restored. "A delightful moment in time perfectly captured," commented reviewer Anna Biagioni Hart in *School Library Journal.* "It's a simple scenario but Scott captures a child's emotions nicely," noted a critic for *Publishers Weekly.*

In 1996, the Shoshone tale that the author referred to years earlier finally came to fruition with the publication, to wide acclaim, of *Brave as a Mountain Lion.* Spider, who lives on a contemporary Shoshone reservation, is afraid of participating in a school spelling bee. But, encouraged by other family members, and finally through his own efforts, to think of himself as "brave as a mountain lion, clever as a coyote, silent as a spider," he wins second place. "Scott knows how to take a universal childhood anxiety and particularize it to the needs of a story," commented Roger Sutton in the *Bulletin of the Center for Children's Books.*

■ Works Cited

Cooper, Ilene, review of *A Brand Is Forever, Booklist,* April 1, 1993, p. 1434.

De Montreville, Doris, and Elizabeth D. Crawford, eds., *Fourth Book of Junior Authors & Illustrators,* H. W. Wilson, 1978.

Hart, Anna Biagioni, review of *Hi, School Library Journal,* July, 1994, p. 89.

Review of *Hi, Publishers Weekly,* May 30, 1994, p. 56.

Review of *Let's Catch a Monster, Publishers Weekly,* October 9, 1967, p. 60.

McDermott, Leone, review of *Grandmother's Chair, Booklist,* November 15, 1990, p. 667.

Review of *Sam, Booklist,* February 15, 1968, p. 702.

Review of *Sam, Booklist,* May 1, 1973, p. 836.

Review of *Someday Rider, Kirkus Reviews,* August 15, 1989, p. 1251.

Stevenson, Deborah, review of *Cowboy Country, Bulletin of the Center for Children's Books,* November, 1993, pp. 98-99.

Strickland, Charlene, review of *Someday Rider, School Library Journal,* December, 1989, p. 88.

Sutherland, Zena, review of *Big Cowboy Western, Bulletin of the Center for Children's Books,* December, 1965, p. 68.

Sutherland, Zena, review of *On Mother's Lap, Bulletin of the Center for Children's Books,* December, 1972, p. 64.

Sutton, Roger, review of *A Brand Is Forever, Bulletin of the Center for Children's Books,* April, 1993, p. 263.

Sutton, Roger, review of *Brave as a Mountain Lion, Bulletin of the Center for Children's Books,* February, 1996, pp. 202-03.

Watson, Elizabeth S., review of *One Good Horse: A Cowpuncher's Counting Book, Horn Book,* July-August, 1990, p. 447.

Watson, Elizabeth S., review of *A Brand Is Forever, Horn Book,* May-June, 1993, p. 330.

Watson, Elizabeth S., review of *Cowboy Country, Horn Book,* November-December, 1993, p. 760.

■ For More Information See

PERIODICALS

Booklist, May 15, 1994, p. 1684.

Bulletin of the Center for Children's Books, November, 1990, p. 70.

Horn Book, November-December, 1992, pp. 741-742; July-August, 1994, p. 445.

Kirkus Reviews, May 15, 1994, p. 706.

Publishers Weekly, July 18, 1990, p. 53; March 23, 1992, p. 71.

School Library Journal, April, 1990, p. 96.*

GEORGE SHANNON

SHANNON, George (William Bones) 1952-

■ Personal

Born February 14, 1952, in Caldwell, KS; son of David W. (a professor) and Doris (Bones) Shannon. *Education:* Western Kentucky University, B.S., 1974; University of Kentucky, M.S.L.S., 1976.

■ Career

Librarian at public schools in Muhlenberg County, KY, 1974-75; Lexington Public Library, Lexington, KY, librarian, 1976-78; professional storyteller and lecturer, 1978—. Guest lecturer at University of Kentucky, 1977. Member, external advisory board, Cooperative Children's Book Center, Madison, WI.

■ Awards, Honors

Notable Book designation, American Library Association, 1981, and Children's Choice Book, International Reading Association/Children's Book Council, 1982, both for *The Piney Woods Peddler;* Friends of American Writers award, 1990, for *Unlived Affections.*

■ Writings

FOR CHILDREN

Lizard's Song, illustrated by Jose Aruego and Ariane Dewey, Greenwillow, 1981, translated as *La Cancion del Lagarto,* Morrow, 1994.
The Gang and Mrs. Higgins, illustrated by Andrew Vines, Greenwillow, 1981.
The Piney Woods Peddler, illustrated by Nancy Tafuri, Greenwillow, 1981.

Dance Away!, illustrated by Jose Aruego and Ariane Dewey, Greenwillow, 1982.
The Surprise, illustrated by Aruego and Dewey, Greenwillow, 1983.
Bean Boy, illustrated by Peter Sis, Greenwillow, 1984.
(Reteller) *Stories to Solve: Folktales from around the World,* illustrated by Sis, Greenwillow, 1985.
Oh, I Love, illustrated by Cheryl Harness, Bradbury Press, 1988.
Sea Gifts, illustrated by Mary Azarian, D. Godine, 1989.
(Reteller) *More Stories to Solve: Fifteen Folktales from around the World,* illustrated by Peter Sis, Greenwillow, 1990.
Dancing the Breeze, illustrated by Jacqueline Rogers, Bradbury Press, 1991.
Laughing All the Way, illustrated by Meg McLean, Houghton, 1992.
Climbing Kansas Mountains, illustrated by Thomas B. Allen, Bradbury Press, 1993.
Seeds, illustrated by Steve Bjorkman, Houghton, 1994.
(Reteller) *Still More Stories to Solve: Fourteen Folktales from around the World,* illustrated by Peter Sis, Greenwillow, 1994.
April Showers, illustrated by Jose Aruego and Ariane Dewey, Greenwillow, 1995.
Heart to Heart, illustrated by Steve Bjorkman, Houghton, 1995.
(Compiler) *Spring: A Haiku Story,* illustrated by Malcah Zeldis, Greenwillow, 1995.
Tomorrow's Alphabet, illustrated by Donald Crews, Greenwillow, 1995.
This Is the Bird, illustrated by David Soman, Houghton, 1996.
(Reteller) *True Lies,* illustrated by John O'Brien, Greenwillow, 1997.

and when he got to the river all his friends were gone.

When confronted by Bear, who wants his feathers for a bed, Duck uses his sense of humor to distract Bear and escape. (From *Laughing All the Way,* written by Shannon and illustrated by Meg McLean.)

FOR YOUNG ADULTS

Unlived Affections, Harper, 1989.

OTHER

Humpty Dumpty: A Pictorial History, Green Tiger Press, 1981.

Folk Literature and Children: An Annotated Bibliography of Secondary Materials, Greenwood Press, 1981.

(With Ellin Greene) *Storytelling: A Selected Annotated Bibliography,* Garland, 1986.

Arnold Lobel (criticism), Twayne, 1989.

(Compiler) *A Knock at the Door,* illustrated by Joanne Caroselli, Oryx Press, 1992.

Contributor of articles and reviews to magazines, including *Horn Book, Catholic Library World, School Library Journal,* and *Wilson Library Bulletin.*

■ Sidelights

Professional storyteller George Shannon combines his interest in folklore and the oral storytelling tradition with his love of literature for children in a series of picture books for the younger set. In addition to several nonfiction works and a series of popular retellings of folktales—*Stories to Solve, More Stories to Solve,* and *Still More Stories to Solve*—Shannon has written such well-received works as *The Piney Woods Peddler, Dancing the Breeze,* and *Climbing Kansas Mountains,* as well as an award-winning young adult novel entitled *Unlived Affections,* which he published in 1989.

Born in Caldwell, Kansas, in 1952, Shannon acquired the knack for making up stories early in life, and by the seventh grade writing his stories down had become a hobby. "I have always been wrapped up in stories and books," Shannon once told *SATA.* "My parents read to me, and I in turn to my younger brothers. Books and family stories filled our home, and going to the library was as common as going to the market." Teachers throughout middle and high school encouraged his efforts at writing, and after entering college, Shannon continued his love affair with books and writing by studying children's literature and, later, library science at Western Kentucky University. He spent several years working as a children's librarian before devoting himself to storytelling and writing his own books for children beginning in 1978.

Shannon's first published work for children, *Lizard's Song,* is the tale of a lizard who sings joyfully of his unique place in the world and teaches other animals to be equally celebratory of their own. A *Publishers Weekly* reviewer praised the picture book, which would later be translated for Spanish-speaking children, calling it "a jolly, amiable fancy about the value of finding one's own niche and being one's own self." *Lizard's Song,* which features the colorful illustrations of Jose Aruego and Ariane Dewey, was quickly followed by other Shannon picture books, many also illustrated by Aruego and Dewey.

The Piney Woods Peddler is an adaptation of the story of "Lucky Hans" collected by the Brothers Grimm. A trader on the road doing business resolves to bring his daughter home a silver dollar at the end of his travels; as his luck wanes, each of his trades brings in less than the one before, leaving him with only a silver dime. Fortunately the young daughter is cheerfully pleased with her father's small gift, in a humorous story that Ethel L. Heins described in *Horn Book* as "a repetitive, lilting tale that incorporates elements of traditional American swapping songs."

"We do what's right.
We play by the rules.
But when the rain comes, we love to dance like fools!"

Unaware of a nearby snake looking for a meal, carefree frogs sing and dance in Shannon's 1995 picture book *April Showers,* illustrated by Jose Aruego and Ariane Dewey.

Fourteen haiku poems were collected and arranged by Shannon to express the wonders of a walk in springtime. (From *Spring: A Haiku Story*, illustrated by Malcah Zeldis.)

Relationships between family members are central to many of Shannon's tales for young people. A father and daughter await the moon in their flower garden in the poetic *Dancing the Breeze*, while *Climbing Kansas Mountains* finds Sam and his dad scaling a grain elevator in their native Kansas, from which height they can see the vast prairie stretching out before them. While Carol Fox found the story "more description than plot," she praised *Climbing Kansas Mountains* in her review for *Bulletin of the Center for Children's Books*, noting that the story's "tone is warm and intimate with childlike language and viewpoint." And in *This Is the Bird*, described by a *Kirkus Reviews* critic as "a moving tribute to familial bonds," a carved wooden bird links generations as it is passed from one family member to another. Close friendship is dealt with in *Seeds*, as young Warren moves away from neighboring artist and gardener Bill, but retains his ties to his friend by planting a garden in Bill's honor. "This is a warm, satisfying story about a different kind of friendship, about loss, and about new beginnings," noted Stephanie Zvirin in her *Booklist* review.

Animal characters take the place of human protagonists in several of Shannon's stories. *Dance Away!* finds Rabbit with so much energy that he out-dances all of his friends; he also out-dances cunning Fox, who plans to trap a rabbit for his supper but who ends up trapped in Rabbit's choreography. And in *Laughing All the Way*, Duck has a pretty awful day, which reaches a low point when Bear decides to pluck the fowl's feathers and make a soft downy bed. Fortunately, Duck keeps his sense of humor, and soon has Bear laughing so hard that he accidentally lets Duck go. "Children who love silliness, wordplay, and colorful language ... will delight in this book," commented Lauralyn Persson in a *School Library Journal* review.

In addition to his books for youngsters, Shannon is the author of a novel for young adults. *Unlived Affections*, which won the Friends of American Writers award in 1990, is the story of eighteen-year-old Willie Ramsey. After the death of his grandmother, who raised him since his mother was killed in a car accident when he was two, Willie is determined to break with his oppressive past, sell everything in the family home, and start a new life at college in Nebraska. While cleaning out his grandmother's things in preparation for the sale, Willie comes upon a trove of old letters, many written by his unknown father to his mother. The letters reveal many things Willie has been told about his family to be untrue: his father did not desert his family but left because he was grappling with his sexual identity; and Willie's mother never told her husband that he had a son. "Shannon has a story to tell, and it is an unusual and moving one, full of secrets, lies, and dreams," commented Betsy Hearne in *Bulletin of the Center for Children's Books*. A *Publishers Weekly* reviewer called the novel's narrative "honest and concise," adding that "readers will be moved by the sensitive portrayal of each character and the tragedies they endure."

When Shannon tells stories before an audience, he explains that it is like "writing out loud," with each telling slightly different, slightly unique. Several of his books have sprung from the stories he has performed in public, repeated out loud many times prior to being committed to paper. An avid journal-keeper and letter-writer, Shannon also collects impressions, thoughts, and ideas that often make their way into his fiction. "I travel frequently to tell stories," he explained to *SATA*, "and always at my side is the dog-eared journal filled with dreams, lines, phrases, plot snatches, and impressions that all feed into the next story I tell and the next book I write."

"Books are forever stacked about my home waiting to be read, reread or returned to various libraries," Shannon also revealed. "My reading matches those genres in which I write and explore: essays, journals, letters, folktales, picture books, and poetry. The picture book has long been of interest to me and I admire its symbiotic matching of words and visuals. The challenge of sharing a complete story in as few words as possible is one I welcome. To me it has a kinship with the sparse oral writing of the masses who authored the rich folk literature I share as a professional storyteller."

"The sounds and rhythms of my stories are of major importance to me," Shannon also explained of his craft, "and I want them to flow on the tongue as if always being said aloud—always new to share. While I do not write poetry, I work to have the finer elements of poetry in my prose." Much of Shannon's brief, intense style he attributes to his work as a professional storyteller in the oral tradition, which he calls "a form of writing but without ink or paper." He explained to *SATA* that "I am forever working toward distilling my thoughts into tightly formed stories for all ages." His interest in concentrated forms of writing drew Shannon to the Japanese poetic form called "haiku"; his collection of fourteen haiku verses in 1996's *Spring: A Haiku Story* has been praised for its ability to interest young children in this subtle poetic form. Imagery and character continue to serve as his main focus: the imagery of folktales created by generations past, and the characters of men and women living between major life events. "Less will always be more," writer/storyteller Shannon maintained, "for it creates the connective bridge between writer and reader as the reader invests himself in the story to create its full life."

■ Works Cited

Fox, Carol, review of *Climbing Kansas Mountains*, *Bulletin of the Center for Children's Books*, January, 1994, p. 168.

Hearne, Betsy, review of *Unlived Affections*, *Bulletin of the Center for Children's Books*, September, 1989, p. 20.

Heins, Ethel L., review of *The Piney Woods Peddler*, *Horn Book*, February, 1982, pp. 36-37.

Review of *Lizard's Song*, *Publishers Weekly*, September 11, 1981, p. 76.

Persson, Lauralyn, review of *Laughing All the Way*, *School Library Journal*, October, 1992, p. 95.

Review of *This Is the Bird*, *Kirkus Reviews*, March 1, 1997, pp. 387-88.

Review of *Unlived Affections*, *Publishers Weekly*, July 14, 1989, p. 80.

Zvirin, Stephanie, review of *Seeds*, *Booklist*, June 1-15, 1994, pp. 1844-45.

■ For More Information See

BOOKS

Sixth Book of Junior Authors and Illustrators, edited by Sally Holmes Holtze, H. W. Wilson, 1989.

PERIODICALS

Booklist, December 1, 1981, p. 506; December 1, 1985, p. 574; February 15, 1991, p. 1203; April 15, 1996, p. 1444.

Bulletin of the Center for Children's Books, October, 1984, pp. 34-35; May, 1991, p. 226; April, 1996, p. 279.

Horn Book, June, 1982, p. 283; September-October, 1990, p. 627; May-June, 1991, pp. 342-43; November-December, 1994, p. 750; May-June, 1995, p. 329.

Junior Bookshelf, August, 1982, p. 129; June, 1983, p. 110; June, 1984, p. 120; February, 1986, p. 29.

Kirkus Reviews, April 1, 1981, p. 431; September 1, 1983, p. 155; August 1, 1989, p. 1168; April 15, 1991, p. 539; July 15, 1994, p. 995; April 15, 1995, p. 563.

New York Times Book Review, July 14, 1996, p. 19.

Publishers Weekly, May 1, 1981, p. 67; August 9, 1993, p. 477; April 1, 1996, p. 76.

School Library Journal, May, 1996, p. 108.*

* * *

SHPAKOW, Tanya 1959(?)-

■ Personal

Education: Graduated from the Rhode Island School of Design.

■ Addresses

Home—Albuquerque, NM.

■ Career

Author and illustrator of children's books.

■ Writings

SELF-ILLUSTRATED

Baba, Knopf, 1989.
On the Way to Christmas, Knopf, 1991.

■ Work in Progress

The Island of the Six-Toed Cats, about fifty-six felines adrift at sea after a hurricane, and *Bear Thanksgiving*, about a missing eight-year-old boy and a bear cub.

■ Sidelights

Tanya Shpakow described the best and worst aspects of illustrating her own children's books to Fran Rogers Krajewski of *Writer's Digest:* "When I write a book, I don't have to wait six months to a year to find out what it's going to look like. At the same time, if I'm disappointed, I can only blame myself for not drawing the characters correctly or not creating just the right atmosphere." One disadvantage, however, is that "when you're blocked, you're *really* blocked," Shpakow continued in the same interview. "If you can't think of how your story should go, you're probably not going to be able to dig yourself out by doodling around and drawing a picture of it.

"The story can become your enemy. What happens is, you sour yourself on all sorts of things in terms of pictures if you're really having a struggle.... But the text must *always* come first.

"If you don't have the text in your mind—not only seeing the characters, but knowing that character's habits, where and how he lives, what he thinks about, who he meets—then you can't draw the pictures."

Shpakow's advice for beginning illustrators is to stay away from "putting a character or an object in the middle of a page, drawing it beautifully—like it's a museum specimen—and letting it go at that. It's beautiful, but it's boring. If you're not showing a lot of movement and activity in a picture, it can be quite dull.

"I try to do a certain number of pictures where there is some kind of space that the child can jump into, so that there's some perspective used in the actual drawing. That way, children can project themselves into the picture plane and feel like they're really there *in* the story."

As regards the written portion of her picture books, Shpakow told Krajewski, "Even though my characters have to experience and get through a trauma or dilemma, I don't ever write stories that are straightforward morality tales. The plot will be related to everyday life, but it can still be fantastical or improbable.

"The fear of being left behind—at a rest stop, in a grocery store, never to be found again—is every kid's worst nightmare, and possibly every adult's. But when I address the abandonment issue, as I did in *On the Way to Christmas*, I don't want it to be an actual child being left behind. I want the story to be less threatening, so I'll write about a teddy bear being blown off a car or, as happens in *The Island of the Six-Toed Cats*, about fifty-six cats set adrift at sea following a hurricane.

"It's easier for children if they can emote along with characters who are safer. ... They can scream and cry and yell and laugh all the way through the stories (which all have happy endings). It makes it an emotionally safe experience for them."

Tanya Shpakow's self-illustrated picture books feature unusual stories accompanied by illustrations that have brought comparisons to Chris Van Allsburg and Susan Jeschke. While her stories are sometimes considered less accomplished than her illustrations, Shpakow's first two works, *Baba* and *On the Way to Christmas,* were generally well received. In *Baba,* a young girl listens to her grandmother's tales of being born in Russia and sold for a penny to the gypsies, from whom she learned to fly. Due to the combination of fantasy and reality, it is not clear if "Baba is flying through the air or attending a Bingo game, and this may confuse or put off some children," remarked Betsy Hearne in the *Bulletin of the Center for Children's Books.* Nonetheless, Marilyn Iarusso, a *School Library Journal* contributor, praised Shpakow's visual depiction of the "mischievous and appealing" Baba in drawings "with dramatic shading and lighting effect." Likewise, a *Kirkus Reviews* critic singled out Shpakow's "eerie" illustrations which, while "clearly influenced by Van Allsburg ... have their own unique, fey humor."

In *On the Way to Christmas,* Walter the teddy bear gets lost when the movers fail to pack him inside the car, a mishap that leads to many adventures before he finds his way back to the little boy with whom he lives. The story is "beautiful," averred Ellen J. Brooks in the *Children's Book Review Service,* full of "suspense, warmth and the magic of Christmas."

■ Works Cited

Review of *Baba, Kirkus Reviews,* September 1, 1989, p. 1332.
Brooks, Ellen J., review of *On the Way to Christmas, Children's Book Review Service,* October, 1991, p. 17.
Hearne, Betsy, review of *Baba, Bulletin of the Center for Children's Books,* January, 1990, pp. 120-21.
Iarusso, Marilyn, review of *Baba, School Library Journal,* January, 1990, p. 90.
Krajewski, Fran Rogers, "Writing—and Illustrating—Children's Picture Books," *Writer's Digest,* April, 1996, pp. 25-27.

■ For More Information See

PERIODICALS

Children's Bookwatch, September, 1991, p. 5.
Language Arts, April, 1990, p. 430.
School Library Journal, October, 1991, p. 33.*

SUSAN SHWARTZ

SHWARTZ, Susan (Martha) 1949-
(Gordon Kendall, a joint pseudonym)

■ Personal

Born December 31, 1949, in Youngstown, OH; daughter of Ralph Bernard (an attorney) and Lillian (Levine) Shwartz. *Education:* Mount Holyoke College, B.A. (magna cum laude), 1972; attended Trinity College, Oxford, 1970-71; Harvard University, M.A., 1973, Ph.D., 1977. *Politics:* "Idiosyncratic." *Religion:* Jewish. *Hobbies and other interests:* Languages (Latin, French, Greek, German, Middle High German, Old French, Old Norse, Old and Middle English), travel, classical music, ballet, opera, parties, shopping, cats, cooking.

■ Addresses

Home and office—One Station Square, Number 306, Forest Hills, NY 11375. *Electronic mail*—s.shwartz @ genie.com or smshwartz @ aol.com. *Agent*—Richard Curtis Associates, 171 East 74th Street, New York, NY 10022.

■ Career

Ithaca College, Ithaca, NY, assistant professor of English, 1977-81; Deutsch, Shea & Evans, New York City, senior writer and researcher, 1981-82; Final Analysis, New York City, junior project director, 1982; BEA Associates, New York City, information coordinator, 1982-87; Donaldson, Lufkin & Jenrette, New York City, financial editor, 1987-88; Prudential Securities, New York City, financial writer/editor and associate vice president, 1994-. Teaching fellow, Harvard University, 1974-77; postdoctoral fellow, Dartmouth College, NH, 1978. Senior Analyst/Editor, Moody's Investors Service. *Member:* Science Fiction Writers of America, Horror

Writers of America, Phi Beta Kappa, Harvard Club of New York.

■ Awards, Honors

Grant from National Endowment for the Humanities, 1978; short story award from *Village Voice,* 1981, for "The Old Man and the C"; also nominated for five Nebula Awards and two Hugo Awards.

■ Writings

SCIENCE FICTION AND FANTASY NOVELS

(With Shariann N. Lewitt, under joint pseudonym Gordon Kendall) *White Wing,* Tor Books (New York City), 1985.
Byzantium's Crown, Popular Library (New York City), 1987.
The Woman of Flowers, Popular Library, 1987.
Queensblade, Popular Library, 1988.
Silk Roads and Shadows, Tor Books, 1988.
Heritage of Flight, Tor Books, 1989.
(With Andre Norton) *Imperial Lady: A Fantasy of Han China,* Tor Books, 1989.
The Grail of Hearts, Tor Books, 1992.
(With Norton) *Empire of the Eagle,* Tor Books, 1993.
Shards of Empire, Tor Books, 1996.
Cross and Crescent, Tor Books, 1997.
(With Joseph Sherman) *Vulcan's Forge,* Simon & Schuster (New York City), 1997.

EDITOR

Hecate's Cauldron (fantasy anthology), DAW Books (New York City), 1982.
Habitats (science fiction anthology), DAW Books, 1984.
Moonsinger's Friends: An Anthology in Honor of Andre Norton, Bluejay (New York City), 1985.
Arabesques: More Tales of the Arabian Nights, Avon (New York City), 1988.
Arabesques II, Avon, 1989.
(With Martin H. Greenberg) *Sisters in Fantasy,* New American Library (New York City), 1995.
(With Greenberg) *Sisters in Fantasy II,* New American Library, 1996.

OTHER

(Contributor) Marion Zimmer Bradley, editor, *Grayhaven,* DAW Books, 1983.

Author of "Facts for Fantasy," a column in *Ares.* Also contributor to magazines and newspapers, including *Science Fiction Review, Feminine Eye, New York Times, Vogue, Washington Post,* and *Cleveland Plain Dealer.*

■ Sidelights

Exploring difficult social issues while using well-developed female characters in important roles, Susan Shwartz, writes *St. James Guide to Science Fiction Writers* contributor Daryl F. Mallett, "has quickly gained attention in the SF and fantasy fields with her somewhat controversial writing." *Heritage of Flight* provides an example of Shwartz's strong heroines and of

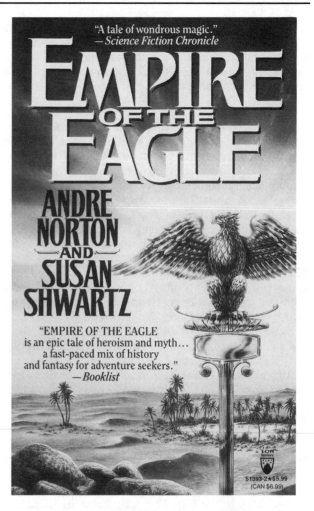

"A tale of wondrous magic."
— *Science Fiction Chronicle*

EMPIRE OF THE EAGLE

ANDRE NORTON AND SUSAN SHWARTZ

"EMPIRE OF THE EAGLE is an epic tale of heroism and myth... a fast-paced mix of history and fantasy for adventure seekers."
— *Booklist*

51393-2 ★ $5.99
(CAN $6.99)

Shwartz and coauthor Andre Norton mingle fantasy and history to portray Roman tribune Quintus and his battle to reclaim the honor of his legions after they are led into slavery in Ch'in China. (Cover illustration by Peter Goodfellow.)

her penchant for dark themes. It tells the story of a band of refugees from a great war between planets. The refugees become marooned on a planet—a planet with an indigenous life-form that threatens the humans. As a result, commander Pauli Yeager is forced to lead her people in an act of genocide. "And when they commit the horrible crime, *Voelkermord,*" explains Mallett, "Pauli shoulders the entire burden."

"I began writing in graduate school after thirteen years of swearing I couldn't write," Shwartz commented in an online interview with Amazon.com. "I was doing a PhD in medieval English at Harvard and learning fast that I would rather write the types of things I read than write footnotes on them." Shwartz cites history and music as primary influences on her work. Her interest in history colors *Empire of the Eagle,* written in collaboration with Andre Norton. Based in part on a historical event (the destruction of the Roman legions under the proconsul Crassus at the battle of Carrhae in 43 B.C.), the novel blends elements of Roman, Chinese, and Indian myth and religion. In the story, remnants of the Roman legions are led into slavery in Ch'in China along the Silk

Road trade route. The Romans soon win the chance to redeem their offended honor in battle. Indian gods (such as Ganesha, the elephant-headed god), and partly-historical figures (such as Draupadi, heroine of the epic poem *The Mahabhrata*) also figure in the action. Candace Smith, reviewing the book for *Booklist,* called it "a fast-paced mix of history and fantasy for adventure seekers." A *Publishers Weekly* commentator added: "Norton and Shwartz weave a curious and convincing tale melding otherworldliness and dire reality."

Another well-received work blending elements of fantasy and history is Shwartz's *Grail of Hearts,* the story of a harlot named Kundry condemned to a life of eternal wandering for irreverent behavior during the crucifixion of Christ at Golgotha. Kundry endures many centuries as the servant of the sorcerer Klingsor, who is driven by a desire to possess the holy grail. Klingsor has Kundry seduce the young knight Amfortas, keeper of the grail, but the two fall in love, causing a series of complex events—including time travel—fueled by Klingsor's anger. Kundry is sent by Klingsor back to the first century, where much of the book's action takes place. *Voice of Youth Advocates* contributor Laura Staley praised the scenes set in ancient Judaea as "vividly realized" and "engrossing," explaining that "the reader can practically smell the sweat and hear the whisper of the lavish silks of the harlots." A *Publishers Weekly* critic similarly asserted that in *Grail of Hearts* Shwartz "has created a strong, eerie and often painful world inhabited by a woman difficult to forget."

One of Shwartz's most recent works, *Shards of Empire,* is a historical fantasy featuring a strong female protagonist. Set in 10th-century Byzantium against a backdrop of warring factions and political intrigue, the novel portrays the relationship between a young soldier named Leo and a brave and beautiful young Jewish woman called Asherah. Describing *Shards of Empire* as "an absorbing look at the customs and prejudices of the time," a *Publishers Weekly* reviewer noted that the "multicultural melting pot of Byzantine society ... gives Shwartz a marvelous setting in which to combine various magics, cultures, religions, and folklores." A *Kirkus Reviews* commentator praised the historical setting as "well-researched, persuasive, and engaging."

Susan Shwartz has commented: "For me, the important things are technical mastery, communicating with people, and the joy of a job done as well as I can. Beyond that, I get a thrill out of seeing my work in print; I never dreamed I'd do it.

"I trained as a medievalist in college and graduate school (don't ask me why), and that meant learning languages. What else did it mean? A dangerous fascination for pure research, with rewriting, and with language and background as games and preoccupations. I find my own academic background to be a help—when it comes to finding a setting for a story—and a hindrance, since it keeps me rewriting and slows down my style. I tend to write four and five drafts of a work before I begin to be satisfied, and I plot slowly. On the other hand, coming

out of a scholarly tradition's been useful for learning my craft.

"What do my works reflect about me? God only knows: that my characters tend to be faced with the consequences of their actions, that I cannot tolerate sloppy sentiment or thinking, that I'm fascinated by completely realized secondary worlds, my own or other writers'."

■ Works Cited

Review of *Empire of the Eagle, Publishers Weekly,* October 18, 1993, pp. 67-68.

Review of *The Grail of Hearts, Publishers Weekly,* November 29, 1991, p. 45.

Mallett, Daryl F., "Susan Shwartz," in *St. James Guide to Science Fiction Writers,* 4th edition, St. James Press, 1996.

Review of *Shards of Empire, Kirkus Reviews,* February 1, 1996, p. 182.

Review of *Shards of Empire, Publishers Weekly,* March 25, 1996, p. 66.

Shwartz, Susan, comments from an online interview, Amazon.com, December 11, 1996.

Smith, Candace, review of *Empire of the Eagle, Booklist,* November 15, 1993, p. 606.

Staley, Laura, review of *The Grail of Hearts, Voice of Youth Advocates,* October, 1992, p. 243.

PERIODICALS

Booklist, June 15, 1989, p. 1783.

Library Journal, August, 1985, p. 121; June 15, 1989, p. 83; December, 1991, p. 202.

Publishers Weekly, June 14, 1985, p. 70; February 19, 1988, p. 82; June 24, 1988, pp. 106-07.

Voice of Youth Advocates, August, 1988, p. 141.

*   *   *

SIROF, Harriet 1930-

■ Personal

Born October 18, 1930, in New York, NY; daughter of Herman (a dress manufacturer) and Lillian (Miller) Hockman; married Sidney Sirof (a psychologist), June 18, 1949; children: Laurie, David, Amy Sirof Bordiuk. *Education:* New School for Social Research, B.A., 1962.

■ Addresses

Home and office—792 East 21st St., Brooklyn, New York, 11210. *Agent*—Jennie Dunham, Russell & Volkening, 50 West 29th St., New York, NY 10001. *Electronic mail*—hsirof @ aol.com (America Online).

■ Career

Remedial reading teacher at elementary schools in Brooklyn, NY, 1962-76; St. John's University, Jamaica, NY, instructor of creative writing, 1976-87; Brooklyn College of the City University of New York, Brooklyn, instructor of writing, 1980—. *Member:* Author's Guild,

Society of Children's Book Writers and Illustrators, New York City Author's Read Aloud Program.

■ Awards, Honors

The Real World was a Junior Library Guild selection.

■ Writings

A New-Fashioned Love Story, Xerox Publications, 1977.
The IF Machine, Scholastic, 1978.
The Junior Encyclopedia of Israel (nonfiction), Jonathan David, 1980.
Save the Dam!, Crestwood House, 1981.
The Real World, Franklin Watts, 1985.
That Certain Smile, Weekly Reader Books, 1986.
Anything You Can Do, Weekly Reader Books, 1986.
The Road Back: Living with a Physical Disability (nonfiction), New Discovery Books, Macmillan, 1993.
Because She's My Friend, Atheneum, 1993.
Bring Back Yesterday, Atheneum, 1996.

Contributor of children's stories and articles to periodicals, including *Alive!, Alpha, Highlights for Children, Know Your World, Merry-Go-Round, More, Rainbow,* and *Read,* and to anthologies, including *"Remember Me" and Other Stories,* 1976, *"The Switch" and Other Stories,* 1976, and *Triple Action Play Book.*

Also contributor of adult fiction to periodicals, including *Colorado Review, Descant, Inlet, Maine Review, New Orleans Review, North American Review, Sam Houston Review, San Jose Studies,* and *Woman,* and to the anthology *Voices of Brooklyn.*

■ Work in Progress

Do You Need to Read?, a nonfiction book for young readers tracing the history and impact of writing and the relevance of reading today; a novel, *The Boy with Half a Brain.*

■ Sidelights

"My life is representative of a generation of women who grew up before the women's movement," Harriet Sirof recently told *SATA.* "I learned to read at the age of four and dreamed of being a writer from the time I was seven. At ten, I was dictating stories to my friend Boopsie, who planned to be a secretary. I started college at seventeen, but left after a year to get married and plunge wholeheartedly into domesticity. I had three children within five years, and writing was relegated to the status of an abandoned childhood fantasy.

"Then, driven by the feeling that something was missing in my life, I returned to school, graduated first in my class, and became a reading teacher. Although I wrote educational materials for my students and published some of them, I was still dissatisfied. Next, I tried my hand at short stories. Sales to the literary quarterlies and the interest of an agent led me to attempt an adult novel.

It took me nearly two years and two thousand discarded pages to discover that it was not for me. Deeply discouraged, I considered giving up writing.

"When I heard that Scholastic was looking for novels for junior high school students with reading problems, it seemed like something I could do. The resulting *The IF Machine* stayed in print for nearly twenty years. It was a short step from *The IF Machine* to mainstream middle grade and young adult novels. I had finally found what I wanted to do. I have since published eight novels and two nonfiction books for young readers.

"My books often grow out of issues in my own life. A few years ago, I was returning from jogging on a freezing winter day when I slipped on a patch of ice. I broke my hip and paralyzed my right leg. As a way of dealing with the accident, I kept a diary during my hospitalization and long rehabilitation. This diary, along with interviews with other people who suffered sudden or progressive disabilities, provided material for *The Road Back: Living with a Physical Disability* and the background for my novel *Because She's My Friend.*"

The Road Back: Living with a Physical Disability presents the stories of Tisha, Steven and Christopher, three teenagers who, for three different reasons, have become physically disabled. Using these individuals as examples, Sirof shows how rehabilitation takes place in the hospital, as an outpatient, or in a rehab center. She introduces the professionals, explaining therapies, schooling, and laws that serve the disabled. The book is "well written," according to *School Library Journal* contributor Martha Gordon, who noted that Sirof has done a "superb job of integrating story and fact." While Colleen Macklin observed in *Voice of Youth Advocates* that the book lacks photos which would have lent a personal touch, she added that "Sirof does a good job of humanizing these three teens while providing teens with a lot of accurate and insightful information about the disabled in America."

Because She's My Friend is another book that deals with disability, but this time the disability is a subplot, a catalyst for the tale of two very different teenagers, Teri and Valerie. Valerie has also suffered a disabling accident, and she meets Teri in the hospital, where the latter is volunteering for the summer. The two are very unlikely friends. Valerie is the only child of affluent, divorced, career-minded parents, with a glamorous life and lots of money. Teri is the youngest of a large Italian-American family. Shy, polite Teri envies Valerie's self-assured brashness, just as Valerie envies Teri's health and supportive family. Told in alternating first-person chapters, the novel chronicles the girls' brief friendship. Teri learns self-confidence from Valerie, while Teri's unconditional friendship rescues Valerie from depression. Reviewers generally hailed this novel as authentic, with a text that is "immediate and convincing," according to Carolyn Noah in *School Library Journal.* Noah added: "Sirof explores the boundaries of friendship and the meaning of courage in a book that's hard to put down." A *Kirkus Reviews* critic similarly concluded: "A strong book, with gritty characters, interesting problems, and a believable outcome."

Speaking of her 1996 novel, *Bring Back Yesterday,* Sirof told *SATA:* "My first foray into fantasy was an answer to the question: What if? I had been an imaginative only child who told myself stories when I was lonely or unhappy. I asked: 'What if something so horrible happened to a girl like my young self that she lost the ability to distinguish between reality and fantasy?' The result was *Bring Back Yesterday.*"

Bring Back Yesterday is the story of thirteen-year-old Lisa, whose parents are killed in an airplane crash. Her new living situation is with her disorganized aunt Alice, who is working out her pain by becoming an activist for airline safety. Unable to cope with her own grief, Lisa retreats into a fantasy world with an old imaginary childhood friend, Rooji. Rooji and Lisa travel back to Elizabethan England where, dressed as boys, they become apprentices at a theater. Events in both worlds begin to parallel each other and Lisa finds she must learn to deal with her sorrow openly and forgive Aunt Alice her eccentricities. A reviewer in *Publishers Weekly* asserted: "Sirof skillfully parallels Lisa's escapist adventures with the events in her real life," bringing her protagonist's troubles to a satisfactory conclusion.

An earlier work, *The Real World,* is another of Sirof's successful forays into adolescence and contemporary family issues. Cady Stanton has grown up in a women's commune, keeping her distance from such frivolous concerns such as boys, makeup, and clothes. Then the father she has never known surfaces and her mother agrees to let Cady spend some time with him and his new family. The life she encounters there is everything that she has been raised to believe is suspect; her father works, while his new wife stays at home with their children. Her father's affluence and traditional household have a profound influence on Cady and she is caught between two worlds. While *Booklist* reviewer Denise M. Wilms finds the adult characters lacking, she notes that "despite the characterization flaws, the story moves well, and its soap-opera developments are likely to keep light fiction readers turning the pages right to the finish."

Sirof's career is a study in perseverance and tenacity. As she recently told *SATA,* "Each new book is a challenge because I try to do something different each time. *Do You Need to Read?* addresses our gains and losses as the electronic media replace books. My novel-in-progress, *The Boy with Half A Brain,* is my first use of a male protagonist. It took me a long time to become a writer. Now I can't imagine a more interesting occupation."

■ Works Cited

Review of *Because She's My Friend, Kirkus Reviews,* August 15, 1993, p. 1081.

Review of *Bring Back Yesterday, Publishers Weekly,* August 12, 1996, p. 84.

Gordon, Martha, review of *The Road Back: Living with a Physical Disability, School Library Journal,* November, 1993, p. 137.

Macklin, Colleen, review of *The Road Back: Living with a Physical Disability, Voice of Youth Advocates,* April, 1994, p. 54.

Noah, Carolyn, review of *Because She's My Friend, School Library Journal,* October, 1993, p. 130.

Wilms, Denise M., review of *The Real World, Booklist,* February 1, 1986, p. 814.

■ For More Information See

PERIODICALS

Booklist, October 15, 1996, p. 415.
Bulletin of the Center for Children's Books, February, 1986, p. 117.
Publishers Weekly, August 2, 1993, p. 82.
School Library Journal, March, 1982, p. 158.
Voice of Youth Advocates, December, 1993, p. 299; April, 1994, p. 54.

*   *   *

SMITH-REX, Susan J. 1950-

■ Personal

Born August 27, 1950, in Philadelphia, PA; daughter of William (in the navy) and Joyce (in the navy; maiden name, Moyer) Kodad; married Jeffrey Smith (a manufacturer), 1972 (divorced, 1992); married James H. Rex (a university vice-president), November 5, 1994; children: Jeffrey, Siri, Adam, Nathan. *Education:* Lock Haven State College, B.S., 1972; Bloomsburg State College, M.Ed., 1973; Shippensburg State College, Supervisor's Certificate in Special Education, 1978; University of South Carolina, Ed.D., 1983. *Politics:* Democrat. *Religion:* Roman Catholic.

■ Addresses

Home—340 Woodside Dr., Winnsboro, SC 29180. *Office*—College of Education, Winthrop University, Rock Hill, SC 29733. *Electronic mail*—SmithSJ @ Winthrop.edu.

■ Career

Winthrop University, Rock Hill, SC, professor of education, 1979—, director of Winthrop's Project for At Risk Initiatives, 1985—, director of Winthrop's Involvement in Nurturing and Graduating Students (WINGS) Program, 1990—. Director, PhoneFriend (talk line for York County children), 1984—; member of board of directors, Charlotte (NC) Drug Education Center, 1989-90; director, York County Parent Educators in the Work Force Program, 1990—. Host of the South Carolina public television programs *Winthrop Challenge,* 1988-91, and *Perceptions,* 1990-91.

SUSAN J. SMITH-REX

■ Awards, Honors

Jefferson Award, WBTV program *Jefferson Pilot,* 1988; South Carolina Human Rights Award, South Carolina School Counselor Association, 1990; Point of Light Award, President George Bush, 1992, for the WINGS Program; grants from federal and state offices for education, health, and human services.

■ Writings

Art, Fine Motor, and Cognitive Ideas for Special Education, Communication Skill Builders, 1985.

(With Kim "Tip" Frank) *Getting a Grip on A.D.D.: A Kid's Guide to Understanding and Coping with Attention Disorders,* illustrated by Jan Hanna Elliott, Educational Media, 1994.

(With Frank) *Getting a Life of Your Own: A Kid's Guide to Understanding and Coping with Family Alcoholism,* Educational Media, 1995.

(With Frank) *Getting over the Blues: A Kid's Guide to Understanding and Coping with Unpleasant Feelings and Depression,* Educational Media, 1996.

(With Frank) *Getting with It,* Educational Media, 1997.

(With Frank) *ADHD: 102 Practical Strategies for Reducing the Deficit,* Youthlight, 1997.

Contributor to journals and newspapers, including *Principals' Journal.*

■ Sidelights

Susan J. Smith-Rex told *SATA:* "After twenty-five years in the field of special education, I have become very interested in helping children better understand different disabilities and 'at risk' issues, so that they can learn to take increased responsibility for reaching their own potential. Four of the six books I've written are for children. The other two offer ideas for parents and teachers to help students learn strategies for success in the mainstream.

"Five of my books were written with Mr. Kim 'Tip' Frank, a guidance counselor in Rock Hill, South Carolina. Our books have been illustrated by either teachers or high school students, who know our audience well. Educational disabilities is a growing field of study, and I am excited to be a part of it through teaching, writing, and parenting."*

* * *

SPUDVILAS, Anne 1951-

■ Personal

Born October 20, 1951, in Heyfield, Victoria, Australia; daughter of Don and Doris Searle; married Ron Spudvilas (an electrician), April 21, 1973; children: Sunny, Rene. *Education:* Attended Geelong Fine Art Studio, Elsternwick College, and Melbourne College of Decoration. *Hobbies and other interests:* Gardening, painting, "haunting second-hand and antique markets."

■ Addresses

Home—25 Meakin St., East Geelong, Victoria 3219, Australia. *Office*—147 Ryrie St., Geelong, Victoria 3220, Australia.

ANNE SPUDVILAS

■ Career

Freelance graphic designer and book illustrator. *Member:* Australian Society of Authors, Geelong Art Gallery.

■ Awards, Honors

Crichton Award, 1996; Doug Moran National Portrait Prize, 1996; Picture Book Honor, Children's Book Council of Australia, 1996, for *The Race.*

■ Illustrator

Christobel Mattingley, *The Race,* Scholastic, 1995.
Margaret Wild, *Big Cat Dreaming,* Penguin, 1996.
Gary Crew, *Bright Star,* Lothian, 1996.

■ Sidelights

Anne Spudvilas told *SATA:* "I've always drawn, as far back as I can remember. My drawing ability led to work on the local newspaper, then to advertising layout and illustration.

"After the births of Sunny and Rene, I studied painting for three years and painted professionally. I had a solo exhibition in 1985 and exhibited at Geelong Art Gallery in 1986. Commissions to paint the first woman mayor of Melbourne and our law courts and police complex followed.

"My introduction to illustration came in 1990, when writer and friend Isobelle Carmody invited me to illustrate the cover of her wonderful book *The Gathering* for Penguin. More covers followed, my confidence was bolstered, and I sent out samples of my work to every children's publisher I could think of. I've had steady work ever since.

"*The Race* was my first picture book, and it is still my favorite, largely I think because I've used my son Rene as a model, and I've always loved painting him. Both Sunny and Rene have modeled for many covers. I have illustrated a lot of covers for teenage fiction—about thirty so far, and friends and family are roped in to model.

"Illustration is a really enjoyable part of my career as a painter. The feedback from children is wonderful. I visit schools quite regularly to talk about my work and demonstrate drawing. Although I'm nervous about going each time, I'm always rewarded by the children themselves, their enthusiasm, questions, and appreciation. Illustration provides an ongoing life for my work that makes it a satisfying area in which to work. At present I am also working on a commissioned portrait of two children and a large painting of my daughter and her best friend, just for me.

"I work predominantly in oils on canvas. I love the clear, brilliant color, resilience, and texture of this medium. I have a studio in Geelong's Centre, about five minutes from home. It's a great place to work: no phone, but plenty happening down in the street below!"

■ For More Information See

PERIODICALS

Australian Book Review, July, 1995, p. 63.
Magpies, July, 1995, p. 21.
Reading Time, May, 1997, p. 26.

*   *   *

STEELE, Mary 1930-

■ Personal

Born November 11, 1930, in Newcastle, New South Wales, Australia; daughter of William H. (a minister) and Frances D. (a homemaker; maiden name, De Chair) Johnson; married Bruce Steele (an academic), 1963; children: one son, one daughter. *Education:* University of Melbourne, B.A. (with honors), 1951, M.A., 1952; University of London, Post-Graduate Certificate in Education, 1960. *Religion:* Anglican. *Hobbies and other interests:* Gardening, choral singing, music, crafts, reading, travel, attending the theater.

■ Addresses

Home—Balwyn, Australia. *Office*—c/o Hyland House Publishing, 387-9 Clarendon St., South Melbourne, Victoria 3205, Australia.

MARY STEELE

■ Career

Office of the Federal Attorney General, Melbourne, Australia, research officer, 1953-54; Melbourne University, Melbourne, tutor, 1955-57; Australian Scientific Liaison Office, London, England, research officer, 1958-59; Monash University, Melbourne, lecturer in English, 1961-62; part-time work as school librarian, university tutor, research assistant, and book reviewer, 1965-80; writer.

■ Awards, Honors

Arkwright was named Australian Junior Book of the Year, Children's Book Council of Australia, 1986.

■ Writings

Arkwright (self-illustrated), Hyland House (South Melbourne, Australia), 1985.
Mallyroots' Pub at Misery Ponds, Hyland House, 1988.
Citizen Arkwright (self-illustrated), Hyland House, 1990.
Featherbys (self-illustrated), Hyland House, 1993, Peachtree Publishers (Atlanta, GA), 1996.
A Bit of a Hitch and Other Stories, Hyland House, 1995.

Work represented in anthologies published in the United States.

■ Work in Progress

Tenterhooks, a novel for young teenagers and preteens; a book about the author's own childhood.

■ Sidelights

Mary Steele told *SATA:* "Words and writing have always been important to me, as I studied language and literature at university and then went on to teach in the same discipline. I didn't attempt to write fiction until I was involved part-time in a school library. My first book was published in 1985, by which time I was nearly fifty-five years old. Since then I have produced a book every two or three years. My busy family life prevents me from writing full-time, so I am not very prolific. This doesn't worry me; there are more than enough books in the world! Encouraged by my publishers, and rather to my surprise (as I am not a trained artist), I illustrated three of my books. Young readers seem to like my pictures, I think because they recognize the work of a fellow amateur.

"I grew up before the advent of television, videos, and computers. Our main entertainment came from simple games, the radio, and reading. I had my own small collection of books, which I read over and over again, and in them I could lose myself in another world. I write for young readers now, hoping that they will find the same entry into that imaginary world and the same companionship. One need never be bored or lonely in the company of a good book—by the fire, in bed, up a tree, on the beach, in the bath, or on a train. Can the same be said of a television or a computer screen?

"My father had a great sense of humor, and our family life has always been pretty hilarious, so writing in a comic vein comes naturally to me. I believe that most children are born with a natural tendency toward fun and laughter but, unless this is nourished, it won't necessarily develop. Serious and pessimistic issues are so often emphasized in children's books these days, and I feel there is a need to lighten up and take an optimistic view. In any case, one can deal most effectively with human follies through humor and satire.

"As a child I had a great menagerie of animals, and most of my stories include animal characters, especially the first one, *Arkwright.* Arkwright is a giant anteater from South America who wants to see the world. He becomes attached to an old sea captain who is sailing to Australia, where he plans to retire. Arkwright behaves like any immigrant as he adjusts to the customs and creatures of his new home. His adventures carried over into a second book, *Citizen Arkwright.*"

■ For More Information See

PERIODICALS

Magpies, March, 1991, p. 2; March, 1994, p. 31.
Publishers Weekly, September 23, 1996, p. 77.

*   *   *

STEVENS, Diane 1939-

■ Personal

Born April 27, 1939, in Berkeley, CA; daughter of Mike (in sales) and Shyrle (a writer; maiden name, Pedlar) Hacker; married Joe Stevens (a psychiatrist), August 27, 1961; children: Scott, Dana, Tracy. *Education:* University of California, Berkeley, B.A., 1960; Our Lady of the Lake University, M.A., 1982. *Hobbies and other interests:* Cooking, skiing, travel, reading, poetry.

■ Addresses

Home—P.O. Box 422, Cambria, CA 93428. *Electronic mail*—fruitheart @ aol.com.

■ Career

Special education teacher, San Antonio, TX, 1970-80; family therapist, San Antonio, 1980-87; writer. *Member:* Society of Children's Book Writers and Illustrators.

■ Awards, Honors

Liza's Blue Moon was chosen Best Children's Book for 1995, Book Publishers of Texas.

■ Writings

Liza's Blue Moon, Greenwillow Books, 1995.

DIANE STEVENS

Liza's Star Wish, Greenwillow Books, 1997.

■ Work in Progress

True Blue, an adult novel.

■ Sidelights

Diane Stevens told *SATA:* "I grew up to the sound of my mother's typewriter. She wrote novels behind that closed door that my brother and I knew not to go near during her working hours. I watched her over the years as she dealt with rejection, always sending her manuscripts out again immediately, before she let herself get too discouraged. Now she is over eighty years old and still writing every day, on a computer instead of the Underwood typewriter. Her book *The Goldminer's Child* was published in 1996, and she now edits my work before I send it out. She has been an inspiration, but more important, she is an example of the kind of commitment it takes to achieve success."

■ For More Information See

PERIODICALS

Booklist, April 1, 1995, p. 1388.
Bulletin of the Center for Children's Books, March, 1995, p. 251.

Kirkus Reviews, March 15, 1995, p. 396.
Publishers Weekly, January 30, 1995, p. 101.
School Library Journal, April, 1995, p. 136.
Voice of Youth Advocates, August, 1995, p. 166.

*   *   *

STRONG, David
See McGUIRE, Leslie (Sarah)

*   *   *

SWANSON, Helen M(cKendry) 1919-

■ Personal

Born October 3, 1919, in Waukesha, WI; daughter of James Banford (a minister) and Helen Amy McKendry; married Neil H. Swanson, Jr. (a minister and writer), August 30, 1941; children: David, Shirley, Kenneth, Howard. *Education:* Cornell College, Mount Vernon, IA, B.A., 1941; Marquette University, Teaching Certificate, 1963. *Politics:* Registered Republican. *Religion:* Protestant. *Hobbies and other interests:* Reading, hiking, birds.

HELEN M. SWANSON (portrait by Jean London).

■ Addresses

Home and office—824 West Pitcher, Nevada, MO 64772.

■ Career

Elementary schoolteacher in Milwaukee, WI, 1964-65, Toledo, OH, 1966-67, and Maui, HI, 1968-82. Chairperson and member of board of directors, Maui Special Learning Center; community volunteer. *Member:* Phi Beta Kappa.

■ Writings

Angel of Rainbow Gulch, Bess Press, 1992.
The Secret of Petroglyph Cave, Bess Press, 1995.
Angel and Tutu, Bess Press, 1997.

Contributor of about a dozen stories to children's magazines.

■ Work in Progress

Ilima Miller, Hapa Haole (tentative title).

■ Sidelights

Helen M. Swanson told *SATA:* "After reading hundreds of children's books to the youngsters in my primary classes, I convinced myself that I could do it, too. My setting was Maui, where I taught local children in an 'up-country' plantation setting; hence, my choice of Angel. He is a young Hawaiian boy being raised in a *hanai* (adopted) family. His grandmother took him in, simply because she was lonely when her husband died.

"Because I hiked all the Hawaiian islands extensively and was constantly involved with the local culture, it was inevitable that I should choose to write what I knew. Angel has now become a three-book series for young readers aged eight to twelve.

"My editor at Bess Press encouraged me to try a 'girl' series, and now I am doing just that.

"In 1990 my husband and I returned to life on the mainland, in Nevada, Missouri, but my head and heart remain in Hawaii."

* * *

SZYDLOW, Jarl
See SZYDLOWSKI, Mary Vigliante

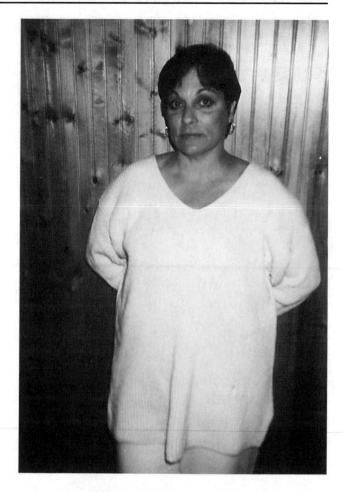

MARY VIGLIANTE SZYDLOWSKI

SZYDLOWSKI, Mary Vigliante 1946-
(Mary Vigliante; Jarl Szydlow, a pseudonym)

■ Personal

Born in 1946; married Frank J. Szydlowski; children: Carrie Ann. *Education:* State University of New York at Albany, B.A. (cum laude), 1971.

■ Addresses

Home—37 Normanside Dr., Albany, NY 12208.

■ Career

Writer. *Member:* Authors Guild, Authors League of America, Science Fiction Writers of America, Society of Children's Book Writers and Illustrators.

■ Writings

FICTION; FOR CHILDREN

I Can't Talk, I've Got Farbles in My Mouth, illustrated by Ray Dirgo, Greene Bark Press (Bridgeport, CT), 1995.

Also author of *Go Away, Julie May,* Trillium Press. Contributor to magazines, including *Young Crusader.*

FICTION; FOR ADULTS

(Under pseudonym Jarl Szydlow) *The Ark* (science fiction novel), Manor Books, 1978.

(As Mary Vigliante) *The Colony* (science fiction novel), Manor Books, 1979.

(As Vigliante) *The Land* (fantasy novel), Manor Books, 1979.

(As Vigliante) *Source of Evil* (science fiction novel), Manor Books, 1980.

Silent Song (novel), Everest House (New York City), 1980.

(As Vigliante) *Worship the Night* (horror novel), Tower Books, 1982.

OTHER

Correspondent, *The Record* (Troy, NY), 1988-91. Contributor to periodicals, including *Show and Tell.*

■ **For More Information See**

PERIODICALS

Booklist, September 1, 1980, p. 34.
Publishers Weekly, May 23, 1980, p. 72.
School Library Journal, May, 1980, p. 80.

T

TATE, Eleanora E(laine) 1948-

◾ Personal

Born April 16, 1948, in Canton, MO; daughter of Clifford and Lillie (Douglas) Tate; raised by her grandmother, Corinne E. Johnson; married Zack E. Hamlett III (a photographer), August 19, 1972; children: Gretchen R. *Education:* Drake University, B.A., 1973.

◾ Addresses

Home—P.O. Box 3581, Morehead City, North Carolina 28557. *Agent*—Charlotte Sheedy, Charlotte Sheedy Literary Agency, 145 West 86th St., New York, NY 10024.

◾ Career

Iowa Bystander, West Des Moines, news editor, 1966-68; *Des Moines Register* and *Des Moines Tribune,* Des Moines, IA, staff writer, 1968-76; *Jackson Sun,* Jackson, TN, staff writer, 1976-77; Kreative Koncepts, Inc., Myrtle Beach, SC, writer and researcher, 1979-81; Positive Images, Inc., Myrtle Beach, SC, president and co-owner (with husband, Zack E. Hamlett III), 1983—.

Contributor to black history and culture workshops in Des Moines, IA, 1968-76; giver of poetry presentations, including Iowa Arts Council Writers in the Schools program, 1969-76, Rust College, 1973, and Grinnell College, 1975; free-lance writer for *Memphis Tri-State Defender,* 1977; guest author of South Carolina School Librarians Association Conference, 1981 and 1982; writer-in-residence, Elgin, SC, Chester, SC, and the Amana colonies, Middle, IA, all 1986. *Member:* National Association of Black Storytellers, Inc. (member of the board, 1988-92, president, 1991-92), Arts in Basic Curriculum Steering Committee, South Carolina Academy of Authors (member of the board, 1987—; vice-president of the board of directors, 1988-90), South Carolina Arts Commission Artists in Education, Concerned Citizens Operation Reach-Out of Horry County, Horry Cultural Arts Council (president of the board of directors, 1990-92); North Carolina Writers Network (member of the board, 1996-97).

◾ Awards, Honors

Finalist, fifth annual Third World Writing Contest, 1973; Unity Award, Lincoln University, 1974, for educational reporting; Community Lifestyles award, Tennessee Press Association, 1977; Bread Loaf Writers Conference fellowship, 1981; "Selected Films for Young Adults," American Library Association, 1985, for film adaptation of *Just an Overnight Guest;* Parents' Choice Award, Parents' Choice Foundation, 1987, for *The Secret of Gumbo Grove;* Presidential Award, National Association of Negro Business and Professional Womens Clubs, Georgetown chapter, 1988; Grand Strand Press Association Award, Second Place, for Social Responsibilities and Minority Affairs, 1988; Notable Children's Book, National Council for the Social Studies/Children's Book Council (NCSS/CBC), 1990, for *Thank You, Dr. Martin Luther King, Jr.!;* Children's Book of the Year selection, Child Study Children's Book Committee, 1990, for *Thank You, Dr. Martin Luther King, Jr.!;* "Pick of the Lists," American Booksellers Association (ABA), 1992, for *Front Porch Stories at the One-Room School,* and 1996, for *A Blessing in Disguise.* Tate was also recognized by the South Carolina House of Representatives in a resolution June 9, 1990, for her literary and community efforts in South Carolina.

◾ Writings

FICTION; FOR YOUNG PEOPLE

Just an Overnight Guest, Dial, 1980.
The Secret of Gumbo Grove, Franklin Watts, 1987.
Thank You, Dr. Martin Luther King, Jr.!, F. Watts, 1990.
Front Porch Stories at the One-Room School, illustrated by Eric Velasquez, Bantam/Skylark, 1992.
(Reteller and compiler) *Retold African Myths,* Perfection Learning, 1992.
A Blessing in Disguise, Delacorte, 1995.

CONTRIBUTOR

Rosa Guy, editor, *Children of Longing,* Bantam, 1970.
Impossible? (juvenile), Houghton, 1972.
Broadside Annual 1972, Broadside Press, 1972.
Communications (juvenile), Heath, 1973.
Off-Beat (juvenile), Macmillan, 1974.
Sprays of Rubies (anthology of poetic prose), Ragnarok, 1975.
(And editor with husband, Zack E. Hamlett III) *Eclipsed* (poetry), privately printed, 1975.
(And editor) *Wanjiru: A Collection of Blackwoman-worth,* privately printed, 1976.
Valhalla Four, Ragnarok, 1977.
Wade Hudson and Cheryl Willis Hudson, compilers, *In Praise of Our Fathers and Our Mothers, a Black Family Treasury by Outstanding Authors and Artists,* Just Us Books, 1997.

OTHER

Contributor of poetry and fiction to periodicals, including *Journal of Black Poetry* and *Des Moines Register Picture Magazine.*

■ **Adaptations**

Just an Overnight Guest was adapted as a film starring Fran Robinson, Tiffany Hill, Rosalind Cash, and Richard Roundtree, Phoenix/ B.F.A. Films & Video, 1983.

■ **Sidelights**

Eleanora E. Tate was born in 1948 in Canton, a small town in northeastern Missouri, where during her early childhood legal segregation was still enforced. She attended first grade in 1954 at the town's one-room grade school for African Americans. The following year her class was integrated into Canton's white school system. Tate has used her experiences as an African American woman to formulate books for both adults and children. Over the course of her career, she has made a special effort to reach young readers on a variety of complex issues, including racial understanding and appreciation, cultural and racial identity in history, neglect and abuse, individual and group pride, and family ties (with a special emphasis on healthy father-daughter relationships). Tate once commented: "I have gotten a thrill out of writing about children. Part of it ... stems from my belief that I had a very happy childhood, with a certain richness to it that I want today's children to share."

Tate's novels for middle graders, each focusing on a young African-American girl, are set in places she knows well. Her first novel, *Just an Overnight Guest,* told from the view of nine-year-old Margie Carson, takes place in Nutbrush, Missouri, a small town modeled after Canton. Margie becomes angry when her mother invites Ethel Hardisen, a disruptive four-year-old who has been abused and neglected, to stay with the family for a night. "Ethel Hardisen!" Margie exclaims in the story, "I hated that trashy little kid.... Some folks said she was half white and other folks said she was half Black. To me she was all bad." Ethel's visit is mysteriously extended,

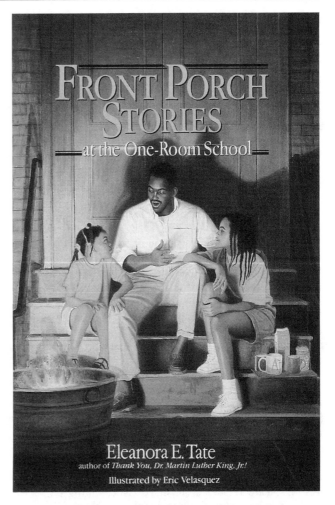

In Eleanora E. Tate's sequel to *Just an Overnight Guest,* Margie's father takes Margie and her cousin to the town's old one-room schoolhouse and tells them stories about his childhood, which not only entertain but also teach something important about their heritage. (Cover illustration by Eric Velasquez.)

despite her bad behavior, and Margie begins to see Ethel as competition for her parents' affection. With the help of her loving father, Margie eventually overcomes her anger and resentment, and learns to accept the now permanent guest whom she discovers is her irresponsible Uncle Jake's daughter. *New York Times Book Review* contributor Merri Rosenberg wrote, "Eleanora Tate does a fine job presenting the emotional complexities of Margie's initiation into adult life's moral ambiguities." In *The Horn Book Magazine,* Celia Morris praised Tate for capturing "the nuances of small-town life, the warmth of a Black family struggling with a problem, and the volatile emotions of a young child."

In her second novel, *The Secret of Gumbo Grove,* the setting is similar to Myrtle Beach, South Carolina. The story, explains Tate, is about an eleven-year-old girl, Raisin Stackhouse, who "loves history, but she can't seem to find any positive Black history in her hometown of Gumbo Grove, South Carolina's most famous oceanside resort, until she stumbles on to an old cemetery owned by her church.... The townspeople aren't too happy with her discovery of the area's history of racial segregation ... because they are ashamed with their own families' past." *Voice of Youth Advocates* contributor Linda Classen considered the book important in giving "a feeling for life in a black community before blacks had rights, which ... not many young people today can comprehend." In the *Bulletin of the Center for Children's Books,* Betsy Hearne called the ending, when Raisin is given a surprise community service award, "a bit tidy," but added that the book "will be satisfying for young readers, who can enjoy this as a leisurely, expansive reading experience."

Also set in Gumbo Grove is Tate's third novel, *Thank You, Dr. Martin Luther King, Jr.!,* a story narrated by fourth-grader Mary Elouise Avery, who yearns to be in the school play about presidents with a conceited, blond-haired classmate whom she idolizes. Instead, she is selected as narrator for the new black history skit, even though she is ashamed of being black and hates being reminded of slavery and Dr. Martin Luther King, Jr. Through the visits of two storytellers and the efforts of her wise grandmother, Mary Elouise comes to appreciate her heritage.

Tate approached this sensitive story with great care. In the *Bulletin of the Center for Children's Books,* Zena Sutherland praised the author for not falling prey to racial stereotyping. "One of the strong points of her story," Sutherland stated, "is that there is bias in both races, just as there is understanding in both." *Booklist* reviewer Denise Wilms echoed Sutherland's sentiments, noting: "Tate tackles a sensitive issue, taking pains to keep characters multidimensional and human."

Tate returns to Nutbrush, Missouri, for her next book, *Front Porch Stories at the One-Room School,* a sequel to *Just an Overnight Guest. Front Porch Stories* finds Margie and Ethel, now three years older, lying around on a hot summer night, so bored that their "life is duller than dirt." Margie's father then takes them on a walk to an old one-room building, formerly the grade school for the town's African-American children. He then begins to tell a number of stories about his childhood, which not only entertain the children but also teach them something important about their heritage. In an afterward to the book, Tate reveals that "most of the stories that the father tells ... are based on my own actual experiences, or on stories I heard and greatly embellished." A *Publishers Weekly* reviewer praised Tate's "evocative language," noting that it "conjures up rural southern life." Moreover, *Front Porch Stories* voices Tate's special concern for father-daughter relationships. Tate once remarked: "It has been said little black boys need fathers. I believe little black girls need fathers. I emphasize that. It's something that hasn't been played up in recent years. I see it every day with my husband and my daughter."

A Blessing in Disguise, Tate's third "Gumbo Grove" novel, confronts the issues of drugs and crime in a small community while featuring the relationship of a girl with her not-so-wise-and-stable father. In this story,

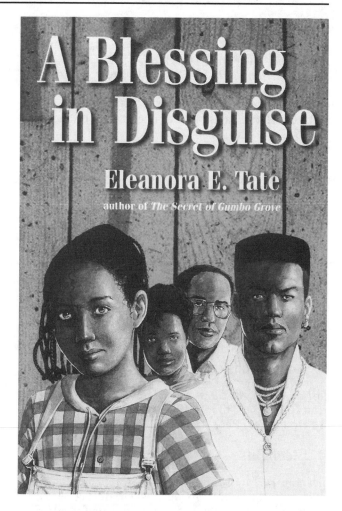

Tate's third "Gumbo Grove" novel relates the story of Zambia Brown and her attempts to gain the affection of her flashy but unstable father. (Cover illustration by Gershom Griffith.)

twelve-year-old Zambia Brown lives with her poor aunt and uncle in the little town of Deacons Neck on the South Carolina coast. Zambia's real father, called Snake, is the shady, drug-dealing owner of a nightclub in Gumbo Grove. Zambia longs to be part of her father's seemingly glamorous life, and is excited when Snake opens another club on her block in Deacons Neck. Her uncle, however, joins with others in a community movement to close the club, causing a rift with Zambia that is healed only when she gains firsthand experience with the consequences of her father's activities. "This novel deals realistically with a small community's battle against drugs and crime and a girl's development of a healthy attitude toward her irresponsible father," maintained *Voice of Youth Advocates* contributor Becky Kornman. Roger Sutton of the *Bulletin of the Center for Children's Books* noted that "the novel is saved from preachiness by Zambia's impulsive, colloquial narration and her true-to-twelve fascination with the night life and its supposed glamour."

Tate has also written poetry, short stories and essays for children that have been published in various collections. Her work for young people has been praised for combining warm family relationships, especially between fathers and daughters, with important themes of awareness and identity, while presenting positive images of black family life, history, and culture. Explaining what has moved her to write for children, Tate once commented: "I would like to add my voice in print, as well as my emotions, to the thought that children's childhoods can be happy if they can learn that they can do anything they set their minds to, if they try."

■ Works Cited

Classen, Linda, review of *The Secret of Gumbo Grove, Voice of Youth Advocates,* August-September, 1987, p. 123.
Review of *Front Porch Stories at the One-Room School, Publishers Weekly,* August 10, 1992, p. 71.
Hearne, Betsy, review of *The Secret of Gumbo Grove, Bulletin of the Center for Children's Books,* June, 1987, p. 199.
Kornman, Becky, review of *A Blessing in Disguise, Voice of Youth Advocates,* April, 1995, p. 28.
Morris, Celia, review of *Just an Overnight Guest, Horn Book,* December, 1980, pp. 643-44.
Rosenberg, Merri, review of *Just an Overnight Guest, New York Times Book Review,* February 8, 1981, p. 20.
Sutherland, Zena, review of *Thank You, Dr. Martin Luther King, Jr.!, Bulletin of the Center for Children's Books,* June, 1990, p. 254.
Sutton, Roger, review of *A Blessing in Disguise, Bulletin of the Center for Children's Books,* February, 1995, p. 216.
Wilms, Denise, review of *Thank You, Dr. Martin Luther King, Jr.!, Booklist,* April 15, 1990, p. 1636.

■ For More Information See

BOOKS

Children's Literature Review, Vol. 37, Gale Research, 1996, pp. 186-93.
Twentieth-Century Young Adult Writers, St. James Press, 1994, pp. 634-35.

PERIODICALS

Booklist, November 1, 1980, p. 408; May 15, 1987, pp. 1450-51; August, 1992, p. 2014.
Bulletin of the Center for Children's Books, October, 1980, p. 42.
Kirkus Reviews, February 15, 1981, p. 215; March 1, 1987, p. 380; February 1, 1990, p. 186; July 15, 1992, p. 926; February 15, 1995, p. 233.
Publishers Weekly, December 5, 1994, p. 77; June 3, 1996, p. 85.
School Library Journal, October, 1980, p. 42; March, 1990, p. 220-21; March, 1992, pp. 163-67.

TIEGREEN, Alan (F.) 1935-

■ Personal

Born July 6, 1935, in Boise, ID; son of a civil servant; married, wife's name Judy (an art teacher); children: Christopher, Carl, Karen. *Education:* University of Southern Mississippi, A.B., 1957; Art Center College of Design, B.P.A., 1961. *Hobbies and other interests:* Music, tennis.

■ Addresses

Home—315 Drexel Ave., Decatur, GA 30030. *Office*—Georgia State University, University Plaza, Atlanta, GA 30303-3044.

■ Career

Artist and illustrator. Georgia State University, professor of art, 1965—. *Exhibitions:* High Museum, Atlanta, GA; Smithsonian Institution, Washington, DC; Knoxville, TN, World's Fair. Permanent installations in Hilton Hotels, Knoxville, TN; Simmons Corporation headquarters, Atlanta, GA.

■ Awards, Honors

National Drawing Society award, 1965; Decatur (GA) Sesquicentennial award, 1972; Georgia Children's Book award, 1974, for *Doodle and the Go-Cart;* Art Directors Club award for illustration; numerous awards for "Ramona" books written by Beverly Cleary.

■ Illustrator

Robert Burch, *Doodle and the Go-Cart,* Viking, 1972.
Beverly Cleary, *Ramona the Brave,* Morrow, 1975.
Eleanor Frances Latimore, *Adam's Key,* Morrow, 1976.
Shirley Rousseau Murphy, *Silver Woven in My Hair,* Atheneum, 1977.
Beverly Cleary, *Ramona and Her Father,* Morrow, 1977.
Cleary, *Ramona and Her Mother,* Dell, 1980.
Cleary, *Ramona Quimby, Age Eight,* Morrow, 1981.
Cleary, *Ramona Forever,* Morrow, 1984.
Cleary, *The Ramona Quimby Diary,* Morrow, 1984.
Cleary, *The Beezus and Ramona Diary,* Morrow, 1986.
Joanna Cole, *Asking about Sex and Growing Up: A Question-and-Answer Book for Boys and Girls,* Morrow, 1988.
Judy Delton, *Blue Skies, French Fries,* Dell,' 1988.
Delton, *Cookies and Crutches,* Dell, 1988.
Delton, *Camp Ghost-Away,* Dell, 1988.
Delton, *Grumpy Pumpkins,* Dell, 1988.
Delton, *Peanut-Butter Pilgrims,* Dell, 1988.
Delton, *The Pooped Troop,* Dell, 1989.
Robert Kimmel Smith, *Bobby Baseball,* Delacorte, 1989.
Judy Delton, *Spring Sprout,* Dell, 1989.
Joanna Cole, compiler, *Anna Banana: 101 Jump-Rope Rhymes,* Morrow, 1989.
Judy Delton, *Huckleberry Hash,* Dell, 1990.

Joanna Cole and Stephanie Calmenson, compilers, *Miss Mary Mack and Other Children's Street Rhymes,* Morrow, 1990.

Judy Delton, *Rosy Noses, Freezing Toes,* Dell, 1990.

Joanna Cole and Stephanie Calmenson, compilers, *The Eentsy, Weentsy Spider: Fingerplays and Action Rhymes,* Morrow, 1991.

Judy Delton, *Lights, Action, Land-Ho!,* Dell, 1992.

Delton, *Pee Wees on Parade,* Dell, 1992.

Joanna Cole and Stephanie Calmenson, *Pat-a-Cake and Other Play Rhymes,* Morrow, 1992.

Cole and Calmenson, compilers, *Pin the Tail on the Donkey and Other Party Games,* Morrow, 1993.

Alex Simmons, *Grounded for Life?,* Troll, 1993.

Simmons, *We Want to Win,* Troll, 1993.

Judy Delton, *Fishy Wishes,* Dell, 1993.

Joanna Cole and Stephanie Calmenson, compilers, *Six Sick Sheep: 101 Tongue Twisters,* Morrow, 1993.

Cole and Calmenson, compilers, *Why Did the Chicken Cross the Road? and Other Riddles, Old and New,* Morrow, 1994.

Judy Delton, *All Dads on Deck,* Bantam, 1994.

Joanna Cole and Stephanie Calmenson, *Crazy Eights and Other Card Games,* Morrow, 1994.

Cole and Calmenson, compilers, *Yours till Banana Splits: 201 Autograph Rhymes,* Morrow, 1995.

Judy Delton, *Teeny Weeny Zucchinis,* Dell, 1995.

Joanna Cole and Stephanie Calmenson, *Bug in a Rug: Reading Fun for Just-Beginners,* Morrow, 1996.

Judy Delton, *Eggs with Legs,* Dell, 1996.

Delton, *Pee Wee Pool Party,* Dell, 1996.

Delton, *Bookworm Buddies,* Dell, 1996.

■ Sidelights

Artist and illustrator Alan Tiegreen, who has provided pictures for the works of several popular children's writers, is best known for his artwork for the award-winning "Ramona" books written by Beverly Cleary. Beginning his career as a book illustrator after working both as an artist and an art professor for several years, Tiegreen believes that bringing texts to life for young readers is one of the most creative and important artistic endeavors. Illustrations for children's books "offer the cream of what's being done in visual communications these days," Tiegreen once stated in *Fifth Book of Junior Authors and Illustrators,* "the place where writers and illustrators can express themselves almost without hindrance."

Born in Boise, Idaho, in 1935, Tiegreen grew up in many different parts of the United States as a result of his father's job with the U.S. government. Nebraska, Alabama, and Ohio all counted as "home" for the budding young artist at one point or another during his boyhood. While interested in both drawing and music, Tiegreen eventually decided to devote his time to art; after graduating from high school, he earned degrees from both the University of Southern Mississippi and Los Angeles' Art Center College of Design.

Completing his formal studies with a Bachelor of Professional Arts degree in 1961, Tiegreen worked at various jobs for several years before joining the art department at Atlanta's Georgia State University, where he has taught painting, drawing, and illustration techniques since 1965. In addition to teaching, Tiegreen is a practicing artist who has exhibited his work throughout the United States. He has been commissioned to create several permanent installations, one a mural in the Atlanta, Georgia, headquarters of Simmons Corporation.

Tiegreen first tried his hand at book illustration when he was approached by the Baptist Home Mission Board and asked to illustrate one of their publications for young readers. He enjoyed the project so much that he began to build an illustration portfolio in his spare time. His break into mainstream children's book publishing came when author Robert Burch became familiar with Tiegreen's work, and requested that the artist create the illustrations for his *Doodle and the Go-Cart.*

While Tiegreen has since worked with a variety of writers, including Robert Kimmel Smith, Alex Simmons, and Joanna Cole, his work with popular children's author Beverly Cleary has garnered the most critical attention. Beginning with 1975's *Ramona The Brave* and continuing through *The Beezus and Ramona Diary,* published in 1986, Tiegreen illustrated seven of Cleary's multi-award-winning titles featuring the irrepressible young Ramona Quimby—"one of the most endearing protagonists of children's fiction," according to *Horn Book* reviewer Ethel L. Heins. Beginning his relationship with Ramona as she grudgingly enters the first grade, Tiegreen follows her humorous trials and tribulations through the third grade, when she and her older sister, now given some independence by their hard-working parents, become bridesmaids and gain a

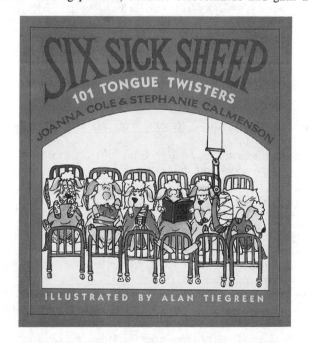

Illustrated by Alan Tiegreen, this collection of popular and lesser known tongue twisters challenges children to test their pronunciation skills.

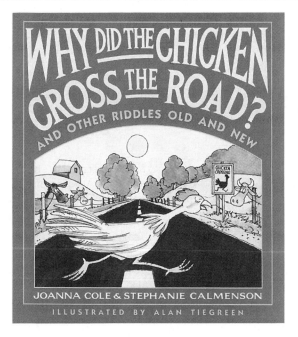

In this book, one of many collaborations between Tiegreen and compilers Joanna Cole and Stephanie Calmenson, over two hundred riddles are reprinted along with a history of riddling and its importance to many cultures.

sense of their futures. From trying to tough out a case of the flu in class to coping with a dad going through a career change, a mom who takes on a full-time job, and an older sister, Beezus, who seems to get more touchy and moody with each passing day, Ramona makes her way through elementary school accompanied by the "engaging drawings of Tiegreen," according to a *Publishers Weekly* reviewer. "The black-and-white sketches skillfully capture Ramona's inimitable style," added *Horn Book* reviewer Mary M. Burns in describing Tiegreen's contribution to the series.

While praised for his own work on the "Ramona" series, Tiegreen offers high commendation for author Cleary. In comments for the *Fifth Book of Junior Authors and Illustrators,* Tiegreen dubbed Cleary's characters "universally appealing," adding: "They embody my feelings when I was a child. I can relate to Ramona's feelings especially. Cleary has an empathy with children and she writes of them with humor and understanding."

In addition to his work with Cleary's Ramona, Tiegreen has also worked on multi-book projects with other authors. Judy Delton's popular "Pee Wee Scouts" series of novels for young readers, which include *Peanut-Butter Pilgrims, The Pooped Troop,* and *Fishy Wishes,* all come under the sway of Tiegreen's adept artistry. Featuring the adventures of the first grade boys and girls in Pee Wee Scout Troop 23, the series is enlivened by Tiegreen's portrayals of the happy-go-lucky six-year-olds as they work on good-deed projects and take traditional scouting trips, but also as the boys end up pitted against the girls, school becomes boring, and an overnight stay results in bouts of homesickness. "The cover and

interior illustrations [are] diverting," noted a *Publishers Weekly* commentator in a review of Delton's *Cookies and Crutches* and *Camp Ghost-Away.*

Tiegreen has also added a level of humor to the many collaborative efforts of Joanna Cole and Stephanie Calmenson. The Cole-Calmenson duo have collected everything from autograph sayings to tongue twisters for the younger set. In his cartoon illustrations for these books, Tiegreen includes people from a variety of ethnic and racial backgrounds, adding to the books' broad-based appeal. His "Springy ink drawings go for the guffaws," commented *Booklist* reviewer Ilene Cooper of the illustrator's work in *Six Sick Sheep: 101 Tongue Twisters.* Pamela K. Bomboy commented in *School Library Journal* that "Amusing black-and-white line drawings add to the appeal" of 1995's *Yours till Banana Splits: 201 Autograph Rhymes.* In reviewing Cole and Calmenson's *Bug in a Rug: Reading Fun for Just-Beginners, Booklist* reviewer Lauren Peterson maintained that "Tiegreen's colorful cartoons, often the most essential component of [each reading] activity, are up to the task. Kids will have fun."

■ Works Cited

Bomboy, Pamela K., review of *Yours till Banana Splits: 201 Autograph Rhymes, School Library Journal,* April, 1995, pp. 122-23.

Burns, Mary M., review of *Ramona and Her Father, Horn Book,* December, 1977, p. 661.

Review of *Cookies and Crutches* and *Camp Ghost-Away, Publishers Weekly,* June 10, 1988, pp. 79-80.

Cooper, Ilene, review of *Six Sick Sheep: 101 Tongue Twisters, Booklist,* March 15, 1993, p. 1318.

Heins, Ethel L., review of *Ramona the Brave, Horn Book,* June, 1975, p. 266.

Peterson, Lauren, review of *Bug in a Rug: Reading Fun for Just-Beginners, Booklist,* September 1, 1996, p. 133.

Review of *Ramona and Her Father, Publishers Weekly,* August 29, 1977, p. 367.

Tiegreen, Alan, as quoted in *Fifth Book of Junior Authors and Illustrators,* edited by Sally Holmes Holtze, H. W. Wilson, 1983, pp. 312-13.

■ For More Information See

PERIODICALS

Booklist, December 15, 1992, p. 740; October 15, 1994, p. 429.

School Library Journal, June, 1989, p. 87; December, 1992, p. 95; April, 1993, p. 128; September, 1994, p. 226.*

*   *   *

TORRES, John A(lbert) 1965-

■ Personal

Born August 18, 1965, in New York, NY; son of Americo, Jr. (a retail manager) and Carmen (Calderon)

Torres; married Julie Perry (a secretary), June 9, 1990; children: Daniel, Jacqueline. *Education:* Fordham University, B.A., 1987. *Politics:* Independent. *Religion:* Roman Catholic.

■ Addresses

Home—2-D Millholland Dr., Fishkill, NY 12524. *Electronic mail*—JohnnyPitt@aol.com (America Online).

■ Career

Writer. Little League coach.

■ Writings

FOR YOUNG PEOPLE

(With Michael J. Sullivan) *Sports Great Darryl Strawberry,* Enslow Publishers, 1990.
(Self-illustrated) *Home-Run Hitters: Heroes of the Four Home-Run Game,* Simon & Schuster, 1995.
Sports Reports: Hakeem Olajuwon, Enslow Publishers, 1997.
Sports Great Jason Kidd, Enslow Publishers, 1997.
Greg Maddux, Lerner Publications, 1997.

■ Work in Progress

Sports Great Oscar De La Hoya, for Enslow Publishers; *Top Ten Three-Point Shooters,* for Enslow; a novel about a sportswriter.

■ Sidelights

John A. Torres told *SATA:* "Ever since I can remember, I have wanted to be a writer. My idol as a child was Ernest Hemingway. Since I also love sports, I tried to combine my two loves: writing and sports. My ultimate dream is to have my novel published and to be able to become a full-time writer. The most important development in my evolution as a writer was when I read [Ernest] Hemingway's *The Old Man and the Sea* during the summer I spent interning at United Press International. That was truly a baptism by fire."

■ For More Information See

PERIODICALS

Horn Book Guide, July, 1990, p. 145; fall, 1995, p. 373.
School Library Journal, November, 1990, p. 124; May, 1995, p. 116.*

* * *

TURNER, Megan Whalen 1965-

■ Personal

Born November 21, 1965, in Fort Sill, OK; daughter of Donald Peyton (a soldier in the U.S. Army) and Nora Courtenay (Green) Whalen; married Mark Bernard Turner (a professor of English), June 20, 1987; children: John Whalen, Donald Peyton. *Education:* University of Chicago, B.A. (with honors), 1987. *Hobbies and other interests:* Cooking, traveling.

■ Addresses

Agent—c/o Greenwillow Books, 1350 Avenue of the Americas, New York, NY 10019.

■ Career

Writer. Harper Court Bookstore, Chicago, IL, children's book buyer, 1988-89; Bick's Books, Washington, DC, children's book buyer, 1991-92. *Member:* Authors Guild.

■ Awards, Honors

Dorothy Canfield Fisher Children's Book Award master list, 1996-97, for *Instead of Three Wishes;* Newbery Honor Book designation, American Library Association, 1997, for *The Thief.*

■ Writings

Instead of Three Wishes, Greenwillow Books (New York City), 1995.
The Thief, Greenwillow Books, 1996.

■ Work in Progress

More novels for children.

■ Sidelights

With just her second published work, Megan Whelan Turner has received one of the highest honors conferred upon an American author of literature for children. *The Thief,* Turner's first novel for young people, was selected by the American Library Association as one of four Newbery honor books for 1997. A suspenseful and witty adventure, Turner's intricately plotted tale revolves around an accomplished thief named Gen, who is released from prison in order to accompany the king's magus on a quest to steal a legendary stone. Turner weaves stories-within-a-story as the charismatic Gen and the magus take turns relating myths and legends to others in their party, and the plot advances rapidly toward what a *Publishers Weekly* reviewer described as "one of the most valuable treasures of all—a twinkling jewel of a surprise ending." *School Library Journal* contributor Patricia A. Dollisch praised Turner's characterization of Gen, adding that the author "does a phenomenal job of creating real people to range through her well-plotted, evenly paced story." Martha V. Parravano of *Horn Book* similarly asserted: "The author's characterization of Gen is simply superb: she lets the reader know so much about him—his sense of humor, his egotism, his loyalty, his forthrightness, his tendency to sulk—and yet manages to hide the most essential information," allowing for the surprise ending.

The stories comprising Turner's debut book, *Instead of Three Wishes,* were also well-received. Aimed at middle-

In her first work, Megan Whalen Turner tells seven stories where very believable magic affects the everyday lives of her characters. (Cover illustration by Jos A. Smith.)

grade readers, Turner's collection contains seven stories in which instances of magic alter the lives of ordinary people. "Turner employs an assortment of folk-and fairytale elements with freshness and ease," noted Roger Sutton of the *Bulletin of the Center for Children's Books,* adding that "her deployment of fantastic elements into realistic settings has a bracing matter-of-factness." *School Library Journal* contributor Jane Gardner Connor maintained: "Turner does a fine job of creating time and place and imbues the selections with a mild humor that will elicit gentle chuckles and smiles." Calling *Instead of Three Wishes* "a fine debut," *Horn Book* reviewer Sarah Guille enthused that the author "combines a shrewd wit with an eye for the endearingly absurd." A *Kirkus Reviews* critic also had high praise for Turner's "auspicious debut," dubbing *Instead of Three Wishes* "an utterly delightful collection."

Inspired by her love of reading, Turner began contemplating a career as a writer at an early age. "When I was ten I read a lot of great books, and when I couldn't easily find more, I decided I would be a writer and write stories of my own, even though it didn't sound as exciting as reading," Turner has commented. "The only

impediment to beginning my career right then was that I couldn't think of anything to write.

"Joan Aiken said she saw stories all around her, prompted by everyday events. She also said (in her bio) that she'd been telling stories since birth and completed her first novel in Latin class when she was seventeen. It took me ten years to come up with an idea and five more to write it down."

■ Works Cited

Connor, Jane Gardner, review of *Instead of Three Wishes, School Library Journal,* September, 1995, p. 204.

Dollisch, Patricia A., review of *The Thief, School Library Journal,* October, 1996, p. 150.

Guille, Sarah, review of *Instead of Three Wishes, Horn Book,* May-June, 1996, p. 337.

Review of *Instead of Three Wishes, Kirkus Reviews,* July 1, 1995, p. 954.

Parravano, Martha V., review of *The Thief, Horn Book,* December, 1996, p. 747.

Gen, an enigmatic thief, is rescued from the king's prison by the royal magus and sent on a treacherous journey to unearth an ancient treasure in this Newbery honor book. (Cover illustration by Walter Gaffney-Kessell.)

Sutton, Roger, review of *Instead of Three Wishes*, *Bulletin of the Center for Children's Books*, October, 1995, p. 72.

Review of *The Thief*, *Publishers Weekly*, October 21, 1996, p. 84.

■ For More Information See

PERIODICALS

Booklist, October 1, 1995, p. 309.
Bulletin of the Center for Children's Books, November, 1996, p. 117.
New York Times Book Review, November 5, 1995, p. 31.
Publishers Weekly, July 24, 1995, p. 66.
Voice of Youth Advocates, June, 1997, p. 114.

* * *

TWEIT, Susan J(oan) 1956-

■ Personal

Surname pronounced "twite"; born September 18, 1956, in Evanston, IL; daughter of Robert C. (a chemist and ornithological researcher) and Joan (a librarian and ornithological researcher; maiden name, Cannon) Tweit; married Richard A. Cabe (an economist and luthier), 1983; children: (stepdaughter) Molly Elizabeth. *Education:* Southern Illinois University, B.A., 1978; graduate study at Colorado State University, 1979-80; graduate study at the University of Wyoming, 1980-83. *Religion:* Quaker. *Hobbies and other interests:* Walking, gardening, knitting, reading mysteries.

■ Addresses

Home—P.O. Box 578, Salida, CO 81201-0578. *Agent*—Jennifer McDonald, Curtis Brown Literary Agency, 1750 Montgomery St., San Francisco, CA 94111. *Electronic mail*—sjtweit @ sni.net.

■ Career

National Park Service, Yellowstone National Park, Mammoth, WY, biological aide, 1976-77; U.S. Forest Service, Shoshone National Forest, Cody, WY, biological technician, 1977-78, vegetation ecologist, 1978-81; University of Wyoming, Women's Resource Center, Laramie, director, 1982-83; Washington State Department of Natural Resources, Olympia, coordinating editor, 1984-87; freelance writer, 1987—; radio commentator for KRWG-FM, New Mexico, 1991—; newspaper columnist for the *Sun News*, Las Cruces, NM, 1992—. Lecturer and speaker at various occasions at locations throughout New Mexico, Utah, and Colorado. Administrative director and cofounder of the Border Book Festival; board member of Antlion Books; clerk for the Las Cruces (NM) Friends Meeting, 1992-94. *Member:* Sin Fronteras/Writers without Borders (founding codirector, 1994-95); PEN Center West, PEN New Mexico; Women Writing the West.

SUSAN J. TWEIT

■ Awards, Honors

United States Department of Agriculture (U.S.D.A.) Award of Merit, 1979; certificate of achievement from the Washington State Department of Natural Resources, 1987; Author of the Year Award from the Branigan Memorial Library in Las Cruces, NM, 1994; Newcomer's Arts Award, Dona Ana Arts Council, Las Cruces, NM, 1996.

■ Writings

FOR CHILDREN; NONFICTION

Meet the Wild Southwest: Land of Hoodoos and Gila Monsters, illustrated by Joyce Bergen, Alaska Northwest Books, 1995.
City Foxes, photographs by Wendy Shattil, Alaska Northwest Books, 1997.

FOR ADULTS; NONFICTION

Grassland and Shrubland Habitat Types of the Shoshone National Forest, U.S. Forest Service (Fort Collins, CO), 1980.
Writers Handbook, Washington State Dept. of Natural Resources (Olympia, WA), 1987.
Pieces of Light: A Year on Colorado's Front Range, Roberts Rinehart, 1990.

The Great Southwest Nature Factbook: A Guide to the Region's Remarkable Animals, Plants, and Natural Features, Alaska Northwest Books, 1992.

Barren, Wild, and Worthless: Living in the Chihuahuan Desert, University of New Mexico Press (Albuquerque, NM), 1995.

Seasons in the Desert: A Naturalist's Notebook, Chronicle Books, 1997.

Contributor to periodicals, including *Sun News, Bloomsbury Review, Hayden's Ferry Review, Sierra, Harrowsmith Country Life, New Mexico,* and *Cricket.*

■ Work in Progress

Seasons on the Pacific Coast: A Naturalist's Notebook, for Chronicle Books; a volume of personal essays (not yet in proposal stage), to be titled *Out of Place; Where Does it Go?,* a picture book for children.

■ Sidelights

Author Susan J. Tweit studied to work in biology, and afterward held positions in Wyoming for the National Park Service and the U.S. Forest Service. While working for the U.S. Forest Service she published her first book about nature, *Grassland and Shrubland Habitat Types of the Shoshone National Forest.* Tweit also penned a *Writers Handbook* in 1987 for her later employers, the Washington State Department of Natural Resources. She became a writer full-time during a year spent in Boulder, Colorado, the setting for her 1990 book, *Pieces of Light: A Year on Colorado's Front Range.* After moving to Las Cruces, New Mexico, Tweit became enamored of the desert Southwest, and many of her books—for both juvenile and adult audiences—concern themselves with this geography. She has recently returned, however, to the home of her heart, the sagebrush country of the Rocky Mountains.

Tweit has commented: "I am a field scientist first, a writer-come-lately. I grew up in a family of naturalists,

Field scientist Tweit follows the unusual life of two foxes raising their kits in the middle of a city graveyard.

and so inevitably evolved into a botanist, studying the form and function of the ecosystems of the arid West. Over time, I came to care less about statistics and results and more about communicating the beauty and magic that I found. I came to understand the power of stories.

"As a writer, I write about what I know. Thus, I tell the stories of our wild relatives, the other inhabitants of the desert where I live, the plants, the animals, the place itself. Like any landscape, the Chihuahuan Desert abounds with lives, with wild neighbors that we often don't notice or don't know. Take the spadefoot toad, a tiny amphibian that appears as if by magic after summer thunderstorms, filling the night with its mating calls, and then vanishing just as quickly when the ephemeral rainwater is gone. Or the shabby-looking creosote bush that by coating itself with a sophisticated protective armor comprised of dozens of smelly and bad-tasting compounds also produces the desert's signature fragrance.

"These stories fascinate me; they are full of wisdom, inventiveness, and the magic that comes of evolution. They tell how even the smallest, most insignificant piece of an ecosystem weaves itself uniquely into the overall pattern. The subjects of my stories are like tiny, bright strands of yarn in a giant tapestry, each a bit of color that you might not notice until it is gone, leaving a void, an empty spot not big, but somehow very wrong, a worrying place like the gap left by a missing tooth. What can these stories possibly mean in today's world of virtual reality and violence? A world where every day, people not so different from you and I drag their belongings about in shopping carts, muttering to themselves, or kill each other for their gang affiliation? A world where most of us no longer remember nature as our home? What relevance do the stories of spadefoot toads and creosote bush have for us?

"They show us where we fit, weaving us back into the immense tapestry that is life on this earth. They remind us that we are not the center of the universe, that our troubles and pains are small in the scheme of things. They teach us that each life, no matter how great or small, how flashy or obscure, has a crucial part in the larger whole. They reassure us that we are not alone, that no matter where we live, we belong to an intricate and diverse community of wild lives, from the tiny algae in the pores of the soil to the regal grizzly bears. There is great wisdom in the stories of these wild relatives, in the elegance of their adaptations to the harsh realities of life. From them we can learn tolerance and humility, respect and even awe, qualities that we sorely need in order to live well with each other and on this earth. I believe that the stories of spadefoot toads and creosote bush are among the most important tales for our times. They bring us home."

■ For More Information See

PERIODICALS

Booklist, March 1, 1996, p. 1180.

V

RACHEL VAIL

VAIL, Rachel 1966-

■ Personal

Born July 25, 1966, in New York, NY; married, husband's name Mitchell; children: Zachary. *Education:* Georgetown University, B.A., 1988.

■ Addresses

Home—New York, NY. *Office*—c/o Writers House, 21 W. 26th Street, New York, NY 10010.

■ Career

Writer. *Member:* Authors Guild.

■ Awards, Honors

Editor's Choice, *Booklist,* 1991, for *Wonder,* and 1992, for *Do-Over;* "Pick of the List," American Booksellers Association, 1991, for *Wonder;* Blue Ribbon designation, *Bulletin of the Center for Children's Books,* 1992, for *Do-Over;* Books for the Teen Age, New York Public Library, 1992, for *Do-Over,* and 1994, for *Ever After;* Best Books, *School Library Journal,* 1996, for *Daring to be Abigail.*

■ Writings

Wonder, Orchard Books (New York City), 1991.
Do-Over, Orchard Books, 1992.
Ever After, Orchard Books, 1994.
Daring to Be Abigail, Orchard Books, 1996.

■ Sidelights

Born in Manhattan, Rachel Vail grew up in New Rochelle, New York. In her youth she never intended to be a writer, but she received the encouragement of various teachers, both in high school and later at Georgetown University, who helped her to develop her talent. In an autobiographical sketch for *Horn Book,* Vail recalls one instructor in particular named Doc Murphy. A theater professor, Murphy encouraged her to focus on the essentials of character. Vail observed, "I think writing would be so much more exciting and less daunting to children if the emphasis were put on the details, the questions that propel the writer to create astonishing, unique characters who, by their juxtaposition with other astonishing, unique characters, make stories happen."

Vail's emphasis on character is apparent in her first novel for children, a coming-of-age story entitled *Wonder.* As 12-year-old Jessica enters seventh grade she

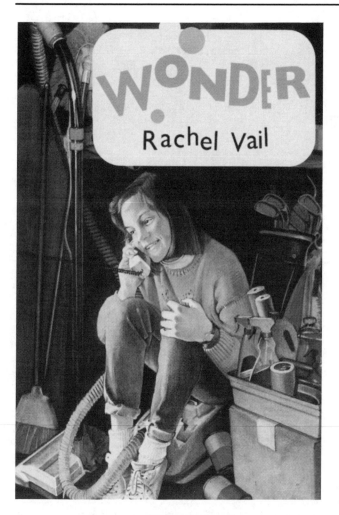

When Jessica enters seventh grade, her best friend and five other girls ostracize her, but she perseveres with determination and encouragement from her first love interest.

finds that she has suddenly become unpopular. Sheila, her former best friend, and five other girls succeed in ostracizing Jessica, giving her the humiliating nickname "Wonder" after one of the girls describes her new polka-dot dress as "a Wonder Bread explosion." With determination, and with the welcome attentions of Conor O'Malley, the object of her first crush, Jessica perseveres. Lauded by critics for its skillful rendering of character, *Wonder* proved to be a highly successful debut novel for its author. "Vail has the measure of this vulnerable age and its painful concern about identity within the group," noted a *Kirkus Reviews* commentator, who added: "Gauche, likable Jess ... is a character to remember." *School Library Journal* contributor Debra S. Gold also spoke favorably of Vail's characterization of her central protagonist in *Wonder,* commenting: "Jessica's first-person account reveals a three-dimensional character with whom readers will laugh and empathize." Deborah Abbott of *Booklist* asserted: "Piercing and funny, Vail's breezy story describes the hazards of junior high, sketched with the emotional chasms universal to the age."

One of Jessica's schoolmates, Whitman Levy, becomes the hero of Vail's next story, *Do-Over.* Eighth-grader Whitman is faced with some severe family problems, including his parents' imminent break-up, while struggling with his first real boy-girl relationships and a part in the school play. Vail balances the comical tale of his various escapades with other thorny issues, including Whitman's discovery that his best friend Doug is a bigot. Eventually the self-conscious and somewhat bewildered Whitman comes to understand how to deal with all that confronts him, in a moment of self-realization while on stage: "I could screw up or I could be amazing, and there's no turning back, no do-overs." Reviewers of Vail's work in *Do-Over* again highlighted her strengths with character and dialog in a number of positive assessments. *School Library Journal* contributor Jacqueline Rose asserted: "Vail is a master at portraying adolescent self-absorption, awkwardness, and fickleness, all with freshness and humor." In the *Bulletin of the Center for Children's Books,* Roger Sutton compared Vail favorably with popular children's writer Judy Blume, writing: "Vail is funnier than Blume, and more moving, partly because of her natural ear for teenaged talk, and partly because she never, ever preaches. This is

Eighth-grader Whitman Levy is faced with some severe family problems, including his parents' imminent break-up, while struggling with his first romance and a part in the school play.

Abigail's newly adopted boldness at summer camp backfires when she takes a foolish dare.

the real thing." Stephanie Zvirin of *Booklist* likewise spoke of the "sharp and genuine" dialog in *Do-Over,* commending Vail's "remarkable talent for capturing so perfectly the pleasure and pain of being thirteen—in a real kids' world."

In her third novel, *Ever After,* Vail employs a new narrative technique, presenting much of her story in the form of diary entries written by 14-year-old Molly. Best friends Molly and Vicky live year-round on a small Massachusetts island. The presence of a new friend, summer visitor Grace, causes Vicky to feel insecure and puts a strain on her relationship with Molly. Vicky's possessiveness begins to disturb Molly, and eventually destroys their friendship when Molly learns that Vicky has been reading her personal journal without permission. "That Vicky and Molly's rift is likely to be permanent ... is just one hallmark of the authenticity of this carefully conceived story," noted a *Publishers Weekly* reviewer. A *Kirkus Reviews* commentator praised *Ever After* as "an unusually immediate portrayal of a thoughtful teen finding her balance among her peers while making peace with her own capabilities." *School Library Journal* contributor Ellen Fader characterized the book as "a breezy, smart-talking novel that explores the ever-fascinating arena of young teen friendship,"

while Hazel Rochman of *Booklist* expressed a common critical refrain when noting that "the contemporary teenage voice is exactly right."

Daring to be Abigail features a narrative format similar to the one that Vail employs in *Ever After.* The story unfolds in the letters of Abby Silverman, an 11-year-old girl who has decided to "reinvent herself" while away at Camp Nashaquitsa for the summer. Her newly-adopted boldness wins the acceptance of her fellow campers, but also seems to require that Abby, now Abigail, forsake Dana, an unpopular girl in her cabin. Although she likes Dana, Abigail succumbs to peer pressure by accepting a dare to urinate in Dana's mouthwash. Unable to stop Dana before she uses the rinse, Abigail is thrown out of the camp, and addresses a final, poignant letter to her dead father, whose apparent disappointment with Abby inflamed her crisis of identity and prompted her efforts at "reinvention." Deborah Stevenson of the *Bulletin of the Center for Children's Books* noted that Abigail's "vulnerability and her poignantly, desperately upbeat letters home will engender reader sympathy and understanding." *Booklist* reviewer Stephanie Zvirin praised Vail for once again being "right on target when it comes to the reality of preadolescent girls, catching how they act and what they say, their nastiness and envy and sweetness, and how confusing it is to long for independence, yet be afraid of the freedom and responsibility that come with it." Lauren Adams, reviewing *Daring to Be Abigail* for *Horn Book,* commented: "As in her other books, Vail displays her talent for capturing the humor and angst of early adolescence; this latest novel ... is her most sophisticated yet."

■ Works Cited

Abbott, Deborah, review of *Wonder, Booklist,* September 1, 1991, p. 54.

Adams, Lauren, review of *Daring to Be Abigail, Horn Book,* May-June, 1996, pp. 337-39.

Review of *Ever After, Kirkus Reviews,* April 1, 1994, pp. 486.

Review of *Ever After, Publishers Weekly,* February 21, 1994, pp. 255-56.

Fader, Ellen, review of *Ever After, School Library Journal,* May, 1994, p. 136.

Gold, Debra S., review of *Wonder, School Library Journal,* August, 1991, p. 196.

Rochman, Hazel, review of *Ever After, Booklist,* March 1, 1994, p. 1254.

Rose, Jacqueline, review of *Do-Over, School Library Journal,* September, 1992, p. 282.

Stevenson, Deborah, review of *Daring to Be Abigail, Bulletin of the Center for Children's Books,* February, 1996, p. 207.

Sutton, Roger, review of *Do-Over, Bulletin of the Center for Children's Books,* December, 1992, pp. 125-26.

Vail, Rachel, "Making Stories Happen," *Horn Book,* May-June, 1994, pp. 301-04.

Review of *Wonder, Kirkus Reviews,* August 8, 1991, p. 1095.

Zvirin, Stephanie, review of *Do-Over, Booklist,* August, 1992, p. 2013.

Zvirin, Stephanie, review of *Daring to Be Abigail,* *Booklist,* March 1, 1996, p. 1184.

■ For More Information See

BOOKS

Seventh Book of Junior Authors and Illustrators, H. W. Wilson, 1996, pp. 323-24.

PERIODICALS

Bulletin of the Center for Children's Books, September, 1991, p. 24.
Horn Book, November-December, 1992, p. 731.
Kirkus Reviews, July 15, 1992, p. 927.
Publishers Weekly, August 9, 1991, p. 58; December 20, 1991, p. 24.
School Library Journal, March, 1996, p. 198.

* * *

VICKERS, Sheena 1960-

■ Personal

Born January 14, 1960, in Durham City, England; daughter of William Forster and Elizabeth (Henderson) Dawson; married James Vickers (a graphic artist). *Education:* Bath Lane Art School, National Diploma in Applied Design and H.N.D., 1982. *Hobbies and other interests:* Walking (Northumberland coastline and Scotland), movies, reading, watercolors, blues music, art galleries.

■ Addresses

Home and office—248 Whitehorse Lane, Sth., Norwood, London, England.

■ Career

Yellow Hammer Studio, London, England, storyboard illustrator, 1982-85; freelance illustrator, 1985—. Designer for Pinewood and Disney film studios in England, 1992-96; creator of children's educational comics.

■ Illustrator

"TIME TREKKERS" SERIES; WITH DAVE BURROUGHS

Antony Mason, *The Time Trekkers Visit the Romans,* Aladdin/Watts, 1995, Copper Beech Books, 1995.
Kate Rignell, *The Time Trekkers Visit the Dinosaurs,* Aladdin/Watts, 1995, Copper Beech Books, 1995.
Antony Mason, *The Time Trekkers Visit the Stone Age,* Aladdin/Watts, 1996, Copper Beech Books, 1996.
Kate Rignell, *The Time Trekkers Visit the Middle Ages,* Aladdin/Watts, 1996, Copper Beech Books, 1996.

■ Work in Progress

Research on world mythology, concentrating on monster and hero/heroine stories.

SHEENA VICKERS

■ Sidelights

Sheena Vickers told *SATA:* "I have always been interested in ancient history and have been lucky enough to visit and live among people of different cultures. I enjoyed researching and illustrating the 'time trekkers' books. They contain a lot of detailed information, as well as a fast-moving time travel story line.

"I think children have a special capacity to take in a lot of detail, if it is presented in an interesting or unusual way. I believe these books not only give the details of events, places, and dates, but they also conjure up the sights, sounds, and smells of the period."*

* * *

VIGLIANTE, Mary
See SZYDLOWSKI, Mary Vigliante

* * *

VOGT, Gregory L.

■ Personal

Born in Milwaukee, WI. *Education:* B.S., M.S., University of Wisconsin at Milwaukee; Ed.D., Oklahoma State University.

■ Career

Writer. National Aeronautics and Space Administration (NASA), aerospace education specialist. Has worked as an eighth-grade science teacher; adjunct assistant professor, Oklahoma State University; educational consultant, National Wildlife Federation; writer/editor, Educational Publications at NASA. Formerly served as executive director of the Discovery World Museum of Science, Economics and Technology in Milwaukee, WI.

■ Writings

Mars and the Inner Planets, Franklin Watts, 1982.
Model Rockets, illustrated by Anne Canevari Green, F. Watts, 1982.
The Space Shuttle, F. Watts, 1983.
A Twenty-Fifth Anniversary Album of NASA, F. Watts, 1983.
Electricity and Magnetism, F. Watts, 1985.
Generating Electricity, F. Watts, 1986.
An Album of Modern Spaceships, F. Watts, 1987.
Halley's Comet: What We've Learned, F. Watts, 1987.
Space Satellites, F. Watts, 1987.
Space Walking, F. Watts, 1987.
Predicting Earthquakes, F. Watts, 1989.
Spaceships, F. Watts, 1989.
Predicting Volcanic Eruptions, F. Watts, 1989.
Space Laboratories, F. Watts, 1989.
Space Explorers, F. Watts, 1990.
Space Stations, F. Watts, 1990.
Forests on Fire: The Fight to Save Our Trees, F. Watts, 1990.
Apollo and the Moon Landing, Millbrook Press, 1991.
Voyager, Millbrook Press, 1991.
Viking and the Mars Landing, Millbrook Press, 1991.
The Hubble Space Telescope, Millbrook Press, 1992.
Magellan and the Radar Mapping of Venus, Millbrook Press, 1992.
Jupiter, Millbrook Press, 1993.
Volcanoes, F. Watts, 1993.
Neptune, Millbrook Press, 1993.
Saturn, Millbrook Press, 1993.
Uranus, Millbrook Press, 1993.
Mars, Millbrook Press, 1994.
Venus, Millbrook Press, 1994.
Pluto, Millbrook Press, 1994.
Mercury, Millbrook Press, 1994.
The Search for the Killer Asteroid, Millbrook Press, 1994.
The Solar System: Facts and Exploration, Twenty-First Century, 1995.
Space Exploration Projects for Young Scientists, F. Watts, 1995.
Asteroids, Comets, and Meteors, Millbrook Press, 1996.
The Sun, Millbrook Press, 1996.
Earth, Millbrook Press, 1996.

■ Sidelights

An aerospace education specialist, Gregory L. Vogt is the author of several books for young people that focus on scientific topics, particularly as they relate to outer

Gregory L. Vogt traces the *Apollo* project from its inception to the moon landing and explains the importance of earlier, preparatory space projects. (From *Apollo and the Moon Landing.*)

space and exploration. For his broad overviews of our solar system and in-depth studies of each planet that comprises it, Vogt has also drawn together information regarding such fascinating earthbound occurrences as volcanos and earthquakes, continuing to spark young imaginations with an interest in science.

Vogt begins to discuss the laws of physics that will fuel his later books on space exploration in 1983's *Model Rockets,* which, although relatively advanced in its technical approach to the subject, was praised by *School Library Journal* reviewer Patricia Homer as "a worthwhile book covering information in a new and interesting way and attempting not only to instruct but to demonstrate." Vogt's other early books for children include *Electricity and Magnetism* and *Generating Electricity,* part of Franklin Watts' "First Book" series of science studies. In *Electricity and Magnetism,* Vogt shows the relationship between the two physical properties, detailing the structure of atoms and tracing the history of experimentation that has led to today's technological advances in these areas. Floyd D. Jury, in his review in *Science Books and Films,* credits Vogt with "reviving some of the mysteries of these fundamental forces of nature that have fascinated inquiring minds for centuries." *Generating Electricity* discusses both the history of society's use of electricity and the development of alternative energy sources in the second half of the twentieth century. To illustrate many of the concepts covered in his book, Vogt includes easy-to-perform experiments, "an inclusion that students should find useful," according to a *Booklist* reviewer.

Vogt has worked as a science teacher, curriculum writer, planetarium lecturer, and as educational consultant to NASA and the National Wildlife Federation. His expertise in the areas of astronomy led to *Mars and the Inner Planets,* the first of many works Vogt has compiled on the Earth's planetary environs. *Mars and the Inner Planets* provides introductions to Mercury, Venus, and Mars, focusing on the astronomer's interest in the planets that surround us and separate us from the sun, theories about the origins of the solar system and each planet's capacity for life, as well as on technological developments that have refuted such theories. Vogt has expanded readers' understanding of each of the planets in our solar system in his works for Millbrook Press's "Gateway Solar System" series, published between 1993 and 1996. In these books Vogt ventures to Jupiter, Saturn, Uranus, Neptune, Pluto, and the Sun itself, exhibiting his characteristic "grasp of matters astronomical with a precise but not overwhelming array of facts, presented in a lively way," according to *School Library Journal* reviewer John Peters. Each of the series' titles includes numerous illustrations, charts, and photographs, a list of sources for further reading, a glossary of terms, and a page of "Quick Facts" about the planet studied, including such information as its distance from the sun, orbital speed, and revolution and rotational periods, all in relation to the earth. A related volume, *Asteroids, Comets, and Meteors,* features recent discoveries of these relatively minute members of our solar system and includes several photographs of asteroids from the Galileo space probe and a discussion of the fragmented comet that collided with Jupiter in 1994.

The topics of the majority of Vogt's books for young readers reflect his interest in the history of the U.S. space program, as well as in the science of aeronautics. In Franklin Watts' "Space Library" series, he focuses on a variety of space-related topics, including *Space Satellites, Space Walking,* and *Space Stations. Space Walking* is devoted to the technological development of both U.S. and Soviet space suits and the training needed to use them. Vogt includes coverage of past space walks as well as plans for future excursions outside spaceships, illustrating his text with numerous full-color photographs. While noting that several books are available on similar topics, Sylvia S. Marantz maintained in *School Library Journal* that none focus "on this specific subject with this coverage and appeal." *Space Explorers* ranges from early dreams of finding men on Mars to the possibility of an expedition to the red planet in the coming century, while *Space Laboratories* engages young readers interested in the history of the Mir space station and Skylab, both volumes through the use of large, colorful formats and "pithy texts," according to *Booklist* reviewer Carolyn Phelan.

Vogt gives full rein to his interest in manned space travel in his contributions to Millbrook Press's "Missions in Space" series. In *Apollo and the Moon Landing,* he begins with President John F. Kennedy's 1961 declaration of intent to land a man on the moon within ten years, and then recounts the *Apollo* project up until the *Apollo 11* mission landed on the Moon in July of 1969 and astronauts Neil Armstrong and Buzz Aldrin became the first men to set foot on the lunar surface. Also including coverage of the preparatory *Mercury* and *Gemini* projects, Vogt includes a timeline of U.S. space flights, as well as a glossary, index, and bibliography. "The author's enthusiasm for his subject and his experience as an educator are evident in his writing," maintained *Appraisal* contributor Maria B. Salvadore, who praised *Apollo and the Moon Landing* for its ability to lead interested young people to further study. Other volumes in the "Missions in Space" series include *Voyager, The Space Shuttle,* and *Magellan and the Radar Mapping of Venus,* which focuses not only on the *Magellan* project, but on earlier flybys by the *Mariner* spacecraft, as well as a Soviet landing by the *Vega* aircraft.

From beyond the clouds, Vogt also comes back to ground zero in several books for young readers that focus on the workings of our home planet. In *Predicting Earthquakes,* he covers several recent temblors, discussing the causes of the earth's sudden movements as they result from continental drift and subduction, while explaining to readers how relatively unpredictable earth tremors can be measured through seismographs to determine their origins and intensity. A related volume, *Predicting Volcanic Eruptions,* brings to life the disasters at Mt. Pelee in 1902 and Mt. St. Helens in 1980 while including a "clear, well-ordered, technical explanation" of each phenomenon, according to *Appraisal* reviewer Helen T. Browne, who commended both volumes for instilling in readers "a healthy regard for the damage each [disaster] can cause." Vogt concentrates more on biological rather than geological matters in 1990's *Forests on Fire: The Fight to Save Our Trees,* as he discusses the role fire plays in a forest ecosystem. Beginning with the great Yellowstone fire of 1988, he examines fire prevention, fire-control techniques, governmental policies as they pertain to large forested areas, and the controversies raging between environmentalists and the National Park Service, which operates under the policy of letting fires go their natural course. Vogt's presentation of the treatment of fire within the U.S. forest system renders it "accessible not only to teens, but to anyone needing a clear exposition of this complex topic," noted Meryl Silverstein in a *School Library Journal* review.

∎ Works Cited

Browne, Helen T., review of *Predicting Earthquakes, Appraisal,* autumn, 1990, pp. 70-71.

Review of *Generating Electricity, Booklist,* March 15, 1986, p. 1088.

Homer, Patricia, review of *Model Rockets, School Library Journal,* January, 1983, p. 74.

Jury, Floyd D., review of *Electricity and Magnetism, Science Books and Films,* May-June, 1986, p. 313.

Marantz, Sylvia S., review of *Space Walking, School Library Journal,* March, 1988, p. 211.

Peters, John, review of *Neptune, Saturn,* and *Uranus, School Library Journal,* November, 1993, p. 121.

Phelan, Carolyn, review of *Space Laboratories, Booklist,* May 15, 1990, p. 1808.

Salvadore, Maria B., review of *Apollo and the Moon Landing, Appraisal,* autumn, 1991, pp. 92-93.

Silverstein, Meryl, review of *Forests on Fire: The Fight to Save Our Trees, School Library Journal,* December, 1990, p. 134.

■ For More Information See

PERIODICALS

Appraisal, fall, 1993, pp. 58-59; spring-summer, 1995, pp. 55-56; winter-spring, 1996, pp. 84-85.

Booklist, July, 1982, p. 1446; January 1, 1983, p. 608; May 15, 1986, p. 1228; January 15, 1988, p. 871; January 1, 1990, pp. 918-19; July, 1990, p. 2096; November 1, 1990, p. 514; March 1, 1991, p. 1376; July, 1994, p. 1992; December 1, 1994, p. 672; December 1, 1995, p. 626.

Kirkus Reviews, February 1, 1991, p. 178.

School Library Journal, February, 1986, p. 91; May, 1986, pp. 110-11; February, 1988, p. 83; January, 1990, p. 125; December, 1991, p. 131; October, 1992, pp. 147-48; May, 1994, p. 127; May, 1996, pp. 127-28; July, 1996, p. 97.*

Science Books and Film, May-June, 1983, pp. 272-73; September-October, 1984, p. 28; November-December, 1986, p. 110; September-October, 1988, p. 35; November-December, 1990, p. 126; October, 1991, p. 213; October, 1992, p. 207; January-February, 1994, pp. 15-16; December, 1995, pp. 267-68.

W

NEIL WALDMAN

WALDMAN, Neil 1947-

■ Personal

Born October 22, 1947, in Bronx, NY; son of Abraham (a businessman) and Jessie (Herstein) Waldman; married Jeri Socol (an elementary schoolteacher), December 20, 1972 (divorced 1988); children: Sarah, Jonathan. *Education:* Rochester Institute of Technology, B.F.A., 1969, M.A., 1970. *Politics:* Liberal. *Religion:* Jewish Reformed. *Hobbies and other interests:* Chess, guitar, classical music, travel, softball.

■ Addresses

Home—54 Rockinchair Rd., White Plains, NY 10607.

■ Career

Writer, artist and illustrator. Freelance illustrator, 1973—; children's book illustrator, 1988—. Has worked as package designer, art teacher, and border guard. Olive farmer in Israel, 1970-73, 1975-76; Linbry Products, Yonkers, NY, art director, 1971; member of faculty, William Paterson College of New Jersey, 1980-81; designer of postage stamps (for governments of Sierra Leone, Grenada, and Antigua), record album covers, book dust covers, and theater posters. *Exhibitions:* Artwork exhibited at galleries in the state of New York, including the Society of Illustrators, New York City. *Member:* Graphic Artists Guild.

■ Awards, Honors

Desi Award, 1980, for a poster for Sylvania; nominated for Grammy Awards from National Academy of Recording Arts and Sciences, 1982 and 1983, for record cover designs; United Nations Poster Award for International Year of Peace, 1986; Parents' Choice Award for storybook, 1990, for *Nessa's Fish;* Washington Irving Award for illustration, 1990, for *Bring Back the Deer,* and 1992, for *The Highwayman;* Christopher Award (ages 8-10), 1991, for *The Gold Coin.*

■ Writings

SELF-ILLUSTRATED

Pitcher in Left Field, Prentice-Hall, 1981.
(And editor) Edgar Allan Poe, *Tales of Terror: Ten Short Stories,* Prentice-Hall, 1985.
The Golden City: Jerusalem's 3000 Years, Atheneum, 1995.
The Never-Ending Greenness, Morrow, 1997.
The Two Brothers: A Legend of Jerusalem, Atheneum, 1997.

ILLUSTRATOR

Walter Harter, *Osceola's Head and Other Ghost Stories,* Prentice-Hall, 1974.

David C. Knight, *The Moving Coffins: Ghosts and Hauntings Around the World,* Prentice-Hall, 1983.

Patricia T. Lowe, *The Runt,* Caedmon, 1984.

Michael Mark, *Toba,* Bradbury, 1984.

David C. Knight, editor, *Best True Ghost Stories of the Twentieth Century,* Prentice-Hall, 1984.

Lee P. Huntington, *Maybe a Miracle,* Coward, 1984.

William Warren, *The Headless Ghost: True Tales of the Unexplained,* Prentice-Hall, 1986.

William Warren, *The Screaming Skull: True Tales of the Unexplained,* Prentice-Hall, 1987.

Jeffrey Prusski, *Bring Back the Deer,* Gulliver/Harcourt, 1988.

(With Bryna Waldman) Sarah Leiberman, *A Trip to Mezuzah Land,* Merkos L'inyonei Chinuch, 1988.

Robert Orkand, *Gates of Wonder: A Prayerbook for Very Young Children,* Central Conference of American Rabbis, 1989.

Mark D. Shapiro, *Gates of Shabbat: Shaarei Shabbat: A New Shabbat Manual for the 1990s,* Central Conference of American Rabbis, 1990.

Alfred Noyes, *The Highwayman,* Harcourt, 1990.

Betty Boegehold, *A Horse Called Starfire,* Bantam, 1990.

Nancy Luenn, *Nessa's Fish,* Atheneum, 1990.

Robert Orkand, Howard Bogot, and Joyce Orkand, *Gates of Awe: Holy Day Prayers for Young Children,* Central Conference of American Rabbis, 1991.

Alma Flor Ada, *The Gold Coin,* Atheneum, 1991.

Ken Kesey, *The Sea Lion: A Story of the Cliff People,* Viking, 1991.

Nancy Luenn, *Mother Earth,* Atheneum, 1992.

William Blake, *The Tyger,* Harcourt, 1993.

Katharine Lee Bates, *America the Beautiful,* Atheneum, 1993.

Sarah Waldman, *Light: The First Seven Days,* Harcourt, 1993.

Nancy Luenn, *Nessa's Story,* Atheneum, 1994.

Barbara Diamond Goldin, *The Passover Journey: A Seder Companion,* Viking, 1994.

Chaim Stern, editor, *On the Doorposts of Your Hose: A Mezuzot Beitecha—Prayers and Ceremonies for the Jewish Home, Hebrew Opening,* Central Conference of American Rabbis, 1994.

Kathi Appelt, *Bayou Lullaby,* Morrow, 1995.

Howard Schwartz, *Next Year in Jerusalem: 3000 Years of Jewish Stories,* Viking Penguin, 1996.

Shulamith Levey Oppenheim, *And the Earth Trembled: The Creation of Adam and Eve,* Harcourt, 1996.

Dorothy Hinshaw Patent, *Quetzal: Sacred Bird of the Cloud Forest,* Morrow, 1996.

■ Sidelights

Neil Waldman once told *SATA:* "I was raised in a house where all the arts were encouraged. I sensed, as a small child, that finger paints and coloring books were more than just fun. They were important tools that led to a road of joy, discovery, and fulfillment.

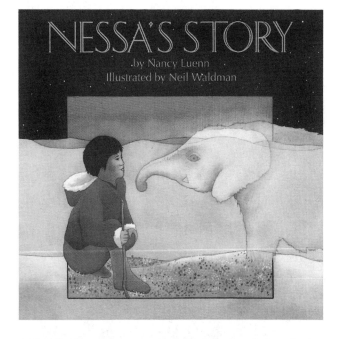

Nessa's Story **portrays an Inuit girl who learns from her grandmother how to participate in the cultural tradition of storytelling.**

"When I entered first grade, I learned very quickly that, within the classroom walls, the arts were 'secondary subjects,' not nearly as important as reading, math and science. I resented this deeply, and unconsciously began to rebel. Through twelve years of school I was considered an 'underachiever.' In fact, I was doing the minimum possible to get by, while working on my art at home.

"When I graduated from high school (near the bottom of my class), I felt as though I had been liberated. I entered an art college, where I spent most of my time drawing and painting. Here, surrounded by other artists for the first time, I began to blossom. Though I'd always known that art was important too, now it was reinforced in my environment. Instead of struggling against the current, I was gliding freely, ever faster and deeper, to places I had never imagined."

Waldman studied illustration and painting at Rochester Institute of Technology. "During and after college there was never a plan for my life," the artist told John Dalmas in the *Sunday Journal-News* (Rockland County, NY). "I wanted to travel since I was a kid and I always wanted to draw and paint. It just never occurred to me I would end up doing what I like for a living." After graduation, Waldman added, "I began to work as an illustrator. This seemed a natural decision, because it would allow me to do what I love most, while earning a living. It was difficult at first, almost like learning a new language. But it was worth it."

Early in his illustration career, Waldman designed postage stamps for Sierra Leone, Granada, Antigua, and many other countries, and won the competition for the U.N. poster representing the International Year of

In *Next Year in Jerusalem: 3000 Years of Jewish Stories,* Howard Schwartz compiles folktales, fairy tales, and legends about the city of Jerusalem and explains the historical significance of the enchanted caves in the story of Joshua depicted here. (Illustrated by Waldman.)

Peace in 1986. He also designed book jackets and magazine covers, but never considered illustrating children's literature until an editor at Gulliver Books approached him about working on a book entitled *Bring Back the Deer,* by Jeffrey Prusski. Illustrating that book changed Waldman's life. Erin Gathrid, the editor at Gulliver, chose Waldman because she had been drawn to work she had seen by him, and felt that it had the same mystical quality as the manuscript for *Bring Back the Deer.* Initially Waldman refused, but Gathrid talked him into reading the manuscript at least five times before he made a decision.

Bring Back the Deer is the story of a young Native American boy's search for identity. When his father goes to hunt for food and doesn't return, the boy follows after him, and in the process discovers the animal spirit inside himself. Waldman recalled for *SATA:* "As I began to read, I felt like I was entering a dark winding cave. By the time I finished reading, I was totally confused. The story left me feeling that I had missed something. If I hadn't promised to read it five times, I would never have looked at it again. But then a strange thing happened. On my second reading, a few things were revealed to me that had escaped me the first time. And when I read it again, I saw even more. By the fifth time, not only did I begin to appreciate it . . . I began to love it."

Though he had never worked on a children's picture book before, he agreed to handle the project. After weeks of difficulty finding the right images, Waldman arranged to meet with Gathrid and Prusski in New York City. Prusski told Waldman of his experience with Shamanism, and how a Native American spirit had written the story through him. "As Jeff continued speaking, I felt myself being transported back . . . back . . . back into the story. Images began flooding my brain. I opened my napkin and began scribbling on it. When I got home later that afternoon, I unfolded the napkin and began to study it. One of my scribblings was the image of two rectangles, one inside the other. I envisioned the main subject of each page within the smaller rectangle, with secondary subjects floating around it. The larger rectangle became the frame for each page. The color within the smaller rectangle would be very bright, to focus the viewer's attention on the central image." After discovering the boy and the grandfather in the tale, "the paintings were flowing effortlessly. Each image was like a roadsign, directing me to whatever came next. I created a tribe, with its own special clothing, dwellings, environment, and even its own language of pictographs. It was as if I was constructing an entire world, which I lived in as I continued to paint."

"I painted intensely for two months," Waldman continued, "and when I finished the book it was clear that my life had changed forever. I knew that I wouldn't be working for advertising agencies or design studios anymore. I wanted to do more picture books. I had tiptoed through the window, and my path lay clearly before me. Like a many colored fan, my life was unfolding before my eyes, revealing colors I had never even dreamed of." A *Publishers Weekly* critic praised Waldman's "splendid debut" in *Bring Back the Deer,* noting that his illustrations "have a lyrical quality that is haunting." Since 1988, when *Bring Back the Deer* was published, Waldman has worked exclusively on children's literature, having illustrated numerous picture books and dust jackets, including seven Newbery or Newbery Honor winners. The book prompted changes in Waldman's personal life as well, as he decided to leave his marriage and embark on a journey of self-discovery.

In 1990, Waldman brought his artistic vision to Alfred Noyes' famous poem *The Highwayman,* which had recently been illustrated twice: once by Charles Mikolaycak and once by Charles Keeping. Unlike his predecessors, Waldman brought a broad palette to the poem, prompting Roger Sutton of the *Bulletin of the Center for Children's Books* to observe: "[Waldman's] colors are often unlikely—plenty of aqua and magenta—but surprisingly effective, as in a moody painting of the highwayman upon his horse, a study in blue and black and gray." A *Publishers Weekly* reviewer characterized Waldman's style in *The Highwayman* as "both abstract and realistic," adding that his watercolors "capture the haunting, tragic spirit of the text." Eleanor K. MacDonald, writing for *School Library Journal,* praised the effect of Waldman's artwork, stating that "the strong sense of atmosphere and dramatic use of design reinforce the melodrama of the story."

In 1993, Waldman illustrated another classic poem, this time William Blake's *The Tyger.* In her *School Library Journal* review, Ruth K. MacDonald described Waldman's acrylic artwork as "modern, highly painterly, and formal." The final picture is a fold-out spread of the "tyger" that covers four pages, with each of the pages leading up to it featuring a section of the larger picture, each reproduced in black and shades of gray. MacDonald stated that "the focus on individual portions of the whole gives readers an opportunity to study *The Tyger* carefully, and to discuss the artist's interpretation."

Nessa's Story, by Nancy Luenn, is the story of an Inuit girl who learns from her grandmother how to participate in the cultural tradition of storytelling. *Booklist* contributor Isabel Schon asserted that Waldman's "original, luminous watercolor paintings," which use a wide range of settings, "are the best part of this story." *School Library Journal* contributor Roz Goodman noted that the "soft, cool colors in a variety of pastel pinks, blues, purples, greens, and browns blend into scenes both realistic and imaginary."

In *Booklist,* Stephanie Zvirin described *The Passover Journey: A Seder Companion* as "a beautiful wedding of the work of two talented individuals" that is "exquisitely designed." Author Barbara Diamond Goldin describes the history behind the Jewish holiday of Passover, and the symbolism behind the Seder meal, eaten in remembrance of the Jews' freedom from slavery in Egypt. Waldman's interpretation of this text features the "geometric borders and pastels characteristic of [his] work" according to Zvirin, and are combined with "stylized classic Egyptian hieroglyphic figures and set against softly tinted pages that actually glow." Hanna B. Zeiger, writing for *Horn Book,* commented that "the page design and stylized illustrations, in pleasing soft pastel colors, help make this book a welcome addition to holiday literature."

Waldman followed his work on *The Passover Journey* with another Jewish-themed book the following year, writing and illustrating *The Golden City: Jerusalem's 3000 Years. School Library Journal* contributor Susan Scheps noted that the book "successfully introduces the panorama of religions and cultures that have formed the city's heritage and created its mystique." A *Kirkus Reviews* critic, on the other hand, maintained that the writing "often overly romanticizes and is entirely subjective about a topic few people can approach objectively." Both reviewers, however, praised Waldman's watercolor and pencil illustrations featuring architecturally accurate portraits of Jerusalem during various time periods in its three-thousand-year history.

In 1995, Waldman lent his talents to a story written by Kathi Appelt, *Bayou Lullaby.* Judy Constantinides, writing in *School Library Journal,* commented that while the verse of this Cajun lullaby is enjoyable, "the true merit of the book lies in Waldman's double-page

acrylic paintings." Waldman's figures are stylized and his palette includes rich jewel tones set against a black background. A *Publishers Weekly* reviewer called *Bayou Lullaby* "an inspired pairing of author and artist."

Turning his attention once again to Jewish themes, Waldman teamed with reteller Howard Schwartz to create a collection of Jewish folktales entitled *Next Year in Jerusalem: 3000 Years of Jewish Stories.* The tales are taken in part from the Talmud and Midrash, some from folklore, and others from mystical or Hasidic sources. Marcia W. Posner wrote in *School Library Journal* that "Waldman has suffused the pages with the peach-colored dawns, golden sunlit days, and turquoise and lavender twilights of Jerusalem." In *Horn Book,* Hanna B. Zeiger observed that "Waldman's watercolor illustrations enhance the handsomely produced volume."

Two more books illustrated by Waldman and published in 1996 deal with ancient myth. *Quetzal: Sacred Bird of the Cloud Forest,* by Dorothy Hinshaw Patent, draws upon Mexican myths of the beautiful bird which inhabits the cloud forests of Mexico and Central America. Waldman employed colored pencil on tinted paper for his illustrations, which according to *School Library Journal* contributor Pam Gosner "are quite lovely, with rich glowing tones." For Shulamith Levey Oppenheim's book *And the Earth Trembled,* based on a traditional Islamic tale of creation, Waldman used the technique of

Waldman's illustration portrays the meeting of Cortes and Moctezuma in Dorothy Hinshaw Patent's depiction of the legend and natural history of the quetzal. (From *Quetzal: Sacred Bird of the Cloud Forest.*)

In his self-illustrated 1997 story, Waldman depicts the beginnings of the reforestation of the Judean hills through the efforts of one young boy who arrives in Israel after escaping the Nazis at the end of World War II. (From *The Never-Ending Greenness*.)

pointillism, which Patricia Lothrop regarded in *School Library Journal* as "well suited to his subject." Lothrop continued: "The pages are brightly colored, the image of the Ibis is appropriately scary, and Paradise is a vision of order in green and blue."

In 1997, Waldman wrote and illustrated another book, *The Never-Ending Greenness*, a story of holocaust survival. In this work, the Jewish narrator reflects on his childhood as he recalls being exiled to a ghetto along with his family at the hands of Nazi soldiers. The family escapes to the surrounding forest, and the boy later realizes his dream of planting trees in Israel. Waldman's story is told in simple language, and his illustrations feature his characteristic stylized palette, utilizing bright blue, orange, pink, and turquoise. A *Publishers Weekly* critic noted that the "reference to Tu b'Shvat ... might commend the book to families who observe that holiday." Betsy Hearne of the *Bulletin of the Center for Children's Books* called *The Never-Ending Greenness* "perfectly paced as an unfolding of personalized history reflected in a life cycle like an unfolding of leaves." Hearne added that the "intensity of the boy's project is magnetic enough to build a bridge of identification with today's young listeners."

■ **Works Cited**

Review of *Bayou Lullaby, Publishers Weekly,* February 13, 1995, p. 77.

Review of *Bring Back the Deer, Publishers Weekly,* October 14, 1988, pp. 71-2.

Constantinides, Judy, review of *Bayou Lullaby, School Library Journal,* April, 1995, p. 97.

Dalmas, John, "Neil Waldman: He Has Designs on Postage Stamps," *Sunday Journal-News* (Rockland County, NY), December 30, 1984.

Review of *The Golden City: Jerusalem's 3000 Years, Kirkus Reviews,* August 1, 1995, p. 1118.

Goodman, Roz, review of *Nessa's Story, School Library Journal,* April, 1994, p. 108.

Gosner, Pam, review of *Quetzal: Sacred Bird of the Cloud Forest, School Library Journal,* October, 1996, p. 138.

Hearne, Betsy, review of *The Never-Ending Greenness, Bulletin of the Center for Children's Books,* June, 1997, pp. 347-48.

Review of *The Highwayman, Publishers Weekly,* September 14, 1990, p. 124.

Lothrop, Patricia (Dooley), review of *And the Earth Trembled: The Creation of Adam and Eve, School Library Journal,* September, 1996, p. 219.

MacDonald, Eleanor K., review of *The Highwayman, School Library Journal,* December, 1990, p. 118.

MacDonald, Ruth K., review of *The Tyger, School Library Journal,* January, 1994, p. 118.

Review of *The Never-Ending Greenness, Publishers Weekly,* February 3, 1997, p. 107.

Posner, Marcia W., review of *Next Year in Jerusalem: 3000 Years of Jewish Stories, School Library Journal,* January, 1996, p. 125.

Scheps, Susan, review of *The Golden City: Jerusalem's 3000 Years, School Library Journal,* November, 1995, p. 94.

Schon, Isabel, review of *Nessa's Story, Booklist,* February 1, 1995, p. 1012.

Sutton, Roger, review of *The Highwayman, Bulletin of the Center for Children's Books,* December, 1990, pp. 95-96.

Zeiger, Hanna B., review of *The Passover Journey: A Seder Companion, Horn Book,* May-June, 1994, p. 334.

Zeiger, Hanna B., review of *Next Year in Jerusalem: 3000 Years of Jewish Stories, Horn Book,* July-August, 1996, p. 472.

Zvirin, Stephanie, review of *The Passover Journey: A Seder Companion, Booklist,* March 1, 1994, p. 1260.*

—*Sketch by Maria Sheler-Edwards*

*   *   *

WASSERSTEIN, Wendy 1950-

■ **Personal**

Born October 18, 1950, in Brooklyn, NY; daughter of Morris W. (a textile manufacturer) and Lola (a dancer;

maiden name, Schleifer) Wasserstein. *Education:* Mount Holyoke College, B.A., 1971; City College of the City University of New York, M.A., 1973; Yale University Drama School, M.F.A., 1976.

■ Addresses

Home—New York, NY. *Agent*—Royce Carlton Inc., 866 United Nations Plaza, Suite 4030, New York, NY 10017.

■ Career

Dramatist and screenwriter. Teacher at Columbia University and New York University, New York City. Actress in plays, including *The Hotel Play,* 1981. Member of artistic board of Playwrights Horizons. *Member:* Dramatists Guild (member of steering committee and women's committee), British American Arts Association (board member), Dramatists Guild for Young Playwrights; WNET (board member), McDowell Colony (board member).

■ Awards, Honors

Joseph Jefferson Award, Dramalogue Award, and Inner Boston Critics Award, all for *Uncommon Women and Others;* grant for playwriting from Playwrights Commissioning Program of Phoenix Theater, c. 1970s; Hale Mathews Foundation Award; Guggenheim fellowship, 1983; grant for writing and for studying theater in England from British-American Arts Association; grant for playwriting from American Playwrights Project, 1988; Pulitzer Prize for drama, Antoinette Perry Award

WENDY WASSERSTEIN

(Tony) for best play from League of American Theatres and Producers, Drama Desk Award, Outer Critics Circle Award, Susan Smith Blackburn Prize, and award for best new play from New York Drama Critics' Circle, all 1989, all for *The Heidi Chronicles;* Outer Critics' Circle Award, 1993, for *The Sisters Rosensweig.*

■ Writings

FOR CHILDREN

Pamela's First Musical, illustrated by Andrew Jackness, Hyperion, 1996.

PLAYS

Any Woman Can't, produced Off Broadway at Playwrights Horizons, 1973.

Happy Birthday, Montpelier Pizz-zazz, produced in New Haven, CT, 1974.

(With Christopher Durang) *When Dinah Shore Ruled the Earth,* first produced in New Haven, CT, at Yale Cabaret Theater, 1975.

Uncommon Women and Others (also see below; first produced as a one-act in New Haven, CT, 1975; revised and enlarged two-act version produced Off Broadway by Phoenix Theater at Marymount Manhattan Theater, November 21, 1977), Avon (New York City), 1978.

Isn't It Romantic (also see below; first produced Off Broadway by Phoenix Theater at Marymount Manhattan Theater, June 13, 1981; revised version first produced Off Broadway at Playwrights Horizons, December 15, 1983), Nelson Doubleday, 1984.

Tender Offer (one-act), first produced Off-Off Broadway at Ensemble Studio Theatre, 1983.

The Man in a Case (one-act; adapted from the short story of the same title by Anton Chekhov), written as part of *Orchards* (anthology of seven one-act plays, all adapted from short stories by Chekhov; produced Off Broadway by the Acting Company at Lucille Lortel Theater, April 22, 1986), Knopf (New York City), 1986.

Miami (musical), first produced Off Broadway at Playwrights Horizons, January, 1986.

The Heidi Chronicles (also see below; produced Off Broadway at Playwrights Horizons, December 11, 1988, produced on Broadway at Plymouth Theatre, March 9, 1989), Dramatists Play Service (New York City), 1990.

The Heidi Chronicles and Other Plays (contains *Uncommon Women and Others, Isn't It Romanic,* and *The Heidi Chronicles*), Harcourt (San Diego), 1990.

The Sisters Rosensweig (produced at Mitzi E. Newhouse Theater, Lincoln Center, October 22, 1992), Harcourt (New York City), 1993.

SCREENPLAYS; FOR TELEVISION

Uncommon Women and Others (adapted from Wasserstein's play of the same title; also see above), Public Broadcasting Service (PBS), 1978.

The Sorrows of Gin (adapted from the short story of the same title by John Cheever), PBS, 1979.

Also author of *'Drive,' She Said*, PBS, and of sketches for the series *Comedy Zone*, CBS-TV, 1984.

OTHER

Bachelor Girls (comic essays), Knopf, 1990.

Author of unproduced film scripts, including (with Christopher Durang) "House of Husbands," adapted from the short story "Husbands"; and a script adapted from the novel *The Object of My Affection* by Stephen McCauley. Contributor of articles to periodicals, including *Esquire*, *New York Times*, and *New York Woman*. Contributing editor, *New York Woman*.

■ Sidelights

In her best-known plays—*Uncommon Women and Others, Isn't It Romantic*, and *The Heidi Chronicles*—dramatist Wendy Wasserstein spotlights college-educated women of the postwar baby boom, who came of age in the late 1960s as feminism was redefining American society. Such women, she suggests, have been torn between a newfound spirit of independence and the traditional values of marriage and motherhood that they were taught as children. Wasserstein has held the attention of theater critics since the late 1970s, when *Uncommon Women* opened to favorable reviews in New York City; in 1989, she received the Pulitzer Prize in drama for *The Heidi Chronicles*. Her first work for children, the picture book *Pamela's First Musical*, invites readers to see Broadway through the eyes of a child.

Born into a New York City family in 1950, Wasserstein attended a series of young women's schools, including the elite Mount Holyoke College, that were marked by social conservatism. She rebelled against the schools' traditions of propriety, preferring instead to cultivate a lively sense of humor. Later, Wasserstein enrolled in graduate courses at New York's City University, studying creative writing under playwright Israel Horovitz and novelist Joseph Heller before gaining a master's degree in 1973. That same year marked Wasserstein's first professional production: *Any Woman Can't*, a bitter farce about a woman's efforts to dance her way to success in a male-dominated environment. The show was presented by a small experimental theater group, Playwrights Horizons, that would later prosper and play a major role in Wasserstein's career.

When Wasserstein graduated from City University, she was unsure of her future. The emergent women's movement brought the prospect of a career in law or business, but Wasserstein was not enthusiastic about these professions. She was drawn to a career as a playwright, a tenuous life made even more so by the growing popularity of television and film. She applied to two prestigious graduate programs, Columbia Business School and Yale Drama School, was accepted by both, and opted for Yale. The leader of Yale's drama program was Robert Brustein, renowned in the American theater community as an advocate of professional discipline and artistic creativity. Wasserstein's classmates at Yale

included Christopher Durang and Albert Innaurato, later to become award-winning playwrights, and Meryl Streep, an actress who later earned acclaim in films.

With Durang's encouragement, Wasserstein became interested in the plays of Anton Chekhov, the celebrated nineteenth-century Russian writer. Wasserstein noted that Chekhov had the objectivity to mock his characters' flaws and delusions; but at the same time, he had the sympathy to portray their hopes and sorrows. The Russian playwright became an enduring role model for Wasserstein. But as she studied the works of famous playwrights, she perceived the same flaw noted by many feminists of the 1970s: such dramatists, predominantly male, had failed to reflect the full range of women's experiences. Female characters, Wasserstein realized, often seemed to be stereotypes such as prostitutes or uncaring mothers. Rarely did they resemble her own women peers, who were striving for professional and emotional fulfillment in a complex and frustrating world. So Wasserstein joined a wave of new women dramatists in America who were determined to bring a broader range of women characters to the stage.

Accordingly, Wasserstein's work at Yale evolved from broad mockery to more subtle portrayals of character. Of her student plays, two are forthright satires: *Happy Birthday, Montpelier Pizz-zazz* shows the social maneuvers at a college party, and *When Dinah Shore Ruled the Earth*, written with Durang, mocks a beauty pageant. But in *Uncommon Women and Others*—which Wasserstein began as her Yale master's thesis—the characters are more complex; and the humor, more low-keyed, is underlain with tension.

Uncommon Women is about a fictional group of Mount Holyoke students who trade quips about men and sex while wondering about their own futures with a mixture of hope and apprehension. As the play makes clear, when feminism reached college campuses in the late 1960s it expanded women's horizons but filled them with uncertainty. The character Rita dominates the play as an outspoken aspiring novelist. As a student she tells her friends that "when we're thirty we're going to be pretty amazing," but she eventually hopes for a "Leonard Woolf" who will, like Virginia Woolf's husband, support her while she perfects her writing. Holly makes a pathetic effort to find a husband on the eve of graduation by phoning a young doctor she once met. He has since married and has forgotten all about her. Surrounding the central characters, each of whom struggles to define herself, are other young women whose self-assurance seems vaguely unsettling by contrast. Leilah, self-contained and inscrutable, makes a cold peace with the world, deciding to become an anthropologist and marry a man from the Middle East. Susie is a booster for outmoded college traditions; Carter, a stereotypical genius who seems guaranteed of success. The play's opening and closing scenes show the central characters at a reunion luncheon a few years after college. Most seem confused and unfulfilled. Rita now asserts that by the age of forty-five they will all be

Ginger married Prince Billy with fifty tapping bridesmaids, fifty leaping men, the trapeze artists, the dancing cats, Chita and her fastest legs, and a reprise of Pamela's favorite song. Then the red velvet curtain came down.

"Bravo! Bravissimo!" The entire audience was on its feet, applauding.

"It's a standing ovation, just as I'd hoped." Aunt Louise was just thrilled that Pamela's first musical had gone so well.

Pamela enjoys her birthday attending a Broadway musical for the first time in award-winning dramatist Wasserstein's picture book. (From *Pamela's First Musical,* illustrated by Andrew Jackness.)

"amazing." Chekhov, Wasserstein later revealed, inspired Rita's funny-sad refrain.

Uncommon Women was first presented at Yale in 1975 as a one-act play. Then Wasserstein rewrote the play in a two-act version and prepared it for the professional stage, receiving encouragement along the way from both Playwrights Horizons and the Eugene O'Neill Playwrights Conference. The finished work received widespread attention from reviewers when it premiered in 1977 under the auspices of Phoenix Theater, a troupe that spotlighted new American plays. *Uncommon Women* soon reached national television as part of the Public Broadcasting Service's *Theatre in America* series.

As Wasserstein established her theater career, she became clearly identified with Playwrights Horizons, which also attracted Durang, Innaurato, and several other well-educated writers of about the same age. Under the growing influence of Andre Bishop, who joined as an administrator in 1975, Playwrights became one of the most critically acclaimed Off-Off Broadway groups of recent times. Bishop wanted the organization and its writers to have lasting professional ties, and it developed such a relationship with Wasserstein. After producing a revised *Isn't It Romantic,* Playwrights Horizons commissioned Wasserstein's next full-length work, *Miami,* a musical comedy about a teenage boy on vacation with his family in the late 1950s. The show received a limited run at the group's theater in early 1986. More successful was Wasserstein's subsequent

full-length play, *The Heidi Chronicles,* which received its New York debut at Playwrights in late 1988.

The Heidi Chronicles was inspired by a single image in Wasserstein's mind: a woman speaking to an assembly of other women, confessing her growing sense of unhappiness. The speaker evolved into Dr. Heidi Holland, an art history professor who finds that her successful, independent life has left her alienated from men and women alike. Most of the play consists of flashbacks that capture Heidi's increasing disillusionment. Starting as a high-school girl, she experiences in turn the student activism of the late 1960s, feminist consciousness-raising of the early 1970s, and the tough-minded careerism of the 1980s. Friends disappoint her: a feminist activist becomes an entertainment promoter, valuing the women's audience for its market potential; a boyfriend becomes a manipulative and selfish magazine editor; a gay male friend tells her that in the 1980s, when gays are dying of AIDS, her unhappiness is a mere luxury. Heidi remains subdued until the play's climactic scene, when she addresses fellow alumnae from a private school for girls. At the end of the play she adopts a baby and poses happily with the child in front of an exhibition of works by Georgia O'Keefe, an acclaimed woman artist. "Heidi's search for self is both mirthful and touching," wrote Mel Gussow of the *New York Times.* Noting Wasserstein's enduring interest in comedy, he observed that "she has been exceedingly watchful about not settling for easy laughter, and the result is a more penetrating play." *The Heidi Chronicles* became Wasserstein's first show to move to a Broadway theater; soon afterwards, the play brought its author the Pulitzer Prize.

Wasserstein and scenic designer Andrew Jackness, a former Yale classmate, made their children's book debuts with *Pamela's First Musical,* for which Jackness furnished the illustrations. "It's a very spare kind of writing," Wasserstein commented of the picture book format in an interview with Richard Donahue for *Publishers Weekly.* "You write it all out, then strip it down to its bones. . . . Writing [*Pamela's First Musical*] was like writing a musical, in that all the big moments go to the drawings—just as a show's big moments go into the songs." In the story, glamorous Aunt Louise takes nine-year-old Pamela into Manhattan for a special birthday treat: lunch at the famed Russian Tea Room and a matinee performance of a Tony Award-winning musical. All of the wonders of a Broadway production are related from the child's wide-eyed perspective, as Pamela delights in the show, the intermission, and an opportunity to meet the performers afterward. A *Kirkus Reviews* critic noted that in *Pamela's First Musical* "Wasserstein captures the thrill of attending a live performance." Of Jackness's accompanying illustrations, a *Publishers Weekly* reviewer wrote: "Splashing across the pages in a frenzy of candy-colored lights, his watercolors capture the hustle and bustle" of the show.

■ Works Cited

Donahue, Richard, "Opening Night," *Publishers Weekly,* April 22, 1996, p. 31.
Gussow, Mel, "A Modern-Day Heffalump in Search of Herself," *New York Times,* December 12, 1988, p. C13.
Review of *Pamela's First Musical, Kirkus Reviews,* April 1, 1996, p. 539.
Review of *Pamela's First Musical, Publishers Weekly,* May 6, 1996, p. 81.

■ For More Information See

BOOKS

Contemporary Literary Criticism, Gale, Volume 32, 1985, Volume 59, 1990.

PERIODICALS

Bulletin of the Center for Children's Books, March, 1996, p. 246.
School Library Journal, April, 1996, p. 120.*

*   *   *

WHYTE, Mary 1953-

■ Personal

Born December 10, 1953, in Cleveland, OH; daughter of Donald Robert (an executive) and Elizabeth Reid (Patton) Whyte; married Smith B. Coleman (a gallery owner), April 23, 1977. *Education:* Temple University, Tyler School of Art, B.F.A., 1976. *Religion:* Christian.

MARY WHYTE

■ Addresses

Home—1007 Embassy Row Way, Johns Island, SC 29455. *Office*—Coleman Fine Art, 45 Hasell St., Charleston, SC 29401.

■ Career

Professional artist, 1976—. *Exhibitions:* Work represented in collections at Bell Atlantic, Easter Seals Society, University of Pennsylvania, and West Chester University; work exhibited in solo and group shows, including those of the American Watercolor Society, Allied Artists of America, Pennsylvania Watercolor Society, South Carolina Watercolor Society, Pennsylvania State Capitol, and Adirondacks National Exhibition of American Watercolors. *Member:* Pennsylvania Watercolor Society, South Carolina Watercolor Society, Philadelphia Watercolor Club, Charleston Artists Guild.

■ Awards, Honors

I Love You the Purplest was chosen as one of the Best Books for 1996 by both *Parents Magazine* and *Child.*

■ Writings

Watercolor for the Serious Beginner (self-illustrated), Watson-Guptill (New York City), 1997.

Contributor to art magazines.

ILLUSTRATOR

Constance W. McGeorge, *Boomer's Big Day,* Chronicle Books (San Francisco, CA), 1994.

McGeorge, *The Snow Riders,* Chronicle Books, 1995.

McGeorge, *Boomer Goes to School,* Chronicle Books, 1996.

Barbara Joosse, *I Love You the Purplest,* Chronicle Books, 1996.

■ Work in Progress

Illustrating children's books for Chronicle Books and Dial; numerous portrait commissions.

■ Sidelights

Mary Whyte told *SATA:* "Art has always been a major focus of my life. I sold my first drawing when I was fourteen years old and had my first solo art exhibition when I was sixteen. My husband and I have an art gallery, Coleman Fine Art, located in the historic district of Charleston, South Carolina.

"I illustrated my first children's book *Boomer's Big Day* in 1994. The book, a collaborative effort with author Constance McGeorge, was inspired by my golden retriever, Boomer. The book prompted the sequel *Boomer Goes to School,* and since then Boomer and I have made many delightful visits to schools and bookstores.

"I live on a barrier island, and from my studio I can hear owls and the faint sound of the ocean. I generally spend forty hours per week in my studio, illustrating books, painting portraits, and writing for artists' magazines. Boomer is always by my side, either under the drawing table asleep, or jangling his leash to tell me it's time for a walk on the beach."

■ For More Information See

PERIODICALS

Booklist, July, 1994, pp. 1955-56; January 1, 1996, pp. 847-48; April 15, 1996, p. 1446; October 15, 1996, p. 436.

Book World, May 8, 1994, p. 18.

Kirkus Reviews, March 15, 1996, p. 450.

Publishers Weekly, April 29, 1996, p. 74; September 16, 1996, p. 82.

School Library Journal, July, 1996, p. 68.

*   *   *

WOODSON, Jacqueline 1964-

■ Personal

Born February 12, 1964, in Columbus, OH. *Education:* Received a B.A. (English).

■ Addresses

Home—Brooklyn, NY. *Agent*—c/o Bantam Doubleday Dell, 1540 Broadway, 20th Fl., New York, NY 10036.

■ Career

Writer. Former faculty member of the Goddard College M.F.A. Writing Program; former fellow at the MacDowell Colony and at the Fine Arts Work Center, Provincetown, MA. Has also worked as a drama therapist for runaway children in New York City.

■ Awards, Honors

Kenyon Review Award for Literary Excellence in Fiction, 1992; Best Books for Young Adults, American Library Association (ALA), 1993, for *Maizon at Blue Hill;* Coretta Scott King Honor Book, ALA, 1995, for *I Hadn't Meant to Tell You This,* and 1996, for *From the Notebooks of Melanin Sun.*

■ Writings

FOR CHILDREN

Martin Luther King, Jr., and His Birthday (nonfiction), illustrated by Floyd Cooper, Silver Burdett, 1990.

We Had a Picnic This Sunday Past, illustrated by Diane Greenseid, Hyperion Books for Children, 1997.

The first title of a trilogy about friends Margaret and Maizon, *Last Summer with Maizon* relates how the girls' friendship is temporarily strained when Maizon attends boarding school and Margaret struggles with the loss of her father. (Cover illustration by Leo and Diane Dillon.)

FICTION; FOR YOUNG ADULTS

Last Summer with Maizon (first book in a trilogy), Delacorte, 1990.

The Dear One, Delacorte, 1991.

Maizon at Blue Hill (second book in a trilogy), Delacorte, 1992.

Between Madison and Palmetto (third book in a trilogy), Delacorte, 1993.

Book Chase ("Ghostwriter" series), illustrated by Steve Cieslawski, Bantam, 1994.

I Hadn't Meant to Tell You This, Delacorte, 1994.

From the Notebooks of Melanin Sun, Scholastic, 1995.

The House You Pass on the Way, Delacorte, 1997.

OTHER

(With Catherine Saalfield) *Among Good Christian Peoples* (video), A Cold Hard Dis', 1991.

Autobiography of a Family Photo (adult novel), New American Library/Dutton, 1994.

(Editor) *A Way Out of No Way: Writing about Growing Up Black in America* (short stories), Holt, 1996.

Contributor to short story collection *Am I Blue?,* edited by Marion Dane Bauer, HarperTrophy, 1994; contributor to *Just a Writer's Thing: A Collection of Prose & Poetry from the National Book Foundation's 1995 Summer Writing Camp,* edited by Norma F. Mazer, National Book Foundation, 1996.

■ Sidelights

Jacqueline Woodson writes about invisible people: young girls, minorities, homosexuals, the poor, all the individuals who are ignored or forgotten in mainstream America. They are the people, as the author writes in a *Horn Book* article, "who exist on the margins." An African American herself, Woodson knows first-hand what it is like to be labelled, classified, stereotyped, and pushed aside. Nevertheless, her stories are not intended to champion the rights of minorities and the oppressed. Rather, they celebrate people's differences. Her characters are not so much striving to have their rights acknowledged as they are struggling to find their own individuality, their own value as people. "I feel compelled to write against stereotypes," says Woodson, "hoping people will see that some issues know no color, class, sexuality. No—I don't feel as though I have a commitment to one community—I don't want to be shackled this way. I write from the very depths of who I am, and in this place there are all of my identities."

Woodson's sense of not really belonging to one community might be grounded in her childhood. During her adolescent years, she moved back and forth between South Carolina and New York City, and "never quite felt a part of either place," according to a *Ms.* article by Diane R. Paylor. But Woodson began to feel "outside of the world," as she explained in *Horn Book,* even before her teen years. The turning point for her came when Richard Nixon resigned the presidency in 1974 and Gerald Ford took his place instead of George McGovern. "McGovern was my first 'American Dream.' Everyone in my neighborhood had been pulling for him."

Maizon's unpleasant experiences with snobbery and racism at a Connecticut boarding school are depicted in this companion volume to *Last Summer with Maizon.* (Cover illustration by Leo and Diane Dillon.)

When Ford stepped into the Oval Office, Woodson felt that she and all of black America had been abandoned. "The word *democracy* no longer existed for me. I began to challenge teachers, and when they couldn't give me the answers I wanted, I became sullen, a loner. I would spend hours sitting underneath the porch, writing poetry and anti-American songs."

Writing soon became Woodson's passion. In the fifth grade, she was the literary editor of her school's magazine. "I used to write on everything," she commented for a Bantam Doubleday Dell Web site. "It was the thing I liked to do the most. I never thought I could have a career as a writer—I always thought it was something I would have to do on the side." Her seventh-grade English teacher encouraged Woodson to write and convinced her that she should pursue whatever career she felt would make her happiest. Deciding that writing was, indeed, what she wanted to do, Woodson endeavored "to write about communities that were familiar to me and people that were familiar to me. I wanted to write about communities of color. I wanted to write about girls. I wanted to write about friendship and all of these things that I felt like were missing in a lot of the books that I read as a child."

Woodson has always had a deep empathy for young girls, who often suffer from low self-esteem in their preteen and adolescent years. "I write about black girls because this world would like to keep us invisible," she wrote in *Horn Book.* "I write about *all* girls because I know what happens to self-esteem when we turn twelve, and I hope to show readers the number of ways in which we are strong." Woodson's first published book, *Last Summer with Maizon,* begins a trilogy about friends Margaret and Maizon. Set in the author's hometown of Brooklyn, the story tells of two eleven-year-olds who are the closest of friends. Their friendship is strained, however, when Margaret's father dies of a heart attack and Maizon goes to boarding school on a scholarship. While her friend is away, Margaret, who is the quieter of the two, discovers that she has a talent for writing. She also finds comfort in her family, who support her in her attempt to deal with her father's death. Maizon, meanwhile, finds that she does not like the almost all-white Connecticut boarding school and returns home after only three months. Glad to be with her loved ones again,

Woodson highlights the tensions between poor and wealthy African Americans through rich twelve-year-old Afeni, whose family takes in a troubled and pregnant teenager from Harlem.

Maizon, along with Margaret, goes to a gifted school in her own neighborhood.

Critics praised *Last Summer with Maizon* for its touching portrayal of two close friends and for its convincing sense of place. Julie Blaisdale, writing in *School Librarian,* also lauded the work for its "positive female characters ... who provide the enduring sense of place and spiritual belonging" in the tale. Roger Sutton of the *Bulletin of the Center for Children's Books,* while generally commending the book, found fault with the way Margaret eases her sadness by writing poetry. "Although underdeveloped," Sutton concluded, "this story will appeal to readers who want a 'book about friends.'" Similarly, *Horn Book* writer Rudine Sims Bishop commented on the story's "blurred focus," but asserted that "the novel is appealing in its vivid portrayal of the characters and the small community they create."

Woodson continues Margaret and Maizon's stories with *Maizon at Blue Hill* and *Between Madison and Palmetto.* The former is not really a sequel but, rather, an "equal" to the first book in the trilogy. *Maizon at Blue Hill* focuses on what happens to Maizon while she is at the Connecticut boarding school. Maizon, who is a very bright girl, likes the academic side of Blue Hill, but she is worried about fitting in socially. Most of the other girls are white and are either snobbish or, at least, not eager to be her friend. Although she is welcomed by a small clique of other black students, Maizon sees this group as rather elitist, too. She decides to return to Brooklyn, where she can comfortably just be herself. An American Library Association Best Book for Young Adults, *Maizon at Blue Hill* has been acclaimed for its strong and appealing characters. "More sharply written than its predecessor, this novel contains some acute characterization," remarked Roger Sutton in *Bulletin of the Center for Children's Books.* Noting that the issues about self-esteem and identity that are addressed in the story spring appropriately from the characters rather than vice versa, *Voice of Youth Advocates* contributor Alice F. Stern asserted: "We are in the hands of a skilled writer here.... Woodson is a real find."

The last book in the trilogy, *Between Madison and Palmetto,* picks up where the first book left off, with Maizon and Margaret entering eighth grade at the academy. Again, Woodson covers a lot of ground in just over one hundred pages, including Margaret's bout with bulimia, issues of integration as the two girls' neighborhood begins to change and white families move in, and the testing of Margaret and Maizon's friendship as Maizon spends more time with another girl named Carolyn. A *Publishers Weekly* reviewer applauded Woodson's gift with characterization, but noted that the effect is "somewhat diluted by the movie-of-the-week problems." In another *Voice of Youth Advocates* review, Alice F. Stern acknowledged that Woodson has "a lot of ground to cover," but noted that "she manages admirably." A *Kirkus Reviews* critic described *Between Madison and Palmetto* as a fine portrayal of a "close-knit community ... [that] comes nicely to life."

In Woodson's Coretta Scott King honor book, wealthy, black Marie befriends poor, white Lena, but must finally reconcile herself to the fact that she cannot relieve the tragedy in Lena's life. (Cover illustration by Jacqueline Woodson.)

In her *Horn Book* article, Woodson grouped her books into two categories: her "good" books, which deal with relationships between family members and friends, and her more controversial books, which address issues of alcoholism, teenage pregnancy, homosexuality, and other issues that skirt the delicate problem of what is "appropriate" for children to read. She reflected on how, after writing her second book, *The Dear One,* the speaking invitations she had formerly received suddenly stopped coming. "Even after *Maizon at Blue Hill,* another relatively 'nice book,' school visits were few and far between. Yet I often wonder, If every book had been like *Last Summer with Maizon,* and I was a young woman with a wedding band on my hand, would I get to visit schools more often?"

The central character of *The Dear One* is twelve-year-old Afeni, a name meaning "The Dear One" in Swahili. Afeni lives in an upper-class African American home and basks in her family's attention. This all changes,

however, when fifteen-year-old Rebecca is invited by Afeni's mother to stay with them. Rebecca, the daughter of an old college friend, is a troubled, pregnant teenager from Harlem. Afeni becomes jealous because she is no longer the center of attention. "But gradually and believably, with the patient support of Afeni's mother and a lesbian couple who are longstanding family friends, the two girls begin to develop mutual trust and, finally, a redemptive friendship," related *Twentieth-Century Children's Writers* contributor Michael Cart.

The Dear One is a unique book in that it deals with tensions not between blacks and whites but between poor and wealthy blacks. Woodson gives a sympathetic portrayal of Rebecca, who is uncomfortable living in what she considers to be a mansion, and who is also reluctant to change her lifestyle. She misses her boyfriend and her family back in Harlem; she envies Afeni and resents the privileges Afeni has been given. The novel also offers a fresh perspective on adult relationships. As Hazel S. Moore noted in *Voice of Youth Advocates,* "The lesbian couple seems to be intact, while the straight couples have divorced and suffered." Marion and Bernadette, the lesbian couple, provide Afeni with wise advice to add to the support she receives from her mother.

Taking things a step further than *The Dear One, I Hadn't Meant to Tell You This* explores a relationship that spans both race and class when Marie, a girl from a well-to-do black family, befriends Lena, whom Marie's father considers to be "white trash." Both girls have problems: Marie's mother has abandoned her family, and Lena is the victim of her father's sexual molestations. Told from Marie's point of view, the book details the twelve-year-old's internal conflicts as she tries to think of how she can help Lena. In the end, Lena, who has been able to find no other viable solutions to her problem, runs away from home, and Marie must accept the fact that there is nothing she can do about her friend's tragedy. Woodson has been praised by critics for not resolving her story with a pat conclusion. Cart commented: "Woodson's refusal to impose a facile resolution on this heartbreaking dilemma is one of her singular strengths as a writer." "Woodson's novel is wrenchingly honest and, despite its sad themes, full of hope and inspiration," concluded a *Publishers Weekly* reviewer.

The issue of homosexuality, which had been peripheral in Woodson's earlier books, comes to the forefront in *From the Notebooks of Melanin Sun* and *The House You Pass on the Way.* Thirteen-year-old Melanin Sun, the central character in the former novel, has a close relationship with his mother, whom he admires as a single working mother who is also putting herself through law school. Their bond is strained, however, when Melanin's mother tells him that she is a lesbian and that she is in love with a white woman. This development makes Melanin question his relationship with his mother, as well as making him wonder about his own sexuality. Torn between his emotional need for his mother and his fear about what her lesbianism implies, Melanin goes through a tough time as his friends also begin to abandon him. Gossip in the neighborhood that Melanin's mother is "unfit" also spreads, making matters even worse. Again, Woodson offers no clear-cut resolution to the story, but by the novel's end Melanin has begun to grow and understand his mother. Critics have praised Woodson's portrayal of Melanin's inner conflicts as being right on the money. As Lois Metzger wrote in the *New York Times Book Review,* "Ms. Woodson, in this moving, lovely book, shows you Melanin's strength and the sun shining through." "Woodson has addressed with care and skill the sensitive issue of homosexuality within the family ... [without] becoming an advocate of any particular attitude," asserted *Voice of Youth Advocates* critic Hazel Moore. In *The House You Pass on the Way,* fourteen-year-old Evangeline, the middle child in a mixed-race family, struggles with feelings of guilt and dismay over her awakening sexual preference. "A provocative topic," noted a *Kirkus Reviews* critic, "treated with wisdom and sensitivity, with a strong secondary thread exploring some of the inner and outer effects of biracialism."

Although most of her works have been aimed at preteen and teenage audiences, Woodson has also written a novel for adults, *Autobiography of a Family Photo,* and a children's picture book, *We Had a Picnic This Sunday Past.* The latter, as with all of the author's work, is about the importance of family, while the former addresses issues of sexuality and sexual behavior for a more mature audience. However, its short length and central coming-of-age theme put *Autobiography of a Family Photo* within the reach of young adult audiences. Told in a series of vignettes spanning the '60s and '70s, the novel is a reminiscence related by an unnamed narrator. Her family has many problems, including her parents' troubled marriage, her brother Carlos's inclination to be sexually abusive, her brother Troy's struggles with homosexuality that compel him to go to Vietnam, and other difficulties. Despite all of this, the narrator survives adolescence, undergoing a "compelling transformation," according to Margot Mifflin in an *Entertainment Weekly* review. However, some critics have contended that the vignettes fail to form a unified whole. A *Kirkus Reviews* contributor, for example, commented: "Chapters build on each other, but the information provided is too scanty to really create any depth." Catherine Bush, writing in the *New York Times Book Review,* complained that the novel focuses too much on the narrator's growing sexual awareness. "I found myself wishing that the narrator's self-awareness and longing could be defined less exclusively in sexual terms," Bush says. Bush concluded, however, that "even in these restrictive terms, the novel is the best kind of survival guide: clear-eyed, gut true."

Woodson has never backed away from portraying truths about life in modern American society. She has written her "good" books about friendship and family that deal with safe, acceptable topics, but she clearly does not shy away from controversial subjects like homosexuality and sexual abuse. Woodson is not trying to force any kind of ideology on her readers, but rather is interested in all kinds of people, especially the socially rejected. "One of the most important ideas I want to get across to my readers," Woodson emphasizes, "is the idea of feeling like you're okay with who you are."

■ Works Cited

Review of *Autobiography of a Family Photo, Kirkus Reviews,* October 1, 1994, pp. 1307-08.

Bantam Doubleday Dell Web Site, "Jacqueline Woodson," http: // www.bdd.com. /forum/bddforum.cgi/ trc/index/wood (April 8, 1997).

Review of *Between Madison and Palmetto, Kirkus Reviews,* December 1, 1993, p. 1532.

Review of *Between Madison and Palmetto, Publishers Weekly,* November 8, 1993, p. 78.

Bishop, Rudine Sims, "Books from Parallel Cultures: New African-American Voices," *Horn Book,* September, 1992, pp. 616-20.

Blaisdale, Julie, review of *Last Summer with Maizon, School Librarian,* November, 1991, p. 154.

Bush, Catherine, "A World Without Childhood," *New York Times Book Review,* February 26, 1995, p. 14.

Cart, Michael, "Jacqueline Woodson," *Twentieth-Century Children's Writers,* 4th edition, edited by Laura Standley Berger, St. James Press, 1995.

Review of *The House You Pass on the Way, Kirkus Reviews,* July 1, 1997, p. 1038.

Review of *I Hadn't Meant to Tell You This, Publishers Weekly,* April 18, 1994, p. 64.

Metzger, Lois, review of *From the Notebooks of Melanin Sun, New York Times Book Review,* July 16, 1995, p. 27.

Mifflin, Margot, review of *Autobiography of a Family Photo, Entertainment Weekly,* April 21, 1995, pp. 50-51.

Moore, Hazel S., review of *The Dear One, Voice of Youth Advocates,* October, 1991, p. 236.

Moore, Hazel S., review of *From the Notebooks of Melanin Sun, Voice of Youth Advocates,* October, 1995, p. 227.

Paylor, Diane R., "Bold Type: Jacqueline Woodson's 'Girl Stories,'" *Ms.,* November-December, 1994, p. 77.

Stern, Alice F., review of *Maizon at Blue Hill, Voice of Youth Advocates,* October, 1992, p. 235.

Stern, Alice F., review of *Between Madison and Palmetto, Voice of Youth Advocates,* June, 1994, p. 95.

Sutton, Roger, review of *Last Summer with Maizon, Bulletin of the Center for Children's Books,* October, 1990, pp. 49-50.

Sutton, Roger, review of *Maizon at Blue Hill, Bulletin of the Center for Children's Books,* December, 1992, p. 128.

Woodson, Jacqueline, "A Sign of Having Been Here," *Horn Book,* November-December, 1995, pp. 711-15.

■ For More Information See

PERIODICALS

Booklist, November 15, 1991, p. 619; July, 1992, p. 1931; March 15, 1993, p. 1344; September 15,

1993, p. 152; February 15, 1994, p. 1072; December 15, 1994, p. 736; January 15, 1995, p. 860; April 1, 1995, pp. 1404, 1412; March 15, 1996, p. 1284.

Bulletin of the Center for Children's Books, September, 1991, p. 26; December, 1993, p. 136; March, 1994, p. 239; July, 1995, p. 401.

Essence, February, 1995, p. 52; April, 1995, p. 56.

Horn Book, November, 1991, p. 746; January, 1994, p. 72; September, 1994, p. 601; July, 1995, p. 468.

Kirkus Reviews, August 1, 1991, p. 1018; October 15, 1992, p. 1318; June 1, 1994, p. 782; May 15, 1995, p. 717.

Ms., July, 1995, p. 75.

New York Times Book Review, July 29, 1990, p. 33; May 10, 1992, p. 21; November 6, 1994, p. 32; April 28, 1996, p. 36.

Publishers Weekly, June 28, 1991, p. 103; January 20, 1992, p. 66; January 4, 1993, p. 74; November 7, 1994, p. 44; May 15, 1995, p. 74; December 11, 1995, p. 71.

School Library Journal, November, 1990, p. 121; June, 1991, p. 129; November, 1992, p. 99; November, 1993, p. 111; May, 1994, p. 136; August, 1995, p. 158.

Voice of Youth Advocates, February, 1991, p. 360; April, 1994, p. 32; June, 1997, p. 114.*

—Sketch by Janet L. Hile